EDITED BY

PAUL BLUMBERG

QUEENS COLLEGE OF THE
CITY UNIVERSITY OF NEW YORK

THE
IMPACT
OF
SOCIAL
CLASS

A Book of Readings

Designed by Carole Fern Halpert

L. C. Card 72-165375
ISBN 0-690-43484-7
Manufactured in the United States of America

2 3 4 5 6 7 8 9 10

THE
IMPACT
OF
SOCIAL
CLASS

A Book of Readings

Thomas Y. Crowell Company New York Established 1834

For My Mother and Ira

CONTENTS

INTRODUCTION

For many reasons, the subject matter of social stratification has been a controversial one in American sociology. The polemical struggle between Marxists and anti-Marxists, both within and outside of the sociological discipline, has often been fought with weapons from the arsenal of stratification. Are social classes necessary and inevitable in society? Is the working class progressive or reactionary? Is struggle or harmony the more basic truth about class relationships under capitalism? Is American society more "open" (i.e., is there greater opportunity for social mobility) than Soviet society? Are social class differences tending to disappear, or are they widening? All these questions, and more, have political as well as scientific importance and, consequently, the arena of social stratification has occasionally become a polemical battlefield, with ideas used as weapons.

There is another source of controversy. Social stratification, by definition, has social inequality as its central concern, and the ideology of American society—at least since the days of Andrew Jackson and probably since the Jeffersonian era—has been based upon strong sentiments of social equality. The whole subject of social inequality goes against the grain of popular opinion that has long been held captive by the pervasive myth of American classlessness. Typical was the remark made to a group of French college students a few years ago by our former ambassador to France, Charles E. Bohlen (a member of the Social Register of Philadelphia) when he said, according to one report, that "not only was the United States a classless society but the revolution in science and technology would soon bring Europe a classless society as well."

Actually, two myths often go hand in hand: first, that America is classless; second, that any man with talent and determination can get to the top. Although these two beliefs continue side by side, they are patently contradictory, for if there is no hierarchy of classes, then there is obviously nothing to get to the top *of*. Contradictions aside, if the ideology of American society were to set the curriculum in our sociology departments, there might not even be a course in social stratification offered. But while sociology is interested in the nature of social ideology, it cannot—if any scientific stature is to be achieved for the discipline—be induced to accept an ideology as necessarily representing an accurate picture of social reality.

What emerges from a study of social stratification in America today, partly reflected in this volume, is a picture of a society that is highly stratified with regard to the distribution of wealth, income, property, prestige, education, opportunity, and power. While these gross inequalities may have been mitigated somewhat in recent decades by the great and increasing wealth of the society as a whole, we nevertheless find a society where social and economic inequality is such as to have consequences for a broad range of people's "life chances," to use Weber's phrase. It is a remarkable testimony to the impact of social class that in the United States, certainly one of the most egalitarian societies in the world, social class can still have an enormous determining effect upon fertility rates, child rearing patterns, marital stability, sexual behavior, work satisfaction, political behavior, cultural tastes, organizational membership, religious beliefs, mental health, and life expectancy—to name just a few areas of life affected by social class.

No wonder, then, that social class is still one of our most important sociological categories and one of the most powerful tools and predictive devices we have in sociology. It is no surprise that social class, however measured, is used and/or controlled for in the vast majority of all survey research done today.

The importance of social class as a predictive tool is enhanced, as we said, by the fact that this predictiveness still holds up in most cases for one of the most egalitarian societies in the world, the United States. And if it is useful here, where class differences have been moderated by an overpowering egalitarian ethos, a highly productive economic system characterized by mass production and standardization of products, and the homogenizing influence of the mass media, then the impact of social class elsewhere must be—and indeed is—even more striking.

I have tried to include in this anthology some of the best material that has been written on social stratification since World War II. In the eight sections of the book, I have attempted to set before the reader some of the major issues in the field of social stratification, which, because of the rather detailed introductions in the text itself, I shall very briefly mention here.

I. Marx and Weber. No contemporary discussion of social stratification is complete without some treatment of the theoretical approaches of Karl Marx and Max Weber, whose works offer alternate images of the class structure of modern society, and whose theoretical world-views—implicitly or explicitly—underlie much of the writing done in the field today.

II. The Relevance of Social Stratification in Modern Society. Here we encounter the debate concerning where modern class structures are headed. Some writers claim social class is slowly being "prosperitied" out of existence, while others assert that there are continuing forces in modern society which, despite absolute rises in the level of living for the population as a whole, still sustain a society with great and seemingly ineradicable amounts of inequality. To my mind, this issue of the destiny of social class in wealthy, so-called "post-industrial" societies is perhaps the single most important question in the field.

III. The Need for Inequality. Section three is concerned with the long-standing debate in sociology over whether social stratification is a necessary, functional feature of all societies, or whether the functions it fulfills could be satisfied by other arrangements, and whether a truly classless society is therefore theoretically possible. Although this debate is presented in modern dress, it is part of an age-old historical controversy between those, on the one hand, who have regarded the social inequality they saw around them as both necessary and just, and those, on the other hand, who have regarded this same social inequality as unnecessary and evil.

IV. Social Class Profiles. In section four we present sketches of various strata in American society: an upper class of New Haven, Connecticut, a national view of the new middle class, a characterization of the American working class, and a lengthy description of a lower class group in the San Francisco Bay area.

V. Subjective Elements: Prestige and Class Consciousness. Social class involves more than objective, material differences among people, with regard, say, to income, wealth, or property. Central to social class is its subjective dimension. And here we examine two aspects of it: the *prestige* that people accord various occupations, and the all-important phenomenon of *class consciousness* or class awareness.

VI. Power and Politics. What are the consequences for political democracy in a society where, though all men are politically equal, they are economically and socially unequal? The first four essays in this section explore this question implicitly, while the last two selections treat the impact of social class upon political values and voting behavior.

VII. Through the Life Cycle. Here we consider some of the major *correlates* of stratification, such as fertility rates and child rearing patterns that are strongly influenced by (correlated to) one's position in the class structure. Social-class analysis ultimately stands or falls by its ability to make predictions about other areas of social life which social class presumably affects.

VIII. Social Mobility. In addition to considering basic causes, measures, and rates of social mobility, this section includes material on some of the usually neglected negative social and psychological consequences of social mobility in modern society.

At the Thomas Y. Crowell Company, I should like to thank Tom Simpson for his valuable advice, assistance, and patience during the preparation of this manuscript, Ed Griffiths, who labored long and hard at the tedious job of accumulating permissions for the collection, and Joan Greene for her conscientious and painstaking guidance of the manuscript through production. For help and encouragement of so many different kinds I could not begin to describe them here, I am grateful to James Perlman, Bernard Karsh, my wife Barbara, Marvin Rosen, Conrad Miller, John Spier, Carol Ann Finkelstein, and Johanna Fortuin. My greatest debt of all, of course, is to the myriad of scholars and writers whose excellent work comprises this volume.

I

MARX
AND
WEBER

1

THE COMMUNIST MANIFESTO

**Karl Marx and
Friedrich Engels**

Sitting down today to write an introduction to *The Communist Manifesto,* written nearly a century and a quarter ago, is a difficult and perplexing task. This is so because one could actually write two separate, contradictory essays. Marxism today is at the same time the most *relevant* and the most *irrelevant* body of theory that attempts to explain the contemporary world. One can dismiss Marxism entirely, as historically interesting but full of fallacies and utterly useless in trying to understand contemporary society. Indeed, most Western social scientists do just this. Or one can claim, along with Sartre, that Marxism is still "the philosophy of our time" and the most important foundation upon which we may understand our world.

The errors in Marx's theory of social class are easy to enumerate; Western social scientists have frequently called them to our attention.

1. The class struggle did not reach such a level of intensity in the advanced Western nations to culminate in an overthrow of capitalism. The capitalist system has proved to be more prosperous, more stable, and more flexible than Marx anticipated. Of course, no one really knows to what extent the prosperity and stability of Western capitalism since the great depression of the 1930's has depended upon war or preparation for war.

2. The working class today, partly because of the increasing wealth and productivity of Western economies, partly because of the success of trade unions, and partly because of the achievements of political democracy and working-class political influence—the working class today is in most nations less than a revolutionary force. In fact, some writers such as S. M. Lipset (see selection 22) consider the working class today as highly conservative. And, indeed, if one wanted to seek out a revolutionary class on the contemporary scene,

SOURCE: Arthur P. Mendel, ed., *Essentials of Marxism* (New York: Bantam Books, 1961).

one might more profitably turn to the universities than to the factories. Nonetheless, as the French revolutionary events of 1968 demonstrated, as well as recent events on the American scene, students are not numerous enough nor so strategically located in the social structure to carry off a revolution alone. The withdrawal of their "services" from society does not deal it a crippling blow. In this sense, we see the usefulness of a Marxian orientation that points to the pivotal role of the working class, partly because of its strategic location and the effect of collective action on the economic life of the nation. And although it is true that workers today generally do not have the revolutionary fervor anticipated by Marx, the French events demonstrated that an old-fashioned revolution is still within the realm of possibility, even in an advanced, industrial country, with the working class playing a key role.

3. We have not had, as Marx expected, a polarization of society into two great antagonistic classes with a small capitalist class at the top and an immense working class at the bottom. Marx did not foresee the rise of a large new salaried middle class (see selection 12) with neither proletarian nor capitalist roots. Marx claimed in the *Manifesto* that the proletarian movement was historically unique because it represented the revolutionary interests of the immense majority of the people. Significantly, though, in the United States in the mid-1950's, the number of middle-class white-collar workers for the first time exceeded the number of manual workers. In that sense, the working class no longer constitutes—and never shall again—the "immense majority" of the population.

4. Marx believed the proletariat to be the motive force of revolution, not simply because it was poor or exploited; so, after all, were derelicts, the unemployed slum proletariat, and much of the peasantry. Nor was it simply because of the strategic location of the working class. Marx, the sociologist, saw the factory, where workers were of necessity gathered together by the employer, as a communications network, a school of revolution, so to speak. There, easy interaction and communication among workers facilitated the recognition of common interests and grievances that first led to the formation of trade unions and later to an ultimate battle, not against individual capitalists, but against the system of capitalism itself.

Marx predicted that revolution would first occur in the most advanced capitalist countries and that the urbanized working class would play a decisive role. Communist revolutions in our century, however, have come to countries that were not the most advanced economically and where the working class has been only weakly developed. Because of the advance of military technology and improvements in transportation and communication, it has become very difficult to begin a revolution and continue to wage it in large cities. The government and the army can easily suppress revolution there. So, the countryside has often become the base of operations for revolutionaries who employ guerrilla warfare to extend the revolution and try to defeat the government and its army on ground strategically more favorable. Theorists of guerrilla warfare, such as Mao Tse-Tung and Che Guevara, have substantially revised Marx's teachings. The setting now is the countryside and there is a new focus on the peasantry, whom Marx often derided as stolid, conservative, and superstitious.

While Western scholars rejoice over Marx's errors, it is impressive that Marxism, or an adaptation of it, provides the world-view of governments that control over a billion people. This, of course, does not prove Marx correct or incorrect, but what other nineteenth-century writer's ideas approximate reality sufficiently to provide on this magnitude the same kind of underlying philosophy, continuing analysis, and interpretation?

Although much of Marx must be discarded today, it nevertheless seems that his fundamental proposition still provides an indispensable point of departure for under-standing the modern world: society is divided into social classes whose relations to one another are often hostile and conflicting. The common conditions of life in each class tend to generate a common world-view. Conflicts between classes often take political as well as economic form, and, as a consequence of the struggle of these classes with one another, important social changes are likely to take place.

Many of the specifics of Marxism remain viable as well. While Marx did not foresee the development of the modern corporation, as such, he did anticipate that under cap-italism, by a kind of economic survival of the fittest, production would become con-centrated in ever fewer but larger and more powerful units. The present bewildering wave of conglomerate corporate mergers in the American economy is but the latest stage in the direction of what Marxists have long called "monopoly capitalism." While this term is undoubtedly an exaggeration, it is nonetheless true that the American economy is increasingly dominated by a few hundred corporate giants, which repre-sent but a tiny fraction of all firms, yet occupy the center of the economic stage.

Along the same lines, Marx was essentially correct in his prediction that the petty bourgeoisie, the small-scale entrepreneur, was destined to lose out in competition with larger capitalists. Marx erred, however, in believing this class would be catapulted into the ranks of the proletariat rather than becoming transformed into a new salaried middle class.

Marx's discussion of the alienation of labor is still of central importance today, and is of continuing interest both to humanists and researchers (see selection 26).

Marx believed that the distribution of income under capitalism—the proportions going to capitalists and workers—would not become more equal. Although it is often asserted that there has been a revolutionary redistribution of income in the United States in this century, several scholars have concluded after a reexamination of the evi-dence that this is not so.* According to these scholars, despite the increasing wealth of the society, the action of trade unions, a whole gamut of welfare state legislation, and progressive taxation, the distribution of income and wealth has remained grossly une-qual and remarkably stable for decades.

Finally, Marx's theory of the state has continuing relevance today. Marx believed that in every society the class that dominated economically also ruled politically, and that the state operated, not impartially, but directly in the interests of the class that controlled the major forms of wealth and property in society. This is obviously not true at all times and places. Popular democracy has greatly complicated the actual ex-ercise of political power and made it much more difficult than ever before for a small economically dominant class to rule. However, the usefulness of Marx's theory lies in its rich suggestiveness as a hypothesis and a model against which reality can be tested and evaluated in each case. Even in contemporary America, where popular democracy is said to be most successful, Marx's theory of the state, modified to be sure, constitutes one of the two major interpretations of power in the country, both on the local and national levels (see selections 17 and 18).

In conclusion, it might be taken as testimony to the continuing importance of Marx that so many of the essays in this volume, published a century and a half after his birth, either implicitly or explicitly take up the issues he raised.

* See Gabriel Kolko, *Wealth and Power in America* (New York: Praeger, 1962); Robert Lamp-man, *The Share of Top Wealth-Holders in National Wealth, 1922–1956* (Princeton, N.J.: Princeton University Press, 1962); Ferdinand Lundberg, *The Rich and the Super-Rich* (New York: Lyle Stuart, 1968).

Bourgeois and Proletarians [1]

The history of all hitherto existing society [2] is the history of class struggles.

Freeman and slave, patrician and plebeian, lord and serf, guild-master [3] and journeyman, in a word, oppressor and oppressed, stood in constant opposition to one another, carried on an uninterrupted, now hidden, now open fight, a fight that each time ended, either in a revolutionary reconstitution of society at large, or in the common ruin of the contending classes.

In the earlier epochs of history, we find almost everywhere a complicated arrangement of society into various orders, a manifold gradation of social rank. In ancient Rome we have patricians, knights, plebeians, slaves; in the Middle Ages, feudal lords, vassals, guild-masters, journeymen, apprentices, serfs; in almost all of these classes, again, subordinate gradations.

The modern bourgeois society that has sprouted from the ruins of feudal society, has not done away with class antagonisms. It has but established new classes, new conditions of oppression, new forms of struggle in place of the old ones.

Our epoch, the epoch of the bourgeoisie, possesses, however, this distinctive feature: It has simplified the class antagonisms. Society as a whole is more and more splitting up into two great hostile camps, into two great classes directly facing each other—bourgeoisie and proletariat.

From the serfs of the Middle Ages sprang the chartered burghers of the earliest towns. From these burgesses the first elements of the bourgeoisie were developed.

The discovery of America, the rounding of the Cape, opened up fresh ground for the rising bourgeoisie. The East-Indian and Chinese markets, the colonization of America, trade with the colonies, the increase in the means of exchange and in commodities generally, gave to commerce, to navigation, to industry, an impulse never before known, and thereby, to the revolutionary element in the tottering feudal society, a rapid development.

The feudal system of industry, in which industrial production was monopolized by closed guilds, now no longer sufficed for the growing wants of the new markets. The manufacturing system took its place. The guild-masters were pushed aside by the man-

---

[1] [Notes by Engels] By "bourgeoisie" is meant the class of modern capitalists, owners of the means of social production and employers of wage-labor; by "proletariat," the class of modern wage-laborers who, having no means of production of their own, are reduced to selling their labor power in order to live.

[2] That is, all *written* history. In 1837, the prehistory of society, the social organization existing previous to recorded history, was all but unknown. Since then Haxthausen [August von, 1792–1866] discovered common ownership of land in Russia, Maurer [Georg Ludwig von] proved it to be the social foundation from which all Teutonic races started in history, and, by and by, village communities were found to be, or to have been, the primitive form of society everywhere from India to Ireland. The inner organization of this primitive communistic society was laid bare, in its typical form, by Morgan's [Lewis H., 1818–1881] crowning discovery of the true nature of the *gens* and its relation to the *tribe*. With the dissolution of these primeval communities, society begins to be differentiated into separate and finally antagonistic classes. I have attempted to retrace this process of dissolution in *The Origin of the Family, Private Property and the State*.

[3] Guild-master, that is a full member of a guild, a master within, not a head of a guild.

ufacturing middle class; division of labor between the different corporate guilds vanished in the face of division of labor in each single workshop.

Meantime the markets kept ever growing, the demand ever rising. Even manufacture no longer sufficed. Thereupon, steam and machinery revolutionized industrial production. The place of manufacture was taken by the giant, modern industry, the place of the industrial middle class, by industrial millionaires—the leaders of whole industrial armies, the modern bourgeois.

Modern industry has established the world market, for which the discovery of America paved the way. This market has given an immense development to commerce, to navigation, to communication by land. This development has, in its turn, reacted on the extension of industry; and in proportion as industry, commerce, navigation, railways extended, in the same proportion the bourgeoisie developed, increased its capital, and pushed into the background every class handed down from the Middle Ages.

We see, therefore, how the modern bourgeoisie is itself the product of a long course of development, of a series of revolutions in the modes of production and of exchange.

Each step in the development of the bourgeoisie was accompanied by a corresponding political advance of that class. An oppressed class under the sway of the feudal nobility, it became an armed and self-governing association in the medieval commune; [4] here independent urban republic (as in Italy and Germany), there taxable "third estate" of the monarchy (as in France); afterwards, in the period of manufacture proper, serving either the semifeudal or the absolute monarchy as a counterpoise against the nobility, and, in fact, cornerstone of the great monarchies in general—the bourgeoisie has at last, since the establishment of modern industry and of the world market, conquered for itself, in the modern representative state, exclusive political sway. The executive of the modern state is but a committee for managing the common affairs of the whole bourgeoisie.

The bourgeoisie has played a most revolutionary role in history.

The bourgeoisie, wherever it has got the upper hand, has put an end to all feudal, patriarchal, idyllic relations. It has pitilessly torn asunder the motley feudal ties that bound man to his "natural superiors," and has left no other bond between man and man than naked self-interest, than callous "cash payment." It has drowned the most heavenly ecstasies of religious fervor, of chivalrous enthusiasm, of philistine sentimentalism, in the icy water of egotistical calculation. It has resolved personal worth into exchange value, and in place of the numberless indefeasible chartered freedoms, has set up that single, unconscionable freedom—Free Trade. In one word, for exploitation, veiled by religious and political illusions, it has substituted naked, shameless, direct, brutal exploitation.

The bourgeoisie has stripped of its halo every occupation hitherto honored and looked up to with reverent awe. It has converted the physician, the lawyer, the priest, the poet, the man of science, into its paid wage-laborers.

---

[4] "Commune" was the name taken in France by the nascent towns even before they had conquered from their feudal lords and masters local self-government and political rights as the "Third Estate." Generally speaking, for the economic development of the bourgeoisie, England is here taken as the typical country, for its political development, France.

The bourgeoisie has torn away from the family its sentimental veil, and has reduced the family relation to a mere money relation.

The bourgeoisie has disclosed how it came to pass that the brutal display of vigor in the Middle Ages, which reactionaries so much admire, found its fitting complement in the most slothful indolence. It has been the first to show what man's activity can bring about. It has accomplished wonders far surpassing Egyptian pyramids, Roman aqueducts, and Gothic cathedrals; it has conducted expeditions that put in the shade all former migrations of nations and crusades.

The bourgeoisie cannot exist without constantly revolutionizing the instruments of production, and thereby the relations of production, and with them the whole relations of society. Conservation of the old modes of production in unaltered form, was, on the contrary, the first condition of existence for all earlier industrial classes. Constant revolutionizing of production, uninterrupted disturbance of all social conditions, everlasting uncertainty and agitation distinguish the bourgeois epoch from all earlier ones. All fixed, fast-frozen relations, with their train of ancient and venerable prejudices and opinions, are swept away, all new-formed ones become antiquated before they can ossify. All that is solid melts into air, all that is holy is profaned, and man is at last compelled to face with sober senses his real conditions of life and his relations with his kind.

The need of a constantly expanding market for its products chases the bourgeoisie over the whole surface of the globe. It must nestle everywhere, settle everywhere, establish connections everywhere.

The bourgeoisie has through its exploitation of the world market given a cosmopolitan character to production and consumption in every country. To the great chagrin of reactionaries, it has drawn from under the feet of industry the national ground on which it stood. All old-established national industries have been destroyed or are daily being destroyed. They are dislodged by new industries, whose introduction becomes a life and death question for all civilized nations, by industries that no longer work up indigenous raw material, but raw material drawn from the remotest zones; industries whose products are consumed, not only at home, but in every quarter of the globe. In place of the old wants, satisfied by the production of the country, we find new wants, requiring for their satisfaction the products of distant lands and climes. In place of the old local and national seclusion and self-sufficiency, we have intercourse in every direction, universal interdependence of nations. And as in material, so also in intellectual production. The intellectual creations of individual nations become common property. National one-sidedness and narrow-mindedness become more and more impossible, and from the numerous national and local literatures there arises a world literature.

The bourgeoisie, by the rapid improvement of all instruments of production, by the immensely facilitated means of communication, draws all nations, even the most barbarian, into civilization. The cheap prices of its commodities are the heavy artillery with which it batters down all Chinese walls, with which it forces the barbarians' intensely obstinate hatred of foreigners to capitulate. It compels all nations, on pain of extinction, to adopt the bourgeois mode of production; it compels them to introduce what it calls civilization into their midst, *i.e.,* to become bourgeois themselves. In a word, it creates a world after its own image.

The bourgeoisie has subjected the country to the rule of the towns. It has created enormous cities, has greatly increased the urban population as compared with the rural, and has thus rescued a considerable part of the population from the idiocy of rural life. Just as it has made the country dependent on the towns, so it has made barbarian and semibarbarian countries dependent on the civilized ones, nations of peasants on nations of bourgeois, the East on the West.

More and more the bourgeoisie keeps doing away with the scattered state of the population, of the means of production, and of property. It has agglomerated population, centralized means of production, and has concentrated property in a few hands. The necessary consequence of this was political centralization. Independent, or but loosely connected provinces, with separate interests, laws, governments and systems of taxation, became lumped together into one nation, with one government, one code of laws, one national class interest, one frontier and one customs tariff.

The bourgeoisie, during its rule of scarce one hundred years, has created more massive and more colossal productive forces than have all preceding generations together. Subjection of nature's forces to man, machinery, application of chemistry to industry and agriculture, steam-navigation, railways, electric telegraphs, clearing of whole continents for cultivation, canalization of rivers, whole populations conjured out of the ground—what earlier century had even a presentiment that such productive forces slumbered in the lap of social labor?

We see then that the means of production and of exchange, which served as the foundation for the growth of the bourgeoisie, were generated in feudal society. At a certain stage in the development of these means of production and of exchange, the conditions under which feudal society produced and exchanged, the feudal organization of agriculture and manufacturing industry, in a word, the feudal relations of property became no longer compatible with the already developed productive forces; they became so many fetters. They had to be burst asunder; they were burst asunder.

Into their place stepped free competition, accompanied by a social and political constitution adapted to it, and by the economic and political sway of the bourgeois class.

A similar movement is going on before our own eyes. Modern bourgeois society with its relations of production, of exchange and of property, a society that has conjured up such gigantic means of production and of exchange, is like the sorcerer who is no longer able to control the powers of the nether world whom he has called up by his spells. For many a decade past the history of industry and commerce is but the history of the revolt of modern productive forces against modern conditions of production, against the property relations that are the conditions for the existence of the bourgeoisie and of its rule. It is enough to mention the commercial crises that by their periodical return put the existence of the entire bourgeois society on trial, each time more threateningly. In these crises a great part not only of the existing products, but also of the previously created productive forces, are periodically destroyed. In these crises there breaks out an epidemic that, in all earlier epochs, would have seemed an absurdity —the epidemic of overproduction. Society suddenly finds itself put back into a state of momentary barbarism; it appears as if a famine, a universal war of devastation had cut off the supply of every means of subsistence; industry and commerce seem to be destroyed. And why? Because there is too much civilization, too much means of subsistence, too much industry, too much commerce. The productive forces at the disposal of society no longer tend to further the development of the conditions of bourgeois property; on the contrary, they have become too powerful for these conditions, by which they are fettered, and no sooner do they overcome these fetters than they bring disorder into the whole of bourgeois society, endanger the existence of bourgeois property. The conditions of bourgeois society are too narrow to comprise the wealth created by them. And how does the bourgeoisie get over these crises? On the one hand by enforced destruction of a mass of productive forces; on the other, by the conquest of new markets, and by the more thorough exploitation of the old ones. That is to say, by paving the way for more extensive and more destructive crises, and by diminishing the means whereby crises are prevented.

The weapons with which the bourgeoisie felled feudalism to the ground are now turned against the bourgeoisie itself.

But not only has the bourgeoisie forged the weapons that bring death to itself; it has also called into existence the men who are to wield those weapons—the modern working class— the proletarians.

In proportion as the bourgeoisie, *i.e.*, capital, is developed, in the same proportion is the proletariat, the modern working class, developed—a class of laborers, who live only so long as they find work, and who find work only so long as their labor increases capital. These laborers, who must sell themselves piecemeal, are a commodity, like every other article of commerce, and are consequently exposed to all the vicissitudes of competition, to all the fluctuations of the market.

Owing to the extensive use of machinery and to division of labor, the work of the proletarians has lost all individual character, and, consequently, all charm for the workman. He becomes an appendage of the machine, and it is only the most simple, most monotonous, and most easily acquired knack, that is required of him. Hence, the cost of production of a workman is restricted, almost entirely, to the means of subsistence that he requires for his maintenance, and for the propagation of his race. But the price of a commodity, and therefore also of labor, is equal to its cost of production. In proportion, therefore, as the repulsiveness of the work increases, the wage decreases. Nay more, in proportion as the use of machinery and division of labor increases, in the same proportion the burden of toil also increases, whether by prolongation of the working hours, by increase of the work exacted in a given time, or by increased speed of the machinery, etc.

Modern industry has converted the little workshop of the patriarchal master into the great factory of the industrial capitalist. Masses of laborers, crowded into the factory, are organized like soldiers. As privates of the industrial army they are placed under the command of a perfect hierarchy of officers and sergeants. Not only are they slaves of the bourgeois class, and of the bourgeois state; they are daily and hourly enslaved by the machine, by the overlooker, and, above all, by the individual bourgeois manufacturer himself. The more openly this despotism proclaims gain to be its end and aim, the more petty, the more hateful and the more embittering it is.

The less the skill and exertion of strength implied in manual labor, in other words, the more modern industry develops, the more is the labor of men superseded by that of women. Differences of age and sex have no longer any distinctive social validity for the working class. All are instruments of labor, more or less expensive to use, according to their age and sex.

No sooner has the laborer received his wages in cash, for the moment escaping exploitation by the manufacturer, than he is set upon by the other portions of the bourgeoisie, the landlord, the shopkeeper, the pawnbroker, etc.

The lower strata of the middle class —the small tradespeople, shopkeepers, and retired tradesmen generally, the handicraftsmen and peasants—all these sink gradually into the proletariat, partly because their diminutive capital does not suffice for the scale on which modern industry is carried on, and is swamped in the competition with the large capitalists, partly because their specialized skill is rendered worthless by new methods of production. Thus the proletariat is recruited from all classes of the population.

The proletariat goes through various stages of development. With its birth begins its struggle with the bourgeoisie. At first the contest is carried on by in-dividual laborers, then by the work people of a factory, then by the operatives of one trade, in one locality, against the individual bourgeois who directly exploits them. They direct their attacks not against the bourgeois conditions of production, but against the instruments of production themselves; they destroy imported wares that compete with their labor, they smash machinery to pieces, they set factories ablaze, they seek to restore by force the vanished status of the workman of the Middle Ages.

At this stage the laborers still form an incoherent mass scattered over the whole country, and broken up by their mutual competition. If anywhere they unite to form more compact bodies, this is not yet the consequence of their own active union, but of the union of the bourgeoisie, which class, in order to attain its own political ends, is compelled to set the whole proletariat in motion, and is moreover still able to do so for a time. At this stage, therefore, the proletarians do not fight their enemies, but the enemies of their enemies, the remnants of absolute monarchy, the landowners, the nonindustrial bourgeois, the petty bourgeoisie. Thus the whole historical movement is concentrated in the hands of the bourgeoisie; every victory so obtained is a victory for the bourgeoisie.

But with the development of industry the proletariat not only increases in number; it becomes concentrated in greater masses, its strength grows, and it feels that strength more. The various interests and conditions of life within the ranks of the proletariat are more and more equalized, in proportion as machinery obliterates all distinctions of labor and nearly everywhere reduces wages to the same low level. The growing competition among the bourgeois, and the resulting commercial crises, make the wages of the workers ever more fluctuating. The unceasing improvement of machinery, ever more rapidly developing, makes their livelihood more and more precarious; the collisions between individual workmen and individual bourgeois take more and more the character of collisions between two classes. Thereupon the workers begin to form combinations (trade unions) against the bourgeoisie; they club together in order to keep up the rate of wages; they found permanent associations in order to make provision beforehand for these occasional revolts. Here and there the contest breaks out into riots.

Now and then the workers are victorious, but only for a time. The real fruit of their battles lies, not in the immediate results, but in the ever expanding union of the workers. This union is furthered by the improved means of communication which are created by modern industry, and which place the workers of different localities in contact with one another. It was just this contact that was needed to centralize the numerous local struggles, all of the same character, into one national struggle between classes. But every class struggle is a political struggle. And that union, to attain which the burghers of the Middle Ages, with their miserable highways, required centuries, the modern proletarians, thanks to railways, achieve in a few years.

This organization of the proletarians into a class, and consequently into a political party, is continually being upset again by the competition between the workers themselves. But it ever rises up again, stronger, firmer, mightier. It compels legislative recognition of particular interests of the workers, by taking advantage of the divisions among the bourgeoisie itself.

Thus the ten-hour bill in England was carried.

Altogether, collisions between the classes of the old society further the course of development of the proletariat in many ways. The bourgeoisie finds itself involved in a constant battle. At first with the aristocracy; later on, with those portions of the bourgeoisie itself whose interests have become antagonistic to the progress of industry; at all times with the bourgeoisie of foreign countries. In all these battles it sees itself compelled to appeal to the proletariat, to ask for its help, and thus, to drag it into the political arena. The bourgeoisie itself, therefore, supplies the proletariat with its own elements of political and general education, in other words, it furnishes the proletariat with weapons for fighting the bourgeoisie.

Further, as we have already seen, entire sections of the ruling classes are, by the advance of industry, precipitated into the proletariat, or are at least threatened in their conditions of existence. These also supply the proletariat with fresh elements of enlightenment and progress.

Finally, in times when the class struggle nears the decisive hour, the process of dissolution going on within the ruling class, in fact within the whole range of old society, assumes such a violent, glaring character, that a small section of the ruling class cuts itself adrift, and joins the revolutionary class, the class that holds the future in its hands. Just as, therefore, at an earlier period, a section of the nobility went over to the bourgeoisie, so now a portion of the bourgeoisie goes over to the proletariat, and in particular, a portion of the bourgeois ideologists, who have raised themselves to the level of comprehending theoretically the historical movement as a whole.

Of all the classes that stand face to face with the bourgeoisie today, the proletariat alone is a really revolutionary class. The other classes decay and finally disappear in the face of modern industry; the proletariat is its special and essential product.

The lower middle class, the small manufacturer, the shopkeeper, the artisan, the peasant, all these fight against the bourgeoisie, to save from extinction their existence as fractions of the middle class. They are therefore not revolutionary, but conservative. Nay more, they are reactionary, for they try to roll back the wheel of history. If by chance they are revolutionary, they are so only in view of their impending transfer into the proletariat; they thus defend not their present, but their future interests; they desert their own standpoint to adopt that of the proletariat.

The "dangerous class," the social scum (*Lumpenproletariat*), that passively rotting mass thrown off by the lowest layers of old society, may, here and there, be swept into the movement by a proletarian revolution; its conditions of life, however, prepare it far more for the part of a bribed tool of reactionary intrigue.

The social conditions of the old society no longer exist for the proletariat. The proletarian is without property; his relation to his wife and children has no longer anything in common with bourgeois family relations; modern industrial labor, modern subjection to capital, the same in England as in France, in America as in Germany, has stripped him of every trace of national character. Law, morality, religion, are to him so many bourgeois prejudices, behind which lurk in ambush just as many bourgeois interests.

All the preceding classes that got the upper hand, sought to fortify their already acquired status by subjecting society at large to their conditions of appropriation. The proletarians cannot become masters of the productive forces of society, except by abolishing their own previous mode of appropriation, and thereby also every other previous mode of appropriation. They have nothing of their own to secure and to fortify; their mission is to destroy all previous securities for, and insurances of, individual property.

All previous historical movements were movements of minorities, or in the interest of minorities. The proletarian movement is the self-conscious, independent movement of the immense majority, in the interest of the immense majority. The proletariat, the lowest stratum of our present society, cannot stir, cannot raise itself up, without the whole superincumbent strata of official society being sprung into the air.

Though not in substance, yet in form, the struggle of the proletariat with the bourgeoisie is at first a national struggle. The proletariat of each country must, of course, first of all settle matters with its own bourgeoisie.

In depicting the most general phases of the development of the proletariat, we traced the more or less veiled civil war, raging within existing society, up to the point where that war breaks out into open revolution, and where the violent overthrow of the bourgeoisie lays the foundation for the sway of the proletariat.

Hitherto, every form of society has been based, as we have already seen, on the antagonism of oppressing and oppressed classes. But in order to oppress a class, certain conditions must be assured to it under which it can, at least, continue its slavish existence. The serf, in the period of serfdom, raised himself to membership in the commune, just as the petty bourgeois, under the yoke of feudal absolutism, managed to develop into a bourgeois. The modern laborer, on the contrary, instead of rising with the progress of industry, sinks deeper and deeper below the conditions of existence of his own class. He becomes a pauper, and pauperism develops more rapidly than population and wealth. And here it becomes evident, that the bourgeoisie is unfit any longer to be the ruling class in society, and to impose its conditions of existence upon society as an overriding law. It is unfit to rule because it is incompetent to assure an existence to its slave within his slavery, because it cannot help letting him sink into such a state, that it has to feed him, instead of being fed by him. Society can no longer live under this bourgeoisie, in other words, its existence is no longer compatible with society.

The essential condition for the existence and sway of the bourgeois class, is the formation and augmentation of capital; the condition for capital is wage-labor. Wage-labor rests exclusively on competition between the laborers. The advance of industry, whose involuntary promoter is the bourgeoisie, replaces the isolation of the laborers, due to competition, by their revolutionary combination, due to association. The development of modern industry, therefore, cuts from under its feet the very foundation on which the bourgeoisie produces and appropriates products. What the bourgeoisie therefore produces, above all, are its own gravediggers. Its fall and the victory of the proletariat are equally inevitable.

2

CLASS, STATUS, PARTY

Max Weber

Many of the writings of the famous German sociologist Max Weber (1864–1920) were directed implicitly against Marxism, and biographers have suggested that in many of his works he is battling with the ghost of Karl Marx. This was certainly true of his most famous work, *The Protestant Ethic and the Spirit of Capitalism,* where Weber attempted to account for the rise of capitalism in the West. In so doing he took direct issue with Marx's theory of historical materialism that attributed the rise of capitalism to the development of the material forces of production and the emergence of a new and powerful bourgeois class. Weber stressed instead the importance of the Protestant Reformation and the role of religious ideas in setting free the incipient forces of capitalism.

SOURCE: Hans H. Gerth and C. Wright Mills, eds. and trans., *From Max Weber: Essays in Sociology* (New York: Oxford University Press, 1946), pp. 180–95. Copyright 1946 by Oxford University Press, Inc. Reprinted by permission of the publisher.

Weber's discussion of social classes is also a challenge to Marxism, though a more modest one, for it is not only quite brief, but also not linked to any greater theoretical scheme—to any theory of politics, economics, or history—as was that of Marx.

Marx's view of class was primarily unidimensional, that is, a single criterion—one's position with respect to the means of production—determined one's position in the stratification order. Weber's view of class is called today *multidimensional;* that is, he saw several different and distinct hierarchies. And, it is Weber's recognition that stratification consists of several possibly independent dimensions that is regarded as his major contribution to the study of social classes.

Weber discussed three major dimensions of stratification systems—class, status, and power.* Weber's definition of class, per se, was very similar to Marx's, though dressed up in slightly different terminology. Essentially, class was an economic category determined by one's "life chances in the market place"—one's source of income and the type of property or skills one possessed.

Where Weber differed from Marx was not in his definition of what a class was, but in the area of class solidarity, class interest, and class consciousness. Weber believed class interests were much less salient and binding than did Marx, akin perhaps to mere interest groups that had a fleeting identity of purpose. Weber argued that the bonds of class membership were essentially weak and that common action of class "members" would be limited to transient economic issues. In this sense, Weber did not believe that classes were communities, that is, cohesive, self-conscious, permanently interacting groups of individuals.

While class for Weber was a strictly objective dimension of stratification, status was a subjective dimension roughly equivalent to prestige, honor, or reputation. And, while class was determined by one's role in the market place, status was determined primarily by one's style of life, how one consumed rather than how one produced. Status groups *were* communities in that they are composed of persons who have similar standing, who recognize each other as social equals, visit in each other's homes, dine together, intermarry, and, in general, travel in the same circles.

But isn't it true that one's class position is the same as one's status position? Isn't it true that a person's occupation or source of wealth or life chances in the market place determines his prestige or status? Isn't status merely the subjective counterpart of class, and if so, what is the purpose of making a distinction between them? Weber's answer is that while class and status are often equal—someone belonging to a very well regarded status group will usually belong to a high economic class—the two are not always identical. Some typical examples might be: an old aristocratic family, once of great wealth, now impoverished; a family of new or recent wealth, with obscure or undistinguished ancestry or perhaps lacking the social accoutrements such as education, manners, or artistic taste; a family of great wealth, but acquired by disreputable means; a wealthy family belonging to a despised ethnic or racial minority; lower white-collar groups whose income is lower than many skilled or even semiskilled manual workers but whose status is higher because they do not engage in manual toil.

It seems especially likely that an old upper class, in its efforts to restrict access to its exclusive circle, will place status barriers between themselves and other wealthy persons who are their class equals. If wealth alone were the criterion for admission to upper-class acceptability, that group might be filled to overflowing, for wealth can be acquired. It is, therefore, insufficient for an upper class to insist upon mere wealth to maintain its traditional exclusiveness. It is common for the upper class to demand

---

* Weber spoke of parties, but we shall call this dimension power, as do most contemporary writers.

things that cannot be bought or acquired in this lifetime, such as ancestry or racial and ethnic purity. These cannot be easily acquired and effectively limit the entry of persons into an old upper class. Only with the passage of time can a wealthy family achieve ancestry. As one parvenu said, bemoaning his inability to be socially accepta- ble: "I want only one thing in life—to be my own grandson."

By stressing that status depended upon style of life, Weber perhaps gave inadequate attention to the fact that one's status in a community could be determined by things other than life style, namely, ancestry, religion, or race. Especially in the higher strata, these things are as important to status as one's manner of living.

Weber was rather vague in his discussion of the third dimension of stratification— power—but again its usefulness is that it once more allows the analysis of those whose status and class positions differ from their power position, however power may be de- fined.

What then is the utility of Weber's multidimensional approach to stratification? First, it demonstrates that there may be several stratification hierarchies, each one in- dependent of the other. Second, it allows one to see that there may be inconsistencies in the placement of persons on these multiple hierarchies, that individuals may oc- cupy different positions in the several hierarchies.

In the last fifteen years or more, the study of positional consistency (referred to as status consistency, congruency, or crystallization) has been a major focus of stratifica- tion research. The guiding idea is that status inconsistency (the ignorant millionaire, the impoverished intellectual, the powerless businessman) is a form of marginality, and that this inconsistency on the several dimensions of the stratification order may breed discontent and resentment. In the perhaps frustrated attempt to equalize his po- sition on a number of stratification hierarchies, the individual may turn to either radi- cal or right-wing political ideologies. Although this multidimensional approach may appeal to sociologists partly out of their unhealthy propensity for the endless multipli- cation of categories of doubtful utility, empirical studies of status inconsistency have produced some suggestive although far from conclusive results. On a broader historical scale, the idea of status inconsistency has been employed to explain a variety of left- and right-wing social movements in America such as nineteenth-century anti-Catholi- cism, the Progressive movement of the early twentieth century, the renewed strength of the Ku Klux Klan in the 1920's, and support for McCarthyism in the 1950's.*

1: Economically Determined Power and the Social Order

Law exists when there is a probability that an order will be upheld by a spe- cific staff of men who will use physical or psychical compulsion with the inten- tion of obtaining conformity with the order, or of inflicting sanctions for in- fringement of it. The structure of every legal order directly influences the dis- tribution of power, economic or other- wise, within its respective community. This is true of all legal orders and not only that of the state. In general, we understand by 'power' the chance of a man or of a number of men to re- alize their own will in a communal action even against the resistance of others who are participating in the action.

'Economically conditioned' power is not, of course, identical with 'power' as

* See Daniel Bell, ed., *The Radical Right* (Garden City, New York: Anchor Books, 1964).

such. On the contrary, the emergence of economic power may be the consequence of power existing on other grounds. Man does not strive for power only in order to enrich himself economically. Power, including economic power, may be valued 'for its own sake.' Very frequently the striving for power is also conditioned by the social 'honor' it entails. Not all power, however, entails social honor: The typical American Boss, as well as the typical big speculator, deliberately relinquishes social honor. Quite generally, 'mere economic' power, and especially 'naked' money power, is by no means a recognized basis of social honor. Nor is power the only basis of social honor. Indeed, social honor, or prestige, may even be the basis of political or economic power, and very frequently has been. Power, as well as honor, may be guaranteed by the legal order, but, at least normally, it is not their primary source. The legal order is rather an additional factor that enhances the chance to hold power or honor; but it cannot always secure them.

The way in which social honor is distributed in a community between typical groups participating in this distribution we may call the 'social order.' The social order and the economic order are, of course, similarly related to the 'legal order.' However, the social and the economic order are not identical. The economic order is for us merely the way in which economic goods and services are distributed and used. The social order is of course conditioned by the economic order to a high degree, and in its turn reacts upon it.

Now: 'classes,' 'status groups,' and 'parties' are phenomena of the distribution of power within a community.

2: Determination of Class-Situation by Market-Situation

In our terminology, 'classes' are not communities; they merely represent possible, and frequent, bases for communal action. We may speak of a 'class' when (1) a number of people have in common a specific causal component of their life chances, in so far as (2) this component is represented exclusively by economic interests in the possession of goods and opportunities for income, and (3) is represented under the conditions of the commodity or labor markets.

It is the most elemental economic fact that the way in which the disposition over material property is distributed among a plurality of people, meeting competitively in the market for the purpose of exchange, in itself creates specific life chances. According to the law of marginal utility this mode of distribution excludes the nonowners from competing for highly valued goods; it favors the owners and, in fact, gives to them a monopoly to acquire such goods. Other things being equal, this mode of distribution monopolizes the opportunities for profitable deals for all those who, provided with goods, do not necessarily have to exchange them. It increases, at least generally, their power in price wars with those who, being propertyless, have nothing to offer but their services in native form or goods in a form constituted through their own labor, and who above all are compelled to get rid of these products in order barely to subsist. This mode of distribution gives to the propertied a monopoly on the possibility of transferring property from the sphere of use as a 'fortune,' to the sphere of 'capital goods'; that is, it gives them the entrepreneurial function and all chances to share directly or indirectly in returns on capital. All this holds true within the area in which pure market conditions prevail. 'Property' and 'lack of property' are, therefore, the basic categories of all class situations. It does not matter whether these two categories become effective in price wars or in competitive struggles.

Within these categories, however, class situations are further differentiated: on the one hand, according to the kind of property that is usable for returns; and, on the other hand, according to the kind of services that can be offered in the market. Ownership of domestic buildings; productive establishments; warehouses; stores; agriculturally usable land, large and small holdings—quantitative differences with possibly qualitative consequences—; ownership of mines; cattle; men (slaves); disposition over mobile instruments of production, or capital goods of all sorts, especially money or objects that can be exchanged for money easily and at any time; disposition over products of one's own labor or of others' labor differing according to their various distances from consumability; disposition over transferable monopolies of any kind—all these distinctions differentiate the class situations of the propertied just as does the 'meaning' which they can and do give to the utilization of property, especially to property which has money equivalence. Accordingly, the propertied, for instance, may belong to the class of rentiers or to the class of entrepreneurs.

Those who have no property but who offer services are differentiated just as much according to their kinds of services as according to the way in which they make use of these services, in a continuous or discontinuous relation to a recipient. But always this is the generic connotation of the concept of class: that the kind of chance in the *market* is the decisive moment which presents a common condition for the individual's fate. 'Class situation' is, in this sense, ultimately 'market situation.' The effect of naked possession *per se,* which among cattle breeders gives the nonowning slave or serf into the power of the cattle owner, is only a forerunner of real 'class' formation. However, in the cattle loan and in the naked severity of the law of debts in such communities, for the first time mere 'possession' as such emerges as decisive for the fate of the individual. This is very much in contrast to the agricultural communities based on labor. The creditor-debtor relation becomes the basis of 'class situations' only in those cities where a 'credit market,' however primitive, with rates of interest increasing according to the extent of dearth and a factual monopolization of credits, is developed by a plutocracy. Therewith 'class struggles' begin.

Those men whose fate is not determined by the chance of using goods or services for themselves on the market, e.g. slaves, are not, however, a 'class' in the technical sense of the term. They are, rather, a 'status group.'

3: Communal Action Flowing from Class Interest

According to our terminology, the factor that creates 'class' is unambiguously economic interest, and indeed, only those interests involved in the existence of the 'market.' Nevertheless, the concept of 'class-interest' is an ambiguous one: even as an empirical concept it is ambiguous as soon as one understands by it something other than the factual direction of interests following with a certain probability from the class situation for a certain 'average' of those people subjected to the class situation. The class situation and other circumstances remaining the same, the direction in which the individual worker, for instance, is likely to pursue his interests may vary widely, according to whether he is constitutionally qualified for the task at hand to a high, to an average, or to a low degree. In the same way, the direction of interests may vary according to whether or not a *communal* action of a larger or smaller portion of those commonly affected by the 'class situation,' or even an association among them, e.g. a 'trade union,' has grown out of the class situation from which the individual may or may not expect promising results. [Communal action refers to that action which is oriented to the feeling of the actors that they belong together. Societal action, on the other hand, is oriented to a rationally motivated adjustment of interests.] The rise of societal or even of communal action from a common class situation is by no means a universal phenomenon.

The class situation may be restricted in its effects to the generation of essentially *similar* reactions, that is to say, within our terminology, of 'mass actions.' However, it may not have even this result. Furthermore, often merely an amorphous communal action emerges. For example, the 'murmuring' of the workers known in ancient oriental ethics: the moral disapproval of the work-master's conduct, which in its practical significance was probably equivalent to an increasingly typical phenomenon of precisely the latest in-

dustrial development, namely, the 'slow down' (the deliberate limiting of work effort) of laborers by virtue of tacit agreement. The degree in which 'communal action' and possibly 'societal action,' emerges from the 'mass actions' of the members of a class is linked to general cultural conditions, especially to those of an intellectual sort. It is also linked to the extent of the contrasts that have already evolved, and is especially linked to the *transparency* of the connections between the causes and the consequences of the 'class situation.' For however different life chances may be, this fact in itself, according to all experience, by no means gives birth to 'class action' (communal action by the members of a class). The fact of being conditioned and the results of the class situation must be distinctly recognizable. For only then the contrast of life chances can be felt not as an absolutely given fact to be accepted, but as a resultant from either (1) the given distribution of property, or (2) the structure of the concrete economic order. It is only then that people may react against the class structure not only through acts of an intermittent and irrational protest, but in the form of rational association. There have been 'class situations' of the first category (1), of a specifically naked and transparent sort, in the urban centers of antiquity and during the Middle Ages; especially then, when great fortunes were accumulated by factually monopolized trading in industrial products of these localities or in foodstuffs. Furthermore, under certain circumstances, in the rural economy of the most diverse periods, when agriculture was increasingly exploited in a profit-making manner. The most important historical example of the second category (2) is the class situation of the modern 'proletariat.'

4: Types of 'Class Struggle'

Thus every class may be the carrier of any one of the possibly innumerable forms of 'class action,' but this is not necessarily so. In any case, a class does not in itself constitute a community. To treat 'class' conceptually as having the same value as 'community' leads to distortion. That men in the same class situation regularly react in mass actions to such tangible situations as economic ones in the direction of those interests that are most adequate to their average number is an important and after all simple fact for the understanding of historical events. Above all, this fact must not lead to that kind of pseudo-scientific operation with the concepts of 'class' and 'class interests' so frequently found these days, and which has found its most classic expression in the statement of a talented author, that the individual may be in error concerning his interests but that the 'class' is 'infallible' about its interests. Yet, if classes as such are not communities, nevertheless class situations emerge only on the basis of communalization. The communal action that brings forth class situations, however, is not basically action between members of the identical class; it is an action between members of different classes. Communal actions that directly determine the class situation of the worker and the entrepreneur are: the labor market, the commodities market, and the capitalistic enterprise. But, in its turn, the existence of a capitalistic enterprise presupposes that a very specific communal action exists and that it is specifically structured to protect the possession of goods *per se,* and especially the power of individuals to dispose, in principle freely, over the means of pro-duction. The existence of a capitalistic enterprise is preconditioned by a specific kind of 'legal order.' Each kind of class situation, and above all when it rests upon the power of property *per se,* will become more clearly efficacious when all other determinants of reciprocal relations are, as far as possible, eliminated in their significance. It is in this way that the utilization of the power of property in the market obtains its most sovereign importance.

Now 'status groups' hinder the strict carrying through of the sheer market principle. In the present context they are of interest to us only from this one point of view. Before we briefly consider them, note that not much of a general nature can be said about the more specific kinds of antagonism between 'classes' (in our meaning of the term). The great shift, which has been going on continuously in the past, and up to our times, may be summarized, although at the cost of some precision: the struggle in which class situations are effective has progressively shifted from consumption credit toward, first, competitive struggles in the commodity market and, then, toward price wars on the labor market. The 'class struggles' of antiquity—to the extent that they were genuine class struggles and not struggles between status groups—were initially carried on by indebted peasants, and perhaps also by artisans threatened by debt bondage and struggling against urban creditors. For debt bondage is the normal result of the differentiation of wealth in commercial cities, especially in seaport cities. A similar situation has existed among cattle breeders. Debt relationships as such produced class action up to the time of Cataline. Along with this, and with an increase in provision of grain for the city by transporting it from the outside, the struggle over the means of sustenance emerged. It centered in the first place around the provision of bread and the determination of the price of bread. It lasted throughout antiquity and the entire Middle Ages. The propertyless as such flocked together against those who actually and supposedly were interested in the dearth of bread. This fight spread until it involved all those commodities essential to the way of life and to handicraft production. There were only incipient discussions of wage disputes in antiquity and in the Middle Ages. But they have been slowly increasing up into modern times. In the earlier periods they were completely secondary to slave rebellions as well as to fights in the commodity market.

The propertyless of antiquity and of the Middle Ages protested against monopolies, pre-emption, forestalling, and the withholding of goods from the market in order to raise prices. Today the central issue is the determination of the price of labor.

This transition is represented by the fight for access to the market and for the determination of the price of products. Such fights went on between merchants and workers in the putting-out system of domestic handicraft during the transition to modern times. Since it is quite a general phenomenon we must mention here that the class antagonisms that are conditioned through the market situation are usually most bitter between those who actually and directly participate as opponents in price wars. It is not the rentier, the share-holder, and the banker who suffer the ill will of the worker, but almost exclusively the manufacturer and the business executives who are the direct opponents of workers in price wars. This is so in spite of the fact that

it is precisely the cash boxes of the rentier, the share-holder, and the banker into which the more or less 'unearned' gains flow, rather than into the pockets of the manufacturers or of the business executives. This simple state of affairs has very frequently been decisive for the role the class situation has played in the formation of political parties. For example, it has made possible the varieties of patriarchal socialism and the frequent attempts—formerly, at least—of threatened status groups to form alliances with the proletariat against the 'bourgeoisie.'

5: Status Honor

In contrast to classes, *status groups* are normally communities. They are, however, often of an amorphous kind. In contrast to the purely economically determined 'class situation' we wish to designate as 'status situation' every typical component of the life fate of men that is determined by a specific, positive or negative, social estimation of *honor*. This honor may be connected with any quality shared by a plurality, and, of course, it can be knit to a class situation: class distinctions are linked in the most varied ways with status distinctions. Property as such is not always recognized as a status qualification, but in the long run it is, and with extraordinary regularity. In the subsistence economy of the organized neighborhood, very often the richest man is simply the chieftain. However, this often means only an honorific preference. For example, in the so-called pure modern 'democracy,' that is, one devoid of any expressly ordered status privileges for individuals, it may be that only the families coming under approximately the same tax class dance with one another. This example is reported of certain smaller Swiss cities. But status honor need not necessarily be linked with a 'class situation.' On the contrary, it normally stands in sharp opposition to the pretensions of sheer property.

Both propertied and propertyless people can belong to the same status group, and frequently they do with very tangible consequences. This 'equality' of social esteem may, however, in the long run become quite precarious. The 'equality' of status among the American 'gentlemen,' for instance, is expressed by the fact that outside the subordination determined by the different functions of 'business,' it would be considered strictly repugnant—wherever the old tradition still prevails —if even the richest 'chief,' while playing billiards or cards in his club in the evening, would not treat his 'clerk' as in every sense fully his equal in birthright. It would be repugnant if the American 'chief' would bestow upon his 'clerk' the condescending 'benevolence' marking a distinction of 'position,' which the German chief can never dissever from his attitude. This is one of the most important reasons why in America the German 'clubby-ness' has never been able to attain the attraction that the American clubs have.

6: Guarantees of Status Stratification

In content, status honor is normally expressed by the fact that above all else a specific *style of life* can be expected from all those who wish to belong to the circle. Linked with this expectation are restrictions on 'social' intercourse (that is, intercourse which is not subservient to economic or any other of business's 'functional' purposes). These restrictions may confine normal marriages to within the status circle and may lead to complete endogamous closure. As soon as there is not a mere individual and socially irrelevant imitation of another style of life, but an agreed-upon communal action of this closing character, the 'status' development is under way.

In its characteristic form, stratification by 'status groups' on the basis of conventional styles of life evolves at the present time in the United States out of the traditional democracy. For example, only the resident of a certain street ('the street') is considered as belonging to 'society,' is qualified for social intercourse, and is visited and invited. Above all, this differentiation evolves in such a way as to make for strict submission to the fashion that is dominant at a given time in society. This submission to fashion also exists among men in America to a degree unknown in Germany. Such submission is considered to be an indication of the fact that a given man *pretends* to qualify as a gentleman. This submission decides, at least *prima facie*, that he will be treated as such. And this recognition becomes just as important for his employment chances in 'swank' establishments, and above all, for social intercourse and marriage with 'esteemed' families, as the qualification for dueling among Germans in the Kaiser's day. As for the rest: certain families resident for a long time, and, of course, correspondingly wealthy, e.g. 'F. F. V., i.e. First Families of Virginia,' or the actual or alleged descendants of the 'Indian Princess' Pocahontas, of the Pilgrim fathers, or of the Knickerbockers, the members of almost inaccessible sects and all sorts of circles setting themselves apart by means of any other characteristics and badges . . . all these elements usurp 'status' honor. The development of status is essentially a question of stratification resting upon usurpation. Such usurpation is the normal origin of almost all status honor. But the road from this purely conventional situation to legal privilege, positive or negative, is easily traveled as soon as a certain stratification of the social order has in fact been 'lived in' and has achieved stability by virtue of a stable distribution of economic power.

7: 'Ethnic' Segregation and 'Caste'

Where the consequences have been realized to their full extent, the status group evolves into a closed 'caste.' Status distinctions are then guaranteed not merely by conventions and laws, but also by *rituals*. This occurs in such a way that every physical contact with a member of any caste that is considered to be 'lower' by the members of a 'higher' caste is considered as making for a ritualistic impurity and to be a stigma which must be expiated by a religious act. Individual castes develop quite distinct cults and gods.

In general, however, the status structure reaches such extreme consequences only where there are underlying differences which are held to be 'ethnic.' The 'caste' is, indeed, the normal form in which ethnic communities usually live side by side in a 'societalized' manner. These ethnic communities believe in blood relationship and exclude exogamous marriage and social intercourse. Such a caste situation is part of the phenomenon of 'pariah' peoples and is found all over the world. These people form communities, acquire spe-

cific occupational traditions of handicrafts or of other arts, and cultivate a belief in their ethnic community. They live in a 'diaspora' strictly segregated from all personal intercourse, except that of an unavoidable sort, and their situation is legally precarious. Yet, by virtue of their economic indispensability, they are tolerated, indeed, frequently privileged, and they live in interspersed political communities. The Jews are the most impressive historical example.

A 'status' segregation grown into a 'caste' differs in its structure from a mere 'ethnic' segregation: the caste structure transforms the horizontal and unconnected coexistences of ethnically segregated groups into a vertical social system of super- and subordination. Correctly formulated: a comprehensive societalization integrates the ethnically divided communities into specific political and communal action. In their consequences they differ precisely in this way: ethnic coexistences condition a mutual repulsion and disdain but allow each ethnic community to consider its own honor as the highest one; the caste structure brings about a social subordination and an acknowledgment of 'more honor' in favor of the privileged caste and status groups. This is due to the fact that in the caste structure ethnic distinctions as such have become 'functional' distinctions within the political societalization (warriors, priests, artisans that are politically important for war and for building, and so on). But even pariah people who are most despised are usually apt to continue cultivating in some manner that which is equally peculiar to ethnic and to status communities: the belief in their own specific 'honor.' This is the case with the Jews.

Only with the negatively privileged

status groups does the 'sense of dignity' take a specific deviation. A sense of dignity is the precipitation in individuals of social honor and of conventional demands which a positively privileged status group raises for the deportment of its members. The sense of dignity that characterizes positively privileged status groups is naturally related to their 'being' which does not transcend itself, that is, it is to their 'beauty and excellence' (χαλο-χάγαδια). Their kingdom is 'of this world.' They live for the present and by exploiting their great past. The sense of dignity of the negatively privileged strata naturally refers to a future lying beyond the present, whether it is of this life or of another. In other words, it must be nurtured by the belief in a providential 'mission' and by a belief in a specific honor before God. The 'chosen people's' dignity is nurtured by a belief either that in the beyond 'the last will be the first,' or that in this life a Messiah will appear to bring forth into the light of the world which has cast them out the hidden honor of the pariah people. This simple state of affairs, and not the 'resentment' which is so strongly emphasized in Nietzsche's much admired construction in the *Genealogy of Morals,* is the source of the religiosity cultivated by pariah status groups. In passing, we may note that resentment may be accurately applied only to a limited extent; for one of Nietzsche's main examples, Buddhism, it is not at all applicable.

Incidentally, the development of status groups from ethnic segregations is by no means the normal phenomenon. On the contrary, since objective 'racial differences' are by no means basic to every subjective sentiment of an ethnic community, the ultimately racial foundation of status structure is rightly and absolutely a question of the concrete individual case. Very frequently a status group is instrumental in the production of a thoroughbred anthropological type. Certainly a status group is to a high degree effective in producing extreme types, for they select personally qualified individuals (e.g. the Knighthood selects those who are fit for warfare, physically and psychically). But selection is far from being the only, or the predominant, way in which status groups are formed: Political membership or class situation has at all times been at least as frequently decisive. And today the class situation is by far the predominant factor, for of course the possibility of a style of life expected for members of a status group is usually conditioned economically.

8: Status Privileges

For all practical purposes, stratification by status goes hand in hand with a monopolization of ideal and material goods or opportunities, in a manner we have come to know as typical. Besides the specific status honor, which always rests upon distance and exclusiveness, we find all sorts of material monopolies. Such honorific preferences may consist of the privilege of wearing special costumes, of eating special dishes taboo to others, of carrying arms—which is most obvious in its consequences—the right to pursue certain non-professional dilettante artistic practices, e.g. to play certain musical instruments. Of course, material monopolies provide the most effective motives for the exclusiveness of a status group; although, in themselves, they are rarely sufficient, almost always they come into play to some extent. Within a status circle there is the question of intermarriage: the interest of the families in the monopolization of potential bridegrooms is at least of equal importance and is parallel to the interest in the monopolization of daughters. The daughters of the circle must be provided for. With an increased inclosure of the status group, the conventional preferential opportunities for special employment grow into a legal monopoly of special offices for the members. Certain goods become objects for monopolization by status groups. In the typical fashion these include 'entailed estates' and frequently also the possessions of serfs or bondsmen and, finally, special trades. This monopolization occurs positively when the status group is exclusively entitled to own and to manage them; and negatively when, in order to maintain its specific way of life, the status group must *not* own and manage them.

The decisive role of a 'style of life' in status 'honor' means that status groups are the specific bearers of all 'conventions.' In whatever way it may be manifest, all 'stylization' of life either originates in status groups or is at least conserved by them. Even if the principles of status conventions differ greatly, they reveal certain typical traits, especially among those strata which are most privileged. Quite generally, among privileged status groups there is a status disqualification that operates against the performance of common physical labor. This disqualification is now 'setting in' in America against the old tradition of esteem for labor. Very frequently every rational economic pursuit, and especially 'entrepreneurial activity,' is looked upon as a disqualification of status. Artistic and literary activity is also considered as degrading work as soon as it is exploited for income, or at least when it is connected with hard physical exertion. An example is the sculptor working like a mason in his dusty smock as over against the painter in his salon-like 'studio' and those forms of musical practice that are acceptable to the status group.

9: Economic Conditions and Effects of Status Stratification

The frequent disqualification of the gainfully employed as such is a direct result of the principle of status stratification peculiar to the social order, and of course, of this principle's opposition to a distribution of power which is regulated exclusively through the market. These two factors operate along with various individual ones, which will be touched upon below.

We have seen above that the market and its processes 'knows no personal distinctions': 'functional' interests dominate it. It knows nothing of 'honor.' The status order means precisely the reverse, viz.: stratification in terms of 'honor' and of styles of life peculiar to status groups as such. If mere economic acquisition and naked economic power still bearing the stigma of its extra-status origin could bestow upon anyone who has won it the same honor as those who are interested in status by virtue of style of life claim for themselves, the status order would be threatened at its very root. This is the more so as, given equality of status honor, property *per se* represents an addition even if it is not overtly acknowledged to be such. Yet if such economic acquisition and power gave the agent any honor at all, his wealth would result in his attaining more honor than those who successfully claim honor by virtue of style of life. Therefore all groups having interests in the status order react with special sharpness precisely against the pretensions of purely economic acquisition. In most cases they react the more vigorously the more they feel themselves threatened. Calderon's respectful treatment of the peasant, for instance, as opposed to Shakespeare's simultaneous and ostensible disdain of the *canaille* illustrates the different way in which a firmly structured status order reacts as compared with a status order that has become economically precarious. This is an example of a state of affairs that recurs everywhere. Precisely because of the rigorous reactions against the claims of property *per se,* the 'parvenu' is never accepted, personally and without reservation, by the privileged status groups, no matter how completely his style of life has been adjusted to theirs. They will only accept his descendants who have been educated in the conventions of their status group and who have never besmirched its honor by their own economic labor.

As to the general *effect* of the status order, only one consequence can be stated, but it is a very important one: the hindrance of the free development of the market occurs first for those goods which status groups directly withheld from free exchange by monopolization. This monopolization may be effected either legally or conventionally. For example, in many Hellenic cities during the epoch of status groups, and also originally in Rome, the inherited estate (as is shown by the old formula for indiction against spendthrifts) was monopolized just as were the estates of knights, peasants, priests, and especially the clientele of the craft and merchant guilds. The market is restricted, and the power of naked property *per se,* which gives its

stamp to 'class formation,' is pushed into the background. The results of this process can be most varied. Of course, they do not necessarily weaken the contrasts in the economic situation. Frequently they strengthen these contrasts, and in any case, where stratification by status permeates a community as strongly as was the case in all political communities of antiquity and of the Middle Ages, one can never speak of a genuinely free market competition as we understand it today. There are wider effects than this direct exclusion of special goods from the market. From the contrariety between the status order and the purely economic order mentioned above, it follows that in most instances the notion of honor peculiar to status absolutely abhors that which is essential to the market: higgling. Honor abhors higgling among peers and occasionally it taboos higgling for the members of a status group in general. Therefore, everywhere some status groups, and usually the most influential, consider almost any kind of overt participation in economic acquisition as absolutely stigmatizing.

With some over-simplification, one might thus say that 'classes' are stratified according to their relations to the production and acquisition of goods; whereas 'status groups' are stratified according to the principles of their *consumption* of goods as represented by special 'styles of life.'

An 'occupational group' is also a status group. For normally, it successfully claims social honor only by virtue of the special style of life which may be determined by it. The differences between classes and status groups frequently overlap. It is precisely those status communities most strictly segregated in terms of honor (viz. the Indian castes) who today show, although within very rigid limits, a relatively high degree of indifference to pecuniary income. However, the Brahmins seek such income in many different ways.

As to the general economic conditions making for the predominance of stratification by 'status,' only very little can be said. When the bases of the acquisition and distribution of goods are relatively stable, stratification by status is favored. Every technological repercussion and economic transformation threatens stratification by status and pushes the class situation into the foreground. Epochs and countries in which the naked class situation is of predominant significance are regularly the periods of technical and economic transformations. And every slowing down of the shifting of economic stratifications leads, in due course, to the growth of status structures and makes for a resuscitation of the important role of social honor.

10: Parties

Whereas the genuine place of 'classes' is within the economic order, the place of 'status groups' is within the social order, that is, within the sphere of the distribution of 'honor.' From within these spheres, classes and status groups influence one another and they influence the legal order and are in turn influenced by it. But 'parties' live in a house of 'power.'

Their action is oriented toward the acquisition of social 'power,' that is to say, toward influencing a communal action no matter what its content may be. In principle, parties may exist in a social 'club' as well as in a 'state.' As over against the actions of classes and status groups, for which this is not necessarily

the case, the communal actions of 'parties' always mean a societalization. For party actions are always directed toward a goal which is striven for in planned manner. This goal may be a 'cause' (the party may aim at realizing a program for ideal or material purposes), or the goal may be 'personal' (sinecures, power, and from these, honor for the leader and the followers of the party). Usually the party action aims at all these simultaneously. Parties are, therefore, only possible within communities that are societalized, that is, which have some rational order and a staff of persons available who are ready to enforce it. For parties aim precisely at influencing this staff, and if possible, to recruit it from party followers.

In any individual case, parties may represent interests determined through 'class situation' or 'status situation,' and they may recruit their following respectively from one or the other. But they need be neither purely 'class' nor purely 'status' parties. In most cases they are partly class parties and partly status parties, but sometimes they are neither. They may represent ephemeral or enduring structures. Their means of attaining power may be quite varied, ranging from naked violence of any sort to canvassing for votes with coarse or subtle means: money, social influence, the force of speech, suggestion, clumsy hoax, and so on to the rougher or more artful tactics of obstruction in parliamentary bodies.

The sociological structure of parties differs in a basic way according to the kind of communal action which they struggle to influence. Parties also differ according to whether or not the community is stratified by status or by classes. Above all else, they vary according to the structure of domination within the community. For their leaders normally deal with the conquest of a community. They are, in the general concept which is maintained here, not only products of specially modern forms of domination. We shall also designate as parties the ancient and medieval 'parties,' despite the fact that their structure differs basically from the structure of modern parties. By virtue of these structural differences of domination it is impossible to say anything about the structure of parties without discussing the structural forms of social domination *per se*. Parties, which are always structures struggling for domination, are very frequently organized in a very strict 'authoritarian' fashion . . .

Concerning 'classes,' 'status groups,' and 'parties,' it must be said in general that they necessarily presuppose a comprehensive societalization, and especially a political framework of communal action, within which they operate. This does not mean that par-ties would be confined by the frontiers of any individual political community. On the contrary, at all times it has been the order of the day that the societalization (even when it aims at the use of military force in common) reaches beyond the frontiers of politics. This has been the case in the solidarity of interests among the Oligarchs and among the democrats in Hellas, among the Guelfs and among Ghibellines in the Middle Ages, and within the Calvinist party during the period of religious struggles. It has been the case up to the solidarity of the landlords (international congress of agrarian landlords), and has continued among princes (holy alliance, Karlsbad decrees), socialist workers, conservatives (the longing of Prussian conservatives for Russian intervention in 1850). But their aim is not necessarily the establishment of new international political, i.e. *territorial,* dominion. In the main they aim to influence the existing dominion.*

---

* The posthumously published text breaks off here. We omit an incomplete sketch of types of 'warrior estates.'

II

THE RELEVANCE
OF SOCIAL
STRATIFICATION
IN MODERN SOCIETY

3

from
CITIZENSHIP AND
SOCIAL CLASS

T. H. Marshall

Whither inequality?

Generally speaking, today there are two schools of thought regarding the trend of social inequality in modern, industrial societies. In the first group are those who support the view that due to a variety of political, economic, and social forces, social-class differences are diminishing, populations are becoming increasingly homogeneous with regard to level of living and style of life, and consequently, the tools and assumptions in the field of social stratification are of decreasing utility in the analysis of modern society.

A second school holds that despite the absolute rise in the material standard of living for most citizens, the distribution of wealth and income in society remains grossly unequal, that there are still great differences in the life style of various groups, that, all things considered, social-class differences are not being overcome, and that modern society can still be analyzed and understood in terms of its division into social classes. In this section we shall present some of the best arguments recently made for each point of view.

We begin with an excerpt from the book *Citizenship and Social Class,* originally presented as a series of lectures at Cambridge in 1949 by the distinguished British sociologist, T. H. Marshall. Although his discussion is based on an analysis of recent British history, Marshall's remarks are applicable to the United States as well as to other Western democracies.

To state his thesis as simply as possible, Marshall argues that for about the last two-and-a-half centuries a silent contest has been waged between the forces of equality and the forces of inequality. This takes the form of a struggle between two major sets of forces: first, the growing

SOURCE: T. H. Marshall, *Citizenship and Social Class* (London: Cambridge University Press, 1950), pp. 91–106. Copyright © 1963 by T. H. Marshall. Reprinted by permission of Doubleday & Company, Inc., and Heinemann Educational Books, Ltd.

strength of political democracy that consistently drives for greater equality for all men; and second, opposing this are certain aspects of our economic institutions that give rise to and sustain great inequality, as people enter into the market place to earn a living and are accordingly rewarded unequally depending upon the positions they occupy.

What are the instruments by which political democracy wages this "war" against inequality? Marshall invokes here the concept of *citizenship* that operates in two ways to diminish inequality. First, the rights of citizenship are gradually extended to more people within the society, and second, the meaning and content of citizenship itself is enlarged and enriched.

In his essay, Marshall speaks of three types of citizenship that have evolved and been extended to all citizens since about the eighteenth century: (1) civil citizenship, consisting of those things associated with our Bill of Rights: freedom of speech, thought, association, religion, equal justice before the law, plus the right to own property and conclude contracts; (2) political citizenship, involving the franchise and the right to run for and hold political office; and (3) social citizenship, including the ever-growing list of benefits associated with the welfare state: universal public education, factory legislation, unemployment insurance, national health care, guaranteed annual income, wars on poverty, and the like.

Tracing their development, Marshall claims that civil, political, and social citizenship evolved respectively during the eighteenth, nineteenth, and twentieth centuries. The major difference between the preindustrial and the modern period is that during the former, class differences were not mitigated by universal rights of citizenship to which all men were entitled; citizenship was highly restricted to those in the upper classes. Thus, political inequality was superimposed upon economic inequality. Today, however, universal rights of citizenship, though admittedly imperfect in their operation, nevertheless apply to all regardless of class. These rights, therefore, tend to level social-class differences. Marshall believes that the progressive development of these rights of citizenship, and the gradual inclusion of more people as full citizens, have done much to eliminate many of the traditional inequalities among men. He believes the forces of equality and democracy will win out against the forces of inequality. ". . . it may be," he concludes, "that the inequalities permitted . . . by citizenship do not any longer constitute class distinctions in the sense in which that term is used for past societies."

The Early Impact of Citizenship on Social Class

So far my aim has been to trace in outline the development of citizenship in England to the end of the nineteenth century. For this purpose I have divided citizenship into three elements, civil, political, and social. I have tried to show that civil rights came first, and were established in something like their modern form before the first Reform Act was passed in 1832. Political rights came next, and their extension was one of the main features of the nineteenth century, although the principle of universal political citizenship was not recognized until 1918. Social rights, on the other hand, sank to vanishing point in the eighteenth and early nineteenth centuries. Their revival began with the development of public elementary education, but it was not until the twentieth century that they attained to equal partnership with the other two elements in citizenship.

I have as yet said nothing about social class, and I should explain here that social class occupies a secondary position in my theme. I do not propose to embark on the long and difficult task of examining its nature and analysing its components. Time would not allow me to do justice to so formidable a subject. My primary concern is with citizenship, and my special interest is in its impact on social inequality. I shall discuss the nature of social class only so far as is necessary for the pursuit of this special interest. I have paused in the narrative at the end of the nineteenth century because I believe that the impact of citizenship on social inequality after that date was fundamentally different from what it had been before it. That statement is not likely to be disputed. It is the exact nature of the difference that is worth exploring. Before going any further, therefore, I shall try to draw some general conclusions about the impact of citizenship on social inequality in the earlier of the two periods.

Citizenship is a status bestowed on those who are full members of a community. All who possess the status are equal with respect to the rights and duties with which the status is endowed. There is no universal principle that determines what those rights and duties shall be, but societies in which citizenship is a developing institution create an image of an ideal citizenship against which achievement can be measured and towards which aspiration can be directed. The urge forward along the path thus plotted is an urge towards a fuller measure of equality, an enrichment of the stuff of which the status is made and an increase in the number of those on whom the status is bestowed. Social class, on the other hand, is a system of inequality. And it too, like citizenship, can be based on a set of ideals, beliefs, and values. It is therefore reasonable to expect that the impact of citizenship on social class should take the form of a conflict between opposing principles. If I am right in my contention that citizenship has been a developing institution in England at least since the latter part of the seventeenth century, then it is clear that its growth coincides with the rise of capitalism, which is a system, not of equality, but of inequality. Here is something that needs explaining. How is it that these two opposing principles could grow and flourish side by side in the same soil? What made it possible for them to be reconciled with one another and to become, for a time at least, allies instead of antagonists? The question is a pertinent one, for it is clear that, in the twentieth century, citizenship and the capitalist class system have been at war.

It is at this point that a closer scrutiny of social class becomes necessary. I cannot attempt to examine all its many and varied forms, but there is one broad distinction between two different types of class which is particularly relevant to my argument. In the first of these, class is based on a hierarchy of status, and the difference between one class and another is expressed in terms of legal rights and of established customs which have the essential binding character of law. In its extreme form such a system divides a society into a number of distinct, hereditary human species—patricians, plebeians, serfs, slaves, and so forth. Class is, as it were, an institution in its own right, and the whole structure has the quality of a plan, in the sense that it is endowed with meaning and purpose and accepted as a natural order. The civilization at each level is an expression of this meaning and of this natural order, and differences between social levels are not differences in standard of living, because there is no common standard by which they can be measured. Nor are there any rights—at least none of any significance—which all share in common.[1] The impact of citizenship on such a system was bound to be profoundly disturbing, and even destructive. The rights with which the general status of citizenship was invested were extracted from the hierarchical status system of social class, robbing it of its essential substance. The equality implicit in the concept of citizenship, even though limited in content, undermined the inequality of the class system, which was in principle a total inequality. National justice and a law common to all must inevitably weaken and eventually destroy class justice, and personal freedom, as a universal birthright, must drive out serfdom. No subtle argument is needed to show that citizenship is incompatible with medieval feudalism.

Social class of the second type is not so much an institution in its own right as a by-product of other institutions. Although we may still refer to 'social status', we are stretching the term beyond its strict technical meaning when we do so. Class differences are not established and defined by the laws and customs of the society (in the medieval sense of that phrase), but emerge from the interplay of a variety of factors related to the institutions of property and education and the structure of the national economy. Class cultures dwindle to a minimum, so that it becomes possible, though admittedly not wholly satisfactory, to measure the different levels of economic welfare by reference to a common standard of living. The working classes, instead of inheriting a distinctive though simple culture, are provided with a cheap and shoddy imitation of a civilization that has become national.

It is true that class still functions. Social inequality is regarded as necessary and purposeful. It provides the incentive to effort and designs the distribution of power. But there is no over-all pattern of inequality, in which an appropriate value is attached, *a priori*, to each social level. Inequality therefore, though necessary, may become excessive. As Patrick Colquhoun said, in a much-quoted passage: 'Without a large proportion of poverty there could be no riches, since riches are the offspring of labour, while labour can result only from a state of poverty. . . . Poverty therefore is a most necessary and indispensable ingredient in society, without which nations and communities could not exist in a state of civilization'.[2] But Colquhoun, while accepting poverty, deplored 'indigence', or, as we should say, destitution. By 'poverty' he meant the situation of a man who, owing to lack of any economic reserves, is obliged to work, and to work hard, in order to live. By 'indigence' he meant the situation of a family which lacks the minimum necessary for decent living. The system of inequality which allowed the former to exist as a driving force inevitably produced a certain amount of the latter as well. Colquhoun, and other humanitarians, regretted this and sought means to alleviate the suffering it caused. But they did not question the justice of the system of inequality as a whole. It could be argued, in defence of its justice, that,

[1] See the admirable characterization given by R. H. Tawney in *Equality*, pp. 121–2.
[2] *A Treatise on Indigence* (1806), pp. 7–8.

although poverty might be necessary, it was not necessary that any particular family should remain poor, or quite as poor as it was. The more you look on wealth as conclusive proof of merit, the more you incline to regard poverty as evidence of failure—but the penalty for failure may seem to be greater than the offence warrants. In such circumstances it is natural that the more unpleasant features of inequality should be treated, rather irresponsibly, as a nuisance, like the black smoke that used to pour unchecked from our factory chimneys. And so in time, as the social conscience stirs to life, class-abatement, like smoke-abatement, becomes a desirable aim to be pursued as far as is compatible with the continued efficiency of the social machine.

But class-abatement in this form was not an attack on the class system. On the contrary it aimed, often quite consciously, at making the class system less vulnerable to attack by alleviating its less defensible consequences. It raised the floor-level in the basement of the social edifice, and perhaps made it rather more hygienic than it was before. But it remained a basement, and the upper stories of the building were unaffected. And the benefits received by the unfortunate did not flow from an enrichment of the status of citizenship. Where they were given officially by the State, this was done by measures which, as I have said, offered alternatives to the rights of citizenship, rather than additions to them. But the major part of the task was left to private charity, and it was the general, though not universal, view of charitable bodies that those who received their help had no personal right to claim it.

Nevertheless it is true that citizenship, even in its early forms, was a principle of equality, and that during this period it was a developing institution. Starting at the point where all men were free and, in theory, capable of enjoying rights, it grew by enriching the body of rights which they were capable of enjoying. But these rights did not conflict with the inequalities of capitalist society; they were, on the contrary, necessary to the maintenance of that particular form of inequality. The explanation lies in the fact that the core of citizenship at this stage was composed of civil rights. And civil rights were indispensable to a competitive market economy. They gave to each man, as part of his individual status, the power to engage as an independent unit in the economic struggle and made it possible to deny to him social protection on the ground that he was equipped with the means to protect himself. Maine's famous dictum that 'the movement of the progressive societies has hitherto been a movement from Status to Contract' [3] expresses a profound truth which has been elaborated, with varying terminology, by many sociologists, but it requires qualification. For both status and contract are present in all but the most primitive societies. Maine himself admitted this when, later in the same book, he wrote that the earliest feudal communities, as contrasted with their archaic predecessors, 'were neither bound together by mere sentiment nor recruited by a fiction. The tie which united them was Contract.' [4] But the contractual element in feudalism co-existed with a class system based on status and, as contract hardened into custom, it

[3] H. S. Maine: *Ancient Law* (1878), p. 170.
[4] ibid., p. 365.

helped to perpetuate class status. Custom retained the form of mutual undertakings, but not the reality of a free agreement. Modern contract did not grow out of feudal contract; it marks a new development to whose progress feudalism was an obstacle that had to be swept aside. For modern contract is essentially an agreement between men who are free and equal in status, though not necessarily in power. Status was not eliminated from the social system. Differential status, associated with class, function, and family, was replaced by the single uniform status of citizenship, which provided the foundation of equality on which the structure of inequality could be built.

When Maine wrote, this status was clearly an aid, and not a menace, to capitalism and the free-market economy, because it was dominated by civil rights, which confer the legal capacity to strive for the things one would like to possess but do not guarantee the possession of any of them. A property right is not a right to possess property, but a right to acquire it, if you can, and to protect it, if you can get it. But, if you use these arguments to explain to a pauper that his property rights are the same as those of a millionaire, he will probably accuse you of quibbling. Similarly, the right to freedom of speech has little real substance if, from lack of education, you have nothing to say that is worth saying, and no means of making yourself heard if you say it. But these blatant inequalities are not due to defects in civil rights, but to lack of social rights, and social rights in the mid-nineteenth century were in the doldrums. The Poor Law was an aid, not a menace, to capitalism, because it relieved industry of all social responsibility outside the contract of employment, while sharpening the edge of competition in the labour market. Elementary schooling was also an aid, because it increased the value of the worker without educating him above his station.

But it would be absurd to contend that the civil rights enjoyed in the eighteenth and nineteenth centuries were free from defects, or that they were as egalitarian in practice as they professed to be in principle. Equality before the law did not exist. The right was there, but the remedy might frequently prove to be out of reach. The barriers between rights and remedies were of two kinds: the first arose from class prejudice and partiality, the second from the automatic effects of the unequal distribution of wealth, working through the price system. Class prejudice, which undoubtedly coloured the whole administration of justice in the eighteenth century, cannot be eliminated by law, but only by social education and the building of a tradition of impartiality. This is a slow and difficult process, which presupposes a change in the climate of thought throughout the upper ranks of society. But it is a process which I think it is fair to say has been successfully accomplished, in the sense that the tradition of impartiality as between social classes is firmly established in our civil justice. And it is interesting that this should have happened without any fundamental change in the class structure of the legal profession. We have no exact knowledge on this point, but I doubt whether the picture has radically altered since Professor Ginsberg found that the proportion of those admitted to Lincoln's Inn whose fathers were wage earners had risen from 0.4 percent. in 1904–8 to 1.8 percent. in 1923–7, and that at this latter date nearly 72 percent. were sons of professional men, high-ranking business men and gentlemen.[5] The decline of class prejudice as a barrier to the full enjoyment of rights is, therefore, due less to the dilution of class monopoly in the legal profession than to the spread in all classes of a more humane and realistic sense of social equality.

It is interesting to compare with this the corresponding development in the field of political rights. Here too class prejudice, expressed through the intimidation of the lower classes by the upper, prevented the free exercise of the right to vote by the newly enfranchised. In this case a practical remedy was available, in the secret ballot. But that was not enough. Social education, and a change of mental climate, were needed as well. And, even when voters felt free from undue influence, it still took some time to break down the idea, prevalent in the working as well as other classes, that the representatives of the people, and still more the members of the government, should be drawn from among the *élites* who were born, bred, and educated for leadership. Class monopoly in politics, unlike class monopoly in law, has definitely been overthrown. Thus, in these two fields, the same goal has been reached by rather different paths.

The removal of the second obstacle, the effects of the unequal distribution of wealth, was technically a simple matter in the case of political rights, because it costs little or nothing to register a vote. Nevertheless, wealth can be used to influence an election, and a series of measures was adopted to reduce this influence. The earlier ones, which go back to the seventeenth century, were directed against bribery and corruption, but the later ones, especially from 1883 onwards, had the wider aim of limiting election expenses in general, in order that candidates of unequal wealth might fight on more or less equal terms. The need for such equalizing measures has now greatly diminished, since working-class candidates can get financial support from party and other funds. Restrictions which prevent competitive extravagance are, therefore, probably welcomed by all. It remained to open the House of Commons to men of all classes, regardless of wealth, first by abolishing the property qualification for members, and then by introducing payment of members in 1911.

It has proved far more difficult to achieve similar results in the field of civil rights, because litigation, unlike voting, is very expensive. Court fees are not high, but counsel's fees and solicitor's charges may mount up to very large sums indeed. Since a legal action takes the form of a contest, each party feels that his chances of winning will be improved if he secures the services of better champions than those employed on the other side. There is, of course, some truth in this, but not as much as is popularly believed. But the effect in litigation, as in elections, is to introduce an element of competitive extravagance which makes it difficult to estimate in advance what the costs of an action will amount to. In addition, our system by which costs are normally awarded to the winner increases the risk and the uncertainty. A man of limited means, knowing that, if he loses, he will have to pay his opponent's costs (after they have been pruned by the Taxing Master) as well as his own, may easily be frightened into accepting an unsatisfactory settle-

[5] M. Ginsberg: *Studies in Sociology*, p. 171.

ment, especially if his opponent is wealthy enough not to be bothered by any such considerations. And even if he wins, the taxed costs he recovers will usually be less than his actual expenditure, and often considerably less. So that, if he has been induced to fight his case expensively, the victory may not be worth the price paid.

What, then, has been done to remove these barriers to the full and equal exercise of civil rights? Only one thing of real substance, the establishment in 1846 of the County Courts to provide cheap justice for the common people. This important innovation has had a profound and beneficial effect on our legal system, and done much to develop a proper sense of the importance of the case brought by the small man —which is often a very big case by his standards. But County Court costs are not negligible, and the jurisdiction of the County Courts is limited. The second major step taken was the development of a poor person's procedure, under which a small fraction of the poorer members of the community could sue *in forma pauperis,* practically free of all cost, being assisted by the gratuitous and voluntary services of the legal profession. But, as the income limit was extremely low (£2 a week since 1919), and the procedure did not apply in the County Courts, it has had little effect except in matrimonial causes. The supplementary service of free legal advice was, until recently, provided by the unaided efforts of voluntary bodies. But the problem has not been overlooked, nor the reality of the defects in our system denied. It has attracted increasing attention during the

last hundred years. The machinery of the Royal Commission and the Committee has been used repeatedly, and some reforms of procedure have resulted. Two such Committees are at work now, but it would be most improper for me to make any reference to their deliberations.[6] A third, which started earlier, issued a report on which is based the Legal Aid and Advice Bill laid before parliament just three months ago.[7] This is a bold measure, going far beyond anything previously attempted for the assistance of the poorer litigants, and I shall have more to say about it later on.

It is apparent from the events I have briefly narrated that there developed, in the latter part of the nineteenth century, a growing interest in equality as a principle of social justice and an appreciation of the fact that the formal recognition of an equal capacity for rights was not enough. In theory even the complete removal of all the barriers that separated civil rights from their remedies would not have interfered with the principles or the class structure of the capitalist system. It would, in fact, have created a situation which many supporters of the competitive market economy falsely assumed to be already in existence. But in practice the attitude of mind which inspired the efforts to remove these barriers grew out of a conception of equality which overstepped these narrow limits, the conception of equal social worth, not merely of equal natural rights. Thus although citizenship, even by the end of the nineteenth century, had done little to reduce social inequality, it had helped to guide progress into

[6] The Austin Jones Committee on County Court Procedure and the Evershed Committee on Supreme Court Practice and Procedure. The report of the former and an interim report of the latter have since been published.

[7] The Rushcliffe Committee on Legal Aid and Legal Advice in England and Wales.

the path which led directly to the egalitarian policies of the twentieth century.

It also had an integrating effect, or, at least, was an important ingredient in an integrating process. In a passage I quoted just now Maine spoke of pre-feudal societies as bound together by a sentiment and recruited by a fiction. He was referring to kinship, or the fiction of common descent. Citizenship requires a bond of a different kind, a direct sense of community membership based on loyalty to a civilization which is a common possession. It is a loyalty of free men endowed with rights and protected by a common law. Its growth is stimulated both by the struggle to win those rights and by their enjoyment when won. We see this clearly in the eighteenth century, which saw the birth, not only of modern civil rights, but also of modern national consciousness. The familiar instruments of modern democracy were fashioned by the upper classes and then handed down, step by step, to the lower: political journalism for the intelligentsia was followed by newspapers for all who could read, public meetings, propaganda campaigns and associations for the furtherance of public causes. Repressive measures and taxes were quite unable to stop the flood. And with it came a patriotic nationalism, expressing the unity underlying these controversial outbursts. How deep or widespread this was it is difficult to say, but there can be no doubt about the vigour of its outward manifestation. We still use those typically eighteenth-century songs, 'God Save the King' and 'Rule Britannia', but we omit the passages which would offend our modern, and more modest, sensibilities. This jingo patriotism, and the 'popular and parliamentary agitation' which Temperley found to be 'the main factor in causing the war' of Jenkins's ear,[8] were new phenomena in which can be recognized the first small trickle which grew into the broad stream of the national war efforts of the twentieth century.

This growing national consciousness, this awakening public opinion, and these first stirrings of a sense of community membership and common heritage did not have any material effect on class structure and social inequality for the simple and obvious reason that, even at the end of the nineteenth century, the mass of the working people did not wield effective political power. By that time the franchise was fairly wide, but those who had recently received the vote had not yet learned how to use it. The political rights of citizenship, unlike the civil rights, were full of potential danger to the capitalist system, although those who were cautiously extending them down the social scale probably did not realize quite how great the danger was. They could hardly be expected to foresee what vast changes could be brought about by the peaceful use of political power, without a violent and bloody revolution. The Planned Society and the Welfare State had not yet risen over the horizon or come within the view of the practical politician. The foundations of the market economy and the contractual system seemed strong enough to stand against any probable assault. In fact, there were some grounds for expecting that the working classes, as they became educated, would accept the basic principles of the system and be content to rely for their protection and progress on the civil rights of citizenship,

[8] C. Grant Robertson: *England under the Hanoverians*, p. 491.

which contained no obvious menace to competitive capitalism. Such a view was encouraged by the fact that one of the main achievements of political power in the later nineteenth century was the recognition of the right of collective bargaining. This meant that social progress was being sought by strengthening civil rights, not by creating social rights; through the use of contract in the open market, not through a minimum wage and social security.

But this interpretation underrates the significance of this extension of civil rights in the economic sphere. For civil rights were in origin intensely individual, and that is why they harmonized with the individualistic phase of capitalism. By the device of incorporation groups were enabled to act legally as individuals. This important development did not go unchallenged, and limited liability was widely denounced as an infringement of individual responsibility. But the position of trade unions was even more anomalous, because they did not seek or obtain incorporation. They can, therefore, exercise vital civil rights collectively on behalf of their members without formal collective responsibility, while the individual responsibility of the workers in relation to contract is largely unenforceable. These civil rights became, for the workers, an instrument for raising their social and economic status, that is to say, for establishing the claim that they, as citizens, were entitled to certain social rights. But the normal method of establishing social rights is by the exercise of political power, for social rights imply an absolute right to a certain standard of civilization which

is conditional only on the discharge of the general duties of citizenship. Their content does not depend on the economic value of the individual claimant. There is therefore a significant difference between a genuine collective bargain through which economic forces in a free market seek to achieve equilibrium and the use of collective civil rights to assert basic claims to the elements of social justice. Thus the acceptance of collective bargaining was not simply a natural extension of civil rights; it represented the transfer of an important process from the political to the civil sphere of citizenship. But 'transfer' is, perhaps, a misleading term, for at the time when this happened the workers either did not possess, or had not yet learned to use, the political right of the franchise. Since then they have obtained and made full use of that right. Trade unionism has, therefore, created a secondary system of industrial citizenship parallel with and supplementary to the system of political citizenship.

It is interesting to compare this development with the history of parliamentary representation. In the early parliaments, says Pollard, 'representation was nowise regarded as a means of expressing individual right or forwarding individual interests. It was communities, not individuals, who were represented.' [9] And, looking at the position on the eve of the Reform Act of 1918, he added: 'Parliament, instead of representing communities or families, is coming to represent nothing but individuals.' [10] A system of manhood and womanhood suffrage treats the vote as the voice of the individual. Political parties organize these voices for

[9] R. W. Pollard: *The Evolution of Parliament*, p. 155.
[10] ibid., p. 165.

group action, but they do so nationally and not on the basis of function, locality, or interest. In the case of civil rights the movement has been in the opposite direction, not from the representation of communities to that of individuals, but from the representation of individuals to that of communities. And Pollard makes another point. It was a characteristic of the early parliamentary system, he says, that the representatives were those who had the time, the means, and the inclination to do the job. Election by a majority of votes and strict accountability to the electors was not essential. Constituencies did not instruct their members, and election promises were unknown. Members 'were elected to bind their constituents, and not to be bound by them'.[11] It is not too fanciful to suggest that some of these features are reproduced in modern trade unions, though, of course, with many profound differences. One of these is that trade union officials do not undertake an onerous unpaid job, but enter on a remunerative career. This remark is not meant to be offensive, and, indeed, it would hardly be seemly for a university professor to criticize a public institution on the ground that its affairs are managed largely by its salaried employees.

All that I have said so far has been by way of introduction to my main task. I have not tried to put before you new facts culled by laborious research. The limit of my ambition has been to regroup familiar facts in a pattern which may make them appear to some of you in a new light. I thought it necessary to do this in order to prepare the ground for the more difficult, speculative, and controversial study of the contemporary scene, in which the lead-

ing role is played by the social rights of citizenship. It is to the impact of these on social class that I must now turn my attention.

Social Rights in the Twentieth Century

The period of which I have hitherto been speaking was one during which the growth of citizenship, substantial and impressive though it was, had little direct effect on social inequality. Civil rights gave legal powers whose use was drastically curtailed by class prejudice and lack of economic opportunity. Political rights gave potential power whose exercise demanded experience, organization, and a change of ideas as to the proper functions of government. All these took time to develop. Social rights were at a minimum and were not woven into the fabric of citizenship. The common purpose of statutory and voluntary effort was to abate the nuisance of poverty without disturbing the pattern of inequality of which poverty was the most obviously unpleasant consequence.

A new period opened at the end of the nineteenth century, conveniently marked by Booth's survey of Life and Labour of the People in London and the Royal Commission on the Aged Poor. It saw the first big advance in social rights, and this involved significant changes in the egalitarian principle as expressed in citizenship. But there were other forces at work as well. A rise of money incomes unevenly distributed over the social classes altered the economic distance which separated these

[11] ibid., p. 152.

classes from one another, diminishing the gap between skilled and unskilled labour and between skilled labour and non-manual workers, while the steady increase in small savings blurred the class distinction between the capitalist and the propertyless proletarian. Secondly, a system of direct taxation, ever more steeply graduated, compressed the whole scale of disposable incomes. Thirdly, mass production for the home market and a growing interest on the part of industry in the needs and tastes of the common people enabled the less well-to-do to enjoy a material civilization which differed less markedly in quality from that of the rich than it had ever done before. All this profoundly altered the setting in which the progress of citizenship took place. Social integration spread from the sphere of sentiment and patriotism into that of material enjoyment. The components of a civilized and cultured life, formerly the monopoly of the few, were brought progressively within reach of the many, who were encouraged thereby to stretch out their hands towards those that still eluded their grasp. The diminution of inequality strengthened the demand for its aboli-

tion, at least with regard to the essentials of social welfare.

These aspirations have in part been met by incorporating social rights in the status of citizenship and thus creating a universal right to real income which is not proportionate to the market value of the claimant. Class-abatement is still the aim of social rights, but it has acquired a new meaning. It is no longer merely an attempt to abate the obvious nuisance of destitution in the lowest ranks of society. It has assumed the guise of action modifying the whole pattern of social inequality. It is no longer content to raise the floor-level in the basement of the social edifice, leaving the superstructure as it was. It has begun to remodel the whole building, and it might even end by converting a skyscraper into a bungalow. It is therefore important to consider whether any such ultimate aim is implicit in the nature of this development, or whether, as I put it at the outset, there are natural limits to the contemporary drive towards greater social and economic equality. To answer this question I must survey and analyse the social services of the twentieth century.

4

THE DECLINE AND FALL OF SOCIAL CLASS

Robert A. Nisbet

Pressing the attack from a slightly different point of view, sociologist Robert Nisbet finds himself in basic agreement with Marshall and argues that social class is really no longer a useful concept in the analysis of American society. While social class was an undeniable reality in the United States during the nineteenth century and even into the early years of this century, and while the non-Western world is to this day clearly stratified, Nisbet argues that changes in American society over the past half-century have all but leveled social-class differences and have thus rendered social-class analysis obsolete. That is to say, it is becoming more and more difficult to understand and explain American society using the terminology, concepts, or world-view of social class.

According to Nisbet, although social-class analysis is increasingly outmoded and its application cumbersome, it is clung to by sociologists for traditional or ideological reasons. For whatever cause, there is an extreme reluctance among scientists to relinquish old theories even when the facts no longer fit them. In an effort to keep social-class analysis relevant, sociologists have, according to Nisbet, resorted to statistical gymnastics whose techniques are more formidable than their findings.

It should be noted that Nisbet's essay first appeared in 1959, at the end of a decade of reputed affluence, and before the "discovery" of poverty in the early 1960's. In our opinion Nisbet glosses over many of the important and continuing elements of inequality in American society; and while the long-range political, economic, and social trends in the United States probably point toward an eventual diminution of class differences, the inequalities that remain are significant enough so that social class continues to be one of the most powerful analytical instruments available to the sociologist. Nisbet's essay is presented here as a forceful and articulate expression of the opposing point of view.

The essential argument of this paper may be stated briefly. It is that the term social class is by now useful in historical sociology, in comparative or folk sociology, but that it is nearly valueless for the clarification of the data of wealth, power, and social status in

contemporary United States and much of Western society in general.

I should emphasize that this position is taken without prejudice to the value of a class society. Despite an overwhelming orientation of social scientists during the past century or two to-

SOURCE: *Pacific Sociological Review*, 2 (Spring 1959), pp. 11–17. Copyright © 1958 by *Pacific Sociological Review*. This essay also appeared in Robert A. Nisbet, *Tradition and Revolt* (New York: Random House, 1968), pp. 105–127. Reprinted by permission of the author and *Pacific Sociological Review*.

ward equalitarianism, the evidence is far from clear that a classless society would be a good society. It may well be that the ideology of equalitarianism, with its components of ever-ready amiability, other-directedness, celebration of the common man, and gravity toward consensus, has much to do with the rampant invasion of privacy and erosion of individuality which have so often made it difficult to hold high the banner of intellectualism and cultural standards in our society. Further, social class has often been a bulwark against political power. Indeed, the historical evidence is clear that in the development of human civilization some astonishing outbursts of creativity have been closely associated with class societies.

But my concern here is not whether a class society is good or bad. The question is, rather, may American society at the present time reasonably and objectively be called a class society? It is well to look first at a few clear-cut definitions of class.

A class society, the anthropologist Goldschmidt writes, is "one in which the hierarchy of prestige and status is divisible into groups each with its own economic, attitudinal, and cultural characteristics and each having differential degrees of power in community decisions." [1] Richard Centers, writing from a more psychological point of view, has emphasized that "a man's class is a part of his ego, *a feeling on his part of belongingness to something; an identification with something larger than himself.*" [2] Halbwachs writes that in a society composed of social classes, "each of these social categories deter-

mines the conduct of its members and imposes definite motivations on them; it stamps each category with such a peculiar and distinctive mark, so forcibly, that men of different classes, even though they live amid the same surroundings and are contemporaries, sometimes strike us as belonging to different species of humanity." [3]

All of these descriptions get at the hard core of social class: class, where it exists, is a tangible relationship; it is substantive, functional, and recognizable through ordinary processes of observation. The proof of existence of a social class worthy of the sociological name should not have to depend upon multi-variate analysis, with correlations generally reaching no higher than .5.

It is of some value, by way of contrast with present confusion, to look back upon the relatively clear and assured view of social class that existed in this country only a half century ago. Recently I treated myself to a re-reading of some of the first-water novels of the turn of the century—by such men as Howells, David Graham Phillips, Dreiser, and Herrick. It is an instructive sociological experience, if only to be reminded that the idea of social class was then as vivid and widely accepted as is today the idea of status mobility. Phrases like "clearly a member of the working class," "by habit and bearing of low class origin," "upper class dress," "of low class mentality and deportment," etc., abound in unambiguous contexts.

Turn to the sociological writings of such men as Cooley, Sumner, and Ross. Here too, along with some penetrating

[1] Walter Goldschmidt, "Social Class in America—A Critical Review," *American Anthropologist,* 52 (October–December, 1950), p. 492.

[2] Richard Centers, *The Psychology of Social Classes,* Princeton: Princeton University Press, 1949, p. 27.

[3] Maurice Halbwachs, *The Psychology of Social Classes,* Glencoe, Ill.: The Free Press, 1958, p. 4.

insights into the nature of social strati-fication, is the unspoken assumption that the reality of class is plain to all, that it needs no substantiation, merely description or analysis. Add to imaginative literature and sociology the lay articles, sermons and orations of the time, and the conclusion is plain that irrespective of the oft-spoken American dream of every man a president, people took class for granted and knew in intimate and daily detail what the content and attributes were of the classes referred to. Despite the ideology of democratic equalitarianism, despite what Tocqueville and Bryce had written about the tenuous character of class lines in the United States, social class, even as recently as 1910, was an understood reality.

How very different is our situation today. It is hard to resist the conclusion that in recent years statistical techniques have had to become ever more ingenious to keep the vision of class from fading away altogether. To this point Arnold Anderson has written cogently: "There is a risk that the search for refined techniques may lead to our unconsciously overlooking the original problem. For example, use of multiple techniques for combining scores on different status scales may yield a valid 'status' score. Social class, however, has traditionally implied membership in groups or quasi-groups." [4] To which I would add that some multiple correlations of status attributes have not only produced sociological monstrosities but, more important, have obscured the data and acted to prevent the appearance of new perspectives in stratification.

Consider for a moment a possible analogy to our preoccupation with social class in the United States: the kinship structure known as the kindred. The kindred is an ancient and real form of association. Almost all human society has been at one time or another based upon it. Even today in the United States the kindred demonstrably exists in our nomenclature, not to mention blood and marital relationships. Further, there are even yet small parts of the United States where the kindred has a certain functional importance; is a recognized part of the culture. Now, I do not think I exaggerate when I say that at least as strong a case can be made out for the role of the kindred as for class in the United States and most of Western culture. But who would bother to make it? Who would seriously treat a small Ozarks community with respect to kindred as a "microcosm of American society," as the place where "all Americans live"? How many social scientists would declare that since *kinship* is an unalterable part of human society, the *kindred* is therefore inevitable and that one's failure to know the interests of his kindred is the result of ideological distortion? And, finally, who would suggest seriously that since kinship is inescapable one had best accept his kindred in the interest of peace of mind?

There is no need to belabor the question. The answer is fairly clear and lies, of course, in the realm of political and social values. Unlike other concepts of sociology that of class has had for a long time certain value overtones to which few if any of us could be insensitive. For most social scientists (preponderantly liberal in political mat-

[4] C. Arnold Anderson, "Recent American Research on Social Stratification." Third Working Conference on Social Mobility and Social Stratification, Amsterdam, 1954; published in *Mens en Maatschappij*, 1955, pp. 321–37.

ters) any denial of the existence of class seemed tantamount to asserting that all Americans have equal opportunity. Too seldom has it occurred to us that the manifest facts of inequality could be placed in other perspectives of stratification.

A historian of ideas with whom I occasionally discuss sociological perplexities tells me that from his point of view the doctrine of social class would seem to have about the same relation to the data of stratification that the Ptolemaic view once had to celestial phenomena. I judge from my colleague's words that by the end of the fifteenth century the Ptolemaic doctrine was not so much wrong as it was tortuous, inefficient and clumsy. Many of the celestial phenomena which the Copernican hypothesis proved able to absorb easily and economically could actually have been handled by the Ptolemaic doctrine in its later form but only, I am informed, by the most extensive use of epicycles and other assumed patterns which neither observation nor reason could justify independently. In the Ptolemaic theory an immense battery of ever new assumptions and modifications of old concepts was necessary to sustain the fundamental view of the universe on which they rested. The new theory simply swept away the vast structure of assumption and concept that had accumulated and worked directly from the data that were given.

Admittedly, the analogy between the Ptolemaic view and the present theory of class is an imperfect one, if only because we are dealing with a doctrine that must perforce be considered *sub specie aeternitatis,* and in this sense was never correct, whereas in the case of social class we have a concept which is historical in content and which as-

suredly has relevance to certain ages and areas of civilization.

But so far as contemporary Western society is concerned, there is clarifying pertinence of the analogy. In the same way that the Ptolemaic theory had to depend increasingly upon more refined analyses and upon the use of concepts and sub-concepts which removed conclusion ever farther from the data actually given, so, I think, does much of the current literature on stratification in the United States. It is not too strong, I think, to say that the concept of class plagues the study of stratification in about the same measure that social systems research would be if we continued to hold to the old primary group-secondary association dichotomy that early American sociology advanced.

Undeniably, class studies based upon community analysis have produced many essential data and, along with these data, many perceptive and valuable insights into the nature of status behavior, affiliation and prestige. But, for the moment leaving aside my fundamental criticism of the non-historical and non-contextual character of these studies, one is forced to conclude that both data and insights too often suffer from a kind of Procrustean adjustment to a conceptual framework that is at once too short and too narrow. It becomes more and more difficult to suppose that the hypothesis of social class would be invoked at the present time in studies of American stratification and power were it not for the deep roots of this hypothesis in the conceptual memory of sociology.

At its extreme, especially in certain of Warner's works, the class perspective has the attributes of a Never Never land: observations carefully sterilized of historical considerations, constructed of self-fulfilling interviews and premises, skillfully extrapolated through use of linear scales and multiple correlations; the whole possessing a certain internal consistency, even credibility, but, on overview, possessing about as much relation to national American society as James Branch Cabell's enchanted land of Poictesme does to Times Square.

II

One reason for the tenacity of class among modern concepts of social science is the lasting impulse it received just after the French Revolution from some of the seminal minds of modern social theory. It was the Revolution— or rather the Conservative reaction to the Revolution—that first made class a preoccupation of modern thinkers. The effects of Revolutionary legislation on such groups as commune, extended family, church and gild were left also on the ancient class structure of France. Such conservatives as Burke, Bonald and Maistre were quick to seize upon class, even as they did family and church, as an essential element of legitimate society. Their overall objective was to bring about a restitution of the old order, in modified form, and to eradicate the equalitarian ideology that the Revolution had produced.

If the Conservatives were the first to make class important in their thinking, the Socialists were quick to follow. Using the same fundamental perspective, the Socialists drew different conclusions and worked toward a very different objective. They too saw class as an essential element of all previous societies including the one that the Revolution had brought into existence. But,

unlike the Conservatives, the Socialists saw *strife* between the classes as an essential element. For them this strife was to become the indispensable dynamic of change continuing in ever more intense fashion until eventually the working class, through its own expansion and through final revolution and seizure of power, would become the sole class, thus bringing to fruition what the political legislation of the French Revolution had only begun.

My concern here is not with a history of the doctrine of class in nineteenth century thought. This has been told often enough. What I wish to emphasize is the extraordinary influence that was levied upon both radical and conservative minds by a particular class system in the early nineteenth century: the English landed class. This remarkable structure, it would appear, served as the prototype, the model, of that concept of class which was to be handed down to the twentieth century. It was Burke, under the spur of his hatred of the revolution in France, who first called the world's attention to the class system in England and to the combination of light and leading that it seemed to represent. Europeans were not slow to pick it up. Even in the French conservative tradition from Bonald through Comte, LePlay, Tocqueville and Taine, the model of English class was a luminous one, underlying many penetrating glimpses into the lives of members of this class.

The relevance of the English landed class to both radical and conservative theories lay in its detachment from any formal system of political law and from any apparent external force. In France and on the Continent in general social classes of the older order had been more nearly of the nature of estates, bounded, reinforced and maintained by laws of the realm. Not so in England. Despite the powerful role that this class played in political affairs, it was not a creature of law and nothing in the English constitution pertained to it.

Time permits only the briefest summary of the characteristics of this class. There was, first, its undifferentiated economic unity founded upon landed property alone. It would be extreme to say that no other forms of property were recognized, but it is fair to note that men who made their fortunes in commerce and business did not usually gain recognition from this class until they had acquired land and based their existence upon it. From generation to generation landed property tended to remain in the same family hands.

Equally notable was the political unity of the class. Economic ownership and political power coalesced almost perfectly. This was to be seen not merely in the overwhelming number of Parliamentary seats that went to members of the landed class and in the astonishing degree of consensus that reigned among them, but in the monopoly they held of administrative functions in local and county government. "The great unpaid," as they were to be called by a later historian, is an apt term. Without formal compensation of any kind, without indeed any position in the law of the land, they performed throughout England the essential tasks of administration including much of the dispensing of justice. It was the generally high sense of responsibility with which the squirearchy operated at local levels—coupled with the absence of the kind of aggressive and independent legal profession that France had produced—that for long restrained a true bureaucracy in England and made of this class a model for all Conservatives.

There was little if any element of caste or even estate. No legal boundaries existed to mark classes and no restrictions of a legal sort prevented others from participating. We know that occasionally men did rise from below to attain influential places in government and society. But they were rare for, although the landed class was not closed, openings were few and could close with extraordinary speed. Overwhelmingly, national politics, local administration, justice and service in the commissioned areas of the armed forces were the functions of this one, socially homogeneous class.

So too was there a high degree of convergence of the various attributes of social status. Excepting for the handful of intellectuals largely concentrated in London, the only people of education were members of this class, and both the public schools and the two great universities were shaped in purpose and result by landed class needs. The norms of what constituted an educated man were universally understood. Language, including accent, could identify a man in a moment as belonging to this class. All were of the Established Church, most of the higher clergy were themselves products of the landed group, and even when they weren't their loyalties to it were strong.

Over the whole structure towered the governing conception of the gentleman. Hard to define in abstract terms, perhaps, the reality of the gentleman was nevertheless as unmistakable and as universal as that of the land itself. In dress, opinion, taste and conviction the landed gentleman set the life style of all that was invested with prestige and power. It was the pervasive image of the gentleman that had so much to do with maintaining the solidarity of this class, with shoring up its political and economic strength, and with making its behavior and desires so universal in England of that day. All of this we know from the countless letters and diaries of the age. The concept of the gentleman is a norm that has not disappeared altogether even yet in England nor in those older parts of the United States where it was carried.

Finally, we should note that this class was functional in all pertinent respects. Between the social attributes of prestige and the realities of economic and political power there was an almost perfect convergence, leading to a degree of solidarity and self-consciousness that could hardly have been exceeded. Criteria of class were clear, easily identifiable and substantially the same everywhere in England. Knowledge of a family's standing with respect to any one of the criteria generally was sufficient to place that family accurately with respect to other criteria. Finally, there was stability of this convergence of attributes from one generation to another. In sum, if it was the social norm of the gentleman that surmounted the structure, it was the monopoly of political power and its deep roots in property that provided the foundations.

I have chosen to describe this class for several reasons. In the first place, better than any definition, it provides a guiding conception of class and a picture of a society that is simply incomprehensible apart from class. Second, it was this class that was to provide the model for Socialist predictions of the course that industrialism would take in the development of its own class structure. And, finally, it is the dwindling, ever more attenuated, survival of this class system that forms the essential perspective of those community studies which emphasize class in twentieth century England and the United States. For, it must not be forgotten, the massive changes in the nineteenth and early twentieth centuries did not everywhere drive out all at once the economic and social characteristics of the older order. What Schumpeter has called the "pre-capitalist strata" remained to give stability to the new order and for a long time to impose its social cultural norms upon emerging functions and statuses.

III

It is sometimes said that Marx's emphasis upon the two classes and the directive role they would take in the future of capitalism was the result of a religious turn of mind which simply transmuted the age old theological myth of the war between good and evil into the conflict between proletariat and capitalist. But this is fanciful and oversimple. The truth is, I believe, that Marx, with the vivid model of the landed class and its fusion of power and prestige in front of him, made the understandable assumption that industrial society would follow, *mutatis mutandis*, the same course of class development. And few today would deny that there was much in the character of the industrialism then emerging to give warrant to the assumption. Even Tocqueville, whose basic values and perspectives were so radically different from Marx's, took almost the same view of industrial society. Both men foresaw a long history of an economic society divided rigidly between an aristocracy of manufacturers set above a kind of peasantry of laborers with conflict between them inevitable.

However plausible this view of the future development of capitalism may have been in Marx's day, it has been grotesquely belied by the facts. The very forces which dissolved the class lines of pre-industrial society acted, in the long run, to prevent any new classes from becoming fixed. National democracy, economic and social pluralism, ethical individualism, and an ever-widening educational front joined to create new patterns of social power and status and to make class obsolete in constantly widening sectors of Western society.

Most of the apparent manifestations of class in industrial society were less the temporary product of the new order itself than they were of the fusion for many years of the new order and the old. Schumpeter is correct in his insistence upon the importance of "pre-capitalist strata" to the early stages of nineteenth century industrialism, but these strata were by no means invariably re-inforcing to capitalism. They could often form the substance of conflict, and their varied patterns were difficult to distinguish from the intrinsic patterns of capitalism itself.

This is true today in many of the underdeveloped areas of the world where class analysis remains essential to an understanding of their political and economic systems. Economic and political power are both set in a clear and homogeneous perspective of social stratification. There is a striking convergence of the attributes of wealth, power and status in such areas as the Middle East and Latin America. But, so far as Western Europe and the United States are concerned, this convergence, this assimilation of economic and political influence within differentiated social classes exists scarcely at all except to a small degree in those areas which have been least touched by the processes of modern democratic-industrial society.

In political terms alone it is possible to see why class could never attain the same significance in modern society that it did in the old. In modern democracies ultimate political power is spread in an unstratified way among voters. Parties, pressure groups and other political associations have become decisive and are more and more difficult to stratify on any general scale. Power tends to be plural; elites are, in Raymond Aron's phrase, divided, not unified. Behind the modern state lies the whole development of political, civil and social rights which have made class rule as difficult as local or sectional tyranny. Equally important has been the mass character of the modern state, reflected both in its values and procedures by the use of ever more direct modes of administration. Finally, the sheer accumulation of economic and social functions by the state, discharged by paid and trained bureaucracies of constantly widening scope, has made impossible the development of any group in contemporary society comparable in political terms to the landed aristocracy. To repeat, class, where it exists, is functional or it is nothing.

In economic terms, there is the profoundly altered relation between property and economic power in modern times. A quarter of a century ago Berle and Means called attention to the structural significance of the divorce between property ownership and corporate control in large areas of the economy. This is a tendency that has only increased and it has been deepened and widened by the appearance of labor leaders and governmental officials who demonstrably wield great economic power and who are even more remote from property ownership. This splitting of the atom of property, to use a phrase of Berle's, has inevitably had far reaching implications to the economic foundations of social class. When economic power derives no longer exclusively from the processes of capital accumulation, or even management, when it is a reflection of positions in the economy which arise from and are sustained by labor and government, the relationship between property and class becomes more and more tenuous.

There is also the massive change from an economy based preponderantly upon primary and secondary sectors to one based increasingly upon tertiary occupations. By 1955, as Seymour Lipset has recently emphasized, tertiary employment had more than doubled over the amount in 1919, totaling 30 million workers compared with 28 million workers in the primary and secondary sectors. "Today over 55 per cent of the labor force is engaged in trade, finance, government, transportation, communication, and service." This has an important relation to social mobility Lipset notes, for throughout American history "the tertiary industries have been the highest paid, followed by the secondary, and finally the primary at the bottom of the scale." [5]

To be sure, quickening social mobility is not inconsistent with the existence of social class, and income differentials among the three sectors do not in themselves negate the possibility of strong class lines. But with a few occupations such as domestic service excepted, it is all too obvious that the majority of jobs falling within the tertiary sector in modern times are not easily subsumed under any class system. Irrespective of high individual mobility in this sector, the job structure itself is too fluctuant, too mobile, to allow classes to form. Finally there is the fact, important to any analysis of class, that the dispersion of productive forces among the three sectors has become more important to the character of our society than the distribution of property.

Equally important has been the deployment of the economy into a large number of functional associations and groups essential to production, distribution and consumption, and which can, only at the risk of fantasy, be arrayed in any unilinear order of hierarchy. For awhile it could be thought that labor unions and consumer-cooperatives were manifestations of lower class position, but anyone who examines carefully the structural position of these, especially the large ones in our economy, not to mention the attitudes of both leadership and rank and file, is increasingly hard put to maintain this position.

As T. H. Marshall has written: "Within the economic structure of society there are many functionally distinct groups, each based on its productive role and the conditions under which it is performed. On some matters the interests of these groups differ; on others they are the same. Associations exist, and spread, for the pursuit of these common interests whenever they arise, and with such degree of combination of groups as they demand. The members of these combining groups differ greatly in social level, and the organizations are for them rationally designed instruments for the

[5] Seymour M. Lipset, "Trends in American Society," to be published in *Concise Guide to Modern Knowledge*, New York: Doubleday, 1959.

achievement of certain specific and limited ends, albeit very important ones. . . . And the associations do not necessarily permeate the whole lives of their members, as social classes do, nor are they always in action; and at times the constituent sub-groups may be more important than the largest aggregate." [6]

There is also the striking change in consumption in modern society. It is not so much the fact of relative abundance, an economic condition on which modern states are increasingly dependent for political success, as it is the general elevation of level of consumption and the disappearance of clear and distinct strata of consumption. The difference between the extremes of wealth and poverty is very great, today as always, but the scale is more continuous and, for the bulk of the population, there has been a compression of the scale. Changes in housing patterns, automobile models, clothing styles, and even food preferences all illustrate this. Given both this compression and continuity, it is unlikely that self-conscious and mutually antagonistic groups will arise.

Whether with respect to consumption or production, then, class lines are exceedingly difficult to discover in modern economic society except in the backwater areas. About the most that research comes up with is that wealthy persons spend their money more freely, choose, when possible, better schools for their children, buy clothes at Brooks or Magnin's, rather than at Penny's, avail themselves of better medical attention, and belong to more clubs. But while all of this is interesting, it says little about anything as substantive as a social class is supposed to be.

The last stand of class as an economic reality appears to be on occupational grounds. If class is linked with production, then occupation must be its chief index. But, to quote again from Marshall, "we find that, in study after study, occupation is used only as an index of social status. Or again, if we turn to studies of the influences of social and economic position (including position in the production system) on political attitudes and behavior—an aspect crucial to the Marxist and Weberian concepts of class—we find that class does not emerge as a substantive social group but is little more than a middle term in the chain that links position to opinion. Richard Centers, for example, writes: 'Just as people who differ in socio-economic position differ in class affiliation, so people who differ in class affiliation differ in turn in politico-economic orientation.' But, when one looks closer, it seems that this 'class affiliation' can hardly be said to have any independent existence, and that no concrete social group can be pointed to which is the 'class' toward which this 'affiliation' is felt." [7]

IV

We come, finally, to the social components of class. It is here that sociologists and anthropologists, especially the Warner school, have demonstrated greatest ingenuity in defense of class as a reality in contemporary American

[6] T. H. Marshall, "General Survey of Changes in Social Stratification in the Twentieth Century," in *Transactions of the Third World Congress of Sociology*, International Sociological Association, 1956, pp. 12–13.

[7] T. H. Marshall, *op. cit.*, pp. 5–6.

life. Through indexes of status characteristics and evaluations of participation in community life, a strong and often imaginative effort has been made to buttress what remains of a perspective that has been declining almost from the time it was first formulated. It is said in effect that even if class conceived as power cannot be demonstrated, life styles and the general preoccupation with social status leave us with self-conscious and culturally implicative classes numbering anywhere from three to ten.

But the evidence here seems to me no more compelling than in the economic and political spheres. I suggest that in the same way that there has been a general disengagement of economic and political power, during the past century and more, from any homogeneous scale of stratification, leaving in its wake plurality and dispersion, so has there been a general disengagement of social status itself from any clearly definable set of ranks. That scales of status exist in our society is incontestable, that they are often of driving concern to individuals is equally incontestable. But social status is at once too continuous within each of the numerous scales of status to make possible any identification of classes that have more than the most restricted or specialized acceptance.

I do not doubt that within a community that is sufficiently isolated from the main currents of national life, sufficiently arrested in terms of historical change, sufficiently homogeneous so far as its economy and government are concerned, a clear and meaningful class system could be discovered. I merely emphasize that to discover such a community today it is necessary to go either to the underdeveloped areas of the world or, in American society, to a few remaining and fast-disappearing pockets of the old order.

It is because social status, like economic and political power, has become disengaged from real lines in modern society, that such novels as *Point of No Return*, *What Makes Sammy Run?*, and John Braine's recent *Room at the Top* are more illuminating so far as status behavior is concerned than the majority of community studies of social class. These novels are concerned with individuals in a mobile society, preoccupied by status considerations exactly *because* classes have been replaced by impersonal levels connected by ever wider channels of vertical mobility. Perhaps I go too far in the last reference; perhaps studies which are only now really beginning will show that channels of mobility are not as wide and congested as I think they are; but as sociologists we cannot overlook the significance of the almost universal *belief* that they are.

In any event, the crucial point here is not the extent of vertical mobility but rather the fact that we are living in a society governed by status, not class, values, and that class lines recede everywhere in almost exact proportion to the reality and urgency of individual status considerations. As a consequence of its disengagement from class, social status has become simultaneously more individual, more autonomous, and is, on any realistic basis, almost as multiple and diverse as is American culture. If I am wrong on this, will someone please rank for me on any linear *class* scale the following individuals: Ted Williams, Ike Williams, G. Mennen Williams, Esther Williams, Mrs. Harrison Williams, and Robin Williams.

Schumpter pointed out in his *Imperialism and Social Classes* that "the family, not the individual person, is the true unit of class and class theory." This is correct, and what has happened to kinship in modern society, both to its structure and to its relation to the larger society, has been closely involved in the shift from social class to social status. Social status does not really imply the existence of groups at all; it can be used with reference to a continuous scale of invidiously valued positions, and it is with this in mind that Goldschmidt has insisted that the "proper figure of speech is not that there are rungs of a ladder; it is rather that there is a chromatic scale of status—a glissando."

There may be still a few communities in the United States where a man's professional, marital and associative choices will be, for as long as he lives in the community of his birth, limited by the level of his family of orientation in almost the same way that one's choices are widened or narrowed by the racial or ethnic group he belongs to. Such communities are few. For, generally, family of orientation is regarded as a marker or starting place by which individuals measure the distance they have moved upward or downward, and, on this matter, I repeat, J. P. Marquand and John Braine have told us more than has Professor Warner.

Admittedly, a status-based society may be as inequalitarian at any given time as one organized in terms of class divisions. Further, it can scarcely be doubted that one's life chances, even his aspirations, will be influenced by the level of his family of orientation. Unquestionably, the sense of personal determination of status will be weaker, on the whole, at the extremes than in middle levels of status, in even the most mobile of societies. Such considerations do not, however, affect the central question of class any more than do the equally vivid facts of inequality of power and wealth in society.

I should say that, nationally, the nearest we come to class consciousness is in what Mozell Hill has called level consciousness. Unlike class consciousness, level consciousness makes for a high degree of individualism with respect to aspirations and life chances; it does not promote feeling of identification or collective involvement. The principal motive of the level conscious individual is to pass up and out of the level in which he finds himself. He is, so to speak, on the make. He lives in an atmosphere of competition that is nourished constantly by education and ideology and by the substantive fact of a shortage of skill in the industrial and professional world. Level consciousness creates awareness of one's differences from others, rather than similarities, and in this respect the individual is constantly moved by distinctions he invents between himself and others, by preoccupation, even anxiety, with these distinctions. As Professor Hill writes, "one by-product of this on the American scene is that people have come to feel that it is not so much a matter of destroying those on a higher level of consumption as it is of acquiring skills, strategies and techniques which will enable one to surmount his level." [8]

It is sometimes said that the failure of individuals to respond accurately to questionnaires which seek to derive a class consciousness corresponding to income level is simply the consequence of "ideological distortion." But, quite apart from the fact that such assertions run the risk of self-sealing and self-fulfilling reasoning, they do not give proper due to the social role of ideol-

---

[8] Mozell Hill in an unpublished manuscript on class and mobility.

ogy. An ideology is not a shadow or representation. It is as real a part of one's social behavior as job or income. As real, and oftentimes more decisive.

The notable unwillingness of substantial numbers of people to concede the existence of class divisions, despite the bait of forced-choice questionnaires and the heavy pull of terminological tradition, is itself a social fact of the highest order. Granted that some uncomfortable economic realities are often obscured by the ideology of classlessness, whether in suburbia or elsewhere, the fact of this refusal to concede the existence of class is itself a powerful influence in preventing differential social statuses from becoming crystallized into classes.

In sum, the concept of social class has been an important, and probably inevitable, first step in the study of differential power and status in society; admittedly, there are non-Western areas of civilization, as well as ages of the past, where the class concept is indispensable to an understanding of power and status; but so far as the bulk of Western society is concerned, and especially the United States, the concept of class is largely obsolete. Any useful inquiry into the distribution of wealth, power and status, and their interactions, will have to be made, I believe, in terms of concepts that are more representative of the actual history of modern political and economic society.

5

THE AFFLUENT WORKER AND THE THESIS OF *EMBOURGEOISEMENT*: SOME PRELIMINARY RESEARCH FINDINGS

John H. Goldthorpe, David Lockwood, Frank Bechhofer, and Jennifer Platt

Much of the argument supporting the view that Western societies are becoming increasingly classless is based on the undeniably growing affluence of the stable, regularly employed working class. As its income increases, the distance between skilled and even semiskilled manual workers, on the one hand, and many segments of the white-collar middle class, on the other hand, tends to diminish. Compare, for example, the income of the following groups in 1970.

SOURCE: *Sociology 1*, no. 1 (January 1967), pp. 11–31. Reprinted by permission of the authors and the Clarendon Press, Oxford.

Median Income of Year-Round, Full-Time Male Workers, 1970

All Occupations	$ 9,184
White Collar	
Professional and Technical Workers	12,255
Self-Employed	20,031
Salaried	11,937
Proprietors, Managers, and Officials	11,665
Salaried Managers and Officials	12,597
Self-Employed Proprietors	7,767
Sales Workers	9,765
Clerical Workers	8,652
Blue Collar	
Skilled Craftsmen	9,253
Semiskilled Operatives	7,644
Unskilled Laborers	6,462
Service	
Service Workers, except Private Household	6,964
Farm	
Farmers and Farm Managers	3,881
Farm Laborers and Foremen	3,355

SOURCE: U.S. Bureau of the Census, *Current Population Reports* Series P-60, No. 78 (Washington, D.C.: U.S. Government Printing Office, 1971).

Here we see that the wages of skilled manual workers exceeded the income of white-collar clerical employees and self-employed small entrepreneurs. The wages of semiskilled factory operatives are not far behind the income of small-scale proprietors, salesmen, and clerical employees.

Whatever the ultimate causes of this phenomenon, whether it be the increasing productivity of the economy, union activity in behalf of workers, or mass production and the standardization of products, it cannot be denied that the overall standard of living of the stable working class is tending to reach middle-class levels.

And yet, it is important not to exaggerate the extent of this phenomenon. There are still millions of workers—black and white—in the South, on the farms, in depressed industries or regions, in nonunionized sectors, in unskilled or service jobs, whose pay remains well below that of even the lowest reaches of the middle class. High working-class incomes are often made by working overtime or by moonlighting. The very *top* working class pay ($10,000–12,000), made by the most highly skilled workers, represents the *bottom* pay for many in substantial middle-class careers (doctors, lawyers, engineers, academics, business executives, and so forth). And the specter of unemployment still hangs mainly over the working class.

Early in 1971, the weekly take-home pay of the average production worker with three dependents was only $109. After spending approximately twenty-five percent of this for house or rent payments, the workers' family has about $3.00 daily per person left over for food, clothing, medicine, transportation, entertainment, and other incidentals. This can scarcely be considered opulence.

Nevertheless, even if we grant a relatively high level of working-class prosperity, those who use the increasing affluence of the working class as proof of their *embour-*

geoisement, or in order to herald a new classless society, engage in too facile an economic determinism. There are many aspects of a working-class job and life that are not significantly affected by growing prosperity. And, as Goldthorpe and his associates indicate in their study of a group of prosperous British workers, a great many distinctive social, cultural, psychological, and political attributes continue to distinguish the modern working class from the middle class, even when their incomes are comparable.

As Goldthorpe points out, for example, even if the workers' income reaches middle-class levels, the frequently alienating nature of the job itself has consequences for working-class life, both on and off the job. Educational differences between workers and the middle class are still significant. These in turn are increasingly important for social-class life styles and subcultures. The worker's son is still less likely to graduate from high school than his middle-class counterpart, or, if he graduates, he is much less likely to go on and to graduate from college. One national study, for example, found that of those graduating from high school in the mid-1960's, only thirty-seven percent of the young people from working-class homes began attending college soon after high school graduation as compared to over sixty-four percent of those from middle-class homes.* This underlines the fact that working-class boys have fewer mobility opportunities than middle-class boys: workers' sons have much less chance of making it into the middle class than middle-class sons have of remaining in the middle class.

In the late 1950's, the American sociologist Bennett Berger studied a group of automobile workers who had recently moved into a California suburb.** Berger examined the extent to which these manual workers, living in a typically middle-class suburban milieu, enjoying a standard of living clearly superior to that of their previous central-city residences, had taken on attributes of the middle class.

His findings paralleled those of Goldthorpe and testify to the *resiliency* of working-class cultural patterns, even at increasing levels of affluence. In short, Berger found in this comfortable working-class suburb traditional working-class cultural patterns such as: limited job mobility aspirations or expectations; emphasis on security or getting by rather than getting ahead; collective mobility via union gains rather than via personal action; little status seeking; loyalty to the Democratic party; identification with the working class more than with any other single class; little reliance on child-rearing experts as a guide in bringing up children; low rates of membership in formal organizations, including infrequent attendance at church and participation in church affairs; little semiformal or formal home entertainment; working-class forms of leisure, relaxation, and esthetic taste in television, books, magazines, movies, and the like.

It is apparent from these and other studies that the working class is *not* becoming extinct, contrary to the glib generalizations often made these days by those who somewhat prematurely seek to celebrate America's classless society.

The theme of 'the affluent worker' is not new: it has been a recurrent one from the earliest years of Western industrial society. It antedates, in fact, the Marxian themes of 'proletarianisation' and the growing impoverishment of the industrial labour force. For example, around the year 1790, John Millar of Glasgow, one of the great Scots forerunners of modern sociology,

* U.S. Bureau of the Census, *Current Population Reports,* Series P-20, No. 185 (Washington, D.C.: U.S. Government Printing Office, 1969).
** Bennett Berger, *Working-Class Suburb: A Study of Auto Workers in Suburbia* (Berkeley, Calif.: University of California Press, 1960).

made the following observations on the society of his day:

> When a country . . . is rapidly advancing in trade, the demand for labourers is proportionately great; their wages are continually rising, instead of soliciting employment, they are courted to accept of it; and they enjoy a degree of affluence and importance which is frequently productive of insolence and licentiousness.
>
> That the labouring people in Britain have, for some time, been raised to this enviable situation is evident from a variety of circumstances, from the high price of labour; from the absurd attempt of the legislature to regulate their wages, and to prevent them from deserting particular employments; from the zeal displayed by the lower orders in the vindication of their political, as well as of their private rights; and, above all, from the jealousy and alarm with which this disposition has, of late, so universally impressed their superiors.[1]

This passage is of interest, and is quoted, not only because of its date. It is also significant because it provides the basic pattern for most subsequent discussion on the matter of the affluent worker. This pattern is as follows. First, reference is made to aspects of economic progress—in Millar's case, the rapid growth of trade and rising demand for labour—which are directly responsible for the spread of prosperity. Secondly, certain consequences of this affluence are postulated for workers' social consciousness and conduct— for Millar, increasing awareness of their social importance, the decline of deference, independence vis-a-vis employers, and so on. Then finally, these developments are in turn related to certain significant features of the current *political* situation—in 1790, the concern of the lower orders to claim political as well as civil rights. In other

words, underlying Millar's observations there is a theory—which he in fact develops more explicitly elsewhere in his work [2]—of the primarily economic determination of political behaviour and institutions, with changes in the objective and subjective aspects of social stratification being seen as a crucial mediating process.

A broadly comparable theory is, of course, central to the work of Marx and Engels. Indeed Millar may well have been an important influence in the development of Marx's sociological thinking.[3] However, on the particular question of the affluent worker, the interesting point is that this theoretical affinity co-exists with a complete reversal of perspective. Millar, as we have seen, regarded the growing affluence of the labouring population as a threat to the established hierarchy of social ranks and to the political system associated with this. For Millar, the affluent worker was a potentially dynamic factor in a relatively stable social order. For Marx and Engels, on the other hand, the more prosperous stratum of the working class was an essentially conservative element, hindering the growth of true working-class consciousness and of a revolutionary working-class movement, and thus holding back the inevitable crisis of capitalist society.

Engels, in particular, gave a good deal of attention to this problem of working-class conservatism in his writings of the 1870's and 1880's.[4] In this he was activated chiefly by the failure of the industrial workers of Great Britain to exploit the new franchise of 1867 and to secure working-class dominance in Parliament. Engels' explanation of this failure emphasized the British worker's craving for 'respectability' and enhanced social status which thus led to a willingness, indeed eagerness, to accept bourgeois social values, life-styles, and political ideas. But Engels then went on to argue further that this process of the *embourgeoisement* of the British working class had itself to be explained by reference to Britain's exceptional economic position in the mid-nineteenth century as the world's leading industrial nation. Only because of this national economic supremacy was it possible for the theory of working class 'immiseration' to be controverted and for a sizeable section of the British labour force to enjoy living standards which were such as to encourage their bourgeois aspirations. In this way, then, in spite of their radically different standpoints, Engels' analysis is very similar to Millar's in its basic form. In their discussion of the affluent worker, both are ultimately interested in a certain political situation; and this they seek to understand in terms of the dynamics of social stratification, which they in turn relate to the secular trend of economic development.

From the end of the nineteenth century, a Marxian, or more accurately, a para-Marxian perspective on the question of the affluent worker has been the dominant one; that is to say, it has been generally argued (or assumed) that affluence is conducive to *embourgeoisement* which itself leads to political conservatism, or at any rate to political apathy, within the working class. During certain periods of labour unrest and socialistic fervour, such arguments may have been somewhat subdued; but, unfailingly, they have re-emerged with conditions of greater economic and political stability. However, one basically important development from the original Marxian position should be noted. With the decline in faith in the predictive aspects of Marx's

thought, *embourgeoisement* has ceased to be regarded as a purely temporary process which would sooner or later be checked and reversed as part of the logic of the auto-destruction of the capitalist system. Rather, it has come to be seen as a permanent and progressive process which is inherent in the 'affluent society' of the modern West and which reflects, in fact, the logic of the long-term evolution of *industrialism*. The industrial society of the future, it has been claimed, will be an essentially 'middle-class' society; as the age of scarcity gives way to the age of abundance, the idea of a working class with its own distinctive way of life, values, and goals is one which becomes increasingly obsolete.[5]

So far as Great Britain is concerned, this new version of the *embourgeoisement* thesis came to particular prominence in course of the last decade. The circumstances which lent it force are now part of the familiar history of these years and we need refer to them here only very briefly. Economically, the 1950's were characterized by a relatively rapid rise in living standards and, most significantly, by a marked growth in the number of 'middle-range' incomes. This resulted in an increasing overlap, in terms of income, between those in white-collar and manual occupations; and, concomitantly, former differences in patterns of consumption were also much reduced as manual workers considerably increased their ownership of consumer durables and, in a growing number of cases, began to buy their own homes. Politically, these same years were ones of undisputed Conservative dominance. The three successive electoral victories of the Conservative party, with rising majorities, were without historical parallel, while the Labour vote showed ominous signs of secular decline. Moreover, there were indications that in the areas of the country which were economically most progressive, this fall in the Labour vote was due to some significant extent to loss of support from among the industrial working class, either through defections or through new voters failing to follow in the traditional pattern.

In these circumstances, then, it can scarcely be regarded as surprising that the thesis of the progressive *embourgeoisement* of the British working class should prove to be an attractive one. The argument that British society was becoming increasingly middle-class provided the obvious means of linking together the outstanding economic and political developments of the period. It was, in fact, an argument accepted by spokesmen of both the right and left, by numerous journalists and social commentators, and by not a few political scientists and sociologists. However, the existence of this general consensus of opinion did not alter the fact—though it may have served to obscure it—that the thesis of 'the worker turning middle-class' lacked any satisfactory validation. It remained merely as an assumption, or at best an inference, which it seemed reasonable to make in interpreting the socio-political situation in Britain at the end of the 1950's. Although the circumstantial evidence might be persuasive, very little *direct* evidence could be presented to support the specific proposition that manual workers and their families were in the process of being assimilated on a relatively large scale into middle-class ways of life and middle-class society.[6]

· · · · ·

This situation may be regarded as the point of departure of the research project on which this paper gives a pre-liminary report. Primarily, the aim of the project was to investigate the thesis of working-class *embourgeoisement* in an empirical way, and with it the generally accepted view of the relationship between working-class affluence and working-class politics in contemporary British society. From the outset we felt, on theoretical grounds, that this view was a highly questionable one. Thus, in planning our project we decided to seek a *locale* for the field research which would be *as favourable as possible* for the validation of the arguments about which we were doubtful. In this way, we gave ourselves the possibility of providing a test of the *embourgeoisement* thesis which might be critical in the sense that if it were to be shown that a process of *embourgeoisement* was *not* in evidence in the case we studied, then there would be strong grounds for arguing that such a process was unlikely to be occurring to any significant extent within British society at large.

This strategy involved, therefore, first, an attempt to specify theoretically what a *locale* of the kind in question would be like; and then, secondly, discovering some adequate real-life approximation. These proved to be no easy matters. Eventually, though, it was decided that the town of Luton would come nearest to meeting our requirements, and for the following major reasons: (i) it was a prosperous and rapidly growing industrial centre in an area of the country now experiencing general economic expansion; (ii) in consequence of this, the town's labour force contained a high proportion of geographically mobile workers; (iii) also in consequence of the town's rapid growth, a high proportion of its population lived in relatively new housing areas; and (iv) the town was somewhat removed from the older industrial regions of the country and was thus not dominated by their traditions of industrial relations and of industrial life generally.[7]

We thus based our research primarily upon a sample of 229 manual workers drawn from the hourly-paid employees of three progressive manufacturing firms sited in Luton.[8] All these firms had advanced personnel and welfare policies and were noted for their good industrial relations records. Our sample was limited to men who were (i) between the ages of 21 and 46; (ii) married; (iii) earning regularly *at least* £17 per week (October 1962); and (iv) resident in the town of Luton itself or adjacent housing areas. The sample was also constructed so as to enable comparisons to be made between workers at different skill levels and involved in different types of production system.[9] For further comparative purposes, we also took a sample of 54 lower-level white-collar workers based on two of the firms. The manual workers were interviewed twice; once at their place of work and then again, together with their wives, in their own homes. The white-collar workers were interviewed at home only.[10]

Our manual workers proved to have a broadly comparable range of incomes to the white-collar workers and also differed little from the latter in their ownership of various high-cost consumer goods and in house ownership. Other characteristics of the manual sample which should be noted were the following: (i) a majority (55 per cent) lived outside of typically working-class localities such as those in the centre of the town or the council estates; (ii) 71 per cent were not natives of Luton or of the Luton district; and (iii) only 13 per cent had ever had the experience of

being unemployed for longer than a month. We would then claim that such a sample could be regarded as one that was reasonably appropriate to our purposes.

We cannot here present anything like a full account of the findings of our research; for apart from obvious limitations of space, the analysis of our material is still incomplete.[11] What we aim to do is to set out some general results which have a direct bearing on what we believe must be regarded as major elements in the *embourgeoisement* thesis. In an earlier paper distinctions were made between the economic, normative, and relational dimensions of change in class structure;[12] and it is in terms of these that the following discussion proceeds. First, we shall be concerned with some basic features of the work situation of the men in our sample. This is a most important aspect of their class situation viewed in economic terms—although one which has tended to be neglected because attention has been focussed on 'affluence' in the sphere of consumption. However, from our standpoint, it is not enough to know that certain manual workers can earn high incomes: what must also be known is under what conditions this affluence is achieved, and their human and social implications. Secondly, in regard to both the normative and relational aspects of class, we present data on the nature and extent of our workers' participation in community life; including data on the further vital but again often neglected question of the extent to which the manual-nonmanual division in work continues to coincide with a major line of status-group demarcation. Then finally, and again under the normative heading, we concentrate on the political attitudes and behaviour of our sample. As we have already observed, political orientations have been the matter of ultimate interest in most discussions of 'the affluent worker' thus far; and it is for this reason that they are singled out for special attention in this paper.

(i) Employment and the Work Situation

An obvious but basic fact about the men in our sample is that they are 'affluent' primarily because of their employment in large-scale, technologically advanced manufacturing enterprises. Their role as wage workers in such enterprises is indeed fundamental to the understanding of their entire social existence. On the one hand, it is through filling this role that they are able to achieve a level of income which makes a 'middle-class' standard and style of living available to them. On the other hand, however, it can be shown that as rank-and-file industrial employees, their typical life experiences and life chances are in several ways significantly different from those of most workers in distinctively 'middle-class' occupations.

To begin with, it could be said that many of the workers with whom we were concerned appear to experience their work as little more than mere *labour;* that is, as an expenditure of effort which offers no reward in itself and which is motivated primarily by the extrinsic reward of payment. It is true that the men performing the more skilled jobs—toolmakers, millwrights, setters—could derive some degree of satisfaction directly from their work. But for the large number of those in the less skilled jobs—in particular, the machinists and assemblers—it was rather the case that their work, as experienced, involved various kinds of *de-*

privation; for example, lack of variety, lack of challenge, lack of autonomy, and often too relatively unpleasant physical conditions.

This situation was indicated by the answers we received to a number of questions in our interview schedule. For instance, of the machinists and assemblers, 60 per cent reported that they found their work monotonous, 84 per cent that it did not command their full attention, and 47 per cent that it was physically tiring. Moreover, we also asked our respondents in a quite general way: 'Did you like any of your other [i.e. previous] jobs more than the one you have now?' In the case of the machinists and assemblers 62 per cent said that they had, as too did 47 per cent of the more skilled men and 44 per cent of the process workers. And the reasons given revealed that overwhelmingly these men assessed previous jobs as being preferable on the grounds of the greater *intrinsic* rewards which they had offered when compared with their present work or, at any rate, because the deprivations they had entailed were less severe. The kinds of jobs most frequently referred to in this respect were either ones at a higher skill or status level than the individual's present work, or jobs in agriculture, transport, services, and other forms of employment which do not usually involve the physiological or psychological rigours of mass-production industry. Over a quarter of the more skilled workers and over three-quarters of the semi-skilled men have held jobs in one or other of these two categories at some earlier time in their working lives.

The implication of these findings is, then, that for a sizeable proportion of the workers in our sample, their attachment to their present employment is mainly of a pecuniary kind. In other words, it would appear that these men have in some way arrived at a decision to abandon work which could offer them some greater degree of immediate satisfaction in order to take a job which enables them to gain a higher level of monetary reward. Confirmation that such an instrumental view of work was in fact the prevalent one, within all groups in the sample, was provided by the answers we received to a further question of a more direct kind. After enquiring of our respondents if they had ever seriously thought of leaving the firms for which they now worked —just under half said they had—we went on to ask: 'What is it, then, that keeps you here?' From the replies which were made, it was clear that by far the most important consideration was the high level of pay which could be earned. This was mentioned by 65 per cent of the more skilled men and by 69 per cent of the semi-skilled workers. Moreover, of the latter 1 in 4 (24 per cent) stated that 'the money' was the *only* reason why they remained in their present employment.[13] By contrast, less than 1 in 3 (29 per cent) of the skilled men and only 1 in 7 (14 per cent) of the semi-skilled made any mention of staying in their present job because they liked the work they did.

When this same question was put to the men in our white-collar sample, a significantly different pattern of response was produced. Only two men out of the 54 said that they stayed in their jobs simply because of the level of pay, and only 30 per cent made any reference to pay at all. On the other hand, liking the work they did was the reason which was most frequently mentioned, being given by 2 white-collar workers out of 5 (39 per cent).[14]

It would appear, then, that for many of the affluent workers we studied, affluence has been achieved only at the cost of having to accept work as an activity largely devoid of immediate reward—as an activity which is chiefly a means to the end of a high level of income and consumer power. In this respect, the more skilled men may be regarded as fortunate in being able to find high-paying jobs which can also offer some opportunity for fulfilling more expressive needs—even though they too, it would seem, still view their work in a largely instrumental way. For the men lacking in skills—or, more accurately, skills in high demand —the road to affluence has often been a much harder one. Most commonly, on our evidence, it has meant taking and holding down jobs which offer higher pay than do most other types of manual work *because of* their inherent strains and deprivations. In this way, therefore, a 'middle-class' standard of income and consumption has been brought within reach; but only through a kind of work which is not typically part of white-collar experience.[15]

Moreover, it may also be observed that the nature of the work they perform is not the only cost of affluence to the men in our sample: the amount of work they do and when they do it are also important considerations. Even with the relatively high rates of pay which they enjoyed, the workers we studied could rarely earn wage packets of upwards of £20 for a normal week's work. For the majority, overtime formed a regular part of their employment and was an essential element in their high standard of living. During the period in which our interviews were being carried out, we estimate that the men in our sample were averaging around 5½ hours overtime per week. This would imply an average working week of from 48 to 50 hours. Furthermore, three-quarters of those in our sample were also permanently on shift work, which is, of course, an increasingly common aspect of employment in modern capital-intensive plants. The majority of the men on shifts were required to do regular periods of night work, while the remainder were on some kind of double day-shift system. In this latter group, those who were favourably disposed towards shift work and those who disliked it were roughly equal in number. But among the men who had to work 'nights', unfavourable attitudes were twice as frequent as favourable ones. The most common complaints of these men were to the effect that night working impaired their physical or psychological well-being, that it led to the disruption of family living, and that it interfered with their leisure and 'social' pursuits.

Systematic overtime and shift working must then be seen as an integral part of the way of life of most of the affluent workers we studied. Not only are these characteristic features of their employment, but they also have consequences for workers' activities outside the factory—consequences of a constraining kind. Moreover, in the particular form in which our workers experience them, such constraints could not be said to figure prominently in the social life of those in white-collar occupations.

Finally, on the theme of employment, there is one other way in which the manual workers with whom we are concerned remain significantly differentiated from most varieties of white-collar man. This is in terms of their chances of advancement—of making a career—within the enterprise in which they work. In general, opportunities for rising from the ranks, whether of manual or nonmanual employees, are known to be contracting in most kinds of business organization. But still, the prospects for office workers, technicians, sales personnel, and so on are appreciably better than are those for men on the shop floor. For the latter, even where their firms follow policies of 'promotion from within'—as our Luton firms attempted to do—the chances of being promoted must inevitably be slight, if only because of the small number of openings which exist in relation to the large number of possible candidates.

Among the manual workers we studied, the fact that advancement within the enterprise was unlikely was fairly well recognized. In reply to a question on our interview schedule, only two men out of our sample of 229 were prepared to rate their chances of promotion even to foreman level as being 'very good'; 37 per cent of the skilled men and 30 per cent of the semi-skilled thought their chances in this respect were 'fairly good', but 37 per cent of the former group and 41 per cent of the latter felt they were 'not too good', and 19 per cent and 25 per cent respectively regarded the position as being 'hopeless'.[16] We also put the following question to our respondents: 'If a worker of ability really put his mind to it, how far up this firm do you think he could get in the end?' The answers we received were clearly influenced by the different 'myths and legends' of the three firms from which our workers came; but overall less than half (45 per cent) believed that such a man would achieve managerial level; 40 per cent thought he would reach a supervisory grade, and most of the remainder (13 per cent) said that he would get nowhere at all.

When comparable questions were put to our white-collar sample, a notably different picture emerged: 63 per cent believed that their chances of promotion to the next highest grade were 'very good' or 'fairly good', as against 37 per cent having more pessimistic views; and similarly, 65 per cent of the sample believed that a rank-and-file white-collar worker with ability and determination would be able to make his way into a managerial position.

These varying assessments of chances of promotion are not only significant in reflecting, as they do, differences in objective life situations: they are important also in the way in which they are associated with marked differences in the entire pattern of aspirations between the two occupational groups in question. For example, among the white-collar workers the greater optimism about promotion coexists with a general desire to achieve advancement within the firm. When asked how they would like the idea of promotion, 87 per cent of the white-collar workers responded positively. By contrast, when the manual workers were asked how they would like the idea of being made a foreman, a positive response was forthcoming from 62 per cent of the more skilled men and from only 43 per cent of the semi-skilled.[17] On the other hand, though, one alternative means of 'getting ahead' had more often been hopefully thought about by the manual workers: nearly two-fifths of the latter (37 per cent) as opposed to one-fifth of the white-collar sample (19 per cent) had seriously considered starting up in business on their own account; and in fact there were 28 men in the manual

sample (12 per cent) who were actually trying to do this at the time or who had tried in the past.

However, undoubtedly the greatest difference of all in this respect lies in the fact that for manual wage workers —whether affluent or not—the main hope for the future cannot be in 'getting ahead' in any of the more usual 'middle-class' senses. Rather, it must rest in the progressive increase of the rewards which they gain *from their present economic role*. Individually, they can certainly help to realize this by being occupationally and geographically mobile—by being prepared to 'follow the money'. And it was clearly in this way that many of the men in our sample had achieved their affluent condition. But even then, to a greater extent than with most white-collar employees, in industry at least, the economic future of these workers still remains dependent upon *collective* means; that is to say, upon trade-union representation and trade-union power.

In this latter connection, two basic points may be anticipated from the fuller treatment of unionism among our affluent workers which we shall present elsewhere. First, our research provides no indication that affluence diminishes the degree of workers' attachment to unionism—although it may well be important in changing the meaning of this adherence. The factories with which we were concerned were, in effect, quite valuable recruiting grounds for the unions in that they attracted a high proportion of workers who were not union members but who subsequently became enrolled; 38 per cent of the men in our sample had become unionists only after taking up their present employment. Secondly, while the large majority of the workers we studied could not be said to be men committed to their union as part of a great socio-political movement or even as a 'fraternity', they nonetheless recognized well enough the practical importance of the union and of union strength in regard to the day-to-day issues of industrial relations—and at shop and factory levels in particular. In brief, one could say that for most of the men in question a union was, at least, an organization to which, as wage workers, it paid them to belong; it had definite instrumental value. The fact that the same could now also be said of an increasing number of nonmanual employees, notably in commerce and administration, cannot be denied. But this, of course is not so much evidence of *embourgeoisement* as of a reverse process in which the work situation of many white-collar employees is becoming in various ways closer to that of their blue-collar counterparts.

(ii) Community Life

As we have already noted, the majority of our sample of affluent workers were not natives of Luton. They were, rather, men who had migrated to the town during the last two decades in search chiefly of higher wages and better housing. We have also observed that more than half now live in areas which could not be described as typically working-class. This is closely associated with the fact that a similar proportion (57 per cent) own or are buying their homes. These characteristics of the sample are then perhaps sufficient in themselves to indicate that many of the men we studied do not share in what is thought of as the 'traditional' pattern of community life among urban industrial workers and

their families; that is, a pattern based upon residential stability and social homogeneity in which kinship and various forms of communal sociability play a dominant part.[18]

On the matter of kinship, this conclusion can be supported more directly by other of our data. For example, as a result of their geographical mobility, a high proportion of the men in our sample had become physically separated from their kin to a degree which made day-to-day contact impossible— and so too had many of their wives. Thus, of those who still had parents alive, only 13 per cent of the men and 18 per cent of the wives had parents living within ten minutes' walk of themselves; and in the case of 56 per cent of the men and 48 per cent of their wives, their parents were all living entirely outside the Luton area. The degree of separation from siblings was slightly less marked, since sometimes they too had moved to Luton. But, even so, only 36 per cent of the couples we studied had a majority of their closer kin (parents, siblings, and in-laws) living in the Luton area. The remaining couples were almost equally divided between those with the majority of their kin living within a 50-mile radius of Luton and those whose kin were for the most part yet further afield.

Given, then, that many of the couples we studied were not members of largely kin-based communities of the traditional working-class kind, the question arises of whether this situation was associated with any shift towards patterns of community life which were more typically middle-class and at the same time with any substantial degree of social mixing with recognizably middle-class persons. For if *embourgeoisement* is a likely concomitant of working-class affluence, then one would expect that middle-class life styles and society would be most readily sought after among those manual workers who, as well as being affluent, have also been freed from the social controls of an established working-class community and, in particular, from the essentially conservative influence of the extended family. The findings of our research which bear on this point are, in detailed form, rather complex: nonetheless, in general terms they are clear enough and they tend to give little support to the thesis of *embourgeoisement,* at least in the crude form in which it has usually been advanced.

The first point to be made is that in spite of the limits set by physical distance, kin were still relatively prominent in the social lives of the couples we studied. As might be expected, for those couples whose closer kin were for the most part in the Luton area, social contacts with kin were far more frequent than those with persons in any other comparable category, such as neighbours, workmates, or other friends. However, even in the case of the other couples—almost two-thirds of the sample—whose kin were mostly outside of Luton, the part which kin played in their social lives was far from negligible. For example, we asked our respondents, both husband and wife: 'Who would you say are the two or three people that you most often spend your spare time with [apart from spouse and children]?' For those couples whose kin were largely in the area, kin made up 41 per cent of the persons named; but still with the remaining couples, 22 per cent of those mentioned were kin nonetheless. Similarly, when we asked wives about the persons they had visited, or had been visited by, during the past week, kin accounted

for 52 per cent of the total for wives in the former group but still for 20 per cent for those in the latter. In the case of those couples who were largely separated from their kin, these findings would, then, suggest one or both of two things: first, that the few kin which these couples had in the Luton area tended to be seen quite often and, second, that fairly close contact was kept with other kin regardless of their distance.[19]

However, what is perhaps of greatest significance about the couples in question is the way in which their relative isolation from kin is compensated for. Primarily, it would seem, the place of the absent kin is taken not by friends chosen from among the community at large but, rather, by *neighbours,* roughly defined as persons living within ten minutes' walk. For instance, in answer to the question on the two or three people with whom spare time was most often spent, neighbours represented 47 per cent of those mentioned but other friends only 12 per cent.[20] Again, on the question of wives' visiting and visitors, neighbours accounted for 54 per cent of those involved and other friends for only 26 per cent. In this connection, a comparison with the white-collar sample is instructive. The white-collar couples, being less mobile, were somewhat less likely to be separated from their kin than the manual sample as a whole; and kin were a clearly more important element in their pattern of sociability than in that of the manual couples who had moved away from the centres of their kinship networks. But the further interesting difference between these two groups was that the white-collar couples, *in spite of* their greater amount of contact with kin,[21] *also* had far more contact with friends who were not neighbours or workmates. Thus, of the persons with whom the white-collar couples spare time was mostly spent, 29 per cent were friends of this kind, and such friends also accounted for 31 per cent of the persons the white-collar wives visited or were visited by.[22]

What this suggests to us is, then, that among the affluent workers we studied, middle-class norms had, as yet at least, only a very limited influence on patterns of sociability. In cases where kinship could not provide the basis of social life, these workers and their wives appeared to turn most readily for support and companionship to those persons who, as it were, formed the next circle of immediate acquaintance—that is, persons living in the same neighbourhood. Making numbers of friends from among people with whom their relationships were not in some degree 'given', in the way that relationships with kin and neighbours are, was still not a highly characteristic feature of their way of life. Compared with the white-collar couples, they were apparently lacking in motivation, and probably also in the requisite skills, for this kind of social exercise.[23]

One further finding from our interviews supports this interpretation. It is a typical feature of middle-class social life that couples entertain each other in their own homes. We therefore asked our respondents how often they had other couples round and who were the people who regularly came. Briefly, what emerged was that the couples in the manual sample did not entertain at home anything like so frequently as did the white-collar couples and, further, that they were more likely to confine such entertaining to their kin. Workmates and neighbours, as well as other friends, were all less often invited than in the case of the white-collar cou-

ples.[24] In other words, it would seem that among our affluent workers middle-class styles of sociability remain less influential than the 'traditional' working-class belief that the home is a place reserved for kin and for very 'particular' friends alone.

Finally, there is the question of how far our affluent workers and their wives were actually involved in what might be regarded as middle-class society. To what extent did white-collar persons figure in their social lives? In this respect, the interpretation of our findings is not very difficult. They point fairly clearly to a considerable degree of status segregation. For example, to revert to our question on persons with whom spare time was mostly spent, 75 per cent of those named by couples in the manual sample were also manual workers and their wives, and only 17 per cent were persons of clearly higher status in occupational terms. Moreover, of the latter, 29 per cent turn out to be kin. We can in fact say that 20 per cent of the couples in our sample find their chief companions entirely among their kin and a further 47 per cent entirely among kin or persons of similar occupational status. On the other hand, only a very small minority—about 7 per cent of the sample—appear to associate predominantly with unambiguously middle-class people.

A similar picture also emerges if we turn from informal relationships to examine participation in formal organizations. Such participation was not at a high level among our affluent workers or their wives, and was significantly lower than in the white-collar sample. For the men, the average number of organizations belonged to (not counting trade unions) worked out at less than 1.5 and for the wives was as low as 0.5. However, more relevant than their number for present purposes was the character of these organizations: they were not of a kind likely to lead to association with middle-class people, or at least not in any intimate way. Predominantly, they were ones either almost entirely working-class in membership—such as working-men's clubs, angling or allotment societies—or, if more mixed in their social composition, organizations which had some fairly specific purpose—religious, charitable, sporting etc.—and a well-defined internal hierarchy. What was largely lacking among couples in the sample was participation in organizations with some middle-class membership but with primarily diffuse, 'social' functions —such as, say, drinking or recreational clubs—or participation in organizations of any kind in which other manual workers and their wives were not in a large majority.

In general, then, one may say that there is little indication that the affluent workers we studied are in process of being assimilated into middle-class society. Nor, in the great majority of cases, do they even appear to see in this a style to be emulated. On our evidence there is thus little need, and little basis, for the hypothesis that nontraditional norms and status aspirations accompany these workers' enjoyment of a relatively high standard of living. Furthermore, the small number of cases where some degree of *embourgeoisement* does appear to be in train suggests that many other factors are involved here apart from that of affluence itself. For the most part, those ways in which the social lives of the men and women in our sample do most obviously diverge from a more traditional working-class pattern are, in our view, largely to be explained as the consequences of job and residential

mobility, and also perhaps of the constraints imposed by overtime and shift working; that is, as the consequences of certain objective conditions of their relatively prosperous existence to which these workers and their wives have been obliged to adapt. And the *direction* of these changes, we would suggest, is not towards 'middle-classness', but rather towards what might be termed a more 'privatized' mode of living.[25] In contrast with the communal and often kin-based sociability of the traditional working-class locality, the characteristic way of life among the couples we studied would appear to be one far more centred on the home and the immediate family; a way of life in which kin and neighbours, although still relatively important, figure in a more selective and limited way, and in which friends and acquaintances in the middle-class style do not, as yet at least, play any major part.[26]

(iii) Political Orientations

It was not the aim of our research to provide a direct test of the argument that growing affluence and the process of *embourgeoisement* were causing national, secular decline in the Labour Party's electoral support among the working class. For this purpose, a very different kind of research design would have been required. With our relatively small sample of affluent workers, we sought not simply to discover the pattern of their voting behaviour but also to set this in its socio-economic context and to form some idea of the *meaning* which party support held for our respondents. However, in presenting our findings in this section some straightforward voting figures are a necessary starting-point and are in themselves not without interest.

At the General Election of 1959, 212 out of our sample of 229 were eligible to vote. Of these 212, 71 per cent reported voting Labour as against 15 per cent Conservative and 3 per cent Liberal, with the remainder abstaining. Some variations in voting occurred between the different occupational groups within our sample, and thus this overall pattern to some degree reflects decisions made in constructing the sample.[27] Nonetheless, even allowing for this and for the fact that our respondents were males in the younger age groups, there can be little doubt on these figures that their level of Labour voting was, to say the very least, not lower than that which has been indicated for manual workers generally on the basis of national surveys; [28] and this, it may be remarked, was at the election in which the effects of working-class affluence were supposed to have told most heavily against the Labour Party. In fact, our data show that to a very large extent our affluent workers have been quite stable in their support of Labour: 69 per cent have been regular Labour voters from 1945 onwards or from whenever they first voted as opposed to 12 per cent being regular Conservative supporters. Moreover, among the remainder—the uncommitted or 'switchers'—there was no trend whatsoever towards greater Conservative voting in course of the 1950's. Finally when our respondents were asked how they intended to vote at the forthcoming general election (1964), the division between the two main parties was again 69 per cent Labour, 12 per cent Conservative. Thus, while the data we are able to produce from our sample may be insufficient in themselves to refute conclusively the thesis

which links working-class affluence with a political shift to the right, they are at all events conspicuously at odds with this and show, at least, that such a shift certainly does not occur in any necessary and automatic way.

Furthermore, that no simple relationship exists between affluence and vote is also indicated by our more detailed analyses. It is true that within our sample there is a tendency for the degree of Conservative voting to rise slightly with the level of both the husband's and the family's income. Again, the percentage of Conservative voters in the 1959 election was higher among those who reported that their standard of living had risen during the last ten years than it was among those who reported no such rise. However, in both of these cases, it turns out that the relationship in question is much reduced —and sometimes even eliminated—if one holds constant various other factors to which we shall shortly turn. The same limitation, it may be added, also applies to the relationship between Conservative voting and house ownership to which several writers have attached particular significance.[29] And moreover, in this case, the association was not in fact a particularly stable one: 15 per cent of the present owner-occupiers in our sample had been regular Conservative voters as against 7 per cent of those who were not owner-occupiers; but only 12 per cent of the former group compared with 11 per cent of the latter were intending to vote Conservative at the next election.

It would then seem fairly clear that the voting patterns of the workers we studied cannot be satisfactorily explained as any kind of straightforward reaction to their affluent condition. The evidence cannot be made to fit such an interpretation. Instead, our findings would suggest a view which, sociologically, makes far more sense. It is that in seeking to understand the voting behaviour of the men in our sample, major emphasis must be placed not on variables relating to their income, possessions, or standard of living generally, but rather on the similarities and differences in their social experiences and social relationships within the main milieux of their daily existence. In other words, one must not jump directly from economic circumstances to political action but should focus one's attention, rather, on the social reality which lies, as it were, behind these circumstances and which at the same time makes the political action meaningful.

Consider, for example, the salient fact that, notwithstanding their affluence, the percentage of men in our sample voting Labour is, if anything, higher than one would expect on the basis of national survey data. In the explanation of this, we would suggest, the most relevant considerations include the following: (i) that the men in question are all manual wage workers employed in large-scale industrial enterprises; (ii) that, as such, they are mostly members of trade unions; [30] (iii) that, in the vast majority of cases (96 per cent), they have been manual wage workers of one kind or another for most of their working lives; and (iv) that, again in the majority of cases, they were brought up in working-class families (68 per cent) and have married the daughters of such families (63 per cent). Given, then, the typical pattern of past experience and prevailing social relationships which these characteristics imply—and which affluence can scarcely affect—a high Labour vote is no longer very surprising. We can understand it as resulting from a complex

of mutually reinforcing traditions and group pressures, exercising their influence at work, in the family, and in the local community.

This interpretation, moreover, can be extended and confirmed if we now turn again to the Conservative minority. Our data reveal, as would be predicted, that these Conservative supporters, apart of course from all being wage workers, do not share to the same extent as the rest of the sample the working-class characteristics which have just been set out. Most notably, they are more likely than the Labour voters to be men who have remained outside the union movement (22 per cent against 11 per cent) or who have become union members only in course of their present employment (67 per cent against 39 per cent); and they would also appear generally more likely to have some connection in one way or another with white-collar society—through coming from a white-collar family or having married into such a family, through having held a white-collar job or having a wife with such a job.[31] It is, then, factors such as these which can modify—sometimes considerably—the relationship between Conservative voting and the economic variables to which we earlier referred. For example, of the non-unionists in the sample, 20 per cent intended voting Conservative in 1964 as compared with only 11 per cent of the union members; and within these two categories no association between income and vote is any longer apparent. Similarly, if we divide up the sample according to the degree of individuals' 'white-collar affiliation', we find that 21 per cent of those in the 'high' group are intending Conservative voters as against 10 per cent in the 'intermediate' group and only 7 per cent in the 'low' group.[32] And once more, income level appears to have no effect on vote when this further factor is held constant. In these ways too, therefore, it becomes evident that the link between affluence and vote is, at most, an indirect and uncertain one. The Conservative voters in our sample illustrate this point no less than the affluent supporters of Labour.

Finally in this section, we turn from the social correlates of party choice to a consideration of the voting behaviour of our respondents from their own point of view. In our interviews, we asked all those who had formed a fairly stable attachment to a party the reason for this; and the analysis of replies we received, in the case of the Labour majority in particular, are an important supplement to the foregoing discussion.

To begin with, the emphasis which we previously gave to certain class characteristics in understanding the high Labour vote in our sample is quite strongly confirmed by Labour supporters' own explanation of their position. By far the most frequent kind of reason given for an attachment to the Labour Party was one phrased in terms of class and of class and family custom: the Labour Party was the party which 'stands for the working class', which 'looks after ordinary working people like us' or, simply, the party which 'working-class people vote for'. In fact, 70 per cent of the 147 regular Labour supporters supplied answers giving reasons in this vein. In a way, therefore, these men would appear to differ little from the mass of Labour voters in the country as a whole. Abrams, for example, has reported on the basis of a national survey, carried out in 1960, that Labour is regarded by the large majority of its adherents as being an essentially 'class' party.[33] To

this extent, then, there is again evidence that affluence has, in itself, done little as yet to erode the class basis of Labour support.

At the same time, though, it is worth noting that the only other kind of explanation which Labour voters at all frequently provided was one which indicated an attachment to the party of a somewhat less affective and more calculative nature. Just under a quarter (24 per cent) gave reasons for their support in terms of particular material advantages which they expected to gain from certain aspects of Labour's policy—in relation, for instance, to social services or the management of the economy. Such a position is not, of course, in any way inconsistent with a sharp awareness of 'class' interests: nonetheless, where an outlook of this kind prevails, the tie to the Labour Party is one which could quite conceivably be broken—even if only temporarily— given circumstances which make Conservative policy appear the more attractive in economic terms. And there are other data from our interviews which suggests this same possibility.[34]

However, it should be added here that it was among the Conservative voters that calculative attitudes of the sort in question were most strongly in evidence. Exactly half of the 24 'stable' Conservative voters stated that they supported this party because they believed that they personally were better off economically under Conservative government or because they felt that the Conservatives had the better men and policies for creating general prosperity. On the other hand, instances of a more traditionalistic attachment to the Conservatives of a 'deferential' kind were rare; and more relevantly from the point of view of the *embourgeoisement* thesis, we were able to find no evidence at all of the 'socially aspiring' Conservative—that is, of the manual worker who votes Conservative because of the higher status which he feels this action serves to symbolize. In this connection, it should be remembered that the Conservative supporters in our sample, to a greater extent than the Labour voters, were likely to be cross-pressured—with white-collar relationships and experience set in opposition to their present role and status as industrial workers. In their case, thus, a largely instrumental view of politics is perhaps to be more expected than any tendency to regard party choice as an attribute of class or status group membership.

. . . . .

Our conclusion to this last section may, we believe, usefully serve as our conclusion to this paper as a whole. The point emerging from the foregoing discussion which carries most general significance is, in our view, the following: that the dynamics of working-class politics cannot be regarded as forming part of any inexorable process of social change deriving from continual rising standards of living. Certainly, the sequence, assumed in much previous discussion, of affluence—*embourgeoisement*—Conservative voting is generally unsupported by our findings. The acquisition by manual workers and their families of relatively high incomes and living standards does not, on our evidence, lead to widespread changes in their social values and life-styles in the direction of 'middle-classness'; neither would it appear to be conducive to a political shift to the right, or in any way incompatible with a continuing high level of support for Labour. 'Middle-classness' is not, after all, simply a matter of money; and politics has never been reducible to a

mere epiphenomenon of economic conditions. The position of a group within a system of social stratification is not decisively determined by the income or possessions of its members, but rather by their characteristic life-chances and experiences and by the nature of their relationships with other groups. And it is in this context that their politics must be understood—a context which changes much more slowly than the relative levels of wages and salaries or patterns of consumption.

Our affluent workers remain, in spite of their affluence, men who live by selling their labour power to their employers in return for wages; and, in all probability, they will still be so at the end of their working days. Again, although they and their families enjoy a standard of living comparable to that of many white-collar families, their social worlds are still to a large extent separate from those of the latter, except where bridges of kinship, or to a lesser degree of neighbourhood, can span the social distance between them. Nor is there much indication that affluence has encouraged the desire to *seek* acceptance in new social milieux at higher status levels. Thus, we would suggest, there is, as yet at least, little basis for expecting any particular change in the political attitudes and behaviour of these workers, apart perhaps from the spread of the more calculative—more rational—outlook to which we have referred.

We do not, of course, seek in this way to rule out the possibility that at some future date, when working-class affluence is more general and of longer standing, it may prove to have political implications of major importance. But in this case, we would argue, what still remains entirely uncertain is what these implications will be. The assumption that they will necessarily favour the Right, and social and political stability, has no firm basis: it may equally well be that by 1990 a latter-day John Millar will be again invoking the affluent worker as the source of social dissent and of political radicalism.

NOTES

1. John Millar, 'The Advancement of Manufactures, Commerce, and the Arts, since the Reign of William III; and the Tendency of this Advancement to diffuse a Spirit of Liberty and Independence', an essay appended to *An Historical View of the English Government from the Settlement of the Saxons in Britain to the Revolution in 1688*, London: Mawman, 1803.

2. See John Millar, *The Origin of the Distinction of Ranks*, London: Murray, 1779; *cf.* also W. C. Lehmann, *John Millar of Glasgow*, Cambridge: Cambridge University Press, 1960, Ch. XI esp.

3. Cf. R. L. Meek, 'The Scottish Contribution to Marxist Sociology' in John Saville (ed.), *Democracy and the Labour Movement; essays in honour of Dona Torr*, London: Lawrence and Wishart, 1954.

4. See, in particular, 'The English Elections', 1874 and 'Trades Unions', 1881; *cf.* also Engels' letters to Marx, 7 October 1858; to Marx, 18 November 1868; to Kautsky 12 September 1882; to Kelley–Wischnewetzky, 10 February 1885; and to Sorge, 7 December 1889. All the above are reprinted in Karl Marx and Frederick Engels, *On Britain*, Moscow: Foreign Languages Publishing House, 1953.

5. For a critical discussion of theories of this kind, see John H. Goldthorpe, 'Social Stratification in Industrial Society' in P. Halmos (ed.), *The Development of Industrial Society*, Sociological Review Monographs, No. 8, Keele, 1964.

6. For an elaboration of this argument, see David Lockwood, 'The "New Working Class"', *European Journal of Sociology*, Tome I, 1960, No. 2, 248–259, and John H. Goldthorpe and David Lockwood, 'Affluence and the British Class Structure', *Sociological Review*, n.s.II (1963), 133–163.

7. The theoretical basis for our choice of Luton will be given in full in our final report on the research. However, further relevant discussion of factors favourable to *embourgeoisement* can be found in David Lockwood and John H. Goldthorpe, 'The Manual Worker: Affluence, Aspiration and Assimilation', paper presented to the Annual Meeting of the British Sociological Association, 1962.

8. Vauxhall Motors Ltd; The Skefko Ball Bearing Co. Ltd; and Laporte Chemicals Ltd.

9. Three different skill levels were represented: 56 men were craftsmen (toolmakers, millwrights and other maintenance men from Skefko and Laporte); 23 were setters (from Skefko); and 150 were semi-skilled production workers. This latter category comprised men in jobs which were characteristic of the main type of production system operating in each of our three firms; viz. Vauxhall assemblers (86) Skefko machinists (41) and Laporte process workers (23). In effect, then, our sample was one of a population made up of men who met the criteria referred to above and who were employed in certain selected occupations in the three firms with which we were concerned. Caution must be exercized in regard to data relating to the sample as a whole in cases where there are marked differences between the occupational groups on which the sample is based; for in these cases 'overall' figures will reflect the weight given to particular groups through variations in our sampling ratios. Where references are made in the text to the sample as a whole without qualification, it may be assumed that inter-occupational differences are not, so far as we can discover, of any great significance.

10. The response rate for the manual workers (i.e. on the basis of the 229 agreeing to both interviews) was 70 per cent and for the white-collar workers, 72 per cent.

11. We would emphasize the preliminary nature of all the findings reported in this paper. The detailed results of our research will be presented in monographs dealing with different aspects of the study—industrial, political etc.—and these monographs will then, it is hoped, provide the basis for a final report aiming at a *vue d'ensemble*.

12. Goldthorpe and Lockwood, 'Affluence and the British Class Structure', pp. 135–6. In general, the 'Note on Concepts and Terminology' appended to 'Affluence and the British Class Structure' has been followed throughout the present text.

13. The factor next most frequently referred to—by 47 per cent of the more skilled men and 33 per cent of the semi-skilled—was that of security; and in many cases it was made clear that the main concern here was with long-run income maximization rather than with the minimum requirement of having a job of some kind. Also worth noting is the fact that those men who said they *had* thought of leaving gave reasons for this in preponderantly *non*-economic terms; less than 1 in 12 (7 per cent) referred to any dissatisfaction with pay. On the other hand, in the reasons given by semi-skilled men, the nature of their work and working conditions figured more prominently than any other source of discontent.

14. Of the 35 white-collar workers who had thought of leaving, poor pay was given as a reason by 9 (26 per cent) and together with the desire for wider job experience was the reason most often mentioned.

15. For a more detailed discussion of the working lives of the assemblers in our sample, see John H. Goldthorpe, 'Attitudes and Behaviour of Car Assembly Workers: a deviant case and a theoretical critique', *British Journal of Sociology*, 17 (1966), 227–244.

16. We asked: 'One way a worker might improve his position is by getting promotion, say, to a foreman's job. If you decided to have a go at this how would you rate your chances of getting to be a foreman? Would you say they were very good, fairly good, not too good or hopeless?' There were 4 'Don't knows'.

17. The white-collar workers were asked: 'What about the idea of promotion? Would you like this very much, quite a lot, not very much, not at all?' The manual workers were asked: 'How about the idea of becoming a foreman? Would you like this very much, quite a lot, not much, not at all?'

18. For a useful survey of the research on the basis of which some generalized picture of the 'traditional' working class way of life may be formed, see Josephine Klein, *Samples from English Cultures,* London: Routledge and Kegan Paul, 1965, vol. I, ch. 4.

19. Even in the case of the third of the sample the majority of whose kin were located more than 50 miles from Luton, the proportion of kin among the persons with whom spare time was most often spent remained at 22 per cent, and kin also accounted for 16 per cent of the wives' visiting partners.

20. The remaining 19 per cent (after adding in the 22 per cent who were kin) were workmates or ex-workmates. The 'neighbours' category includes 'ex-neighbours'; i.e. persons whom the respondents first came to know when they were living within ten minutes' walk.

21. Kin accounted for 31 per cent of the persons with whom the white-collar couples reported most often spending their spare time, and for 28 per cent of the wives' visiting partners.

22. As against 15 per cent and 41 per cent respectively who were neighbours. The remaining persons mentioned by the white-collar couples as leisure time companions were workmates.

23. In regard to the comparisons which we have made both between the white-collar couples and the manual couples who are largely separated from their kin and between the latter group and the other manual couples, it should be noted that no

great differences occur in the actual *numbers* of persons mentioned either as
leisure time companions or as wives' visiting partners. Thus, to think in terms of
the 'substitution' of neighbours (rather than of other friends) for absent kin would
appear appropriate.

24. The questions asked were: 'How about having other couples round, say for a meal,
or just for the evening: how often would you say you do this, on average?' and then
'Who is it you have round—are they friends, relatives or who?' 15 per cent of the
manual sample as against 7 per cent of the white-collar sample said that they never
had couples round, and 54 per cent as against 76 per cent said they entertained in
this way once a month or more. Of the couples entertained by the manual workers,
57 per cent were kin compared with 45 per cent in the case of white-collar workers.

25. Cf. Goldthorpe and Lockwood, 'Affluence and the British Class Structure', pp.
150–155.

26. As evidence of the degree of 'privatization' within the sample it may be noted that
on the question of the two or three people with whom spare time was most often
spent, 7 per cent of the couples could not mention even one person in this connection and 21 per cent could only mention one between them. The average number referred to by husband and wife *together* was under three. Again, in the case of visits
made by and to the wives, the range of persons involved appears much narrower
than that suggested in most studies of the 'traditional' worker. Only 3 per cent of the
wives mentioned seeing more than 6 people in this way during the past week, and
51 per cent mentioned only one person or none at all.

27. The Labour vote in the five main occupational groups was as follows: craftsmen,
76 per cent; setters, 52 per cent; process workers, 77 per cent; machinists, 76 per cent;
assemblers, 68 per cent. Similar variation occurs in all other voting data referred to
subsequently.

28. See, for example, the data presented in Robert R. Alford, *Party and Society,* London: John Murray, 1963, ch. 6 and Appendix B.

29. See, for example, Mark Abrams *et al., Must Labour Lose?,* London: Penguin Books,
1960, pp. 42–43.

30. Overall, 87 per cent of the sample were union members. All the setters and machinists belonged to a union and so too did 88 per cent of the craftsmen, 78 per cent
of the process workers and 79 per cent of the assemblers.

31. Of the Conservative voters, 45 per cent had white-collar connections in at least two
of these ways—through both their parents or parents-in-law and through their own
or their wives' occupational experience. The corresponding figure for the Labour
voters was 23 per cent. (These figures and those in the text relate to intended vote, 1964).

32. The 'high' group comprized men with white-collar connections through both their
parents or parents-in-law and through their own or their wives' occupational experience; those in the 'intermediate' group had connections in one or other of these
ways; and those in the 'low' group had no such connections.

33. Op. cit., pp. 12–14.

34. For example, in reply to a question on whether it would make any difference which
party won the next election, a third of the intending Labour voters felt that it
would not. And when attention was in this way directed to proximate and current issues, even those who felt that the election result would make a difference tended to
see this largely in terms of social welfare and other economic 'pay-offs' which they
might expect from a Labour victory, rather than in terms of 'the working class in
power' or the implementation of socialist ideas.

6

THE WITHERING AWAY OF CLASS:
A CONTEMPORARY MYTH

J. H. Westergaard

In this section we have been discussing what might be called the equality thesis: the idea that social class differences in Western societies are dissolving with the gradual spread of equality. Although we have attempted to balance the arguments on both sides, in a sense they cannot be. The contest is uneven because the pervasive egalitarianism of American society has given rise to an elaborate mythos of equality, carried by the mass media, that has so saturated the society that it has gained a general acceptance among both students and the public at large. According to these popular beliefs —which are all contrary to fact—most rich men in America began at the bottom; there is far more social mobility in the United States than elsewhere; there has been a radical redistribution of income in this country in the last few decades; the progressive income tax is a great leveler, soaking the rich and benefiting the poor; and the ownership of corporate stock is widely and equitably distributed among all groups of the population.*

With regard to the latter, for example, the president of the New York Stock Exchange, echoing the general belief, said a few years ago that "the creation of a *people's capitalism* in the United States is an economic landmark without parallel." Buttressing such statements are visions of coupon-clipping workers sharing broadly in the ownership of the factories in which they work, and statistical data demonstrating the growth in the number of shareholders from 1.5 million in 1900 to over 30 million in 1970.

What is ignored, of course, in the general celebration of American equality are the detailed facts such as the following table provides showing the distribution of stock according to occupation that give the lie to such claims. As shown, the vast majority of working men own no corporate stock whatsoever, a far cry from the much publicized image of people's capitalism. Ignored in the rhetoric of people's capitalism and similar egalitarian notions are the multimillionaire stockowners whose wealth and holdings are as formidable as they are unrecognized. A detailed study in the early 1960's revealed the following mammoth holdings: the late Richard K. Mel-

---

* For the mobility myth, for example, see Seymour M. Lipset and Reinhard Bendix, *Social Mobility in Industrial Society* (Berkeley: University of California Press, 1960), as well as the introduction to selection 30. For the redistribution myth, see the books by Kolko and Lampman mentioned in the footnotes to the introduction to the *Communist Manifesto*. For the income tax myth, see Kolko and Philip M. Stern, *The Great Treasury Raid* (New York: Random House, 1962).

SOURCE: Perry Anderson and Robin Blackburn, eds., *Towards Socialism* (Ithaca, N.Y.: Cornell University Press, 1966), pp. 77–95, 104–8. Reprinted by permission of Cornell University Press and the *New Left Review*.

Stock Ownership and Occupation, 1970

Occupation of Shareholder	Percent of Each Group Who Are Individual Shareholders
Professionals and Technical Workers	56
Managers, Officials, and Proprietors	49
Clerical and Sales Workers	24
Craftsmen and Foremen	13
Service Workers	6
Operatives and Laborers	5
Farmers and Farm Laborers	5

SOURCE: Computed from the New York Stock Exchange 1970 Census of Share-owners and U.S. Bureau of the Census, *Statistical Abstract of the United States* (Washington, D.C.: U.S. Government Printing Office, 1970), p. 225.

lon held, in addition to $2 million of Gulf Oil stock, $51 million of stock in the Mellon National Bank and Trust Company, $71 million of Alcoa, and $18 million of General Motors stock; Allen P. Kirby, besides his other holdings, owned $46 million of Alleghany Corporation stock, $6.5 million of New York Central Railroad stock, and $25 million of F. W. Woolworth; Lammot du Pont Copeland held $47 million of du Pont stock and $62 million of Christiana Securities Company stock; William L. McNight of Minnesota Mining and Manufacturing held $167 million of 3-M stock; Thomas J. Watson of IBM and his immediate family held about $52 million in IBM stock; Henry Ford, 2nd, owned $85 million of Ford stock; and the late Billy Rose owned $10 million of stock in AT&T.* This listing of giant stockowners whose holdings are truly staggering could go on and on, but it is meant to suggest only one fact: the enormous concentration of stock ownership in the United States. It has been estimated that a mere one percent of all American adults hold approximately 71 percent of the nation's corporate stock and own fully 28 percent of all the nation's wealth.

Just as *wealth* in this country is very unequally distributed, so too is *income*. For example, while the median income of fully employed American men was about $6,800 in 1966, and the income of full-time agricultural workers was $2,600, the chairman of General Motors in that year was paid $926,978, not including income earned from other sources. In 1968, the chairman of Chrysler Corporation earned a salary of $200,-000 plus other compensation of $430,700 for a total of $630,700. Earlier in the decade the forty-three highest paid men in American industry were earning annual salaries which ranged from a "low" of $250,000 to a high of over $550,000. These amounts did not include additional compensation in the form of expense accounts, deferred payments, pension plans, or stock options which companies increasingly made use of to reduce the tax bite on high executive compensation.

Taking the country as a whole, the top 20 percent of the nation's families currently receive about 41 percent of total personal income, while the poorest 20 percent receive only about 5 percent of personal income. It should be noted that there has been no appreciable change in this distribution at least since the end of World War II, and, as mentioned earlier, many scholars doubt that very much significant change has taken place at all during most of this century.

* For a more complete listing of enormous shareholders, see Jean Crockett and Irwin Friend, *Characteristics of Stock Ownership,* most accessibly summarized in the *New York Times,* September 13, 1963, Western edition.

It is this kind of data that stock the arsenal of those who deny the validity of the equality thesis. And in the present selection, British social scientist J. H. Westergaard discusses these continuing inequalities of wealth and income in Britain and the United States, and directly confronts many of the crucial arguments put forward by proponents of the equality thesis.

The years since the early 1950's have echoed with the claim that the old class structure of capitalism is steadily dissolving. The labels attached to that new order of society which is believed to be emerging from the ruins of the old—the 'welfare state', the 'affluent society', the 'home-centred society', the 'mass society', 'post-capitalism', and so on—have become the clichés of contemporary debate. Their variety and imprecision indicate some of the uncertainties of diagnosis and prognosis. Evaluations, too, have differed widely: reactions to the trends discerned range from triumph to despondency. But the descriptions offered of current trends generally have much in common: the assertion that the old sources of tension and class conflict are being progressively eliminated or rendered irrelevant; that the structure of contemporary Western societies is being recast in a mould of middle class conditions and styles of life; that these developments signal 'the end of ideology'. Such notions in turn are infused with a sense of a social fluidity which is felt to fal-

sify past characterizations of capitalism.

Yet arguments and evidence alike have often been taken for granted, rather than stated precisely and scrutinized carefully. Rhetoric has obscured both links and gaps in the chain of reasoning. Hunches, impressions and assumptions have been given parity with facts. Minor changes have been magnified into major ones, uncertain indications into certain proof. Evidence consistent with several interpretations has been treated as if only one were possible. The labelling of trends has been extended into a labelling of sceptics as 'fundamentalists', their criticisms dismissed as the product of a psychological inability or unwillingness to recognize a changing reality. These are reasons enough for even a cursory review of the main themes and postulates of the fashionable interpretations of mid-twentieth century capitalism and its allegedly dissolving class structure, as they have been formulated especially in Britain and the United States.[1]

Whatever their variations, these interpretations hinge on two basic as-

[1] The following are examples of recent literature, differing greatly in approach, emphasis and interpretation, in which the thesis is stated or implied that capitalism has been fundamentally transformed and that its class structure is being eroded or rendered innocuous: C. A. R. Crosland, *The Future of Socialism*, 1956; J. Strachey, *Contemporary Capitalism*, 1956; T. H. Marshall, *Citizenship and Social Class*, 1950; D. Butler and R. Rose, *The British General Election of 1959*, 1960; M. Abrams *et al.*, *Must Labour Lose?* 1960; F. Zweig, *The Worker in an Affluent Society*, 1961; R. Dahrendorf, *Class and Class Conflict in Industrial Society*, 1959; J. K. Galbraith, *American Capitalism*, 1956; D. Bell, *The End of Ideology*, 1961; K. Mayer, 'Diminishing Class Differentials in the United States', *Kyklos*, vol. 12, no. 4, 1959; R. A. Nisbet, 'The Decline and Fall of Social Class', *Pacific Sociolog. Rev.*, Spring 1959. This is only a small, and in some respects haphazard, selection; but it illustrates varying expressions of a thesis which has been postulated, or simply assumed as self-evident, in a great deal of recent socio-political commentary.

sumptions. The first is that the substantive inequalities of earlier capitalism are both diminishing and losing their former significance. The second is that, for these or other reasons, radical dissent is progressively weakened as new patterns of living and aspiration negate or cut across the older class-bound horizons and loyalties. Substantive inequalities are reduced, it is argued, by a continuous redistribution of wealth and the extension of economic security; by a growth in the numbers and importance of occupations in the middle ranges of skill and reward; by a progressive narrowing of the inequalities of opportunity for individual advancement; and by a widening diffusion of power or influence. In so far as power remains concentrated, it no longer derives from the accumulation of private property, but from control over bureaucratic organizations of diverse kinds—public at least as much as private—in which authority is divorced from wealth. Thus two crucial dimensions of inequality no longer coincide. In so far as inequalities remain in the chances of wealth, health, security and individual advancement, these disparities lose their psychological (and, it is often implied, their moral) force as sources of conflict because, with steadily rising levels of living and a widening base of common rights of 'citizenship', their effects are confined to a continuously narrowing area of life. Analysis and speculation concerning the cultural, psychological and political repercussions of these changes have, of course, focused primarily on the manual working class, whose homogeneity and distinctive character, it is argued, are being eroded. Among manual workers, according to one interpretation, old loyalties of class are being replaced by

new preoccupations with status: a former unity of industrial and political interest is dispelled by a growing sensitivity to invidious distinctions of social prestige and subtle variations in the styles of life, by which everyday patterns of social acceptance and rejection are symbolized. Alternatively, workers' aspirations are seen to focus more and more narrowly upon the home and the immediate family, a concern with material achievement predominating that involves little or no concomitant preoccupation with the rituals of status or with the ideological orientations of class. In either version, loyalties of the world of work are replaced by loyalties of the hearth; the values and perspectives of the labour market are replaced by those of the consumers' market; a faith in collective action is replaced by a reliance on individual achievement or family security; in short, an ethos traditionally thought of as middle class is assumed to be spreading widely among manual workers. In addition, it is sometimes argued or implied, new dividing lines of cultural distinction or political tension are coming to the fore which bear no relation to the old divisions of economic class or social status: for instance, between adults and adolescents, the latter inhabiting a distinctive 'teen-age culture' of their own; between 'high-brows' or 'egg-heads' and the 'masses,' irrespective of social position; between the old, the retired and those living on fixed incomes, on the one hand, and earners—employers and employees alike—on the other hand; between people in their role as producers and (somewhat schizophrenically, it would seem) in their role as consumers; between professionals and 'organization men' in both private and public administration; and so on.

The general tenor of these arguments is familiar; the balance within them between truth and falsehood, fact and speculation, plausibility and implausibility, much less so.

1. Inequalities of Wealth

In its simplest form, the 'post-capitalist' thesis postulates a continuous tendency towards the reduction of inequalities in the distribution of income and wealth.[2] In particular, it is pointed out, incomes as recorded in the reports of tax authorities and official surveys have shown a fairly marked convergence towards the middle ranges since the late 1930's. This argument can be challenged on two major scores. The first, as critics both in Britain and in the United States have emphasized, is that in part at least the reduction in measured income inequality merely reflects an increased use of devices to reduce the heavier tax liabilities of the wartime and post-war period. Such devices involve the conversion of real income into forms which escape normal rates of income tax—and which do not appear as income in the usual sources of information. There are no means of assessing the full amount of income

which thus goes unrecorded. But since such devices are more readily available to those with relatively high incomes in general, and to private business in particular, the net result is an understatement of income inequality in current data.[3] In fact, the few attempts made to adjust the data, in such a way as to make allowance for some of the distortions resulting from tax evasive devices, have indicated a much milder redistribution of effective income than usually assumed—and one confined largely or exclusively to the 1940's.

The second objection relates to this last point. Even when no allowance is made for the effects of tax evasion, such reduction in the inequality of incomes as can be traced in both British and American analyses is in the main a phenomenon of the Second World War and the years immediately around it. Signs of any consistent narrowing of income disparities in the recorded data during the decades before then are slight and uncertain; and if account is taken of the probability that means of tax evasion were further developed and more elaborately institutionalized in the 1950's, this last decade or so may well have witnessed a slight regression towards a distribution of effective in-

---

[2] The discussion in this section draws, *inter alia*, on the following analyses of trends in the distribution of income and wealth: for Britain, H. F. Lydall, 'The Long-Term Trend in the Size Distribution of Incomes', *J. Royal Statist. Soc.*, series A, vol. 122, no. 1, 1959; *idem, British Incomes and Savings*, 1955; *idem* and D. G. Tipping, 'The Distribution of Personal Wealth in Britain', *Bull. Oxford Univ. Inst. Statistics*, Feb. 1961; J. A. Brittain, 'Some Neglected Features of Britain's Income Levelling', *Amer. Econ. Rev.*, May 1960; J. L. Nicholson, 'Redistribution of Income in the United Kingdom', in C. Clark and D. Stuvel (eds.), *Income and Wealth: series X*, 1964; R. M. Titmuss, 'The Social Division of Welfare', in his *Essays on the Welfare State*, 1958; T. Lynes, *National Assistance and National Prosperity*, 1962; for the United States, S. Kusnetz and E. Jenks, *Shares of Upper Income Groups in Income and Savings*, 1953; R. J. Lampman, *The Share of Top Wealth Holders in National Wealth, 1922–1956*; H. F. Lydall and J. B. Lansing, 'A Comparison of the Distribution of Personal Income and Wealth in the United States and Great Britain', *Amer. Econ. Rev.*, March 1959; G. Kolko, *Wealth and Power in America*, 1962; H. P. Miller, *Trends in the Incomes of Families and Persons in the United States, 1947 to 1960*, 1963; *idem, Rich Man, Poor Man*, 1964.

[3] For a detailed examination of the variety of devices available for tax evasion in Britain, see R. M. Titmuss, *Income Distribution and Social Change*, 1962.

come more unequal than in the 1940's. This may remain uncertain. But it is clear that such reductions of income inequality as have occurred are both limited in extent, and very largely the result of the special demands of the wartime economy and of policies introduced at or around the time of the war.

There are factors, it is true, which might be expected to make for a general, longer-term trend towards income equalization: the decreased proportion of unskilled and casual workers in the labour force, as well as other changes in occupational structure; diminished pay differentials of skill, sex and age; an increased progression in the rates of income tax. In the latter case, however, the redistributive effects are limited—perhaps indeed neutralized—by the continued importance of nonprogressive forms of taxation, by the regressive operation of income tax allowances, and by the adoption of tax evasive devices.[4] In general, moreover, except in the 1940's the redistributive effects of these and other factors seem not to have been sufficient substantially to outweigh other long-run factors working in the opposite direction: among these, the increased proportion of old and retired people in the population, coupled with the fact that—at least in Britain—the real incomes of retired people dependent on public support have not kept up with general increases in income. This might seem to suggest a shift in the nature of income inequality—from disparities between classes and occupations to disparities between age groups. Indeed, such an interpretation is frequently implied,

and fits in with the general thesis of a dissolving class structure. But it is essentially misleading. Poverty in old age is not a general phenomenon of the retired—but of those who in retirement have neither property income nor the proceeds of private (though tax-supported) pension schemes to rely on. The burden of poverty—on a contemporary definition of the term—has been shifted progressively into the tail-end of working class and lower middle class life; but it remains a problem of those classes.

The inequality of incomes is thus maintained in part through differential access to fringe benefits and tax-free sources of income generally. Old disparities take on new forms appropriate to the corporate economy of the mid-twentieth century. But, despite a drop during the 1940's in the reported ratio of income from capital to earned income, property ownership remains a potent, direct source of income inequality; especially so, if regard is paid to effective rather than nominal income. And the distribution of private property remains strikingly unequal. In Britain in the mid-1950's, two-fifths of all private property were estimated to be in the hands of only 1 per cent of the adult population, four-fifths in the hands of only 10 per cent. Concentration was still more extreme forty years earlier; but such diffusion as has taken place—and the estimate may overstate its extent—has only marginally affected the bulk of the population. Legal ownership of private corporate business is especially highly concentrated, four-fifths of all share capital being held by only 1 per cent of the

---

[4] Some remarkable recent calculations suggest that, both in Britain and the United States, there may be hardly any progression in the proportionate incidence of all forms of taxation combined as between different levels of income. See Clark and Peters, 'Income Redistribution: Some International Comparisons', in Clark and Stuvel (eds.), *op. cit.*

adult population, and nearly all the rest by another 9 or 10 per cent. The concentration of private property in the United States is not quite so extreme—the result in part, no doubt, of a wider diffusion of home ownership and a rather larger surviving element of small-scale enterprise, especially farming; but it is still very marked. In the middle 1950's, 1 per cent of the adult population owned a quarter of all private property. Moreover, the American figures show no substantial and consistent decline in the unequal distribution of property over time; and despite a slightly greater diffusion of shareholding, the concentration of legal ownership of private business corporations follows much the same general pattern as in Britain.[5]

Thus the argument that a continuous trend towards income equalization and a wide diffusion of property are dissolving the class structure of capitalist society can hardly be sustained. Nor, therefore, can any weakening of the 'radical consciousness' be attributed to such forces. This is not to say that the significance of the economic divisions characteristic of capitalism remains unchanged. It is obvious that the much milder character of the trade cycle since the 1930's has reduced the insecurities of working class life—even though the manual worker is still more exposed to the risk of short-time working and of redundancy, cyclical or technological, than others; and even though unemployment has increased in the last decade, especially in the United States. It is clear, too, that the extension of general social services— while their redistributive effects are commonly exaggerated—has released personal income for expenditure in

other fields, shifting the effect of income differentials from the 'more essential' towards the 'less essential' areas of consumption. Even so, such enlargement of the basic rights of 'citizenship' has been neither an automatic nor a continuous process. In the recent history of both Britain and the United States, it is essentially a phenomenon of the 1930's and the 1940's. The last decade and more have seen little or no extension of such policies: in Britain, indeed, regression in some respects; while in the United States measures introduced primarily during the New Deal have left vast areas of basic social security or insecurity—health and housing in particular—to the more or less unrestricted play of market forces, property interests and private charity, in a manner reminiscent of the late nineteenth century Britain.

The mitigation of the effects of inequality through an extension of citizenship rights and economic security has thus depended—as it does in the future—on the assertion of a 'radical consciousness'. Overall levels of living have, of course, also risen, as a consequence of forces of a more continuous and less directly policy-determined character: the long-run, though intermittent, upward trend in productivity; and (a factor often neglected) the spread of the small-family pattern, involving a curtailment of some of the traditional fluctuations in the economic cycle of the working class family, and the shift of relative poverty largely to a single phase of the cycle, that of old age.

In short, inequalities of income and property have been only marginally reduced. But they operate in areas of expenditure increasingly removed from

[5] See also E. B. Cox, *Trends in the Distribution of Stock Ownership*, 1963.

those of bare subsistence living, and against a background of generally rising average levels of real income. It may well be, therefore, that the persistent inequalities of wealth are coming to assume a different significance in the eyes of those who remain 'more unequal than others'. The visibility of economic inequality may diminish, obscured by past and prospective rises in the overall levels of living. Persistent disparities may be veiled, too, if their effects are felt increasingly late in life rather than in the early stages of a worker's career. Resentment may diminish, or change in character, as inequality is relevant more to the 'frills' of life than to essentials of survival.

Arguments to this effect are, in fact, implicit or explicit in a number of the more sophisticated versions of the 'post-capitalist' thesis. They point, not so much to a transformation of the economic structure of class as such, as to a transformation of the conditions relevant to the formation and direction of class consciousness: it is not the inequalities of class that have been reduced, but their 'transparency'. But in this shift from an economic and institutional analysis of class structure to a psychological analysis of class perceptions, assumptions are involved which are neither self-evidently true nor yet often enough made explicit. Of these, the most central—and a very simple one—is the premise that what the observer regards as 'frills' will also generally be so regarded. It cannot be realistically denied—though it may be forgotten—that 'standards' of living, in the sense of notions about what constitutes a tolerable or reasonable level of living, are not fixed, but tend to rise *more or less* concomitantly with actual levels of living. The logic of the 'post-capitalist' thesis then requires that this

should be 'less' rather than 'more'. It implies the assumption, either that the rise in actual levels of living generally keeps one step ahead of, or on a par with, the rise in the standards or expectations which people set themselves; or that any discrepancy in the other direction will be insufficient to generate the degree of tension which in the past was a major component of political radicalism and industrial militancy. Indeed, the argument that class consciousness among working class people is being progressively replaced by an increased concern with status, or by a 'home-centred' preoccupation with sheer material achievement, appears to postulate that any such excess of expectations over the level of living which can actually be achieved at any given time will provide, not a potential for social protest, but only an incentive for further individual effort within the limits of the existing economic and political order—a spur to efficient conformity.

Such postulates and assumptions, however, need much more explicit statement and concrete evidence than they have hitherto been given. Political trends in the post-war Western world are no proof of their accuracy; for those trends cannot be described simply in terms of a progressive reduction of class conflict; nor, in so far as they can, are they amenable to plausible explanation only in terms of the kind of arguments outlined above. Again, no proof is provided by the numerous studies, impressionistic observations and inspired conjectures which have pointed to heightened material aspirations and an increased adoption of 'middle class' standards of living among workers. Doubt arises, not about the general truth of such observations, but about their interpretation. The notion that workers must somehow 'catch' middle class values and orientations when they adopt spending habits that earlier were possible only for middle class people is, of course, naïve in the extreme.[6] It is hardly necessary to belabour the point that the process by which the luxuries of yesterday become the necessities of today, and in turn are replaced by new luxuries, is a long-standing one, and one whose end does not seem in sight. What is important, however, is that the process may be changing its character —and not necessarily in the directions assumed in fashionable commentary. For it is arguable, indeed plausible, that the luxuries of today are increasingly widely seen as the necessities— not of tomorrow or a remoter future, but of today also; that the prerogatives of one class are increasingly demanded as the rights of all; in short, that the rate of increase in standards or expectations of living is accelerating faster than the rate of increase in actual levels of living. Ordinary standards of aspiration may to a growing extent be set by the levels in fact achieved only by the prosperous minority—through direct comparison, or under the impact of advertising and the mass media generally. Indeed, the dynamics of the contemporary capitalist economy requires such a sustained pressure for consumption, as the defenders of advertising are prone to stress.

If this is so, then the nature of class structure is certainly changing. The character of individual classes as 'quasi-communities', as partially separate sub-cultures each with its own fairly distinctive set of norms, standards and aspirations, will be loosening. Parochial, tradition-bound ceilings on hopes and demands in the various strata and groups of the working class will be in process of replacement by a common, 'middle class' yardstick of material achievement. Though not a new phenomenon, the probable contemporary acceleration of the process is significant. This, in a sense, is precisely what the apologists for contemporary capitalism claim is happening; yet the conclusions they draw need by no means follow. Precisely opposite conclusions are equally, or even more, plausible. For while the common 'middle class' yardstick is continually being raised, the levels of material achievement which it prescribes are perpetually, and by very definition, beyond the reach of the bulk of the population. The persistent economic inequalities thus guarantee a built-in tension between goals and the objective possibilities of achieving them. Whether tension is translated into political radicalism, or finds other forms of expression, is a separate question, and will be briefly discussed later. Its answer will depend in part on non-economic factors. But if the analysis is correct, it is clear that in at least one respect the potential for class conflict in contemporary capitalist societies, far from decreasing, may instead be growing.

2. Inequalities of Opportunity

It is a major theme of much contemporary commentary that Western societies are becoming steadily more 'fluid'. Not only is it believed that economic and

[6] For a cogent critique of this and a number of other assumptions embedded in the postulate of working class 'embourgoisement', see D. Lockwood, 'The "New Working Class" ', *European J. Sociology*, vol. 1, no. 2, 1960; *idem* and J. Goldthorpe, 'Affluence and the British Class Structure', *Sociolog. Rev.*, vol. 11, 1963.

other distinctions between the social strata are getting blurred; but movement between the strata is assumed to be more frequent than before, the opportunity for such movement more equally distributed. The internal homogeneity, the external distinctiveness and the hereditary character of the working class are being weakened, so it is argued—as individuals increasingly acquire rather than inherit their class position; and as in any case the continuous growth in numbers of white collar jobs provides new openings for upward social mobility. Assertions along these lines are common—even in general socio-political commentaries by social scientists who, in their role as technical specialists, must recognize the flimsiness of the evidence.[7]

For in fact the evidence flatly contradicts some of the formulations of this thesis; and it leaves others open to serious doubt. First, so far as can be seen, overall inequalities of opportunity for social ascent and descent have not been reduced in either Britain or the United States during this century—or, for that matter, in most other Western countries for which information is available. In comparison, for instance, with the son of a professional or a business executive, the odds against a manual worker's son achieving professional status, or just a middle-class job in general, have remained very much as they were at the turn of the century. More adequate data might alter the detailed picture, but hardly the general conclusion. Most of the evidence relates, of course, to the experience of people fairly well advanced in their careers—not to today's younger generation. But data on the distribution of educational opportunity in contemporary Britain, and on post-war trends of social mobility in the United States, do not suggest any prospect of striking changes in the future.[8]

Secondly, however, it may be argued that *relative* inequalities of opportunity between those born in different classes matter less than *absolute* chances of advancement: the absolute chance, say, which a working class boy has of climbing out of the class in which he starts life. If changes in the occupational structure (or other changes) substantially increase such absolute chances of upward mobility—even if the same changes improve the career prospects of those born higher up the social scale, and relative opportunity thus remains as unequal as before—this could be significant in reducing the degree to which working class status is, and appears to be, permanent and hereditary. In fact, shifts in occupational structure have occurred, and are still occurring, which could appear to justify some such expectations. The general consequences of these shifts need separate discussion. But their net effect on social mobility has been to increase upward movement no more than at most rather margin-

[7] Among the studies on which the following discussion is based are: D. V. Glass (ed.), *Social Mobility in Britain*, 1956; N. Rogoff, *Recent Trends in Occupational Mobility*, 1953; articles in *Amer. Sociolog. Rev.* by E. Chinoy (April 1955), G. Lenski (Oct. 1958) and E. Jackson and H. J. Crockett (Feb. 1964); G. Carlsson, *Social Mobility and Class Structure*, 1955; K. Svalastoga, *Prestige, Class and Mobility*, 1959; S. M. Miller, *Comparative Social Mobility*, vol. ix, no. 1 of *Current Sociology*, 1960; S. M. Lipset and R. Bendix, *Social Mobility in Industrial Society*, 1959.

[8] See E. Jackson and H. J. Crockett, 'Occupational Mobility in the United States', *Amer. Sociolog. Rev.*, Feb. 1964; and the references in footnote 9 on page 93 below.

ally. The evidence is patchy and not all of a piece. Nevertheless, there has been no sign of any marked expansion in the chances of climbing up the social scale.

This is not to say that the Western capitalist countries are 'closed' societies —Britain any more than the United States, despite the old stereotypes. There is a good deal of movement of individuals between the different strata, even though much of this movement covers fairly short distances in social space, involves shifts within either the manual or the non-manual group far more often than between them, and is characterized by sharp and persistent inequalities in the distribution of opportunities. The point is that, partially 'open' as they are, these industrial societies have not become *more* open during this century. Factors which might have been expected to alter rates of mobility over time seem either to have been insignificant in effect, or to have cancelled each other out. Educational opportunities, for example, have been extended. But their extension, in large measure, has benefited all classes. Inequalities of educational opportunity remain marked—at the higher levels of education generally provided today in comparison with the past. The educational qualifications normally required at any given point of the occupational scale have simply been raised. It is true that the overall expansion of education has been accompanied by some reduction in the inequalities of educational opportunity. But this—a slow trend, so far as Britain is concerned, and one not noticeably accelerated after 1944—has occurred to a more limited degree than is usually assumed; so limited, that its consequences have evidently been roughly neutralized by concomitant restrictions on social mobility through channels other than the educational system.[9] These restrictions are often forgotten; but the increasing emphasis on the role of education in social recruitment is a direct reflection of them. In particular, with the professionalization, bureaucratization and automation of work, appointment to jobs in the middle and higher reaches of the occupational scale comes to depend more on school, college and university qualifications than on personal qualities and experience acquired at work. The frequency of social mobility has not been significantly increased; but its incidence is steadily more confined to a single phase of the life cycle. If the individual is to be socially mobile, he must be so during his years of formal education: the chances of promotion or demotion, once he has entered on his adult working career, are almost certainly narrowing. The position of the adult manual worker—and to a growing extent, that of the routine grade

[9] See A. Little and J. H. Westergaard, 'The Trend of Class Differentials in Educational Opportunity in England and Wales'. *Brit. J. Sociology*, Dec. 1964. See also the various major special studies of the distribution of educational opportunity in post-war Britain: J. Floud *et al.*, *Social Class and Educational Opportunity*, 1956; R. K. Kelsall, *Report on an Enquiry into Applications for Admission to Universities*, 1957; Ministry of Education, Central Advisory Council, *Early Leaving*, 1954; *idem*, *15 to 18*, 1959–60 (Crowther report); Committee on Higher Education, *Higher Education: Report* and *Appendices I and II*, 1963; and especially, J. W. B. Douglas, *The Home and the School*, 1964. Cf. also D. V. Glass, 'Education and Social Change in Modern England' in M. Ginsberg (ed.), *Law and Opinion in England in the 20th Century*, 1959. For some United States data, see, e.g., D. Wolfle, *America's Resources of Specialized Talent*, 1954.

clerical worker—becomes a more, not a less, permanent one.[10]

Nevertheless, it might be argued, this very change in the character of social mobility may alter people's perceptions of the chances of advancement. Mobility becomes more of an institutionalized process. The educational system is geared to it. Career opportunities become more predictable, as they come to depend more on a formalized kind of scholastic achievement. 'Elbows', 'string-pulling', connections and luck will matter less. In consequence, the chances of rising in the social scale may *seem* to be greater, even though they are not; and failure may be accepted with more resignation, if it is the result of a 'fair' process of selection. The argument, however, is double-edged. Failure may be the more unacceptable, if accepting it means to recognize one's intellectual 'inferiority'. Moreover, the very institutionalization of education as the royal road to success is likely to increase expectations to the point where they will come into conflict with the harsh reality of existing limitations on opportunity. There again, the question turns on psychological imponderables, about which very little is known. But there is good reason to believe that the demand for education is spreading well down the social scale. In part, indeed, this is a logical reaction to the growing importance of formal education as the main channel of social mobility: as the adult worker's hopes of promotion for himself become still more evidently unreal, aspirations focus instead upon the children's prospects. Be that as it may, such heightened recognition of the importance of education is another example of a weakening of the old cultural distinctions between the classes. But precisely as workers increasingly share 'middle class' aspirations for the education and future careers of their children, so the existing limitations and persistent inequalities of educational opportunity must result in the frustration of those aspirations as the common experience. Such frustration may be the harder to bear, because the condemnation of both parents and children to permanently inferior status is more final and irreversible than before.

The strength of the various factors involved is still unknown. The balance of probabilities, and the forms in which frustrated aspirations might find expression, are thus uncertain. Yet the conclusion stands that in this field, too, the potential for social protest is at least as likely to be growing as to be declining. Contemporary capitalism generates a tension between aspirations increasingly widely shared and opportunities which, by the very nature of the class structure, remain restricted and unequally distributed.

[10] Evidence suggesting a decline over time in the proportion of industrial managers or directors who reached their positions by promotion from low-grade clerical or manual jobs can be found for Britain in: Acton Society Trust, *Management Succession*, 1956; R. V. Clements, *Managers: A Study of Their Careers in Industry*, 1958; C. Erickson, *British Industrialists: Steel and Hosiery, 1850–1950*, 1959. The Civil Service has shown increased recruitment of administrative class officials by promotion from the lower ranks (R. K. Kelsall, *Higher Civil Servants in Britain*, 1955), but is probably a special case. R. Bendix, *Work and Authority in Industry*, 1963, *inter alia* summarizes some American data on trends in the recruitment of industrial management.

3. Changes in Occupational Structure

The share of white collar jobs in total employment has been growing throughout this century. Commentators have often exaggerated the implications of this trend hitherto. They have tended to underplay the facts, for instance, that the very marked 'white collar trend' in the United States in large measure has reflected a general shift from agricultural to urban employment; that the occupational composition of the male labour force has been very much less affected than that of the female labour force, within which 'white blouse' work has replaced domestic service as the dominant form of employment; and that the expansion of the 'tertiary sector' of the economy has increased the relative number, not only of white collar jobs, but also to a small extent of non-domestic service jobs, many of them low-paid and demanding little skill. It is true, nevertheless, that shifts in occupational structure overall have involved a fall in the share of unskilled and casual work, and a rise in the share of both semi-skilled manual and various kinds of black-coated work.[11] Moreover, much of the commentary has been directed to the future rather than the past. Not only will the 'white collar trend' continue for some time; but automation in industry is likely to produce a sizeable growth in the numbers of skilled workers and technicians, in place of that growth in the numbers of semi-skilled workers which in the past has been associated with the mechanization of industry and its conversion to conveyor-belt production. These prospects have been widely hailed as yet another source of capitalist social stability: a strengthening of the centre in place of 'polarization'.

There is, however, considerable room for doubt about such complacently enthusiastic interpretations.[12] The balance between the two trends— of automation, with its increased demand for skill and technical expertise, and of continuing mechanization of the older kind, with its increased employment of semi-skilled workers—is still uncertain, and may remain so for some time to come. The adoption of automation is likely to be a slow and uneven business. The relevant criteria, of course, will be profitability, not work satisfaction through 'job enlargement' for its own sake. Since capitalist economic organization provides no mechanisms for the sharing of gains and losses, resistance to automation from small business may be, and from trade unions will be, considerable. Labour resistance, indeed, is certain to grow if the American pattern of recent years

[11] Shifts in occupational structure can be more accurately traced for the United States than for Britain; see, e.g., U.S. Bureau of Census, *Occupational Trends in the United States, 1900–1950*, 1958. Official British classifications of occupations have changed a good deal over time. But it is fairly clear that the approximate two-to-one ratio of manual to non-manual workers in the male population of 1951 represented only a rather limited relative decline of the manual element during this century. When the relevant 1961 Census figures are available they may show some acceleration of the rate of decline. For one estimate of the growth of 'middle class' occupations, see A. L. Bowley, *Wages and Income of the United Kingdom Since 1860*, 1937.

[12] The work of G. Friedmann includes admirably balanced and careful assessments of the implications of technological change for labour; see his *Industrial Society: The Emergence of the Human Problems of Automation*, 1955, and *The Anatomy of Work*, 1962.

spreads—the paradox of high unemployment rates persisting during a boom. There is a danger here for the working class movement: of a division between those—the unskilled and workers in the declining industries—most affected by technological unemployment, and those whose labour is at a high premium in the changing market. But the unpredictability, and the potentially sweeping character, of the incidence and effects of automation may reduce that danger, if not eliminate it. Technological innovation thus generates tension of the very kind that, allegedly, is a matter of the past. And since the source of such tension is inherent in capitalist economic organization, it can only be overcome through extensive public intervention of the kind that, allegedly again, is a contemporary irrelevancy. If both the fruits and the sacrifices involved in automation are to be shared, they must be socialized: the case against private property and private economic control is underlined. Technological innovation may be inhibited, too, as it is at present, by shortages of skilled labour and technical expertise. But in so far as these shortages are overcome through extension of education and training, the premiums which the new skills can command in the labour market will diminish. Whether 'job enlargement' through automation will decrease political radicalism by increasing work satisfaction is unpredictable; for the relationship between work satisfaction and class consciousness remains as yet virtually unexplored. But in economic terms, any 'middle class' potential of the new 'aristocracy of labour' rests on conditions in the labour market which

happen now to be favourable, but which may well not continue to be so.

In general, the 'optimistic' evaluations of current and prospective shifts in occupational structure are based on a static view of the relative rewards, prestige and conditions associated with different occupations. Premiums for scarce skills are implicitly assumed to persist, even if the scarcity itself is unlikely to do so. White collar work is implicitly assumed to retain its traditional status and characteristics, even though the expansion of such work is almost certainly also changing its traditional features. The rationalization, mechanization and perhaps even the partial automation of clerical work will accentuate the division between controllers and supervisors, on the one hand, and routine black-coated operatives, on the other. If so, the latter increasingly are reduced to the status of bureaucratic counterparts of the semi-skilled manual workers of industry. There has, no doubt, already been a long-standing trend in that direction, but a slow one. It is likely to be accelerated, and to gain greater significance, as the traditional compensation of routine clerical work disappears: that of a reasonable chance of promotion. The forces which now tend to block previous channels of upward mobility for those who start their careers in low-grade white collar jobs have already been discussed. Whether these and related changes will—at last—result in a social and political identification of routine clerical workers with the manual working class is a moot point. Their long history of middle-class associations allows room for doubt.[13] The changes in their status, conditions and

[13] D. Lockwood's *The Black-coated Worker: A Study in Class Consciousness*, 1958, is an acute and elegant analysis of the roots of white collar workers' longstanding social and political separation from the manual working class. See also C. W. Mills, *White Collar*, 1951.

prospects could produce other reactions—in particular circumstances, as recent historical precedents suggest, considerably less pleasant ones. The point remains that to interpret the continuing expansion of white collar work as a uniform strengthening of the 'stable' middle strata of society is to apply a yardstick of decreasing contemporary relevance.

· · · · ·

4. Class Culture and Class Solidarity

Point for point the evidence underlines the same broad conclusion: the structural inequalities of capitalist society remain marked. Disparities of economic condition, opportunity and power persist—modified, if at all, only within fairly narrow limits. There is no built-in automatic trend towards diminishing class differentials. But it does not necessarily follow that the persistent, objective lines of class division will also be, or continue to be, the lines within which consciousness of class takes shape or across which conflict occurs. That there need be no such neat correspondence is very clear from the example of the United States. It is the claim of many contemporary commentators that Britain, and Western Europe generally, are now going the way of North America in this respect. Among arguments in support of

this claim are those which stress a lessened significance or visibility of inequality—as the old insecurities of working class life are reduced or eliminated; as overall levels of living increase; as opportunities for individual social mobility, while not increased, become institutionalized through the system of formal education. The conclusion, as I have tried to show, in no obvious way follows from the facts. But other arguments have emphasized rather a general erosion of the cultural distinctiveness of working class life, and of those features of the local environment from which, it is assumed, class consciousness among workers has traditionally derived its strength. Old loyalties to kin, locality and traditional patterns of life are on the wane; and so, it has been implied (especially in contributions to the debate from the 'new left'), the basis for class cohesion and political radicalism is dissipated. A 'sense of classlessness' or of middle-class identification replaces former values of solidarity.[14]

Though the evidence is far from adequate, there is no reason to doubt that in a number of respects working class 'patterns of culture' are changing, and becoming less distinctive in the process. It seems reasonable to assume that those features of working class life will be weakening which, in the past, were conditioned primarily by low absolute levels of living, extreme insecurity and marked local or social isolation. There

---

[14] These assumptions have often been made in an implicit, rather than an explicit, fashion. See, however, S. Hall, 'A Sense of Classlessness', *Universities and Left Review*, Autumn 1958 (also the criticism by R. Samuel, 'Class and Classlessness', *ibid.*, Spring 1959); F. Zweig, *The Worker in an Affluent Society*, 1961; D. Butler and R. Rose, *The British General Election of 1959*, 1960; R. Williams, *The Long Revolution*, 1961. In the background to this debate there have been such studies of, or commentaries upon, traditional working class 'community' life as M. Young and P. Willmott, *Family and Kinship in East London*, 1957, and R. Hoggart, *The Uses of Literacy*, 1957. F. Pappenheim, *The Alienation of Modern Man: An Interpretation Based on Marx and Tönnies*, 1959, is relevant to this debate at a much more abstract, general and theoretical level. See also footnote 6 on page 91.

are indications in that direction.[15] Class differentials in mortality, for example, seem to have been diminishing at certain points, or assuming a more complex pattern than before, although the relative disparities in infant mortality in Britain have hitherto remained remarkably constant. Class differentials in fertility have recently narrowed substantially in the United States and some other countries. British data have so far shown only the most uncertain of hints of a similar change; but it seems plausible that it may occur here, too. Indeed, it is not inconceivable that the familiar gradient of fertility may be reversed. If working class people increasingly adopt the same kind of material and educational aspirations as middle class people, while persistent inequalities prevent them from realizing those aspirations, they may reduce the size of their families below the middle class norm. There are signs of some such reversal in Norway, for example. Whatever the trends in fertility differentials, the absolute size of family has, of course, been considerably reduced in the working class, as it has in the middle class. This by itself has undoubtedly played a major part in transforming the general character of working class family life. A traditional urban British pattern of fairly strong extended ties of kinship, coupled with a rather marginal domestic role for the man within the nuclear family, may well have been the result of material poverty and economic insecurity, the sharp fluctuations in the economic cycle of the family associated with high fertility, and local isolation of working class communities. Though this pattern persists, it is giving way to one closer to contemporary middle class family norms. This process seems more likely to be a long-standing secular trend, resulting from the reduced significance of the underlying causes, than the product primarily of post-war suburbanization, as has been suggested. But suburbanization has also been pointed to as part of a more general change in working class residential distribution and conditions of life, to which wide significance has been attached. The closed, homogeneous, one-industry, one-class, one-occupation community, familiar from earlier industrialism, is no longer typical. Suburbs and new towns are taking the place of the old mining villages, textile districts and dockside areas. And, through these and other changes, the street, the pub, the working-men's club are losing their importance as centres of local social contact, in a world where working class families lead increasingly 'home-centred' lives.

There is as yet no certainty about the extent and pace of all such changes in working class culture and environment. The main dispute, however, is not about the facts, but about their implications. Sweeping social and political deductions have been drawn, with

---

[15] Evidence for some of the following points will be found in: General Register Office, *Registrar General's Decennial Supplement for England and Wales, 1951: Occupational Mortality*, 1954, 1958; J. N. Morris and J. A. Heady, 'Social and Biological Factors in Infant Mortality', *Lancet*, 12th Feb.–12th March, 1955; A. J. Mayer and P. Hauser, 'Class Differentials in Expectation of Life at Birth', in R. Bendix and S. M. Lipset, *Class, Status and Power*, 1953; D. V. Glass and E. Grebenik, *The Trend and Pattern of Fertility in Great Britain*, Royal Commission on Population Papers, vol. 6, 1954; Census of England and Wales, 1951, *Fertility Report*, 1959; National Bureau Committee for Economic Research, *Demographic and Economic Change in Developed Countries*, 1958; R. Freedman *et al.*, *Family Planning, Sterility and Population Growth*, 1959; C. F. Westoff *et al.*, *Family Growth in Metropolitan America*, 1961.

gay abandon but little documentation. Not only has it become almost fashionable to deplore the dilution of traditional working class culture *per se*—a reaction which reflects an odd, conservative nostalgia for a way of life moulded by insecurity, local seclusion and crude deprivation, both material and mental. But this 'cultural dilution' has also, not infrequently, come to be equated with an alleged decline of class consciousness, and its replacement by narrow preoccupations of status and 'respectability' or by sheer apathy. No substantial evidence has been offered for this equation: it has been assumed, not proven. Underlying it, there is commonly a premise which deserves explicit examination. This is an assumption that the kind of working class unity which finds expression in industrial, or more especially in political, action draws its nourishment from the simpler and more intimate loyalties of neighbourhood and kin. Consequently, it is postulated, as the latter are weakened so the former declines. The assumption is highly questionable. For it implies that the solidarity of class—which is societal in its sweep, and draws no nice distinctions between men of this place and that, this name and that, this dialect and that—is rooted in the kind of parochial solidarity which is its very antithesis. To doubt the implied identity between the two antitheses is not to deny that sectional loyalties of region and occupation have contributed in the past to the formation of wider loyalties of class; but the permanence of that contribution has depended upon a transcendence of the original narrow basis of solidarity. Thus the developing labour movement has in many cases drawn special strength from the workers of such locally cohesive, homogeneous communities as the mining valleys of Britain and the timber districts of Scandinavia (though not in this century, for instance, from the mill towns of Lancashire to any marked extent); and the industries located in communities of this kind are still characterized by a comparatively high incidence of strike action.[16] Yet, at the political level especially, the collective force of the labour movement grew precisely as the local isolation of these and other working class communities declined. The two trends are not just fortuitously coincidental, but logically related. For the growth of a nation-wide movement—uniting, say, miners of South Wales with shipyard workers of Clydeside and others throughout the country—entailed of necessity a widening of horizons, and the displacement (if not a total suppression) of local and sectional loyalties by commitment to a common aim, however uncertainly defined. In sociological jargon, the 'particularistic' ties of neighbourhood, kin and regional culture provide no adequate basis for the maintenance of the 'universalistic' loyalties involved in class political action.

This historical widening of once parochial horizons also entailed the progressive abandonment of aims and aspirations restricted by static, traditional definitions. Past experience and purely local criteria no longer set the limits to individual or collective ambition. The standards of comparison by which workers judged their own condition and their children's future increasingly were raised, increasingly were shared,

---

[16] See, e.g., C. Kerr and A. Siegel, 'The Inter-industry Propensity to Strike', in A. W. Kornhauser *et al., Industrial Conflict*, 1954.

and increasingly reflected the conditions and prospects which industrial capitalism offered the more prosperous minority. Working class adoption of 'middle class' aspirations is thus no new phenomenon. Nor therefore can the process in its contemporary dress, or the general attenuation of traditional working class culture of which it is part, be regarded as one which must necessarily induce social complacency and political paralysis. On the contrary, precisely because it involves an inbuilt discrepancy between common demands and the unequal distribution of means for their fulfilment, it provides a continuing potential for social protest; the more so, the more 'middle class' demands become the norm.

7

THE "EQUALITY" REVOLUTION

Herbert J. Gans

In spite of continuing inequality, let us grant for a moment the premise of those who speak of a growing classlessness in American society. Let us agree for the sake of argument with those who say that we are now entering a technologically sophisticated post-industrial society, in which the old economic preoccupations—such as the problems of production, the adequate and equitable distribution of goods, the universal satisfaction of material needs, and so on—if not completely solved, are now capable of easy solution.

If we grant this premise, does this necessarily mean that the social-class dynamic has gone completely out of American society? We naturally assume that widespread affluence is a force for complacency and apathy, and conversely, that social unrest is associated with economic deprivation. Should we not therefore expect a new period of social harmony and stability in American society based on growing affluence and economic equality?

Not necessarily. First of all, in an egalitarian setting, such as American society, as inequality gradually narrows, what happens is that the inequalities that remain become increasingly disruptive and unacceptable. As sociology students have long been taught, discontent is based not so much on absolute as on relative levels of deprivation. Sociologist Philip Wexler, for example, has observed that in the highly egalitarian milieu of the Israeli kibbutzim, the mere fact that one member may have, over and above his fellows, a simple subscription to a newspaper, may become a real source of dissension. As equality approaches, remaining inequities become magnified and a source of as great or greater discontent than previous gross inequities. This helps to explain the current indignation and anger over continued poverty in America, although the poor

SOURCE: The *New York Times Magazine* (November 3, 1968), p. 36. Copyright © 1968 by the New York Times Company. Reprinted by permission of the author and the *New York Times*.

in our midst today are probably at least as well off as the poor ever were before in this country and perhaps better off than the poor elsewhere. Likewise, the movement for Negro equality has increased in ferocity as the prospects for equality become ever greater.

Moreover, as equality begins to approach, those whose position in society has traditionally been high often resent the incursions from below and may take political or economic action to prevent them. Recent strikes of white collar and professional workers in Sweden and Israel, for example, have been based largely on the fear that the working class is too successfully closing the traditional income gap between itself and the middle class; and much social turmoil ensues in the struggle to preserve this distance.

What is perhaps even more important in the dynamics of unrest in an egalitarian society is revealed in the waves of protest that have swept college campuses with growing severity since the Free Speech Movement at Berkeley in 1964. What is unique about current unrest is that it is based on *affluence* and is led by the affluent. Several studies have shown that white campus activists are predominantly sons and daughters of middle- and upper-class parents rather than from working-class families. Unlike any preceding generation, they have never known economic want or insecurity and, unlike their parents, have no memories or fears of economic depression. Having taken affluence for granted all their lives and living in a society rich enough so that by working just part time they can manage to live adequately if not luxuriously in its interstices, these students are uniquely characterized by their relative indifference to or even contempt of the traditional economic values of industrial society, career, security, and material gratifications. A *Fortune* magazine study published in 1969 revealed that of the country's 6.7 million college students, about 40 percent—fully three million—were "defined . . . mainly by their lack of concern about making money."

Used to taking the affluent society for granted, these students are able to put the old social class career motives behind them. They are seeking to go *beyond affluence* and to direct their protests against the more subtle expressions of inequalities and inequities in other areas of American life. The entire counter-culture phenomenon, as discussed in such popular works as Theodore Roszak's *The Making of a Counter Culture* and Charles Reich's *The Greening of America,* is based in large measure upon youthful reaction to the kinds of material affluence that their parents' generation struggled for and achieved. In this sense, affluence, or classlessness, if you will, has become a real force for social change. Naturally, there are the old economic concerns focusing on the poor white and black, but mainly, as the older issues of economic inequality are put behind them, students and others are free to turn their crusade for equality toward other noneconomic areas. In this selection, sociologist Herbert Gans discusses other kinds of inequities that are becoming a focus for the " 'equality' revolution."

Someday, when historians write about the nineteen-sixties, they may describe them as the years in which America rediscovered the poverty still in its midst and in which social protest, ranging from demonstrations to violent uprisings, reappeared on the American scene. But the historians may also note a curious fact, that the social protest of the sixties has very little to do with poverty. Most of the demonstrators and marchers who followed Martin Luther King were not poor; the college students who have been protesting and sitting-in on campus are well-to-do, and even the participants in the ghetto uprisings of the last few years—although hardly affluent—were not drawn from the poorest sectors of the ghetto.

The social protest of the nineteen-sixties has to do with *inequality,* with the pervasive inequities remaining in American life. So far the demand for greater equality has come largely from the young and the black, but I wish to suggest that in the years to come, America will face a demand for more equality in various aspects of life from many other types of citizens—a demand so pervasive that it might well be described as the "equality revolution."

This demand will take many forms. Some will ask for *equality,* pure and simple; others will press for more *democracy,* for greater participation in and responsiveness by their places of work and their governments; yet others will ask for more *autonomy,* for the freedom to be what they want to be and to choose how they will live. All these demands add up to a desire for greater control over one's life, requiring the reduction of the many inequities—economic, political and social —that now prevent people from determining how they will spend their short time on this earth.

Ever since the Declaration of Independence decreed that all men are created equal, Americans have generally believed that they were or could be equal. Of course, the Constitution argued by omission that slaves were unequal, and we all know that many other inequities exist in America. Undoubtedly, the most serious of these is economic.

About a fifth of the country lives on incomes below the so-called Federal "poverty line" of $3,300 for an urban family of four, and the proportion is higher if the population not counted by the last census (14 per cent of all Negro males, for example) is included. An additional 7 per cent of households, earning between $3,300 and $4,300 a year, are considered "near poor" by the Social Security Administration. Altogether, then, probably about a third of the country is living at or below the barest subsistence level—and about two-thirds of this population is white.

Moreover, despite the conventional description of America as an affluent society, few of its citizens actually enjoy affluence. The Bureau of Labor Statistics estimates that an urban family of four needs $9,376 a year (and more than $10,000 in New York City) for a "modest but adequate standard of living"; but in 1966, 69 per cent of American families with two children were earning less than $10,000. (Their median income was $7,945, although a recent City University study showed the median income of New York families in 1966 to be only $6,684—and those of Negroes and Puerto Ricans to be $4,754 and $3,949 respectively.)

Even $9,400 is hardly a comfortable income, and it is fair to say that today the affluent society includes only the 9 per cent of Americans who earn more than $15,000 a year. Everyone else still worries about how to make ends meet, particularly since the standards of the good life have shot up tremendously in the last two decades.

Of course, income levels have also risen in the last 20 years, and an income of $9,400 would classify anyone as rich in most countries. Even the earnings of America's poor would constitute affluence in a country like India. But comparisons with the past and with other countries are irrelevant; people do not live and spend in the past or in other countries, and what they earn must be evaluated in terms of the needs and wants identified as desirable by the mass media and the rest of American culture. Undoubtedly an advertising man or a college professor who earns $15,000 is in the richest 1 per cent of all the people who ever lived, but this fact does not pay his mortgage or send his children to school. And if *he* has economic problems, they are a thousand times greater for the poor, who have much the same wants and hopes, but must make do with $3,000 a year or less.

The extent of economic inequality is also indicated by the fact that the richest 5 per cent of Americans earn 20 per cent of the nation's income; but the bottom 20 per cent earn only 5 per cent of the income. Although this distribution has improved immeasurably since America's beginnings,* it has not changed significantly since the nineteen-thirties. In other words, the degree of economic inequality has not been affected by the over-all increase in incomes or in gross national product during and after World War II.

There are other kinds of economic inequality in America as well. For example, most good jobs today require at least a bachelor's degree, but many families still cannot afford to send their children to college, even if they are not poor. Job security is also distributed unequally. College professors have tenure and are assured of life-time jobs; professionals and white-collar workers earn salaries and are rarely laid off, even in depressions; factory workers, service workers and migrant farm laborers are still paid by the hour, and those not unionized can be laid off at a moment's notice.

Economic inequality goes far beyond income and job security, however. Some executives and white-collar workers have a say in how their work is to be done, but most workers can be fired for talking back to the boss (and are then ineligible for unemployment compensation). Generally speaking, most work places, whether they are offices or factories, are run on an autocratic basis; the employee is inherently unequal and has no more right to determine his work, working conditions or the policy of his work place than the enlisted man in the Army. He is only a cog in a large machine, and he has about as much influence in deciding what he will do as a cog in a machine. Our schools are similarly autocratic; neither in college nor in elementary and high school do students have any significant rights in the classroom; they are unequal citizens who must obey the teacher if they are to graduate.

The poor suffer most from these inequalities, of course. They hold the least secure jobs; they are least often union members; if they are on welfare, they can be made penniless by displeasing the social workers in charge of their cases. And being poor, they pay more for everything. It is well known that they pay more for food (sometimes even at supermarkets) and for furniture and other consumer goods; they also pay more for hospital care, as a recent study in New Haven indicates. They even pay more when they gamble. Affluent Americans can gamble in the stock market, where it is difficult to lose a lot of money except in the wildest speculation. The poor can afford only to play the numbers, where the chance of a "hit" is about 1 in 600, and if they prefer not to participate in an

---

* For example, University of Michigan historian Sam Warner reports in "The Private City" that among the minority of Philadelphians affluent enough to pay taxes in 1774, 10 per cent owned 89 per cent of the taxable property.

illegal activity, they can play the New York State Lottery, where the chance of winning is only about 1 in 4,000.

Political inequality is rampant, too. Although the Supreme Court's one-man, one-vote decision will eventually result in voting equality, the individuals who contribute to a candidate's election campaign will have far more political influence than others.

Ordinary citizens have few rights in actual practice; how many can afford to argue with policemen, or hire good lawyers to argue their cases, or make their voices heard when talking to their elected representatives? This year's political conventions [1968] have indicated once again that the rank-and-file delegates (including those named by political bosses or rigged state conventions) have little say in the choosing of Presidential candidates or platforms. Even the person who is included in a sample of the now-so-important public-opinion polls cannot state his opinion if the pollster's questions are loaded or incorrectly worded.

Finally, there are many kinds of inequality, autocracy and lack of autonomy of which most Americans are not even aware. In many cities, for instance, high-speed mass-transit lines rarely serve poorer neighborhoods and really good doctors and lawyers are available only to the wealthy. Rich or poor, not many people have a say in the choice of TV programs they are shown or in the rates they are charged by electric companies; and who can escape from the poisons in the air?

In a large and complex society, inequality and the lack of control over one's life are pervasive and are often thought to be inevitable by-products of modernity and affluence. We are learning, however, that they are not inevitable—that there can be more equality, democracy and autonomy if enough people want them.

In the past, when most people earned just enough to "get by," they were interested mainly in higher incomes and did not concern themselves with equality or autonomy in their everyday lives. For example, the poor took—and still will take—any jobs they could get because they needed the money to pay for the week's food and the month's rent. Working-class and lower-middle-class people were, and are, only slightly more able to choose; they take whatever job will provide the most comfortable lives for themselves and their families. But in the upper-middle class, the job is expected to offer personal satisfactions, and upper-middle-class people gravitate to the jobs and careers that provide more equality and autonomy. The huge increase in graduate-school enrollments suggests that many college students want the personal freedom available in an academic career; their decreasing interest in business careers indicates that they may be rejecting the autocracy and lack of autonomy found in many large corporations.

Today, as more people approach the kind of economic security already found in the affluent upper-middle class, they are beginning to think about the noneconomic satisfactions of the job and of the rest of life; as a result, aspirations for more equality, democracy and autonomy are rising all over America.

Some manifestations of "the equality revolution" are making headlines today, particularly among students and blacks. Whatever the proximate causes of college protests and uprisings, the students who participate in them agree on two demands: the right to be treated as adults—and therefore as equals—and the right to participate in the governing of their schools. Though the mass media have paid most attention to the more radical advocates of these demands, equality and democracy are sought not just by the Students for a Democratic Society but by an ever-increasing number of liberal and even conservative students as well.

Similar demands for equality and democracy are being voiced by the young people of the ghetto. Only a few years ago, they seemed to want integration, the right to become part of the white community. Today, recognizing that white America offered integration to only a token few and required with it assimilation into the white majority, the young blacks are asking for equality instead. When they say that black is beautiful, they are really saying that black is equal to white; when the ghetto demands control of its institutions, it asks for the right to have the same control that many white neighborhoods have long had.

And although the call for "participatory democracy" is voiced mainly by young people of affluent origins in the New Left, a parallel demand is manifesting itself among the young blue-collar supporters of Governor Wallace. What they are saying, in effect, is that they are tired of being represented by middle-class politicians; they want a President who will allow the working class to participate in the running of the Federal Government and will get rid of the upper-middle-class professionals who have long dominated the formulation of public policies, the people whom the Governor calls "pseudointellectuals."

Many other instances of the equality revolution are less visible, and some have not made the headlines. For example, in the last two generations, wives have achieved near equality in the family, at least in the middle class; they now divide the housework with their husbands and share the decision-making about family expenditures and other activities. Today, this revolution is being extended to the sexual relationship. Gone is the day when women were passive vessels for men's sexual demands; they are achieving the right to enjoy sexual intercourse.

Children have also obtained greater equality and democracy. In many American families, adolescents are now free from adult interference in their leisure-time activities and their sexual explorations, and even preteens are asking to be allowed their own "youth culture."

Man's relationship to God and the church is moving toward greater equality, too. The minister is no longer a theological father; in many synagogues and Protestant churches, he has become the servant of his congregation, and the unwillingness of many Catholics to abide by the Pope's dictates on birth control hides other, less publicized, instances of the rejection of dogma that is handed down from on high. The real meaning of the "God is Dead" movement, I believe, is that the old conception of God as the infallible autocrat has been rejected.

In the years to come, the demand for more equality, democracy and autonomy is likely to spread to many other aspects of life. Already, some high-school students are beginning to demand the same rights for which college students are organizing, and recipients of public welfare are joining together to put an end to the autocratic fashion in which their payments are given to them. Public employees are striking for better working conditions as well as for higher wages; teachers are demanding more freedom in the classroom and—in New York—the right to teach where they choose; social workers want more autonomy in aiding their clients, and policemen seek the right to do their jobs as they see fit, immune from what they call "political interference." The right of the individual to determine his job is the hallmark of the professional, and eventually many workers will seek the privileges of professionalism whether or not they are professional in terms of skills.

Eventually, the equality revolution may also come to the large corporations and government agencies in which more and more people are working. One can foresee the day when blue-collar and white-collar workers demand a share of the profits and some voice in the running of the corporations.

Similar changes can be expected in the local community. Although the exodus to suburbia took place primarily because people sought better homes and neighborhoods, they also wanted the ability to obtain greater control over governmental institutions. In the last 20 years, the new suburbanites have overthrown many of the rural political machines that used to run the suburbs, establishing governments that were responsive to their demands for low taxes and the exclusion of poorer newcomers. In the future, this transformation may spread to the cities as well, with decentralized political institutions that respond to the wants of the neighborhood replacing the highly centralized urban machines.

Consumer behavior will also undergo change. The ever-increasing diversity of consumer goods represents a demand for more cultural democracy on the part of purchasers, and the day may come when some people will establish consumer unions and cooperatives to provide themselves with goods and services not offered by large manufacturers. Television viewers may unite to demand different and perhaps even better TV programs and to support the creation of UHF channels that produce the types of quality and minority programming the big networks cannot offer.

It is even possible that a form of "hippie" culture will become more popular in the future. Although the Haight-Ashbury and East Village hippies have degenerated into an often-suicidal drug culture, there are positive themes in hippiedom that may become more acceptable if the work-week shrinks and affluence becomes more universal; for example: the rejection of the rat race, the belief in self-expression as the main purpose of life, the desire for a more communal form of living and even the idea of drug use as a way to self-understanding. In any case, there is no reason to doubt that many people will want to take advantage of a "square" form of the leisurely hippie existence—now available only to old people and called retirement—while they are still young or middle-aged. This day is far off and by then marijuana is likely to have achieved equality with liquor as America's major elixir for temporary escape from reality and inhibition.

These observations suggest that the future will bring many kinds of change to America, producing new ideas that question beliefs and values thought to be sacrosanct. Who, for example, imagined a few years ago that the ghetto would reject the traditional goal of integration or that college students would rise up against their faculties and administrations to demand equal rights? Thus, nobody should be surprised if in the next few years adolescents organize for more freedom in their high schools or journalists decide that their editors have too much power over their work.

These demands for change will, of course, be fought bitterly; protests will be met by backlash and new ideas will be resisted by old ideologies.

Today many argue that college students are still children and should not be given a voice in college administration, just as many say that women do not really need orgasms or that men who help their wives at home are becoming effeminate. Undoubtedly, the defenders of outmoded traditions will argue sincerely and with some facts and logic on their side, but processes of social change have little to do with sincerity, facts or logic. When people become dissatisfied with what they have and demand something better they cannot be deterred by facts or logic, and the repression of new ideas and new modes of behavior is effective only in the very short run.

But perhaps the most intense struggle between new ideas and old ideologies will take place over America's political philosophy, for a fundamental change is taking place in the values which guide us as a nation. In a little-noticed portion of the "Moynihan Report," Daniel P. Moynihan pointed out that the civil rights struggle, which had previously emphasized the achievement of liberty, particularly political liberty from Jim Crow laws, would soon shift to the attainment of equality, which would allow the "distribution of achievements among Negroes roughly comparable to that of whites."

Moynihan's prediction was uncannily accurate with respect to the civil rights struggle, and I would argue, as he does, that it will soon extend to many other struggles as well and that the traditional belief in liberty will be complemented and challenged by a newly widespread belief in the desirability of equality.

Since America became a nation, the country has been run on the assumption that the greatest value of all is liberty, which gives people the freedom to "do their own thing," particularly to make money, regardless of how much this freedom deprives others of the same liberty or of a decent standard of living. Whether liberty meant the freedom to squander the country's natural resources or just to go into business for oneself without doing harm to anyone else, it was the guiding value of our society.

Today, however, the demand for liberty is often, but not always, the battle cry of the "haves," justifying their right to keep their wealth or position and to get more. Whether liberty is demanded by a Southern advocate of states' rights to keep Negroes in their place or by a property owner who wants to sell his house to any white willing to buy it, liberty has become the ideology of the more fortunate. In the years to come, the "have-nots," whether they lack money or freedom, will demand increasingly the reduction of this form of liberty. Those who ask for more equality are not opposed to liberty *per se,* of course; what they want is sufficient equality so that they, too, can enjoy the liberty now virtually monopolized by the "haves."

The debate over liberty vs. equality is in full swing, and one illuminating example is the current argument about the negative income tax and other forms of guaranteed annual incomes for the underpaid and the poor. The advocates of guaranteed annual incomes want greater equality of income in American society; the opponents fear that the liberty to earn as much as possible will be abrogated. However, neither side frames its case in terms of equality or liberty. The advocates of a guaranteed annual income rely on moral argument, appealing to their fellow Americans to do away with the immorality of poverty. The opponents charge that a guaranteed annual income will sap the incentive to work, although all the evidence now available suggests that professors and other professionals who have long had virtually guaranteed annual incomes have not lost their incentive to work, that what saps incentive is not income but the lack of it.

Being poor makes people apathetic and depressed; a guaranteed income would provide some emotional as well as economic security, raise hopes, increase self-respect and reduce feelings of being left out, thus encouraging poor people to look for decent jobs, improve family living conditions and urge their children to work harder in school. A guaranteed annual income may reduce the incentive to take a dirty and underpaid job, however, and at the bottom of the debate is the fear of those who now have the liberty to avoid taking such jobs that less-fortunate Americans may be given the same liberty.

In the years to come, many other arguments against equality will develop. We have long heard that those who want more equality are radicals or outside agitators, seeking to stir up people thought to be happy with the way things are. This is clearly nonsensical, for even if radicals sometimes lead the drive for more equality, they can succeed only because those who follow them are dissatisfied with the status quo.

Another argument is that the demand for more equality will turn America into a society like Sweden, which is thought to be conformist, boring and suicidal, or even into a gray and regimented society like Russia. But these arguments are nonsensical, too, for there is no evidence that Swedes suffer more from ennui than anyone else, and the suicide rate—high in all Scandinavian countries save Norway— was lower in Sweden at last counting than in traditionalist Austria or Communist Hungary and only slightly higher than the rate in *laissez-faire* West Germany or pastoral Switzerland. And current events in the Communist countries provide considerable evidence that the greater economic equality which some of these countries have achieved does not eliminate the popular desire for freedom and democracy.

But perhaps the most frequently heard argument is that the unequal must do something to earn greater equality. This line of reasoning is taken by those who have had the liberty to achieve their demands and assumes that the same liberty is available to everyone else. This assumption does not hold up, however, for the major problem of the unequal is precisely that they are not allowed to earn equality—that the barriers of racial discrimination, the inability to obtain a good education, the unavailability of good jobs or the power of college presidents and faculties make it impossible for them to be equal. Those who argue for earning equality are really saying that they want to award it to the deserving, like charity. But recent events in the ghettos and on the campuses have shown convincingly that no one awards equality voluntarily; it has to be wrested from the "more equal" by political pressure and even by force.

Many of the changes that make up the equality revolution will not take place for a generation or more, and how many of them ever take place depends on at least three factors: the extent to which the American economy is affluent enough to permit more equality, the extent to which America's political institutions are able to respond to the demands of the unequal, and—perhaps most important—the extent to which working-class and lower-middle-class Americans want more equality, democracy and autonomy in the future.

If the economy is healthy in the years to come, it will be able to "afford" more economic equality while absorbing the costs of such changes as the democratization of the workplace, increased professionalism and more worker autonomy. If automation and the currently rising centralization of American industry result in the disappearance of jobs, however, greater equality will become impossible and people will fight each other for the remaining jobs. This could result in a bitter conflict between the "haves" and the "have-nots" that might even lead to a revolution, bringing about formal equality by governmental edict in a way not altogether different from the Socialist and Communist revolutions of the 20th century. But that conflict between the "haves" and the "have-nots" could also lead to a right-wing revolution in which the "haves," supported by conservatives among the "have-nots," would establish a quasi-totalitarian government that would use force to maintain the existing inequalities.

Although the likelihood of either a left-wing or a right-wing revolution is probably small, even a gradual transformation toward greater equality is not likely to be tranquil. More equality for some means a reduction in privilege for others, and more democracy and autonomy for some means a loss of power for others. Those who have the privilege and the power will not give them up without a struggle and will fight the demand for more equality with all the economic and political resources they can muster. Even today, such demands by only a small part of the black and young population have resulted in a massive backlash appeal for law and order by a large part of the white and older population.

Moreover, whenever important national decisions must be made, American politics has generally been guided by majority rule or majority public opinion, and this has often meant the tyranny of the majority over the minority. As long as the unequal are a minority, the structure of American politics can easily be used to frustrate their demands for change. The inability of the Federal Government to satisfy the demands of the Negro population for greater equality is perhaps the best example. In the future, the political structure must be altered to allow the Government to become more responsive to minority demands, particularly as the pressure for equality grows.

Whether or not such governmental responsiveness will be politically feasible depends in large part on how working-class and lower-middle-class Americans feel about the equality revolution. They are the ruling majority in America, and if they want more equality, democracy and autonomy, these will be achieved—and through peaceful political methods. If the two classes remain primarily interested in obtaining more affluence, however, they will be able to suppress demands for equality by minorities, especially those demands which reduce their own powers and privileges. No one can tell now how these two classes will feel in the future, but there is no doubt that their preferences will determine the outcome of the equality revolution.

Still, whatever happens in the years and decades to come, the equality revolution is under way, and however slowly it proceeds and however bitter the struggle between its supporters and opponents, it will continue. It may succeed, but it could also fail, leaving in its wake a level of social and political conflict unlike any America has ever known.

What I have written so far I have written as a sociologist, trying to predict what will occur in coming generations. But as a citizen, I believe that what will happen ought to happen, that the emerging demand for more equality, democracy and autonomy is desirable. Too many Americans, even among the nonpoor, still lead lives of quiet desperation, and the good life today is the monopoly of only a happy few. I think that the time has come when unbridled liberty as we have defined it traditionally can no longer be America's guiding value, especially if the right to liberty deprives others of a similar liberty. But I believe also that there is no inherent conflict between liberty and equality; that the society we must create should provide enough equality to permit everyone the liberty to control his own life without creating inequality for others, and that this, when it comes, will be the Great Society.

III

THE NEED
FOR INEQUALITY

8

SOME PRINCIPLES OF STRATIFICATION

Kingsley Davis and Wilbert E. Moore

9

SOME PRINCIPLES OF STRATIFICATION: A CRITICAL ANALYSIS

Melvin M. Tumin

We present here two essential positions in the most heated and continuous debate waged in recent times in the field of social stratification: is social inequality functionally necessary in society? The functional theory of stratification presented by Kingsley Davis and Wilbert Moore fits into the general theory of functionalism common in anthropology and sociology. In its simplest terms, functionalism makes an implicit or explicit analogy between society and a biological organism. The function of the liver, heart, and lungs is the contributions these organs make to the maintenance of the organism. Society is regarded in this light as consisting of functional and interrelated parts. Functionalism analyzes basic social institutions, such as the family, religion, the class structure, and so on by asking what part these institutions play in the maintenance and continuity of society. As the anthropologist A. R. Radcliffe-Brown stated long ago, "The *function* of any recurrent activity such as the punishment of a crime . . . is the part it plays in the social life as a whole and therefore the contribution it makes to the maintenance of the structural continuity."

Although functionalism has enjoyed an unprecedented vogue of popularity in American sociology, it has been criticized on many grounds. First, it tends to be ahistorical. It does not encourage a search for origins, development, or historical roots, but is mainly concerned with current function. In its theoretical justification for the neglect of history, it perhaps furthers the already excessive parochialism of contemporary sociologists. Second, functionalism has been criticized for its preoccupation with the static element in society, with its attention focused on functional integration, continuity, and social equilibrium. Especially in a world torn by conflict and change, functionalism has come under increasing attack. Third, functionalism has traditionally been criticized for having a politically conservative bias; for whereas conservatives are likely

113

to say "whatever is, is good," functionalists are inclined to argue—though they deny it—that whatever is tends to be *functional*.

In essence, what has fueled this interminable debate over the functional necessity of stratification are its political implications, political in the broadest sense. It should be remembered that American sociology is part of American society and, as such, it is in many ways a product of the values of American life. In certain fields, among them social stratification, sociology has at times taken on a markedly political, ideological, or polemical tone. Stratification is, after all, concerned with the distribution of wealth, power, and prestige in society, and these are highly charged political issues. Thus, one cannot really expect a subject matter so close to the everyday political battles to be completely above the fray.

Inequality goes back to the very beginnings of human society; almost from the moment when there was an economic surplus, some men took more for themselves and left others with less. And down through the ages, when men, having witnessed this inequality, thought and wrote about their society, they have reacted in one of two ways: they have either defended this inequality or they have damned it.* Those who have praised it have done so according to a myriad of principles: that inequality is god-given, that it is an inevitable consequence of the inborn inequality of men, that it helps society to operate smoothly, and so on. To take a recent, rather unusual example, T. S. Eliot believed that a strong, stable, hereditary upper class was essential in order to protect, preserve, and transmit the enormous artistic and cultural heritage of Western civilization. Only a firmly established, insulated upper class, he argued, possesses the leisure, the training, the education, the means, and the inclination to serve as guardians of the cultural tradition for the entire society. Destruction of the upper class means a possible destruction of the carriers of Western culture.

The debate over functionalism brings together in contemporary sociological dress the age-old exponents of the two traditional views: those who see inequality in society as necessary, desirable, and inevitable, and those who regard inequality as basically unjust and remediable.

Long after the school of functionalism has been forgotten, perhaps the essay by Davis and Moore will be remembered as one of the last cogent arguments in the historical tradition which defends social inequality. Over the years this essay has drawn a barrage of criticism and support. Of the criticism, probably none is as definitive as the one presented here by Melvin Tumin.

■ Kingsley Davis and Wilbert E. Moore

In a previous paper some concepts for handling the phenomena of social inequality were presented.[1] In the present paper a further step in stratification theory is undertaken—an attempt to show the relationship between stratification and the rest of the social order.[2]

Starting from the proposition that no society is "classless," or unstratified, an effort is made to explain, in functional terms, the universal necessity which calls forth stratification in any social system. Next, an attempt is made to explain the roughly uniform distribution

* See Gerhard Lenski, *Power and Privilege: A Theory of Social Stratification* (New York: McGraw-Hill, 1966), ch. 1.

SOURCE: *American Sociological Review*, vol. 10, no. 2 (April 1945), pp. 242–49. Reprinted by permission of the authors and the American Sociological Association.

of prestige as between the major types of positions in every society. Since, however, there occur between one society and another great differences in the degree and kind of stratification, some attention is also given to the varieties of social inequality and the variable factors that give rise to them.

Clearly, the present task requires two different lines of analysis—one to understand the universal, the other to understand the variable features of stratification. Naturally each line of inquiry aids the other and is indispensable, and in the treatment that follows the two will be interwoven, although, because of space limitations, the emphasis will be on the universals.

Throughout, it will be necessary to keep in mind one thing—namely, that the discussion relates to the system of positions, not to the individuals occupying those positions. It is one thing to ask why different positions carry different degrees of prestige, and quite another to ask how certain individuals get into those positions. Although, as the argument will try to show, both questions are related, it is essential to keep them separate in our thinking. Most of the literature on stratification has tried to answer the second question (particularly with regard to the ease or difficulty of mobility between strata) without tackling the first. The first question, however, is logically prior and, in the case of any particular individual or group, factually prior.

The Functional Necessity of Stratification

Curiously, however, the main functional necessity explaining the universal presence of stratification is precisely the requirement faced by any society of placing and motivating individuals in the social structure. As a functioning mechanism a society must somehow distribute its members in social positions and induce them to perform the duties of these positions. It must thus concern itself with motivation at two different levels: to instill in the proper individuals the desire to fill certain positions, and, once in these positions, the desire to perform the duties attached to them. Even though the social order may be relatively static in form, there is a continuous process of metabolism as new individuals are born into it, shift with age, and die off. Their absorption into the positional system must somehow be arranged and motivated. This is true whether the system is competitive or non-competitive. A competitive system gives greater importance to the motivation to achieve positions, whereas a non-competitive system gives perhaps greater importance to the motivation to perform the duties of the positions; but in any system both types of motivation are required.

If the duties associated with the various positions were all equally pleasant to the human organism, all equally important to societal survival, and all equally in need of the same ability or talent, it would make no difference who got into which positions, and the problem of social placement would be greatly reduced. But actually it does make a great deal of difference who gets into which positions, not only because some positions are inherently more agreeable than others, but also because some require special talents or training and some are functionally more important than others. Also, it is essential that the duties of the positions be performed with the diligence that their importance requires. Inevitably, then, a society must have, first, some kind of rewards that it can use as inducements, and, second, some way of distributing these rewards differentially according to positions. The rewards and their distribution become a part of the social order, and thus give rise to stratification.

One may ask what kind of rewards a society has at its disposal in distributing its personnel and securing essential services. It has, first of all, the things that contribute to sustenance and comfort. It has, second, the things that contribute to humor and diversion. And it has, finally, the things that contribute to self-respect and ego expansion. The last, because of the peculiarly social character of the self, is largely a function of the opinion of others, but it nonetheless ranks in importance with the first two. In any social system all three kinds of rewards must be dispensed differentially according to positions.

In a sense the rewards are "built into" the position. They consist in the "rights" associated with the position, plus what may be called its accompaniments or perquisites. Often the rights, and sometimes the accompaniments, are functionally related to the duties of the position. (Rights as viewed by the incumbent are usually duties as viewed by other members of the community.) However, there may be a host of subsidiary rights and perquisites that are not essential to the function of the position and have only an indirect and symbolic connection with its duties, but which still may be of considerable importance in inducing people to seek the positions and fulfil the essential duties.

If the rights and perquisites of different positions in a society must be unequal, then the society must be stratified, because that is precisely what stratification means. Social inequality is thus an unconsciously evolved device by which societies insure that the most important positions are conscientiously filled by the most qualified persons. Hence every society, no matter how simple or complex, must differentiate persons in terms of both prestige and esteem, and must therefore possess a certain amount of institutionalized inequality.

It does not follow that the amount or type of inequality need be the same in all societies. This is largely a function of factors that will be discussed presently.

The Two Determinants of Positional Rank

Granting the general function that inequality subserves, one can specify the two factors that determine the relative rank of different positions. In general those positions convey the best reward, and hence have the highest rank, which (a) have the greatest importance for the society and (b) require the greatest training or talent. The first factor concerns function and is a matter of relative significance; the second concerns means and is a matter of scarcity.

DIFFERENTIAL FUNCTIONAL IMPORTANCE

Actually a society does not need to reward positions in proportion to their functional importance. It merely needs to give sufficient reward to them to insure that they will be filled competently. In other words, it must see that less essential positions do not compete successfully with more essential ones. If a position is easily filled, it need not be heavily rewarded, even though important. On the other hand, if it is important but hard to fill, the reward must be high enough to get it filled anyway. Functional importance is therefore a necessary but not a sufficient cause of high rank being assigned to a position.[3]

DIFFERENTIAL SCARCITY OF PERSONNEL

Practically all positions, no matter how acquired, require some form of skill or capacity for performance. This is implicit in the very notion of position, which implies that the incumbent must, by virtue of his incumbency, accomplish certain things.

There are, ultimately, only two ways in which a person's qualifications come about: through inherent capacity or through training. Obviously, in concrete activities both are always necessary, but from a practical standpoint the scarcity may lie primarily in one or the other, as well as in both. Some positions require innate talents of such high degree that the persons who fill them are bound to be rare. In many cases, however, talent is fairly abundant in the population but the training process is so long, costly, and elaborate that relatively few can qualify. Modern medicine, for example, is within the mental capacity of most individuals, but a medical education is so burdensome and expensive that virtually none would undertake it if the position of the M.D. did not carry a reward commensurate with the sacrifice.

If the talents required for a position are abundant and the training easy, the method of acquiring the position may have little to do with its duties. There may be, in fact, a virtually accidental relationship. But if the skills required

are scarce by reason of the rarity of talent or the costliness of training, the position, if functionally important, must have an attractive power that will draw the necessary skills in competition with other positions. This means, in effect, that the position must be high in the social scale—must command great prestige, high salary, ample leisure, and the like.

HOW VARIATIONS ARE TO BE UNDERSTOOD

In so far as there is a difference between one system of stratification and another, it is attributable to whatever factors affect the two determinants of differential reward—namely, functional importance and scarcity of personnel. Positions important in one society may not be important in another, because the conditions faced by the societies, or their degree of internal development, may be different. The same conditions, in turn, may affect the question of scarcity; for in some societies the stage of development, or the external situation, may wholly obviate the necessity of certain kinds of skill or talent. Any particular system of stratification, then, can be understood as a product of the special conditions affecting the two aforementioned grounds of differential reward.

Major Societal Functions and Stratification

RELIGION

The reason why religion is necessary is apparently to be found in the fact that human society achieves its unity primarily through the possession by its members of certain ultimate values and ends in common. Although these values and ends are subjective, they influence behavior, and their integration enables the society to operate as a system. Derived neither from inherited nor from external nature, they have evolved as a part of culture by communication and moral pressure. They must, however, appear to the members of the society to have some reality, and it is the role of religious belief and ritual to supply and reinforce this appearance of reality. Through belief and ritual the common ends and values are connected with an imaginary world symbolized by concrete sacred objects, which world in turn is related in a meaningful way to the facts and trials of the individual's life. Through the worship of the sacred objects and the beings they symbolize, and the acceptance of supernatural prescriptions that are at the same time codes of behavior, a powerful control over human conduct is exercised, guiding it along lines sustaining the institutional structure and conforming to the ultimate ends and values.

If this conception of the role of religion is true, one can understand why in every known society the religious activities tend to be under the charge of particular persons, who tend thereby to enjoy greater rewards than the ordinary societal member. Certain of the rewards and special privileges may attach to only the highest religious functionaries, but others usually apply, if such exists, to the entire sacerdotal class.

Moreover, there is a peculiar relation between the duties of the religious official and the special privileges he enjoys. If the supernatural world governs the destinies of men more ultimately than does the real world, its earthly representative, the person through whom one may communicate with the supernatural, must be a powerful individual. He is a keeper of sacred tradition, a skilled performer of the ritual, and an interpreter of lore and myth. He is in such close contact with the gods that he is viewed as possessing some of their characteristics. He is, in short, a bit sacred, and hence free from some of the more vulgar necessities and controls.

It is no accident, therefore, that religious functionaries have been associated with the very highest positions of power, as in theocratic regimes. Indeed, looking at it from this point of view, one may wonder why it is that they do not get *entire* control over their societies. The factors that prevent this are worthy of note.

In the first place, the amount of technical competence necessary for the performance of religious duties is small. Scientific or artistic capacity is not required. Anyone can set himself up as enjoying an intimate relation with deities, and nobody can successfully dispute him. Therefore, the factor of scarcity of personnel does not operate in the technical sense.

One may assert, on the other hand, that religious ritual is often elaborate and religious lore abstruse, and that priestly ministrations require tact, if not intelligence. This is true, but the technical requirements of the profession are for the most part adventitious, not related to the end in the same way that science is related to air travel. The priest can never be free from competition, since the criteria of whether or not one has genuine contact with the supernatural are never strictly clear. It is this competition that debases the priestly position below what might be expected at first glance. That is why priestly prestige is highest in those societies where membership in the profession is rigidly controlled by the priestly guild itself. That is why, in part at least, elaborate devices are utilized to stress the identification of the person with his office—spectacular costume, abnormal conduct, special diet, segregated residence, celibacy, conspicuous leisure, and the like. In fact, the priest is always in danger of becoming somewhat discredited—as happens in a secularized society—because in a world of stubborn fact, ritual and sacred knowledge alone will not grow crops or build houses. Furthermore, unless he is protected by a professional guild, the priest's identification with the supernatural tends to preclude his acquisition of abundant worldly goods.

As between one society and another it seems that the highest general position awarded the priest occurs in the medieval type of social order. Here there is enough economic production to afford a surplus, which can be used to support a numerous and highly organized priesthood; and yet the populace is unlettered and therefore credulous to a high degree. Perhaps the most extreme example is to be found in the Buddhism of Tibet, but others are encountered in the Catholicism of feudal Europe, the Inca regime of Peru, the Brahminism of India, and the Mayan priesthood of Yucatan. On the other hand, if the society is so crude as to have no surplus and little differentiation, so that every priest must be also a cultivator or hunter, the separation of the priestly status from the others has hardly gone far enough for priestly prestige to mean much. When the priest actually has high prestige under these circumstances, it is because he also performs other important functions (usually political and medical).

In an extremely advanced society built on scientific technology, the priesthood tends to lose status, because sacred tradition and supernaturalism drop into the background. The ultimate values and common ends of the society tend to be expressed in less anthropomorphic ways, by officials who occupy fundamentally political, economic, or educational rather than religious positions. Nevertheless, it is easily possible for intellectuals to exaggerate the degree to which the priesthood in a presumably secular milieu has lost prestige. When the matter is closely examined the urban proletariat, as well as the rural citizenry, proves to be surprisingly god-fearing and priest-ridden. No society has become so completely secularized as to liquidate entirely the belief in transcendental ends and supernatural entities. Even in a secularized society some system must exist for the integration of ultimate values, for their ritualistic expression, and for the emotional adjustments required by disappointment, death, and disaster.

GOVERNMENT

Like religion, government plays a unique and indispensable part in society. But in contrast to religion, which provides integration in terms of sentiments, beliefs, and rituals, it organizes the society in terms of law and authority. Furthermore, it orients the society to the actual rather than the unseen world.

The main functions of government are, internally, the ultimate enforcement of norms, the final arbitration of conflicting interests, and the overall planning and direction of society; and externally, the handling of war and diplomacy. To carry out these functions it acts as the agent of the entire people, enjoys a monopoly of force, and controls all individuals within its territory.

Political action, by definition, implies authority. An official can command because he has authority, and the citizen must obey because he is subject to that authority. For this reason stratification is inherent in the nature of political relationships.

So clear is the power embodied in political position that political inequality is sometimes thought to comprise all inequality. But it can be shown that there are other bases of stratification, that the following controls operate in practice to keep political power from becoming complete: (a) The fact that the actual holders of political office, and especially those determining top policy must necessarily be few in number compared to the total population. (b) The fact that the rulers represent the interest of the group rather than of themselves, and are therefore restricted in their behavior by rules and mores designed to enforce this limitation of interest. (c) The fact that the holder of political office has his authority by virtue of his office and nothing else, and therefore any special knowledge, talent, or capacity he may claim is purely incidental, so that he often has to depend upon others for technical assistance.

In view of these limiting factors, it is not strange that the rulers often have less power and prestige than a literal enumeration of their formal rights would lead one to expect.

WEALTH, PROPERTY, AND LABOR

Every position that secures for its incumbent a livelihood is, by definition, economically rewarded. For this reason there is an economic aspect to those positions (e.g., political and religious) the main function of which is not economic. It therefore becomes convenient

for the society to use unequal economic returns as a principal means of controlling the entrance of persons into positions and stimulating the performance of their duties. The amount of the economic return therefore becomes one of the main indices of social status.

It should be stressed, however, that a position does not bring power and prestige *because* it draws a high income. Rather, it draws a high income because it is functionally important and the available personnel is for one reason or another scarce. It is therefore superficial and erroneous to regard high income as the cause of a man's power and prestige, just as it is erroneous to think that a man's fever is the cause of his disease.[4]

The economic source of power and prestige is not income primarily, but the ownership of capital goods (including patents, good will, and professional reputation). Such ownership should be distinguished from the possession of consumers' goods, which is an index rather than a cause of social standing. In other words, the ownership of producers' goods is, properly speaking, a source of income like other positions, the income itself remaining an index. Even in situations where social values are widely commercialized and earnings are the readiest method of judging social position, income does not confer prestige on a position so much as it induces people to compete for the position. It is true that a man who has a high income as a result of one position may find this money helpful in climbing into another position as well, but this again reflects the effect of his initial, economically advantageous status, which exercises its influence through the medium of money.

In a system of private property in productive enterprise, an income above what an individual spends can give rise to possession of capital wealth. Presumably such possession is a reward for the proper management of one's finances originally and of the productive enterprise later. But as social differentiation becomes highly advanced and yet the institution of inheritance persists, the phenomenon of pure ownership, and reward for pure ownership, emerges. In such a case it is difficult to prove that the position is functionally important or that the scarcity involved is anything other than extrinsic and accidental. It is for this reason, doubtless, that the institution of private property in productive goods becomes more subject to criticism as social development proceeds toward industrialization. It is only this pure, that is, strictly legal and functionless ownership, however, that is open to attack; for some form of active ownership, whether private or public, is indispensable.

One kind of ownership of production goods consists in rights over the labor of others. The most extremely concentrated and exclusive of such rights are found in slavery, but the essential principle remains in serfdom, peonage, encomienda, and indenture. Naturally this kind of ownership has the greatest significance for stratification, because it necessarily entails an unequal relationship.

But property in capital goods inevitably introduces a compulsive element even into the nominally free contractual relationship. Indeed, in some respects the authority of the contractual employer is greater than that of the feudal landlord, inasmuch as the latter is more limited by traditional reciprocities. Even the classical economics recognized that competitors would fare unequally, but it did not pursue this fact to its necessary conclusion that, however it might be acquired, unequal control of goods and services must give unequal advantage to the parties to a contract.

Technical Knowledge

The function of finding means to single goals, without any concern with the choice between goals, is the exclusively technical sphere. The explanation of why positions requiring great technical skill receive fairly high rewards is easy to see, for it is the simplest case of the rewards being so distributed as to draw talent and motivate training. Why they seldom if ever receive the highest rewards is also clear: the importance of technical knowledge from a societal point of view is never so great as the integration of goals, which takes place on the religious, political, and economic levels. Since the technological level is concerned solely with means, a purely technical position must ultimately be subordinate to other positions that are religious, political, or economic in character.

Nevertheless, the distinction between expert and layman in any social order is fundamental, and cannot be entirely reduced to other terms. Methods of recruitment, as well as of reward, sometimes lead to the erroneous interpretation that technical positions are economically determined. Actually, however, the acquisition of knowledge and skill cannot be accomplished by purchase, although the opportunity to learn may be. The control of the avenues of training may inhere as a sort of property right in certain families or classes, giving them power and prestige in consequence. Such a situation adds an artificial scarcity to the natural scarcity of skills and talents. On the other hand, it is possible for an opposite situation to arise. The rewards of technical position may be so great that a condition of excess supply is created, leading to at least temporary devaluation of the rewards. Thus "unemployment in the learned professions" may result in a debasement of the prestige of those positions. Such adjustments and readjustments are constantly occurring in changing societies; and it is always well to bear in mind that the efficiency of a stratified structure may be affected by the modes of recruitment for positions. The social order itself, however, sets limits to the inflation or deflation of the prestige of experts: an over-supply tends to debase the rewards and discourage recruitment or produce revolution, whereas an under-supply tends to increase the reward or weaken the society in competition with other societies.

Particular systems of stratification show a wide range with respect to the exact position of technically competent persons. This range is perhaps most evident in the degree of specialization. Extreme division of labor tends to create many specialists without high prestige since the training is short and the required native capacity relatively small. On the other hand it also tends to accentuate the high position of the true experts—scientists, engineers, and administrators—by increasing their authority relative to other functionally important positions. But the idea of a technocratic social order or a government or priesthood of engineers or social scientists neglects the limitations of knowledge and skills as a basic for performing social functions. To the extent that the social structure is truly specialized the prestige of the technical person must also be circumscribed.

Variation in Stratified Systems

The generalized principles of stratification here suggested form a necessary preliminary to a consideration of types of stratified systems, because it is in terms of these principles that the types must be described. This can be seen by trying to delineate types according to certain modes of variation. For instance, some of the most important modes (together with the polar types in terms of them) seem to be as follows:

A. THE DEGREE OF SPECIALIZATION

The degree of specialization affects the fineness and multiplicity of the gradations in power and prestige. It also influences the extent to which particular functions may be emphasized in the invidious system, since a given function cannot receive much emphasis in the hierarchy until it has achieved structural separation from the other functions. Finally, the amount of specialization influences the bases of selection. Polar types: *Specialized, Unspecialized.*

B. THE NATURE OF THE FUNCTIONAL EMPHASIS

In general when emphasis is put on sacred matters, a rigidity is introduced that tends to limit specialization and hence the development of technology. In addition, a brake is placed on social mobility, and on the development of bureaucracy. When the preoccupation with the sacred is withdrawn, leaving greater scope for purely secular preoccupations, a great development, and rise in status, of economic and technological positions seemingly takes place.

Curiously, a concomitant rise in political position is not likely, because it has usually been allied with the religious and stands to gain little by the decline of the latter. It is also possible for a society to emphasize family functions—as in relatively undifferentiated societies where high mortality requires high fertility and kinship forms the main basis of social organization. Main types: *Familistic, Authoritarian* (*Theocratic* or sacred, and *Totalitarian* or secular), *Capitalistic.*

C. THE MAGNITUDE OF INVIDIOUS DIFFERENCES

What may be called the amount of social distance between positions, taking into account the entire scale, is something that should lend itself to quantitative measurement. Considerable differences apparently exist between different societies in this regard, and also between parts of the same society. Polar types: *Equalitarian, Inequalitarian.*

D. THE DEGREE OF OPPORTUNITY

The familiar question of the amount of mobility is different from the question of the comparative equality or inequality of rewards posed above, because the two criteria may vary independently up to a point. For instance, the tremendous divergences in monetary income in the United States are far greater than those found in primitive societies, yet the equality of opportunity to move from one rung to the other in the social scale may also be greater in the United States than in a hereditary tribal kingdom. Polar types: *Mobile* (open), *Immobile* (closed).

E. THE DEGREE OF STRATUM SOLIDARITY

Again, the degree of "class solidarity" (or the presence of specific organizations to promote class interests) may vary to some extent independently of the other criteria, and hence is an important principle in classifying systems of stratification. Polar types: *Class organized, Class unorganized.*

External Conditions

What state any particular system of stratification is in with reference to each of these modes of variation depends on two things: (1) its state with reference to the other ranges of variation, and (2) the conditions outside the system of stratification which nevertheless influence that system. Among the latter are the following:

A. THE STAGE OF CULTURAL DEVELOPMENT

As the cultural heritage grows, increased specialization becomes necessary, which in turn contributes to the enhancement of mobility, a decline of stratum solidarity, and a change of functional emphasis.

B. SITUATION WITH RESPECT TO OTHER SOCIETIES

The presence or absence of open conflict with other societies, of free trade relations or cultural diffusion, all influence the class structure to some extent. A chronic state of warfare tends to place emphasis upon the military functions, especially when the opponents are more or less equal. Free trade, on the other hand, strengthens the hand of the trader at the expense of the warrior and priest. Free movement of ideas generally has an equalitarian effect. Migration and conquest create special circumstances.

C. SIZE OF THE SOCIETY

A small society limits the degree to which functional specialization can go, the degree of segregation of different strata, and the magnitude of inequality.

Composite Types

Much of the literature on stratification has attempted to classify concrete systems into a certain number of types. This task is deceptively simple, how-

ever, and should come at the end of an analysis of elements and principles, rather than at the beginning. If the preceding discussion has any validity, it indicates that there are a number of modes of variation between different systems, and that any one system is a composite of the society's status with reference to all these modes of variation. The danger of trying to classify whole societies under such rubrics as *caste, feudal,* or *open class* is that one or two criteria are selected and others ignored, the result being an unsatisfactory solution to the problem posed. The present discussion has been offered as a possible approach to the more systematic classification of composite types.

REFERENCES

1. Kingsley Davis, "A Conceptual Analysis of Stratification," *American Sociological Review.* 7: 309–32, June, 1942.
2. The writers regret (and beg indulgence) that the present essay, a condensation of a longer study, covers so much in such short space that adequate evidence and qualification cannot be given and that as a result what is actually very tentative is presented in an unfortunately dogmatic manner.
3. Unfortunately, functional importance is difficult to establish. To use the position's prestige to establish it, as is often unconsciously done, constitutes circular reasoning from our point of view. There are, however, two independent clues: (a) the degree to which a position is functionally unique, there being no other positions that can perform the same function satisfactorily: (b) the degree to which other positions are dependent on the one in question. Both clues are best exemplified in organized systems of positions built around one major function. Thus, in most complex societies the religious, political, economic, and educational functions are handled by distinct structures not easily interchangeable. In addition, each structure possesses many different positions, some clearly dependent on, if not subordinate to, others. In sum, when an institutional nucleus becomes differentiated around one main function, and at the same time organizes a large portion of the population into its relationships, the *key* positions in it are of the highest functional importance. The absence of such specialization does not prove functional unimportance, for the whole society may be relatively unspecialized; but it is safe to assume that the more important functions receive the first and clearest structural differentiation.
4. The symbolic rather than intrinsic role of income in social stratification has been succinctly summarized by Talcott Parsons, "An Analytical Approach to the Theory of Social Stratification," *American Journal of Sociology.* 45: 841–862, May, 1940.

■ Melvin M. Tumin *

The fact of social inequality in human society is marked by its ubiquity and its antiquity. Every known society, past and present, distributes its scarce and demanded goods and services unequally. And there are attached to the positions which command unequal amounts of such goods and services certain highly morally-toned evaluations of their importance for the society.

The ubiquity and the antiquity of such inequality has given rise to the assumption that there must be something both inevitable and positively functional about such social arrangements.

Clearly, the truth or falsity of such an assumption is a strategic question for any general theory of social organization. It is therefore most curious that the basic premises and implications of the assumption have only been most casually explored by American sociologists.

The most systematic treatment is to be found in the well-known article by Kingsley Davis and Wilbert Moore, entitled "Some Principles of Stratification." [1] More than twelve years have passed since its publication, and though it is one of the very few treatments of stratification on a high level of generalization, it is difficult to locate a single systematic analysis of its reasoning. It will be the principal concern of this paper to present the beginnings of such an analysis.

The central argument advanced by Davis and Moore can be stated in a number of sequential propositions, as follows:

1. Certain positions in any society are functionally more important than others, and require special skills for their performance.

2. Only a limited number of individuals in any society have the talents which can be trained into the skills appropriate to these positions.

3. The conversion of talents into skills involves a training period during which sacrifices of one kind or another are made by those undergoing the training.

4. In order to induce the talented persons to undergo these sacrifices and acquire the training, their future positions must carry an inducement value in the form of differential, i.e., privileged and disproportionate access to the scarce and desired rewards which the society has to offer. [2]

5. These scarce and desired goods consist of the rights and perquisites attached to, or built into, the positions, and can be classified into those things which contribute to (a) sustenance and comfort, (b) humor and diversion, (c) self-respect and ego expansion.

6. This differential access to the basic rewards of the society has as a consequence the differentiation of the prestige and esteem which various strata acquire. This may be said, along with the rights and perquisites, to constitute institutionalized social inequality, i.e., stratification.

7. Therefore, social inequality among

* The writer has had the benefit of a most helpful criticism of the main portions of this paper by Professor W. J. Goode of Columbia University. In addition, he has had the opportunity to expose this paper to criticism by the Staff Seminar of the Sociology Section at Princeton. In deference to a possible rejoinder by Professors Moore and Davis, the writer has not revised the paper to meet the criticisms which Moore has already offered personally.

SOURCE: *American Sociological Review*, vol. 18, no. 4 (1953), pp. 387–94. Reprinted by permission of the author and the American Sociological Association.

different strata in the amounts of scarce and desired goods, and the amounts of prestige and esteem which they receive, is both positively functional and inevitable in any society.

Let us take these propositions and examine them *seriatim*.[3]

1. Certain positions in any society are more functionally important than others and require special skills for their performance.

The key term here is "functionally important." The functionalist theory of social organization is by no means clear and explicit about this term. The minimum common referent is to something known as the "survival value" of a social structure.[4] This concept immediately involves a number of perplexing questions. Among these are: (a) the issue of minimum vs. maximum survival, and the possible empirical referents which can be given to those terms; (b) whether such a proposition is a useless tautology since any *status quo* at any given moment is nothing more and nothing less than everything present in the *status quo*. In these terms, all acts and structures must be judged positively functional in that they constitute essential portions of the *status quo;* (c) what kind of calculus of functionality exists which will enable us, at this point in our development, to add and subtract long and short range consequences, with their mixed qualities, and arrive at some summative judgment regarding the rating an act or structure should receive on a scale of greater or lesser functionality? At best, we tend to make primarily intuitive judgments. Often enough, these judgments involve the use of value-laden criteria, or, at least, criteria which are chosen in preference to others not for any sociologically systematic reasons

but by reason of certain implicit value preferences.

Thus, to judge that the engineers in a factory are functionally more important to the factory than the unskilled workmen involves a notion regarding the dispensability of the unskilled workmen, or their replaceability, relative to that of the engineers. But this is not a process of choice with infinite time dimensions. For at some point along the line one must face the problem of adequate motivation for *all* workers at all levels of skill in the factory. In the long run, *some* labor force of unskilled workmen is as important and as indispensable to the factory as *some* labor force of engineers. Often enough, the labor force situation is such that this fact is brought home sharply to the entrepreneur in the short run rather than in the long run.

Moreover, the judgment as to the relative indispensability and replaceability of a particular segment of skills in the population involves a prior judgment about the bargaining-power of that segment. But this power is itself a culturally shaped *consequence* of the existing system of rating, rather than something inevitable in the nature of social organization. At least the contrary of this has never been demonstrated, but only assumed.

A generalized theory of social stratification must recognize that the prevailing system of inducements and rewards is only one of many variants in the whole range of possible systems of motivation which, at least theoretically, are capable of working in human society. It is quite conceivable, of course, that a system of norms could be institutionalized in which the idea of threatened withdrawal of services, except under the most extreme circumstances, would be considered as absolute moral anathema. In such a case, the whole notion of relative functionality, as advanced by Davis and Moore, would have to be radically revised.

2. Only a limited number of individuals in any society have the talents which can be trained into the skills appropriate to these positions (i.e., the more functionally important positions).

The truth of this proposition depends at least in part on the truth of proposition 1 above. It is, therefore, subject to all the limitations indicated above. But for the moment, let us assume the validity of the first proposition and concentrate on the question of the rarity of appropriate talent.

If all that is meant is that in every society there is a *range* of talent, and that some members of any society are by nature more talented than others, no sensible contradiction can be offered, but a question must be raised here regarding the amount of sound knowledge present in any society concerning the presence of talent in the population.

For, in every society there is some demonstrable ignorance regarding the amount of talent present in the population. *And the more rigidly stratified a society is, the less chance does that society have of discovering any new facts about the talents of its members.* Smoothly working and stable systems of stratification, wherever found, tend to build-in obstacles to the further exploration of the range of available talent. This is especially true in those societies where the opportunity to discover talent in any one generation varies with the differential resources of the parent generation. Where, for instance, access to education depends upon the wealth of one's parents, and where wealth is differentially distributed, large segments of the population

are likely to be deprived of the chance even to *discover* what are their talents.

Whether or not differential rewards and opportunities are functional in any one generation, it is clear that if those differentials are allowed to be socially inherited by the next generation, then, the stratification system is specifically dysfunctional for the discovery of talents in the next generation. In this fashion, systems of social stratification tend to limit the chances available to maximize the efficiency of discovery, recruitment and training of "functionally important talent." [5]

Additionally, the unequal distribution of rewards in one generation tends to result in the unequal distribution of motivation in the succeeding generation. Since motivation to succeed is clearly an important element in the entire process of education, the unequal distribution of motivation tends to set limits on the possible extensions of the educational system, and hence,. upon the efficient recruitment and training of the widest body of skills available in the population. [6]

Lastly, in this context, it may be asserted that there is some noticeable tendency for elites to restrict further access to their privileged positions, once they have sufficient power to enforce such restrictions. This is especially true in a culture where it is possible for an elite to contrive a high demand and a proportionately higher reward for its work by restricting the numbers of the elite available to do the work. The recruitment and training of doctors in modern United States is at least partly a case in point.

Here, then, are three ways, among others which could be cited, in which stratification systems, once operative, tend to reduce the survival value of a society by limiting the search, recruitment and training of functionally important personnel far more sharply than the facts of available talent would appear to justify. It is only when there is genuinely equal access to recruitment and training for all potentially talented persons that differential rewards can conceivably be justified as functional. And stratification systems are apparently *inherently antagonistic* to the development of such full equality of opportunity.

3. The conversion of talents into skills involves a training period during which sacrifices of one kind or another are made by those undergoing the training.

Davis and Moore introduce here a concept, "sacrifice" which comes closer than any of the rest of their vocabulary of analysis to being a direct reflection of the rationalizations, offered by the more fortunate members of a society, of the rightness of their occupancy of privileged positions. It is the least critically thought-out concept in the repertoire, and can also be shown to be least supported by the actual facts.

In our present society, for example, what are the sacrifices which talented persons undergo in the training period? The possibly serious losses involve the surrender of earning power and the cost of the training. The latter is generally borne by the parents of the talented youth undergoing training, and not by the trainees themselves. But this cost tends to be paid out of income which the parents were able to earn generally by virtue of *their* privileged positions in the hierarchy of stratification. That is to say, the parents' ability to pay for the training of their children is part of the differential *reward* they, the parents, received for their privileged positions in the society. And to charge this sum up against sacrifices

made by the youth is falsely to perpetrate a bill or a debt already paid by the society to the parents.

So far as the sacrifice of earning power by the trainees themselves is concerned, the loss may be measured relative to what they might have earned had they gone into the labor market instead of into advanced training for the "important" skills. There are several ways to judge this. One way is to take all the average earnings of age peers who did go into the labor market for a period equal to the average length of the training period. The total income, so calculated, roughly equals an amount which the elite can, on the average, earn back in the first decade of professional work, over and above the earnings of his age peers who are not trained. Ten years is probably the maximum amount needed to equalize the differential.[7] There remains, on the average, twenty years of work during each of which the skilled person then goes on to earn far more than his unskilled age peers. And, what is often forgotten, there is then still another ten or fifteen year period during which the skilled person continues to work and earn when his unskilled age peer is either totally or partially out of the labor market by virtue of the attrition of his strength and capabilities.

One might say that the first ten years of differential pay is perhaps justified, in order to regain for the trained person what he lost during his training period. But it is difficult to imagine what would justify continuing such differential rewards beyond that period.

Another and probably sounder way to measure how much is lost during the training period is to compare the per capita income available to the trainee with the per capita income of the age peer on the untrained labor market during the so-called sacrificial period. If one takes into account the earlier marriage of untrained persons, and the earlier acquisition of family dependents, it is highly dubious that the per capita income of the wage worker is significantly larger than that of the trainee. Even assuming, for the moment, that there is a difference, the amount is by no means sufficient to justify a lifetime of continuing differentials.

What tends to be completely overlooked, in addition, are the psychic and spiritual rewards which are available to the elite trainees by comparison with their age peers in the labor force. There is, first, the much higher prestige enjoyed by the college student and the professional-school student as compared with persons in shops and offices. There is, second, the extremely highly valued privilege of having greater opportunity for self-development. There is, third, all the psychic gain involved in being allowed to delay the assumption of adult responsibilities such as earning a living and supporting a family. There is, fourth, the access to leisure and freedom of a kind not likely to be experienced by the persons already at work.

If these are never taken into account as rewards of the training period it is not because they are not concretely present, but because the emphasis in American concepts of reward is almost exclusively placed on the material returns of positions. The emphases on enjoyment, entertainment, ego enhancement, prestige and esteem are introduced only when the differentials in these which accrue to the skilled positions need to be justified. If these other rewards were taken into account, it would be much more difficult to dem-

onstrate that the training period, as presently operative, is really sacrificial. Indeed, it might turn out to be the case that even at this point in their careers, the elite trainees were being differentially rewarded relative to their age peers in the labor force.

All of the foregoing concerns the quality of the training period under our present system of motivation and rewards. Whatever may turn out to be the factual case about the present system—and the factual case is moot—the more important theoretical question concerns the assumption that the training period under *any* system must be sacrificial.

There seem to be no good theoretical grounds for insisting on this assumption. For, while under any system certain costs will be involved in training persons for skilled positions, these costs could easily be assumed by the society-at-large. Under these circumstances, there would be no need to compensate anyone in terms of differential rewards once the skilled positions were staffed. In short, there would be no need or justification for stratifying social positions on *these* grounds.

4. In order to induce the talented persons to undergo these sacrifices and acquire the training, their future positions must carry an inducement value in the form of differential, i.e., privileged and disproportionate access to the scarce and desired rewards which the society has to offer.

Let us assume, for the purposes of the discussion, that the training period is sacrificial and the talent is rare in every conceivable human society. There is still the basic problem as to whether the allocation of differential rewards in scarce and desired goods and services is the only or the most efficient way of recruiting the appropriate talent to these positions.

For there are a number of alternative motivational schemes whose efficiency and adequacy ought at least to be considered in this context. What can be said, for instance, on behalf of the motivation which De Man called "joy in work," Veblen termed "instinct for workmanship" and which we latterly have come to identify as "intrinsic work satisfaction"? Or, to what extent could the motivation of "social duty" be institutionalized in such a fashion that self interest and social interest come closely to coincide? Or, how much prospective confidence can be placed in the possibilities of institutionalizing "social service" as a widespread motivation for seeking one's appropriate position and fulfilling it conscientiously?

Are not these types of motivations, we may ask, likely to prove most appropriate for precisely the "most functionally important positions"? Especially in a mass industrial society, where the vast majority of positions become standardized and routinized, it is the skilled jobs which are likely to retain most of the quality of "intrinsic job satisfaction" and be most readily identifiable as socially serviceable. Is it indeed impossible then to build these motivations into the socialization pattern to which we expose our talented youth?

To deny that such motivations could be institutionalized would be to overclaim our present knowledge. In part, also, such a claim would seem to derive from an assumption that what has not been institutionalized yet in human affairs is incapable of institutionalization. Admittedly, historical experience affords us evidence we cannot afford to ignore. But such evidence cannot legitimately be used to deny absolutely the possibility of heretofore untried alternatives. Social innovation is as important a feature of human societies as social stability.

On the basis of these observations, it seems that Davis and Moore have stated the case much too strongly when they insist that a "functionally important position" which requires skills that are scarce, "must command great prestige, high salary, ample leisure, and the like," if the appropriate talents are to be attracted to the position. Here, clearly, the authors are postulating the unavoidability of very specific types of rewards and, by implication, denying the possibility of others.

5. *These scarce and desired goods consist of rights and perquisites attached to, or built into, the positions and can be classified into those things which contribute to (a) sustenance and comfort; (b) humor and diversion; (c) self-respect and ego expansion.*

6. *This differential access to the basic rewards of the society has as a consequence the differentiation of the prestige and esteem which various strata acquire. This may be said, along with the rights and perquisites, to constitute institutionalized social inequality, i.e., stratification.*

With the classification of the rewards offered by Davis and Moore there need be little argument. Some question must be raised, however, as to whether any reward system, built into a general stratification system, must allocate equal amounts of all three types of reward in order to function effectively, or whether one type of reward may be emphasized to the virtual neglect of others. This raises the further question regarding which type of emphasis is likely to prove most effective as a differential inducer. Nothing in the known facts about human motivation impels us to favor one type of reward over the other, or to insist that all three types of reward must be built into the positions in comparable amounts if the position is to have an inducement value.

It is well known, of course, that societies differ considerably in the kinds of rewards they emphasize in their efforts to maintain a reasonable balance between responsibility and reward. There are, for instance, numerous societies in which the conspicuous display of differential economic advantage is considered extremely bad taste. In short, our present knowledge commends to us the possibility of considerable plasticity in the way in which different types of rewards can be structured into a functioning society. This is to say, it cannot yet be demonstrated that it is *unavoidable* that differential prestige and esteem shall accrue to positions which command differential rewards in power and property.

What does seem to be unavoidable is that differential prestige shall be given to those in any society who conform to the normative order as against those who deviate from that order in a way judged immoral and detrimental. On the assumption that the continuity of a society depends on the continuity and stability of its normative order, some such distinction between conformists and deviants seems inescapable.

It also seems to be unavoidable that in any society, no matter how literate its tradition, the older, wiser and more experienced individuals who are charged with the enculturation and socialization of the young must have more power than the young, on the assumption that the task of effective socialization demands such differential power.

But this differentiation in prestige between the conformist and the deviant is by no means the same distinction as that between strata of individuals each of which operates *within* the normative order, and is composed of adults. The *latter* distinction, in the form of differentiated rewards and prestige between social strata is what Davis and Moore, and most sociologists, consider the structure of a stratification system. The *former* distinctions have nothing necessarily to do with the workings of such a system nor with the efficiency of motivation and recruitment of functionally important personnel.

Nor does the differentiation of power between young and old necessarily create differentially valued strata. For no society rates its young as less morally worthy than its older persons, no matter how much differential power the older ones may temporarily enjoy.

7. Therefore, social inequality among different strata in the amounts of scarce and desired goods, and the amounts of prestige and esteem which they receive, is both positively functional and inevitable in any society.

If the objections which have heretofore been raised are taken as reasonable, then it may be stated that the only items which any society must distribute unequally are the power and property necessary for the performance of different tasks. If such differential power and property are viewed by all as commensurate with the differential responsibilities, and if they are culturally defined as *resources* and not as rewards, then no differentials in prestige and esteem need follow.

Historically, the evidence seems to be that every time power and property are distributed unequally, no matter what the cultural definition, prestige and esteem differentiations have tended to result as well. Historically, however, no systematic effort has ever been made, under propitious circumstances, to develop the tradition that each man is as socially worthy as all other men so long as he performs his appropriate tasks conscientiously. While such a tradition seems utterly utopian, no known facts in psychological or social science have yet demonstrated its impossibility or its dysfunctionality for the continuity of a society. The achievement of a full institutionalization of such a tradition seems far too remote to contemplate. Some successive approximations at such a tradition, however, are not out of the range of prospective social innovation.

What, then, of the "positive functionality" of social stratification? Are there other, negative, functions of institutionalized social inequality which can be identified, if only tentatively? Some such dysfunctions of stratification have already been suggested in the body of this paper. Along with others they may now be stated, in the form of provisional assertions, as follows:

1. Social stratification systems function to limit the possibility of discovery of the full range of talent available in a society. This results from the fact of unequal access to appropriate motivation, channels of recruitment and centers of training.

2. In foreshortening the range of available talent, social stratification systems function to set limits upon the possibility of expanding the productive resources of the society, at least relative to what might be the case under conditions of greater equality of opportunity.

3. Social stratification systems function to provide the elite with the political power necessary to procure acceptance and dominance of an ideology which rationalizes the *status quo*, whatever it may be, as "logical," "natural" and "morally right." In this manner, social

stratification systems function as essentially conservative influences in the societies in which they are found.

4. Social stratification systems function to distribute favorable self-images unequally throughout a population. To the extent that such favorable self-images are requisite to the development of the creative potential inherent in men, to that extent stratification systems function to limit the development of this creative potential.

5. To the extent that inequalities in social rewards cannot be made fully acceptable to the less privileged in a society, social stratification systems function to encourage hostility, suspicion and distrust among the various segments of a society and thus to limit the possibilities of extensive social integration.

6. To the extent that the sense of significant membership in a society depends on one's place on the prestige ladder of the society, social stratification systems function to distribute unequally the sense of significant membership in the population.

7. To the extent that loyalty to a society depends on a sense of significant membership in the society, social stratification systems function to distribute loyalty unequally in the population.

8. To the extent that participation and apathy depend upon the sense of significant membership in the society, social stratification systems function to distribute the motivation to participate unequally in a population.

Each of the eight foregoing propositions contains implicit hypotheses regarding the consequences of unequal distribution of rewards in a society in accordance with some notion of the functional importance of various positions. These are empirical hypotheses, subject to test. They are offered here only as exemplary of the kinds of consequences of social stratification which are not often taken into account in dealing with the problem. They should also serve to reinforce the doubt that social inequality is a device which is uniformly functional for the role of guaranteeing that the most important tasks in a society will be performed conscientiously by the most competent persons.

The obviously mixed character of the functions of social inequality should come as no surprise to anyone. If sociology is sophisticated in any sense, it is certainly with regard to its awareness of the mixed nature of any social arrangement, when the observer takes into account long as well as short range consequences and latent as well as manifest dimensions.

Summary

In this paper, an effort has been made to raise questions regarding the inevitability and positive functionality of stratification, or institutionalized social inequality in rewards, allocated in accordance with some notion of the greater and lesser functional importance of various positions. The possible alternative meanings of the concept "functional importance" has been shown to be one difficulty. The question of the scarcity or abundance of available talent has been indicated as a principal source of possible variation. The extent to which the period of training for skilled positions may reasonably be viewed as sacrificial has been called into question. The possibility has been suggested that very different types of motivational schemes might conceivably be made to function. The separability of differentials in power and property considered as resources appropriate to a task from such differentials considered as rewards for the performance of a task has also been suggested. It has also been maintained that differentials in prestige and esteem do not necessarily follow upon differentials in power and property when the latter are considered as appropriate resources rather than rewards. Finally, some negative functions, or dysfunctions, of institutionalized social inequality have been tentatively identified revealing the mixed character of the outcome of social stratification, and casting doubt on the contention that

> Social inequality is thus an unconsciously evolved device by which societies insure that the most important positions are conscientiously filled by the most qualified persons.[8]

REFERENCES

1. *American Sociological Review*, X (April, 1945), pp. 242–249. An earlier article by Kingsley Davis, entitled, "A Conceptual Analysis of Stratification," *American Sociological Review*, VII (June, 1942), pp. 309–321, is devoted primarily to setting forth a vocabulary for stratification analysis. A still earlier article by Talcott Parsons, "An Analytical Approach to the Theory of Social Stratification," *American Journal of Sociology*, XLV (November, 1940), pp. 849–862, approaches the problem in terms of why "differential ranking is considered a really fundamental phenomenon of social systems and what are the respects in which such ranking is important." The principal line of integration asserted by Parsons is with the fact of the normative orientation of any society. Certain crucial lines of connection are left unexplained, however, in this article, and in the Davis and Moore article of 1945 only some of these lines are made explicit.
2. The "scarcity and demand" qualities of goods and services are never explicitly men-

tioned by Davis and Moore. But it seems to the writer that the argument makes no sense unless the goods and services are so characterized. For if rewards are to function as differential inducements they must not only be differentially distributed but they must be both scarce and demanded as well. Neither the scarcity of an item by itself nor the fact of its being in demand is sufficient to allow it to function as a differential inducement in a system of unequal rewards. Leprosy is scarce and oxygen is highly demanded.

3. The arguments to be advanced here are condensed versions of a much longer analysis entitled, *An Essay on Social Stratification*. Perforce, all the reasoning necessary to support some of the contentions cannot be offered within the space limits of this article.

4. Davis and Moore are explicitly aware of the difficulties involved here and suggest two "independent clues" other than survival value. See footnote 3 on p. 244 of their article.

5. Davis and Moore state this point briefly on p. 248 but do not elaborate it.

6. In the United States, for instance, we are only now becoming aware of the amount of productivity we, as a society, lose by allocating inferior opportunities and rewards, and hence, inferior motivation, to our Negro population. The actual amount of loss is difficult to specify precisely. Some rough estimate can be made, however, on the assumption that there is present in the Negro population about the same range of talent that is found in the white population.

7. These are only very rough estimates, of course, and it is certain that there is considerable income variation within the so-called elite group, so that the proposition holds only relatively more or less.

8. Davis and Moore, *op. cit.,* p. 243.

10

DIFFERENTIATION IN COLLECTIVE SETTLEMENTS

Y. Talmon-Garber

In his criticism of the functional theory of stratification, Tumin suggests that Davis and Moore were perhaps being unduly ethnocentric in not considering other forms of work motivation that might inspire individuals, besides the limited set of rewards that they outlined.

Probably the most widespread and successful attempt in the modern world to create a community based on equality in which the motivations for work involve ideals of social service and communal responsibility rather than personal aggrandizement and considerations of personal wealth, rank, or power, are the Israeli kibbutzim. Begun in

SOURCE: *Scripta Hierosolymitana*, 3 (1956), pp. 153–78. Reprinted by permission of S. Talmon.

Palestine sixty years ago by Jewish immigrants from eastern Europe, there were by the end of 1968 some 232 kibbutzim with a total population of over 93,000.

From the point of view of social stratification, there were two important ideological characteristics of the original kibbutz movement.

1. While human differences and inequality were recognized, what was unique about the kibbutz experiment was its attempt to construct a set of social institutions that would diminish the natural inequalities among men. This egalitarianism has taken the following major forms: (a) a uniform standard of living for all members and absence of individual payment for work; (b) rotation of jobs, especially leadership positions and menial tasks, in order to avoid a permanent association of men and jobs and the invidious rankings which might naturally follow therefrom; (c) democratic control of the kibbutz through election of leaders and widespread participation of the members on committees.

Most societies, instead of reducing the natural inequalities among men, magnify them, so that personal inequality is reenforced by economic, social, and political inequality. The continuing ideal of the kibbutz is to play down what is felt to be undesirable forms of inequality and to try to base relationships on considerations of fraternity rather than on hierarchy.

2. A second ideological feature of the kibbutz movement was that humble agricultural toil became infused with positive value. The early Zionists who came to Palestine believed that the Jewish occupational structure in the Diaspora (lands of the dispersion) was abnormal. Jews were concentrated in commerce, finance, and business —all urban, petty bourgeois occupations, none basic to life itself such as manual work and especially agriculture. The idea was prevalent that the Jewish occupational structure was somehow parasitic and that the only way to "restructure" or "productivize" Jewish occupational life along more normal lines was to settle Jews in a land of their own where they would be forced to engage in the whole spectrum of occupations common to man. Agriculture, from which Jews had been separated for so long, was seen as the most productive and honorable occupation open to man. On the other hand, white-collar occupations in business, commerce, and finance were looked upon with some disdain, for they were seen as less important to life and a carry-over from the Diaspora culture. The so-called "religion of labor" was thus unique for it reversed the traditional status hierarchy and accorded higher position to manual than to nonmanual labor. Although much of the original zeal for manual toil has dwindled today, it still has its hold and undercuts, to a certain extent, the high status that might otherwise accrue to executive and managerial positions on the kibbutz.

What the Israeli sociologist Talmon-Garber was concerned with in her study of a half-dozen kibbutzim in the 1950's is *the continuing struggle on the collectives between the inexorable forces of bureaucratization inherent in modern life, on the one hand, and the principles of equality and classlessness, on the other*. The forces of bureaucratization consist of two kinds of pressures: (a) in the interests of "efficiency," gradually to allow the most able leaders to hold power permanently; thus, elite positions become hardened and exclusive; and (b) the gradual accumulation by these permanent leaders of miscellaneous privileges and benefits, such as a higher standard of living, high status, and enhanced power. If the forces of bureaucratization ultimately prevail, then, of course, the kibbutz will become stratified and the experiment in classlessness will have failed. Talmon-Garber's tentative conclusion is that while some concessions have been made to the forces of bureaucracy, in the manner of longer tenure for those in leadership positions, for example, there are numerous counterforces which are resisting bureaucratization. In short, the issue is not settled and the struggle continues.

In their sixty-year history, however, the collectives have demonstrated a number of things. First, the kibbutz experiment suggests that it is possible to motivate people to work—at least in small communities—without the use of material incentives. Those who invoke either "human nature" or functional necessity, and claim that it violates human or social needs for men to work without material inducement have to explain the obvious economic and technical success of the collectives. Second, the kibbutzim have demonstrated that social organization is possible with no appreciable personal inequality with respect to wealth or property. The collectives have not fallen apart; in this sense, classlessness does seem possible. Third, on a small scale at least, it seems possible to create a community with a minimum of inequality of power among individuals.

Finally, the kibbutzim suggest that while it is possible to *reduce* status differences among people, it is extremely difficult if not impossible to eradicate them completely. Of all the social inequalities in society, differences in status are the most difficult to level. While it is possible to equalize wealth and property or to reduce large inequalities of power, especially in small communities, it is extremely difficult to make people equal with respect to reputation. As Talmon-Garber points out, in spite of the pervasive egalitarianism of the kibbutz, some people (though not necessarily the formal leaders) command more respect and have higher status than others.

Perhaps this lends credence to the functional theory of Talcott Parsons who argues that it is impossible to create a society with status equality. His argument, in brief, is that every social system must have a set of values, that is, things that are regarded as more or less desirable than others. Some societies, for example, may put positive value on intelligence, ingenuity, hard work, and thrift; while other societies may stress piety, generosity, patience, reticence, and otherworldliness. It follows that those people who in their lives most closely approximate the positive values of their particular society will command higher status than those who do not. Thus, status inequality seems to be built into every society by virtue of its value system.

Introduction

The purpose of this paper is the description and analysis of an explorative research project on élite formation in Collective Settlements in Israel.[1] The study of social differentiation in these Collectives provides an opportunity to observe differentiation as it appears within a primary group based on spontaneous solidarity and on an intense identification with equalitarian values. The establishment of a comprehensive

[1] The main features of the Collective settlements (Kvuzot or Kibbutzim) are: common ownership of all property except for a few personal belongings, communal organization of production, consumption, and care of children. The community is run as a single economic unit and a single household. The family has ceased to be an autonomous group from the point of view of the division of labour. Husband and wife have independent jobs. Main meals are taken in the communal dining-hall. Members' needs are provided for by communal institutions on an equalitarian basis. All income goes into the common treasury. Each member gets only a very small annual cash allowance for personal expenses. In most Collectives, children live apart from their parents and are looked after by members assigned to this task. They spend a few hours every day with their parents and siblings, but from their birth on they sleep, eat and study in special children's houses. Each age-group leads its own life and has its autonomous arrangements.

The settlements are governed by a general assembly, which convenes every week or every fort-

social structure and the development of sub-systems within that structure entail a process of routinization. Formalization and differentiation are the two main aspects of this process. The original basic homogeneity is disrupted by the division of labour, the articulation of the authority structure, the crystallization of various solidary sub-groups, and the establishment and growth of families. In this paper we propose to discuss the relation between élite formation and the consolidation of other solidary sub-groups.

The allocation of jobs in the Collectives was originally based on the assumption that, except for a few tasks which required highly specialized training and considerable experience, every member would be able to perform any given task. The Collectives insisted on frequent job-changes, and especially so in the managerial and leadership positions. The necessity for specialization and the exigencies of running a comparatively big enterprise have resulted in a partial retreat from the original assumption. Considerations of efficiency have overruled the principle of job rotation in many spheres of social and economic life in the Collectives. The tendency towards a more articulated and more stable division of labour is discernible in the assignment of jobs as well as in election to public office. There is evidence of the emergence of a stable and distinct élite.

The crystallization of solidary sub-groups is another aspect of the process of differentiation. The groups of settlers who join the original founders of each community at different stages of its development very often remain distinguishable from the founders. Sometimes these sub-groups assimilate and become completely integrated. Most of them, however, retain their identity and constitute semi-separate sub-groups within the framework of the Collectives.

Processes of élite formation and of crystallization of solidary sub-groups appear in varying degrees in all Collectives. Hardly any attempt has as yet been made to examine the extent of differentiation and to account for it in terms of a general theory of stratification.

The first research in this direction was made by E. Rosenfeld in her study, "Stratification in a Classless Society." [2] Her main conclusions are as follows:

A. In spite of the absence of economic differentiation, we find two clearly crystallized social strata in the Collectives. The differences of rank between the emerging strata are based on the objectively defined attributes of managerial positions in work or administration and on seniority. Leaders and managers are recruited from the sub-group of old-timers; these old-timer managers and leaders make up the upper stratum. The lower stratum is heterogeneous, and is composed of old-timers and newcomers and of responsi-

---

night, by a council and various committees. Each Collective is affiliated to one of the main four Collective Movements.

The founders of each Collective settle as a group. Additional groups and individuals join them afterwards. The groups are generally organized in various youth movements and undergo training in longer-established Collectives.

Collectives may vary in size from 40–50 members of a newly founded settlement to larger and older ones with a population of over 1000. There were 227 Collectives in Israel in 1952 with a total population of 69,039.

[2] E. Rosenfeld, "Stratification in a Classless Society," *American Sociological Review* (March 1952).

ble, permanent workers as well as temporary ones. The significant distinction, in terms of the balance of rewards and the role played in the process of change, obtains between the upper stratum on the one hand and the whole rank and file on the other.

B. Allocation of rewards. E. Rosenfeld employs the typology of rewards proposed by K. Davis and W. Moore, namely (a) Sustenance and Comfort; (b) Humour and Diversion; (c) Self-respect and Ego-expansion. No special rights as to sustenance and comfort are attached to managerial-leadership positions, but upper-stratum members are privileged to some extent as to humour and diversion, and highly privileged as to self-respect and ego-expansion.

C. Differences in living conditions and reward-balance in each stratum create two types of vested interests with regard to institutional change. Those more directly exposed to disfunctional consequences of the Collective systems have a stake in pressure for change, while those experiencing more directly its functional aspects want to preserve the system in its entirety. Members of the underprivileged lower stratum demand a higher standard of living and more independence of communal institutions. The privileged upper stratum is "conservative" and opposes these demands.

The importance of E. Rosenfeld's study lies not so much in its conclusions as such, as in *the basic hypothesis of correlation between the balance of rewards, extent of differentiation and trends of institutional change.* This hypothesis was the basis of further examination of the process of differentiation in the Collectives.

I. Elite Formation

The extent of consolidation of a leader-manager élite and its relation to other sub-groups were examined in an explorative research in six Collectives.[3] A careful study of this problem entailed:

A. A working definition of the leader-manager élite.
B. The setting up of a systematic framework for the examination of the degree of consolidation of sub-groups.
C. Change of the typology of rewards.
D. Analyses of the emergence of the élite in terms of balance of rewards.

We included in the leader-manager élite [4] all members engaged in work organization and overall administra-

[3] This paper is a summary of the results of an explorative research project on Collective Settlements in Israel which was conducted by the Sociological Research Seminar of the Hebrew University. Our sample is not representative. The conclusions are therefore tentative and will be re-examined in further research. I wish to express my gratitude to the students who participated in this research, to Mr. E. Ron, who did a considerable part of the field work, and Mr. A. Ezioni, who assisted me in the summing up of the first stage of our project. I also wish to thank Mrs. R. Weinberger, Dr. S. N. Eisenstadt, Mr. J. Ben-David and Dr. J. Katz for their comments.

The Chair of Co-operation of the Hebrew University provided us with the funds for conducting this research. I am grateful to Mr. H. Viteles, Lecturer in Co-operation, for his generous help.</br>
[4] In this research we concentrated chiefly on the élite of leaders and managers. A full analysis of the élite in the Collectives will entail examination of (a) the technical-professional élite and (b) the ideological-cultural élite in each Collective on the one hand, and on the other, an examination of (a) the élite of the Collective movements and (b) representatives of the Collectives in the country-wide élite.

tion, and in direction of the community.

A. Holders of key public offices (treasurer, secretaries for internal and external affairs, work-allocator, etc.).

B. Managers of the main branches of production (e.g. Dairy, Sheepfold, Vegetable-garden, Citrus groves, Green fodder, Dry farming, or Industries, if any).

C. Managers of consumption and services (manageress of the communal kitchen-dining hall, laundry, clothing store-room, children's houses, etc.).

D. All members of the council (usually including most of those in A).

E. All members of the central economic committee (usually including some of B).

F. Chairmen of other important committees (health, housing, recreation, education, etc.).

Key public offices and managerial positions are full-time jobs. Chairmen and members of all committees carry out their public functions in their spare time. Nomination to any of these jobs and offices is subject to the approval of one of the main committees or to the ratification of the general assembly.

Examination of the institutional framework and of the members' evaluation of the relative importance of the various management-leadership offices led to a classification of élite positions into two sub-categories. In the sub-category of *primary* élite positions we included the key office-holders, all members of the council and all members of the central economic committee. In the *secondary* élite we included the branch managers and the chairmen of the important committees. The range of activity in secondary élite positions is limited. It is the holders of primary élite positions who co-ordinate and direct the community as a whole. Their influence is pervasive and continuous.

The extent of consolidation of the élite and of the sub-groups was assessed by examination of the following aspects:

A. Representation.

B. Turnover and mobility patterns.

C. Formal and informal leadership.

D. Exclusiveness in interpersonal relations.

E. Attitudes towards basic ideological issues.

The analysis of representation, of the rate of turnover and of mobility patterns applies to the last seven years. Analyses of informal leadership, of the network of interpersonal relations, and of ideology deal with members who were actually in office at the time of our study as well as with members who were found to be alternative candidates for nomination and were only temporarily out of élite positions.

REPRESENTATION

The main sub-categories examined as to their representation in the élite were those based on (a) former membership in a youth-movement group or in an agricultural training group; (b) seniority of stay in the settlement; and (c) country of origin. In all the Collectives included in our sample, representation is not proportionate, and in some of them we found one sub-category which had considerably more representatives in the élite than any of the others. The tendency towards monopolization is more marked in primary élite positions than in secondary ones.

In none of the Collectives did we find a monopolization of most of the élite positions. Nomination is based on a policy of gaining the widest possible participation and representation of the members in the Collective's public life on the one hand, and on the necessity for continuity and efficiency on the other. Some time may pass until individual newcomers or a minority "ethnic" group cease to be peripheral and begin to participate in communal affairs. There are some signs of the blocking of channels of recruitment. There are sub-groups which remain passive and almost unrepresented. It should be stressed, however, that the élite is as a rule heterogeneous and that most major sub-categories and sub-groups are represented in it to some extent.

Length of stay in the Collectives proved to be an important determinant of degree of representation, but it was not the only one. Country of origin and former membership in a youth movement or training group often counterbalance and attenuate the influence of seniority. Both have marked effects on representation. A strong tendency towards monopolization appeared only in Collectives where the categories obtained by considering each of the main criteria overlap. Reinforcing determinants of differentiation were found to be correlated with highly disproportionate representation. Cross-cutting categories and basic homogeneity as to degree of indoctrination and as to way of life counterbalance monopolization.

Turnover and Mobility Patterns

Consolidation of the élite as a closed and stable group depends on a considerable slowing down of the turnover in élite positions. The upper-stratum hypothesis assumes permanent membership in the élite. Examination of the rates of rotation and a follow-up of mobility patterns during the seven years covered by our study modify this assumption in many respects.

The trend towards longer tenure appears in leadership and managerial offices as well as in other jobs. In each of the Collectives in our sample we found a number of office-holders who were almost permanent members of the élite. Some occupy one of the central positions most of the time. Others pass from one élite position to another and are hardly ever out of élite positions. Some of the key offices rotate among a limited number of experts who take turns and hold these offices alternately. Nor is it uncommon for members in key positions to hold a number of positions at a time. Terms of office are often longer than they used to be. On the other hand, it should be stressed that the rate of turnover in élite positions is considerably more rapid than it is in any other sphere. The number of members who are considered indispensable, and consequently occupy one élite position or another most of the time, is small—no more than a few members in each Collective. There is no uniform rate of turnover in all élite positions and there are considerable and significant differences between the sub-categories of key offices. Figures adduced here substantiate these conclusions and indicate the main trends of development in this respect.[5]

Tenure of office in the council (which is the main executive body) is comparatively short. Most members of

---

[5] The figures quoted here pertain to the terms of tenure in one of the Collectives in our sample. We chose this Collective because we reached a more exact method of examining turnover while analyzing it. Terms of tenure in the other Collectives are essentially not very different from those cited here.

the council hold office for one year, some for two years. A longer tenure of office is rare. Only a few of the members in office at the time of our project had been in the council previously during the seven-year period covered by our examination. The average continuous term of duty is about 1.4 years. The discontinuous term of duty is 1.6 years.

Tenure of office in the main economic committee is longer than in the council. The average continuous term of office there is 1.9 years. A number of the present members of this committee have held office in it once or even twice previously during the last seven years. The discontinuous average term of office is thus longer than the continuous one—2.5 years.

The full-time public offices are the most important élite positions. The average continuous tenure was found to be 1.7 years. The secretary for internal affairs does not hold his job for more than one year as a rule. The treasurer has the maximum tenure in this category—three years. The average discontinuous tenure in these positions is 2.3 years.

The average continuous tenure in all the primary élite positions mentioned above is 1.9 years. The average discontinuous tenure in this category is 2.6 years.

The highest average continuous tenure was found in the management of the branches of production—2.9 years. Average discontinuous tenure is 3.3 years. Maximum continuous tenure is 6.2 years.

Tenure in consumption and services is much shorter. The average continuous tenure is 1.9 years. Average discontinuous tenure is 2.2 years. Maximum tenure is 3.6 years.

Chairmen of committees have an av-

erage continuous term of 1.9 years. The average discontinuous tenure is about the same.

The average continuous term in the secondary élite positions when they are considered as a whole is 2.6 years. The average discontinuous tenure is 3.1 years.

Members of committees other than the council and the economic committee, who were not included in the élite, have an average continuous tenure of 1.6 years and a discontinuous one of 2.2 years.

To sum up, tenure in primary élite positions is thus shorter than in secondary élite positions. Movement in and out of high office and in and out of a given range of offices is considerable.

The trend towards bureaucratization is partly counterbalanced by institutional devices which check the formation of a leading group which would be permanently in power. Assignment to office by election, limited tenure, and the division of responsibilities among many semi-independent committees, encourage wide-spread participation and prevent the consolidation of a rigid authority structure.

Examination of mobility patterns indicates the importance of the committees in this respect. 30 or 40 per cent of all community members serve on one of the committees. It is in these committees that newcomers get their initial experience in management and gradually attain recognition. Even when the committees are fairly inactive and have little influence on community affairs, they serve as channels of mobility. Key positions are entrusted to members who make their mark in the committees. Movement from secondary to important committees is considerable. The committees are important stepping-stones in advancement to élite positions.

Examination of jobs and public offices held by the present members of the élite during the past seven years reveals recurring patterns: (a) Alternating periods of productive manual work and full-time public office. Periodic abstention from public office and return to productive work is not so prevalent as it used to be, but still occurs quite often. (b) Transfer to semi-professional jobs such as that of accountant, teacher and mechanic. (c) Recurring temporary terms of office in élite positions outside the settlement. Members of the Collectives are very often nominated to temporary terms of offices in the Collectives' country-wide organizations (which deal with common political, administrative and cultural matters), in youth movements, in the political parties, in the Army and in Government institutions. Holders of élite positions outside the community are recruited mainly from the active and influential office-holders in each community.

Examination of the changes in voluntary public office in committees reveals frequent and recurring movement from secondary to important positions and vice versa, as well as retreat to temporary inactivity. Members who have once occupied important élite positions are not allowed to remain inactive for long. They generally return to public office after a period of inactivity, but not necessarily to one of the main positions.

The examination of rates of rotation and of mobility patterns leads to the conclusion that turnover in élite positions is still considerable. The constant increase in membership in these communities, their economic expansion, the scarcity of competent, experienced managers among newcomers and the

growing emphasis on efficiency, inevitably lead to a slowing down of the rates of replacement. The trend towards bureaucratization of management and leadership is partly counterbalanced by the following factors:

A. Routinization of tasks.
B. Intensive vocational training.
C. Recruitment to élite positions outside the community.
D. Difficulties of recruitment.

The Collectives have by now evolved established ways of dealing with many problems. Rules of procedure, binding laws and regulations and definite routines are to be found in many spheres of activity. Some of the tasks which required a great deal of personal skill and initiative in the first phases of communal development have by now become matters of routine.

Quite a number of members have gained experience in the course of their work and have specialized in certain spheres of social and economic organization. Many members have attended special intensive courses in their respective fields of interest, while others have been sent for training and experience to longer established Collectives. The number of candidates for some of the jobs and public offices increases gradually, and the nomination committee is able to change the personnel of some of the committees and to replace some of the office-holders without seriously undermining efficiency.

Another important factor is the assignment of members of the Collectives to élite positions in the wider institutional framework. The Collectives occupy an élite position in the more comprehensive community and have all sorts of vested interests in outside bodies. They are highly represented in many country-wide organizations and institutions. As mentioned above, candidates for élite positions outside the community are chosen mainly from those holding élite positions within the community. Recruitment to élite positions in outside bodies speeds up replacement and prevents the blocking of channels of mobility within each community.

The difficulties of recruitment are of crucial importance in this context. In all the Collectives in our sample we have found both assumed and sincere reluctance to accept the responsibility of certain major positions. Only in rare cases does a member accept nomination without protest. It has become an almost accepted procedure for candidates to try to prove that they are either unsuited to the position, or are unable to accept it. Some of these refusals should not be taken too seriously and are just a way of proving that one does not covet authority. Ceremonial refusal is quickly overcome and has little effect on recruitment.[6] In many cases, however, refusals are sincere and candidates cannot be easily prevailed upon to accept the position offered. Some of the positions are by no means easy to fill, and members accept them only on condition that their tenure be limited. Office-holders insist on their right to return to their former occupations and refuse to remain in public office longer than one term at a time. Obstinate refusals are very rare and the nomination committee generally manages to persuade the candidates to take on responsibility. In some cases, however, it is necessary to bring informal pressure to bear and the candidate accepts nomination only after long discussion and an assembly decision. There are marked differences in the incidence of refusals and reluctance to assume office. Refusals and withdrawal from management of production and from membership in economic committees are not frequent. Difficulties in recruitment are much more prevalent in nominations to positions in management of consumption and services, in social committees, and in some of the central key positions.

Tendencies to temporary withdrawal and refusals to hold office for more than a term at a time, speed up replacement and counterbalance bureaucratization.

ELITE AND INFORMAL LEADERSHIP

The distinctive characteristics of the élite were further clarified by examination of the relations between élite and informal leadership. In the category of informal leaders we included all the influential members who did not hold any official élite position at the time of our study. The distinction between formal and informal leadership is not clear-cut in a Collective. Elite positions are not highly formalized and office-holders have a direct and constant contact with most of the members. Moreover, the distinction is temporary in most cases. The multiplicity of offices, the emphasis on wide-spread participation and the tendency towards withdrawal from office, result in speedy recruitment of any member who is felt to wield some influence on his fellow-members for some reason or other. Members who have acquired a reputation as efficient managers or as influential leaders are not allowed to stay away from office for long. Sooner

---

[6] The ceremonial nature of some of the refusals may be clearly seen in the following quotation: "The nomination committee decided to nominate me principal of the school. I objected in accordance with what has become our generally accepted custom." This member accepted the appointment after a short discussion.

or later they are called upon to accept responsibility and are assigned to one of the élite offices. Informal leaders who were not assigned to office for a comparatively long period were to be found only in Collectives with very disproportionate representation. The leaders of under-represented sub-groups in these Collectives wield considerable influence in their own sub-group, but do not hold any élite position. The extended non-participation of informal leaders in the élite indicates a strong tendency towards monopolization.

A clear-cut and long-term distinction between formal and informal leadership is rare, but even in Collectives which try to avoid blocking their channels of mobility there is no complete overlapping of the two categories. Some types of influential leaders are more highly represented in the élite than others. The growing emphasis on economic problems and on efficiency, for example, has entailed a growing representation of managers and experts in the élite. Quite a number of members who had been prominent leaders in their youth movements or training groups did not occupy élite positions in the community at the time of our study. Some of them took up work in various branches of production or in teaching, and were active in the social committees, i.e. health, recreation, education, etc. Others turned to activity in the country-wide movement and spent varying periods outside their communities. Very few of the élite office-holders appeared on the list of members who were considered to be the most faithful adherents of the Collective's ideals. Most of those who fulfil the function of giving friendly advice or sympathy in cases of personal strain or difficulty are not office-holders. Another type of unrepresented or under-represented leader is the opinion leader, whose main unofficial function is to appraise the working of communal institutions. Opinion leaders usually express their approval or disapproval in informal conversation and less often in the general assembly. They praise and criticize and attain positions of recognized leadership in this respect.

Their pervasive influence is based on their special position in the community. (a) Opinion leaders are, as a rule, permanent and successful workers in highly respected occupations such as agricultural branches, child care and medical service. The approval and esteem they gain as able workers in important occupations reinforce their interpersonal influence. The disapproval of malcontents, who are marginal, does not carry much weight with their fellow-members. (b) Most opinion leaders are in opposition to the office-holders, but they do not unite and make no concerted attempt to replace them. Most of them avoid assignment to public offices as much as possible. They seem independent and impartial because they do not covet positions of authority. Their reputation remains intact because they do not have to stand the severe test of bearing the responsibility of key positions. Opinion leaders direct, form and express public opinion and gain considerable influence.

INTERPERSONAL RELATIONS

Closure in informal association is one of the main indices of the crystallization of status groupings. A close scrutiny of participants in both spontaneous and planned informal parties and an analysis of patterns of visiting on weekdays and holidays, clearly indicate a high degree of closure in interpersonal relations between the sub-groups. The more intimate attachments of each individual and each family are confined in many cases either within the bounds of the sub-groups or within the confines of a sub-category comprising a number of sub-groups.

In all the Collectives in our sample we found a small clique comprising some of the office-holders and a number of informal leaders. Members of this small informal group meet quite often and discuss community affairs. In most cases it is an amorphous and unstable group. In two of the Collectives it was clearly discernible and wielded considerable influence. Membership in the clique is definitely not a family affair. The family friends of the members of this group do not, for the most part, belong to the group itself. It is perhaps significant that the casual, as well as the planned, meetings of the clique are as a rule held in one of the public buildings or in the room of one of the bachelors and not in the family rooms. Informal relations in the clique tend to be distinct from family relations.

The clique is a small group. Only a few élite members are included in it. Consideration of the élite as a whole clearly indicates that there is no break in social relations between the élite and the rank and file. Most members of the élite do not visit each other frequently after working hours. There is a considerable amount of tension between some of them, especially those who hold one élite position or another most of the time. Quite a number of them try as much as possible to avoid close contact with other élite members. Most élite office-holders establish their more intimate friendships with members of their own sub-groups who are not members of the élite. They maintain closer and more intimate relations with members of their own sub-groups who do not hold any élite positions than with office-holders who are members of other sub-groups. The line dividing the élite from other members is not an important one from the point of view of interpersonal relations. Diffuse informal relations tend, on the whole, to be segregated and insulated from the more formal and functionally specific relations entailed in élite positions. The élite is not a separate and exclusive status group.

IDEOLOGY AND DISTINCTIVE ROLE IN THE PROCESS OF CHANGE

The dynamic relations between the ideological cleavage and the dual social division was examined by an opinion study dealing with the basic issues of communal life. The main emphasis of our inquiry was put on attitudes towards proposals which would redefine the relations of the individual and the family towards communal institutions, and which would raise the standards of living.

Differences of opinion cut across the élite rank and file division in all the Collectives in our sample. The "innovators," who demand less dependence on communal institutions and a higher standard of living, are by no means confined to the rank and file. The proportion of "conservatives," i.e. those who remain true to the initial ideals of the revolutionary phase of the movement, is as a rule higher in the élite than in the rank and file, but quite a number of élite office-holders are "innovators." In two of the Collectives the "innovators" have gained ascendancy and are in the majority.

Differences of opinion cut across the distinctions between the sub-groups as well, but the sub-groups seem to be more homogeneous ideologically than the élite. In two Collectives the most conservative sub-groups are composed of newcomers who have very little representation in the élite. Most members of these sub-groups are young, single and highly indoctrinated with the rather stoic, self-denying ideals of the Collective movement. They strongly disapprove of the tendency of most of the old-timers to press for less privation, more privacy and more independence. In four Collectives the old-timers are more conservative than the newcomers. Unlike the newcomers mentioned above, the newcomers in these Collectives had very little ideological training prior to their joining the Collectives. Country of origin, seniority, age, sex and family status have a very marked effect on opinions on basic ideological issues, but the main variable seems to be the nature of ideological training and the degree of indoctrination in youth movements and training groups.

Of special interest in this context are the opinions expressed by élite office-holders from the under-represented sub-groups. Representatives of the "conservative" sub-groups mentioned above are on the whole, staunch adherents of the "conservative" trend and protest against the leniency of other élite office-holders. In Collectives in which the under-represented sub-group was composed mainly of "innovators," we found two different constellations. In two of these Collectives most of the recognized leaders of the under-represented sub-group accept the views of the majority of the over-represented sub-groups and try to inculcate their values in their own sub-groups. They identify themselves with the old-timers and are hardly aware of the disparity between the sub-groups. In the two re-maining Collectives the situation is quite different. Most of the recognized leaders of the under-represented sub-groups hold the same views as the majority of the members of their own sub-group. They identify themselves with their sub-group and represent its views in the élite. They are acutely conscious of the differences between sub-groups.

The differences in the degree to which the mobile members of under-represented sub-groups identified themselves with their membership group, were found to be correlated to the degree of monopolization of élite positions by the over-represented sub-group and to the degree of closure in inter-personal relations. In the Collectives where the over-represented group was also the reference group of the leaders of under-represented sub-groups, we found open channels of mobility and less closure in the relations between members of different sub-groups. The leaders of under-representd sub-groups participate freely in all informal activities and have fairly close contacts with other élite office-holders. The awareness of differentiation and identification with a membership group were found to be correlated to monopolization and to the gap in social relations. An analysis of diversity of opinion and identification in only terms of the dual division between the élite and other members failed completely. Any attempt to deal with change without taking into consideration the degree of indoctrination and the degree of participation, yields a grossly oversimplified and distorted picture.

II. Allocation of Rewards

The attempt to account for the specific characteristics of the élite in the Collectives brings us to the problem of rewards.

TYPOLOGY

In our analysis of the allocation of rewards we shall not use the Davis and Moore typology. This typology is vague and not exhaustive. It is unrelated to basic-system functions. The categories are moreover on different levels of analysis. Henceforth we will distinguish between:

A. *Means-objects* put at the disposal of the actor which he may use as he pleases.

B. *Objects of direct gratification* either purely expressive or expressive-evaluative in emphasis.

C. *Relational rewards*—rewards derived from institutionally regulated attitudes of actors towards one another.

Relational rewards are further classified in terms of the two-pattern variables of affectivity-neutrality, and specificity-diffuseness yielding four basic types of relational rewards.

The neutral relational rewards are:
A. *Approval* of specific achievement.
B. Diffuse ascriptive *esteem.*

The affective relational rewards are:
C. Specific affective *response.*
D. *Diffuse affective acceptance.*

In our treatment of the problem of rewards we followed T. Parsons,[7] but found it necessary to modify his typology and his definition of the terms to some extent.

Our analysis differs from that of T. Parsons in two important respects. Parsons does not take into account the significance of means-objects as rewards to the actor. He makes a clear-cut distinction between facilities which are primarily instrumental and rewards which are primarily expressive, and includes all means-objects in the category of facilities. It seems to us that a line should be drawn between facilities which are allocated to the actor for the performance of his role, and means-objects which are put at his disposal and which he may use as he chooses. The budget put at the disposal of a department director for the carrying out of the tasks relating to his office is a facility, while the salary paid him for his work is a reward. The specific authority which is allocated to office-holders for the execution of their tasks is a facility. Diffuse authority which is not restricted to the execution of tasks and which the office-holder may use for furthering personal ends, should be considered a reward. Means-objects motivate and sanction adequate performance. Means-objects which are put at the disposal of the actor and which he may use as he pleases, are included in the category of rewards.

Another distinction which is implicit in Parsons' analysis and which is made explicit in our typology, is a distinction between relational and non-relational rewards. The relational rewards are derived from positive attitudes of alter. They imply mutually oriented attitudes. Both means-objects and objects of direct gratification are inherently

[7] T. Parsons, *Working Papers*, chap. 5, Free Press, 1953. *Social System*, pp. 414–428, Free Press, 1951. "Revised Analytical Approach to Social Stratification," *Class Status and Power*, edited by S. Lipset and R. Bendix, pp. 91–128, Free Press, 1953.

partly independent of the interaction process. Parsons over-emphasizes the conspicuous-expressive aspect of style of life and treats non-relational rewards as symbolic manifestations of attitudes. He seems to imply that one enjoys a steak or a concert mainly because they symbolize and express social status. Objects may have expressive significance which is not derived from, and is at least partly independent of, the attitudes of other actors.

The typology delineated here is analytical and the meaning of concrete rewards depends on their significance in any situation of action.

The discussion of the typology is of necessity schematic and abstract. The meaning of the categories as well as the usefulness of the typology as a tool of analysis will be clarified in the course of concrete analysis.

Our examination of the allocation of rewards is based on discussion of the problem of recruitment to élite positions. We resorted to reports on the working of nomination committees and put special emphasis on the reasons given for reluctance to assume office and for resignation from office. We asked office-holders to describe their sources of satisfaction and the difficulties inherent in their jobs. Considerable light was thrown on our problem by analysis of cases of disputes and conflicts between élite members, and between them and ordinary members.

Non-Relational Rewards

The distinctive features of the system of rewards in the Collectives are the almost complete absence of means-rewards and the essentially non-stratified distribution of direct gratifications. There is no payment for service. The standard of living is basically homogeneous. Any differences in standard of living between individual members are based on universalistic ascriptive principles such as age, sex, family status, state of health and seniority. The gradual allocation of better housing and of more furniture and equipment according to these principles brings about some differentiation in the standard of living. A marked gap between the highest and the lowest standards and a low rate of equalization of housing-facilities and personal amenities result in considerable, though not permanent, inequality. However, the differences in standard of living are unrelated to a hierarchy of positions or to a degree of achievement.

A major disadvantage entailed in holding élite positions is the loss of leisure. Sessions of committees take place after work hours.[8] Office-holders very often work from early morning till late at night. Elite members have less free time than the rank and file.

There are a few small informal advantages attached to holding office. Office-holders have easier access to Collective institutions and may get somewhat better service. Elite members whose work entails frequent travel to town can save part of the money they get for personal expenses and buy little presents for their families. They have a little more cash, more opportunities for recreation, and more freedom of movement. These advantages are of no small importance in the strict and equalitarian organization of the Collectives. Elite members, however, are not the only ones who enjoy these privileges.

---

[8] Lack of free time and unwillingness to lose touch with the family are the main reasons given for reluctance to accept nomination. It is not easy to discover the real meaning and significance of these standard statements.

Most senior members have easy access to communal institutions and have no difficulty in getting what is due to them. Anybody who works outside the community gets a small additional allowance for personal expenses. Drivers get the same sum as office-holders. The special advantages are not exclusively attached to élite positions. They cannot serve as indicators of social position and as symbols of status.

Authority is another source of both means and direct gratifications. Members of the Collectives are dependent on Collective institutions for the satisfaction of their needs. Legitimate power means partial independence. Office-holders have the right to direct others. They have their say and wield considerable influence in their sphere of competence. Office-holders who actually direct the policy of the whole community have wide-ranging authority.

Analysis of our material brings out quite clearly that authority is a fairly important reward. Very few admitted it openly, but immunity from over-dependence and legitimate power of direction seem to be sources of direct gratification. Office-holders are not very outspoken about it, but it crops up on many occasions.

The significance of authority as a source of rewards should not, however, be exaggerated. It is not of primary importance in the reward scheme. Basically, authority is defined in the Collectives as a facility, and not as a reward. Authority is specific and limited. There is a strict prohibition against exercise of authority outside the prescribed bounds of one's own sphere of competence and against utilizing it for personal ends. There is no rigid authority structure and very few direct and effective sanctions. The office-holders depend on voluntary co-operation. They have difficulties in work relations in their own sphere of activity, and in co-ordinating affairs with other managers. The office-holders can do very little about these difficulties. If disobedience and lack of co-ordination become serious, they can only refer the problem to one of the committees or to the general assembly. Authority is limited in both range and efficacy. Furthermore, (as will be shown in the analyses of relational rewards) the evaluation of authority is ambivalent, and high authority does not necessarily lead to high prestige.[9]

RELATIONAL REWARDS

The strict limitation of the allocation of non-relational rewards enhances the importance of relational rewards.

A. NEUTRAL AFFECTIVE REWARDS: Voluntary public service is one of the main values of the Collective movement. Holders of élite positions who volunteer for service and work hard on behalf of the Community win the respect of their fellow-members. The esteem accorded to them is, however, not unambiguous.

In evaluating different positions the main emphasis used to be on productive labour—mainly agriculture. The exigencies of running a complex and specialized enterprise have resulted in

---

[9] The difficulties which result from the ambivalence of authority and the lack of a clear hierarchy are reflected in the comment: "There is no fixed hierarchy. It all depends on personal influence. Holders of office wield either too much influence or, what is more common, too little." "One hesitates to assert one's authority and demand obedience. After all, what right have I to tell another person what to do?"

a shift in the relative importance of the bases of evaluation. The aversion towards authority-positions in management and administration is much weaker. Most members evaluate élite positions highly, but the bias against them has not disappeared completely, and is still operative to some extent. Authority positions (especially those which are divorced from manual labour) are still imbued with some ambiguity. So tenacious are the tenets of equalitarian ethics that there is considerable reluctance to discuss invidious evaluation except in an oblique and indirect fashion. Most members feel hesitant and a bit confused when dealing with this subject. Very rarely did we get a whole-hearted, ungrudging and unreserved high evaluation of élite positions as such. Elite members are somewhat apologetic and on the defensive when asked to evaluate the relative importance of élite positions. Analysis of our material makes it quite clear that the scale of differential evaluation is not unequivocal, and that esteem gained by holding position is therefore not free from ambiguity.

Another factor is of crucial importance in this context. The social standing of members is determined mainly by the assessment of personal qualities, the assessment of the degree of conformity to norms, and the evaluation of achievement, and not so much by the extrinsic invidious value attached to a position as such. The main emphasis used to be on personal qualities and conformity. The growing importance attached to economic success has considerably enhanced the importance of achievement. The main emphasis has shifted in many cases to approval according to standards of efficiency. Elite positions provide ample opportunity for proving one's abilities by the successful fulfilment of roles. Office-holders are in the center of public attention and success in their office is rewarded by general recognition. Competent office-holders are accorded approval and rise in the hierarchy. The reward gained is in some cases considerable. The emphasis on approval, and not on ascriptive esteem, is, however, a source of strain. The temporary and shifting placement according to specific achievement results in basic insecurity. Many office-holders felt that they had to be constantly proving themselves, that their activities were constantly being scrutinized and criticized. Sharp criticism is one of the main reasons given for withdrawal from office.

The absence of symbols of status and excellence and the prevalence of the equalitarian pattern of behaviour should also be mentioned. There are very few easily perceptible indices of either esteem or approval. Successful holders of important positions are praised in informal conversation. The reputation they have gained by serving their community is very often commented upon and some of them are treated with genuine respect. There is, however, no institutionalized and public expression of deference. There are no ritualized salutations, no honorific titles, no order of precedence at any public meeting. Deferential behaviour is almost completely ruled out. There are no exemptions from burdensome tasks and no special immunities. Elite members serve in the communal kitchen and in the communal dining-hall on Saturdays and holidays just like all the other members. Differences are toned down, and members who have higher status make a special point of behaving simply and as inconspicuously as possible. Invidious distinctions are suppressed, since patterns of behaviour are focused around the denial of differences.

B. AFFECTIVE REWARDS: The attempt to develop a comprehensive and full-fledged social structure on the basis of primary group relations entails an emphasis on affective relational rewards. Hence the importance attached to response in reciprocal relations and to acceptance by fellow-members. Diffuse sympathy, solidarity and identification with the community are the core of the reward system.

Elite office-holders are responsible for the main spheres of communal organization. Directly or indirectly they influence the overall direction of the community. Their central position helps them to preserve a wider perspective. They can grasp the community as a whole and identify themselves with it. Those who are recruited to élite positions outside the community develop solidary relations with the country-wide élite. Acceptance in the élite of the more comprehensive community may become a source of affective rewards. The weakening and contraction of solidary relations within the community is the main problem which besets the office-holders in this sphere.

Preoccupation with public affairs involves the inevitable sacrifice of more intimate relations. Office-holders have very little time left for their families and close friends. Their families see very little of them and have to forego their company most of the time. The estrangement is acutely felt by the families of office-holders. Public office held by one member of the family confers on other members of his family neither a perceptibly higher standard of living nor a marked rise in social standing. There is *some* transfer of the esteem gained by the élite member to his relatives. The immediate family shares, to some extent, the social standing attained by one of its members, but the emphasis on personal qualities and personal contribution precludes the consolidation of the family as an undifferentiated status group. Individuals are not identified with their families and are assessed mainly according to their own individual merits. Thus there is little compensation for the temporary estrangement from the family which results from holding public office.

The estrangement from family and friends is sometimes accompanied by isolation in wider-range relations. Loss of acceptance is caused mainly by a certain discrepancy between the norms which define the approved behaviour in interpersonal relations and the functional consideration of efficiency. Office-holders have to act in an authoritative way. They have to decide between conflicting claims and to disregard personal considerations. The decisions which they reach are often disapproved of by many members, so that they can hardly avoid friction and disputes. Considerable success very often means conflict and estrangement.[10] Many of the most competent office-holders, who are accorded high esteem and approval, are not liked. Only a few of them appear on the list of the most popular and well-liked members; most

---

[10] On loss of acceptance: "Why should I quarrel with my friends?" or "Why should I quarrel with my fellow-members?" are among the most prominent reasons given for resignations. The discrepancy between approval and acceptance is clearly expressed in the following quotation: "Our treasurer and secretary are exceptionally able and competent. They really work wonders. But between you and me, considered as *people*, they're not worth much. Nobody likes them particularly." Reservations of this kind appear quite often.

of them have a high social position but are somewhat isolated. The gain in esteem and approval may very well be counterbalanced by the loss of acceptance.

The loss of diffuse solidarity is serious and is acutely felt because of the low incidence of segregation between relations in different spheres of interaction. Most social relations are limited to the one inclusive community. There is no secluded and semi-closed sphere of family relations. Daily activities involve proximity, constant interaction, and complex co-ordination. It is difficult to draw a line between different spheres of interaction and to avoid tension. Diffuse friendly relations have special significance in this context.

The growth of the settlement and its economic expansion introduce a significant change in this respect. The growing differentiation between different spheres of activity and the increase in the number of members and sub-groups entail some segregation between complexes of relations. Heterogeneity was found to be more important than the number of members and the mere size of the settlement. Crystallization of sub-groups is of crucial significance in this respect. These sub-groups may become competing foci of intensive primary relations and may replace the inclusive community as the main reference group. Office-holders very often consider themselves, and are also considered to be, representatives of the sub-groups. They protect themselves from criticism by limiting their relations with members of other sub-groups. The cohesive sub-group thus becomes the main source of security. The intense solidarity of the sub-group may counterbalance the loss of acceptance incurred by the holding of office

in élite positions. Tension is isolated by limiting the range of face-to-face contacts and by the segregation of diffuse and more intimate social relations from specific work relations.

To sum up: Office-holders are slightly privileged as to means-objects and immediate gratifications. Office-holders who have proved their ability by competent and efficient performance of their role get approval. They have comparatively high status. These gains are partly counter-balanced by the loss of leisure, the ambivalence of esteem and insecurity of approval, the absence of symbolization of status, and the decrease of acceptance. Increase of esteem awarded to élite positions, greater segregation between spheres of interaction and the growing representation of the Collectives in the country-wide élite, considerably increase the reward gains of the office-holders.

REWARD BALANCE IN DIFFERENT ELITE POSITIONS

Up to this point we have dealt with the balance of rewards of the élite as a whole, but the balance of rewards in élite positions is not uniform. There are perceptible and significant variations between the rewards allocated to different types of élite positions.

The reward balance of *managers of production* branches is more positive than that of managers of consumption and services. Branches of production are highly evaluated and are put at the top of the esteem-scale. Management in this sphere is not divorced from manual labour. The authority exercised by managers of production is based on expert knowledge and experience. Success in the performance of their roles is clearly expressed by higher production and higher income. It is readily recognized and easily estimated. Members who do not work in the same branch and are not experts know very little about it. The number of members who know enough to criticize is therefore quite limited. In some of the branches of production, especially those which enjoy the highest esteem, we found solidary work-groups. "We-consciousness," intensive informal relations between members, and specific patterns of behaviour characterize those work-groups. Members of the work-group appear very often in the assembly as a united body. They have common interests in respect to the allocation of money investment, machines and manpower, and support the demands which the manager makes on their behalf. The need to present a united front in out-group relations often outweighs inner tensions. The backing of a cohesive work-group is an important factor of stability in the recruitment of managers of production.

The evaluation of *consumption and services* is, generally speaking, lower than that of production. Managers in these spheres have close contacts with most of the members and serve them in conditions of relative scarcity. Norms of distribution are not always clear. The decision as to the specific needs of the individual often rests with the manager. Vagueness of norms and the difficulty of dealing with special cases are sources of friction and numerous disputes. Faulty performance affects each member directly and is therefore easily discernible. There is comparatively little specialization in this sphere and every member considers himself competent to criticize the managers; there are very few criteria of success. Work-groups are not as solidary as work-groups in the branches of production.

The *full-time central élite positions* are very highly evaluated. Some of these positions, however, entail a considerable amount of tension and ambivalence. Office-holders in these positions are not engaged in productive manual labour. They are held responsible for the proper functioning of all communal institutions. They are at the center of public opinion and any serious complaint is as a rule directed against them.[11] Authority structure is not very clearly articulated. Overall co-ordination depends on the ability of office-holders to mediate between conflicting claims and to reach working agreements. Insubordination to overall direction and non-co-operation between managers seem to be more prevalent than disobedience within the work-group. There are no clear standards of performance and no distinctive and easily recognizable indices of success.

There are more sources of tension in *social* committees than in purely *economic* ones. Two main difficulties are inherent in holding public office as chairmen of the social committees, namely: Roles are relatively unstructured and friction ensues from decisions on personal problems. Isolation of tension is difficult because of the constant contact with a comparatively large number of members.

The analysis of reward balance in élite positions has made it quite clear that the élite is not an undifferentiated

---

[11] One of the secretaries for internal affairs complained: "I am the lightning rod in my community, the person to whom all complaints are addressed."

unit from the point of view of allocation of rewards, and that élite positions are not devoid of tension. It seems significant that the incidence of withdrawal from office, and to some extent the length of tenure as well, are correlated to the variation in reward balance and to the degree of tension in different types of élite positions. As mentioned above, there is much more reluctance to assume office and to continue holding it for a long time in the management and organization of consumption and services, in social committees and in key central offices than in the management of production branches and economic committees. Short tenure in positions which require both marked ability and experience (such as the central key positions) is directly related to the degree of ambivalence, insecurity and estrangement. The diversity of reward balance in different élite positions and a concomitant considerable amount of tension, explain why there is so slight a tendency towards the consolidation of a united and exclusive group of active and influential members permanently in power. The meagre compensation for estrangement and the need to isolate tension, account for the tendency of segregation between functionally specific relations and the more diffuse and more intimate social relations.

The analysis of the balance of rewards in élite positions has proved to be an important instrument for the discovery of sources of satisfaction and foci of tension. The extension of the analysis to all institutionalized roles and the examination of the balance of rewards in all other sub-groups will enable us to achieve a more adequate understanding of the process of differentiation.

III. Conclusions

The main conclusions of our explorative research are:

A. Any attempt to analyze our material in terms of the dual division between élite and non-élite failed completely.

B. The integration of solidary sub-groups on the basis of seniority in the community, country of origin and former membership in a youth movement and/or training group is stronger than the integration on the basis of functional position in the élite. The élite is not a solidary and closed status group.

C. Reinforcing criteria of differentiation and overlapping categories enhance marked differentiation and closure of the sub-groups. Crosscutting categories and small differences as to degree of indoctrination and as to way of life enhance wide-spread participation.

D. The absence of a marked tendency towards the consolidation of a united and closed élite is related to the diversity of reward-balance in different élite positions and to the considerable strain entailed in some of these positions.

E. The increase of esteem accorded to key positions, the growing segregation of relations in different spheres of interaction, and growing representation in the country-wide élite entail a considerable reward gain and enhance the integration of the élite.

F. The analysis of the relation between differentiation and the trends of institutional change should be based on:
a. Examination of the degree of indoctrination.
b. Examination of the extent of monopolization of élite positions.

c. Examination of the range of informal participation.

d. Examination of balance of rewards in all institutionalized roles.

The conclusions summarized here are tentative. Our sample is not representative, and it may well be that one conclusion or another does not apply to all Collectives. The main emphasis in this summary is on the examination of our basic hypotheses and on the setting up of a systematic framework for further research.

IV

SOCIAL-CLASS PROFILES

11

THE UPPER CLASS OF NEW HAVEN

August B. Hollingshead and Frederick C. Redlich

Although America has never had a titled aristocracy, this is not to say that we lack a coherent upper class, based upon wealth, ancestry, breeding, and ethnic purity, with definite aristocratic values.

In this selection by August Hollingshead, one of the pioneers of stratification research in the United States, and his colleague, psychiatrist Frederick Redlich, we are given a social profile of the upper class of New Haven, Connecticut, in the early 1950's. As part of a comprehensive study of the relationship between social class and mental illness in New Haven, the researchers conducted a large number of interviews with residents in order to obtain a clear picture of the class structure of the community. On the basis of an analysis of these interviews, Hollingshead decided that the community could most accurately be divided into five major social classes, the same number he had utilized in his book *Elmtown's Youth*, a well-known study of the impact of social class on the young people of a small Illinois community. The major indicators of social class for Hollingshead which comprised his so-called Index of Social Position, involved the weighted ranking of three items: the location of the family's residence, plus the occupation and formal education of the head of the household.

The upper class in New Haven—termed simply class I—comprises only about 3 percent of the population. Within class I, however, there are two groups, a core group of old upper-class families whose position rests not simply upon wealth, but upon lineage and tradition, and a fringe group of newly rich or ethnic rich—the proverbial *arrivistes* or *nouveaux riches.* Some scholars, such as W. Lloyd Warner, of whom Hollingshead was an early collaborator, saw sufficient distinctions between these two elements of the

SOURCE: *Social Class and Mental Illness: A Community Study* (New York: John Wiley & Sons, 1958), pp. 69–85. Reprinted by permission of the publisher.

upper class to warrant dividing them into two separate classes: an upper upper and a lower upper class. But whether one sees them as part of the same class or of two separate classes, it is important to note the age-old tension and competition between the two, as the fringers strive for acceptance into the inner circle and the core group attempts to maintain its exclusiveness.

This distinction between the old and new rich is most pronounced in the East and South, and least pronounced in the West where, because of the relative recency of settlement, the roots of the old rich do not go so far back. Thus, Los Angeles, the second largest city in the country, still does not have a *Social Register,* that exclusive listing of America's "best" families, while Buffalo, New York, a much smaller city, has had one for years.

Although Hollingshead treats here merely the upper class of one medium sized Eastern city, and though it might be inferred that this upper class is thoroughly self-contained, it has been argued that the American upper class is becoming a truly *national* upper class, rather than being merely a series of separate local, metropolitan, small town, or rural upper classes.* It has become nationalized in terms of interaction, cohesion, friendship patterns, marriages, and the like.

Of course, it must not be thought that every member of the American upper class is acquainted with every other. For if, as G. William Domhoff asserts, the American upper class consists of merely .5 percent of the total population, that still means, with a total U.S. population base of some 200 million, an upper class of one million persons, considerably larger than anyone's circle of friends or acquaintances! Nevertheless, it is true that since the end of the nineteenth century, the American upper class has been transformed from a series of isolated and local upper classes into a more interconnected and interacting national upper class. The forces which are responsible for the nationalization of the upper class include:

1. the emergence of the national corporation and the interconnections among them via interlocking directorates;

2. the preparatory school. Studies of the social and geographical origins of prep school students show that they come from upper-class homes from all over the country. This tends to unify the upper class, or sectors of it, and provides a uniquely homogeneous socializing instrument;

3. the ivy league schools. Again, studies have shown that, as with the prep schools, the ivy league colleges, despite a certain democratization and recruitment from other classes, continue to provide a locus for the commingling of the young upper class on a national scale;

4. the exclusive upper-class urban clubs (such as New York's Knickerbocker Club, San Francisco's Pacific Union Club, and Boston's Somerset Club) which provide a sheltered meeting ground for members of America's upper class;

5. resorts and vacation spots. In his book, *The Last Resorts,* Cleveland Amory indicates that certain vacation spots cater to an upper-class clientele from all over the country. Obviously, here friends are made, courtships develop, and so forth; and

6. marriage patterns. Analyses of marriage announcements in the society pages of newspapers across the country demonstrate that all this previous interaction pays off, that is, the upper-class marriage market is national in scope.

Every generation, aristocratic prophets of doom foretell the early demise of the upper class. The old ways are crumbling; new money is pushing in; the younger generation is marrying outside its sheltered walls; inflation, taxes, and the imponderables

---

* See C. Wright Mills, *The Power Elite* (New York: Oxford University Press, 1956); G. William Domhoff, *Who Rules America?* (Englewood Cliffs, New Jersey: Prentice-Hall, 1967).

of the economy are eroding its life style; and so on. While such predictions have always proven false and unduly alarmist, there have been certain developments in American society that pose something of a challenge to the old, insulated upper class.

1. The continuing push of egalitarianism and democracy in the United States often makes the aristocratic traditions and exclusiveness of the upper class seem outmoded and absurd, objects of ridicule rather than emulation. Middle-class college students, for example, are unfailingly amused by any discussion of the pretensions and potlatching of contemporary debutante parties.

2. The old, hereditary upper class is threatened somewhat by the beginning of racial and social-class integration of its institutions such as prep schools, ivy league colleges, clubs, and the like. In other areas of American life, integration makes sense in terms of the democratic ethos, but the major function of upper-class institutions is to segregate, to keep people out, and to maintain the purity of the class. Integration defeats this very purpose.

3. The rising standard of living of the population in general and the upper middle class in particular threatens the existence of material status symbols. Status symbols, after all, are only effective if they are exclusive. The automobile, once a status symbol because it was relatively scarce and expensive, has now utterly lost its magic, simply because of its universal dissemination. Because of the rising standard of living across the board, there are very few material status symbols left, i.e., objects that confer status because they are economically out of reach of most of the population. Aside from extravagant housing, private jet aircraft, yachts, Paris originals, and a few other exotic items, most things—or ingenious imitations—are becoming attainable by most stably employed Americans on liberal credit terms.

4. Finally, the aristocracy of birth in the United States is more and more challenged by the aristocracy of *talent,* those of whatever social origins who have managed to achieve eminence in American life, as actors, musicians, writers, artists, scientists, athletes, and so on. A dual status system now exists and the elite of talent is strengthened in its status claims because it harmonizes so well with the ethic of achievement in American society. This rivalry between the elite of birth and of talent is probably stronger now than ever before, but has always existed, and is well illustrated by a note Beethoven was reputed to have sent after he had endured public humiliation by one Prince Lichnowsky:

> *Prince!*
> *What you are, you are by accident of birth. What I am, I am through myself. There have been and will be thousands of princes. There is only one Beethoven.*

Status Awareness

Each respondent in the control sample was asked a series of questions designed to elicit his awareness of status. The first question asked was: "Do you think classes exist in the community?" The second was: "What things determine one's class?" Each respondent made his own decision as to his belief in classes and the criteria that placed a person in a class. After responses were recorded from these questions, the interviewer asked, "To what class would you say you belong?" The interviewer then read slowly eight choices: "upper," "upper-middle," "middle," "lower-middle," "working," "lower," "do not know," and "I do not believe in classes."

The direct questions on "class" brought into focus incongruity between a person's response to a question involving values in the publicly professed dimensions of the culture, particularly if it involves democratic beliefs, and his actions in situations involving in-group codes. A class I matron, who was startled by the questions but who identified herself as "upper" class, provided insight into this facet of the social ethic with the acid comment, "One does not speak of classes; they are felt." In spite of such incongruities, over 98 percent of the class I respondents think there are "social classes" in the community: 37 percent identify with the "upper" class, 56 percent classify themselves as "upper-middle" class, and 5 percent as "lower-middle" class. The remaining 2 percent do not believe in classes.

Whereas class status brings its members into contact with one another in many functional relationships in the maintenance of the community's general social life, ethnic and religious differences segment the 3.4 percent of the community's population placed in class I (by the Index of Social Position) into internally organized, almost self-contained, social worlds. A *core group,* composed of pacesetting, commonly recognized "old families," enjoys the highest prestige and power positions in the status system. Revolving around it are satellite groups composed of persons who have "arrived" recently in the business and professional worlds and, in the words of an *arriviste,** "Yale professors who try to play the game on $10,000 a year." Although there are distinct differences in the ability of different groups to "play the game," all groups respect and, in many ways, emulate those who sometimes satirically

are referred to by members of fringe groups as "proper New Haveners." "Proper New Haveners" are truly "at the summit" of local "society." Members of these families have been at the summit for two, three, and more generations, and some have been in the "nuclear group" since colonial times.

Fifty-three percent of the adults in this class are stable through two and more generations and 47 percent are upward mobile from their parental families. Stable members of the core group possess a complex subculture which aspirants must acquire before they are admitted into the group. Those who are accorded "accepted" status are the "gatekeepers"; they decide which "new people" are invited into their exclusive organizations. Conversely, the gatekeepers "drop the black ball" on those they do not approve.

Economic Orientation

Executives and professional men head class I families. Those in business are major office holders, such as on boards of trustees, presidents, vice-presidents, secretaries, and treasurers in the larger industries, construction and transportation companies, stores, banks, brokerage houses, and utilities. Two thirds of the men in the professions are in independent practice—lawyers, physicians, engineers, architects, and certified public accountants; the other one third are salaried—professors, clergymen, and engineers for the most part. A few executives receive from $40,000 to $50,000 a year, but more earn from $20,000 to $30,000. The modal range for mature

---

* By *"arrivistes"* we mean persons who are upward mobile, who have achieved class I positions through their own efforts rather than by inheritance, usually in the current generation. The connotation of unscrupulousness usually associated with the word does not apply in these discussions.

free professionals is from $20,000 to $25,000 per year. However, the median reported family income, where the male head is the only one gainfully employed, is $10,000. This median is conditioned in large part by the presence of Yale University and its large, comparatively low-paid faculty, as well as the presence of young professionals, widows, and retired people in the sample. In the 8 percent of the households where a wife is engaged in business or a profession, the median income is $15,025 a year.

Families in the core group are, on the whole, wealthy, but there are large differences in their economic positions. A few families are multimillionaires; other families may possess only a quarter- to a half-million dollars. The wealth of the core group has been inherited by two, three, and more generations, whereas that of the *arrivistes* has been acquired during the present or previous generation. Inherited wealth is accorded a higher social value within the core group than "made money." Several generations of inherited wealth attest to the genuineness of the patina on the family's pecuniary escutcheon. A family which possessed the ability to make money in the first place, and to hold it and add to it through the generations, has demonstrated its "true" worth.

A cardinal principle in established families is that capital funds should not be squandered. Each generation should live on income only and add to capital by conservative management. Squandering of capital funds results in the next generation's being faced with the problem of earning its living. An inherited income assures a high standard of living without undue effort of a family head to support his family of procreation. Men are expected to look after their inheritances and those of their wives, but estate managers may be employed and trust departments of large banks relied upon for counsel, if not actual management of securities, trusts, and properties. A man should have an occupation or a profession, although he may not rely too heavily upon it for income. Income from inherited wealth supplemented by income from salaries and fees earned by the male head is the most general pattern.

Persons with private incomes are careful to see that the dollar sign is muted on their possessions and on the things they do. The dollar sign and interest in the dollar sign are stigmata of newly rich strivers. Individuals who accumulate wealth view money as *the* requisite of high social position; those who have inherited wealth look to other things as the sine qua non of position. The core group is not ostensibly interested in money, but a substantial income is necessary to their way of life. This point was brought to our attention sharply by an elderly member of a distinguished family who, in response to a question on income, reported with indignation, "We have it."

Ethnic Origin

Persons able to pass the core group's test of financial means are faced with a more crucial barrier—the lineage test. Lineage is used to protect the group from "social climbers" who are attempting to reach "the summit" on the basis of personal achievement. The upward mobile nuclear family with the right ethnic background is the most serious threat to privileged position, and they are a target for the group's hostile and biting remarks. For example, a

man in the core group was discussing local families and their estates when the interviewer commented on the purchase of an estate by an *arriviste* of mixed Irish and Yankee descent in the respondent's neighborhood. The respondent, who was interviewed in his office, straightened in his chair, tapped the desk with a forefinger, and stated emphatically, "Money does not count up there (a hill in a suburb covered with estates). Family background, who you are—these are the things that count." This man overlooks the simple fact that these families could not live on their estates without wealth. An *arriviste* may manage to purchase an estate "on the hill" and be isolated from the social life of the families who accept one another as equals. The question of who one is, ethnically, places acceptance in the group in a different dimension of the social structure from economic competence. A person is able to do something about his role and function in the economic system, but he is powerless in the ethnic dimension of his life. Here he is dependent upon his ancestors.

The core group ascribes a different and lower status to persons from disapproved ethnic backgrounds—Jews, Irish, Italians, Greeks, Poles, and others from southern and eastern Europe. Core group members tend to lump these national origin groups together; all are undesirable. An industrial leader, when asked why New Haven has such a diverse population, stated, "I should say largely it was an overflow of great tidal waves of these races—Italians, Irish, Jews, Germans, and so on—reaching New York and sliding on to the next place. These races are very gregarious, and they are coaxed easily by a roll of money." A prominent core group matron thought that the "Ital-

ians just swarmed into this area. It seemed to be the happy hunting ground. New Haven has become an Italian colony. It's amazing." Another emphasized, "The Poles and Italians gave us our vicious gangs." A prominent attorney accused the "Jewish traders" of "gobbling up fine old companies in trouble" and continuing "their Sheeney ways."

Chronologically, wealth comes first; then one's family background is discovered, and the importance of wealth is pushed into the background. The number of generations a family has been prominent *and* resident in the community is important to the elderly arbiters of power and status. This point was well put by a distinguished matriarch while we were discussing the importance of some families in the life of the city over a number of generations. Such a family was named as an illustration. The respondent closed her eyes, thought for a few moments, and resumed the discussion with, "The ——— are not really old New Haveners. They first settled in Saybrook (a pioneer settlement on the Connecticut coast) in the 1640s, but the family did not move to New Haven until 1772." The core group is composed of extended families who trace their ancestry directly to the colonial period and then to England, Scotland, the Netherlands, or to French Huguenot refugees. These well-known "old Yankees" represent 59 percent of this stratum. Persons of Irish descent, who through the years have accumulated wealth and established family positions but have maintained their identifications with the Roman Catholic Church, are a group apart and compose 11 percent of this class. Descendants of other immigrant stocks—German (6 percent), Scandinavian (2 percent), and Italian

(9 percent)—who are accumulating wealth through business enterprise and successful professional practices, represent other subgroups. Jews (13 percent) represent a separate hierarchy from the Gentile groups. German-Jewish families as a rule occupy higher prestige positions in the Jewish segment of class I than Jews of Polish and Russian descent.

Religious Affiliation

Ethnic origins and religious affiliations are highly correlated. Viewed over-all, the three major religious groups are divided as follows: Protestants—61 percent, Roman Catholics—24 percent, Jews—13 percent, and mixed or no affiliation—2 percent. Within the Protestant group, 61 percent of the families are Congregationalists, 17 percent are Episcopalians, 7 percent are Lutherans, 5 percent are Baptists, 2 percent are Methodists, and other denominations comprise the remaining 7 percent. In each religious group—Protestant, Catholic, and Jewish—the membership is concentrated in a small number of congregations. For example, there are 24 Congregational churches in the community, but over 93 percent of the core group members belong to three of these churches. Episcopalians are clustered in 2 of 19 parishes in the area, and Roman Catholics are concentrated in 4 parishes. Among Jews, the greatest clustering is in the Reformed congregation. As Russian and Polish Jews have moved upward in the class structure, they have left the Orthodox and Conservative congregations and affiliated with the Reformed Temple founded by German Jews who came to the community a century ago. As these *arrivistes* have become affiliated with the Temple, the descendants of its Germanic founders have tended to withdraw from its affairs except for important ritualistic occasions and high holy days.

Although 98 percent of the respondents claim affiliation with three religions, from 8 to 33 percent are not members of any specific congregation and do not attend services. For practical purposes, these people are "unchurched." Approximately 25 percent of Protestant men and women and 38 percent of Jewish men and women have no congregational ties; only 15 percent of the Roman Catholic men and 8 percent of the women are in this category. These people probably had nominal connections with their claimed denominations at one time in their lives, but currently they are outside the religious participation pattern. The percentage of "unchurched" persons is significantly higher in class I in comparison with the other strata. The "unchurched" men and women in each major religion are upward mobile in significantly larger numbers than those who are stable socially. However, a considerable number of upward mobile persons function actively in selected churches and thereby aid their mobility strivings in a positive way.

Religious identification rather than affiliation and active participation is a salient factor in the organization of this stratum's social life. If a person is identified as a Jew, most Gentile doors are closed to him; moreover if he is a Roman Catholic, lines are drawn around him in Protestant circles, but not so openly. Conversely, Jews and Roman Catholics react in negative ways to Protestants. The three parallel hierarchies of Protestant, Catholic, and Jew, around which the social life of the community, at all levels, is organized, have crystallized in class I with signal force. A core group member made this very clear when he stated, in response to a question about his relationships with Jews, "We have business dealings with them. I sometimes sit next to an eminent Hebrew at a business luncheon." When asked if Hebrews were ever invited into his home, he bristled and said coldly, "In my living room there is never a Hebrew, no matter how eminent he is in professional or business life. Hebrews know."

A distinguished member of a prominent Jewish family described in detail how his family has been discriminated against in its attempts to be accepted into "restricted" clubs and associations. With particular reference to having the "black ball dropped" on his application for membership in a beach club, he remarked with feeling, "My ass is not good enough to sit on their sand."

A housewife whose husband changed his name legally from an easily recognizable Polish-Jewish one to a distinguished New England Yankee one about thirty years ago in the hope that it would enable him, in her words, "to cross over," told how this move failed. They then joined the Temple and became leaders in the Jewish community. She feels strongly that her religion is her "social gospel" but it does not help her make contact with the "white Protestants" who are "the privileged group in New Haven society."

A male member of the "privileged group" who was nominally a Congregationalist but attended church on Easter, Christmas, and only a few other times, did not think religion was too important in his way of life. He commented, "The churches are becoming women's and children's organizations, and, outside of paying the bills, the men don't seem to have much control."

Education

Class I is the most highly educated segment of the population. The median years of school completed by the male heads of families is 17.6. The median for the wives is 14.4 years. One wife in five has the same amount of education as her husband; 43 percent of the husbands have had at least four years more education than their wives, but only 7 percent of the wives have had at least one more year of education than their husbands. The distinct difference in the amount of education between husbands and wives is an outstanding characteristic of this class.

Formal schooling, after the eighth grade, normally is received in a private institution patterned after the English public school. Secondary education in a public school is frowned upon by all segments of the core group; many in this stratum refuse to send their children to the public schools from the earliest years. The core group families send their sons to distinguished New England boarding schools where they spend from four to six years preparing for an Ivy League College. Daughters are sent to well-known boarding schools to prepare them for entrance into a select women's college. Families who cannot afford to send their children to boarding schools enter them in one of the accepted single-sex day schools in the community.

The country day and boarding schools are staffed by an elite corps of headmasters and headmistresses of approved Yankee lineages and Protestant faiths, from "upper class" families, who were educated in the aristocratic-value system and are dedicated to preserving and transmitting it. They may close the educational gates to persons who cannot pass both the means and lineage tests, but other criteria are used to justify such actions. They attempt to hire teachers with backgrounds similar to theirs; as this is difficult today, their staffs tend to be made up of upward mobile individuals who have identified with the core group's value system.

Private secondary schooling is preparatory, if not a requisite, to entrance into a one-sex "name" college. The "big three," Yale, Harvard, and Princeton, are the dominant preference for men. The smaller men's colleges occupy secondary positions in the local value hierarchy—Amherst, Williams, Dartmouth, Brown, and Wesleyan. Women should be sent to Smith, Vassar, Wellesley, Bryn Mawr, Mount Holyoke, or Radcliffe to be acceptable in the social world under discussion. Coeducational private colleges such as Swarthmore or Oberlin are respectable but do not carry prestige. Attendance at a state university marks a man or a woman as an *arriviste;* the state university graduate is at best a "fringer" in the elite groups. The vast majority of the upward mobile family heads, whether from old American stock or ethnic groups, were trained in whole or in part at state universities, but they generally do everything within their means to see that their children attend private secondary schools and name colleges.

Lessons to teach the individual how to act in various social situations and how to use leisure time in approved ways are extremely important in the way of life of this stratum. Professional functionaries who sell their skills and talents to class I families run classes for ballroom dancing, tennis, golf, sailing, music, and so on. Several years of formal training in leisure-time pursuits prepare the young person for the core

group's way of life, as well as the parallel one prevailing among the fringe groups.

Family Constellation

The nuclear group of husband, wife, and dependent children constitutes the primary family and common household unit. This group normally passes through a family cycle which begins with marriage, extends through the childbearing and child-rearing years, and ends in old age through the death of one of the parental pair. Each marriage brings into being a new family cycle. Upon the birth of their first child, the nuclear pair becomes a family of procreation, but for the child this family of origin is his family of orientation. Thus, each individual who marries and rears children has a family of orientation and a family of procreation.

Each nuclear family is related to a number of other nuclear families by consanguineal and affinal ties. Also, each family in the kin group occupies a position in the status system which may be the same or different from the others. The differences are produced by the mobility of some families. This movement of the individual nuclear family in the status system, while it is approved and often lauded as "the American way," has important effects on kin group relations.

One's ancestors and relatives count for more in the core group than what one has achieved in one's own lifetime. Background is stressed most heavily when it comes to the crucial question of whom a member may marry. One of the perennial problems of the established family is the control of the marriage choices of its young men. Young women can be controlled more easily because of the more sheltered life they lead and their more passive role in courtship. The relative passivity of the female, coupled with sex exploitation of females from lower social positions by high level males that sometimes leads to marriage, results in a significant number of old maids in established families. Strong emphasis on family background leads to the selection of marriage mates from within the old-family group in an exceptionally high percentage of cases and, if not from the old-family group, then from the new-family segment of this stratum. The degree of kinship solidarity, combined with intraclass marriages, results in comparative stability in the class, in the extended kin group, and in the nuclear family within it.

The core group family is basically an extended kin group, solidified by lineage and a heritage of common experience in the communal setting. A complicated network of consanguineal and affinal ties unites nuclear families of orientation and procreation into an ingroup that rallies when its position is threatened by the behavior of one of its members, particularly where out-marriage is involved; this principle will be illustrated later. The nuclear family is viewed as only a part of a broader kin group that includes the consanguineal descendants of a known ancestral pair, plus kin brought into the group by marriage. Divorce is avoided if possible; when it occurs the entire family looks upon it as a disgrace, if not a scandal. The solidarity of the kin group is markedly successful in keeping divorce to a minimum. The ratio of widows and widowers to divorced persons is 27 to 1. This is the highest ratio in the population.

An important factor in the established family's ability to maintain its position through several generations is its economic security. Usually a number of different nuclear families within a kin group are supported, in part at least, by income from a family estate held in trust. Also, because of the practice of intramarriage within the core group, it is not unusual for a family to be the beneficiary of two or more estates held in trust. For example, one extended family group is the beneficiary of a trust established a century ago that yields something over $300,000 annually after taxes. This income is divided among 37 different nuclear families descended from the founder, 28 of whom live in the home community; 23 of these families are beneficiaries of one other trust fund, and 14 receive income from two or more other trust funds. These different nuclear families regard themselves as part of the "Scott" family; moreover, they are so regarded by other established families, as well as by persons lower in the status system who know something of the details of the family history.

The Scott family has maintained its social position for more than two centuries by a combination of property ownership, educational, legal, and political leadership, and control of marriages. Its members are proud that it has never had a non-Protestant marriage in seven generations; only five divorces have been traced, but these are not mentioned; one desertion has been hinted but not confirmed.

The family tradition of Protestant intermarriages had a severe test in recent years. A son of one nuclear family, who had spent four years in the Armed Forces in World War II, asked a class II Catholic girl to marry him. The engagement was announced by the girl's family to the consternation of the Scott family, who immediately brought pressure on the boy to "break off the affair." After several months of family and class pressure against the marriage, the young man "saw his error" and broke the engagement. A year later he married a family-approved girl from one of the other "old" families in the city. Today he is an officer in his wife's family's firm, and his father has built him a fine suburban home.

This case illustrates a number of characteristics typical of the established core group family. It is stable, extended, tends to pull together when its position is threatened—in this instance by an out-marriage—exerts powerful controls on its members to ensure that their behavior conforms to family and class codes, and provides for its members economically by trust funds and appropriate positions.

The *arriviste* family is characterized most decisively by phenomenal economic or professional success during a short interval of time. Its meteoric rise in the social system is normally the personal triumph of the nuclear head of the family. If the head is a businessman, he is busy making a "million bucks"; the family purchases the symbols associated with the wealthy American family: a large house, fine furniture, big automobiles, and expensive clothes. The new tycoon knows the power of money in the market place, and he often attempts to buy high position in the status system. In a professional family, the head is intent on making a "name" in his profession and acquiring some wealth. His family follows the same general pattern of purchasing the outward symbols of success but in a more modest fashion. The

new family is able to meet the means test, but not the lineage test of the established families. Consequently, it is generally systematically excluded from membership in the cliques and associations of greatest prestige. This is resented especially by the wife and children, but less often by the tycoon or professional man.

The new family is unstable in comparison with the established family. It lacks the security of accepted position at the top of the local status system—a position that will come only with time; it cannot be purchased. The stabilizing influence exerted by an extended family group, as well as friends, on the deviant individual is absent. Then too, the adults in the new family are self-directing, full of initiative, believe in the freedom of the individual, and rely upon themselves rather than upon a kin group. (Many upwardly mobile individuals break with their kin groups to aid their mobility.) The result is, speaking broadly, conspicuous expenditure, insecurity, and family instability. Thus, we find divorces, broken homes, and other symptoms of disorganization in a significantly large number of new families. The ratio of widows and widowers to divorced persons is only 5 to 1; this is significantly lower than in the core group. In like manner, the percentage of children under 17 years of age living in broken homes is decidedly higher in the new families (18 percent versus 3.4 percent). Because new families are so conspicuous in their consumption and behavior, they become, in the judgment of the general population, symbolic of "upper class" actions and values to the resentment of established families who generally frown upon such behavior.

Family Homes

Single-family houses valued by the tax assessor from $30,000 to $50,000 are owned by 81 percent of their occupants; 95 percent are valued for tax purposes at above $20,000, and some homes are valued above $100,000. The "small" house has 8 to 10 rooms, whereas a "large" one may have 25 to 30 rooms. The modal house has from 12 to 15 rooms. It is located on spacious, carefully landscaped grounds designed to give privacy and is set off by the beauty of the structure in the "best" residential areas. These tend to be hills and ridges in the suburban towns, but there are still "pockets" of fine homes in the city. To be socially correct, and to enhance one's prestige, a second home is essential for core group families. It is a "cottage" located at fashionable beaches along Long Island Sound, the Maine Coast, on Cape Cod, or one of the offshore islands, for example, Martha's Vineyard. If a family prefers the mountains, their "cottage" is found in exclusive areas of the Berkshire, White, or Green Mountains. Summer "cottages" are generally in colonies protected by incorporated private associations whose members decide who may buy into the area or to whom an owner may rent his "cottage." Some are small homes of 5 rooms, but others are estates of 15 to 20 rooms with large landscaped grounds, multiple-car garages, a small stable, and a tennis court.

The family seat, or town house, is occupied from nine to ten months each year. The "cottage" is used during the summer, usually from Fourth of July until Labor Day. This is The Season when a family is expected to be out of town. Core group families usually own or have access to a third home—the lodge. The lodge is occupied for only two or three weeks during the year: a fishing lodge in Maine or New Brunswick during the trout season; a hunting lodge in the same areas during the deer, moose, and bear seasons. The fishing and hunting lodges are owned privately, but the owners generally belong to an association so that large areas of water or land can be controlled at relatively nominal costs to each member. Some of these sportsmen's associations are a century old, and have members in the same family to the fourth and fifth generations.

Exclusiveness is attained in the "best" areas by rigid zoning requirements which insure a certain amount of uniformity in the size of the grounds and the structures. These areas are separated from adjacent areas by shrubbery and large lawns. Within the home, entertainment rooms are separated from the bedrooms, and the family quarters are isolated from servants' quarters. The accent is upon privacy for the family and its individual members in and around the home. The day of many servants has passed but a family normally has either one full-time or a part-time cleaning woman, and often both. A domestic cleaning service may do the heavy house-cleaning each week, and a complete house-cleaning two, three, or four times a year. The housewife does a good bit of the day-to-day light housekeeping—shopping and other maintenance chores—but the heavy work is done ordinarily by hired help. When a core group family is pinched financially, it places a higher value on a part-time servant than on expensive entertaining and expensive automobiles. The home grounds are landscaped and maintained by contract gardeners; only families with the larger estates employ a full-time gardener. However, families try to keep the servant complex intact through the one maid-of-all-work, even if she is employed part-time, and specialists who do contract work, such as washing windows and polishing floors.

An automobile is a necessity, but a few conservative individuals do not own and have never learned to drive one. At least 99 percent of the families own one automobile, and over half own two. The preferred family car is a Cadillac, but Chryslers, Oldsmobiles, Buicks, and station wagons of the more popular brands are acceptable. The car tends to be under three years of age; some families will drive automobiles for ten years or more, but they are carefully polished and maintained. If the family owns a country place, it is customary to letter its name on the station wagon. Another folkway is to possess a two- or three-numbered marker (license plates in Connecticut are markers and they are permanent) or to have only one's initials on the marker. A family with two initials on its marker usually rates higher than one with three or four letters. One family owns several automobiles; each marker in the three generations represented has one given initial of a family member and the initial of the family's surname. The ceremonial car of the family head, a custom-built black Cadillac sedan, bears the initials of a noted ancestor who lived a century ago.

The Club System

A family's class status can be determined most accurately by its club memberships because the private clubs of the area are graded according to the prestige of their members. Conversely, a man, woman, or a nuclear family is ranked by those conversant with the elite's system of values in terms of the clubs to which one belongs. Memberships in appropriate clubs are evidence of validated status and they symbolize for the initiated "who one is." Socially acceptable people belong to approved clubs; those who are unacceptable or have been in the community too short a time to have established a "toe hold" do not hold memberships. All private clubs are self-perpetuating associations, managed by a board of governors, the inner circle who represent the value structure of those in power in the club. The members and the board of governors in particular determine who is admitted; in sum, they are the gatekeepers of the accepted elite.

Three distinct types of clubs characterize this stratum: the one-sex club, the family club, and the special interest club. "Gentlemen's" and "ladies'" clubs represent the first type. The family club is designed to meet the social and recreational needs for all family members. The special interest club is for persons with particular tastes and hobbies. Three "gentlemen's" clubs maintain club houses where the members may meet, relax, read, have a drink at the private bar, or eat with their equals. Two of these clubs are "exclusive"; the acknowledged members of the core group, the Gentile professional and business elites, are divided between them. No exclusive "ladies'" club maintains a club house. Their members meet in private homes, parish houses, or other clubs. The most exclusive one meets in the home of some member. It has no name other than the one its members have traditionally accorded themselves, namely, Our Society. This is truly a core group of equals where memberships are passed down from mothers to daughters and daughters-in-law with few exceptions. There are a half-dozen acceptable family clubs in the community, but Gentile members of the core group are concentrated in one, the *arrivistes* are clustered in another, professional families in two others, and Jewish *arrivistes* and professionals in another. Several yacht, fishing, hunting, and beach clubs are maintained by Gentile families; in like manner groups of Jewish families maintain beach and country clubs.

Some 97 percent of the class I families have at least one club membership and 75 percent belong to two or more clubs. The husband belongs to a men's club, the wife to a ladies' club, and the family to a family club. A relatively small number of leisure time interests are represented in the special interest clubs—tennis, golf, polo, sailing, fishing, and hunting among the men and the raising of flowers and purebred livestock or thoroughbred horses among both sexes.

Mass communication media reach class I persons in a selective way. Practically every home is equipped with a radio, but only 50.5 percent owned television sets as late as the fall of 1952. Among the television set owners, there are sharp differences between the core group and the *arrivistes*. Only one third of the core group own television sets—usually these are families with younger children. Over four out of five *arriviste* families own television sets, large and expensive ones. Television viewing is very selective among core group adults; they are partial to drama, serious music, and news programs. The *arrivistes* too view these programs but they include also variety, comedy, and quiz programs.

The local evening newspaper is subscribed to by 99 percent of class I householders. In addition, 26 percent subscribe to the local morning newspaper. Both of these daily newspapers are owned and published by the same family. Approximately 51 percent of the class I families subscribe to *The New York Times* regularly, and 26 percent receive *The New York Herald Tribune*. News magazines, like *Time* and *U.S. News and World Report,* reach 31 percent of the homes; 17 percent of the homes receive trade or professional journals; 39 percent subscribe to such educational and literary magazines as *Harper's, The New Yorker,* and *Saturday Review*. At least four such "quality" magazines come into over 53 percent of the class I homes.

Philanthropy

A sense of social obligation in relation to those they "fear are not so fortunate" is a commonly held value among mature individuals. Both men and women spend hundreds of hours each year serving on the boards of many welfare organizations. They set policy, raise money, and hire and fire personnel as the occasion demands. Their only compensation is the knowledge that someone has to be responsible for these community activities. Generous amounts of money are given to the United Fund, special charities, the hospital, and various health drives like the March of Dimes and the Heart Fund. The younger women, in particular, give freely of their time and generously of their money to help maintain philanthropic activities sponsored by each of the seven Junior Leagues or associations of similar type. Support of the symphony, art center, schools, and colleges are also prominent in the obligation pattern of this stratum.

The Social Ethic

Formal recognition of a Gentile family's position in the elite is achieved by inclusion in the *Social Directory;* over 95 percent of class I Gentile families are listed, but less than 5 percent of class I Jewish families. Listing in the *Directory* is a symbol of acceptance into the higher brackets of the class structure, but not into the inner circle. A family must belong to the Cotillion or the Assembly to be in the inner circle. This requires the possession of all the traits that make a "lady" or a "gentleman" by local standards. The means, the lineage, and the breeding tests must be passed before a family is acceptable to the core group. Elements in the breeding test include "character," "good manners," "personal grooming," and evidence of "culture." Pretense is a cardinal sin; to pretend is as vulgar as an attempt to buy one's way. One must never accept hospitality unless he can return it in the same spirit it was given. Proper clothes for the occasion are stressed heavily. Personal grooming is important for both sexes at all times and at all ages. A woman may acquire the finest imported gowns but have a mouthful of crooked teeth and a "blatant Midwestern voice" which mark her origins and block her efforts to be accepted. In sum, the cardinal characteristics of this stratum's cultural pattern include wealth, lineage, and "good breeding." There are no substitutes; those who enjoy the coveted qualities of high status and acceptability possess this trinity; those who aspire to be ac-

cepted in the core group must acquire them. A distinguished elderly gentleman whose ancestors were founders of a western Massachusetts city has lived in the city for over 70 years. While discussing the "New Haven" attitude he observed, "If my grandchildren live to be old men and women, they may be looked upon as New Haveners," by those we have referred to as "proper New Haveners."

A salient characteristic of some numbers of the core group is an ardent amateur's interest in avocations such as sailing, polo, golf, breeding of purebred livestock, and the collection of book plates. Their assured private incomes enable them to indulge their hobbies and idiosyncrasies to an extent undreamed of by middle and working class persons. Their whimsical personalities combined with wide experiences make many of them delightful sophisticates and charming companions.

Summary

Class I is composed of the community's business and professional leaders. Its members live in those areas of the community generally regarded as the "best"; the male heads are college graduates, usually from famous private institutions; their wives have completed from one to four years of college. Incomes are the highest of any stratum, and many families are wealthy; often their wealth is inherited. This is true particularly of a core group of interrelated families who have lived in the area for several generations. Members of the core group are descendants of the pioneers who settled in New England three centuries ago. These families dominate the private clubs that

play so prominent a part in this
group's use of leisure time. The core
group family is stable, secure, and,
from the viewpoint of its values, socially responsible for its members and
the welfare of the community.

The core group's business and professional supremacy is challenged by
the upward mobile *arrivistes*. Men and
women in this segment of class I are
educated, able, aggressive, and, in a
word, leaders. Relations between the
core group members and *arrivistes* represent an area of tension, particularly
in social affairs and community activities. The upward mobile families are

"new people" to the community; most
are descendants of "old immigrants,"
but some are from "new immigrant"
stocks. The nuclear family is not as stable as the core group family; separations, divorces, and remarriages are not
too unusual. We infer that separations
and divorces are evidences of "acting
out" inner tensions, associated with
their mobility and feelings of rejection
by the core group. Although the *arrivistes* are still a minority in class I,
many core group members feel threatened by them and the vigorous leadership they show in community affairs.

12

THE NEW MIDDLE CLASS

C. Wright Mills

C. Wright Mills was not the first to make the crucial distinction between the *old* and
the *new* middle class, but it is his book, *White Collar*, from which this selection is
taken, that stands today, twenty years after its first publication, as the definitive work
on the emergence of this distinctive class. It is the development of the new middle
class, and the transformation of society which underlies it, that remains one of the
most important facts of the stratification system of the United States, and other industrialized countries as well.

As the reader will recall, Marx made essentially two predictions regarding the fate
of the lower-middle class. First, he anticipated that this group would lose out in competition with larger capitalists. The small businessman would be broken and the
economy would become increasingly concentrated and transformed into a kind of
monopoly capitalism, as later Marxists termed it. Secondly, Marx predicted that
this petty bourgeoisie, having been bankrupted and displaced by this economic law
of the survival of the fittest, would sink inexorably into the proletariat. Thus, society
would be polarized into two opposing groups with little if any buffer between

SOURCE: *White Collar: The American Middle Classes* (New York: Oxford University Press, 1951),
pp. 63–76. Copyright © 1956 by Oxford University Press, Inc. Reprinted by permission of the
publisher.

them: a small group of capitalists at the top, and an immense working class at the bottom.

What can we say of Marx's predictions? In brief, Marx may be considered half right and half wrong. As Mills demonstrates—and the trends Mills cites to 1940 have continued unabated to this day—with the rise of the giant corporation there has been a sharp decline in the economic importance of this so-called old middle class. This class is defined in terms of its modest ownership of some means of production: a small shop, a factory, a farm, or a professional practice.

Now, while it is true that economic enterprise has become increasingly concentrated at the expense of this old middle class, the displaced members of this class have emphatically not been catapulted into the Marxian proletariat. Instead, a whole new class of people has been created, really neither fish nor fowl. They are not old-fashioned entrepreneurs, for they do not own the companies for which they work; but, on the other hand, neither are they wage workers in the strictest sense. They are, instead, members of a new salaried middle class, a heterogeneous group including salaried professionals and technical workers (such as teachers, social workers, and engineers), managers (but not owners) at all levels, sales people in and out of stores, and clerical and office workers of all kinds.

It is this new middle class of salaried white-collar employees that has shown and will continue to show the greatest dynamism in advanced societies, especially when compared with the declining old middle class and the working class that, in the United States, is beginning to shrink slowly.

What accounts for the remarkable rise of the new middle class; how did the species come into existence? It was not simply a matter of a change in the occupational preferences of individual persons in the labor force, that Robert Jones decides, for example, to become a bank clerk instead of a factory worker. Rather, the growth of this class reflects basic changes in the structure of American society, especially rising productivity of the economy, the transformation of property, and the growing role of government.

Rising productivity of the economy has affected the composition of the class structure. First, increasing agricultural productivity, reflected in tremendous improvements in machinery, fertilizers, the development of new seeds and breeds, means that fewer farmers are needed to feed more people. In 1820, one farmer could feed only four persons; today one farmer can grow food for 42 persons. The result: a tremendous decline in the farm population, today under 5 percent of the labor force as compared to 38 percent at the turn of the century.

The same holds true in the industrial sector. In industry after industry, automation and other technical advances have boosted output while reducing the number of men on the production line.

With the decline in numbers of those engaged in production, on the farms and in the factories, comes a rise in other kinds of occupations, corresponding to the increasing complexity and sophistication of the economy: jobs in trade, service, in professional, technical, managerial, sales, and clerical fields.

A second factor in the rise of this new middle class is the transformation of property. The United States is no longer a nation of small businesses and farms but a nation of gigantic bureaucratic organizations. We have now a kind of economic collectivism represented by the major corporations, not a socialist but a private collectivism. And along with the changes in the size of economic organizations the social class composition of the country has changed accordingly. From a nation of small, independent property owners—the old middle class—we have become a nation of employees, people who work for a large organization, public or private, either as wageworkers or as members of the growing new middle class.

In the chapter presented here, Mills discusses the traditional bases upon which white-collar workers claimed higher status than wageworkers. Mills later suggests that many of the sources of white-collar prestige are breaking down and that in certain respects the lower ranks of the new middle class are being leveled down to that of the working class. In brief, some of these threats to white-collar status are: (1) the convergence of white-collar and blue-collar income; (2) the narrowing of the education gap between white-collar and blue-collar workers; (3) factory-like conditions of work for white-collar employees in automated offices; (4) the breakdown of racial and ethnic exclusiveness of white-collar workers and the entry of large numbers of women into white-collar fields; and (5) the increasingly working-class origins of new middle-class people, as sons and daughters of workers enter lower white-collar occupations.

All this points tentatively in the direction of a kind of status proletarianization of the lower new middle class. Of course, Marxists have claimed all along that the new middle-class man—especially in the lower ranks—is only a special kind of proletarian, similar in almost all ways to the wageworker—source of income, approximate level of income, employee status, and so on—and that working-class consciousness would probably develop among this group. For many years this seemed more a pious hope than anything else, and even Mills himself wrote off the political possibilities of the white-collar class, viewing them as hopelessly privatized and "inactionary" politically. Nevertheless, recent developments in American society have raised the distinct possibility that many elements of the white-collar class (or the "new working class" as they are lately called), may be becoming radicalized and class conscious to an extent unanticipated just a few years ago.* Many of these people are employed by local governments (as teachers, social workers, etc.) and have been victimized by the bankruptcy and squalor of the public sector, and have consequently become among the most militant trade unionists in the country.

Many white-collar people have been radicalized by the contradiction between the humanistic college education they received, and the kinds of regimented, alienating, and—to them—meaningless jobs that are available to them in the corporate world after college. Many graduates are further alienated by being unable to find work at all, as unemployment at the start of the post-Vietnam era begins to affect educated workers as well as the traditional working class. And finally, many of them have been drawn into political thinking by the time of troubles through which America is struggling, politicized by pressing issues of the day: the war, civil rights, women's liberation, ecology, the counter-cultural revolution, and so on.

The change from old middle-class to new middle-class dominance has had important implications for American social character. In the nineteenth-century days of old middle-class hegemony, what were the character traits that one had to have to succeed in business—in terms of the ideology of capitalism anyway? They were, following Weber's discussion, hard work, diligence, thrift, and rugged individualism. Perhaps one of the last of this old middle-class breed was the late S. S. Kresge who worked his way up from a poor boyhood on a Pennsylvania farm to become a fabulously wealthy owner of a chain store empire. Kresge so embodied the old middle-class virtues that he was perhaps a caricature of them. He strenuously opposed smoking, drinking, and card playing, considering them wasteful of a man's time, money, health, and energy; despite his wealth he was incredibly thrifty in his personal spending habits, refusing to play golf because he claimed he could not afford to lose the golf balls,

---

* See, e.g., Richard Flacks, "Strategies for Radical Social Change," *Social Policy*, 1 (March/April, 1971), 7–14.

wearing his suits until they were threadbare, and driving his automobiles until "the wheels fell off." Accounting for his success, he said: "I think I was successful because I saved and because I heeded good advice. I worked—and I didn't work only eight hours a day, but sometimes eighteen hours a day." The one hobby he indulged himself throughout his long life was his beekeeping. But even this had a moral: "My bees," he recalled, "always reminded me that hard work, thrift, sobriety and an earnest struggle to live an upright Christian life are the first rungs of the ladder of success."

Today, the old middle-class ethic is dying out, in reality if not in rhetoric. Especially the old virtues of rugged individualism have been replaced by the ethic of conformity and fitting in. More and more people today are working with other people, not with things, manipulating persons, not objects. And, perhaps more important, the road to success today lies in climbing the corporate or government hierarchy. The old middle-class man was his own boss and could go his own way; the new middle-class man depends for his success upon his personality and carefully attuning his behavior to the expectations of colleagues and superiors.

There has always been a strain of conformity in American life, noted by early observers of the American scene, such as Tocqueville, partly perhaps a consequence of popular democracy and egalitarianism. There is no question, however, that the rise of the salaried new middle-class man working for the large organization stimulated a new emphasis on conformity, being well liked, pleasing others, adjusting, and developing the proper personality, that was entirely foreign to the classic American traits of rugged individualism characteristic of the old captains of industry of an earlier era. And an entire bookshelf of sociology, social criticism, and popular literature arose after World War II analyzing this new social character: *The Lonely Crowd, The Organization Man, Life in the Crystal Palace, The Man in the Grey Flannel Suit, The Pyramid Climbers, How to Succeed in Business without Really Trying,* and many more.

In the early nineteenth century, although there are no exact figures, probably four-fifths of the occupied population were self-employed enterprisers; by 1870, only about one-third, and in 1940, only about one-fifth, were still in this old middle class. Many of the remaining four-fifths of the people who now earn a living do so by working for the 2 or 3 per cent of the population who now own 40 or 50 per cent of the private property in the United States. Among these workers are the members of the new middle class, white-collar people on salary. For them, as for wage-workers, America has become a nation of employees for whom independent property is out of range. Labor markets, not control of property, determine their chances to receive income, exercise power, enjoy prestige, learn and use skills.

1. Occupational Change

Of the three broad strata composing modern society, only the new middle class has steadily grown in proportion to the whole. Eighty years ago, there were three-quarters of a million middle-class employees; by 1940, there were over twelve and a half million. In that period the old middle class increased 135 per cent; wage-workers, 255 per cent; new middle class, 1600 per cent.*

* In the tables in this section, figures for the intermediate years are appropriately graded; the change has been more or less steady.

The Labor Force	1870	1940
Old Middle Class	33%	20%
New Middle Class	6	25
Wage Workers	61	55
Total	100%	100%

The employees composing the new middle class do not make up one single compact stratum. They have not emerged on a single horizontal level, but have been shuffled out simultaneously on the several levels of modern society; they now form, as it were, a new pyramid within the old pyramid of society at large, rather than a horizontal layer. The great bulk of the new middle class are of the lower middle-income brackets, but regardless of how social stature is measured, types of white-collar men and women range from almost the top to almost the bottom of modern society.

The managerial stratum, subject to minor variations during these decades, has dropped slightly, from 14 to 10 per cent; the salaried professionals, displaying the same minor ups and downs, have dropped from 30 to 25 per cent of the new middle class. The major shifts in over-all composition have been in the relative decline of the sales group, occurring most sharply around 1900, from 44 to 25 per cent of the total new middle class; and the steady rise of the office workers, from 12 to 40 per cent. Today the three largest occupational groups in the white-collar stratum are schoolteachers, salespeople in and out of stores, and assorted office workers. These three form the white-collar mass.

New Middle Class	1870	1940
Managers	14%	10%
Salaried Professionals	30	25
Salespeople	44	25
Office Workers	12	40
Total	100%	100%

The Middle Classes	1870	1940
Old Middle Class	85%	44%
Farmers	62	23
Businessmen	21	19
Free Professionals	2	2
New Middle Class	15%	56%
Managers	2	6
Salaried Professionals	4	14
Salespeople	7	14
Office Workers	2	22
Total Middle Classes	100%	100%

White-collar occupations now engage well over half the members of the American middle class as a whole. Between 1870 and 1940, white-collar workers rose from 15 to 56 per cent of the middle brackets, while the old middle class declined from 85 to 44 per cent.

Negatively, the transformation of the middle class is a shift from property to no-property; positively, it is a shift from property to a new axis of stratification, occupation. The nature and well-being of the old middle class can best be sought in the condition of entrepreneurial property; of the new middle class, in the economics and sociology of occupations. The numerical decline of the older, independent sectors of the middle class is an incident in the centralization of property; the numerical rise of the newer salaried employees is due to the industrial mechanics by which the occupations composing the new middle class have arisen.

2. Industrial Mechanics

In modern society, occupations are specific functions within a social division of labor, as well as skills sold for income on a labor market. Contemporary divisions of labor involve a hitherto unknown specialization of skill: from arranging abstract symbols, at

$1000 an hour, to working a shovel, for $1000 a year. The major shifts in occupations since the Civil War have assumed this industrial trend: as a proportion of the labor force, fewer individuals manipulate *things,* more handle *people* and *symbols.*

This shift in needed skills is another way of describing the rise of the white-collar workers, for their characteristic skills involve the handling of paper and money and people. They are expert at dealing with people transiently and impersonally; they are masters of the commercial, professional, and technical relationship. The one thing they do not do is live by making things; rather, they live off the social machineries that organize and co-ordinate the people who do make things. White-collar people help turn what someone else has made into profit for still another; some of them are closer to the means of production, supervising the work of actual manufacture and recording what is done. They are the people who keep track; they man the paper routines involved in distributing what is produced. They provide technical and personal services, and they teach others the skills which they themselves practice, as well as all other skills transmitted by teaching.

As the proportion of workers needed for the extraction and production of things declines, the proportion needed for servicing, distributing, and co-ordinating rises. In 1870, over three-

	1870	1940
Producing	77%	46%
Servicing	13	20
Distributing	7	23
Co-ordinating	3	11
Total employed	100%	100%

fourths, and in 1940, slightly less than one-half of the total employed were engaged in producing things.

By 1940, the proportion of white-collar workers of those employed in industries primarily involved in the production of things was 11 per cent; in service industries, 32 per cent; in distribution, 44 per cent; and in co-ordination, 60 per cent. The white-collar industries themselves have grown, and within each industry the white-collar occupations have grown. Three trends lie back of the fact that the white-collar ranks have thus been the most rapidly growing of modern occupations: the increasing productivity of machinery used in manufacturing; the magnification of distribution; and the increasing scale of co-ordination.

The immense productivity of mass-production technique and the increased application of technologic rationality are the first open secrets of modern occupational change: fewer men turn out more things in less time. In the middle of the nineteenth century, as J. F. Dewhurst and his associates have calculated, some 17.6 billion horsepower hours were expended in American industry, only 6 per cent by mechanical energy; by the middle of the twentieth century, 410.4 billion horsepower hours will be expended, 94 per cent by mechanical energy. This industrial revolution seems to be permanent, seems to go on through war and boom and slump; thus 'a decline in production results in a more than proportional decline in employment; and an increase in production results in a less than proportional increase in employment.'

Technology has thus narrowed the stratum of workers needed for given volumes of output; it has also altered the types and proportions of skill needed in the production process. Know-how, once an attribute of the mass of workers, is now in the machine and the engineering elite who design it. Machines displace unskilled workmen, make craft skills unnecessary, push up front the automatic motions of the machine-operative. Workers composing the new lower class are predominantly semi-skilled: their proportion in the urban wage-worker stratum has risen from 31 per cent in 1910 to 41 per cent in 1940.

The manpower economies brought about by machinery and the large-scale rationalization of labor forces, so apparent in production and extraction, have not, as yet, been applied so extensively in distribution—transportation, communication, finance, and trade. Yet without an elaboration of these means of distribution, the wide-flung operations of multi-plant producers could not be integrated nor their products distributed. Therefore, the proportion of people engaged in distribution has enormously increased so that today about one-fourth of the labor force is so engaged. Distribution has expanded more than production because of the lag in technological application in this field, and because of the persistence of individual and small-scale entrepreneurial units at the same time that the market has been enlarged and the need to market has been deepened.

Behind this expansion of the distributive occupations lies the central problem of modern capitalism: to whom can the available goods be sold? As volume swells, the intensified search for markets draws more workers into the distributive occupations of trade, promotion, advertising. As far-flung and intricate markets come into being, and as the need to find and create even more markets becomes urgent, 'middle men' who move, store, finance, promote, and sell goods are knit into a vast network of enterprises and occupations.

The physical aspect of distribution involves wide and fast transportation networks; the co-ordination of marketing involves communication; the search for markets and the selling of goods involves trade, including wholesale and retail outlets as well as financial agencies for commodity and capital markets. Each of these activities engage more people, but the manual jobs among them do not increase so fast as the white-collar tasks.

Transportation, growing rapidly after the Civil War, began to decline in point of the numbers of people involved before 1930; but this decline took place among wage-workers; the proportion of white-collar workers employed in transportation continued to rise. By 1940, some 23 per cent of the people in transportation were white-collar employees. As a new industrial segment of the U.S. economy, the communication industry has never been run by large numbers of free enterprisers; at the outset it needed large numbers of technical and other white-collar workers. By 1940, some 77 per cent of its people were in new middle-class occupations.

Trade is now the third largest segment of the occupational structure, exceeded only by farming and manufacturing. A few years after the Civil War less than 5 out of every 100 workers were engaged in trade; by 1940 almost 12 out of every 100 workers were so employed. But, while 70 per cent of those in wholesaling and retailing were free enterprisers in 1870, and less than 3 per cent were white collar, by 1940, of the people engaged in retail trade 27 per cent were free enterpris-

ers; 41 per cent white-collar employees.

Newer methods of merchandising, such as credit financing, have resulted in an even greater percentage increase in the 'financial' than in the 'commercial' agents of distribution. Branch banking has lowered the status of many banking employees to the clerical level, and reduced the number of executive positions. By 1940, of all employees in finance and real estate 70 per cent were white-collar workers of the new middle class.

The organizational reason for the expansion of the white-collar occupations is the rise of big business and big government, and the consequent trend of modern social structure, the steady growth of bureaucracy. In every branch of the economy, as firms merge and corporations become dominant, free entrepreneurs become employees, and the calculations of accountant, statistician, bookkeeper, and clerk in these corporations replace the free 'movement of prices' as the co-ordinating agent of the economic system. The rise of thousands of big and little bureaucracies and the elaborate specialization of the system as a whole create the need for many men and women to plan, co-ordinate, and administer new routines for others. In moving from smaller to larger and more elaborate units of economic activity, increased proportions of employees are drawn into co-ordinating and managing. Managerial and professional employees and office workers of varied sorts—floorwalkers, foremen, office managers—are needed; people to whom subordinates report, and who in turn report to superiors, are links in chains of power and obedience, co-ordinating and supervising other occupational experiences, functions, and skills. And all over the economy, the proportion of clerks of all sorts has increased:

from 1 or 2 per cent in 1870 to 10 or 11 per cent of all gainful workers in 1940.

As the worlds of business undergo these changes, the increased tasks of government on all fronts draw still more people into occupations that regulate and service property and men. In response to the largeness and predatory complications of business, the crises of slump, the nationalization of the rural economy and small-town markets, the flood of immigrants, the urgencies of war and the march of technology disrupting social life, government increases its co-ordinating and regulating tasks. Public regulations, social services, and business taxes require more people to make mass records and to integrate people, firms, and goods, both within government and in the various segments of business and private life. All branches of government have grown, although the most startling increases are found in the executive branch of the Federal Government, where the needs for co-ordinating the economy have been most prevalent.

As marketable activities, occupations change (1) with shifts in the skills required, as technology and rationalization are unevenly applied across the economy; (2) with the enlargement and intensification of marketing operations in both the commodity and capital markets; and (3) with shifts in the organization of the division of work, as expanded organizations require co-ordination, management, and recording. The mechanics involved within and between these three trends have led to the numerical expansion of white-collar employees.

There are other less obvious ways in which the occupational structure is shaped: high agricultural tariffs, for example, delay the decline of farming as an occupation; were Argentine beef allowed to enter duty-free, the number of meat producers here might diminish. City ordinances and zoning laws abolish peddlers and affect the types of construction workers that prevail. Most states have bureaus of standards which limit entrance into professions and semi-professions; at the same time members of these occupations form associations in the attempt to control entrance into 'their' market. More successful than most trade unions, such professional associations as the American Medical Association have managed for several decades to level off the proportion of physicians and surgeons. Every phase of the slump-war-boom cycle influences the numerical importance of various occupations; for instance, the movement back and forth between 'construction worker' and small 'contractor' is geared to slumps and booms in building.

The pressures from these loosely organized parts of the occupational world draw conscious managerial agencies into the picture. The effects of attempts to manage occupational change, directly and indirectly, are not yet great, except of course during wars, when government freezes men in their jobs or offers incentives and compulsions to remain in old occupations or shift to new ones. Yet, increasingly the class levels and occupational composition of the nation are managed; the occupational structure of the United States is being slowly reshaped as a gigantic corporate group. It is subject not only to the pulling of autonomous markets and the pushing of technology but to an 'allocation of personnel' from central points of control. Occupational change thus becomes more conscious, at least to those who are coming to be in charge of it.

3. White-Collar Pyramids

Occupations, in terms of which we circumscribe the new middle class, involve several ways of ranking people. As specific activities, they entail various types and levels of *skill*, and their exercise fulfils certain *functions* within an industrial division of labor. These are the skills and functions we have been examining statistically. As sources of income, occupations are connected with *class* position; and since they normally carry an expected quota of prestige, on and off the job, they are relevant to *status* position. They also involve certain degrees of *power* over other people, directly in terms of the job, and indirectly in other social areas. Occupations are thus tied to class, status, and power as well as to skill and function; to understand the occupations composing the new middle class, we must consider them in terms of each of these dimensions.

'Class situation' in its simplest objective sense has to do with the amount and source of income. Today, occupation rather than property is the source of income for most of those who receive any direct income: the possibilities of selling their services in the labor market, rather than of profitably buying and selling their property and its yields, now determine the life-chances of most of the middle class. All things money can buy and many that men dream about are theirs by virtue of occupational income. In new middle-class occupations men work for someone else on someone else's property. This is the clue to many differences between the old and new middle classes, as well as to the contrast between the older world of the small propertied entrepreneur and the occupational structure of the new society. If the old middle class once fought big property structures in the name of small, free properties, the new middle class, like the wage-workers in latter-day capitalism, has been, from the beginning, dependent upon large properties for job security.

Wage-workers in the factory and on the farm are on the propertyless bottom of the occupational structure, depending upon the equipment owned by others, earning wages for the time they spend at work. In terms of property, the white-collar people are *not* 'in between Capital and Labor'; they are in exactly the same property-class position as the wage-workers. They have no direct financial tie to the means of production, no prime claim upon the proceeds from property. Like factory workers—and day laborers, for that matter—they work for those who do own such means of livelihood.

Yet if bookkeepers and coal miners, insurance agents and farm laborers, doctors in a clinic and crane operators in an open pit have this condition in common, certainly their class situations are not the same. To understand their class positions, we must go beyond the common fact of source of income and consider as well the amount of income.

In 1890, the average income of white-collar occupational groups was about double that of wage-workers. Before World War I, salaries were not so adversely affected by slumps as wages were but, on the contrary, they rather steadily advanced. Since World War I, however, salaries have been reacting to turns in the economic cycles more and more like wages, although still to a lesser extent. If wars help wages more because of the greater flexibility of wages, slumps help salaries because of their greater inflexibility. Yet after each war era, salaries have never regained their previous advantage over wages. Each phase of the cycle, as well as the progressive rise of all income groups, has resulted in a narrowing of the income gap between wage-workers and white-collar employees.

In the middle 'thirties the three urban strata, entrepreneurs, white-collar, and wage-workers, formed a distinct scale with respect to median family income: the white-collar employees had a median income of $1,896; the entrepreneurs, $1,464; the urban wage-workers, $1,175. Although the median income of white-collar workers was higher than that of the entrepreneurs, larger proportions of the entrepreneurs received both high-level and low-level incomes. The distribution of their income was spread more than that of the white-collar.

The wartime boom in incomes, in fact, spreads the incomes of all occupational groups, but not evenly. The spread occurred mainly among urban entrepreneurs. As an income level, the old middle class in the city is becoming less an evenly graded income group, and more a collection of different strata, with a large proportion of lumpen-bourgeoisie who receive very low incomes, and a small, prosperous bourgeoisie with very high incomes.

In the late 'forties (1948, median family income) the income of all white-collar workers was $4,000, that of all urban wage-workers, $3,300. These averages, however, should not obscure the overlap of specific groups within each stratum: the lower white-collar people—sales-employees and office workers—earned almost the same as skilled workers and foremen,* but more than semi-skilled urban wage-workers.

In terms of property, white-collar people are in the same position as wage-workers; in terms of occupational income, they are 'somewhere in the middle.' Once they were considerably above the wage-workers; they have become less so; in the middle of the century they still have an edge but the over-all rise in incomes is making the new middle class a more homogeneous income group.

As with income, so with prestige: white-collar groups are differentiated socially, perhaps more decisively than wage-workers and entrepreneurs. Wage earners certainly do form an income pyramid and a prestige gradation, as do entrepreneurs and rentiers; but the new middle class, in terms of income and prestige, is a superimposed pyramid, reaching from almost the bottom of the first to almost the top of the second.

People in white-collar occupations claim higher prestige than wage-workers, and, as a general rule, can cash in their claims with wage-workers as well as with the anonymous public. This fact has been seized upon, with much justification, as the defining characteristic of the white-collar strata, and although there are definite indications in the United States of a decline in their prestige, still, on a nation-wide basis, the majority of even the lower white-collar employees—office workers and salespeople—enjoy a middling prestige.

The historic bases of the white-collar employees' prestige, apart from superior income, have included the similarity of their place and type of work to those of the old middle-classes' which has permitted them to borrow prestige. As their relations with entrepreneur and with esteemed customer have be-

---

* It is impossible to isolate the salaried foremen from the skilled urban wage-workers in these figures. If we could do so, the income of lower white-collar workers would be closer to that of semi-skilled workers.

come more impersonal, they have borrowed prestige from the firm itself. The stylization of their appearance, in particular the fact that most white-collar jobs have permitted the wearing of street clothes on the job, has also figured in their prestige claims, as have the skills required in most white-collar jobs, and in many of them the variety of operations performed and the degree of autonomy exercised in deciding work procedures. Furthermore, the time taken to learn these skills and the way in which they have been acquired by formal education and by close contact with the higher-ups in charge has been important. White-collar employees have monopolized high school education—even in 1940 they had completed 12 grades to the 8 grades for wage-workers and entrepreneurs. They have also enjoyed status by descent: in terms of race, Negro white-collar employees exist only in isolated instances —and, more importantly, in terms of nativity, in 1930 only about 9 per cent of white-collar workers, but 16 per cent of free enterprisers and 21 per cent of wage-workers, were foreign born. Finally, as an underlying fact, the limited size of the white-collar group, compared to wage-workers, has led to successful claims to greater prestige.

The power position of groups and of individuals typically depends upon factors of class, status, and occupation, often in intricate interrelation. Given occupations involve specific powers over other people in the actual course of work; but also outside the job area, by virtue of their relations to institutions of property as well as the typical income they afford, occupations lend power. Some white-collar occupations require the direct exercise of supervision over other white-collar and wage-workers, and many more are closely attached to this managerial cadre. White-collar employees are the assistants of authority; the power they exercise is a derived power, but they do exercise it.

Moreover, within the white-collar pyramids there is a characteristic pattern of authority involving age and sex. The white-collar ranks contain a good many women: some 41 per cent of all white-collar employees, as compared with 10 per cent of free enterprisers, and 21 per cent of wage-workers, are women.* As with sex, so with age: free enterprisers average (median) about 45 years of age, white-collar and wage-workers, about 34; but among free enterprisers and wage-workers, men are about 2 or 3 years older than women; among white-collar workers, there is a 6- or 7-year difference. In the white-collar pyramids, authority is roughly graded by age and sex: younger women tend to be subordinated to older men.

The occupational groups forming the white-collar pyramids, different as they may be from one another, have certain common characteristics, which are central to the character of the new middle class as a general pyramid overlapping the entrepreneurs and wage-workers. White-collar people cannot be adequately defined along any one possible dimension of stratification—skill, function, class, status, or power. They are generally in the middle ranges on each of these dimensions and on every descriptive attribute. Their position is more definable in terms of their relative differences from other strata than in any absolute terms.

* According to our calculations, the proportions of women, 1940, in these groups are: farmers, 2.9%; businessmen, 20%; free professionals, 5.9%; managers, 7.1%; salaried professionals, 51.7%; salespeople, 27.5%; office workers, 51%; skilled workers, 3.2%; semi-skilled and unskilled, 29.8%; rural workers, 9.1%.

On all points of definition, it must be remembered that white-collar people are not one compact horizontal stratum. They do not fulfil one central, positive *function* that can define them, although in general their functions are similar to those of the old middle class. They deal with symbols and with other people, co-ordinating, recording, and distributing; but they fulfil these functions as dependent employees, and the skills they thus employ are sometimes similar in form and required mentality to those of many wage-workers.

In terms of property, they are equal to wage-workers and different from the old middle class. Originating as propertyless dependents, they have no serious expectations of propertied independence. In terms of income, their class position is, on the average, somewhat higher than that of wage-workers. The overlap is large and the trend has been definitely toward less difference, but even today the differences are significant.

Perhaps of more psychological importance is the fact that white-collar groups have successfully claimed more prestige than wage-workers and still generally continue to do so. The bases of their prestige may not be solid today, and certainly they show no signs of being permanent; but, however vague and fragile, they continue to mark off white-collar people from wage-workers.

Members of white-collar occupations exercise a derived authority in the course of their work; moreover, compared to older hierarchies, the white-collar pyramids are youthful and feminine bureaucracies, within which youth, education, and American birth are emphasized at the wide base, where millions of office workers most clearly typify these differences between the new middle class and other occupational groups. White-collar masses, in turn, are managed by people who are more like the old middle class, having many of the social characteristics, if not the independence, of free enterprisers.

13

THE WORKING CLASS SUBCULTURE: A NEW VIEW

S. M. Miller and Frank Riessman

In their studies of class structure, sociologists have discovered that the further away an individual is from a particular class, the more difficulty he has in making fine gradations within that class and between adjacent classes. Thus, lower-class persons have a tendency to lump everyone together at the level of the upper middle and above, and consider them all identically remote.

SOURCE: *Social Problems*, vol. 9, no. 1 (Summer 1961), pp. 86–97. Reprinted by permission of the authors and the Society for the Study of Social Problems.

Here we have a direct parallel between social distance and physical distance. Seen from the ground, two airplanes may appear to be on a collision course, although there may be thousands of feet separating them. Likewise from the air, a four story and a six story building may appear to be the same size, though any walker in the city can easily distinguish between them.

Looking at the class structure from their position in the middle or upper middle class, sociologists have often been guilty of the same errors as their respondents. Frequently in the literature the terms working class and lower class are used almost interchangeably. Sociologists have thus unwittingly validated the principle that they have discovered; from their fairly high and secure vantage point they have often been unable to make fine distinctions at the lower end of the class structure.

In addition to criticizing other sociological views of workers, S. M. Miller and Frank Riessman in this essay clearly distinguish the working class from the lower class beneath it, and take a hardheaded and realistic look at some of the major subcultural themes of the stable working class in America.

A decade and a half ago the working class was depicted by Allison Davis and Robert J. Havighurst [1] as permissive and indulgent toward their children and free of the emotional strain of impulse-inhibition which characterized the middle class in the United States. Indeed, it was felt by many that the middle class had much to envy and imitate in the working class.[2] This romantic view of the working class has faded. It is now asserted that the working class (usually termed the "lower class") is incapable of deferring gratification [3] and consequently unable to make major strides in improving their conditions. Frequently accompanying this view is the belief that this lower class is "immoral," "uncivilized," "promiscuous," "lazy," "obscene," "dirty," and "loud." [4] With the rising plane and standard of living of workers has come the argument that workers are middle class in their outlook and desires; [5] the

[1] Allison Davis and Robert J. Havighurst, "Social Class and Color Differences in Child Rearing," *American Sociological Review*, 11 (December, 1946), pp. 698–710.

[2] Cf. David Riesman in his introduction to Ely Chinoy's *Automobile Workers and the American Dream* (New York: Random House, 1955).

[3] Louis Schneider and Sverre Lysgaard, "The Deferred Gratification Pattern: A Preliminary Study," *American Sociological Review*, 18 (April, 1953), pp. 142–9.

[4] These adjectives are taken from Rodman who then goes on to declare: "Lantz, Centers, Warner *et al.*, Hollingshead, Drake and Cayton, West, and David, Gardner and Gardner make it clear that this is the way the lower class is viewed within the United States, the Henriques and Braithwaite studies make it clear that this is the way the lower class is viewed within the West Indies." Hyman Rodman, "On Understanding Lower-Class Behaviour," *Social and Economics Studies*, 8 (December, 1959). Other authors state: "One of the most venerable stereotypes has been that applied by middle-class people to lower-class people. The qualities have from time to time included lack of thrift, intellectual inferiority, habitual dirtyness, licentiousness, and many that have derogatory implications." Robert R. Sears, Eleanor E. Maccoby, and Harry Levin, *Patterns of Child Rearing* (Evanston: Row, Peterson and Company, 1957), p. 442. We have isolated five types of stereotypes of workers—anomic, depraved, incapable of deferring gratification, class conscious and middle-class oriented; these are discussed in S. M. Miller and Frank Riessman, "Images of Workers," a paper presented to the Eastern Sociological Society, New York, 1957.

[5] Daniel Bell, *The End of Ideology* (Glencoe: Free Press, 1959), and in various issues of *Fortune* magazine. On the other hand, see his path-breaking article, "The Subversion of Collective Bargaining," *Commentary*, March, 1960.

difficulties in attaining full middle-class status lead to juvenile delinquency on the part of those youth who fall back into the working and lower classes [6] and to authoritarianism on the part of those who rise into the middle class.[7] Recently, a further vigorous blow has felled any notions of desirable characteristics of workers: their economic liberalism is not paralleled by political liberalism for workers are said to be more authoritarian in outlook than are members of the middle class.[8] The free, spontaneous worker is now seen as an aggressive, authoritarian, yet fettered person.

The cyclothymic views of workers are more fitting as a topic in the sociology of knowledge than they are in the analysis of what workers actually believe and practice. In other work, we have criticized in some detail a number of prevailing interpretations of workers —the middle-class image,[9] the non-deferred gratification pattern,[10] the authoritarian view.[11] By the nature of criticism, we have not been able to present our view of what workers are like, for they are not simply the negative or opposite of prevailing views.

For example, because it is demonstrated that workers' behavior is not consistently characterized by an inability to postpone gratifications, we cannot therefore conclude that a major characteristic of the working class is *having* a deferred gratification pattern. It may very well be that the whole issue of deferred gratification does not have special relevance to workers' lives. The concept might stem from a sociocentric point of view, where the middle-class observer, in a sense, says, "If I were in the workers' boots, I wouldn't postpone gratification; I would enjoy myself while I could in the present and not worry about a future which is pretty vague and hopeless anyway." This thinking does not arise out of the context in which workers' behavior takes place, but rather is imposed upon it. In other words, the entire concept of deferred gratification may be inappropriate to understanding the essence of workers' lives.

In this paper, we can only present a few elements of what we believe is a more realistic picture of workers. This analysis is severely compressed and truncated in this presentation and it might be helpful therefore to indicate at the outset an important element of our general orientation. Our stress is much more on cognitive and structural factors than on the more commonly cited affectual and motivational ones. The nature of the conditions of working-class lives (jobs, opportunities, family structure) affects behavior more than has been frequently realized; similarly, modes of understanding the environment can be more important than

---

[6] Albert Cohen, *Delinquent Boys: The Culture of the Gang* (Glencoe: Free Press, 1955).

[7] Joseph Greenblum and Leonard I. Pearlin, "Vertical Mobility and Prejudice: A Socio-Psychological Analysis," in Reinhard Bendix and Seymour Martin Lipset, eds., *Class, Status and Power* (Glencoe: Free Press, 1953).

[8] Seymour Martin Lipset, *Political Man: The Social Bases of Politics* (Garden City: Doubleday & Company, 1960), Chapter IV.

[9] S. M. Miller and Frank Riessman, "Are Workers Middle Class?" *Dissent*, Fall, 1961.

[10] S. M. Miller, Arthur Seagull, and Frank Riessman, "The Deferred Gratification Pattern: A Critical Appraisal," in L. Ferman *et al*, eds., *Poverty in America* (Ann Arbor: University of Michigan Press, 1965).

[11] S. M. Miller and Frank Riessman, " 'Working-Class Authoritarianism': A Critique of Lipset," *British Journal of Sociology*, 13 (September, 1961), pp. 263–76.

deep-seated personality factors in behavioral patterns. (For example, workers' low estimates of opportunities and high expectations of risk and loss may be more crucial in the unwillingness to undertake certain long-term actions than personality inadequacies involved in a presumed inability to defer gratification.) This is not to argue that motivational-psychological-affectual variables are unimportant but that they have been overstressed while cognitive and structural variables have been underemphasized. The recognition of the importance of the internal life of man has sometimes overshadowed the significance of the more manifest aspects of his existence.

Our definition of working class is simple: regular members of the non-agricultural labor force in manual occupations. Thus, we exclude the "lower class," irregular working people, although the analysis has some relevance to the lower class as will be mentioned below. One of the greatest sources of difficulties in understanding non-upper and non-middle class behavior is that social scientists have frequently used the omnibus category of "lower class" to encompass the stable, and frequently mobile, fairly high income skilled workers, the semi-skilled factory worker, the worker in varied service trades, the unskilled worker and the irregular worker. This collection is probably more a congeries of fairly disparate groups than a category with similar life chances and circumstances. It is especially important to distinguish the seg-ment which has irregular employment (and "voluntary" withdrawals from the labor force), unskilled jobs in service occupations (and is largely Negro and Puerto Rican now) from the other groupings, which are larger and have more of a commonness to them.

This latter group of regular workmen we call "working class" despite the reluctance of many social scientists today to use this historic term; the opprobrious term "lower class" might be applied to the irregular segment although it would probably be better all around if a less invidious term (perhaps "the unskilled") were employed.

The reluctance to make the distinction between "working class" and "lower class," despite useful discussions by Kahl [12] and others, not only is a topic worthy of independent study, but leads to error. For example, Hollingshead and Redlich in their important study have been interpreted as finding that the lower the class, the higher the rate of mental illness. Close examination of their data reveal, however, that the working class, Class IV, is closer to the upper and middle classes, Classes I, II and III, than to the lower class, Class V. Classes I through IV are similar, while Class V is quite dissimilar from all the other classes, including the working class.[13]

Within the working class, we are primarily interested in the *stable* working-class subculture. We believe there is considerable variation within the working class,[14] but the differences probably are variations upon the

---

[12] Joseph A. Kahl, *The American Class Structure* (New York: Rinehart and Company, 1959), pp. 205 ff.

[13] For the original report, see A. B. Hollingshead and Frederick C. Redlich, *Social Class and Mental Illness* (New York: John Wiley and Sons, 1958). The point above is taken from S. M. Miller and Elliot G. Mishler, "Social Class, Mental Illness, and American Psychiatry," *Milbank Memorial Fund Quarterly*, XXXVII (April, 1959), pp. 174–99.

[14] Robert Blauner, in his thoughtful paper, "Industrial Differences in Work Attitudes and Work Institutions," points out important differences among workers in different industries. Bennett

theme of the stable working-class pattern. While we think in terms of working-class subcultures, and, to some extent, lower-class subcultures, a key to understanding them, we believe, is likely to be the *stable* working-class subculture.

Phenotypes, Genotypes and the Middle Class

Our analysis is aimed at developing *themes* in working-class life. Thus, we are interpreting the *meaning* of findings rather than reporting new findings. We have utilized the published materials commonly employed plus our own interviews and observations of working-class people.

A major inadequacy in explanations of the working-class life style has been the failure to explain behavior in terms of genotypes. For example, in attitudinal polls in which similar questions are asked of middle- and working-class people, many differences are revealed between the two groups. But what is the meaning of the replies? For example, if workers agree with the statement, "Communists should be imprisoned," does it mean that they are especially unaccepting of civil liberties or that they are punitive towards those whom they see as criminals, and that they

consider punishment an effective deterrent and a just reward for wrongdoing? They may be wrong in all respects, but does their attitude reflect fundamentally a rejection of Bill of Rights thinking or a punitive attitude which has as one of its results in a specific situation the denial of civil liberties? Emphasis on the phenotype, civil liberties, may obscure the basic dynamics of the attitude in stressing a Bill of Rights little known to workers.[15]

Another illustration of phenotypic analysis was the tendency of Davis and Havighurst to denote long breast-feeding as belonging in the cluster they termed permissive child-care. This may have been accurate for the middle class since long breast-feeding is associated there with the *ideology* of permissiveness: indulgence, reliance on love, child-centered, etc. It is not for the working class because long breast-feeding is not related genotypically to the permissive child-rearing *ideology* in that class.[16]

A second major difficulty in explaining working-class life is the preoccupation with comparing it with the middle class.[17] The comparisons have perhaps inevitably a pejorative tone so that, for example, at one time those critical of the middle class could charge it with having poor child care compared to the more spontaneous workers. It ap-

Berger, *Working Class Suburb* (Berkeley: University of California Press, 1960) believes there are differences in attitudes among workers of "Arkie" and "Okie" backgrounds, and workers of a non-rural background. A variety of studies show the importance of educational differences among workers, a factor with which we are very concerned. See Frank Riessman, *Workers' Attitudes Towards Participation and Leadership*, unpublished Ph.D. dissertation in social psychology, Columbia University, 1955.

[15] Cf. David Joseph Bordua, *Authoritarianism and Intolerance, A Study of High School Students*, unpublished Ph.D. thesis, Department of Social Relations, Harvard University, 1956, pp. 228, 237, 239.

[16] Evelyn Millis Duvall, "Conceptions of Parenthood," *American Journal of Sociology*, LII (November, 1946), pp. 193–203. Cf. Martha Wolfenstein, "The Emergence of Fun Morality," *Journal of Social Issues*, VII, No. 4 (1951), pp. 15–25.

[17] Hyman Rodman, *op. cit.*

pears that some of the critics of this view have moved to the other pejorative extreme and are now critical of working-class child care and rather uncritically praising of the middle-class style of child care.[18]

A difficulty then in analyzing the working class has been this value shift to a more positive orientation towards the middle class and therefore a more critical view of the working class. As one class ascends in approval the other descends because the two classes are seen in a contrapuntal and judgmental relationship.

Another difficulty is that the middle class has apparently changed considerably in various ways so that comparisons involving the middle class are frequently of official norms rather than actual practices, of old norms rather than present norms. For example, it is frequently said that many working-class children of talent do not go on to college because they lack the ability to defer gratification, an ability the college-bound middle-class youth display. Is it really true today in the prosperous middle-class youth culture of the United States that most middle-class youth are deferring gratification when they go to college? More likely, many

look upon it in anticipation and retrospect as coming closest in their total experiences to the realization of gratifications.[19] Frequently, it seems that the working class is compared with an inner-directed, economically marginal middle class of yore than with an "acting-out," "other-directed," "affluent" middle class of today. The shifts in the middle class, murky as they are, make it especially difficult and dubious to use it as a yardstick for elucidating (and frequently evaluating) working-class life.

Basic Themes

Before discussing a few of the themes which we think are basic in working-class life, we present a brief overall picture of what we believe are the essential characteristics of the stable American worker today.

He is traditional, "old fashioned," somewhat religious, and patriarchal.[20] The worker likes discipline, structure, order, organization and directive, definite (strong) leadership, although he does not see such strong leadership in opposition to human, warm, informal,

[18] Cf. Urie Bronfenbrenner, "Socialization and Social Class through Time and Space," in E. E. Maccoby, T. M. Newcomb and E. L. Hartley, eds., *Readings in Social Psychology* (New York: Henry Holt, 1958).

[19] Some of us who have been through the mill of graduate school may feel, as suggested to us by Harold Wilensky, that we, at least, have deferred gratification! On the other hand, Allison Davis' discussion of "the graduate or medical student who is largely dependent upon his own earnings . . ." is certainly out-of-date for at least the medical student. Allison Davis, "Socialization and Adolescent Personality," in G. E. Swanson, T. M. Newcomb and E. L. Hartley, eds., *Readings in Social Psychology* (New York: Henry Holt, 1952), p. 530.

[20] The cross-class F-scale studies uniformly show that workers are more likely than middle-class individuals to support the statement that "the most important thing a child should learn is obedience to his parents." Maccoby and Gibbs have pointed out that workers strongly demand respect and obedience from their children. Eleanor E. Maccoby, Patricia K. Gibbs, *et al.*, "Methods of Child Rearing in Two Social Classes," in William E. Martin and Celia Burns Stendler, eds., *Readings in Child Development* (New York: Harcourt Brace and Company, 1954), pp. 380–96. Riessman's data indicate that not only parents but older people in general are to be obeyed and respected. See Frank Riessman, *op. cit.*, also Duvall, *op. cit.*

personal qualities.[21] Despite the inadequacy of his education, he is able to build abstractions, but he does so in a slow, physical fashion.[22] He reads ineffectively, is poorly informed in many areas, and is often quite suggestible, although interestingly enough he is frequently suspicious of "talk" and "new fangled ideas."

He is family centered; most of his relationships take place around the large, extended, fairly cooperative family.[23] Cooperation and mutual aid are among his most important characteristics.[24]

While desiring a good standard of living, he is not attracted to the middle-class style of life with its accompanying concern for status and prestige.[25]

He is not class conscious although aware of class differences. While he is somewhat radical on certain economic issues, he is quite illiberal on numerous matters, particularly civil liberties and foreign policy.[26]

The outstanding weakness of the worker is lack of education. Strongly desiring education for his children, he shows considerable concern about their school work, although he feels estranged and alienated from the teacher and the school, as he similarly feels alienated from many institutions in our society.[27] This alienation is expressed in a ready willingness to believe in the corruptness of leaders and a general negative feeling toward "big shots."

He is stubborn in his ways, concerned with strength and ruggedness, interested in mechanics, materialistic, superstitious, holds an "eye for an eye" psychology, and is largely uninterested in politics.

Stability and Security

We suspect that one of the central determinants in working-class life is the striving for stability and security.[28] External and internal factors promote instability and insecurity. Chief among the external factors is unemployment and layoff. Prosperity has of course

[21] Frank Riessman, op. cit., passim.

[22] For a review of the relevant literature, see Frank Riessman, Education and the Culturally Deprived Child (New York: Harper and Brothers, 1961).

[23] Floyd Dotson, "Patterns of Voluntary Association Among Urban Working Class Families," American Sociological Review, 16 (October, 1951), pp. 687–93. "In at least 15 of the 50 families, leisure time activities of the husbands and wives were completely dominated by the kin group. In another 28 families, regular visiting patterns with relatives constituted a major, although not exclusive, form of social activity." (p. 691) Also see p. 693.

[24] August B. Hollingshead, "Class Differences in Family Stability," in Bendix and Lipset, op. cit., p. 290. A similar point is made by Allison Davis, Burleigh B. Gardner and Mary R. Gardner, Deep South (Chicago: University of Chicago Press, 1941), p. 111. Also see John Useem, Pierre Tangent, and Ruth Useem, "Stratification in a Prairie Town," American Sociological Review, 7 (June, 1942), p. 334.

[25] The relevant literature is discussed in Miller and Riessman, "Are Workers Middle Class?", op. cit.

[26] The Centers' findings can be interposed to support the first sentence of the paragraph despite Centers' mode of analysis. Richard Centers, The Psychology of Social Classes (Princeton: Princeton University Press, 1949). Cf. Ralf Dahrendorf, Class and Class Conflict in Industrial Society (Stanford: Stanford University Press, 1959), pp. 288–289. On civil liberties and foreign policy, see Lipset, op. cit.

[27] Riessman, Education and the Culturally Deprived Child, has a discussion of some of the relevant literature.

[28] Hollingshead, op. cit., pp. 290–1.

barred the anguish of the prolonged depression of the 1930's, but the danger of occasional layoffs of some duration is not remote during the usually shaky prosperity conditions which are interlarded with episodes of recession, plant relocation, industry decline and strikes.[29]

Chief among the internal factors promoting instability are family discord, including divorce and desertion, intergenerational conflict, and the desire for excitement.

Coping with the instability threats becomes a dominant activity within the working-class family. Many practices, such as mutual aid and cooperation, extended family perspectives, are important as adjustive mechanisms. "Getting by" rather than "getting ahead" in the middle-class self-realization and advancement sense is likely to be dominant.[30] For example, the limited desire to become foremen is partly a result of the economic insecurity resulting from the loss of job seniority in case of a layoff.[31]

Part of the ambivalence toward obtaining a college education reflects the same emphasis on security. Even a highly talented working-class youth is not sure what he can do with a college diploma, and he may fear the disruption of his familial, community and peer group security.[32]

The poll data indicating the unwillingness of workers to take economic risks and their greater concern for jobs with security, is part of the same pattern of a striving for stability.[33]

Traditionalism

The American working class is primarily a migrant group; not only have people come from European farms and rural settlements to American factories but they also have migrated from America's rural life to the industrial scene.[34] Traditional practices, once thought to be infrequent in urbanized, industrialized, nuclear-oriented families, are very strong in working-class families.[35] The pattern is patriarchal, extended (with many relevant cousins, grandparents, and aunts and uncles) and delineated by sharply separated sex roles. The family is not child-centered (or child-dominant or dominating), but parent-centered and controlled. Traditional values of automatic obedience by

---

[29] Charles H. Hession, S. M. Miller and Curwen Stoddart, *The Dynamics of the American Economy* (New York: Alfred A. Knopf, 1956), Chapter 11.

[30] Joseph A. Kahl, *op. cit.*, pp. 205–210.

[31] Ely Chinoy, *op. cit.*, and Charles R. Walker, *Steeltown* (New York: Harper and Brothers, 1950), have data showing the considerable reluctance of workers to become foremen.

[32] The initial attraction of many working-class youth to engineering is partly due to the apparently concrete and clear nature of the work and the presumed definiteness of the education for a particular type of job. Motivating working-class youth to go to college may require an expansion and sharpening of working-class children's interpretation of the job market.

[33] Centers, *op. cit.*, p. 62.

[34] Lloyd Reynolds, *Labor Economics and Labor Relations* (New York: Prentice-Hall, Inc., 1949), pp. 7–23.

[35] Recent literature, particularly Weinstein and Axelrod, have pointed out that traditional practices are more widespread than previously thought in the middle class. The lack of differences between middle-class and working-class respondents reported in the studies may be due to the lack of sensitive instruments. While our analysis is not necessarily based on the notion of greater traditional and extended practices in working-class than in middle-class families, we believe that these practices assume a greater importance in the overall activities of the former.

children are expected to be the norm even if not always observed in practice.[36]

One probable consequence of this is that workers seem to be more authoritarian than they probably are. For while on the F-scale type of test, they tend to be "conventional," a characteristic of the authoritarian according to Adorno et al., it is doubtful, as we have tried to argue elsewhere,[37] that this conventionalism means the same in both the middle and working class.

The worker also has a traditional attitude toward discipline which again may be confused with authoritarianism. All the child-rearing data indicate that workers utilize physical punishment as a basic discipline technique. In the eyes of the worker punishment discourages people from wrong-doing whether the punishment is inflicted upon them or upon others who serve as "examples." There is also a "rightness" about punishment for a misdeed, for punishment is the other side of responsibility for one's actions. Thus, for example, acceptance of the death penalty may not be the result of a sado-masochistic character structure but the product of a belief in the efficacy of punishment in deterring others from misdeeds and in the value of attaching responsibility to people's actions.[38] Workers consequently do not easily accept the notion that an individual is not responsible for his crimes because of his emotional state at the time of their occurrence.

Intensity

We believe that one of the most neglected themes in working-class life and one of the most difficult to understand and interpret is that of intensity. This intensity is expressed in a number of different ways. It is found in the areas in which workers have belief and emotional involvement. While there are numerous areas about which workers are confused, and lacking in opinion (e.g., the high percentage of "no answer" and "don't know" on public opinion polls), there are important spheres in which they have definite convictions, and indeed, are highly stubborn. Their beliefs about religion, morality, superstition, diet, punishment, custom, traditional education, the role of women, intellectuals, are illustrative here. Many of these attitudes are related to their traditional orientation and they are held unquestioningly in the usual traditional manner. They are not readily open to reason and they are not flexible opinions.

Other possible sources of this intensity may be their physical (less symbolic) relation to life,[39] their person centeredness (to be discussed below), and their lack of education.

Person-Centered

Threaded through much of working-class life is a person-centered theme. On one level this theme has an infor-

---

[36] Duvall, op. cit.

[37] Miller and Riessman, " 'Working-Class Authoritarianism': A Critique of Lipset," op. cit. Also, our "Social Class, Education and Authoritarianism," a paper presented to the American Sociological Society, Washington, 1957.

[38] Cf. Bordua, op. cit.

[39] The discussion by Miller and Swanson on the "motoric" orientation of workers is one of the most suggestive in the literature. Daniel R. Miller and Guy E. Swanson, Inner Conflict and Defense (New York: Henry Holt and Company, 1960).

mal, human quality, of easy, comfortable relationship to people where the affectionate bite of humor is appreciated. The factory "horse-play," the ritualistic kidding, is part of this although by no means all of it. It is an expressive component of life.[40]

At another level, it is the importance of personal qualities. One learns more from people than from books, it is said. At a political level, the candidate as a decent, human person is more important than the platform.[41]

In the bureaucratic situation, the worker still tends to think of himself as relating to people not to roles and invisible organizational structure. This orientation is an aspect of particularism, the reaction to persons and situations in terms of their personal qualities and relations to oneself rather than in terms of some universal characteristics of their social position. The neighbor or workmate who gets ahead is expected "not to put on airs"; he should like the "old gang" and accept them despite his new position. An individual is expected to transcend his office. A foreman is a s.o.b. not because he has stresses and demands on the job which force him to act forcibly and harshly, but because of his personal qualities. Contrariwise, one of the top executives is frequently regarded as one who would help the rank-and-file workers if he had the chance, because *he* is a "nice guy"; putting him in the stresses of a new position would not force him to act as others in that position have acted.[42] It is the man not the job that makes for behavior; this attitude is not a class-conscious one, far from it. Another example of particularism is the juvenile delinquent who reacts positively to the social worker or therapist who seems to be interested in him beyond the call of professional duty.

Pragmatism and Anti-Intellectualism

With workers, it is the end-result of action rather than the planning of action or the preoccupation with means that counts. An action that goes astray is not liked for itself; it has to achieve the goal intended to be satisfactory.[43] It is results that pay off. While this orientation has an anti-intellectual dimension, it does somewhat reduce the reliance on personality (person-centered theme) by its emphasis on results. Workers like the specific action, the clear action, the understood result. What can be seen and felt is more likely to be real and true in the workers' perspectives, which are therefore likely to be limited. The pragmatic orientation of workers does not encourage them to see abstract ideas as useful. Education, for what it does for one in terms of opportunities, may be desirable but abstract intellectual speculation, ideas which are not rooted in the realities of the present, are not useful, indeed may be harmful.

On the other hand, workers often have an exaggerated respect for the ability of the learned. A person with intellectual competence in one field is frequently thought to be a "brain"

---

[40] *Ibid.*

[41] Cf. Lipset, *op. cit.*, pp. 285–6.

[42] S. M. Miller, *Union Structure and Industrial Relations: A Case Study of a Local Labor Union*, unpublished Ph.D. thesis, Princeton University, 1951.

[43] Melvin L. Kohn, "Social Class and the Exercise of Parental Authority," *American Sociological Review*, 24 (June, 1959), pp. 364–5.

with ability in all fields; partly this is due to the general abstract nature of ideas regardless of field. If a real obstacle comes up, they may expect "the brain" to have a ready solution for it, even if they may not be willing to adopt it.

At first glance, the anti-words orientation may appear to be incompatible with the possible appeal of the charismatic. But it is not. For the charismatic are charismatic because they can be emotional and expressive, qualities not usually associated with abstract ideas. Also, the charismatic leader may promise "pie in the sky" but it is a very concrete, specific set of ingredients with a clear distribution of the pie.

Excitement

Another component in workers' lives is the appreciation of excitement, of moving out of the humdrum. News, gossip, new gadgets, sports, are consequently very attractive to workers. To some extent, the consumership of workers—the desire to have new goods, whether television sets or cars—is part of this excitement dimension. The excitement theme is often in contradiction with the traditional orientation.

It is worth noting that different subgroups within the working class may favor one theme rather than another. Thus younger groups, and especially juvenile delinquents, are probably much more attracted to the excitement theme, are more alienated and less traditional. On the other hand, workers with a more middle-class orientation are probably less alienated, more traditional and pragmatic.

Parsimony and Variation

In the preceding remarks we have touched only very fleetingly on a few themes of working-class life and ignored other important themes, like co-operation and a physical orientation, almost completely. While we can sum up our analysis in a relatively few descriptive adjectives, such as person centered, traditional, pragmatic, etc., we have been unable to develop a parsimonious conceptualization, such as a non-deferred gratification pattern which attempts to explain by this single formulation or theme a vast array of behavior. Perhaps the simplest shorthand, if one wishes to use it, would be Parsons'; employing his criteria, we could say that workers are particularistic rather than universalistic, affective rather than neutral, ascriptive rather than achievement-minded, diffuse in definition of role rather than specific. But this summary may obscure more than it reveals.

Indeed, our analysis contains a number of themes which may, in part, be in opposition to each other. For example, traditionalism and alienation have certain conflicting features, as do pragmatism and person centeredness, and the resulting strains and adjustive mechanisms are important to analyze.

Let us make just two points to indicate the general value of the orientation that we have only sketchily presented here: (1) It may be possible to understand other working-class and lower-class styles by looking for sources of variation from the stable working-class pattern. (2) The development of the stable working-class style among lower-class and working-class youth might be the goal of educational and other socializing and remedial forces rather than instilling the middle-class value structure.

Variations of Working-Class Culture

By stating that we are describing the *stable* worker we imply that there are other worker subcultures. We feel that the stable worker has been relatively ignored in the emphasis on the "underprivileged," "lower class," unskilled, irregular worker and the middle-class oriented worker. By understanding the stable worker, important leads are provided for understanding other subcultural variations.

The unskilled, irregular (read "lower class") worker lacks the disciplined, structured and traditional approach of the stable worker and stresses the excitement theme. He does less to cope with insecurity and instability. In the large industrial and commercial centers today the lower-class style of life (as distinct from the stable working-class style) is found particularly among peoples relatively new to industrial and urban life: Negroes, Puerto Ricans, transplanted Southern whites. They have not been able so far to make the kind of adjustment that stable workers have. Frequently, they have special problems not only of discrimination but of fairly menial (service) jobs at low pay, extremely poor housing and considerable overcrowding. Some children of stable workers do not develop the stable pattern and assume the lower-class style. A few children of middle-class parents become lower class: they have unskilled jobs and adopt the low-

er-class style of life. But the bulk of individuals with the lower-class style come from those who are children of unskilled workers and of farmers, thus including many of the ethnic people of whom we spoke earlier.[44]

Another deviant group from the main working-class pattern are those workers who are very much concerned with achievement of success for children and for the symbols of success in consumership. In many cases the families are secure and stable and have been able to make a workable accommodation to the stresses of their lives. But this is not enough for the middle-class orientation; in many cases there is a vague opportunity and motivational factor present.

Those of working-class origins who do move into the middle class and into the middle-class style of life are likely to have a middle-class cross-pressure in that they more frequently than other working-class children have relatives who were or are middle class. Their grandparents may have been middle class; their parents though in working-class occupations are more likely to have more education than is typical in the working class and to have other attributes of middle-class life.[45] If we may give a literary example, in *Sons and Lovers,* the hero, brought up in a mining community, had a working-class father but his mother was a teacher and came from a middle-class community. Undoubtedly, the hero, whose life follows that of D. H. Lawrence, received motivation from her to move into literary activities and probably also some early direct help in reading and school. The motivational fac-

---

[44] The data to support this assertion can be computed from the two American studies detailed in the appendix to S. M. Miller, "Comparative Social Mobility," *Current Sociology,* 1961.

[45] Cf. the remarks of Kaare Svalastoga in "Report of the Fifth Working Conference on Social Stratification and Social Mobility," International Sociological Association, 1960.

tor is important but it is likely linked to the background and experiential factor of grandparental and paternal activities.

We have discussed these two styles in different ways. The lower-class style is considered to be the inability to develop an adequate measure of coping with the environment so that some degree of security and stability ensues. The origin of the middle-class style would seem to emerge from the stable pattern. A working-class family would likely first go through a stable period of accommodation before it or the children developed middle-class orientations. *It is not intrinsic in the stable pattern that a middle-class orientation emerge but the stable stage would seem to be a necessary step in most cases for the development of a middle-class orientation.*

Other variations in the subculture of workers exist. Religious, ethnic, educational, and regional factors are important in producing deviations from the pattern we have described.

The Stable Style as Goal

Explicitly as well as implicitly, many agents of educational and other institutions that deal with working-class and lower-class youth attempt to "middle-classize" them. When any effort is extended toward the juvenile delinquent, it is usually with this orientation. Such endeavors are largely a failure because the middle-class outlook is alien to the experiences, prospects and values of these youth. Possibly there is a better

chance of emphasizing working-class values; for example cooperation—as happens in group therapy—rather than vocational success in middle-class terms. We recognize that it is not easy to develop some of the working-class values but they are probably much easier to develop than the middle-class ones. In addition, emphasis on the former may develop a more favorable attitude on the part of the youth to both the institution and its agents than does the insistence on the middle-class values.

A basic value question is involved here: Do we attempt to make the middle-class style a model for all to follow? Or do we adopt a rigid cultural relativity position that the lower class has a right to its way of life regardless of the social effects? Or do we attempt to develop what appear to be the most positive elements, from the point of view of society and the individuals involved, of the styles of life closest to them? While we have some doubts about the answer, the possibility of the stable working-class style as the goal adds a new dimension to a deep problem that deserves more forthright scrutiny than it has received.

Our attempts at interpreting working-class life will undoubtedly prove inadequate. But we are certain that without an attempt at analyzing the contexts and the genotypes of working-class behavior and attitude, the *description* (and there is faulty description) and interpretation of working-class life will remain a reflex of social scientists' changing attitudes toward the middle class.

14

CHARACTERISTICS OF THE LOWER-BLUE-COLLAR CLASS

Albert K. Cohen and Harold M. Hodges, Jr.

There are two prevailing approaches to the study and understanding of lower-class life today. One might be termed the culture of poverty approach, associated with the work of the late anthropologist Oscar Lewis and others. According to this view, the various social classes do not share a common value system, and many of the crucial values of the higher strata are not accepted by the lower strata. Lower-class culture is seen as playing a major role in keeping the poor where they are and contributing to a self-defeating vicious circle. Typical values of the lower class often mentioned (with implicit contrasts to middle-class patterns) include the inability to defer gratification, overwhelming apathy, low levels of aspirations, little emphasis on education, an orientation to security rather than risk, and the like. Such characteristics are perpetuated by being passed on from father to son, involving the lower class in a kind of unbreakable pathological chain that is transmitted as part of the learning and socialization process. This approach tends to see lower-class culture as the key to the problems of this class, and it is often argued that changes in values and culture are central to improvement in its condition. The emphasis tends to be on personal counseling, guidance, and other psychological techniques to attack what are considered to be self-defeating values and behavior patterns.

The other major approach to the study of lower-class life is less likely to concede the existence of a separate, autonomous value system which is primarily responsible for the condition of this group. This approach tends to emphasize the essential similarity in the values of all classes. To the extent that distinctive lower-class values are recognized, they are regarded mainly as adaptations of the values of the higher strata to the imperatives of lower-class life. That is, this perspective attempts to demonstrate how the conditions of life in the lower class, the inescapable facts of poverty, and the limited opportunity to escape from it, have created and sustained certain values. Many of these values, it is argued, are a logical response to the objective conditions of life in the lower class. Apathy, for example, can be an effective psychological protection against repeated failure. The often-condemned unwillingness of the lower class to defer gratification (to save or to plan) can be seen simply as a response to the unpredictability of life. During wartime, when life becomes as uncertain for all classes as it always is for the lower class, the philosophy of living for the moment suddenly becomes well-nigh universal.

According to this approach, what is keeping the lower-class man at the bottom is not so much his values as the conditions of his workaday life which inevitably produce

SOURCE: *Social Problems*, vol. 10, no. 4 (Spring 1963), pp. 303–8, 309, 310, and 315–34. Reprinted by permission of the authors and the Society for the Study of Social Problems.

certain cultural responses in an effort to cope with and adapt to the circumstances of failure and adversity. These values are perpetuated, not simply by transmission from father to son, but by the fact that the sons, in their own lives, are confronted with the same problems as their fathers before them and thus respond similarly. Remedial action implicit in this approach naturally stresses social rather than individual action, with the emphasis on changing the structure of social and economic opportunities for the lower class, with the expectation that values will eventually respond to changed material conditions.

It is this second approach that sociologists Cohen and Hodges are inclined to favor in their discussion of a group of lower-class persons in the San Francisco Bay area. First describing the setting of lower-class life, they go on to analyze distinctive values of the lower class, always attempting to account for these values in terms of the daily life experiences of the lower-class man himself.*

This paper deals with the characteristics of the "lower-blue-collar" or "lower-lower" class. (For brevity, we shall use the conventional abbreviations, "LL," "UL," etc., in referring to the various classes.) Our data are drawn from the findings of a comprehensive study of social class on the San Francisco Peninsula, under the direction of Harold M. Hodges. One purpose of the present paper is to contribute to our descriptive knowledge of the LL class. Its main purpose, however, is to suggest theory to account for some of the characteristics of that class.[1]

A complete and detailed report of all the findings obtained in the Peninsula research will be presented in a later

---

* For an introduction to the debate over the culture of poverty concept, see Oscar Lewis, "The Culture of Poverty," in *La Vida* (New York: Vintage Books, 1968), pp. xlii–lii; Walter B. Miller, "Lower Class Culture as a Generating Milieu of Gang Delinquency," *Journal of Social Issues*, 14 (April 1958), pp. 5–19; Herbert H. Hyman, "The Value Systems of Different Classes," in R. Bendix and S. M. Lipset, eds., *Class, Status, and Power*, 2nd ed. (New York: The Free Press, 1966), pp. 488–99. Critiques include: Charles A. Valentine, *Culture and Poverty: Critique and Counter-Proposals* (Chicago: University of Chicago Press, 1968); Elliot Liebow, *Tally's Corner: A Study of Negro Streetcorner Men* (Boston: Little, Brown, 1967); Robert Merton, "Social Structure and Anomie," in *Social Theory and Social Structure* (Glencoe, Ill.: The Free Press, 1957), pp. 131–60; S. M. Miller and Frank Riessman, "'The Culture of Poverty': A Critique," in *Social Class and Social Policy* (New York: Basic Books, 1968), pp. 52–66; Hyman Rodman, "The Lower Class Value Stretch," *Social Forces*, 42 (December 1963), pp. 205–15.

[1] This study resembles, in one way or another, those of (1) Knupfer, (2) Inkeles, (3) Walter Miller, and (4) S. M. Miller and Frank Riessman, all of whom are cited below. However, (1), (2), and (4) are based on data which have in turn been derived from numerous studies by different investigators on different populations. Furthermore, (1) is primarily concerned with description or portraiture; (2) is concerned with testing a set of inferences from theory; (3) is a brilliant attempt to characterize lower-class culture in terms of six "focal concerns" but does not deal systematically with their dependence upon current life conditions of the class; (4) is primarily concerned with the characteristics of the "stable working class." The present study is based on a single population; it is primarily concerned with the lower-lower class and with explanation; and our interpretations are frankly *post facto* attempts to make sense of our data. Reference must also be made to the comprehensive and well-known writings on the characteristics of the social classes by W. Lloyd Warner and A. B. Hollingshead. No attempt will be made to cite all these authors at every point where they might be relevant; their relevance is too pervasive.

publication by Hodges. In the present paper we shall be concerned only with those findings with respect to which the lower-blue-collar stratum differs, to a statistically significant degree, from all other strata. Even on this level we shall not attempt to be complete; otherwise the paper would be prohibitively long. We have not, however, knowingly omitted any findings that would tend to contradict our descriptive generalizations or to impair the plausibility of our interpretations. This, however, is a matter of judgment. When the full data are published, others will no doubt see some implications in them for the present subject that we do not. The reader will note, however, that the findings are in general consistent with previous research. Those that are peculiar to this study usually concern attributes or response patterns whose linkage to the lower-blue-collar class has not been the subject of previous research.

In the section immediately following we briefly describe the sampling and instruments. Then we set out what seem to us four crucial aspects of the workaday roles and experiences of the LL. Following that, we set forth what we believe to be the most important characteristics of the "typically LL" adaptation to these roles and experiences —important in the sense of setting the framework for the next and longest section of this paper, the presentation and interpretation of the research findings.

We assume that the LL's behavior and attitudes depend on his roles and experiences in a variety of ways, some of them relatively simple and direct, some complex and indirect. In this sense we are eclectic. The general emphasis in our interpretations, however, is on moving from the structurally patterned life conditions of the adult LL,

via a variety of processes or mechanisms, to the data. This contrasts with the characteristic emphases of two other approaches. One is to account for behavior and attitudes as consequences of class-typed child-rearing practices. For example, one might study the way "extrapunitiveness" depends upon child rearing, and the relationship of the relevant child-rearing practices to social class. In contrast, we would be interested in the way the characteristic problems, opportunities and expectations of the LL's workaday roles and relationships might conduce to a tendency to project blame outwards; we will assume without argument that if such tendencies are a natural outgrowth of the performance of lower-class roles, they will also acquire a certain amount of subcultural support and validation among lower-class persons, and will somehow become communicated, through one mechanism or another, in the child-rearing process.

The other contrasting approach is to start from a few master traits, tendencies, needs, or orientations that define an overall personality configuration, and to show how the data about behavior and attitudes make sense as manifestations or implications of such a configuration. We do not question that the several components or ingredients of personality, however they may be conceptualized, are accommodated to or integrated with one another in some sort of system; in fact, this mode of reasoning is implicit throughout this paper. Again, however, our *emphasis* is on the way *the configuration itself* is intelligible as a product of the life conditions. The configurationist or "basic personality structure" approach, while it maximizes sensitivity to the way differences in behavior depend on differences in the internal structure of personalities, may divert attention from the way those same differences in behavior may depend on differences in the situation of action. In short, although your "intropunitiveness" and my "extrapunitiveness" *may* reflect "deep" trends in our respective personalities, we start with no such assumptions, and we are interested in exploring *first* how these styles of imputing blame are respectively encouraged by the kinds of social relationships we are characteristically involved in.

Sampling and Instruments [2]

Primary sources of the data were six sets of self-administered questionnaires, three open-ended questionnaires, and one Rorschach schedule. Left with respondents by student interviewers, the questionnaires were designed to elicit information relating to approximately thirty basic variables.[3] These pertained to such diverse matters as infant training and child rearing, religious values, self concepts, status concern, career orientations, familistic loyalties, sex norms, leisure time activities, and various "attitudes" for which there were available standardized scales.

The project involved six waves of interviewing, and each respondent filled out one of the nine schedules utilized. Aside from the Rorschach and open-ended procedures, the questionnaire

items were largely limited to the forced-choice type.

Approximately 2600 male heads of families residing in three tiers of counties (San Francisco, San Mateo, and Santa Clara) comprised the sample. The sample in turn consisted of a series of sub-samples resident in contiguous sub-areas. Each sub-sample received one or more questionnaires. Within each sub-area every hundredth residence within every fifth census tract was contacted.[4] Responses to control items repeated in questionnaires administered to different sub-samples did not differ significantly in their distribution by social class. Nor did the responses of Negro and Mexican-American respondents to selected items differ significantly from the responses of non-ethnic respondents. On the basis of these preliminary tests, we did not deem it necessary to control for ethnicity on the remaining items. The rate of non-response (refusals) consistently ranged between 18 and 22 per cent in each tract.[5] Not-at-home respondents were eliminated from the population after two unsuccessful calls, and interviews were then obtained from the nearest adjacent households.

The rationale for the choice of this particular geographic area and use of such a cross-sectional technique was the desire to tap both an urban and a suburban population, and to test whether the response patterns by class differed

---

[2] This description of the data-gathering phase of the research has been kept as brief as possible. A fuller description of the instruments and procedures can be obtained by writing to Harold M. Hodges, Department of Sociology, San Jose State College, San Jose, California.

[3] These were derived from the most frequently posited class-linked traits in the literature (experimental and theoretical).

[4] In order to insure sufficient representation from each class level, a stratified random sampling procedure was employed for the final two interview waves.

[5] Slightly more than 50 per cent of the initial non-respondents filled out questionnaires in subsequent follow-up analyses; comparison of their questionnaire responses with those of the original respondents yielded no statistically significant differences.

in these two types of areas. Since no significant differences did obtain between subjects in the different communities sampled, it was decided to treat all the respondents as a single sample. The final sample was believed to be highly representative of the social class divisions encompassed by this area. (Although representativeness in occupational and educational terms was sought in the randomized selection of respondents and census tracts, the "class level" of each respondent was determined on the basis of a modified version of A. B. Hollingshead's "Two-Factor Index of Social Position." [6])

Class differentials in responses were assessed by means of the chi-square test. The .05 level of confidence was employed.

The LL's Life-Situation

SIMPLIFICATION OF THE EXPERIENCE WORLD

The LL has experienced a relatively narrow range of objects and situations and of perspectives from which to define, classify and evaluate them. In comparison with other strata, the various stages of the LL's career have not subjected him to expectations nor provided him with opportunities to move in a variety of social and cultural worlds, with correspondingly various roles, styles of living, aspirations and perspectives. His workaday roles entail less complex and heterogeneous role sets, less various and novel interests to be encountered and balanced, less diverse criteria and expectations to which he must be responsive. This is not true only of his experience world insofar as

it is directly shaped by his work roles. He is also relatively exempt from the expectation that he assume and he has fewer opportunities to assume "public service" roles and the perspectives that go with them. Not only his direct but also his vicarious experience is limited. His meager education, the relative inutility to his workaday roles of information about diverse, remote events, and the limitation of his circle of intimates, on and off the job, to people very like himself neither facilitate nor encourage vicarious encounters with other, contrasting worlds.

POWERLESSNESS

More precisely, we have in mind here "powerlessness in the universalistic-achievement sector," *i.e.,* in those interaction settings in which goods, services and status are dependent upon the assumption and performance of impersonal, functionally specific roles, insulated from claims based upon particularistic ties or membership in ascribed categories. Societies differ in the extent to which facilities and rewards are distributed in accordance with such impersonal mechanisms; our society approaches one pole. If we mean by power, in this context, the ability to manipulate such mechanisms to realize one's goals, the LL is relatively powerless. He is powerless because his bargaining power is weak: he is the most easily replaceable, the marginal utility of his contribution to the productive process is least, his skills are the least esteemed, and he has the least access to and control over strategically important information. He is powerless also because, as one moves down the status hierarchy in the work situation,

[6] A. B. Hollingshead, *Two-Factor Index of Social Position,* New Haven: privately printed, 1957.

the institutionalized definitions of the work role progressively narrow the range of autonomous decision and of aspects of the work situation that are subject to negotiation until, at the pole approached by the LL's position, the alternatives are limited to simple compliance, withdrawal, or rebellion.

Deprivation

By this we mean poverty of resources relative to felt needs and levels of aspiration. It cannot, of course, be taken for granted that deprivation in this sense is more sharply felt at the lower levels of the status hierarchy. Since the upper limits of the level of aspiration are, in principle, indefinitely expansible, it is possible to feel deprived at any level. Furthermore, there operates a countertendency to curtail the level of aspiration in accordance with the levels of realistic expectation. However, there is evidence, both from our own study [7] and from others,[8] that the LL is chronically more deprived, in our sense, than persons on other status levels. This felt or experienced deprivation is consistent with what we might expect, especially in a society such as ours. (a) Our culture stresses, to an un-

usual degree, both the right and the moral obligation of members of all classes to "better themselves," and the propriety of maximizing one's "universe of comparison," that is, the range of persons with whom one might legitimately compare himself. (b) Ours is an economy that is dependent, to an exceptional degree, upon mass markets; to a corresponding degree, vast energies and resources are directed to the stimulation and elevation of levels of aspiration. (c) Not only does our culture emphasize the meritoriousness of upward mobility; we do, as a matter of fact, have a relatively high rate of upward mobility from all class levels. This means that the LL, although his actuarial probabilities of upward mobility, measured either in income or status, may be small, has some knowledge of persons *starting from the same initial level* who have "gotten ahead." The significance of this lies here: Persons who are relatively removed from our workaday world and the groups with whom we identify will be relatively weak as reference objects. We ordinarily compare ourselves with people whom we perceive to be "like ourselves." But if those whom we perceive to be like ourselves come to acquire

[7] For example, more of the LL than of any other stratum answered "very much" or "somewhat" (rather than "not at all") to *all* the parts of the following question: "Do you feel that you have fallen short—or might fall short—of your hopes, dreams, and ideals in any of the following: (a) in obtaining the amount or kind of education (schooling) you desire (b) in doing the sort of work (job) you enjoy most (c) in living in the sort of home and neighborhood you had hoped for (d) in enjoying as happy a marriage and home life as you had dreamed of (e) in earning the amount of income (money) you had hoped to (f) in saving or setting aside enough money for the future (g) in making headway (or success) in your work (job or occupation) (h) in enjoying life as much as you had hoped you would."

[8] See Alex Inkeles, "Industrial Man: The Relation of Status to Experience, Perception, and Value," *American Journal of Sociology*, 66 (July, 1960), pp. 1–31 for a review of the relevant survey literature. For a review of studies focusing on work satisfaction, see Robert Blauner, "Work Satisfaction and Industrial Trends in Modern Society," Reprint No. 151, Institute of Industrial Relations, University of California, Berkeley, 1960, reprinted from Walter Galenson and Seymour M. Lipset, editors, *Labor and Trade Unionism*, New York: John Wiley and Sons, 1960.

larger shares of income, deference, and power, while we stay behind, it is difficult to preserve, without ambivalence, a stably low level of aspiration.

INSECURITY

By this we mean the irregular and unpredictable occurrence of deprivation. (By contrast, the inmate of a correctional institution may experience deprivation without corresponding insecurity.) No society and no social level is immune to the "aleatory element"— to sickness, death, disability, injury to person or property through "acts of God," entanglements with the law and all manner of unanticipated "trouble" —all making extraordinary demands upon one's resources. But insecurity, as distinct from chronic deprivation, besets the life of the LL to a greater degree than it does the members of other strata. (a) The probability of occurrences, such as those enumerated, making extraordinary demands upon his resources is greater. (b) His resources are more meager, they are more rapidly expended to meet current needs, and hence there is less left over to deal with "emergencies." (c) His resources, such as they are, are more subject to unpredictable loss or diminution, because of the instability of his job and because of the paucity of alternative or supplementary sources of income. (d) Our society has, to be sure, established roles and structures to cope with the aleatory element: medicine, public and private charities, unemployment agencies and unemployment compensation, social work, etc. However, these services too are administered through functionally specific roles constrained by legislative and institutional requirements. Either the services must be paid for, or

the availability of "free" services to which one has legitimate title depends upon his ability to move knowledgeably and skillfully through impersonal and bureaucratic channels. The LL, because of the simplification of his experience world, lacks the requisite knowledge and skills and consequently assurance and optimism, and the very instrumentalities of his society that are consciously designed to alleviate his insecurity are often awkward and cumbersome for him to manipulate.

The Lower-Blue-Collar Adaptation

The task of the LL is to evolve a way of life that will reduce his insecurity and enhance his power in ways that do not depend on achievement in the universalistic sector and on command of a rich and sophisticated variety of perspectives. He can do this by forging a network of relationships, with people similarly circumstanced, that is in some ways like a mutual insurance scheme. People linked by such a network provide one another with a sense of status and worth, and also with aid and support in time of need, without regard to fluency, leverage or merit in the formally organized world of work and among the anonymous incumbents of public bureaucracies. Such a network differs from a conventional insurance scheme in that the kinds of benefits to which one is entitled are not specified in advance by any kind of contract or enumeration but consist broadly of "help in time of trouble"; it differs also in that one's contributions to the scheme are not specified with respect to kind, quantity or periodicity but consist of "doing whatever he can" whenever another is in need.[9] If one has a sufficiently extensive network of such relationships, and he has honored his obligations in the past, there is probably someone to whom he can turn if he should ever need help in paying for an operation, meeting burial expenses, finding a place to live, evading a process server, or putting up the children until he is "back on his feet." Title to these benefits is not tied to incumbency of specific roles, approaches through prescribed channels, or conformity to legalistic requirements. On the contrary, the relationships are valued precisely because they are not hedged about by such conditions. In sum, the distinguishing characteristics of such relationships are that they are diffuse, reciprocal, durable, and particularistic. They will define for us a "solidary" relationship.

The LL will tend to move, so far as possible, within such a world of solidary familiars. Within this world he can move with some confidence, some security, some sense of trust, and with dignity. Outside this world he feels weak, uncertain, disparaged and distrustful. The tendency to classify people as either inside or outside this network of particularistic solidarities will, therefore, have a peculiar saliency for the LL...

Findings and Interpretations

FAMILY AND KINSHIP

We shall present our data on family visiting in tabular form, rather than merely summarize them in the text as will be our practice elsewhere in this paper, for reasons that will be apparent when we turn to the results of other studies.

As can be seen from Tables 1, 2 and 3, our LL subjects say they interact more with relatives both absolutely and also relative to their interaction with other categories. Furthermore, we found that our LL's relatives typically live nearby; almost one-half—in comparison to one-in-ten middle class subjects—claim close relatives living within a four-block radius of their own dwellings. This propinquity of kin obtains whether the LL is a long-time resident of his neighborhood or a recent migrant. At the same time, our data suggest that family life is more unstable and strife-ridden. The LL's are more likely to circle "2" or more in answer to our question: "Of your five closest friends, how many have had one or more marriages broken (by divorce, annulment, separation, or desertion)?" To the question, "What is (or was) the usual relationship between *wife* and mother-in-law?", the LL's more often choose one of the two responses (out of five) at the "negative" pole, *i.e.*, "extreme disharmony and friction" or "so much disharmony they don't even speak."

These data, so far as they go, are consistent with what we would expect in the light of the reasoning in the preceding section, although this reasoning would not require that the LL's have an *absolutely* higher rate of interaction with kin than the other strata. However, the implications of the findings of other studies are not so clearcut.

[9] See Donald E. Muir and Eugene A. Weinstein, "The Social Debt: An Investigation of Lower-Class and Middle-Class Norms of Social Obligation," *American Sociological Review*, 27 (August, 1962), p. 538.

TABLE 1. Item: "Roughly how many times *a month* do you (husband and wife) visit: neighbors ....; relatives ....; other friends ....?"

Stratum	N	Mean visits (relatives) per month
Upper middle	100	2.07
Lower middle	223	3.36
Upper lower	231	3.30
Lower lower	97	4.06

P: LL vs. UL < .001; LL vs. all < .001

TABLE 2. Item: "Who are the people you have over to your home (for parties or night-time visits) *most* frequently or often (check one): (a) neighbors; (b) relatives; (c) friends from work; (d) friends you've met elsewhere?"
N's responding:

Stratum	(a) "Neighbors"	(b) "Relatives"	(c) "Friends (work)"	(d) "Friends (elsewhere)"	Totals	% (b)
UM	12	18	24	59	113	16
LM	5	15	21	31	72	21
UL	16	49	12	42	119	41
LL	6	24	2	9	41	59

P for Response "b" (Relatives) only: LL vs. UL < .01; LL vs. all < .001

TABLE 3. Item: "Of your *four* closest friends who live in this area—those you most often have over to your home or whom you visit—how many are *relatives* (of either husband or wife): none ....; one ....; two ....; three ....; all four ....?"

Stratum	N	Mean	Per cent answering "3" or "all"
Upper middle	144	0.65	22
Lower middle	285	0.81	28
Upper lower	135	1.28	42
Lower lower	101	1.70	56

P: LL vs. UL = .05; LL vs. all = .001

PARTICIPATION IN VOLUNTARY ASSOCIATIONS

Consistent with the findings of other studies,[10] the LL participated least in voluntary associations. He *belonged* to fewer organizations including the fraternal, church-related and trade-union associations in which his UL counterpart participated relatively heavily, and he was the most likely to *attend* no organization meetings at all. (In general,

[10] The literature is reviewed in Charles R. Wright and Herbert H. Hyman, "Voluntary Association Memberships of American Adults: Evidence from National Sample Surveys," *American Sociological Review*, 23 (June, 1958), pp. 284–294.

differences in participation between LL and UL were greater than those between UL and LM.)

We may suppose that people invest their energies in such participation for two sorts of reasons: first, because they feel that they have a stake in the goals of the organization and that their own participation is instrumental to the attainment of those goals and, second, because they derive satisfaction from the social relationships that they enjoy by virtue of participation. On both these counts, the LL's motivation to participate should be expected to be low.

Voluntary organizations characteristically, although in varying degrees, are concerned with the affairs of a larger community. To be able to appreciate these concerns assumes an ability to envisage events relatively remote from the immediate concrete situation and a relationship between such events and one's own destiny. The severe limitation of the experience world makes it difficult for the LL to think in these terms. In comparison to other strata, his image of the world outside his immediate concrete situation is fragmentary, uncertain, and obscure. Except in the case of organizations like labor unions, where the payoffs are relatively immediate, direct and tangible, it is difficult for him to visualize the relationship between the goal-directed activities of the organization and his own interests. And finally, as we shall argue below, even though he values the goals of the organization and believes in giving it generalized "support," he does not feel that his influence within the organization is great enough that his active participation would make any important difference in how things turn out.

The satisfactions that derive from participation itself consist largely of respect and deference, which in turn are linked to the exercise of power, the occupation of honorific positions, and the quality of performance of one's organizational roles. These latter, in turn, rest upon the possession of relevant skills and personal qualities: knowledge about the goals of the organization and the aspects of the larger social scene that are relevant to the attainment of those goals; fluency in discussion and argumentation; special combinations of discipline, restraint, initiative and sensitivity that are necessary to perform successfully in committee operations; certain technical skills: parliamentary, clerical, bookkeeping, fiscal. These are the same kinds of skills and personal qualities that the LL, in comparison to other strata, has the least opportunity to acquire, cultivate and practice in the world of work and the universalistic-achievement sector.

We should expect rather, as we have argued, that the LL will seek the attainment of his goals, whatever they may be, and the satisfactions of social interaction through a network of particularistic, highly personal relationships, and assume a "passive," "apathetic" attitude toward involvement in relatively formal organizations whatever their goals. It is of interest that Dotson,[11] who also finds the lower class to be less involved in voluntary associations, points out (1) that they *are* very much involved in active forms of participation with kin and close-knit non-kin cliques, and (2) that where they *are*

[11] Floyd Dotson, "Patterns of Voluntary Association Among Urban Working-Class Families," *American Sociological Review*, 16 (October, 1951), pp. 687–693.

involved in voluntary associations, it is with the least formal—e.g., athletic and church-related groups.

PREFERENCE FOR THE FAMILIAR

One of the clearest outcomes of this study is an image of the LL as one who is reluctant to meet new people and new situations, to form new social relationships, and above all to initiate interaction with strangers. On the contrary, he values and seeks out, more than anybody else, the routine, the familiar, the predictable. Our findings on this matter are worth reporting rather fully because of the light they add to current controversy about the meaning of "other-directedness" and about where, if anywhere, among the various social strata this property principally resides.

> LL's more often agreed with the following statements: "I am not the sort of person who enjoys starting a conversation with strangers on a bus or train"; "It is easiest not to speak to strangers until they speak to you"; "I don't enjoy going to large parties where there are many people I don't know"; "[I much prefer] sticking with my old friends" [to making new friends]; [main reason doesn't want to change job:] "having to get acquainted with new people"; "I find it hard to 'warm up' to most of the people I meet—to feel close to them and enjoy their company." Our instruments also included Rorschach items and some open-ended questions. Unfortunately, the Ns on these instruments were too small to permit separate analysis of the LL and UL responses. These were, accordingly, combined, but some of the results do seem pertinent and worth reporting. Rorschach responses of combined-lower-class subjects were most often interpreted, on blind reading: "finds it especially trying to ad-

> just to new people and new situations." To the open-ended question, "What things bother you most in everyday life?", these subjects most often answered to the effect that things and people are too unpredictable, they prefer the routinized and familiar. To the question: "who do you prefer as friends," they most often answered "relatives" and "neighbors."

It seems clear that this neophobia does not express an *indifference* to "popularity" and "acceptance." In this respect, the LL is at least as "other-directed" as any of the other strata:

> LL's most strongly agreed with the statements: "One of the most important things that can be taught a child is how to get along with others—how to mix well, make friends easily, and be popular"; "It is more worthwhile to be popular, well-liked, and friendly than it is to get ahead in the world at the risk of making enemies and being disliked"; "It is difficult, when in a crowd of strangers, not to be concerned about how I look to them—about the sort of impression I am making." When asked to note the "things in life which worry you most," LL's and UL's combined most often mentioned things akin to "being well-liked by fellows at work," or "by others."

The LL is not the citadel of old-fashioned "inner-directedness":

> LL's agree most often: "If a person has strong but unpopular likes or dislikes, he should keep them to himself instead of letting others know how he feels"; "It is hard for me to speak out and say what I think if I have to run the risk of being taken for an 'oddball' or character."

The hypotheses most consistent with *all* of the foregoing findings are these: the LL cares greatly what others think of him; he lacks confidence in his ability to say and do "the right things" in encounters with strangers; he is therefore anxious and uncomfortable in such encounters; and he seeks comfort and security in a circle of "old-shoe" relationships. His description of the qualities he values in friends *and in himself* is consistent with the foregoing.

> He agrees most often that "the personality he admires most in others is 'strong, quiet, calm.' " (More often than members of any other stratum, he tells us that the movie actor he most admires is John Wayne.) To open-ended questions, LL's and UL's combined most often list as qualities they would most like to have in their closest friends: "quiet," "calm," "easy-going," "not loud"; and as qualities they would most like to have in themselves: "quiet," "calm," "steady," "reliable."

In short, the LL likes people (and presumably his friends like people) who don't "rock the boat," who don't make excessive demands upon a limited capacity to shift perspectives and adopt new roles.

This relative inflexibility of role-taking, which is implied in the simplification of the LL's experience world, would seem to be central to the entire pattern of response. Indeed, the LL agrees most often with the statement: "I find it difficult to 'change my personality' easily when talking with various sorts of people." This discussion is, in a way, an extension and documentation of the theme of the preceding sections, the dependence of the LL upon kin and old friends. . . .

ANTI-INTELLECTUALITY

The LL expressed least admiration of intellectuals, professors, writers and artists. Typically, indeed, he treated them with disdain or suspicion. From lists of occupations he was least likely to choose occupations in these categories as representing what he would want to be if he had to start life over again, or to list them among the four occupations he would rate highest in prestige. Those who expressed a hope that their sons or daughters might go to college were more interested than were the other levels in the practical, financially remunerative aspects of education as compared to its esthetic or intellectual aspects. LL's most disliked symphonic, ballet and operatic music. They most strongly agreed that the country would be better off if people tried to "be more 'down to earth' and less intellectual and 'high-brow.' " They were most likely to indicate that they "would probably be deeply hurt" if they "were to learn that friends or acquaintances secretly thought they were 'too intellectual' (high-brow or 'egghead')." They most strongly agreed that "Our government would be sounder and better run if there were fewer intellectuals involved in it and more hard-headed, down-to-earth businessmen." They reacted most negatively to what, from their standpoint, are "highbrow" television programs (quiz shows, plays, panels).

It would seem natural that people should be distrustful of what they do not understand, disdainful of skills they do not possess, and threatened by modes of reasoning and interaction in which they cannot participate creditably. The more general formulation that underlies these assumptions is that people tend to disvalue standards of evaluation whose application would result in the disparagement of the self. This interpretation of the LL's anti-intellectuality would seem to fit well with the general argument of this paper. It is also likely that art and intellectuality are most disdained in the lower classes because these classes are most preoccupied with masculinity—indeed, according to Walter Miller "masculinity" is one of the "focal concerns" of "lower-class culture"—and art and intellectuality are tainted with connotations of femininity.

Some might argue that the association between class and anti-intellectuality, although real, depends in turn upon certain parameters of the American cultural scene: (1) American culture as a whole has a certain "practical," utilitarian, anti-intellectual bias, and in certain Old World cultures men of learning command much higher respect, even in the lower classes, than in the United States. (2) The sex-role symbolism that attaches to art and intellectuality is, if not peculiarly American, especially strong in our society. We will not examine the merits of these contentions here. Any more thorough consideration of the issue would, however, have to take into account Lipset's vigorous criticism of the view that intellectuals are less esteemed in the United States than in other countries.[12] . . .

Authoritarianism

Our LL subjects agreed most strongly with Adorno F-Scale items. This scale is often interpreted as a scale of authoritarianism. Needless to say, this interpretation is open to some question. However, Christie, in his critical re-examination of the literature bearing on the behavioral correlates of F-Scale scores, concludes that "the reports available on social behavior of individuals accepting these items indicate that they behave in a manner which is characteristically authoritarian." He also concludes that "the relevant research indicates a sizeable negative correlation between scores on the F-Scale and various measures related to socio-economic status."[13] In any case, we wish to emphasize that the face implications of the F-Scale for authoritarianism are less ambiguous for some items than for others, and that our imputation of authoritarian trends is based primarily upon items that emphasize rather explicitly the necessity for leaders to be strict, the division of people into two classes: the weak and the strong, the importance of obedience and respect for authority in children, and a belief in harsh and punitive repression of deviants. The last point is additionally supported by several other items in our questionnaire not derived from the F-Scale. Finally, mention should be made of Lipset's comprehensive review of the evidence, from a variety of sources, of "working-class authoritarianism."[14]

We offer three distinct, but complementary, kinds of interpretations.

1. The first is essentially that offered by Lipset,[15] who argues, in effect, that "working-class authoritarianism" is not so much a primary commitment to authoritarianism *per se,* as it is a special manifestation of a more general characteristic. To wit, "other things being equal, [the working class] will prefer

---

[12] Seymour M. Lipset, *Political Man,* Garden City: Doubleday and Company, 1960, pp. 323 ff; Seymour M. Lipset and Reinhard Bendix, *Social Mobility in Industrial Society,* Berkeley and Los Angeles: University of California Press, 1960, p. 111.

[13] Richard Christie and Marie Jahoda, eds., *Studies in the Scope and Method of "The Authoritarian Personality,"* Glencoe: The Free Press, 1954, pp. 149–194.

[14] Seymour M. Lipset, *Political Man,* Garden City: Doubleday and Company, 1960, pp. 97–130.

[15] *Ibid.*

the least complex alternative." This preference would seem to follow from the simplification of the experience world. People who, by comparison with members of other social levels, have had little occasion and less necessity to assume, on any given issue, a variety of perspectives, to envisage a variety of possibilities, to take into account and attempt to balance a variety of interests might be expected to develop a characteristic style of decision-making —namely, to proceed directly to simple, unqualified, easily comprehended solutions. And the least complex alternative is usually the authoritarian one. It means you have to answer only one question: Whose word goes? There is no simpler way of resolving an issue.

2. However, the experience world of the LL is not only simpler than that of the other strata; it is also qualitatively different in respects that, it seems to us, must make a difference in the ways power and authority are perceived and evaluated. In the world of work above all, but not only there, the LL is most likely to confront others in the role of a subordinate subject to express demands. These demands are likely to have the following characteristics. (a) They are formulated in relatively concrete terms: *"Do this"*—rather than in terms of broad goals, to be implemented in ways that commend themselves to his discretion. He is not expected, to the same degree as members of other strata, to "exercise judgment," which means to weigh and balance alternatives, consider the circumstances, and reconcile conflicting principles. (b) The demands are less likely to be justified or rationalized to him in terms of more ultimate goals or principles. The authority of those who issue the demands is supposed to be enough to legitimize them. (c) The alternatives, when confronted with these demands, are few: compliance or defiance or, in some cases, withdrawal.[16]

A job inevitably involved a hierarchy of authority. There was always a boss, and it was accepted shipyard dogma that it was the worker's place to do what the boss commanded and to do it without hesitation or question. "What a fellow learns on his first job, if he learns nothing else," I was told by an old-timer "is to take the boss's orders and to keep his own mouth shut. I used to try and tell a boss if I knew he was wrong about a job, but after being tossed out on my ear a time or two, I soon learned better. Now I do the thing just like the foreman tells me to, even if I'm sure it will get torn down and have to be put in different when the real big shots come snooping around. The way I figure it, that's the boss's worry and none of mine." (p. 397)

Archibald is at pains to point out that, although servility toward the boss was accompanied by much antagonism and criticism, nobody ever questioned the legitimacy or inevitability of the *system,* of the idea of an hierarchical structure of power and privilege.

In short, role relationships are more likely for the LL to be defined in terms of somebody responsible for making decisions and giving orders, and somebody responsible for carrying them out. Putting it more bluntly still, the decisive question in "real life" situations is,

[16] See the excellent review by Blauner, *op. cit.,* pp. 342–349, of the literature on the patterning of control, responsibility, autonomy, etc., in working-class occupations. See also Katherine Archibald, "Status Orientations among Shipyard Workers," in Reinhard Bendix and Seymour M. Lipset, eds., *Class, Status and Power,* Glencoe: The Free Press, 1953, pp. 395–403, for a vivid description of attitudes toward authority among shipyard workers.

for the LL, more than for anybody else, "Who's boss?" We are assuming that the pervasiveness of this kind of experience in the social world of the LL produces a generalized set or disposition to conceptualize issues and to resolve them in terms of power and authority.

3. One other consideration seems to us relevant: the degree of symbolic fusion of *status* and *authority*. By "status" we understand here the show of respect by one party to another. People who exercise authority or power over others are likely to command respect from the others as well, but the extent to which these are correlated as incidents of the same role relationships can vary considerably. The ability psychologically to differentiate between status and authority or power should vary, presumably, with the extent to which they are, in one's experience, *de facto* fused or differentiated.

In comparison to the world of the blue-collar class, and especially the lower-blue-collar class, the world of the middle-class person is more likely to be one in which differentials of status are not associated with corresponding differences in authority. The whole sphere of the learned professions, for example, and the sphere of "technical staff" in industry, government and commerce is a sphere of relatively high status accorded to people with prized abilities or people who occupy valued roles, but who do not necessarily exercise conspicuous authority over others. To put it differently, their ability to command respect does not depend upon or correlate strongly with their ability to issue commands, to inflict sanctions or grant indulgences. This dissociation in actual experience facilitates the conceptual distinguishing between authority and status.

This is less true in the lower-class world—or the same world from the perspective of the lower-class person. The status-graded relationships most familiar to the LL—e.g., relationships with employers, landlords, work supervisors, law enforcement officials—are more likely to be correlated with gradations of power. Although the powerful are not always respected, they can usually exact at least the outward show of respect; and the respected are usually powerful. Under these conditions we should expect a less complete differentiation of power and status, on a symbolic or perceptual level, than in the middle class. This means that status without power will be felt as dubious and uncertain status. To deny the right of a person to exercise power will be felt as a denial of status. Contrariwise, the effective exercise of power, the show of compliance by others, will be the most effective validation of status.

If this is so, we should expect that the LL, to a greater extent than other classes, will tend to measure status by power, and to validate his own claim to status, where he feels entitled to it, by asserting a claim to power. An illustration will be provided in our discussion in the section on "patriarchy."

Insofar as this mechanism operates, it should produce "authoritarianism" in the specific sense of *a tendency to take a person's power as a measure of his status;* and, as a psychological corollary of this, a tendency to claim power in proportion to one's claim to status.

INTOLERANCE

Although the study's LM stratum proved least forgiving of violations of what we may call "conventional morality"—*i.e.,* hetero-sexual misconduct, drunkenness and swearing—the LL was most harsh in condemnation of other sorts of deviants: the atheist, the homosexual, the "un-American," the radical, the artist-intellectual. But it was above all toward the ethnic minority group that he directed his animosity. Whether assessed in terms of a modified Bogardus ethnic distance, the Adorno "E-Scale," or standardized measures of ethnic and racial intolerance, this lower-blue-collar antipathy was consistently apparent. We suggest two mechanisms to link this with the life conditions of the LL stratum.

1. The LL's tendency, of which we have already spoken, to the simplification of alternatives would include, with reference to the world of social objects, simplified categorization in terms of in-group and out-group, "we" and "they," such that people fall unambiguously in the one or the other. In addition to a general tendency to categorize dichotomously and unequivocally, a further implication of the preference for the simple is a reduction of incongruity, in the sense of the assignment of people to a "favorable" category on one modality and to an "unfavorable" category on another. Such assignment implies seeing the same people from different perspectives, which, we have argued, does not come so easily to the LL as to middle-class persons.

2. In our remarks on "anti-intellectuality" we offered the proposition that "people tend to disvalue standards of evaluation whose application would result in the disparagement of the self." Therefore, where a culture provides a set of possible criteria for evaluating persons, sub-groups will tend to develop subcultural emphases on those criteria on which they fare relatively well and to de-emphasize those criteria on which they do poorly. They will grasp, so to speak, at status straws, and make much of them. We have also said that the LL's claim to status on the basis of universalistic, achievement-related criteria are weak, relative to the claims of the other strata. It follows that the LL will tend to de-emphasize these criteria and to place relatively more emphasis on the "ascriptive" components of social identity, like race, nationality, and ethnicity. If this line of reasoning is correct, the "prejudice" of the LL is not *in spite of* the "American creed" but partly *in consequence of* it. The "American creed" implies one kind of criterion for measuring the worth of a person. The more consistently it is applied, the worse does the LL fare, and the greater his tendency to seek *other* bases for differential evaluation in our cultural tradition, bases that will yield different results and go part way toward redressing the balance. This would then be a special case of a component of a cultural value system generating behavior and attitudes incongruent with those same values.

Pessimism-Insecurity

"A body just can't take nothing for granted; you just have to live from day to day and hope the sun will shine tomorrow." No theme more consistently runs through the pattern of the LL's responses and distinguishes him from the others. In his view, nothing is certain; in all probability, however, things will turn out badly as they generally have in the past. The theme stands out most clearly in his agreement with Srole "Anomie" items—e.g., "Nowadays a person has to live pretty much for today and let tomorrow take care of itself"; "In spite of what some people say, the lot of the average man is getting worse, not better"; "It's hardly fair to bring children into the world with the way things look for the future"; and so on.[17]

From one point of view, there is nothing less problematical than this pattern of response. After all, we have described the LL as powerless, deprived, and insecure. Are not these responses of his simply a realistic recognition of his life situations and his life chances?

However, one could also argue as follows: The LL's world view is disproportionately black. After all, lots of LL's can and do, by steady work habits, self-discipline and frugality, achieve a higher and more dependable income, reduce their vulnerability to the aleatory element, move into the upper-blue-collar class, and, in general, render their own lives and prospects less bleak. The actual situation of the LL is, to be sure, an unhappy one, but this is determined only in part by his objective insecurity and powerlessness; it is also determined by his *adaptation to* that insecurity and powerlessness, by a style of life marked by improvidence, unsteady work habits, and other characteristics calculated to insure his continued occupancy of what Knupfer calls his "underdog" status. In short, his world view is not a realistic perception. It is, rather, a rationalization of failure and frustration that are attributable as much to his personal limitations as to his objective circumstances; it is also a self-fulfilling prophecy, for the belief motivates a style of life that insures the experience of failure and frustration.

It would be hard to prove that either the "pessimistic" or "optimistic" view of things is more realistic. It is true that some LL's do "make it," and often as a result of rational, disciplined effort. The LL has seen others "of his own kind" achieve what, from his perspective, is a tolerable situation of security and comfort. So there is an objective basis for "optimism." On the other hand, we have already remarked that the actuarial probability for any given LL to "better himself" is probably small; at any rate the probability that the pay-off will be commensurate with the effort and discipline is problematic. There is, then, an objective basis for "pessimism" as well.[18] Furthermore, if a LL makes the more optimistic assumption and the corresponding commitments of his slender resources to "bettering himself," and is *then* thwarted, the sense of disappointment, frustration, and pessimism can be even more poignant. It could be argued, then, that the "pessimistic" world view is also *adaptive* for most LL's, in that it tends to inhibit the development of levels of expectation that are likely to be disappointed, and therefore to protect them against the consequent frustration.

The LL's world view is also a defense against moral criticism. The assumption that it is possible to "better oneself" and that one's misfortune is self-inflicted and a sign of one's lack of moral fibre runs deep in the American cultural tradition. From the standpoint of many of his fellow citizens, including many of his "respectable" upper-blue-collar neighbors, the LL is a failure; his failure creates the presumption that he is morally inadequate; and his style of life provides his critics with "objective evidence" of his moral inadequacy. A view of the world in which

---

[17] For comparative data see Inkeles, *op. cit.*, pp. 18–31 ("The Mastery-Optimism Complex").

[18] Lipset and Bendix, *Social Mobility in Industrial Society*, Chs. VI and VII.

the role of chance is selectively noted and exaggerated both justifies his style of life and explains the distribution of the world's goods in ways that do not reflect on his moral adequacy.

If we are correct, then, we have all the essential terms of a vicious circle: (1) A set of life conditions characterized by powerlessness, deprivation and insecurity. (2) The adoption of a view of the world as bleak and uncertain, partly a matter of realistic perception and partly an adaptive protection against disappointment. (3) On the basis of this world-view, the adoption of a style of life characterized by "improvidence," etc. (4) In consequence of the style of life, the more certain recurrence of the experience of powerlessness, deprivation and insecurity. (5) A further intensification of the pessimistic world view, partly on the basis of the fact that things *did* turn out badly after all, and partly to protect the self against the criticism of having brought about one's plight through one's own moral defect.

MISANTHROPY

LL's, more than the members of any other stratum, are cynical and distrustful. For example, disproportionate numbers of LL's "strongly agreed" with these Rosenberg Misanthropy items (which we cite, not because they come from a scale labelled "Misanthropy" but because of their *prima facie* connotations): "many people are out to cheat or outwit others, and if you don't watch yourself, people are liable to take advantage of you"; "nine people out of ten are basically selfish and more inclined to look out for themselves than they are to help others"; "you have to be careful with strangers; very few can be trusted and many are

inclined to take advantage of your weakness and generosity." This "people are no good" theme was substantiated by responses to several other items. Economic and occupational success, they most often agreed, is accomplished by "friends or connections," "luck or chance," "pull or manipulating," or "cheating or underhanded dealing" (in contrast to "daring and taking risks," "education" or "hard, day-by-day work"). They most often agree that television repairmen, politicians, doctors, auto mechanics, butchers, union officials and businessmen are not trustworthy. The LL's image of the world resembles a jungle. We suggest two sources of this image.

1. The more obvious of these sources is simply realistic perception of the fact that he *is* an object of exploitation. The LL is, by virtue of his relative powerlessness, the least able of all our subjects to protect himself against exploitation. Among persons, each of whom has something valuable to withhold from the other, or is in a position to inflict some damage upon the other, or is in a position to invoke the agencies of the law for the protection of his rights and the redress of grievances, a certain mutual consideration tends to prevail and the more obvious types of fraud and coercion to be tempered. In brief, when the powerful deal with the powerful, it pays, within limits, to observe the rules of the game to which they claim to subscribe, and the assumption that people can be trusted and that they mean what they say is a more realistic assumption than when the powerful deal with the weak. Furthermore, among those who are least powerful—whose own resources are least and who enjoy only fitful and imperfect protection under the ragged edges of the umbrella of justice—the

vulnerability to force, fraud and exploitation of all kinds *from members of their own stratum* is great. Negro neighborhoods in American communities in which people are left to settle their own disputes, as long as they do not infringe upon the interests of white people, provide a particularly clear-cut example. Although the LL's image of the world no doubt often exaggerates the component of malice and treachery, his cynicism and distrust cannot be dismissed as "projective," in contrast to a more "realistic" view of people as good and benevolent.

2. The foregoing interpretation is couched in the crudest terms of power and the presence or absence of countervailing power. We suggest also that this "misanthropy" reflects a certain moral attitude toward the world.

The middle-class world—the world of bureaucratic office, business, government and the professions—is a world whose effective functioning depends very largely upon the operation of a more-or-less universalistic ethic. It is a world where relationships among people must be governed very largely by expectations attached to functionally specific roles, without regard to the extent or the depth of their relationships to one another in other roles and in other contexts. Those whose status, livelihood and fortunes depend most profoundly upon their achievements within such a system will have a common stake in supporting such a universalistic ethic; they will themselves feel most bound by it and most expect others to be bound by it; and, as a matter of fact, their experience in their dealings with one another will testify to the existence of such an ethic.

The LL, by contrast, has a relatively small investment in the "universalistic-achievement" sector of society. It is the

sector in which he fares poorly, in which he moves awkwardly, which he can least exploit to his own advantage, and which provides him with little security. We have argued above that security, for him, lies in a close circle of people he can trust, people whose obligations are *to him as a person* and not as an incumbent of a functionally specific role. The LL's stake, therefore, is in a morality of particularistic loyalties and reciprocities.

What we are suggesting is that "misanthropy" is not merely a picture, in the mind of the LL, of the universe as a kind of amoral, Hobbesian jungle, but a way of classifying people that is implied in a particularistic morality. For the LL, a decisive feature of his world is that it consists of friends and strangers. Your friends will stand by you, as you are obligated to stand by them. Strangers are not to be trusted (although it is assumed that they too are bound by obligations to *their* friends), nor do you expect them to trust you. But most people are strangers. In sum, we are suggesting that what our research instruments may have tapped is not a unitary, pervasive, characterologically rooted distrust of all humanity, but *one* facet of the LL's particularistic morality.

It is interesting that, notwithstanding his misanthropy, however we choose to interpret that expression, the LL is also *credulous* in the sense that he most readily accepts the written or printed word at its face value. Of all our subjects he least often indicates that he finds it hard "to believe in the truth of most television commercials I see" or the truth of magazine or newspaper advertisements or television commercials stating that "most doctors agree that Brand X is best." It is one thing to feel a generalized distrust in human beings, their motives and their claims; it is another to form an attitude on a specific claim or message *where one has few independent criteria for evaluating the content of the message, little awareness of specific alternatives, and little disposition to weigh evidence.* It is one of the best established findings of social psychology that "suggestibility" and "gullibility" are maximized when the cognitive field is "unstructured," *i.e.,* when the actor has no independent frame of reference for forming a judgment. Needless to say, the availability of such independent frames of reference depends heavily on the richness of one's direct and vicarious experience.

EXTRAPUNITIVENESS

This caption suggests another perspective from which to view the findings we have discussed under "pessimism" and "misanthropy." In the psychological literature, the term suggests a fund of aggression that accumulates in response to frustration, and which has to "go somewhere," either inward or outward. People "high on extrapunitiveness" characteristically "handle their aggression" by "directing it outwards"; intropunitive people direct it inwards. We make no assumption here about the psychohydraulics of aggression. We are concerned, however, with the visible datum that, when things go wrong, some people more characteristically "pin responsibility" on themselves, others on circumstances outside themselves. This becomes fairly explicit in the disproportionately frequent agreement of LL subjects with the statement: "When things go wrong at

home or work I find it easy to blame others instead of myself." We have few items that go to the issue as straightforwardly as this, but certainly our data as a whole strongly suggest that LL's find it easier to impute the fault for faulty outcomes to something outside the self.

We have already referred to the function that such a view of things may perform by helping to protect the self against criticism. However, it is important to point out that this "extrapunitiveness" of the LL may also "reflect social reality" in a fairly direct way—the social reality in this case being the actual distribution of authority and responsibility when people come together in inter-class relationships.

We take our lead from Henry and Short, *Suicide and Homicide.* Where blame will be perceived to lie, they suggest, depends on the objects to which it may legitimately be imputed. This, in turn, depends on "the strength of external restraint over behavior."

As the role of others in the determination of behavior increases, the right to blame others for unfortunate consequences also increases. When the role of the self in determining behavior is great relative to the role of others, the self must bear responsibility for the consequences of behavior.[19]

In contrast to lower-class persons, middle-class persons are more likely to be required by their roles to relate to others either as superordinates, as colleagues, or as independent operators. The important thing about these roles is that the expectations that attach to them are not merely expectations of conscientious performance of detailed assignments received from others, but

---

[19] Andrew F. Henry and James F. Short, Jr., *Suicide and Homicide,* Glencoe: The Free Press, 1954, p. 103.

that they are expectations that one will, without minute directives, close supervision, or threats of punishment, exercise good judgment, make appropriate decisions, and carry them out. In short, one is expected to provide his own discipline and assume responsibility for his decisions and their consequences. The legitimacy of one's claims to middle-class roles rests, as a matter of fact, largely upon the claim —albeit an implicit one—that one is capable of such initiative, decision, self-direction and self-discipline. To assert such a claim, however, is to deny to oneself the right to blame others for things that go wrong.

As we have said under "Authoritarianism," the typical roles of the LL require that he take not only his cues but his directives from others. More important in the present context, he has a *right* to clear, explicit and detailed instructions and, when he is done, to "await further orders." What he has to do, when he is to do it, when he is through, how his work is to be coordinated with that of others are, in fact and as a matter of legitimate expectation, largely determined by others. He is perceived, and he tends to perceive himself, as the instrument through which other people's decisions are implemented. An important corollary is that successful or socially valued outcomes of his labors are likely to be credited to the wisdom or judgment of some superordinate echelon. In short, the expectations attaching to his roles facilitate for the LL, in a way that they do not for middle-class persons, the assignment of blame to others when things go wrong.

PATRIARCHY

Lower-blue-collar men agreed most often with the statement, "Men should make the really important decisions in the family." Let us take agreement with this statement as our operational definition of "patriarchy." We must then distinguish this from the actual, operative structure of decision and control in the home, for LL subjects also report that LL women actually take the major share of responsibility for budgeting, bill-paying and child-care —to a greater degree, in fact, than is true in the other class levels.[20]

Elizabeth Bott suggests that the inconsistency is only apparent and that the "patriarchal" sentiments of lower-class male "heads" are really expressive of a family with a rather rigid division of labor in which each parent has authority and responsibility in his own sphere. Her argument is especially interesting because it relates this division of labor to the kinds of social networks we discussed in the section on kinship.

. . . If both husband and wife come to marriage with such close-knit networks, and if conditions are such that the previous pattern of relationships is continued, the marriage will be superimposed on these pre-existing relationships, and both spouses will continue to be drawn into activities with people outside their own elementary family (family of procreation). . . . Rigid segregation of conjugal roles will be possible because each spouse can get help from people outside. . . . If husband and wife come to marriage with . . . loose-knit networks or if conditions are such that their networks become loose-knit after marriage, they must seek in each other

[20] There is another sense, which we shall not discuss here, in which the LL's are most "patriarchal": they agree most strongly with statements affirming that women are out of their place in the world of business and politics and that the proper place of women is in the home.

some of the emotional satisfactions and help with familial tasks that couples in close-knit networks can get from outsiders. Joint organization becomes more necessary for the success of the family as an enterprise.[21]

Therefore, Bott argues, the common tendency to describe the working-class family as both "male-authoritarian" (or "patriarchal") and as "mother-centered" is not paradoxical. They are, indeed, both, depending upon the functional area which one is attending to. James H. Robb comments on the disagreement as to who is the "real head" of the working-class family.

> . . . The disagreement seems to be based on a sharp division of labour between men and women and a difference of opinion as to which role is to be regarded as the more important. One consequence of the man's economic importance is that so long as he remains in work he can claim, if he wishes, almost complete exemption from all other tasks connected with the family. Again, it is essential for the well-being of the family that he should be kept as fit for work as possible. Therefore, he tends to get first consideration . . . in the comforts and amenities of the home. . . . On the other hand, his abdication from responsibility for activities within the home leaves his wife in a central position as far as closer relationships within the household are concerned.[22]

In any case, it is clear from these and other descriptions of lower-class family life that the lower class male is *not* a patriarch within the ordinary connotations of the term. At the same time we are left with a strong feeling that the repetition of the themes of "woman's place" and "the man is (or should be)

boss" expresses more than a simple recognition of a division of labor. It might be that if we had items that discriminated sentiments about the relative authority of husband and wife in different spheres, we would have obtained differences that are not revealed by responses in the form of agreement and disagreement with the "blanket" statement put to our subjects. Pending such more discriminating research, however, it seems to us reasonable to assume, on the basis of responses to our own questionnaire item and impressionistic reports of lower-class family life, that the LL male really feels that he *should be* the boss, the ultimate authority, in his household in a general and not a functionally circumscribed sense.

We suggest that, if there is any validity to our argument that status and power tend to be psychologically fused for the LL subject, the LL parent, and especially the male, will have a "compulsive" need to affirm, and from time to time to exert, his power in the household. The male will tend to equate respect for his role as husband and father with *compliance* with his will. This does not mean that he will attempt to run the household; he will leave that to his wife. But he will need from time to time to make a demonstration of his power, to be ascendant in a contest of will in order to reassure himself of his status. In most matters concerning the internal affairs of the household, however, effective power will be actually wielded by the wife, not because she would be more successful in a showdown, but because, by the husband's default, she is left in effective command most of the time. If the

[21] Elizabeth Bott, *Family and Social Network*, London: Tavistock Publications, 1957, p. 60.

[22] James H. Robb, *Working-Class Anti-Semite, A Psychological Study in a London Borough*, London: Tavistock Publications, 1954, p. 60.

arguments of Bott and Robb are supplemented by these considerations, it could take us much farther toward reconciling the facts concerning the *de facto* distribution of power in the LL household and what LL subjects say on questionnaires and in interviews.

Toughness

LL subjects were more "tough-minded" on selected items from Eysenck's T-Scale.[23] We are not here concerned, however, with interpreting scores on Eysenck's "T-factor," which are compounded from responses to 32 scale items. We limit ourselves to a consideration of three connotations of the term "toughness" which are sufficiently distinct to merit separate consideration and which are based on responses to both Eysenck and other items in our questionnaires.

1. There is "tough-mindedness" in the sense of subscribing to a "dog-eat-dog" ideology, expressed in agreement with this questionnaire item: "If a person hopes to get ahead in this world he can't help stepping on others' toes, and he can't let this bother him." This item is representative of several other items to the same effect, to all of which the LL agrees more frequently than do subjects of any other level. This is, of course, an aphorism, a formula, part of the LL's "vocabulary of motives," not necessarily a description of what he does, and it must be interpreted guardedly. There is good reason to believe that it is often qualified, implicitly because it is taken for granted, by a phrase to this effect: "excepting, of course, certain kinsmen and good friends." Interpreted in this way, it be-

comes another expression of the LL's particularistic orientation to the social universe, and there is little more that need be said that we have not said under our discussion of "misanthropy."

2. A second connotation is not so much a callous indifference to the woes of others as an ability to "take it," whether "it" is physical pain, suffering, or a sea of troubles. We have two items, with which the LL's most frequently agree, that seem to tap this sentiment: "A really strong man doesn't let his feelings or emotions show," and "One of the most important things that a teen-age boy should learn is how to 'take it' without crying." If men ever make virtues of necessity, we should certainly expect toughness in this sense to be accounted a virtue among the LL's. We expect this, however, not only because the occupational tasks of the LL require stamina, fortitude, and endurance, and because he is subject to deprivation and insecurity, but also because his value to those who depend on him—his fellow workers, his family, and friends—depends on his ability to "take it."

3. Finally, there is a third connotation of "toughness": a general posture of truculent self-assertiveness, defiance, "don't-push-me-around" touchiness. The LL's agree most frequently that "No really strong or manly man will let other people push him around." This kind of toughness is exaggerated and romanticized in many lower-class folk heroes and movie and TV criminals, who are eventually destroyed, to be sure, and whose toughness itself may be the instrument of their destruction; however, there is something about

[23] H. J. Eysenck, *The Psychology of Politics*, London: Routledge and Kegan Paul, 1954, Chs. IV and V and pp. 276–280; *The Structure of the Human Personality*, London: Methuen, 1953, Ch. VII.

their refusal to grovel to any man and their contempt for the trouble they invite that apparently elicits a kind of fascination and even admiration in their audiences. "Toughness," in this sense, is apparently equivalent to Miller's "autonomy," one of his six "focal concerns" of "lower-class culture." [24] However, we have also described the LL as "authoritarian," as tending to conceive of social relationships as naturally hierarchical, in which there is always somebody who dominates and somebody who is dominated. It may even be true, as Miller himself suggests, that the LL's overt insistence upon autonomy "runs counter to an implicit seeking out of highly restrictive social environments where rules, regulations, and edicts exert close control over all his behavior." [25] Perhaps this duality will seem less contradictory if we view the matter in the light of certain aspects of role theory.

Any set of people who share similar life conditions and who interact intimately with one another are likely also to develop characteristic common ways of classifying and symbolizing one another and themselves—*i.e.*, a role system. These categories or roles will not be random but will constitute a public codification of socially recognized ways of adapting to the characteristic life situations of the group and the problems of adjustment that they pose. Thus, in prisons there develop systems of argot roles, a classification of social types according to the way people adapt to the characteristic deprivations, frustrations and opportunities of the inmate world.[26] This set of roles is, *among people so circumstanced,* the psychologically salient set of possibilities in terms of which people may be coded, and therefore the set of selves and public identities from which people may choose.

We have said that one of the pervasive characteristics of the social world of the LL is hierarchically structured authoritarian relationships, in which the LL is confronted with more or less peremptory demands. It is distinctive of these relationships that they minimize the possibility of expressing individuality and achieving an identity through the exercise of responsible discretion or initiative. We would expect that the possible ways of dealing with such authoritarian relationships will constitute central concerns in the LL's world and that they will become embodied in a psychologically salient set of role possibilities.

We have already suggested two polar types of response to the authoritarian relationship. One is compliance, obedience, surrender of autonomy; in short, one can build a self around the role of the "good soldier." This is one of the ways the possibilities of the relationship can be exploited for the enhancement of the self, at the same time that it has the tangible gain of minimizing "trouble." The polar alternative to this is "toughness" in the sense in which we are now using it. This is the refusal to surrender autonomy, ranging from outright defiance to surly or sullen compliance, by which one serves public notice that one's will has not been broken.

[24] Walter B. Miller, "Lower-Class Culture as a Generating Milieu of Gang Delinquency," *The Journal of Social Issues,* 14, No. 3 (1958), pp. 12–13.

[25] William C. Kvaraceus, Walter B. Miller, *et al., Delinquent Behavior: Culture and the Individual,* Washington: National Education Association, 1959, p. 67.

[26] Gresham L. Sykes and Sheldon H. Messinger, "The Inmate Social System," in Richard A. Cloward, *et al., Theoretical Studies in the Social Organization of the Prison,* Social Science Research Council Pamphlet 15, New York: Social Science Research Council, 1960, Ch. I.

Whatever the gains of this role, it obviously has its costs; it invites "trouble." We therefore find also various compromises and combinations constructed out of the materials of compliance and resistance: putting up a show of resistance and allowing oneself to be overcome by superior force, or complying for the most part but occasionally "blowing up" in the face of some "provocation." Another possibility is "playing it cool" *i.e.*, compliance with authority but making it clear to one's self and one's peers that this compliance is purely expedient and does not rest on respect for authority or on ego-involvement in conformity. A closely related alternative, which fuses subtly into "playing it cool," is "conning" the powers that be—that is, disarming their suspicion by the show of compliance or deference, and exploiting the consequent trust. Of all these, the openly belligerent posture is perhaps the least common because it is the most dangerous, and perhaps for that very reason the most "heroic."

But the most common compromise of all, probably, is to *perform* in the style of one role but to talk in the style of another, in a muted or not-quite-serious way where it is dangerous, and more boldly when the situation permits. Much of the "toughness" of the LL and his insistence on autonomy is undoubtedly "tough talk" that is very different from his performance and that makes it possible for him to enjoy some of the gratifications of more than one pattern of adaptation to authority.

CONSUMPTION PATTERNS

The prevailing market value of the LL's car, television, and basic appliances averages almost 20 per cent higher than the average value of equivalent upper-blue-collar possessions, despite a median family income that is fully one-third lower. A number of explanations readily suggest themselves. However, the very surfeit of explanations should make one wary. Furthermore, the dangers of a middle-class ethnocentric bias, always great, are nowhere greater than here. The middle-class person's attitude toward the spending patterns of the LL is frequently a combination of patronizing amusement, moral indignation, envy, and resentment. It would be surprising if this attitude did not color the motivations that are imputed to the LL, or even distort the perception of the facts about spending themselves.

Perhaps the most popular explanation of the LL's spending is that it is a compensatory response to status insecurity. We are dealing here with that stratum whose claim to status in the larger social system on the basis of generally valued attainments or positions is weakest. A disproportionate investment of his slender resources in "loud," showy, expensive artifacts, especially those touted by the mass media, would be the most efficient "status equalizer." (A higher percentage of LL's own Cadillacs—no doubt mostly secondhand—than of any other level.)

An alternative line of thinking would suggest that the differences among the social classes are not as great as they appear to be. It could be that the important difference between the middle class, for example, and the LL, is that the middle class spends substantial amounts on innumerable details of their backdrops and accoutrements: clothes, cosmetics, car, house, lawn and garden, curtains, rugs, silver, objets d'art, gourmet foods, etc., and that they spend it for much the same reasons as the LL, but attribute this spending to taste and breeding. It could be that the LL, having so much less money to dispose of for "status spending," can get a larger net status dividend by concentrating his spending on a few expensive, highly visible objects, rather than by spending small sums on each of a larger number of "cheap," inconspicuous objects. In brief, it may be that the marginal status utility, so to speak, of the consumer dollar may be maximized in different ways depending on the total amount that is available to be expended.

There is no question but that possessions are enviable, and their display brings status. But the possibility also suggests itself that the "disproportionate" expenditure on "creature comforts" is not altogether an expression of striving for status or need for reassurance thereof. It could be also that it is a simple and logical implication of the LL's pessimistic world view that we have described. If one despairs of materially improving his status, if husbanding one's resources seems futile, if scrimping and economizing determine the future much less than do "the breaks," if nothing seems certain but the present, then the resources one has are "freed" to be spent in ways that promise immediate gratification. What the middle-class person might censor as "improvidence" might appear to the LL as a sensible way to live in an uncertain world.

Whatever explanation we favor, we must come to terms with the additional fact that the LL seems to have defaulted his pride in his home. With more "leisure" time available than any other stratum, he seldom effects the simplest of repairs or improvements, nor does he often boast of a garden or even a lawn. Certainly the "home" is a "status symbol" par excellence. If the LL is so preoccupied with status, why does he invest so little in this highly visible symbol? Why do the other classes, and notably the middle class, presumably less anxious about status, invest so much of both their money and their time in defining, beautifying, cultivating and improving the home? Let us speculate on this, at the cost of adding to our surfeit of hypotheses.

It may be that the contrast between the LL's valuation of cars and appliances *versus* his valuation of housing is a spurious contrast. In the case of cars and appliances we were speaking of an attitude toward the *purchase* of consumption goods; in the latter case, we were speaking primarily of an attitude toward the *care and husbandry* of property once acquired. It may be that the same "improvident" style of life—a low level of rational, deliberate, disciplined planfulness—expresses itself in *both* spending patterns *and* "care" patterns. Our data do not permit us to generalize about patterns of care regarding cars and appliances, but it may be that, were such data available, they would reveal the same casualness about care as obtains with respect to housing. On the other social levels, by contrast, what we may have is a generalized pattern of careful husbandry of property that expresses itself in housing but also in all other classes of possessions.

However, there is one further possibility that we cannot ignore. If the house, and especially its external visage, is a symbol, what precisely does it symbolize? Surely the house, to a greater degree than any other possession, symbolizes the status and the "personality" of the *family* that occupies it. It is a presentation of a *collective* self, of the common identity of the conjugal family. The more highly its members value this common identity to the exclusion of other identities, the more their self-conceptions are at stake in the public image and reputation of the conjugal unit, and the fewer the competing solidarities, the more willing they will be to lavish money and time and work on the preservation and enhancement of the visage they present in common. Where the conjugal family is seen as and is in fact a precarious entity we should expect a greater reluctance to invest so heavily in this presentation of the collective self.

We are not prepared ourselves to do more than offer these speculations. Hopefully they will provide the materials from which it may be possible to construct an adequate theory of the distinctive consumption patterns of the LL.

Cautions and Qualifications

1. This paper does not present a "portrait of the underdog." It is specifically concerned with the respects in which the LL *differs to a statistically significant degree* from the other strata. Our comparisons do not necessarily contrast a majority of the LL's with a majority of each of the other strata. Viewed from another perspective, many of the "characteristically LL" responses of this study would turn out to be differences in emphasis on a set of common cultural themes.

2. Our statistical treatment does not deal with the range of variation within the LL stratum, nor with the extent to which the same subjects are responsible for the differences obtained on different comparisons. Both for the sake of descriptive knowledge and of the advancement of theory, it would be useful also to investigate *patterns of adaptation within the same stratum*. It is entirely probable that we would find a number of distinct patterns or internally consistent response systems. These differences might represent alternative adaptations to the same circumstances, adaptations to differences in life conditions within the same stratum, or adaptations to the impact of the characteristically LL life conditions on different ethnic or other subcultures.

3. Had we concentrated on certain sub-groups within the LL stratum, or had we studied LL's in some other setting, our findings might have turned out somewhat differently. For example, much of our discussion has concerned the relationship between characteristics of the conjugal family and characteristics of the social networks. When Young and Willmott [27] followed their lower-class families from Bethnal Green to a housing estate in the suburbs, where husband and wife are isolated from their kin and lifelong friends and neighbors, they observed significant changes in the relationships between the spouses. Elizabeth Bott [28] points out that there is a relationship between "connectedness of the social network" and family patterns, but that the relationship between social class and connectedness, and therefore between class and family patterns, is much looser, and she suggests some of the variations in life situations within a social class that might affect the relationship between connectedness and social class. Furthermore, we do not know in what ways class differences may be affected by conditions peculiar to the San Francisco Bay Area—e.g., the proportion of recent arrivals in the population, the

[27] Bott, *op. cit.*, Chs. VIII–X.
[28] *Ibid.*, Ch. IV.

rate of geographical mobility within the area, the rapidity of growth and change. One wonders especially what might be the effect of a relatively high and expanding overall level of prosperity, in which different classes might share differently, and the LL's, perhaps, least of all. It is beyond the purview of this paper to explore all these factors and their consequences, but it is important to call them to the attention of the reader.

4. For the sake of making a point, many of our comparisons are overdrawn. For example, although we have made much of "deficiency in role-taking ability," it would be flying in the face of common experience to assume that LL's are clods incapable of seeing more than one perspective. The "peasant shrewdness" of the lower classes is not "animal cunning" as contrasted to "role-taking ability." It is a pejorative term for role-taking ability. The skills employed by the servant, whether faithfully to serve or craftily to manipulate the master, are role-taking skills. The ability of the lower-caste Negro to adapt to the demands of the upper-caste white, to conform to the etiquette of race relations and at the same time to retain some sense of autonomy, demands no small skill in role-taking. "Conning," an art at which many LL's, but not LL's alone, are adept, is role-taking in the service of morally dubious ends, but it is role-taking *par excellence*.[29] In short, to take our descriptions literally, even though those descriptions point to real and important differences, is to subscribe to a caricature.

5. It is worth repeating that this paper is concerned with the lower blue-collarite, not the blue-collar or "working" class in general. The findings reported here, with exceptions noted, contrast the LL to his upper-blue-collar compatriots as well as to members of the other strata. The stably employed, economically secure, relatively prosperous working class—such as the Ford workers described by Bennett Berger—live under a very different set of life conditions. Indeed, Berger suggests that "what Warner calls the 'upper lower class' . . . has less in common with the 'lower lower class' than with the 'lower middle class.' "[30]

6. Reference should be made to the problem of comparing questionnaire and interview responses by subjects of different social classes. It is possible that, in some respects, class differences may be minimized by a tendency of subjects of all classes to give "approved" or "conventional" responses. It is also possible, however, that differences may be exaggerated in certain respects. If it is correct that LL's, compared with the other strata, are in general more prone to formulate their beliefs and feelings—whatever their actual complexity and subtlety—in stereotyped, folk expressions, if they are more inclined to see one side of an issue *at a time* and less inclined to qualify their responses in order to register nuances and mixed feelings, we may expect that the verbal formulations they produce or select will render less faithfully the actual complexity of their feelings than is true of the other strata. In brief, it is possible that inter-

---

[29] See Daniel Glaser, "A Note on the 'Differential Mediation of Social Perception as a Correlate of Social Adjustment,' " *Sociometry*, 20 (June, 1957), pp. 156–160.

[30] Bennett M. Berger, *Working-Class Suburb*, Berkeley and Los Angeles: University of California Press, 1960, p. 96.

view and questionnaire techniques are more likely, when applied to LL respondents than when applied to respondents of the other strata, to produce caricatures in which the half-tones and shadings, present in the subject, are obliterated in the image.

7. Are there, among the LL themes we have delineated, a dominant few, closely linked to the life conditions, which in turn determine the remainder? Have we, indeed, performed a kind of informal factor analysis? Retrospectively, a few themes do seem to stand out as relatively prepotent: e.g., a poverty of perspectives, a preference for particularistic relationships, a tendency to view the self as a victim of circumstances beyond one's control. However, we leave open the question of what conception of the personality is most adequate to the actual complexity of the relationships among the characteristics we have discussed. Nor do we here attempt to deal systematically with the difficult theoretical problems of the relationship between two axes, so to speak, of explanation: (1) the derivation of "attitudes" or "components" of personality from a set of life conditions, and (2) the dependence of these attitudes upon one another as members of the same personality system.

8. Closely related to the foregoing questions is the question: What are the implications of the LL's questionnaire responses for his conduct in concrete situations? Does each personality "contain" a bundle of themes that operate *en bloc* across a range of life situations, and that maintain a fairly constant strength relative to each other, or does each vary in saliency according to the situation? Or is it better to think of the "attitudinal" data produced by our subjects as a "vocabulary of motives," which limits the way they can define situations and the kinds of responses they can make intelligible or acceptable to themselves, but a vocabulary of which they can still make selective and discriminating use according to the requirements of the self and the situation? Or are we dealing with a set of more-or-less shared perspectives according to which a certain repertoire of roles or social personalities comes to make sense, roles that may then be "activated" and brought into play selectively according to the opportunities, alternatives and challenges provided by the social situation? In this view, an individual might shift from the role of the good soldier to the truculent tough to the loyal friend to the patriarchal autocrat to the big sport as the situation changes without moving out of a family of compatible roles, some of which, however, would be more central to the self than others. But these large questions, too, are among the unfinished business of this paper.

V

SUBJECTIVE
ELEMENTS:
PRESTIGE AND CLASS
CONSCIOUSNESS

15

OCCUPATIONAL PRESTIGE IN THE UNITED STATES, 1925–63

Robert W. Hodge,
Paul M. Siegel, and
Peter H. Rossi

The study of occupational prestige presented here is a replication of the pioneering nationwide survey conducted in 1947 by the National Opinion Research Center (NORC). The authors here compare their study with earlier ones, especially the 1947 NORC survey and discuss to what extent there have been changes in the prestige of American occupations in the last several decades.

What determines the prestige of an occupation? Why do some jobs inspire the highest veneration while others are regarded as degrading and unworthy? What are the criteria that people implicitly use in rating the occupations of those around them?

In a study of the race and class system of a remote mountain community in Brazil, the American anthropologist, Marvin Harris, has described a status system that is strikingly similar to our own. Describing the ranking of occupations in this small Brazilian town, Harris says:

> *Those who are* completely dependent upon the strength and endurance of their own physical powers—*like the farmers, the water carriers, the woodcutters, etc.—are at the bottom of the list. The artisan whose crafts demand a* special skill *in addition to sheer physical effort rank slightly higher. Higher still are the storekeepers and commercial travellers who combine a minimum of physical with* a certain intellectual effort. *Still higher are* those who command the labor of others—*the landlord farmers who do no work in the fields, and the owners of large workshops who merely supervise production. Those who own large machines like trucks or a flour mill share this level. Owners of special professional monopolies, the doctor, the lawyer or dentist who control the destinies and welfare of others, rank still higher. The top place belongs to those who command both the labor and the*

SOURCE: *American Journal of Sociology*, 70 (November 1964), 286–302. Reprinted by permission of the University of Chicago Press.

*destinies of a large part of the community—the politicians, mayor, councilmen, and political party leaders.**

Obviously, this is not a perfect description of the occupational ranking system in the United States; nevertheless, what strikes one here is the similarity of the ranking criteria in both societies.** It is true, for example, that "those who are completely dependent upon the strength and endurance of their own physical powers" command but little respect in American society. Long ago, in his *Theory of the Leisure Class,* Thorstein Veblen incisively described how honest physical toil, regardless of how important it might be for society—cleaning streets, collecting garbage, mining coal, harvesting crops, unloading ships—has come to be defined as almost dehumanizing. It is as if mankind were struggling to disguise its resemblance to the beasts, and anyone whose occupation requires merely the expenditure of brute strength is too reminiscent of man's association to the rest of the animal kingdom and is thereby despised for this unpleasant reminder.

If an occupation demands a certain manual skill in addition to sheer physical strength, the standing of that occupation will be enhanced somewhat, but there are limits to the prestige of manual work, regardless of skill, because of the stigma attached to physical toil. The use of intellectual rather than physical powers on the job raises the prestige of an occupation considerably, but the difference between high and low status is not merely the difference between brain work and brawn work, for there are other, perhaps more important, criteria that involve the possession and use of *power.* As Harris says, those who command the labor of other people—who give orders on the job rather than having to obey them—command high regard. And, those who control the destinies of other people are likely to receive the deference of the community.

Looking at the ranking of occupations on pages 237–41, one can readily see the operation of these principles. Although there are exceptions, manual workers are generally concentrated below those who are able to avoid physical labor on the job. The three lowest ranking occupations not only demand physical toil, but involve work that is either considered dirty (garbage collector, street sweeper), or socially demeaning (shoeshiner). For manual workers, status increases generally with level of skill, but the stigma of manual labor means that even the highest ranking workers (railroad engineer, electrician) achieve a position no higher than 39 out of 90 occupations.

Those whose work involves considerable intellectual effort rank high: scientists, college professors, chemists, and so forth. And those who control the labor and/or the destinies of others also hold high position: miscellaneous government officials, corporate directors, large employers, and army officers. The top two occupations may be seen as involving crucial control over different aspects of man's destiny. The highest ranking occupation, U. S. Supreme Court justice, is the occupation that most closely resembles the Christian view of God: the supreme judge of us all. And the physician, of course, possesses great control over the physical destiny of his fellows.

Whether this pattern of ranking is the consequence of some kind of cross-cultural "law," or whether it is subject to change or reversal, is still a matter of dispute. In any

---

* Marvin Harris, "Race Relations in Minhas Velhas, A Community in the Mountain Region of Central Brazil," in Charles Wagley, ed., *Race and Class in Rural Brazil* (N.Y.: UNESCO, 1952), p. 66, emphasis added.

** International comparisons of occupational prestige have revealed very great similarities in ranking around the world. See Robert W. Hodge, Donald J. Treiman, and Peter H. Rossi, "A Comparative Study of Occupational Prestige," in R. Bendix and S. M. Lipset, eds., *Class, Status, and Power,* 2nd ed. (New York: The Free Press, 1966).

case, a fairly rigid hierarchy of occupational prestige is a continuing source of inequality in societies that in other ways may be becoming less stratified.

The research reported in this paper represents an attempt to add historical depth to the study of the prestige of occupations in the United States. It reports mainly on a replication conducted in 1963 of the National Opinion Research Center's well-known 1947 study of the prestige positions accorded to ninety occupations by a national sample of the American adult population.[1] We also deal with several fragmentary earlier studies, which together with the two main NORC studies, provide a rough time series going back to 1925. Since the two NORC studies were not replications of the earlier ones, we shall dwell mainly on change and stability in the prestige of occupations during the period from 1947 to 1963.

The prestige hierarchy of occupations is perhaps the best studied aspect of the stratification systems of modern societies. Extensive empirical studies have been undertaken in a variety of nations, socialist and capitalist, developed and underdeveloped. Intensive analyses have been undertaken of results of particular studies searching for the existence of disparate prestige hierarchies held by subgroups within nations.[2] Despite rather extensive searches conducted by a variety of techniques, it appears that occupational-prestige hierarchies are similar from country to country and from subgroup to subgroup within a country. This stability reflects the fundamental but gross similarities among the occupational systems of modern nations. Furthermore, knowledge about occupations and relatively strong consensus on the relative positions of occupations are widely diffused throughout the populations involved.

The consensus within and among populations on the prestige positions of occupations leads one to expect that there will be considerable stability over time in the positions of particular occupations. Industrialization has proceeded to different points in the several countries whose prestige hierarchies have been studied without seriously affecting the relative positions of occupations in the countries involved. Cross-sectional comparisons between different countries at different stages of indus-

[1] The replication was undertaken as the first stage of a larger project supported by a National Science Foundation grant (NSF G85, "Occupations and Social Stratification") aimed at providing definitive prestige scores for a more representative sample of occupations and at uncovering some of the characteristics of occupations which generate their prestige scores. The replication was undertaken as the first step in the research program to determine whether appreciable shifts occurred in prestige scores in the time period 1947–63 so that the effects of improvements in technical procedures could be sorted out from effects of historical changes in any comparisons which would be undertaken between the 1947 study and the more definitive researches presently under way.
[2] See, e.g., Kaare Svalastoga, *Prestige, Class and Mobility* (Copenhagen: Gyldendal, 1959), pp. 43–131; C. A. Moser and J. R. Hall, "The Social Grading of Occupations," in D. V. Glass (ed.), *Social Mobility in Britain* (London: Routledge & Kegan Paul, 1954), pp. 29–50; and Albert J. Reiss, Jr., Otis Dudley Duncan, Paul K. Hatt, and Cecil C. North, *Occupations and Social Status* (New York: Free Press of Glencoe, 1961). The last-mentioned volume contains the major analyses of the 1947 North-Hatt-NORC study of occupational prestige.

trial evolution suggest that it would be erroneous to expect any considerable change in the *prestige* structure of a single country over time, even though that country might be experiencing appreciable changes in *occupational* structure. We can only expect to observe changes on the order of those previously found between two nations at different stages of economic development.

On the other hand, there are cogent reasons for expecting that changes in occupational structure will be reflected, at least ultimately, in corresponding changes in the prestige positions of occupations. The prestige position of an occupation is apparently a characteristic generated by the way in which the occupation is articulated into the division of labor, by the amount of power and influence implied in the activities of the occupation, by the characteristics of incumbents, and by the amount of resources which society places at the disposal of incumbents. (Other factors are undoubtedly at work, but these are the most obvious.) Hence, as occupations shift in these respects over time, corresponding adjustive shifts in prestige positions can be anticipated.

Considerable changes have occurred since 1947 in the occupational structure and labor force of the United States. The long-term trend in the growth of professional and scientific occupations persisted and was even accelerated during this period. Governmental and popular concern over the numbers and quality of our professional and technical manpower was expressed in a great expansion of our universities as well as in more attention being given lower levels of schooling. The proportion of the labor force devoted to agricultural pursuits declined along with unskilled and heavy labor

components. This was also the period during which automation continued to expand, raising a serious question as to whether the American labor force could absorb both workers freed from jobs eliminated by technological progress and the large cohorts of postwar births now beginning to enter the labor force. Mention must be made of the stepped-up drive for equality on the part of Negroes, although we cannot tarry here to examine it. The question at issue is whether changes in the occupational structure have been reflected in shifts in the prestige of occupations between the two points in time.

On the basis of our empirical knowledge concerning the stability under a variety of conditions of the hierarchy of occupational prestige, we can support an expectation that there will be relatively few changes in the positions of occupations as we proceed from the 1947 to the 1963 study. On the basis of what seems to be a reasonable model of how these prestige positions have been generated, we expect somewhat more in the way of changes. Neither point of view produces very precise expectations for we need to know what is an acceptable level of stability (or change) either to conform to or to negate each expectation.

One further problem plagues interpretation of any comparisons such as this study envisages: Consider a set of occupational titles for which we have an aggregate prestige rating at two points in time; the difference between these ratings can be attributed either to a general increase in the amount of prestige in the occupational system or to an increase in the prestige of the aggregate of occupations in the set and a corresponding decrease in the prestige of some occupations not in the set. There is no conceivable way of choosing between these interpretations with the present data.

In view of the large number of professional occupations included in the NORC list, it may well be the case that in the aggregate the ninety occupations stood higher in the prestige hierarchy in 1963 than in 1947. If prestige is regarded as a "commodity" that behaves like the payoff in a "zero-sum" game, then, to be sure, what one set of occupations gains another must lose. But the NORC titles might get higher ratings in 1963 than 1947 because there is, all told, a greater amount of prestige in the system. If the latter is the case, the ninety NORC titles may get higher ratings and at the same time a smaller share of all prestige and a lower place in the total prestige hierarchy.[3]

These remarks are perhaps sufficient to alert the reader to the ambiguities which characterize the study of occupational prestige. Indeterminacies encountered in the study of a set of occupations are, of course, duplicated when the focus is upon a single occupation. It is for this reason that our focus is largely on the ordering of the ninety NORC occupational titles in two time periods and not upon changes in the prestige of particular occupations. All indications of changes in occupational prestige revealed here are of necessity relative to the set of ninety titles under consideration. These occupations exhaust our universe, and changes in their prestige are assumed to indicate restructuring of the relative prestige of the occupations under consideration.

Methods and Procedures

A small-scale replication of the 1947 study was undertaken in the spring of 1963. In order properly to compare the replication with the original, it was necessary to replicate the study using procedures as nearly identical as possible with those of the earlier study. The same question was used to elicit ratings, and the ninety job titles were rated in the same orders (using rotated blocks) in the same way. Most of the items (with the exception of those that were historically obsolete) were repeated. Even the sample was selected according to the outmoded quota sampling methods employed in 1947. The few new items included in the restudy were placed in the questionnaire after the occupational ratings.

Because of the stability of prestige positions of occupations from subgroup to subgroup in the 1947 study, it was felt that a relatively small national sample would be sufficient for the replication. In all a total of 651 interviews was collected according to quota sampling methods from a national sample of adults and youths.[4]

---

[3] This point is perhaps more clearly illustrated with a more familiar commodity: money income in dollars. It is fairly easy to see how a group could receive a smaller proportion of all income over time, but at the same time have greater income because there is more income to spread between groups.

[4] Justification for our claim that 651 cases suffice to give a reliable intertemporal comparison can be derived from examination of sampling error estimates based on the assumption of a random sample. Such estimates indicate that confidence limits at the 0.90 level for $p=0.50$ and $N=651$ are 0.47 and 0.53. For $N=60$ (smaller than any subgroup used in this paper) the corresponding error estimates are 0.39 and 0.61. Thus for even relatively small subgroups any dramatic changes are likely to be detected, although it must be clearly understood that error estimates for quota sampling are only approximated by assuming that formulas for random samples apply.

As in the 1947 study, occupational ratings were elicited by asking respondents to judge an occupation as having *excellent, good, average, somewhat below average,* or *poor* standing (along with a "don't know" option) in response to the item: "For each job mentioned, please pick out the statement that best gives *your own personal opinion* of the *general standing* that such a job has."

One indicator of prestige position is the proportion of respondents (among those rating an occupation) giving either an "excellent" or a "good" response. Another measure which can be derived from a matrix of ratings by occupation requires weighting the various responses with arbitrary numerical values: We can assign an excellent rating a numerical value of 100, a good rating the value of 80, an average rating the value of 60, a somewhat below average rating the value of 40, and a poor rating the value of 20. Calculating the numerical average of these arbitrarily assigned values over all respondents rating the occupation yields the NORC prestige score. This latter measure has received rather widespread use despite arbitrariness in the numerical weights assigned to the five possible ratings.[5]

The ratings and derived scores for each of the ninety occupations obtained in 1947 and in 1963 are shown in Table 1. We present the findings in such detail because of their intrinsic interest. However, the bulk of the analysis contained in this paper is more concerned with characteristics of the distributions of these ratings than with the positions of particular occupations.

Congruities in Occupational Prestige: 1947–63

The major result of the 1963 restudy is dramatically summarized in the product-moment correlation coefficient of .99 between the scores in 1947 and the scores in 1963. The linear regression of the 1963 on the 1947 scores is given by

$$Y = 0.97X + 2.98,$$

a result which indicates that there is very little regression toward the mean and a slight net upward shift in scores.[6] (Here and elsewhere in the text boldface symbols are used to represent regression estimates.)

The high over-all correlation in the total set of occupations is matched by high correlations within subsets of occupations. If we group occupations into professional occupations, other non-manual occupations, and manual occupations, as in Table 2, we can see that the regression lines within the three groups are quite similar.[7]

---

[5] The reader will observe that the correlation between the two ways of ordering occupations need not be unity. Of the two measures mentioned above, the proportion of excellent or good ratings enjoys some advantages over the NORC prestige scores. Its range and variance are somewhat larger than the NORC prestige scores, which tend to obscure differences between occupations in the middle of the prestige hierarchy. However, the two measures are, in fact, highly intercorrelated ($r = .98$) and the advantages of the proportion of excellent or good ratings over the NORC prestige scores are largely statistical in nature. Throughout this paper, the bulk of our analysis employs the NORC prestige scores—a decision based largely on the wide use and popularity of the prestige scores derived from the original 1947 study.

[6] When the NORC scores are ranked, we find a Spearman rank-order correlation of .98 between the 1947 and 1963 ranks.

[7] The hypothesis that a common regression line fits all groups may be rejected at the 0.07 level of confidence, as indicated by the F-ratio resulting from an analysis of covariance.

TABLE 1. Distributions of Prestige Ratings, United States, 1947 and 1963

Occupation	March, 1947								June, 1963							
	Per Cent						NORC Score	Rank	Per Cent						NORC Score	Rank
	Excellent*	Good	Average	Below Average	Poor	Don't Know†			Excellent‡	Good	Average	Below Average	Poor	Don't Know§		
U.S. Supreme Court Justice	83	15	2	—	—	3	96	1	77	18	4	1	1	1	94	1
Physician	67	30	3	—	—	1	93	2.5	71	25	4	—	—	1	93	2
Nuclear physicist	48	39	11	1	1	51	86	18	70	23	5	1	1	10	92	3.5
Scientist	53	38	8	1	—	7	89	8	68	27	5	—	1	2	92	3.5
Government scientist	51	41	7	1	—	6	88	10.5	64	30	5	—	1	2	91	5.5
State governor	71	25	4	—	—	1	93	2.5	64	30	5	—	1	1	91	5.5
Cabinet member in the federal government	66	28	5	1	—	6	92	4.5	61	32	6	1	1	2	90	8
College professor	53	40	7	—	—	1	89	8	59	35	5	—	1	1	90	8
U.S. representative in Congress	57	35	6	1	1	4	89	8	58	33	6	2	—	2	90	8
Chemist	42	48	9	1	—	7	86	18	54	38	8	—	—	3	89	11
Lawyer	44	45	9	1	1	1	86	18	53	38	8	—	1	—	89	11
Diplomat in the U.S. foreign service	70	24	4	1	1	9	92	4.5	57	34	7	1	1	3	89	11
Dentist	42	48	9	1	—	—	86	18	47	47	6	—	—	—	88	14
Architect	42	48	9	1	—	6	86	18	47	45	6	—	—	2	88	14
County judge	47	43	9	1	—	1	87	13	50	40	8	1	—	1	88	14
Psychologist	38	49	12	1	—	15	85	22	49	41	8	1	—	6	87	17.5
Minister	52	35	11	1	1	1	87	13	53	33	13	—	1	1	87	17.5
Member of the board of directors of a large corporation	42	47	10	1	—	5	86	18	42	51	6	1	—	1	87	17.5

* Bases for the 1947 occupational ratings are 2,920 less "don't know" and not answered for each occupational title.

† Base is 2,920 in all cases.

‡ Bases for the 1963 occupational ratings are 651 less "don't know" and not answered for each occupational title.

§ Base is 651 in all cases.

— Less than 0.5 per cent.

SOURCE OF THE 1947 DISTRIBUTIONS: Albert J. Riess, Jr., and others, *Occupations and Social Status* (New York: Free Press of Glencoe, 1963), Table ii-9.

TABLE 1. (*Cont.*)

Occupation	March, 1947								June, 1963							
	Per Cent						NORC Score	Rank	Per Cent						NORC Score	Rank
	Excellent*	Good	Average	Below Average	Poor	Don't Know†			Excellent‡	Good	Average	Below Average	Poor	Don't Know§		
Mayor of a large city	57	36	6	1	—	1	90	6	46	44	9	1	1	1	87	17.5
Priest	51	34	11	2	2	6	86	18	52	33	12	2	1	6	86	21.5
Head of a department in a state government	47	44	8	—	1	3	87	13	44	48	6	1	1	1	86	21.5
Civil engineer	33	55	11	1	—	5	84	23	40	52	8	—	—	2	86	21.5
Airline pilot	35	48	15	1	1	3	83	24.5	41	48	11	1	1	1	86	21.5
Banker	49	43	8	—	—	1	88	10.5	39	51	10	1	—	—	85	24.5
Biologist	29	51	18	1	1	16	81	29	38	50	11	—	—	6	85	24.5
Sociologist	31	51	16	1	1	23	82	26.5	35	48	15	1	1	10	83	26
Instructor in public schools	28	45	24	2	1	1	79	34	30	53	16	1	—	—	82	27.5
Captain in the regular army	28	49	19	2	2	2	80	31.5	28	55	16	2	—	1	82	27.5
Accountant for a large business	25	57	17	1	—	3	81	29	27	55	17	1	1	—	81	29.5
Public school teacher	26	45	24	3	2	—	78	36	31	46	22	1	1	—	81	29.5
Owner of a factory that employs about 100 people	30	51	17	1	1	2	82	25.5	28	49	19	2	1	1	80	31.5
Building contractor	21	55	23	1	—	1	79	34	22	56	20	1	—	—	80	31.5
Artist who paints pictures that are exhibited in galleries	40	40	15	3	2	6	83	24.5	28	45	20	5	2	4	78	34.5
Musician in a symphony orchestra	31	46	19	3	1	5	81	29	25	45	25	3	1	3	78	34.5
Author of novels	32	44	19	3	2	9	80	31.5	26	46	22	4	2	5	78	34.5
Economist	25	48	24	2	1	22	79	34	20	53	24	2	1	12	78	34.5

TABLE 1. (Cont.)

Occupation	March, 1947 Per Cent Excellent*	Good	Average	Below Average	Poor	Don't Know†	NORC Score	Rank	June, 1963 Per Cent Excellent‡	Good	Average	Below Average	Poor	Don't Know§	NORC Score	Rank
Official of an international labor union	26	42	20	5	7	11	75	40.5	21	53	18	5	3	5	77	37
Railroad engineer	22	45	30	3	—	1	77	37.5	19	47	30	3	1	1	76	39
Electrician	15	38	43	4	—	1	73	45	18	45	34	2	—	—	76	39
County agricultural agent	17	53	28	2	—	5	77	37.5	13	54	30	2	1	4	76	39
Owner-operator of a printing shop	13	48	36	3	—	2	74	42.5	13	51	34	2	—	2	75	41.5
Trained machinist	14	43	38	5	—	2	73	45	15	50	32	4	—	—	75	41.5
Farm owner and operator	19	46	31	3	1	1	76	39	16	45	33	5	—	1	74	44
Undertaker	14	43	36	5	2	2	72	47	16	46	33	3	2	3	74	44
Welfare worker for a city government	16	43	35	4	2	4	73	45	17	44	32	5	2	2	74	44
Newspaper columnist	13	51	32	3	1	5	74	42.5	10	49	38	3	1	1	73	46
Policeman	11	30	46	11	2	1	67	55	16	38	37	6	2	—	72	47
Reporter on a daily newspaper	9	43	43	4	1	2	71	48	7	45	44	3	1	1	71	48
Radio announcer	17	45	35	3	—	2	75	40.5	9	42	44	5	1	1	70	49.5
Bookkeeper	8	31	55	6	—	1	68	51.5	9	40	45	5	1	—	70	49.5
Tenant farmer—one who owns livestock and machinery and manages the farm	10	37	40	11	2	1	68	51.5	11	37	42	8	3	1	69	51.5
Insurance agent	7	34	53	4	2	2	68	51.5	6	40	47	5	2	—	69	51.5
Carpenter	5	28	56	10	1	—	65	58	7	36	49	8	1	—	68	53
Manager of a small store in a city	5	40	50	4	1	1	69	49	3	40	48	7	2	—	67	54.5

TABLE 1. (Cont.)

Occupation	March, 1947 Per Cent						NORC Score	Rank	June, 1963 Per Cent						NORC Score	Rank
	Excellent*	Good	Average	Below Average	Poor	Don't Know†			Excellent‡	Good	Average	Below Average	Poor	Don't Know§		
A local official of a labor union	7	29	41	14	9	11	62	62	8	36	42	9	5	4	67	54.5
Mail carrier	8	26	54	10	2	1	66	57	7	29	53	10	1	—	66	57
Railroad conductor	8	30	52	9	1	1	67	55	6	33	48	10	3	—	66	57
Traveling salesman for a wholesale concern	6	35	53	5	1	2	68	51.5	4	33	54	7	3	2	66	57
Plumber	5	24	55	14	2	1	63	59.5	6	29	54	9	2	—	65	59
Automobile repairman	5	21	58	14	2	—	63	59.5	5	25	56	12	2	—	64	60
Playground director	7	33	48	10	2	4	67	55	6	29	46	15	4	3	63	62.5
Barber	3	17	56	20	4	1	59	66	4	25	56	13	2	1	63	62.5
Machine operator in a factory	4	20	53	20	3	2	60	64.5	6	24	51	15	4	1	63	62.5
Owner-operator of a lunch stand	4	24	55	14	3	1	62	62	4	25	57	11	3	1	63	62.5
Corporal in the regular army	5	21	48	20	6	3	60	64.5	6	25	47	15	6	2	62	65.5
Garage mechanic	4	21	57	17	1	—	62	62	4	22	56	15	3	—	62	65.5
Truck driver	2	11	49	29	9	—	54	71	3	18	54	19	5	—	59	67
Fisherman who owns his own boat	3	20	48	21	8	7	58	68	3	19	51	19	8	4	58	68
Clerk in a store	2	14	61	20	3	—	58	68	1	14	56	22	6	—	56	70
Milk route man	2	10	52	29	7	1	54	71	3	12	55	23	7	1	56	70
Streetcar motorman	3	16	55	21	5	2	58	68	3	16	46	27	8	2	56	70
Lumberjack	2	11	48	29	10	8	53	73	2	16	46	29	7	3	55	72.5
Restaurant cook	3	13	44	29	11	1	54	71	4	15	44	26	11	—	55	72.5
Singer in a nightclub	3	13	43	23	18	6	52	74.5	3	16	43	24	14	3	54	74
Filling station attendant	1	9	48	34	8	1	52	74.5	2	11	41	34	11	—	51	75

TABLE 1. (*Cont.*)

| Occupation | March, 1947 | | | | | | | | June, 1963 | | | | | | | |
| | Per Cent | | | | | | NORC | | Per Cent | | | | | | NORC | |
	Excellent *	Good	Average	Below Average	Poor	Don't Know †	Score	Rank	Excellent ‡	Good	Average	Below Average	Poor	Don't Know §	Score	Rank
Dockworker	2	7	34	37	20	8	47	81.5	2	9	43	33	14	3	50	77.5
Railroad section hand	2	9	35	33	21	3	48	79.5	3	10	39	29	18	2	50	77.5
Night watchman	3	8	33	35	21	1	47	81.5	3	10	39	32	17	1	50	77.5
Coal miner	4	11	33	31	21	2	49	77.5	3	13	34	31	19	2	50	77.5
Restaurant waiter	2	8	37	36	17	1	48	79.5	2	8	42	32	16	—	49	80.5
Taxi driver	2	8	38	35	17	1	49	77.5	2	8	39	31	18	1	49	80.5
Farm hand	3	12	35	31	19	1	50	76	3	12	31	32	22	—	48	83
Janitor	1	7	30	37	25	1	44	85.5	1	9	35	35	19	1	48	83
Bartender	1	6	32	32	29	4	44	85.5	1	7	42	28	21	2	48	83
Clothes presser in a laundry	2	6	35	36	21	2	46	83	2	7	31	38	22	1	45	85
Soda fountain clerk	1	5	34	40	20	2	45	84	—	5	30	44	20	1	44	86
Sharecropper—one who owns no live-stock or equipment and does not manage farm	1	6	24	28	41	3	40	87	1	8	26	28	37	2	42	87
Garbage collector	1	4	16	26	53	2	35	88	2	5	21	32	41	1	39	88
Street sweeper	1	3	14	29	53	1	34	89	1	4	17	31	46	1	36	89
Shoe shiner	1	2	13	28	56	2	33	90	—	3	15	30	51	2	34	90
Average	22	31	30	11	7	4	70	—	22	32	29	11	6	2	71	—

TABLE 2. Regressions within Subsets of Occupations

Occupation Group	Regression Coefficient	Regression Constant	Correlation
Total, all occupations ($n=90$)	0.97	2.98	.99
Professional, including one title duplicated for validation purposes ($n=33$)	1.05	−3.61	.96
One non-manual occupations ($n=21$)	0.92	5.85	.98
All manual occupations, including one craft occupation duplicated for validation purposes and two military titles ($n=21$)	1.00	2.00	.99
Farm occupations ($n=4$); not computed	—	—	—

The very slight effect of grouping occupations is shown again in Figure 1, where the three within-group regression lines are plotted over the range of the 1947 NORC scores contained within each group. The three lines nearly coincide over the observed range of the NORC scores and do not appreciably depart from the line $Y = X$ (where the 1963 and the 1947 scores are equal).

The gross similarity between the 1947 and the 1963 NORC scores tends to overshadow some interesting small changes revealed by the data. Thus, in Figure 1 the regression line for blue-collar occupations lies above (and, in fact, parallels) the line $Y = X$. Consequently, one infers that all blue-collar occupations had slightly higher scores in 1963. For professionals and other white-collar workers, however, the pic-

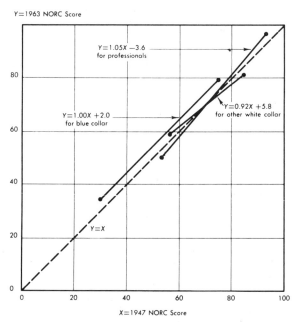

FIGURE 1. Regressions of 1963 NORC Score on 1947 NORC Score within Occupational Groups.

ture is more complex, since the within-group regression lines for these two broad groupings cross over the line $Y = X$. Consequently, in the case of professionals, those particular occupations with the highest prestige scores in 1947 (largely scientific and free professional occupations) slightly increased their scores, whereas those professional occupations with relatively low prestige in 1947 (marginal professional occupations such as "singer in a nightclub") receive somewhat lower scores. Among "other white-collar occupations" the situation is reversed. That is, from the within-group regression line we see that the other white-collar occupations with highest prestige in 1947 (largely managerial and political occupations) tended on the average to decline slightly, whereas lower white-collar occupations slightly increased in prestige.[8]

One other point is brought out sharply by Figure 1 and deserves mention. Since the within-occupational-group regression lines are plotted only for the range of 1947 scores observed within the group, one can easily see the appreciable overlap in scores between professional, other white-collar, and blue-collar occupations. Although these divisions are often employed by social scientists as though they represented fundamental class barriers,[9] Figure 1 makes clear that no such barrier can be

detected on the basis of occupational prestige. The cleavage between white-collar and blue-collar—if it exists at all —is based not so much upon matters of societal evaluation as perhaps upon the character of dress and work in the three groups.

All in all the preceding results indicate a striking similarity between the structure of the 1947 and the 1963 NORC scores. While we shall subsequently document a number of systematic shifts in the prestige of specific occupational groups, it is abundantly clear that these shifts are small and did not produce any substantial re-ordering of the relative prestige of the ninety occupations under consideration here.

There are several good reasons for this observed stability. First, relative differential educational requirements, monetary rewards, and even something as nebulous as the functional importance of occupations are not subject to rapid change in an industrial society.[10] Second, any dramatic shifts in the prestige structure of occupations would upset the dependency which is presumed to hold between the social evaluation of a job, its educational prerequisites, its rewards, and its importance to society. Finally, instabilities would further ambiguities or status inconsistencies if the prestige structure were subject to marked and rapid change.

[8] There is a slight increase in the ability of the within-group regression lines to predict the direction of changes in scores between 1947 and 1963, as compared with the regression line for the total set. Correct predictions about the directions of change can be made by the over-all regression in 60.5 per cent of the cases and by the within-group regression lines in 62.8 per cent of them, an increase in efficiency of 5.8 per cent.

[9] This is, e.g., the major distinction employed in a recent comparative study of occupational mobility (Seymour Martin Lipset and Reinhard Bendix, *Social Mobility in Industrial Society* [Berkeley: University of California Press, 1959]).

[10] For a discussion of this point see Otis Dudley Duncan, "Properties and Characteristics of the Socio-economic Index," in Reiss *et al., op. cit.*, pp. 152–53. A correlation of .94 was found between an aggregate measure of the income of an occupation in 1940 and a similar indicator in 1950; a correlation of .97 was found between the proportion of high-school graduates in an occupation in 1940 and the same measure in 1950.

Indeed, the meaning of achievement, career, seniority, and occupational mobility would be fundamentally altered if occupational prestige were subject to large-scale changes. No small amount of intragenerational mobility between prestige classes would, for example, be induced solely by the changing structure of occupational prestige *even though individuals did not change their occupations over time.*

. . . . .

Occupational Prestige Since 1925

Since the appearance of George S. Counts's pioneering 1925 study of occupational prestige, a number of readings have been taken on the distribution of occupational prestige. These studies have utilized a variety of different measurement techniques and different types of samples of raters, college students being quite popular. However, there is evidence that the over-all structure of prestige is invariant under quite drastic changes in technique.[11] Furthermore, one of the major findings of the original 1947 NORC survey was that all segments of the population share essentially the same view of the prestige hierarchy and rate occupations in much the same way.[12] With these findings in mind, we may utilize se-

lected prestige studies conducted since 1925 to ascertain whether any substantial changes in the prestige structure of occupations have occurred since that date.

A pre-World War II and post-Depression bench mark is provided by the investigations of Mapheus Smith, who provides the mean ratings of one hundred occupations as rated by college and high-school students in the academic years 1938–39, 1939–40, and 1940–41. The rating technique used by Smith differs considerably from that employed in the NORC study. Respondents were originally required to *rank* occupations according to how far an average incumbent would be seated from the guest of honor at a dinner honoring a celebrity and then to *rate* the occupations on a 100-point scale of prestige (according to the rater's personal estimation).[13]

A pre-Depression bench mark of occupational prestige is provided by Counts's study, which provides rankings of forty-five occupations according to their "social standing." The data were collected from high-school students, high-school teachers, and college students.[14] Unlike the NORC and Smith studies, rankings rather than ratings were obtained by Counts. Counts provides rankings for six groups of respondents, and a continuous type variable can be derived by taking the average rank of an occupation over the six

---

[11] One study, e.g., requested respondents to sort seventy of the occupations in the NORC list into groups of *similar* occupations. The respondent was then asked to order the groups of similar occupations he had formed into social levels. Nevertheless, a rank-order correlation of .97 was found between scores derived from this study and scores obtained from the 1947 NORC study (see John D. Campbell, "Subjective Aspects of Occupational Status" [unpublished Ph.D. thesis, Harvard University, 1952], chap. ii).

[12] Reiss *et al., op. cit.,* pp. 189–90.

[13] Mapheus Smith, "An Empirical Scale of Prestige Status of Occupations," *American Sociological Review,* VIII (April, 1943), 185–92.

[14] George S. Counts, "The Social Status of Occupations: A Problem in Vocational Guidance," *School Review,* XXXIII (January, 1925), 16–27.

groups, weighting for the number of respondents in each group.

These four studies, then, provide an opportunity to examine occupational prestige since 1925. A fairly large number of titles are shared in common between each pair of studies, so that the number of titles utilized in any given comparison is larger than the total number of titles that have been rated in many prestige studies.[15]

Product-moment correlations between the prestige ratings of occupations common to each pair of studies are presented in Table 3, together with

from adjacent points in time. That no substantial changes are observed over a span of approximately 40 years is a bit more surprising and is further evidence of constraints toward the stability of prestige hierarchies.

. . . . .

Conclusions

The theme of this paper has been accurately captured by an eminent pathologist who remarked of biochemical phenomena: "Universal instability of

TABLE 3. Correlations Between Occupational Prestige Ratings at Selected Time Periods, 1925–63 *

Study and Time Period	C	S	X	Y
C (Counts's mean ranks, 1925)	—	.968	.955	.934
S (Smith's mean ratings, *ca.* 1940)	23	—	.982	.971
X (NORC scores, 1947)	29	38	—	.990
Y (NORC scores, 1963)	29	38	90	—

* Correlations placed above diagonal; no. of matching titles placed below diagonal.

SOURCES: George S. Counts, "The Social Status of Occupations: A Problem in Vocational Guidance," *School Review*, XXXIII (January, 1925), 20–21, Table 1; Mapheus Smith, "An Empirical Scale of Prestige Status of Occupations," *American Sociological Review*, VIII (April, 1943), 187–88, Table I; National Opinion Research Center, "Jobs and Occupations: A Popular Evaluation," *Opinion News*, IX (September 1, 1947), 3–13. See text for details.

the number of matching titles. It is evident from the data presented in Table 3 that *there have been no substantial changes in occupational prestige in the United States since 1925.* The lowest correlation observed is .934, and this occurs between the 1963 NORC scores and the mean ranks derived from the 1925 study of Counts. In view of the high correlation between 1947 and 1963 NORC scores, it is not particularly surprising that high correlations are found between any pair of studies

constituents seems to be compatible with a stability and even monotony of organized life." [16] Such is the picture one gleans of occupational structures from the present endeavor. Between 1947 and 1963 we are fully aware that many *individual* changes in occupation were under way as men advanced in their career lines, retired, or entered the labor force. Yet, despite the turnover of incumbents, occupational morphology, at least insofar as prestige is concerned, remained remarkably sta-

[15] See, e.g., the national studies cited by Alex Inkeles and Peter H. Rossi, "National Comparisons of Occupational Prestige," *American Journal of Sociology*, LXI (January, 1956), 329–39.

[16] René Dubos, *The Dreams of Reason: Science and Utopias* (New York: Columbia University Press, 1961), p. 124.

ble. To be sure, systematic patterns of change could be detected, but one would miss the import of this paper if one failed to recognize that these changes were minor relative to the over-all stability. The view developed here is that a stable system of occupational prestige provides a necessary foundation to which individuals may anchor their careers.

System maintenance is, however, only part of the story. Small, but nevertheless systematic, changes can be de-tected between 1947 and 1963. In some cases these changes appear to be attributable to increasing public knowledge of occupations, but it was suggested that any complete understanding of prestige shifts and their causes would require a time series pertaining to the standing of particular occupations. The present study is a step in that direction. Our purposes will be adequately accomplished if others are stimulated to make periodic readings of, as it were, the occupational weather.

16

from
THE PSYCHOLOGY OF SOCIAL CLASSES

Richard Centers

It is commonly assumed that American workers are not and have never been particularly class conscious; much less so, for example, than European workers. And indeed, the assertion of a low level of class consciousness in the United States has been a traditional explanation for the failure of socialism on our shores. Part of the empirical evidence for the lack of class consciousness of the American worker was a series of public opinion polls taken in the late 1930's and early 1940's which purported to demonstrate that at least 80 percent of the American public considered themselves members of an enormous middle class.

Shortly after World War II, the psychologist Richard Centers conducted a national survey of 1,000 white males, challenging both the methodology and the findings of these earlier polls that had gained wide currency. Centers came to his study armed with what he called an "interest group theory of classes." Clearly adopting Marxian ideas, Centers suggested that persons who occupy the same position in the "economic processes of society" (namely, those who share a common position vis-à-vis the means of production) were likely to share: (1) certain political, economic, and social attitudes; and (2) an awareness or consciousness of membership in a particular social class.

In his book, *The Psychology of Social Classes*, Centers boldly set forth his findings,

SOURCE: Richard Centers, *The Psychology of Social Classes: A Study of Class Consciousness* (Princeton, N.J.: Princeton University Press, 1949), pp. 30–33, 55–57, 76–77, 85, 87, and 107–9. Copyright 1949 by Princeton University Press. Reprinted by permission of the publisher.

which contradicted previous studies, and claimed to find *a great deal of class consciousness* in America. Although its conclusions have often been criticized, the book stands as a pioneer work in the empirical study of social stratification and class consciousness in the United States. We present here brief excerpts from the book in which Centers criticizes previous studies of class consciousness, argues for a four-class model (upper, middle, *working,* and lower), assesses the political attitudes of various occupational groups, and describes the high degree of class consciousness that he found among his respondents.

How class conscious *are* Americans? Of course, the answer depends ultimately on how the term is defined. If you define it in the strict Marxian sense—do workers recognize themselves as members of a great proletariat, do they have a revolutionary vision of a classless society which their political solidarity will bring about—then the answer is obviously no, Americans are not class conscious. Also, most Americans are not very likely to use social class labels in ordinary conversation.*

This does not mean, however, that Americans are not aware of social class differences among people. Centers' study was only one of the first of many to demonstrate that, when presented with social class terms, Americans are able to understand and use them. But, because of our egalitarian ideology, Americans are reluctant to use social class labels spontaneously. However, although sociological terms are not used generally by the public to refer to social class, colorful, meaningful, and sometimes euphemistic substitutes are used to convey essentially the same thing. The concerns and conversations of Americans are shot through with social class content. Getting ahead, making good, moving up in the world, making something of yourself, social climber, high-class, high society, trash, no-account, ne'er do well, people from the other side of the tracks—these are just a few of the innumerable expressions with social class connotations that Americans habitually use.

Nevertheless, it must be admitted that social class identification is not now a paramount aspect of the thinking of most Americans; class is not a salient and vital aspect of their sense of identity. In this sense, Centers exaggerated the amount of class consciousness in America. Because he forced his respondents to choose among a given set of categories, he stacked the cards, so to speak, and called forth responses which were latent and probably not a crucial aspect of people's sense of who they are. Furthermore, the only study in recent years to replicate Centers' study found a decrease in the proportion of respondents identifying with the working class (down from 51 percent to 34 percent).**

Nevertheless, as we know, social class is still highly predictive of political attitudes and behavior, and in this sense Americans are class conscious. And apparently, when people are forced to choose among a number of social classes, there is a significant correspondence between their objective social class position in society and their subjective identification.

* For a thorough survey of the subject, on which this discussion is partly based, see Joseph Kahl, *The American Class Structure* (New York: Holt, Rinehart and Winston, 1957), chap. 6.
** Robert W. Hodge and Donald J. Treiman, "Class Identification in the United States," *American Journal of Sociology,* 73 (March, 1968), pp. 535–47. By adding upper middle to the list of class choices, the researchers did not duplicate Centers' method precisely and this may partially account for the falloff in working class identification.

Some Prior Research and the Tasks of the Present Enquiry

Though there would seem to be considerable support for the interest group theory of class consciousness, the class identification data gathered by the *Fortune* surveys, by Gallup and by Cantril seemed to contradict this interest group view. Gallup, in a 1939 survey, found 88 per cent of the people saying they were middle class, while only 6 per cent claimed membership in either the upper or lower classes. *Fortune's* data, collected in 1940, showed 79 per cent of people identifying themselves with the middle class, and Cantril's analysis of 1941 data concerning the relation between income group and social class identification discovered almost nine-tenths, or 87 per cent, of people saying they were middle social class. Cantril also found that almost three-fourths asserted that they belonged to a middle income group. The correlation between social class and income group, though positive, was only .49, however, with 43 per cent of the people regarding their social class as one or more steps higher than their income level. A later report, which treated the same data in relation to occupational stratification, while showing some stratum differences in the expected direction, nevertheless indicated that a majority of the American people within each of eight occupational groups identified themselves with the middle social class, that nearly nine out of every ten business executives, white collar, or skilled workers, farmers, or professional people so identified themselves, while five out of six of the semiskilled, unskilled workers or servants made the same identification.

Although these findings appeared to be explained in part as the effect of a very high aspiration level which might tend to induce a person to identify himself with those above him in socioeconomic status, they stood in sharp conflict with the findings of the attitude studies, with those of Kornhauser in particular, and lent little support to an interest-group view of class structure. The conflicts and differences in viewpoint that were found to exist would seem to be merely *intra-class differences of view* rather than differences of outlook between definitely separate classes. They would seem to be differences in the main between segments or sectors of a great middle class to which the majority of persons in our culture conceived themselves to belong. And there would thus be little relation between the two aspects of class consciousness, that is, between politico-economic interests or orientations and the feeling of belongingness to a class typically sharing those interests and orientations.

To the writer, the acceptance of such a view seemed premature and unwarranted, primarily because the class system in which the individual was asked to place himself, though logically or conceptually a meaningful one, was, nevertheless, not a very realistic one, for it did not take adequate account of the class names actually in use among the population, particularly the manual labor section of it. People of this stratum, at least as known through general observation, typically refer to themselves as the "working class," or as the "working people," or as the "working class of people," and as "labor," or the "laboring class of people." The term lower class, which is often used by social scientists to designate this stratum, has gained no wide currency, probably because it implies too much inferiority. Being a worker, on the other hand, far from being universally looked down upon, may even indicate a valued attribute or virtue.

The conviction that it was primarily the terminology that was faulty in the identification studies was strengthened by the discovery that approximately 25 per cent of factory workers and a somewhat lesser number of general and farm laborers had replied to the effect that they used the terms working or laboring class when the 1940 *Fortune* survey had asked: "What word do you use to name the class in America you belong to?" [1]

Fortune's survey hastily concluded that because these people in the main later chose the name middle class, when they were requested to reply in terms of *only* upper, middle or lower, that they were, therefore, really middle class after all. It could as easily have been inferred, instead, that they were merely avoiding the term "lower class."

It was decided that the major task of the present study should be a review of the whole matter of class consciousness as this might bear upon the interest group hypothesis of class alignment. It was decided to reexamine the phenomena of class identification under a new condition that permitted the individual to choose among not only "upper," "middle," and "lower," but among these and "working class" as well, and also to inquire again into some of the basic politico-economic attitudes that are characteristically regarded as indices of class feeling or class interest.

· · · · ·

Politico-Economic Orientations of Occupational Strata

There are two sets of psychological data sought and secured by this research that outrank all others in impor-

tance. These are the individual's class identification and his politico-economic orientation. It is these two variables that in the theoretical literature on social classes have figured most prominently as indices to a person's class consciousness.

The latter variable, the individual's politico-economic orientation (attitudes, beliefs and behavior) has traditionally been considered even more significant a manifestation of class consciousness than his group identification, to judge from the space in the literature devoted to its description. It may be that this is merely because theorists have not properly appreciated the significance of the feeling of belongingness until fairly recently, or it may simply be that group loyalties and identifications have been less observable. In any case, the consideration of politico-economic orientations first seems appropriate enough a place to begin an analysis of class psychology.

Conservatism-Radicalism

One question to be asked and answered with respect to an interest group concept of class is this: Do persons of differing status and role in the economic order (e.g. occupational strata) characteristically distinguish themselves from one another by the possession of differing points of view with respect to important political and economic issues? Are some characteristically demanding radical and fundamental changes while others typically assert the correctness of things as they are? In short, are some occupational strata radical and opposed in point of view to other occupational strata who are conservative?

An examination of the data pre-

[1] A large proportion of *Fortune's* respondents, 27.5 per cent, replied that they did not know.

sented in Table 1 reveals at once that such differences are indeed present. Whereas almost nine-tenths—87 per cent—of large business owners and managers are either conservative or ultra conservative [2] in political and economic orientation, only about one-fifth—21 per cent—of semi-skilled manual workers are so oriented. Again, although 55.5 per cent of large businessmen can be described as ultra conservative, only 2.5 per cent of unskilled workers can be found in this category. These differences are, furthermore, not confined to the urban strata alone, but are manifested between the rural occupational strata as well. The differences as far as ultra-conservatism is concerned [3] are significant between any manual group and any business, professional or white collar group. Some differences are significant within the business, professional and white collar set of categories; but though the gradation toward less ultra-conservatism is clearly continued within the manual groups, differences are not statistically significant within this set of strata.

The gradation in this occupational hierarchy from the conservative to the radical viewpoint is marked and for the most part in regular progression. The polarity of opinion is striking testimony to the antagonistic views that have been commonly supposed to exist. . . .

Class Identifications— The American Class Structure

. . . The discovery of what names the people of the several social classes in our culture distinguish themselves by is of prime importance in considerations of class theory. The determination of what names *are* in actual use has not proved an easy task, as has been pointed out in previous discussion. In framing a question on class identification for the present study it has also been indicated before that the writer built upon what knowledge had been gained before. It was considered unnecessary to repeat the exploratory work of the *Fortune* survey, which had asked an open-answer type of question, for public attitude surveys based on cross sections of the total population characteristically achieve quite similar results, and *For-*

[2] [Editor's note: Centers determined the political views of his respondents on the basis of their answers to a conservatism-radicalism (C-R) battery of six questions he put to them: whether they believed America was truly a land of opportunity; whether workers should have more power in government; whether basic industries should be nationalized; whether they preferred the basic principles of the welfare state over those of laissez-faire; whether they usually sided with workers or employers during strikes; and whether they believed that workers were generally treated fairly by their employers.] It will be recalled that a person is described as *ultra conservative* if five or more of his responses to the questions in the six-item C-R battery were in the conservative direction. An individual is classified as a plain *conservative* if three or more of his responses were conservative in character and there were at least two more such conservative responses than any possible number of radical answers. A person is defined as an *ultra radical* if five or more of his six answers were radical in nature. One is called simply a *radical* here if three or more of his replies were radical and outnumbered any possible conservative answers to the extent of two or more. All other persons are designated as *indeterminate*.

[3] In tests for significance between groups in this report usually only one response category is used. Although one could, of course, use more, it would appear superfluous to do so in most cases. Also, in all cases the significance tests for the two rural strata are limited to comparisons between them only.

TABLE 1. Attitude Differences of Occupational Strata: Conservatism-Radicalism

	N	% Ultra Conservative	% Conservative	% Indeterminate	% Radical	% Ultra Radical	For "Ultra Conservative" Differences Are Significant Between
NATIONAL*	1097	22.5	27.9	27.3	13.5	8.8	
Urban							
A. All Business, Professional, and White Collar	430	35.8	31.9	21.4	7.0	3.9	A & B†
B. All Urban Manual *(Detailed Groupings for A and B)*	414	7.5	21.0	33.1	22.7	15.7	B & A
1. Large Business	54	55.5	31.5	11.1	0.0	1.9	1 & 4,5,6,7
2. Professional	73	30.2	39.7	19.2	4.1	6.8	2 & 3,5,6,7
3. Small Business	131	45.8	28.2	17.6	6.9	1.5	3 & 2,4,5,6,7
4. White Collar	172	24.4	31.4	28.5	10.5	5.2	4 & 1,3,5,6,7
5. Skilled Manual	163	12.2	26.4	34.4	17.2	9.8	5 & 1,2,3,4
6. Semi-skilled Manual	174	5.2	16.1	29.3	28.7	20.7	6 & 1,2,3,4
7. Unskilled Manual	77	2.5	20.8	39.0	20.8	16.9	7 & 1,2,3,4
Rural							
C. Farm Owners and Managers	153	32.8	35.9	24.8	3.9	2.6	C & D‡
D. Farm Tenants and Laborers	69	11.7	31.9	30.4	18.8	7.2	D & C

* Figures for the national population include a few persons who either could not be classified as to occupation or who were classified as "Protective Service" (e.g. members of the armed or police forces).

† The two *major* urban strata are compared for significance only with each other.

‡ The two *rural* strata are compared for significance only with each other.

251

tune's question, "What word do you use to name the class in America you belong to?", had gained the information necessary for the formulation of a question designed to more rigidly structure the identifications into a system. Since *Fortune* had found that the terms *middle class* and *working* (or *laboring*) *class* were the most frequently used of all, it was clear that these, along with the terms *upper class* and *lower class,* which (together with apparently equivalent terms) constituted the next most frequent responses, should constitute the alternatives for the question used in the present study.

Members of the cross section were asked: "If you were asked to use one of these four names for your social class, which would you say you belonged in: the middle class, lower class, working class or upper class?" The answers will convincingly dispel any doubt that Americans are class conscious, and quite as quickly quell any glib assertions like *Fortune's* "America Is Middle Class."

Not only do all but an insignificant minority admit of membership in some class, but over half of our people (51 per cent) say they belong to the working class (Table 2). Given the opportunity now to claim membership in any of four different classes, only about half as many claim to belong to the middle

class as have been found calling themselves middle class in previous studies. Whereas the latter have shown, characteristically, figures of from 80 to 90 per cent, only 43 per cent of people now say they are middle class. . . .

Class Identifications of Occupational Strata

. . . What is the relation between people's present occupational status and their class membership? An answer is found in Table 3.

Nearly three-quarters of all business, professional and white collar workers identify themselves with the middle or upper classes. An even larger proportion of all manual workers, 79 per cent, identify, on the other hand, with the working and lower classes. Within the detailed urban occupational categories there is the same sort of gradation displayed as that shown for politico-economic orientations in the last chapter. But now, somewhat more than in the usual case, there is also a definite and sharp break to be discerned in the difference in the identifications of white collar workers as compared to those of skilled manual workers. The former, despite such trends as those reported above, still tends to be a middle class

TABLE 2. Class Identifications of a National Cross Section of White Males (July 1945) (N = 1,097)

Per Cent Saying	
Upper Class	3
Middle Class	43
Working Class	51
Lower Class	1
Don't Know	1
"Don't Believe in Classes"	1

TABLE 3. Psychological Differences of Occupational Strata: Class Identification

Q23a. If you were asked to use one of these four names for your social class, which would you say you belonged in: the Middle Class, Lower Class, Working Class, or Upper Class?

Occupation	N	% Upper Class	% Middle Class	% Working Class	% Lower Class	% Don't Know	% Don't Believe in Classes	% Total Upper and Middle	For "Total Upper and Middle" Differences Are Significant Between
Urban									
A. All Business, Professional, and White Collar	430	4	70	23	0.2	1.2	1.8	74	A & B
B. All Manual Workers	414	1	20	77	1.7	0.3	—	21	B & A
(Detailed Groupings for A and B)									
1. Large Business	54	13	78	7	—	2.0	—	91	1 & 3,4,5,6,7
2. Professional	73	4	81	10	—	1.0	4.0	85	2 & 4,5,6,7
3. Small Business	131	3	70	24	—	1.5	1.5	73	3 & 1,5,6,7
4. White Collar	172	2	61	34	0.6	0.6	1.8	63	4 & 1,2,5,6,7
5. Skilled Manual	163	2	26	71	1.0	—	—	28	5 & 1,2,3,4,6
6. Semi-skilled	174	1	14	83	1.0	1.0	—	15	6 & 1,2,3,4,5
7. Unskilled	77	—	18	75	7.0	—	—	18	7 & 1,2,3,4
Rural									
C. Farm Owners and Managers	153	3	42	51	1.0	3.0	—	45	C & D
D. Farm Tenants and Laborers	69	2	16	73	2.0	7.0	—	18	D & C

group, the latter to be, in heavy majority, a working class one.[4]

. . . . .

Summary Review of Occupation and Class Consciousness

Does a person's status and role with respect to the economic order of society
give rise in him to a complex or pattern of attitudes, interests and beliefs as
well as to a consciousness of membership in a group which shares those attitudes, interests and beliefs as this
interest group theory demands?

If this is the case, then one should
expect to find large differences in people's politico-economic orientations or
attitudes, to conform to their differences in status and role. *Such differences are found.* [Earlier] the differences in conservatism-radicalism were
shown to have a positive and substantial relationship to people's economic
status and role as that status and role
was indicated by occupational position.
Especially striking were the differences
in conservatism-radicalism to be seen
between large business owners and
managers on the one hand and the unskilled and semi-skilled manual workers on the other. All this is in complete
accord with theory. . . .

But what of that other aspect of the
theory; that which implies that persons
occupying different positions with respect to the processes of production
and exchange should have different
class affiliations? Here, too, facts are in
essential harmony with the trend to be
expected. An examination of the class
affiliations of occupational strata as
shown by Table 3 confirms theoretical
expectation, and confirms it in substantially the same way as has already been
found to be the case with respect to attitudes. People at opposite poles of the
occupational order have such widely
different class identifications that there
can be no mistaking the fact that the
members of the strata at the top of the
occupational order, in overwhelming
majority, declare themselves to be
members of classes to which only small
minorities of the lowest occupational
strata will claim membership. The con-
verse is equally true, or nearly so at
least. Lower stratum people do not in
any great numbers identify themselves
with the same social classes as higher
placed persons do. Also, "members" of
strata in the middle of the array, as
might be expected, again, have divided
loyalties. Single strata such as white
collar workers or skilled manual workers, though showing a difference in
class affiliation between themselves that
is so large as to approach the kind of
cleavage that some students of modern
social classes have anticipated, nevertheless betray the intermediate character of their positions by less solidarity
of affiliation within their given stratum
being shown. The cleavage toward stratum polarities with respect to class
identification has clearly advanced even
farther than it has with respect to politico-economic attitudes, and is essentially similar in character.

---

[4] Preliminary analysis of data on the class identifications of women indicates that these generalizations apply to women as well as men. The occupation-class relationships appear substantially
the same, regardless of the sex of the sample.

VI

POWER
AND
POLITICS

17

THE STUDY OF LOCAL COMMUNITY POWER

Arnold M. Rose

18

THE HIGHER CIRCLES

C. Wright Mills

19

WHO HAS THE POWER?

David Riesman,
Nathan Glazer,
and Reuel Denney

There is no question more basic to the understanding of any society than the relationship between social class and political power. In the current sociological literature which treats the question of political power, either at the local or the national level, two major interpretations of the distribution of power compete for acceptance.

The *elitist* view claims that power, either on the local or national scene, is exercised essentially by a small group that rules, directs, manipulates, or controls in its own interests. The elitist model is important for social stratification because part of the ruling elite is usually said to consist of the dominant economic forces in the community. The elitist model, then, tends to be neo-Marxist in its orientation for it sees a crucial tie-in between economic and political power, and is alert to the manner in which economic power is translated into political power.

The *pluralist* model, more in the liberal than the radical tradition, does not see power as concentrated exclusively among a small elite group, but regards it as far more diffused and fragmented throughout the society. According to this view, a great multitude of autonomous groups competes with one another for the realization of its interests. The game is not fixed and the outcome is not a foregone conclusion. The political process is characterized by shifting alliances and changing constellations of forces, depending upon the issues, and the victors in the struggle change also with the issues themselves, with the outcome depending upon the complex, workings of a competitive system.

The three essays that begin this section are taken from books that illustrate this debate between elitists and pluralists. Since Robert and Helen Lynd published their pioneering study of Middletown in 1925, there have been literally dozens of sociological investigations of American communities. Not all of them have focused on social stratification or the relationship of stratification to political power in the community. But many of them have; and many of these studies have differed in the ways they have studied power in the community. The first selection in this group is from *The Power Structure,* a book by the late sociologist Arnold Rose. Rose, who was inclined to favor the pluralist view, analyzes here the different methods by which power in the local community has been investigated; he assesses the strengths and weaknesses of each method, and suggests the relationship of each method to elitist and pluralist theory.

The second selection is taken from the controversial and widely read *The Power Elite* by C. Wright Mills (whom we have seen before in a selection from *White Collar*). Mills, the iconoclastic radical who, like Thorstein Veblen and Charles Beard before him so upset his academic colleagues, was at his death the hero of the emerging New Left. Nearly five years before President Eisenhower warned of the growing influence of the so-called military-industrial complex,* Mills disturbed the universe with his analysis of the national power structure. Since World War II, he argued, a triumvirate of political, corporate, and military elites, whose lives intersect in their common interests, similar social class backgrounds, and the enormous power that they wield, has come to dominate a society which is increasingly stalemated at the "middle levels of power" and which consists of an atomized, impotent, and manipulated mass of citizens at the bottom.

The third essay is taken from David Riesman's (et al.) well-known work, *The Lonely Crowd.* While some of the material and references are clearly out of date—the work was originally published in 1952—this brief essay illustrates extremely well the pluralist idea. While Mills sees the important decisions made increasingly at the top by an exclusive and unified elite, Riesman sees a more open and fluid situation, with the give and take of so-called veto groups which permeate the society. His is a much more diversified structure, with many autonomous power sources jockeying for strategic advantage. In this view, as opposed to elitist theory, social class is not central in the struggle for political power.

■ Arnold M. Rose

As Linton Freeman and his associates have demonstrated, the method of study of local community power has in large part determined the outcome of the research, and the several approaches identify different groups of actors as powerful.[1] Polsby has remarked that "What social scientists presume to be the case will in great measure influence the design and even the outcome of their research."[2] There is an interrelation of the definition of

* The phrase is attributed to Malcolm Moos, now president of the University of Minnesota.

[1] Linton C. Freeman, Thomas J. Faxaro, Warner Bloomberg, Jr., and Morris H. Sunshine, "Locating Leaders in Local Communities: A Comparison of Some Alternative Approaches," *American Sociological Review,* 28 (October 1963), 797. Although they use the term "leader," it is obvious it refers to the same phenomenon discussed here as "power."

[2] Nelson W. Polsby, *Community Power and Political Theory* (New Haven: Yale University Press, 1963), p. 6.

variables in the research, the actual research strategy, and the outcome of the investigation. The multitude of definitions has led to a number of methods,[3] and a variety of results. In order to compare the outcomes of any two studies, it is imperative that the interrelation and co-determination of these three factors be kept constantly in mind. In general there may be said to be three methods of research in local community power studies—the positional, the reputational, and the decision-making approaches—although there are variations within each approach.

The *positional approach* to the study of community power assumes that "an actor's power is closely correlated with his position in an official or semi-official hierarchy."[4] This method searches for the "potential power-offices in the community's institutionalized economic, political, and/or civic structures."[5]

We can affix the names of the people who occupy these offices, and we can say that here are the people who speak for the major institutional sectors of the community. Therefore, they surely must be the power-holders of this community,

the people that are most influential in initiating and sanctioning policy.[6]

The great advantage of this method is its simplicity. Aside from the task of defining which positions in the community are "on top," this approach presents the researcher with few, if any, procedural problems; it "employs objective, verifiable social characteristics of specified individuals," and "assumes that the power structure consists largely of those persons who belong in some selected social category."[7] This very simplicity, however, also is the basis of the many disadvantages of positional analysis, which all accrue from "the shaky assumption on which it rests, for formal position is not necessarily correlated with power."[8]

There is a complete disregard for those not occupying formal, official positions, and therefore, no distinction between authority and control.[9] As sociologists have long known, the informal social structure is often as important as, or more important than, the formal structure.

It should be mentioned that a strict positional analysis is rarely, if ever, employed as the sole method in community power studies, but rather as an

[3] For a description of the various methods see Robert A. Dahl, *Modern Political Analysis* (Englewood Cliffs, N.J.: Prentice-Hall, 1963), pp. 52–3; Peter H. Rossi, "Community Decision Making," *Administrative Science Quarterly,* 1 (March 1957), 425; Linton C. Freeman, *et al.,* "Locating Leaders," pp. 791–8; and Sethard Fisher, "Community-Power Studies: A Critique," *Social Research,* 29(4) (Winter 1962), 449–66.

[4] Dahl, *Analysis,* p. 52.

[5] Delbert Miller, quoted in conversation by Howard J. Ehrlich, "Power and Democracy: A Critical Discussion," in William V. D'Antonio and Howard J. Ehrlich (eds.), *Power and Democracy in America* (Notre Dame, Ind.: University of Notre Dame Press, 1961), p. 99; also Robert O. Schulze and Leonard U. Blumberg, "The Determination of Local Power Elites," *American Journal of Sociology,* 63 (November 1957), 291.

[6] Quoted from Delbert Miller (see preceding note).

[7] Fisher, "Community-Power Studies," pp. 449–50.

[8] Dahl, *Analysis,* p. 52. "The positional approach also assumes a connection between social position and social behavior, that is, if one knows the former one can make reliable inferences about the latter" (Fisher, "Community-Power Studies," p. 450).

[9] Harold D. Lasswell, Daniel Lerner, and C. Easton Rothwell, *The Comparative Study of Elites* (Stanford, Calif.: Stanford University Press, 1952), pp. 7–8.

adjunct to other methods. In some studies, after the power structure is identified by other means, it is compared with a list of occupants of formal positions to determine the extent of their participation. In other studies, lists of occupants of positions in different institutional sectors are compared to determine the amount of overlap. Finally, the lists are used as a preliminary step in both the reputational and decision-making methods which are discussed below. In any event, formal position is usually regarded as only one of many possible resources in determining an actor's potential for affecting the behavior of others. It is generally assumed that there are also power-holders who do not formally hold office in the major institutions and associations.

Currently the most widely employed approach to the study of community power, and consequently the one subjected to the most penetrating examination and criticism, is the *reputational approach*. In general, the procedure is to "determine community-power structures on the basis of judgments by community members who are considered 'knowledgeable' about community life. These 'judges' select names from lists of potential candidates based on imputed degrees of influence. Those persons most frequently selected according to the given criteria are said to constitute the power structure." [10]

Most of these power-reputation or power-attribution studies stem from the work of Floyd Hunter in Regional City.[11] One of his most severe critics, Nelson Polsby, acknowledges that "the work of Floyd Hunter dominates the contemporary scene," [12] and all those who use this approach realize their debt to his pioneering work. It is therefore useful to examine the specific manner in which Hunter went about identifying the power structure of Regional City.

In essence, Hunter's method was simple—if you want to know about power in a community, ask people who are active in the community. Hunter first got "basic lists of power personnel" for Atlanta, Georgia:

> The Community Council in Regional City (Atlanta), a council of civic organizations, provided preliminary lists of leaders in community affairs. The Chamber of Commerce provided business leaders of establishments employing more than 500 employees and of financial houses doing the largest volume of clearances. The League of Women Voters provided lists of local political leaders who had at least major governmental committee chairmanship status. Newspaper editors and other civic leaders provided lists of society leaders and leaders of wealth.[13]

Hunter then created a panel of 14 "judges"—on what basis *they* were selected Hunter does not tell us—and asked for their opinions as to who "were top leaders on each of the lists thus provided." [14] Through the use of

[10] Fisher, "Community-Power Studies," p. 451. See also Freeman, *et al.,* "Locating Leaders," p. 793; Raymond E. Wolfinger, "A Plea for a Decent Burial," *American Sociological Review,* 27 (December 1962), 842; Rossi, "Community Decision Making," pp. 427–9; Dahl, *Analysis,* pp. 52–3; Ehrlich, "A Critical Discussion," pp. 99–100.

[11] Floyd Hunter, *Community Power Structure, A Study of Decision Makers* (Garden City, N.Y.: Doubleday, 1963).

[12] Polsby, *Political Theory,* p. 45.

[13] Hunter, *Community Power Structure,* p. 261.

[14] Ibid.

these judges, Hunter practically nullifies the usefulness of the previous lists he gathered, except to put some limits on the judges, for it is the judges who select the 40 "top influentials." These in turn were interviewed and asked, "If a project were before the community that required a *decision* by a group of leaders—leaders that nearly everyone would accept—which *ten* on the list of forty would you choose?"[15] By counting the votes that each person received, Hunter designated the 12 highest as the "upper-limits personnel." This was confirmed by constructing a sociogram of the mutual choices made, indicating that the "upper-limits personnel" rarely voted for people outside that group.

Having located the "power personnel" of Atlanta, Hunter proceeded to interview them extensively to determine how this power structure worked. At the top of the "power structure" in Atlanta, Hunter found, was a small group of men who made the important decisions for the community. "The test for admission to this circle of decision-makers is almost wholly a man's position in the business community in Regional City."[16] These policy-makers initiate policy. Once a policy has been decided at this level, the policy-makers "move out of the picture" and turn the project over to men in the "under-structure" (professionals, association staff, political figures, etc.) who then see that the policy formulated above is executed.[17] On some projects the policy group may "designate" a number of its members to direct its execution.[18]

How is policy made in Regional City? At one point Hunter specifically states that "the popular notion of men plotting behind the scenes is a fictional illusion. . . ."[19] Nonetheless, even with this explicit disclaimer, the picture of policy-making in Atlanta that he paints is very much one of conspiracy and "behind the scenes" activity. For example, Hunter tells us that "The 'top-flight' meetings—those of high policy nature—are held in private clubs or private homes."[20] And, "The fact that the under-structure personnel do not frequent the clubs is in itself one of the subtle exclusion devices. The 'boys' of the Grandview Club are known to make policy decisions within the confines of the club dining rooms which eventually filter down to the community under-structure."[21]

Hunter quotes at length from James Treat, the individual in the "power structure" who was able to "manipulate" the governor of the state.[22] Treat describes how the policy-makers held a meeting at the Grandview Club where one "crowd" initiated the project of an International Trade Council. Treat goes on:

There is one detail I left out, and it is an important one. We went into that meeting with a board of directors picked. The constitution was all written, and the man who was to head the council as executive was named. . . . a fellow who will take advice.[23]

At this meeting of policy-makers, the details are worked out and money is raised to get the project started. Up to this point the matter has been kept entirely within the circle of decision-makers, as Treat indicates.

[15] Ibid. p. 63 (italics Hunter's).   [16] Ibid. p. 78.   [17] Ibid. p. 98.   [18] Ibid. p. 94.
[19] Ibid. p. 178.   [20] Ibid. p. 16.   [21] Ibid. p. 193.   [22] Ibid. p. 160.
[23] Ibid. p. 171.

The public doesn't know anything about the project until it reaches the stage I've been talking about. After the matter is financially sound, then we go to the newspapers and say *there is a proposal for consideration*.[24]

Hunter has quoted Treat at length not because he feels this is an exceptional incident, but rather because he feels that Treat's "description is applicable to many similar situations in the community."[25] But it is not only through the use of their wealth that the top leaders are able to initiate policies and have them carried through, for there are few if any who have the power to resist top leaders.

The method of handling the relatively powerless under-structure is through the pressures previously described—warnings, intimidations, threats, and in extreme cases violence. In some cases the method may include isolation from all sources of support for the individual, including his job, and therefore his income. The principle of "divide and rule" is applicable in the community, as it is in larger units of political patterning, and it is effective.[26]

Largely because Hunter concluded that Atlanta was ruled by a small clique of decision-makers who made community policies from behind the scenes and in their own interests, the "reputational method" was identified with conclusions of a "power elite" (to use C. Wright Mills's term). As a result, criticisms of the reputational method have often been criticisms of findings of "power elites."

In fact, however, while the reputational method may tend to discover "power elites" where there are none, it only does so when the researcher himself is predisposed toward finding a "pyramidal power structure." As the pluralist critics of Hunter have pointed out,[27] there is much evidence in his study to indicate that a cohesive group of policy-makers, who wield most of the power in the community and make all the important decisions, simply does not exist.

In the first place, Hunter's particular use of the reputational method which *tended* to indicate a cohesive ruling elite was a result of Hunter's expectations. Hunter asked his 40 leaders selected by his panel of judges, "If a project were before the community that required *decision* by a group of leaders —leaders nearly everyone would accept —which *ten* on the list of forty would you choose?"[28] Assume for the moment that there are different leaders on different issues as the pluralists suggest. While we do not know how the judges or the top leaders interpreted the question, hopefully we would find on the list the top leaders in different "issue-areas." We now have a list of "key influentials." The problem is whether the people named on this list are influential across the board or whether each person on the list is very influential in one area and not at all in other areas. But by asking the general question as Hunter does, he cannot distinguish between the two structures of leadership and, in fact, by artificially combining the names of these people on one list he presents the illusion of a cohesive elite.

In addition to the panel-of-experts

---

[24] Ibid, p. 172 (italics mine).
[25] Ibid. p. 170.
[26] Ibid. p. 241.
[27] See, for example, Nelson W. Polsby, *Political Theory*, pp. 115–56.
[28] Hunter, *Community Power Structure*, p. 63 (italics Hunter's).

method used by Hunter, other reputational researchers have employed the "snowball" or "cobweb" technique—in which a number of individuals selected at random name the leaders who, in their turn, are interviewed and asked for additional names—and the community sampling method.[29] As mentioned above, the most popular panel-of-experts method employs positional analysis as an intervening step.

The reputational approach introduces a new dimension in the study of power. In addition to power as a potential for control and power as control itself, one must now recognize power reputations as a new, distinct class of variables. The relationship among these three variables is by no means clear, although even reputational researchers, such as D'Antonio and Form, call attention to the importance of the distinction.[30] Power as control is usually determined by examining the decision-making process; power as a potential for control may be determined by locating the person in various formal hierarchies; and power reputations are determined by asking judges who they think is powerful. It should be mentioned that most reputational researchers do not consider the reputation itself as the goal of their study, but as an index of power as either potential or actual control. For example, Hunter uses "power" to describe "the acts of men going about the business of moving other men to act in relation to themselves or in relation to organic or inorganic things,"[31] while D'Antonio and Form define it as the ability to control the decision-making process.[32] Thus reputations for power have been employed as indices of both potential and actual behavior, although many of the researchers confuse the indices with the definition of power they give lip service to when it comes to interpreting their findings.

Where reputations are used as an index of actual behavior, critics argue that it is more meaningful to study the behavior itself. Polsby claims that what is being determined by this method is the identity of those persons who have the reputation for being influential. This reputation can be divided into "the part which is justified by behavior and the part which is not so justified."[33] That is, "asking about rep-

---

[29] A. Alexander Fanelli, "A Typology of Community Leadership Based on Influence and Interaction Within the Leader Subsystem," *Social Forces*, 34(4) (May 1956), 333; Schulze and Blumberg, "Local Power Elites," p. 292; Robert E. Agger, "Power Attributions in the Local Community," *Social Forces*, 34(4) (May 1956), 322–31.

[30] William V. D'Antonio and William H. Form, *Influentials in Two Border Cities* (Notre Dame, Ind.: University of Notre Dame Press, 1965), pp. 11–12; J. R. Lawrence, "In the Footsteps of Community Power," *American Political Science Review*, 55 (December 1961), 819–20; Howard J. Ehrlich, "The Reputational Approach to the Study of Community Power," *American Sociological Review*, 26(6), (December 1961), 927; Raymond E. Wolfinger, "Reputation and Reality in the Study of Community Power," *American Sociological Review*, 25 (October 1960), 636.

[31] Hunter, *Community Power Structure*, p. 2.

[32] D'Antonio and Form, *Influentials*, pp. 11–12.

[33] Nelson W. Polsby, "Three Problems in the Analysis of Community Power," *American Sociological Review*, 24 (December 1959), 796–7. "The problem that has always bothered me about the reputational method is its latent circularity. . . . How do you know whether they are influentials? What is the test of it? Do you ask of other people whether they are influential, and how do you test the projections of these other people? This could go on *ad infinitum*. I do not see it as an objective test by which we know whether the people who finally get on his list are influential or not. Speaking rigorously, all we could say would be that [we have] a

utations is asking at a remove about behavior. . . . It can be cogently argued that the researcher should therefore make it his business to study behavior directly and not rely on second-hand opinions." [34] Where, on the other hand, reputations are used as an index of power thought of as a *potential* of control, such potential must be evaluated alongside other bases for potential, such as formal position.

This distinction is seen by Ehrlich as explaining Wolfinger's criticism of the reputational method which calls attention to the fact that those identified as influential by that method often lose out to comparatively un-influential people when they confront each other in the community. Wolfinger, he maintains, is concerned with the exercise of power, while the reputational approach focuses on potential power. Thus he says, "If it can be demonstrated that this power potential, as determined by the reputational method, is indeed exercised, then presumably Wolfinger and those of us equally concerned, would accept the validity of this approach. Without such demonstration, I must concur with him that the reputational approach may be telling us nothing or very little about the objective structure of power and decision-making in the local community." [35] Wolfinger had noted a "troublesome tendency for the 'bigwigs' depicted

as the rulers of Seattle, Atlanta, etc., to be defeated by plebeians who never made the reputational hit parade," [36] and, in a reply to Ehrlich, argues that this cannot be explained by claiming that the method measures potential, not exercised, power. According to Wolfinger, if the reputational method measures potential rather than exercised power, it requires "not merely that the respondents be accurate observers and generalizers, a task that demonstrably is too much for many of them, but that they be such profound students of politics that they can identify the bases of power in the community and the possession of these resources by the townspeople. This assumption is so clearly fallacious that to explicate it is to disprove it." [37] Reputations for power can indeed be said to describe the *perceived* distribution of power in the local community, and depending on the purposes of the study, this may be useful in helping to describe the local power system. If, for example, it can be shown that the way in which the power structure is perceived helps determine the way in which people react to it, reputations for power will definitely provide a useful variable in the study of power. For example, Vidich and Bensman comment on a dominant leader working behind the scenes in a small town called Springdale. All groups and individuals overestimate

list of people who have reputations for influence—and we could never say anything more than that, for this is actually all we know." Dahl, quoted in Ehrlich, "A Critical Discussion," pp. 101–2; see also M. Herbert Danzger, "Community Power Structure: Problems and Continuities," *American Sociological Review*, 29 (October 1964), p. 707.

[34] Polsby, "Three Problems," p. 797. "In the study of community power, as in other areas of sociology, the examination of intentions, reputations, and attributions is to be applauded. The interpretations we assign to these 'meanings' must, however, always be modulated and enriched by our knowledge of the behavior which accompanies them." Nelson W. Polsby, "The Sociology of Community Power : A Reassessment," *Social Forces*, 37 (March 1959), 236.

[35] Ehrlich, "The Reputational Approach," 926–7.

[36] Wolfinger, "A Plea for a Decent Burial," pp. 844–5.

[37] Ibid.

his authority, but by this very fact they increase his power since they act on the basis of their estimation.[38]

Few reputational researchers would accept the relegation of the technique to this comparatively minor role in community power studies, and fewer still would agree with Agger that it is "simply a heuristic device at this stage of theoretical development."[39] To accept such a view would leave them open for Wolfinger's criticism that their approach is "little more than a methodologically elaborate variant of the older procedure of asking insiders."[40] However, to then charge, as Wolfinger does, that these researchers believe their method to be "a sufficient tool to study the distribution of political power in a community,"[41] would seem too extreme, for reputational studies have increasingly employed positional and decision-making analyses to supplement their descriptions.

One of the basic assumptions of the reputational method seems to be that power is exercised behind the scenes and that it is next to impossible to obtain an accurate picture of the structure of power by attending to overt behavior. Thus the researcher must rely on the inside information supplied to him by a panel of knowledgeable community members: "The 'real' leaders are always held to be 'behind' who-

ever is revealed as the community leadership as the result of firsthand digging."[42] For example, Hunter describes men of power in Regional City enforcing their decisions "by persuasion, intimidation, coercion, and, if necessary, force. Because of these elements of compulsion, power-wielding is often a hidden process. The men involved do not wish to become identified with the negative aspects which the process implies."[43] Polsby charges that this assumption of covert leadership often leads researchers "to disbelieve their senses, and to substitute unfounded speculation for plain fact."[44] Another reason the top power-holders may not be directly observable stems from the fact that they may not choose to exercise their power because less powerful individuals, who are involved in the decision-making process, will act in accordance with the general interests of the top power-holders. They may become active only when directly challenged.[45] One danger underlying the assumption that power is exercised covertly is what Robert Dahl has referred to as the "fallacy of infinite regression." If observable behavior is not to be regarded as a reliable index of power, then one must search behind the scenes for centers of power behind the actors who carry out the drama on stage. Once these covert power-holders are identified, by whatever method, the

---

[38] Arthur J. Vidich and Joseph Bensman, *Small Town in Mass Society* (Princeton: Princeton University Press, 1958), p. 277.

[39] Agger, "Power Attributions," p. 331.

[40] Wolfinger, "Reputation and Reality," p. 637.

[41] Ibid. p. 638.

[42] Nelson W. Polsby, "Three Problems," p. 797.

[43] Hunter, *Community Power Structure*, p. 24; also Robert O. Schulze, "The Role of Economic Dominants in Community Power Structure," *American Sociological Review*, 23 (February 1958), 7.

[44] Nelson W. Polsby, "Power in Middletown: Fact and Value in Community Research," *Canadian Journal of Economics and Political Science*, 26(4) (November 1960), 602–3.

[45] See Danzger's discussion of salience of goals in Chapter II.

question immediately presents itself whether there may not be other covert power-holders behind these, and others yet behind them, and so on. There would seem to be no way to prevent this infinite regression of power to ever more concentrated covert centers. That this problem is a real one is demonstrated by the fact that Hunter, among others, is at times "forced to interject that the votes of the informed informants do not accurately describe the ranking of power in the community because some of the most powerful people prefer not to participate directly in the processes of leadership." [46] If the judgments of community knowledgeables are incorrect, there must be some standard against which they are being measured, and this standard is all too often provided by the judgment of the researcher himself. Many reputational researchers do accept the judgments of their panels, however, and thus are not subject to this particular criticism.

Critics of the reputational approach have also turned their attention to the question of the validity of the entire panel-of-experts method. Polsby calls into doubt the special expertise of such a panel in uncovering behind-the-scenes power activity. Schulze and Blumberg compared the judgments of three different panels in "Cibola," Michigan, and discovered a high degree of consensus "as to the overall composition of the local elite of power and influence." [47] According to Polsby, this "effectively denies the panel's special knowledge and renders the test for expertise—assuming the unlikely possi-

bility that one could be devised—moot." [48] A diligent observer would not be beyond compiling a comparable list, by more direct methods, of facts that are apparently not as covert as was assumed.

Danzger suggests comparing the results obtained through reputational analysis with those obtained through other techniques to determine the former's validity. If the findings are similar, it is claimed, the reputational method is validated. [49] Schulze and Blumberg report that the power structure they uncovered by the reputational technique differed significantly from that determined by superordinate position in either the economic or political-civic institutions. [50] On the other hand, Linton Freeman and his associates found that in Syracuse the leaders uncovered by the positional and reputational approaches were essentially the same. These leaders "enjoy the reputation for top leadership" and head "the largest and most actively participating business, industrial, governmental, political, professional, educational, labor, and religious organizations. . . . In view of their formal command over the institutional structure and the symbolic value of their status as indexed by reputation, these individuals may be called the Institutional Leaders of Syracuse." [51]

Herein is demonstrated a dilemma faced by the reputational method. If a reputational analysis yields a power structure similar to that revealed by the positional approach, or for that matter any more direct approach, its

[46] Danzger, "Community Power Structure," p. 713.
[47] Schulze and Blumberg, "Local Power Elites," p. 293.
[48] Polsby, *Political Theory*, pp. 51–2.
[49] Danzger, "Community Power Structure," pp. 708–9.
[50] Schulze and Blumberg, "Local Power Elites," pp. 292–3.
[51] Freeman, *et al.*, "Locating Leaders," p. 797.

critics denounce its claim to expert, inside knowledge, for if it appears that power is not exercised covertly, there is thus no need to employ an indirect method of study. If, however, reputational analysis yields a power structure different from anything determined by more direct methods, its critics claim there is no basis for validation. The absence of an acceptable criterion is characteristic of most, if not all, measures of validity, and thus this is not a shortcoming peculiar to the present case. Since the reputational technique claims to divulge information that is inaccessible by direct observation or by more direct methods, it should be expected to yield different results. In comparing their results to those obtained by other methods, and by accepting concurrence of results as a validation of their method, reputational researchers have implicitly denied the special competence their method is supposed to possess.

Another criticism directed at the reputational approach concerns the accuracy with which the judges perceive power relations. Even granting the questionable assumption that panels of experts are necessary to uncover hidden power relations, this criticism questions the judges' ability to "report political phenomena accurately." [52] The most vocal critics of power reputation studies—Dahl, Polsby, and Wolfinger—report that their study of New Haven reveals that "eminent citizens often were ill-informed about policy-making situations in which they had been deeply involved." [53] Their general argument is that "some people distort reality, that some who should know what is going on don't, and that others accept gossip as gospel and pass it on as the latter." [54] D'Antonio et al. reply that "it is, of course, equally true that some people do not distort reality, that some do indeed know what is going on and that others can discern gossip from gospel." [55] Ehrlich's rebuttal admits that a sole reliance on reputational methods may yield an inaccurate picture of the power structure, but that other means of research are neither logically nor empirically excluded to those who use the reputational approach: "If it is true that those who have used the reputational method have employed it as the sole source of their data, then this may well be a deficiency in their research design but not in the reputational method per se." [56] Another charge, that it is impossible to tell whether or not the respondent and the researcher share the same definition of power, is certainly not peculiar to this method or this area of study, but applies as well to all areas of social research. [57]

Critics have also charged that the "reputational method is particularly susceptible to ambiguity resulting from respondents' confusion of status and

---

[52] Wolfinger, "Reputation and Reality," p. 640; Fisher, "Community-Power Studies," pp. 462–4, 466.

[53] Ibid., pp. 842–43; also Wolfinger, "Reputation and Reality," pp. 641–2; Robert A. Dahl, "Equality and Power in American Society," in William V. D'Antonio and Howard J. Ehrlich (eds.), Power and Democracy in America (Notre Dame, Ind.: University of Notre Dame Press, 1961), p. 76.

[54] William V. D'Antonio, Howard J. Ehrlich, and Eugene C. Erickson, "Further Notes on the Study of Community Power," American Sociological Review, 27 (December 1962), 849.

[55] Ibid.

[56] Ehrlich, "The Reputational Approach," p. 926.

[57] Ibid.

power." [58] As mentioned above, a preliminary positional analysis has accompanied many reputational studies. From these lists of position-holders, such as those Hunter compiled of business, government, civic, and society institutions, the judges select community leaders, and through a further process of self-selection, the list is reduced. It seems odd that a method designed to probe beneath the surface of visible power relations should begin with the persons most visible to any observer, and it is from this list that the powerful are to be drawn. The judges are presented with the lists and instructed, by Hunter, for example, to "place in rank order, one through ten, ten persons from each list of personnel—who in your opinion are the most influential persons in the field designated— influential from the point of view of ability to lead others. . . . If there are persons . . . you feel should be included in the ranking order of ten rather than the ones given, please include them." [59] The implication would seem to be that the lists already contained the names of almost all possible influentials, and upon the statements of the judges would depend only their relative ranking. D'Antonio and Form depart from this aspect of Hunter's technique by providing judges with no lists of names, but asking them only to name the persons they thought most influential in certain areas. [60] If those who appear on reputational lists of influentials are chosen from lists of position-holders, it ought to be no shock that positional and reputational analyses often identify the same persons. Although D'Antonio and Form claim that their judges did not automatically call an individual influential because he had an important office, and tended rather to evaluate performance, expected performance, and resources and their use, they mention elsewhere their focus on the community's leaders who are "the influentials, the men of high position." [61]

Danzger and Rossi independently note the likelihood of reputational judges basing their estimates on formal position or organizational participation, and Wolfinger claims that the difficulty is further compounded by the low esteem in which labor leaders, municipal officials, and local politicians are held, as well as their usually lower socio-economic status, compared to businessmen and leaders of charitable organizations. [62] If reputational studies reveal nothing more than status hierarchies, then their use in measuring power must wait upon the specification of the relationship between status and power.

Another closely related question pertaining to the reputational technique is the variability of power. Lasswell and Kaplan believe that "political phenomena are only obscured by the pseudo-

[58] Wolfinger, "Reputation and Reality," p. 640; Fisher, *et al.*, "Community-Power Studies," pp. 462–4, 466.

[59] Hunter, *Community Power Structure*, p. 256.

[60] D'Antonio and Form, *Influentials*, pp. 256–7. On their return trip to El Paso and Ciudad Juarez, in an attempt to estimate the stability of the list of influentials obtained three years earlier, D'Antonio and Form presented the judges with the earlier list of influentials and instructed them to add or subtract names. No explanation is given for this change in technique, which may have biased the results. See pp. 265–6 of their book.

[61] Ibid. pp. 127–8, 1.

[62] M. Herbert Danzger, "Community Power Structure," pp. 710–11; Rossi, "Community Decision Making"; Wolfinger, "Reputation and Reality," p. 640.

simplification attained with any unitary conception of power as being always and everywhere the same." [63] Power derives from and rests on many different bases, and critics have charged that the reputational approach is concerned with a general category of community power that is unrealistic. Wolfinger and Polsby claim that the technique assumes a person's power to be equal for all issues, whereas, they assert, it may actually vary according to the issue. In addition, a person may be given a high general power ranking because "he is perceived to be very influential on a particular issue which is either currently important to the community or salient to the respondent." [64] Even in accepting the premise that an individual's power varies with the issue, Ehrlich denies that a general power ranking across all issues is misleading, although he is uncertain as to what it would yield.[65] This criticism loses much of its force when reputational studies are able to report findings of restricted as well as general spheres of influence. D'Antonio and Form, for example, report that business and politics were generally perceived to be independent spheres of influence,[66] and Delbert Miller finds that "relatively stable groups of leaders are identified with certain institutional sectors of the community through which they express common interest." [67] Certainly, critics cannot claim that the reputational approach is logically denied the possibility of uncovering differing scopes and spheres of influence, although the early studies using this approach were deficient in this regard.

A number of points of dispute have arisen over the length and composition of the list of community influentials compiled by reputational studies and the interpretation of the work of Floyd Hunter in particular. Hunter's rather arbitrary decision to limit the size of the list to 40 in order to reduce it to manageable size is unfortunate because it has often given the reader "the sense of a supreme military headquarters in which forty top strategists arrive at a consensus on what is to be done, and of a series of lesser commanders." [68] Wolfinger charges Hunter with assuming what he set out to prove: "that no more than 40 people were the rulers of Atlanta, possessed more power than the rest of the population, and comprised its 'power structure.'" [69] This seems a rather inflated accusation since it is by no means clear exactly what Hunter meant to say. In the most recent publication employing the reputational approach, D'Antonio and Form *assume* that a small number of persons were crucial in decision-making.[70] Both this and Hunter's study depend on the

[63] Harold D. Lasswell and Abraham Kaplan, *Power and Society* (New Haven: Yale University Press, 1950), p. 92.

[64] Wolfinger, "Reputation and Reality," p. 638; Polsby, "Sociology of Community Power," pp. 232–6.

[65] Ehrlich, "The Reputational Approach," p. 926.

[66] D'Antonio and Form, *Influentials*, pp. 67–68.

[67] Delbert C. Miller, "Decision-making Cliques in Community Power Structures: A Comparative Study of an American and an English City," *American Journal of Sociology*, 64 (November 1958), 306; also Agger, "Power Attributions," p. 323.

[68] Herbert Kaufman and Victor Jones, "The Mystery of Power," *Public Administration Quarterly*, 14 (Summer 1954), 205–12.

[69] Wolfinger, "Reputation and Reality," pp. 642–3; also Polsby, *Political Theory*, p. 49.

[70] D'Antonio and Form, *Influentials*, pp. 58–9.

agreement of judges, which to Polsby is no more than statistical artifact, to determine how many top leaders there are.[71] Both studies also report that they did not identify all the influentials and that some persons so identified may not be influential.[72] This leads Polsby to argue that the efficiency and economy of the reputational method are quite beside the point if it becomes necessary to inquire as to the relationship between the reputational list and the real world: "clearly, all of the principal actors in specified community decisions will have to be on the lists." [73] D'Antonio and his colleagues disagree, stating that the necessity of having an exhaustive list depends on the use to be made of it. If, for example, the purpose is to measure perceived power or to determine public opinion on a community issue, the exhaustiveness of the list is irrelevant. However, they concur with Polsby that the list itself tells very little, is meant to be only the starting point of the study, and is meant to reveal only a part of the power structure.[74] These researchers—who started by using the reputational method much as Hunter did—finished their last work by coming close to accepting a severely restricted range of application for the reputational method, and

subjecting it to the charge that it is nothing more than a report of public opinion on politics.

Another example of the dispute over the nature of power is revealed by Polsby's charge that the names on D'Antonio and Erickson's list of influentials bear rather a fortuitous relationship to the actual exercise of power. The influentials opposed one another on a variety of issues, often bitterly, and there were always influentials on the losing side in a conflict. D'Antonio finds the accusation unwarranted by observing that 23 of 25 key influentials on the list were actually involved in the decision-making process. Exercise of influence for Polsby seems to be actual realization of will in a conflict over a community issue, while for D'Antonio it involves rather participation in the determination of a community decision with an opportunity to realize one's will. Robert Dahl consents to referring to those who appear on the reputation lists as "influentials," but wishes to reserve the term "dominants" for the victors in a conflict.[75]

D'Antonio and his associates also reply to a further charge by Wolfinger that reputational researchers rarely ask for respondents' perceptions of specific events and prefer not to probe past

[71] Polsby, *Political Theory*, p. 49.

[72] Hunter, *Community Power Structure*, p. 61; D'Antonio and Form, *Influentials*, pp. 242–3.

[73] Nelson W. Polsby, "Community Power: Some Reflections on the Recent Literature," *American Sociological Review*, 27 (December 1962), 838–9. "It has been pointed many times that such a list, even if it is exhaustive and accurate, does not tell us all we need to know in order to make a description of the ways in which community decisions get made. Further, the steps which must be taken to ensure the exhaustiveness and accuracy of such a list render the list itself superfluous. Worse yet, the time and effort associated with putting together a list of this kind directs the attention of researchers away from the problems of describing the political order and toward certifying the list's adequacy. In any event, the question of the adequacy of the list seems to come first."

[74] D'Antonio, *et al.*, "Further Notes," p. 851.

[75] Dahl, quoted in Ehrlich, "A Critical Discussion," p. 110; see discussion of Danzger's distinction between power and dominance above. See also Wolfinger, "A Plea for a Decent Burial," p. 843. For the exchange between Polsby and D'Antonio see Polsby, "Some Reflections," p. 839; and D'Antonio, *et al.*, "Further Notes," p. 851.

their general attitudes toward power. Even Hunter's original study examined certain specific issues.[76] Commenting on Hunter's treatment of issues, Rossi states that "the range of issues with which the power structure concerns itself is delimited by example," and since the total set of issues is unspecified, "the impact of the power structure on the life of the community is hard to assess." [77] Polsby also claims that Hunter's choice of issues is extremely biased and based more upon a desire to confirm his theory than on any objective measure.[78] Later, it will be shown that Polsby and others that advocate a decision-making approach face the very same criticism in attempting to provide an objective basis for a choice as to which community decisions to examine.

Much has been written concerning Floyd Hunter's conclusions about the power structure of Regional City. Rarely do two interpreters agree as to exactly what Hunter meant to say. Perhaps the simplest statement of Hunter's conclusions can be found in his own words.

> The top group of the power hierarchy has been isolated and defined as comprised of policy makers. These men are drawn largely from the businessmen's class in Regional City. They form cliques or crowds, as the term is more often used in the community, which formulate policy. Committees for formulation of policy are commonplace, and on community-wide issues policy is channeled by a "fluid committee structure" down to institutional, associational groupings through a lower-level bureaucracy which executes policy.[79]

Hunter presents data that repeatedly emphasize the close relations that hold among those in the top power group, and it is not without reason that many who have read *Community Power Structure* find merit in Herson's statement that "Hunter unveils a structure of community power that is essentially pyramidal, economic, and—given the consensus, interaction, and almost total control at the top—monolithic." [80] Hunter explicitly denied presenting anything more than a rudimentary power pyramid: "I doubt seriously that power forms a single pyramid with any nicety in a community the size of the Regional City. There are *pyramids* of power in this community which seem more important to the present discussion than *a* pyramid." [81] Nevertheless, the picture that time and again emerges from Hunter's descriptions is strikingly similar to Herson's characterization. Lane provides an excellent summary of Hunter's most telling "findings": [82]

> The techniques whereby these dominant families control the political life of the

---

[76] D'Antonio, *et al.*, pp. 850–51.

[77] Rossi, "Community Decision Making," p. 429.

[78] Polsby, *Political Theory*, p. 54.

[79] Hunter, *Community Power Structure*, p. 111.

[80] Lawrence J. R. Herson, "In the Footsteps of Community Power," *American Political Science Review*, 55 (December 1961), 820; see also Delbert C. Miller, "Decision-Making Cliques in Community Power Structures: A Comparative Study of an American and an English City," *American Journal of Sociology*, 64 (November 1958), pp. 299, 307–9. Hunter's findings are directly contradicted in a later study of Atlanta—the city he studied—by M. Kent Jennings: *Community Influentials: The Elites of Atlanta* (New York: Free Press, 1964).

[81] Hunter, *Community Power Structure*, p. 62 (italics Hunter's).

[82] Robert E. Lane, *Political Life* (Glencoe, Ill.: Free Press, 1959), pp. 257–8.

community are intricate and varied. By their leverage over the economic institutions of the community, they can exercise sanctions over many of the civic leaders and professional people in town; they can intimidate workers through the control over their jobs; they control the credit institutions of the community and can influence such matters as admission to a hospital or a mortgage on a house; they generally control the local press and radio; they subsidize the party (or parties) of their choice and hence influence their selection of candidates. . . .

The political organizations are so completely dominated by the power interests (i.e. business elite) . . . that there is little hope of adequate expression being fostered by them at this time.

They control admission to the prestige associations and clubs; they set the patterns of approved behavior and opinion. . . . Hunter speaks of the great "silence found in the mass of the citizenry of Regional City."

Some studies following Hunter's method have found a similar condition of monolithic business dominance in the power structure,[83] while D'Antonio and Form and Miller suggest a continuum of power structures ranging from a highly stratified business-dominated pyramid to a "ring of institutional representatives functioning in relatively independent roles."[84] The role of the business community will be discussed in more detail later.

Of an even more controversial nature is the question of the relative solidarity and uniqueness of purpose of the top power group, i.e. whether or not it is legitimate to call this group

an elite. The term "elite" has been used often throughout the literature on community power and with hardly more precision than in the case of "power." Perhaps the most commonly used meaning is that of a group of persons at the top of the hierarchy. A definition so general and all-inclusive loses a great deal of utility, and some authors have found it necessary to redefine and delimit the term. Polsby's definition of an elite is a group of persons, always less than a majority, selected by other than majority vote, standing at the apex of the pyramid of community power, and exercising influence over a wide range of community issues.[85] The question becomes, in this context, to what extent have reputational studies revealed the existence of a "power elite" in American communities. It has already been mentioned that although Hunter qualifiedly disavows parts of the definition and nowhere specifically mentions a power elite, many scholars who have read his work have been left with the impression that a power elite was what he meant to imply.

A closely related issue is whether the use of the reputational method necessarily implies the existence of some type of power elite. Polsby asserts that the question reputational researchers put to their informants, essentially, "Who runs this community?" is somewhat like "Have you stopped beating your wife?" in that "virtually any response short of total unwillingness to answer will supply the researcher with a 'power elite' along the lines presupposed" by his theory.[86] D'Antonio, et

---

[83] Orrin E. Klapp and L. Vincent Padgett, "Power Structure and Decision-Making in a Mexican Border City," *American Journal of Sociology*, 65(4) (January 1960), 401–2; Schulze and Blumberg, "Local Power Elites," p. 293; Rossi ("Community Decision Making," pp. 429–30) comments that influence based on economic strength is especially effective in certain circumstances, for example on civic associations dependent on voluntary financial contributions.

[84] D'Antonio and Form, *Influentials*, pp. 222–3; Miller, "Decision-Making Cliques," p. 310.

[85] Polsby, *Political Theory*, p. 10.

[86] Ibid. p. 113.

al., reply that if such were the case, the reputational literature ought be "replete with depictions of American communities as controlled by small, solidary elites." [87] They find, rather, a variety of community power structures suggested by the literature. In rebuttal, Polsby maintains that he, Wolfinger, and Dahl have urged that all matters of existence, shape, durability, and inclusiveness of a community power structure be regarded as empirical questions not subject to *a priori* settlement by definition and denies that he has asserted "that there is a logical relationship between this tendency, a tendency to use the reputational method, and a tendency to discover a power elite." [88] Polsby further remarks that he and his colleagues to not deny the power-elite hypothesis in the abstract, but that their evidence for New Haven contradicts it: "We have, in fact, argued that there is scant evidence to support a conclusion that American communities are run by power elites, and some evidence which tends to refute this conclusion." [89]

Findings from other reputational studies are inconclusive and conflicting as to whether anything approaching an elite is characteristic of the power structure. Schulze and Blumberg, although not mentioning the term "elite," report that their leadership group constituted a "closely knit friendship group which exercised substantial—if not always decisive—control over the community's decisions," [90] while D'Antonio and Form report that "in a dynamic metropolitan American community, there is little probability that a single co-ordinated power elite controls all the decisions in the community," and their data for El Paso and Ciudad Juarez fail to document the existence of a solidary, unified influence system. [91] Evidently, whether or not Polsby can be said to have made the statement, the use of the reputational technique does not necessarily predispose the researcher to find a power elite.

Two other specific criticisms of the reputational technique made primarily by Wolfinger ought to be mentioned. The charge has been made that the reputational approach assumes and reports a static distribution of power: "Shifting distribution of power, whether the result of elections or of other factors, presents a problem in political analysis which appears to be unsolvable by the power-attribution method." [92] From the different descriptions of power structures that have emerged, this criticism would seem to apply only to specific instances in which the method was employed and thus would not be characteristic of the method itself. For example, Miller, as cited above, envisions a structure into which power-holders from different institutional sectors enter and from which they exit according to the issue involved. [93] Elsewhere, Wolfinger charges that Hunter's decision to carry out a "separate (but not equal) study of the Negro sub-community," results in a picture of segregated power structures whereas recent news reports clearly in-

[87] D'Antonio, *et al.*, "Further Notes," pp. 852–3.

[88] Polsby, "Some Reflections," pp. 838–41.

[89] Ibid. p. 841.

[90] Schulze and Blumberg, "Local Power Elites," p. 296.

[91] D'Antonio and Form, *Influentials*, pp. 222–3, 128–9.

[92] Wolfinger, "Reputation and Reality," p. 644.

[93] Hunter also says that "the personnel of the pyramid would change depending upon what needs to be done at a particular time" (p. 66). However, he does seem to imply, as do others who use this approach, that the structure, in this case a pyramid, is relatively fixed.

dicate that "Atlanta Negroes are neither powerless nor isolated from the city's political life." [94] D'Antonio, *et al.,* point out that Hunter's research was carried out from 1951 to 1953, and the Supreme Court school desegregation decision—"which was undoubtedly the springboard for recent Negro protest activities—was not delivered until May 1954." [95] In spite of this, however, his defenders are unable to explain why Hunter virtually ignored the fact that the power holders repeatedly were forced to bargain with other elements in the city, the Negro population included.

The most attractive qualities of the reputational approach are its transportability and its economy of operation: "Like Henry Ford, Floyd Hunter has found the secret of mass production, and today's builder of community power models no longer need build each model over an attenuated time period, beginning labor with a refining of raw materials." [96] Herson feels that an ultimate conclusion as to the merits of reputational studies is, at present, not easily reached: "The power data now being accumulated by Hunter's method ought be viewed as a mound of smelter's ore, offering promise of further refinement and use." [97] Wolfinger's evaluation, as might be expected, is less favorable: "Ten years have passed since Floyd Hunter wrote *Community Power Structure.* In this time neither Hunter nor any of his legion of champions and imitators has produced a val-

idation of the reputational method, while its critics have piled up a mass of refutations. We would do well to bury the reputational method and go on to more valid research techniques and more meaningful questions." [98] Those who continue to employ the reputational approach are convinced that questions on methodology are legitimate and that there is no doubt that more needs to be known about the precision, stability, and congruence of the research operations of power studies. However, they claim "the evidence is not yet in. Neither Wolfinger nor Polsby has provided sufficient evidence to warrant Mr. Wolfinger's necrology." [99]

The third approach to the study of community power to be examined here is the *decision-making process* or *issue-analysis* approach. It eschews both position and reputation as effective means of ascertaining the power structure or generalizing about power, and stresses the actual determination of community decisions and the persons involved in making them: "The process of decision-making is recognized as the nucleus of the phenomenon of power and it is this process that is the object of research." [100] Participation in community decisions is not to be equated with power, but the researcher must, rather, weigh the activities of different participants in decisions and then, by means of an operational definition, appraise their relative power. Dahl considers this operationalism, however crude it

---

[94] Wolfinger, "A Plea for a Decent Burial," p. 844.

[95] D'Antonio, *et al.,* "Further Notes," p. 850.

[96] Herson, "In the Footsteps of Community Power," pp. 821, 818–19.

[97] Ibid. p. 825.

[98] Wolfinger, "A Plea for a Decent Burial," p. 847; see also Polsby, *Political Theory,* p. 56; Kaufman and Jones, "The Mystery of Power," p. 208.

[99] D'Antonio, *et al.,* "Further Notes," p. 849; Ehrlich, "The Reputational Approach," p. 927.

[100] Fisher, "Community-Power Studies," pp. 452–3. Also Rossi, "Community Decision Making," p. 425; and Dahl, *Analysis,* pp. 52–3.

may be, as the method's greatest advantage, and other researchers have commented on its effectiveness in representing the realities of community power.[101] Although the reputational approach has received a considerable amount of attention and criticism, the decision-making approach has received comparatively little of either.[102] Among the more serious difficulties in its application would seem to be its complexity and the resultant necessity of severely limiting the number and range of issues studied, the exclusion of the researcher from spontaneous and private discussions concerning power, and the determination of criteria by which decisions are to be chosen for examination.

D'Antonio and Form have pointed out that there is no way to know whether all important issues become publicized enough for the researcher to become sufficiently aware of them. In a similar vein, Fisher suggests that the decision-making process is only one of a complex, interwoven set of community processes, and that to fully understand one process requires knowledge of the others. Even if it were possible to identify most important issues and to become sufficiently acquainted with the process of resolving them, there would remain the problem of choosing which of the universe of important decisions are typical, and thus those whose examination would provide a valid basis for generalization to the decision-making process in general.[103] Dahl believes it impossible to specify the universe of issues in a community with any great degree of exactness. He suggests selecting sectors of issues, the question of whose importance would arouse little dissent, and sampling issues from these sectors. Since it is difficult to know what a representative sample would mean here, "all that can really be said at the end of the research is that in these sectors this is the pattern of influence found." [104] However, unless the issues chosen from a particular sector can be shown to be representative of that sector, there may be scant evidence for claiming even as much as Dahl does.[105] Dahl continues by saying that it matters little what specific issues are chosen as long as three or four different sectors are concentrated on in order to determine whether or not influence is specialized in relation to different sectors. If this pattern of specialization can be shown to exist, "at least it becomes clear, if nothing else is known, that there isn't a single homogeneous power elite." [106] Delbert Miller charges that no real pattern emerges in decision-making studies because the

---

[101] Dahl, *Analysis*, p. 53; Fisher, "Community-Power Studies," p. 454; Freeman, *et al.*, "Locating Leaders," pp. 792–3.

[102] D'Antonio, *et al.*, "Further Notes," p. 853.

[103] Ibid.; D'Antonio and Form, *Influentials*, p. 131; Fisher, "Community-Power Studies," p. 454. "The field studies of most complicated decisions have not been very valuable. The very complexity and apparent uniqueness of the processes they have unveiled makes generalization going beyond the specific issues studied very hazardous" (Rossi, "Community Decision Making," p. 436).

[104] Dahl, quoted in Ehrlich, "A Critical Discussion," p. 105.

[105] Dahl claims that "once the sector to be examined has been selected, it is no longer so difficult to choose the specific issues or decisions in a somewhat non-arbitrary but not entirely defensible way." (Ibid. p. 106). There has yet to be devised a method for choosing decisions in much more than an arbitrary manner, even if the sector has already been determined.

[106] Ibid.; also Polsby, "A Reassessment," p. 233.

usual technique has been to examine "given issues that are currently running," which "only takes a little slice out of the power-structure; . . . the only way to get a pattern for a community is to watch a whole series of issues, which takes a very long time," and which no researcher who takes this approach, according to Miller, has yet accomplished.[107] Miller is concerned that "Professor Dahl may be deceived by a spatter of non-salient issues which cannot display the true structure of community power." [108] In fact, however, Linton Freeman and his associates have studied decision-making in 39 issues, carefully selected from a comprehensive list of 250 issues, in Syracuse over a five-year period.[109]

Freeman and his associates have called attention to the fact that the decision-making method often includes individuals who, although present when a decision is made, had little or no impact on the decision. However, "this seems preferable to the likelihood of excluding important influentials." [110] In view of this consideration, as in the case of the reputational technique, the question must be put to the proponents of the decision-making method as to what exactly is the relationship between the list of influentials they provide and the actual wielding of power as they define it.

Perhaps a more fundamental criticism of the decision-making or issues-analysis method is that it selects *controversial* issues or sources of data from which the power of participating groups is to be inferred. It thus ignores the "settled," "institutional," or "non-controversial" exercises of power, in which it is more than likely that dominant groups have their way without opposition, because no weaker group finds it worthwhile to make an issue when the strong likelihood is that it will lose. Sometimes, of course, noncontroversial decisions reflect real consensus throughout the community, and occasionally they reflect a preponderance of public opinion which no special interest group finds it practical to oppose. But possibly more often, such noncontroversial decisions reflect the community's acquiescence in the strategically planned decisions taken by some powerful groups, at least temporarily cohesive among themselves. This does not say, of course, that the powerful groups are always the economic elite, the top businessmen; they may on occasion be the labor unions, the government administration, a coalition of other "experts," the combined clergy of the community. In any case, there is no "issue"; a policy decision is announced to the public and there is no negative reaction; and there is no contest of forces for the decision-making investigator to investigate. At the extreme, this situation was probably common in the old-fashioned "company town" once ruled by a single business, but the elitist and monolithic character of power in this situation would not be caught by the issues-analyst if he consistently employed his method. More typically, the situation was regularly reflected, until the past five years, in the uncontested relegation of Negroes to

[107] Miller, quoted in Ehrlich, "A Critical Discussion," pp. 100–101.
[108] Ibid., pp. 106–7.
[109] Linton C. Freeman, Warner Bloomberg, Jr., Stephen P. Koff, Morris H. Sunshine, and Thomas J. Fararo, *Local Community Leadership* (Syracuse, N.Y.: Syracuse University College, 1960).
[110] Freeman, *et al.*, "Locating Leaders," pp. 792–3.

paper very impt +

subordinate positions in the community; a coalition of white people—often a minority of the total population in Southern communities—were the power elite in this case.

. . . . .

As to the elitist versus pluralist patterns of community power that emerge from the use of the reputational method and the decision-making (or "issue-analysis") method, respectively, there is an increasing awareness among students that the power structure varies with the type of community. Instead of studying only one community and generalizing from it to power structures generally, recent students have compared two or more communities, and have ranked the communities along an elitist-pluralist continuum. This makes for such perspicacious and balanced studies as those by Presthus,[111] D'Antonio and Form,[112] and Clelland and Form.[113] In general, the older, smaller towns and cities, especially in the South, have an elitist, oligarchic power structure, with the top business-

men in all the important decision-making positions, while the more industrialized cities have a pluralist, competitive power structure, in which the top businessmen are usually less powerful on non-economic issues than are political leaders, professionals of one specialty or another, and association directors and presidents. In both cases, however, decision-making is carried on by a small minority of the population—about 0.3 per cent in Syracuse in the study of Linton Freeman et al., and between 0.4 and 0.6 per cent in the two New York towns studied by Presthus—but in a framework in which the interests of organized groups and the voting public are taken into account. In both cases, some of the major decisions affecting the communities are made outside the communities—by the state and federal governments mainly, by nationally based corporations and trade unions in some cases—although this fact is most often ignored by the investigators of local community power structure.

■ C. Wright Mills

The powers of ordinary men are circumscribed by the everyday worlds in which they live, yet even in these rounds of job, family, and neighborhood they often seem driven by forces they can neither understand nor govern. 'Great changes' are beyond their control, but affect their conduct and outlook none the less. The very frame-

work of modern society confines them to projects not their own, but from every side, such changes now press upon the men and women of the mass society, who accordingly feel that they are without purpose in an epoch in which they are without power.

But not all men are in this sense ordinary. As the means of information

[111] Robert Presthus, *Men at the Top* (New York: Oxford University Press, 1964).

[112] D'Antonio and Form, *Influentials*.

[113] Donald A. Clelland and William H. Form, "Economic Dominants and Community Power: A Comparative Analysis," *American Journal of Sociology*, 69 (March 1964), 511–21.

SOURCE: C. Wright Mills, *The Power Elite* (New York: Oxford University Press, 1956), Chapter 1.

and of power are centralized, some men come to occupy positions in American society from which they can look down upon, so to speak, and by their decisions mightily affect, the everyday worlds of ordinary men and women. They are not made by their jobs; they set up and break down jobs for thousands of others; they are not confined by simple family responsibilities; they can escape. They may live in many hotels and houses, but they are bound by no one community. They need not merely 'meet the demands of the day and hour': in some part, they create these demands, and cause others to meet them. Whether or not they profess their power, their technical and political experience of it far transcends that of the underlying population. What Jacob Burckhardt said of 'great men,' most Americans might well say of their elite: 'They are all that we are not.' [1]

The power elite is composed of men whose positions enable them to transcend the ordinary environments of ordinary men and women; they are in positions to make decisions having major consequences. Whether they do or do not make such decisions is less important than the fact that they do occupy such pivotal positions: their failure to act, their failure to make decisions, is itself an act that is often of greater consequence than the decisions they do make. For they are in command of the major hierarchies and organizations of modern society. They rule the big corporations. They run the machinery of the state and claim its prerogatives. They direct the military establishment. They occupy the strategic command posts of the social structure, in which are now centered the effective means of the power and the

wealth and the celebrity which they enjoy.

The power elite are not solitary rulers. Advisers and consultants, spokesmen and opinion-makers are often the captains of their higher thought and decision. Immediately below the elite are the professional politicians of the middle levels of power, in the Congress and in the pressure groups, as well as among the new and old upper classes of town and city and region. Mingling with them, in curious ways which we shall explore, are those professional celebrities who live by being continually displayed but are never, so long as they remain celebrities, displayed enough. If such celebrities are not at the head of any dominating hierarchy, they do often have the power to distract the attention of the public or afford sensations to the masses, or, more directly, to gain the ear of those who do occupy positions of direct power. More or less unattached, as critics of morality and technicians of power, as spokesmen of God and creators of mass sensibility, such celebrities and consultants are part of the immediate scene in which the drama of the elite is enacted. But that drama itself is centered in the command posts of the major institutional hierarchies.

1

The truth about the nature and the power of the elite is not some secret which men of affairs know but will not tell. Such men hold quite various theories about their own roles in the sequence of event and decision. Often they are uncertain about their roles, and even more often they allow their fears and their hopes to affect their assessment of their own power. No matter how great their actual power, they tend to be less acutely aware of it than of the resistances of others to its use. Moreover, most American men of affairs have learned well the rhetoric of public relations, in some cases even to the point of using it when they are alone, and thus coming to believe it. The personal awareness of the actors is only one of the several sources one must examine in order to understand the higher circles. Yet many who believe that there is no elite, or at any rate none of any consequence, rest their argument upon what men of affairs believe about themselves, or at least assert in public.

There is, however, another view: those who feel, even if vaguely, that a compact and powerful elite of great importance does now prevail in America often base that feeling upon the historical trend of our time. They have felt, for example, the domination of the military event, and from this they infer that generals and admirals, as well as other men of decision influenced by them, must be enormously powerful. They hear that the Congress has again abdicated to a handful of men decisions clearly related to the issue of war or peace. They know that the bomb was dropped over Japan in the name of the United States of America, although they were at no time consulted about the matter. They feel that they live in a time of big decisions; they know that they are not making any. Accordingly, as they consider the present as history, they infer that at its center, making decisions or failing to make them, there must be an elite of power.

On the one hand, those who share this feeling about big historical events

assume that there is an elite and that its power is great. On the other hand, those who listen carefully to the reports of men apparently involved in the great decisions often do not believe that there is an elite whose powers are of decisive consequence.

Both views must be taken into account, but neither is adequate. The way to understand the power of the American elite lies neither solely in recognizing the historic scale of events nor in accepting the personal awareness reported by men of apparent decision. Behind such men and behind the events of history, linking the two, are the major institutions of modern society. These hierarchies of state and corporation and army constitute the means of power; as such they are now of a consequence not before equaled in human history—and at their summits, there are now those command posts of modern society which offer us the sociological key to an understanding of the role of the higher circles in America.

Within American society, major national power now resides in the economic, the political, and the military domains. Other institutions seem off to the side of modern history, and, on occasion, duly subordinated to these. No family is as directly powerful in national affairs as any major corporation; no church is as directly powerful in the external biographies of young men in America today as the military establishment; no college is as powerful in the shaping of momentous events as the National Security Council. Religious, educational, and family institutions are not autonomous centers of national power; on the contrary, these decentralized areas are increasingly shaped by the big three, in which developments

of decisive and immediate consequence now occur.

Families and churches and schools adapt to modern life; governments and armies and corporations shape it; and, as they do so, they turn these lesser institutions into means for their ends. Religious institutions provide chaplains to the armed forces where they are used as a means of increasing the effectiveness of its morale to kill. Schools select and train men for their jobs in corporations and their specialized tasks in the armed forces. The extended family has, of course, long been broken up by the industrial revolution, and now the son and the father are removed from the family, by compulsion if need be, whenever the army of the state sends out the call. And the symbols of all these lesser institutions are used to legitimate the power and the decisions of the big three.

The life-fate of the modern individual depends not only upon the family into which he was born or which he enters by marriage, but increasingly upon the corporation in which he spends the most alert hours of his best years; not only upon the school where he is educated as a child and adolescent, but also upon the state which touches him throughout his life; not only upon the church in which on occasion he hears the word of God, but also upon the army in which he is disciplined.

If the centralized state could not rely upon the inculcation of nationalist loyalties in public and private schools, its leaders would promptly seek to modify the decentralized educational system. If the bankruptcy rate among the top five hundred corporations were as high as the general divorce rate among the thirty-seven million married couples, there would be economic catastrophe

on an international scale. If members of armies gave to them no more of their lives than do believers to the churches to which they belong, there would be a military crisis.

Within each of the big three, the typical institutional unit has become enlarged, has become administrative, and, in the power of its decisions, has become centralized. Behind these developments there is a fabulous technology, for as institutions, they have incorporated this technology and guide it, even as it shapes and paces their developments.

The economy—once a great scatter of small productive units in autonomous balance—has become dominated by two or three hundred giant corporations, administratively and politically interrelated, which together hold the keys to economic decisions.

The political order, once a decentralized set of several dozen states with a weak spinal cord, has become a centralized, executive establishment which has taken up into itself many powers previously scattered, and now enters into each and every cranny of the social structure.

The military order, once a slim establishment in a context of distrust fed by state militia, has become the largest and most expensive feature of government, and, although well versed in smiling public relations, now has all the grim and clumsy efficiency of a sprawling bureaucratic domain.

In each of these institutional areas, the means of power at the disposal of decision makers have increased enormously; their central executive powers have been enhanced; within each of them modern administrative routines have been elaborated and tightened up.

As each of these domains becomes

enlarged and centralized, the consequences of its activities become greater, and its traffic with the others increases. The decisions of a handful of corporations bear upon military and political as well as upon economic developments around the world. The decisions of the military establishment rest upon and grievously affect political life as well as the very level of economic activity. The decisions made within the political domain determine economic activities and military programs. There is no longer, on the one hand, an economy, and, on the other hand, a political order containing a military establishment unimportant to politics and to money-making. There is a political economy linked, in a thousand ways, with military institutions and decisions. On each side of the world-split running through central Europe and around the Asiatic rimlands, there is an ever-increasing interlocking of economic, military, and political structures.[2] If there is government intervention in the corporate economy, so is there corporate intervention in the governmental process. In the structural sense, this triangle of power is the source of the interlocking directorate that is most important for the historical structure of the present.

The fact of the interlocking is clearly revealed at each of the points of crisis of modern capitalist society—slump, war, and boom. In each, men of decision are led to an awareness of the interdependence of the major institutional orders. In the nineteenth century, when the scale of all institutions was smaller, their liberal integration was achieved in the automatic economy, by an autonomous play of market forces, and in the automatic political domain, by the bargain and the vote. It was then assumed that out of the imbalance and friction that followed the limited decisions then possible a new equilibrium would in due course emerge. That can no longer be assumed, and it is not assumed by the men at the top of each of the three dominant hierarchies.

For given the scope of their consequences, decisions—and indecisions—in any one of these ramify into the others, and hence top decisions tend either to become co-ordinated or to lead to a commanding indecision. It has not always been like this. When numerous small entrepreneurs made up the economy, for example, many of them could fail and the consequences still remain local; political and military authorities did not intervene. But now, given political expectations and military commitments, can they afford to allow key units of the private corporate economy to break down in slump? Increasingly, they do intervene in economic affairs, and as they do so, the controlling decisions in each order are inspected by agents of the other two, and economic, military, and political structures are interlocked.

At the pinnacle of each of the three enlarged and centralized domains, there have arisen those higher circles which make up the economic, the political, and the military elites. At the top of the economy, among the corporate rich, there are the chief executives; at the top of the political order, the members of the political directorate; at the top of the military establishment, the elite of soldier-statesmen clustered in and around the Joint Chiefs of Staff and the upper echelon. As each of these domains has coincided with the others, as decisions tend to become total in their consequence, the leading men in each of the three domains of power—the warlords, the corporation chieftains, the political directorate—tend to come together, to form the power elite of America.

2

The higher circles in and around these command posts are often thought of in terms of what their members possess: they have a greater share than other people of the things and experiences that are most highly valued. From this point of view, the elite are simply those who have the most of what there is to have, which is generally held to include money, power, and prestige—as well as all the ways of life to which these lead.[3] But the elite are not simply those who have the most, for they could not 'have the most' were it not for their positions in the great institutions. For such institutions are the necessary bases of power, of wealth, and of prestige, and at the same time, the chief means of exercising power, of acquiring and retaining wealth, and of cashing in the higher claims for prestige.

By the powerful we mean, of course, those who are able to realize their will, even if others resist it. No one, accordingly, can be truly powerful unless he has access to the command of major institutions, for it is over these institutional means of power that the truly powerful are, in the first instance, powerful. Higher politicians and key officials of government command such institutional power; so do admirals and generals, and so do the major owners and executives of the larger corporations. Not all power, it is true, is anchored in and exercised by means of such institutions, but only within and through them can power be more or less continuous and important.

Wealth also is acquired and held in and through institutions. The pyramid of wealth cannot be understood merely in terms of the very rich; for the great inheriting families, as we shall see, are now supplemented by the corporate institutions of modern society: every one of the very rich families has been and is closely connected—always legally and frequently managerially as well—with one of the multi-million dollar corporations.

The modern corporation is the prime source of wealth, but, in latter-day capitalism, the political apparatus also opens and closes many avenues to wealth. The amount as well as the source of income, the power over consumer's goods as well as over productive capital, are determined by position within the political economy. If our interest in the very rich goes beyond their lavish or their miserly consumption, we must examine their relations to modern forms of corporate property as well as to the state; for such relations now determine the chances of men to secure big property and to receive high income.

Great prestige increasingly follows the major institutional units of the social structure. It is obvious that prestige depends, often quite decisively, upon access to the publicity machines that are now a central and normal feature of all the big institutions of modern America. Moreover, one feature of these hierarchies of corporation, state, and military establishment is that their top positions are increasingly interchangeable. One result of this is the accumulative nature of prestige. Claims for prestige, for example, may be initially based on military roles, then expressed in and augmented by an educational institution run by corporate executives, and cashed in, finally, in the political order, where, for General Eisenhower and those he represents, power and prestige finally meet at the very peak. Like wealth and power, prestige tends to be cumulative: the more of it you have, the more you can get. These values also tend to be translatable into one another: the wealthy find it easier than the poor to gain power; those with status find it easier than those without it to control opportunities for wealth.

If we took the one hundred most powerful men in America, the one hundred wealthiest, and the one hundred most celebrated away from the institutional positions they now occupy, away from their resources of men and women and money, away from the media of mass communication that are now focused upon them—then they would be powerless and poor and uncelebrated. For power is not of a man. Wealth does not center in the person of the wealthy. Celebrity is not inherent in any personality. To be celebrated, to be wealthy, to have power requires access to major institutions, for the institutional positions men occupy determine in large part their chances to have and to hold these valued experiences.

3

The people of the higher circles may also be conceived as members of a top social stratum, as a set of groups whose members know one another, see one another socially and at business, and so, in making decisions, take one another into account. The elite, according to this conception, feel themselves to be, and are felt by others to be, the inner circle of 'the upper social classes.' [4] They form a more or less compact social and psychological entity; they have become self-conscious members of a social class. People are either accepted into this class or they are not, and there is a qualitative split, rather than merely a numerical scale, separating them from those who are not elite. They are more or less aware of themselves as a social class and they behave toward one another differently from the way they do toward members of other classes. They accept one another, understand one another, marry one another, tend to work and to think if not together at least alike.

Now, we do not want by our definition to prejudge whether the elite of the command posts are conscious members of such a socially recognized class, or whether considerable proportions of the elite derive from such a clear and distinct class. These are matters to be investigated. Yet in order to be able to recognize what we intend to investigate, we must note something that all biographies and memoirs of the wealthy and the powerful and the eminent make clear: no matter what else they may be, the people of these higher circles are involved in a set of overlapping 'crowds' and intricately connected 'cliques.' There is a kind of mutual attraction among those who 'sit on the same terrace'—although this often becomes clear to them, as well as to others, only at the point at which they feel the need to draw the line; only when, in their common defense, they come to understand what they have in common, and so close their ranks against outsiders.

The idea of such ruling stratum implies that most of its members have similar social origins, that throughout their lives they maintain a network of informal connections, and that to some degree there is an interchangeability of

position between the various hierarchies of money and power and celebrity.
We must, of course, note at once that if
such an elite stratum does exist, its social visibility and its form, for very
solid historical reasons, are quite different from those of the noble cousin-
hoods that once ruled various European nations.

That American society has never
passed through a feudal epoch is of decisive importance to the nature of the
American elite, as well as to American
society as a historic whole. For it
means that no nobility or aristocracy,
established before the capitalist era, has
stood in tense opposition to the higher
bourgeoisie. It means that this bourgeoisie has monopolized not only
wealth but prestige and power as well.
It means that no set of noble families
has commanded the top positions and
monopolized the values that are generally held in high esteem; and certainly
that no set has done so explicitly by inherited right. It means that no high
church dignitaries or court nobilities,
no entrenched landlords with honorific
accouterments, no monopolists of high
army posts have opposed the enriched
bourgeoisie and in the name of birth
and prerogative successfully resisted its
self-making.

But this does *not* mean that there
are no upper strata in the United
States. That they emerged from a 'middle class' that had no recognized aristocratic superiors does not mean they remained middle class when enormous
increases in wealth made their own superiority possible. Their origins and
their newness may have made the
upper strata less visible in America
than elsewhere. But in America today
there are in fact tiers and ranges of
wealth and power of which people in
the middle and lower ranks know very

little and may not even dream. There
are families who, in their well-being,
are quite insulated from the economic
jolts and lurches felt by the merely
prosperous and those farther down the
scale. There are also men of power who
in quite small groups make decisions of
enormous consequence for the underlying population.

The American elite entered modern
history as a virtually unopposed bourgeoisie. No national bourgeoisie, before
or since, has had such opportunities
and advantages. Having no military
neighbors, they easily occupied an isolated continent stocked with natural resources and immensely inviting to a
willing labor force. A framework of
power and an ideology for its justification were already at hand. Against
mercantilist restriction, they inherited
the principle of *laissez-faire;* against
Southern planters, they imposed the
principle of industrialism. The Revolutionary War put an end to colonial
pretensions to nobility, as loyalists fled
the country and many estates were broken up. The Jacksonian upheaval with
its status revolution put an end to pretensions to monopoly of descent by the
old New England families. The Civil
War broke the power, and so in due
course the prestige, of the ante-bellum
South's claimants for the higher esteem.
The tempo of the whole capitalist development made it impossible for an
inherited nobility to develop and en-
dure in America.

No fixed ruling class, anchored in
agrarian life and coming to flower in
military glory, could contain in America the historic thrust of commerce and
industry, or subordinate to itself the
capitalist elite—as capitalists were subordinated, for example, in Germany
and Japan. Nor could such a ruling
class anywhere in the world contain

that of the United States when industrialized violence came to decide history. Witness the fate of Germany and Japan in the two world wars of the twentieth century; and indeed the fate of Britain herself and her model ruling class, as New York became the inevitable economic, and Washington the inevitable political capital of the western capitalist world.

4

The elite who occupy the command posts may be seen as the possessors of power and wealth and celebrity; they may be seen as members of the upper stratum of a capitalistic society. They may also be defined in terms of psychological and moral criteria, as certain kinds of selected individuals. So defined, the elite, quite simply, are people of superior character and energy.

The humanist, for example, may conceive of the 'elite' not as a social level or category, but as a scatter of those individuals who attempt to transcend themselves, and accordingly, are more noble, more efficient, made out of better stuff. It does not matter whether they are poor or rich, whether they hold high position or low, whether they are acclaimed or despised; they are elite because of the kind of individuals they are. The rest of the population is mass, which, according to this conception, sluggishly relaxes into uncomfortable mediocrity.[5]

This is the sort of socially unlocated conception which some American writers with conservative yearnings have recently sought to develop. But most moral and psychological conceptions of the elite are much less sophisticated, concerning themselves not with individuals but with the stratum as a

whole. Such ideas, in fact, always arise in a society in which some people possess more than do others of what there is to possess. People with advantages are loath to believe that they just happen to be people with advantages. They come readily to define themselves as inherently worthy of what they possess; they come to believe themselves 'naturally' elite; and, in fact, to imagine their possessions and their privileges as natural extensions of their own elite selves. In this sense, the idea of the elite as composed of men and women having a finer moral character is an ideology of the elite as a privileged ruling stratum, and this is true whether the ideology is elite-made or made up for it by others.

In eras of equalitarian rhetoric, the more intelligent or the more articulate among the lower and middle classes, as well as guilty members of the upper, may come to entertain ideas of a counter-elite. In western society, as a matter of fact, there is a long tradition and varied images of the poor, the exploited, and the oppressed as the truly virtuous, the wise, and the blessed. Stemming from Christian tradition, this moral idea of a counter-elite, composed of essentially higher types condemned to a lowly station, may be and has been used by the underlying population to justify harsh criticism of ruling elites and to celebrate utopian images of a new elite to come.

The moral conception of the elite, however, is not always merely an ideology of the overprivileged or a counter-ideology of the underprivileged. It is often a fact: having controlled experiences and select privileges, many individuals of the upper stratum do come in due course to approximate the types of character they claim to embody. Even when we give up—as we must—

the idea that the elite man or woman is born with an elite character, we need not dismiss the idea that their experiences and trainings develop in them characters of a specific type.

Nowadays we must qualify the idea of elite as composed of higher types of individuals, for the men who are selected for and shaped by the top positions have many spokesmen and advisers and ghosts and make-up men who modify their self-conceptions and create their public images, as well as shape many of their decisions. There is, of course, considerable variation among the elite in this respect, but as a general rule in America today, it would be naïve to interpret any major elite group merely in terms of its ostensible personnel. The American elite often seems less a collection of persons than of corporate entities, which are in great part created and spoken for as standard types of 'personality.' Even the most apparently free-lance celebrity is usually a sort of synthetic production turned out each week by a disciplined staff which systematically ponders the effect of the easy ad-libbed gags the celebrity 'spontaneously' echoes.

Yet, in so far as the elite flourishes as a social class or as a set of men at the command posts, it will select and form certain types of personality, and reject others. The kind of moral and psychological beings men become is in large part determined by the values they experience and the institutional roles they are allowed and expected to play. From the biographer's point of view, a man of the upper classes is formed by his relations with others like himself in a series of small intimate groupings through which he passes and to which throughout his lifetime he may return. So conceived, the elite is a set of higher circles whose members are selected, trained and certified and permitted intimate access to those who command the impersonal institutional hierarchies of modern society. If there is any one key to the *psychological* idea of the elite, it is that they combine in their persons an awareness of impersonal decision-making with intimate sensibilities shared with one another. To understand the elite as a social class we must examine a whole series of smaller face-to-face milieux, the most obvious of which, historically, has been the upper-class family, but the most important of which today are the proper secondary school and the metropolitan club.[6]

5

These several notions of the elite, when appropriately understood, are intricately bound up with one another, and we shall use them all in this examination of American success. We shall study each of several higher circles as offering candidates for the elite, and we shall do so in terms of the major institutions making up the total society of America; within and between each of these institutions, we shall trace the interrelations of wealth and power and prestige. But our main concern is with the power of those who now occupy the command posts, and with the role which they are enacting in the history of our epoch.

Such an elite may be conceived as omnipotent, and its powers thought of as a great hidden design. Thus, in vulgar Marxism, events and trends are explained by reference to 'the will of the bourgeoisie'; in Nazism, by reference to 'the conspiracy of the Jews'; by the petty right in America today, by reference to 'the hidden force' of Communist spies. According to such notions of the omnipotent elite as historical cause, the elite is never an entirely visible agency. It is, in fact, a secular substitute for the will of God, being realized in a sort of providential design, except that usually non-elite men are thought capable of opposing it and eventually overcoming it.*

The opposite view—of the elite as impotent—is now quite popular among liberal-minded observers. Far from being omnipotent, the elites are thought to be so scattered as to lack any coherence as a historical force. Their invisibility is not the invisibility of secrecy but the invisibility of the multitude. Those who occupy the formal places of authority are so checkmated—by other elites exerting pressure, or by the public as an electorate, or by constitutional codes—that, although there may be upper classes, there is no ruling class; although there may be men of power, there is no power elite; although there may be a system of stratification, it has no effective top. In the extreme, this view of the elite, as weakened by compromise and disunited to the point of nullity, is a substitute for impersonal collective fate; for, in this view, the decisions of the visible men of the higher circles do not count in history.**

Internationally, the image of the omnipotent elite tends to prevail. All good events and pleasing happenings are quickly imputed by the opinion-makers to the leaders of their own nation; all bad events and unpleasant experiences are imputed to the enemy abroad. In both cases, the omnipotence of evil rulers or of virtuous leaders is assumed. Within the nation, the use of such rhetoric is rather more complicated: when men speak of the power of their own party or circle, they and their leaders are, of course, impotent; only 'the people' are omnipotent. But, when they speak of the power of their opponent's party or circle, they impute to them omnipotence; 'the people' are now powerlessly taken in.

More generally, American men of power tend, by convention, to deny that they are powerful. No American runs for office in order to rule or even govern, but only to serve; he does not become a bureaucrat or even an official, but a public servant. And nowadays, as I have already pointed out, such postures have become standard

---

* Those who charge that Communist agents have been or are in the government, as well as those frightened by them, never raise the question: 'Well, suppose there are Communists in high places, how much power do they have?' They simply assume that men in high places, or in this case even those in positions from which they might influence such men, do decide important events. Those who think Communist agents lost China to the Soviet bloc, or influenced loyal Americans to lose it, simply assume that there is a set of men who decide such matters, actively or by neglect or by stupidity. Many others, who do not believe that Communist agents were so influential, still assume that loyal American decision-makers lost it all by themselves.

** The idea of the impotent elite is mightily supported by the notion of an automatic economy in which the problem of power is solved for the economic elite by denying its existence. No one has enough power to make a real difference; events are the results of an anonymous balance. For the political elite too, the model of balance solves the problem of power. Parallel to the market-economy, there is the leaderless democracy in which no one is responsible for anything and everyone is responsible for everything; the will of men acts only through the impersonal workings of the electoral process.

features of the public-relations programs of all men of power. So firm a part of the style of power-wielding have they become that conservative writers readily misinterpret them as indicating a trend toward an 'amorphous power situation.'

But the 'power situation' of America today is less amorphous than is the perspective of those who see it as a romantic confusion. It is less a flat, momentary 'situation' than a graded, durable structure. And if those who occupy its top grades are not omnipotent, neither are they impotent. It is the form and the height of the gradation of power that we must examine if we would understand the degree of power held and exercised by the elite.

If the power to decide such national issues as are decided were shared in an absolutely equal way, there would be no power elite; in fact, there would be no *gradation* of power, but only a radical homogeneity. At the opposite extreme as well, if the power to decide issues were absolutely monopolized by one small group, there would be no gradation of power; there would simply be this small group in command, and below it, the undifferentiated, dominated masses. American society today represents neither the one nor the other of these extremes, but a conception of them is none the less useful: it makes us realize more clearly the question of the structure of power in the United States and the position of the power elite within it.

Within each of the most powerful institutional orders of modern society there is a gradation of power. The owner of a roadside fruit stand does not have as much power in any area of social or economic or political decision as the head of a multi-million-dollar fruit corporation; no lieutenant on the line is as powerful as the Chief of Staff in the Pentagon; no deputy sheriff carries as much authority as the President of the United States. Accordingly, the problem of defining the power elite concerns the level at which we wish to draw the line. By lowering the line, we could define the elite out of existence; by raising it, we could make the elite a very small circle indeed. In a preliminary and minimum way, we draw the line crudely, in charcoal as it were: By the power elite, we refer to those political, economic, and military circles which as an intricate set of overlapping cliques share decisions having at least national consequences. In so far as national events are decided, the power elite are those who decide them.

To say that there are obvious gradations of power and of opportunities to decide within modern society is not to say that the powerful are united, that they fully know what they do, or that they are consciously joined in conspiracy. Such issues are best faced if we concern ourselves, in the first instance, more with the structural position of the high and mighty, and with the consequences of their decisions, than with the extent of their awareness or the purity of their motives. To understand the power elite, we must attend to three major keys:

I. One, which we shall emphasize throughout our discussion of each of the higher circles, is the psychology of the several elites in their respective milieux. In so far as the power elite is composed of men of similar origin and education, in so far as their careers and their styles of life are similar, there are psychological and social bases for their unity, resting upon the fact that they are of similar social type and leading to the fact of their easy intermingling. This kind of unity reaches its frothier apex in the sharing of that prestige that is to be had in the world of the celebrity; it achieves a more solid culmination in the fact of the interchangeability of positions within and between the three dominant institutional orders.

II. Behind such psychological and social unity as we may find, are the structure and the mechanics of those institutional hierarchies over which the political directorate, the corporate rich, and the high military now preside. The greater the scale of these bureaucratic domains, the greater the scope of their respective elite's power. How each of the major hierarchies is shaped and what relations it has with the other hierarchies determine in large part the relations of their rulers. If these hierarchies are scattered and disjointed, then their respective elites tend to be scattered and disjointed; if they have many interconnections and points of coinciding interest, then their elites tend to form a coherent kind of grouping.

The unity of the elite is not a simple reflection of the unity of institutions, but men and institutions are always related, and our conception of the power elite invites us to determine that relation. Today in America there are several important structural coincidences of interest between these institutional domains, including the development of a permanent war establishment by a privately incorporated economy inside a political vacuum.

III. The unity of the power elite, however, does not rest solely on psychological similarity and social intermingling, nor entirely on the structural coincidences of commanding positions and interests. At times it is the unity of a more explicit co-ordination. To say that these three higher circles are in-

creasingly co-ordinated, that this is *one* basis of their unity, and that at times —as during the wars—such co-ordination is quite decisive, is not to say that the co-ordination is total or continuous, or even that it is very sure-footed. Much less is it to say that willful co-ordination is the sole or the major basis of their unity, or that the power elite has emerged as the realization of a plan. But it is to say that as the institutional mechanics of our time have opened up avenues to men pursuing their several interests, many of them have come to see that these several interests could be realized more easily if they worked together, in informal as well as in more formal ways, and accordingly they have done so.

6

It is not my thesis that for all epochs of human history and in all nations, a creative minority, a ruling class, an omnipotent elite, shape all historical events. Such statements, upon careful examination, usually turn out to be mere tautologies,[7] and even when they are not, they are so entirely general as to be useless in the attempt to understand the history of the present. The minimum definition of the power elite as those who decide whatever is decided of major consequence, does not imply that the members of this elite are always and necessarily the history-makers; neither does it imply that they never are. We must not confuse the conception of the elite, which we wish to define, with one theory about their role: that they are the history-makers of our time. To define the elite, for example, as 'those who rule America' is less to define a conception than to state one hypothesis about the role and power of

that elite. No matter how we might define the elite, the extent of its members'
power is subject to historical variation.
If, in a dogmatic way, we try to include
that variation in our generic definition,
we foolishly limit the use of a needed
conception. If we insist that the elite
be defined as a strictly co-ordinated
class that continually and absolutely
rules, we are closing off from our view
much to which the term more modestly
defined might open to our observation.
In short, our definition of the power
elite cannot properly contain dogma
concerning the degree and kind of
power that ruling groups everywhere
have. Much less should it permit us to
smuggle into our discussion a theory of
history.

During most of human history, historical change has not been visible to
the people who were involved in it, or
even to those enacting it. Ancient
Egypt and Mesopotamia, for example,
endured for some four hundred generations with but slight changes in their
basic structure. That is six and a half
times as long as the entire Christian
era, which has only prevailed some
sixty generations; it is about eighty
times as long as the five generations of
the United States' existence. But now
the tempo of change is so rapid, and
the means of observation so accessible,
that the interplay of event and decision
seems often to be quite historically visible, if we will only look carefully and
from an adequate vantage point.

When knowledgeable journalists tell
us that 'events, not men, shape the big
decisions,' they are echoing the theory
of history as Fortune, Chance, Fate, or
the work of The Unseen Hand. For
'events' is merely a modern word for
these older ideas, all of which separate
men from history-making, because all
of them lead us to believe that history

goes on behind men's backs. History is
drift with no mastery; within it there is
action but no deed; history is mere
happening and the event intended by
no one.[8]

The course of events in our time depends more on a series of human decisions than on any inevitable fate. The
sociological meaning of 'fate' is simply
this: that, when the decisions are innumerable and each one is of small consequence, all of them add up in a way no
man intended—to history as fate. But
not all epochs are equally fateful. As
the circle of those who decide is narrowed, as the means of decision are
centralized and the consequences of decisions become enormous, then the
course of great events often rests upon
the decisions of determinable circles.
This does not necessarily mean that the
same circle of men follow through from
one event to another in such a way
that all of history is merely their plot.
The power of the elite does not necessarily mean that history is not also
shaped by a series of small decisions,
none of which are thought out. It does
not mean that a hundred small arrangements and compromises and adaptations may not be built into the
going policy and the living event. The
idea of the power elite implies nothing
about the process of decision-making as
such: it is an attempt to delimit the social areas within which that process,
whatever its character, goes on. It is a
conception of who is involved in the
process.

The degree of foresight and control
of those who are involved in decisions
that count may also vary. The idea of
the power elite does not mean that the
estimations and calculated risks upon
which decisions are made are not often
wrong and that the consequences are
sometimes, indeed often, not those in-

tended. Often those who make decisions are trapped by their own inadequacies and blinded by their own errors.

Yet in our time the pivotal moment does arise, and at that moment, small circles do decide or fail to decide. In either case, they are an elite of power. The dropping of the A-bombs over Japan was such a moment; the decision on Korea was such a moment; the confusion about Quemoy and Matsu, as well as before Dienbienphu were such moments; the sequence of maneuvers which involved the United States in World War II was such a 'moment.' Is it not true that much of the history of our times is composed of such moments? And is not that what is meant when it is said that we live in a time of big decisions, of decisively centralized power?

Most of us do not try to make sense of our age by believing in a Greek-like, eternal recurrence, nor by a Christian belief in a salvation to come, nor by any steady march of human progress. Even though we do not reflect upon such matters, the chances are we believe with Burckhardt that we live in a mere succession of events; that sheer continuity is the only principle of history. History is merely one thing after another; history is meaningless in that it is not the realization of any determinate plot. It is true, of course, that our sense of continuity, our feeling for the history of our time, is affected by crisis. But we seldom look beyond the immediate crisis or the crisis felt to be just ahead. We believe neither in fate nor providence; and we assume, without talking about it, that 'we'—as a nation —can decisively shape the future but that 'we' as individuals somehow cannot do so.

Any meaning history has, 'we' shall have to give to it by our actions. Yet the fact is that although we are all of us within history we do not all possess equal powers to make history. To pretend that we do is sociological nonsense and political irresponsibility. It is nonsense because any group or any individual is limited, first of all, by the technical and institutional means of power at its command; we do not all have equal access to the means of power that now exist, nor equal influence over their use. To pretend that 'we' are all history-makers is politically irresponsible because it obfuscates any attempt to locate responsibility for the consequential decisions of men who do have access to the means of power.

From even the most superficial examination of the history of the western society we learn that the power of decision-makers is first of all limited by the level of technique, by the *means* of power and violence and organization that prevail in a given society. In this connection we also learn that there is a fairly straight line running upward through the history of the West; that the means of oppression and exploitation, of violence and destruction, as well as the means of production and reconstruction, have been progressively enlarged and increasingly centralized.

As the institutional means of power and the means of communications that tie them together have become steadily more efficient, those now in command of them have come into command of instruments of rule quite unsurpassed in the history of mankind. And we are not yet at the climax of their development. We can no longer lean upon or take soft comfort from the historical ups and downs of ruling groups of previous epochs. In that sense, Hegel is correct: we learn from history that we cannot learn from it.

For every epoch and for every social structure, we must work out an answer to the question of the power of the elite. The ends of men are often merely hopes, but means are facts within some men's control. That is why all means of power tend to become ends to an elite that is in command of them. And that is why we may define the power elite in terms of the means of power—as those who occupy the command posts. The major questions about the American elite today—its composition, its unity, its power—must now be faced with due attention to the awesome means of power available to them. Caesar could do less with Rome than Napoleon with France; Napoleon less with France than Lenin with Russia; and Lenin less with Russia than Hitler with Germany. But what was Caesar's power at its peak compared with the power of the changing inner circle of Soviet Russia or of America's temporary administrations? The men of either circle can cause great cities to be wiped out in a single night, and in a few weeks turn continents into thermonuclear wastelands. That the facilities of power are enormously enlarged and decisively centralized means that the decisions of small groups are now more consequential.

But to know that the top posts of modern social structures now permit more commanding decisions is not to know that the elite who occupy these posts are the history-makers. We might grant that the enlarged and integrated economic, military, and political structures are shaped to permit command decisions, yet still feel that, as it were, 'they run themselves,' that those who are on top, in short, are determined in their decisions by 'necessity,' which presumably means by the instituted roles that they play and the situation of these institutions in the total structure of society.

Do the elite determine the roles that they enact? Or do the roles that institutions make available to them determine the power of the elite? The general answer—and no general answer is sufficient—is that in different kinds of structures and epochs elites are quite differently related to the roles that they play: nothing in the nature of the elite or in the nature of history dictates an answer. It is also true that if most men and women take whatever roles are permitted to them and enact them as they are expected to by virtue of their position, this is precisely what the elite need *not* do, and often do not do. They may call into question the structure, their position within it, or the way in which they are to enact that position.

Nobody called for or permitted Napoleon to chase *Parlement* home on the 18 *Brumaire,* and later to transform his consulate into an emperorship.[9] Nobody called for or permitted Adolf Hitler to proclaim himself 'Leader and Chancellor' the day President Hindenburg died, to abolish and usurp roles by merging the presidency and the chancellorship. Nobody called for or permitted Franklin D. Roosevelt to make the series of decisions that led to the entrance of the United States into World War II. It was no 'historical necessity,' but a man named Truman who, with a few other men, decided to drop a bomb on Hiroshima. It was no historical necessity, but an argument within a small circle of men that defeated Admiral Radford's proposal to bomb troops before Dienbienphu. Far from being dependent upon the structure of institutions, modern elites may smash one structure and set up another in which they then enact quite different roles. In fact, such destruction and creation of institutional structures, with all their means of power, when events seem to turn out well, is just what is involved in 'great leadership,' or, when they seem to turn out badly, great tyranny.

Some elite men *are*, of course, typically role-determined, but others are at times role-determining. They determine not only the role they play but today the roles of millions of other men. The creation of pivotal roles and their pivotal enactment occurs most readily when social structures are undergoing epochal transitions. It is clear that the international development of the United States to one of the two 'great powers'—along with the new means of annihilation and administrative and psychic domination—have made of the United States in the middle years of the twentieth century precisely such an epochal pivot.

There is nothing about history that tells us that a power elite cannot make it. To be sure, the will of such men is always limited, but never before have the limits been so broad, for never before have the means of power been so enormous. It is this that makes our situation so precarious, and makes even more important an understanding of the powers and the limitations of the American elite. The problem of the nature and the power of this elite is now the only realistic and serious way to raise again the problem of responsible government.

7

Those who have abandoned criticism for the new American celebration take readily to the view that the elite is impotent. If they were politically serious, they ought, on the basis of their view, to say to those presumably in charge of American policy: [10]

'One day soon, you may believe that you have an opportunity to drop a bomb or a chance to exacerbate further your relations with allies or with the Russians who might also drop it. But don't be so foolish as to believe that you really have a choice. You have neither choice nor chance. The whole Complex Situation of which you are merely one balancing part is the result of Economic and Social Forces, and so will be the fateful outcome. So stand by quietly, like Tolstoy's general, and let events proceed. Even if you did act, the consequences would not be what you intended, even if you had an intention.

'But—if events come out well, talk as though you had decided. For then men have had moral choices and the power to make them and are, of course, responsible.

'If events come out badly, say that *you* didn't have the real choice, and are, of course, not accountable: *they*, the others, had the choice and they are responsible. You can get away with this even though you have at your command half the world's forces and God knows how many bombs and bombers. For you are, in fact, an impotent item in the historical fate of your times; and moral responsibility is an illusion, although it is of great use if handled in a really alert public relations manner.'

The one implication that can be drawn from all such fatalisms is that if fortune or providence rules, then no elite of power can be justly considered a source of historical decisions, and the idea—much less the demand—of responsible leadership is an idle and an irresponsible notion. For clearly, an impotent elite, the plaything of history, cannot be held accountable. If the elite of our time do not have power, they cannot be held responsible; as men in a difficult position, they should engage our sympathies. The people of the United States are ruled by sovereign fortune; they, and with them their elite, are fatally overwhelmed by consequences they cannot control. If that is so, we ought all to do what many have in fact already done: withdraw entirely from political reflection and action into a materially comfortable and entirely private life.

If, on the other hand, we believe that war and peace and slump and prosperity are, precisely now, no longer matters of 'fortune' or 'fate,' but that, precisely now more than ever, they are controllable, then we must ask—controllable by whom? The answer must be: By whom else but those who now command the enormously enlarged and decisively centralized means of decision and power? We may then ask: Why don't they, then? And for the answer to that, we must understand the context and the character of the American elite today.

There is nothing in the idea of the elite as impotent which should deter us from asking just such questions, which are now the most important questions political men can ask. The American elite is neither omnipotent nor impotent. These are abstract absolutes used publicly by spokesmen, as excuses or as boasts, but in terms of which we may seek to clarify the political issues before us, which just now are above all the issues of responsible power.

There is nothing in 'the nature of history' *in our epoch* that rules out the pivotal function of small groups of decision-makers. On the contrary, the structure of the present is such as to make this not only a reasonable, but a rather compelling, view.

There is nothing in 'the psychology of man,' or in the social manner by which men are shaped and selected for and by the command posts of modern society, that makes unreasonable the view that they do confront choices and that the choices they make—or their failure to confront them—are history-making in their consequences.

Accordingly, political men now have every reason to hold the American power elite accountable for a decisive range of the historical events that make up the history of the present.

It is as fashionable, just now, to suppose that there is no power elite, as it was fashionable in the thirties to suppose a set of ruling-class villains to be the source of all social injustice and public malaise. I should be as far from supposing that some simple and unilateral ruling class could be firmly located as the prime mover of American society, as I should be from supposing that all historical change in America today is merely impersonal drift.

The view that all is blind drift is largely a fatalist projection of one's own feeling of impotence and perhaps, if one has ever been active politically in a principled way, a salve of one's guilt.

The view that all of history is due to the conspiracy of an easily located set of villains, or of heroes, is also a hurried projection from the difficult effort to understand how shifts in the structure of society open opportunities to various elites and how various elites take advantage or fail to take advantage of them. To accept either view—of all history as conspiracy or of all history as drift—is to relax the effort to understand the facts of power and the ways of the powerful.

8

In my attempt to discern the shape of the power elite of our time, and thus to give a responsible meaning to the anonymous 'They,' which the underlying population opposes to the anonymous 'We,' I shall begin by briefly examining the higher elements which most people know best: the new and the old upper classes of local society and the metropolitan 400. I shall then outline the world of the celebrity, attempting to show that the prestige system of American society has now for the first time become truly national in scope; and that the more trivial and glamorous aspects of this national system of status tend at once to distract attention from its more authoritarian features and to justify the power that it often conceals.

In examining the very rich and the chief executives, I shall indicate how neither 'America's Sixty Families' nor 'The Managerial Revolution' provides an adequate idea of the transformation of the upper classes as they are organized today in the privileged stratum of the corporate rich.

After describing the American statesman as a historical type, I shall attempt to show that what observers in the Progressive Era called 'the invisible government' has now become quite visible; and that what is usually taken to be the central content of politics, the pressures and the campaigns and the congressional maneuvering, has, in considerable part, now been relegated to the middle levels of power.

In discussing the military ascendancy, I shall try to make clear how it has come about that admirals and generals have assumed positions of decisive political and economic relevance, and how, in doing so, they have found many points of coinciding interests with the corporate rich and the political directorate of the visible government.

After these and other trends are made as plain as I can make them, I shall return to the master problems of the power elite, as well as take up the complementary notion of the mass society.

What I am asserting is that in this particular epoch a conjunction of historical circumstances has led to the rise of an elite of power; that the men of the circles composing this elite, severally and collectively, now make such key decisions as are made; and that, given the enlargement and the centralization of the means of power now available, the decisions that they make and fail to make carry more consequences for more people than has ever been the case in the world history of mankind.

I am also asserting that there has developed on the middle levels of power, a semi-organized stalemate, and that on the bottom level there has come into being a mass-like society which has little resemblance to the image of a society in which voluntary associations and classic publics hold the keys to power. The top of the American system of power is much more unified and much more powerful, the bottom is much more fragmented, and in truth, impotent, than is generally supposed by those who are distracted by the middling units of power which neither express such will as exists at the bottom nor determine the decisions at the top.

NOTES

1. Jacob Burckhardt, *Force and Freedom* (New York: Pantheon Books, 1943), pp. 303 ff.

2. Cf. Hans Gerth and C. Wright Mills, *Character and Social Structure* (New York: Harcourt, Brace, 1953), pp. 457 ff.

3. The statistical idea of choosing some value and calling those who have the most of it an elite derives, in modern times, from the Italian economist, Pareto, who puts the central point in this way: 'Let us assume that in every branch of human activity each individual is given an index which stands as a sign of his capacity, very much the way grades are given in the various subjects in examinations in school. The highest type of lawyer, for instance, will be given 10. The man who does not get a client will be given 1—reserving zero for the man who is an out-and-out idiot. To the man who has made his millions—honestly or dishonestly as the case may be—we will give 10. To the man who has earned his thousands we will give 6; to such as just manage to keep out of the poor-house, 1, keeping zero for those who get in. . . . So let us make a class of people who have the highest indices in their branch of activity, and to that class give the name of *elite.*' Vilfredo Pareto, *The Mind and Society* (New York: Harcourt, Brace, 1935), par. 2027 and 2031. Those who follow this approach end up not with one elite, but with a number corresponding to the number of values they select. Like many rather abstract ways of reasoning, this one is useful because it forces us to think in a clear-cut way. For a skillful use of this approach, see the work of Harold D. Lasswell, in particular, *Politics: Who Gets What, When, How* (New York: McGraw-Hill, 1936); and for a more systematic use, H. D. Lasswell and Abraham Kaplan, *Power and Society* (New Haven: Yale University Press, 1950).

4. The conception of the elite as members of a top social stratum, is, of course, in line with the prevailing common-sense view of stratification. Technically, it is closer to 'status group' than to 'class,' and has been very well stated by Joseph A. Schumpeter, 'Social Classes in an Ethnically Homogeneous Environment,' *Imperialism and Social Classes* (New York: Augustus M. Kelley, Inc., 1951), pp. 133 ff., especially pp. 137–47. Cf. also his *Capitalism, Socialism and Democracy,* 3rd ed. (New York: Harper, 1950), Part II. For the distinction between class and status groups, see *From Max Weber: Essays in Sociology* (trans. and ed. by Gerth and Mills; New York: Oxford University Press, 1946). For an analysis of Pareto's conception of the elite compared with Marx's conception of classes, as well as data on France, see Raymond Aron, 'Social Structure and Ruling Class,' *British Journal of Sociology,* vol. I, nos. 1 and 2 (1950).

5. The most popular essay in recent years which defines the elite and the mass in terms of a morally evaluated character-type is probably José Ortega y Gasset's, *The Revolt of the Masses,* 1932 (New York: New American Library, Mentor Edition, 1950), esp. pp. 91 ff.

6. 'The American elite' is a confused and confusing set of images, and yet when we hear or when we use such words as Upper Class, Big Shot, Top Brass, The Millionaire Club, The High and The Mighty, we feel at least vaguely that we know what they mean, and often do. What we do not often do, however, is connect each of these images with the others; we make little effort to form a coherent picture in our minds of the elite as a whole. Even when, very occasionally, we do try to do this, we usually come to believe that it is indeed no 'whole'; that, like our images of it, there is no one elite, but many, and that they are not really connected with one another. What we must realize is that until we *do* try to see it as a whole, perhaps our im-

pression that it may not be is a result merely of our lack of analytic rigor and sociological imagination.

The first conception defines the elite in terms of the sociology of institutional position and the social structure these institutions form; the second, in terms of the statistics of selected values; the third, in terms of membership in a clique-like set of people; and the fourth, in terms of the morality of certain personality types. Or, put into inelegant shorthand: what they head up, what they have, what they belong to, who they really are.

In this chapter, as in this book as a whole, I have taken as generic the first view—of the elite defined in terms of institutional position—and have located the other views within it. This straight-forward conception of the elite has one practical and two theoretical advantages. The practical advantage is that it seems the easiest and the most concrete 'way into' the whole problem—if only because a good deal of information is more or less readily available for sociological reflection about such circles and institutions.

But the theoretical advantages are much more important. The institutional or structural definition, first of all, does not force us to prejudge by definition that we ought properly to leave open for investigation. The elite conceived morally, for example, as people having a certain type of character is not an ultimate definition, for apart from being rather morally arbitrary, it leads us immediately to ask *why* these people have this or that sort of character. Accordingly, we should leave open the type of characters which the members of the elite in fact turn out to have, rather than by definition select them in terms of one type or another. In a similar way, we do not want, by mere definition, to prejudge whether or not the elite are conscious members of a social class. The second theoretical advantage of defining the elite in terms of major institutions, which I hope this book as a whole makes clear, is the fact that it allows us to fit the other three conceptions of the elite into place in a systematic way: (1) The institutional positions men occupy throughout their lifetime determine their chances to get and to hold selected values. (2) The kind of psychological beings they become is in large part determined by the values they thus experience and the institutional roles they play. (3) Finally, whether or not they come to feel that they belong to a select social class, and whether or not they act according to what they hold to be its interests—these are also matters in large part determined by their institutional position, and in turn, the select values they possess and the characters they acquire.

7. As in the case, quite notably, of Gaetano Mosca, *The Ruling Class* (New York: McGraw-Hill, 1939). For a sharp analysis of Mosca, see Fritz Morstein Marx, 'The Bureaucratic State,' *Review of Politics,* vol. i, 1939, pp. 457 ff. Cf. also Mills, 'On Intellectual Craftsmanship,' April 1952, mimeographed, Columbia College, February 1955.

8. Cf. Karl Löwith, *Meaning in History* (Chicago: University of Chicago Press, 1949), pp. 125 ff. for concise and penetrating statements of several leading philosophies of history.

9. Some of these items are taken from Gerth and Mills, *Character and Social Structure,* pp. 405 ff. On role-determined and role-determining men, see also Sidney Hook's discussion, *The Hero in History* (New York: John Day, 1943).

10. I have taken the idea of the following kind of formulation from Joseph Wood Krutch's presentation of the morality of choice. See *The Measure of Man* (Indianapolis: Bobbs-Merrill, 1954), p. 52.

■ David Riesman, Nathan Glazer, and Reuel Denney

The Veto Groups

The shifting nature of the lobby provides us with an important clue as to the difference between the present American political scene and that of the age of McKinley. The ruling class of businessmen could relatively easily (though perhaps mistakenly) decide where their interests lay and what editors, lawyers, and legislators might be paid to advance them. The lobby ministered to the clear leadership, privilege, and imperative of the business ruling class.

Today we have substituted for that leadership a series of groups, each of which has struggled for and finally attained a power to stop things conceivably inimical to its interests and, within far narrower limits, to start things. The various business groups, large and small, the movie-censoring groups, the farm groups and the labor and professional groups, the major ethnic groups and major regional groups, have in many instances succeeded in maneuvering themselves into a position in which they are able to neutralize those who might attack them. The very increase in the number of these groups, and in the kinds of interests "practical" and "fictional" they are protecting, marks, therefore, a decisive change from the lobbies of an earlier day. There is a change in method, too, in the way the groups are organized, the way they handle each other, and the way they handle the public, that is, the unorganized.

These veto groups are neither leader-groups nor led-groups. The only leaders of national scope left in the United States today are those who can placate the veto groups. The only followers left in the United States today are those unorganized and sometimes disorganized unfortunates who have not yet invented their group.

Within the veto groups, there is, of course, the same struggle for top places that goes on in other bureaucratic setups. Among the veto groups competition is monopolistic; rules of fairness and fellowship dictate how far one can go. Despite the rules there are, of course, occasional "price wars," like the jurisdictional disputes of labor unions or Jewish defense groups; these are ended by negotiation, the division of territory, and the formation of a roof organization for the previously split constituency. These big monopolies, taken as a single group, are in devastating competition with the not yet grouped, much as the fair-trade economy competes against the free-trade economy. These latter scattered followers find what protection they can in the interstices around the group-minded.[1]

Each of the veto groups in this pat-

---

[1] It should be clear that monopolistic competition, both in business and politics, *is* competition. People are very much aware of their rivals, within and without the organization. They know who they are, but by the very nature of monopolistic competition they are seldom able to eliminate them entirely. While we have been talking of fair trade and tolerance, this should not obscure the fact that for the participants the feeling of being in a rivalrous setup is very

SOURCE: David Riesman, Nathan Glazer, and Reuel Denney, *The Lonely Crowd*, abr. ed. (Connecticut: Yale University Press, 1961), pp. 213–23. Copyright © 1950, 1953, 1961 by Yale University Press. Reprinted by permission of the publisher.

tern is capable of an aggressive move, but the move is sharply limited in its range by the way in which the various groups have already cut up the sphere of politics and arrayed certain massive expectations behind each cut. Both within the groups and in the situation created by their presence, the political mood tends to become one of other-directed tolerance. The vetoes so bind action that it is hard for the moralizers to conceive of a program that might in any large way alter the relations between political and personal life or between political and economic life. In the amorphous power structure created by the veto groups it is hard to distinguish rulers from the ruled, those to be aided from those to be opposed, those on your side from those on the other side. This very pattern encourages the inside-dopester who can unravel the personal linkages, and discourages the enthusiast or indignant who wants to install the good or fend off the bad. Probably, most of all it encourages the new-style indifferent who feels and is often told that his and everyone else's affairs are in the hands of the experts and that laymen, though they should "participate," should not really be too inquisitive or aroused.

By their very nature the veto groups exist as defense groups, not as leadership groups. If it is true that they do "have the power," they have it by virtue of a necessary mutual tolerance. More and more they mirror each other in their style of political action, including their interest in public relations and their emphasis on internal harmony of feelings. There is a tendency for organizations as differently oriented

as, say, the Young Socialists and the 4-H Club, to adopt similar psychological methods of salesmanship to obtain and solidify their recruits.

This does not mean, however, that the veto groups are formed along the lines of character structure. As in a business corporation there is room for extreme inner-directed and other-directed types, and all mixtures between, so in a veto group there can exist complex symbiotic relationships among people of different political styles. Thus a team of lobbyists may include both moralizers and inside-dopesters, sometimes working in harness, sometimes in conflict; and the constituency of the team may be composed mainly of new-style political indifferents who have enough literacy and organizational experience to throw weight around when called upon. Despite these complications I think it fair to say that the veto groups, even when they are set up to protect a clear-cut moralizing interest, are generally forced to adopt the political manners of the other-directed.

In saying this I am talking about the national scene. The smaller the constituency, of course, the smaller the number of veto groups involved and the greater the chance that some one of them will be dominant. Thus, in local politics there is more indignation and less tolerance, just as even the *Chicago Tribune* is a tolerant paper in comparison with the community throwaways in many Chicago neighborhoods.

The same problem may be considered from another perspective. Various groups have discovered that they can

strong. Indeed, they face the problem of so many other-directed people: how to combine the appearance of friendly, personalized, "sincere" behavior with the ruthless, sometimes almost paranoid, envies of their occupational life.

go quite far in the amorphous power situation in America without being stopped. Our society is behaviorally open enough to permit a considerable community of gangsters a comfortable living under a variety of partisan political regimes. In their lack of concern for public relations these men are belated businessmen. So are some labor leaders who have discovered their power to hold up the economy, though in most situations what is surprising is the moderation of labor demands—a moderation based more on psychological restraints than on any power that could effectively be interposed. Likewise, it is sometimes possible for an aggressive group, while not belonging to the entrenched veto-power teams, to push a bill through a legislature. Thus, the original Social Security Act went through Congress, so far as I can discover, because it was pushed by a devoted but tiny cohort; the large veto groups including organized labor were neither very much for it nor very much against it.

For similar reasons those veto groups are in many political situations strongest whose own memberships are composed of veto groups, especially veto groups of one. The best example of this is the individual farmer who, after one of the farm lobbies has made a deal for him, can still hold out for more. The farm lobby's concern for the reaction of other veto groups, such as labor unions, cuts little ice with the individual farmer. This fact may strengthen the lobby in a negotiation: it can use its internal public relations problems as a counter in bargaining, very much as does a diplomat who tells a foreign minister that he must consider how Senator so-and-so will react. For, no matter what the other-directedness of the lobby's leaders, they cannot

bind their membership to carry out a public relations approach. Many labor unions have a similar power because they cannot control their memberships who, if not satisfied with a deal made by the union, can walk off or otherwise sabotage a job.

In contrast, those veto groups are often weaker whose other-directed orientation can dominate their memberships. Large corporations are vulnerable to a call from the White House because, save for a residual indignant like Sewell Avery, their officials are themselves other-directed and because, once the word from the chief goes out, the factory superintendents, no matter how boiling mad, have to fall into line with the new policy by the very nature of the centralized organization for which they work: they can sabotage top management on minor matters but not, say, on wage rates or tax accounting. As against this, the American Catholic Church possesses immense veto-group power because it combines a certain amount of centralized command—and a public picture of a still greater amount—with a highly decentralized priesthood (each priest is in a sense his own trade association secretary) and a membership organization of wide-ranging ethnic, social, and political loyalties; this structure permits great flexibility in bargaining.

These qualifications, however, do not change the fact that the veto groups, taken together, constitute a new buffer region between the old, altered, and thinning extremes of those who were once leaders and led. It is both the attenuation of leaders and led, and the other-oriented doings of these buffers, that help to give many moralizers a sense of vacuum in American political life.

The veto groups, by the conditions

their presence creates and by the requirements they set for leadership in politics, foster the tolerant mood of other-direction and hasten the retreat of the inner-directed indignants.

IS THERE A RULING CLASS LEFT?

Nevertheless, people go on acting as if there still were a decisive ruling class in contemporary America. In the postwar years, businessmen thought labor leaders and politicians ran the country, while labor and the left thought that "Wall Street" ran it, or the "sixty families." Wall Street, confused perhaps by its dethronement as a telling barometer of capital-formation weather, may have thought that the midwestern industrial barons, cushioned on plant expansion money in the form of heavy depreciation reserves and undivided profits, ran the country. They might have had some evidence for this in the fact that the New Deal was much tougher with finance capital—e.g., the SEC and the Holding Company Act—than with industrial capital and that when, in the undistributed profits tax, it tried to subject the latter to a stockholder and money-market control, the tax was quickly repealed.

But these barons of Pittsburgh, Weirton, Akron, and Detroit, though certainly a tougher crowd than the Wall Streeters, are, as we saw earlier, coming more and more to think of themselves as trustees for their beneficiaries. And whereas, from the point of view of labor and the left, these men ran the War Production Board in the interest of their respective companies, one could argue just as easily that the WPB experience was one of the congeries of factors that have tamed the barons. It put them in a situation where they had to view their company from the point of view of "the others."

Despite the absence of intensive studies of business power and of what happens in a business negotiation, one can readily get an impressionistic sense of the change in business behavior in the last generation. In the pages of *Fortune,* that excellent chronicler of business, one can see that there are few survivals of the kinds of dealings—with other businessmen, with labor, with the government—that were standard operating practice for the pre-World War I tycoons. Moreover, in its twenty-year history, *Fortune* itself has shown, and perhaps it may be considered not too unrepresentative of its audience, a steady decline of interest in business as such and a growing interest in once peripheral matters, such as international relations, social science, and other accoutrements of the modern executive.

But it is of course more difficult to know whether character has changed as well as behavior—whether, as some contend, businessmen simply rule today in a more subtle, more "managerial" way. In "Manager Meets Union" Joseph M. Goldsen and Lillian Low have depicted the psychological dependence of a contemporary sales manager on the approval of the men under him, his willingness to go to great lengths, in terms of concessions, to maintain interpersonal warmth in his relations with them, and his fierce resentment of the union as a barrier to this emotional exchange.[2] As against this, one must set the attitude of some of the auto-supply companies whose

[2] "Manager Meets Union: A Case Study of Personal Immaturity," *Human Factors in Management,* ed. S. D. Hoslett (Parkville, Missouri: Park College Press, 1946), p. 77.

leadership still seems much more craft-oriented than people-oriented and therefore unwilling to make concessions and none too concerned with the emotional atmosphere of negotiations. Likewise, the General Motors-UAW negotiations of 1946, as reported in print, sound more like a cock-fight than a Platonic symposium, although in Peter Drucker's *Concept of the Corporation,* a study of General Motors published in the same year, there is much evidence of management eagerness to build a big, happy family.

Power, indeed, is founded, in a large measure, on interpersonal expectations and attitudes. If businessmen feel weak and dependent, they do in actuality become weaker and more dependent, no matter what material resources may be ascribed to them. My impression, based mainly on experiences of my own in business and law practice, is that businessmen from large manufacturing companies, though they often talk big, are easily frightened by the threat of others' hostility; they may pound the table, but they look to others for leadership and do not care to get out of line with their peer-groupers. Possibly, attitudes toward such an irascible businessman as Sewell Avery might mark a good dividing line between the older and the newer attitudes. Those businessmen who admire Avery, though they might not dare to imitate him, are becoming increasingly an elderly minority, while the younger men generally are shocked by Avery's "highhandedness," his rebuff of the glad hand.

The desire of businessmen to be well thought of has led to the irony that each time a professor writes a book attacking business, even if almost nobody reads it, he creates jobs in industry for his students in public relations, trade association work, and market research!

While the Black Horse Cavalry of an earlier era held up businessmen by threatening to let pass crippling legislation desired by anti-business moralizers, today many honest intellectuals who would not think of taking a bribe hold business or trade association jobs because their clients have been scared, perhaps by these very men, into taking cognizance of some actual or imaginary veto group. Since a large structure is built up to woo the group, no test of power is made to see whether the group has real existence or real strength. Understandably, ideologies about who has power in America are relied upon to support these amiable fictions which serve to provide the modern businessman with an endless shopping list, an endless task of glad-handing. This is a far cry, I suggest, from the opportunistic glad-handing of the wealthy on which Tocqueville comments; very likely, what was mere practice in his day has become embedded in character in ours.

Businessmen, moreover, are not the only people who fail to exploit the power position they are supposed, in the eyes of many observers, to have. Army officers are also astonishingly timid about exercising their leadership. During the war one would have thought that the army would be relatively impervious to criticism. But frequently the generals went to great lengths to refrain from doing something about which a congressman might make an unfriendly speech. They did so even at times when they might have brushed the congressman off like an angry fly. When dealing with businessmen or labor leaders, army officers were, it seemed to me, astonishingly deferential; and this was as true of the West Pointers as of the reservists. Of course, there were exceptions, but in many of the situations where the armed services made concessions to propitiate some veto group, they rationalized the concessions in terms of morale or of postwar public relations or, frequently, simply were not aware of their power.

To be sure, some came to the same result by the route of a democratic tradition of civilian dominance. Very likely, it was a good thing for the country that the services were so self-restrained. I do not here deal with the matter on the merits but use it as an illustration of changing character and changing social structure.

All this may lead to the question: well, who really runs things? What people fail to see is that, while it may take leadership to start things running, or to stop them, very little leadership is needed once things are under way—that, indeed, things can get terribly snarled up and still go on running. If one studies a factory, an army group, or other large organization, one wonders how things get done at all, with the lack of leadership and with all the featherbedding. Perhaps they get done because we are still trading on our reserves of inner-direction, especially in the lower ranks. At any rate, the fact they do get done is no proof that there is someone in charge.

There are, of course, still some veto groups that have more power than others and some individuals who have more power than others. But the determination of who these are has to be made all over again for our time: we cannot be satisfied with the answers given by Marx, Mosca, Michels, Pareto, Weber, Veblen, or Burnham, though we can learn from all of them.

There are also phenomena in this vast country that evade all of them (and surely, too, evade my collaborators and me). One example is the immense power, both political and economic, possessed by Artie Samish, allegedly the veto-group boss of California. Samish is a new-type lobbyist, who represents not one but scores of interests, often competing ones, from truckers to chiropractors, and who plays one veto group off against others to shake them down and strengthen his own power: he has learned how the other-orientation of the established veto groups will lead them to call still other groups into being through his auspices. Since the old-line parties have little power in California, there is no way of reaching a clear-cut decision for or against a particular veto group through the party system; instead, the state officials have become dependent on Samish for electoral support, or at least nonopposition, through his herded groups of voters and their cash contributions; moreover, he knows how to go directly to the people through the "democratic" plebiscite machinery.[3]

Carey McWilliams has observed that Samish's power rests both on the peculiar election machinery of the state and on the fact that no one industry or allied group of industries, no one union,

---

[3] Ironically enough, but typically enough, Samish craves the one power he does not have: social power in the society-page sense. A poor boy in origin, he can make or break businessmen and politicians but cannot get into the more exclusive clubs. And while consciously he is said to despise these social leaders whom he can so easily frighten and manipulate, he cannot purge himself of the childhood hurts and childhood images of power that make him vulnerable to their exclusion of him. In this, of course, he resembles other and better-known dictators.

I have drawn on Carey McWilliams, "Guy Who Gets Things Done," *Nation*, CLXIX (1949), 31–33; and Lester Velie, "Secret Boss of California," *Collier's*, CXXIV (August 13, 20, 1949), 11–13.

one ethnic group or region, is dominant. The situation is very different in a state like Montana, where copper is pivotal, and one must be either for the union or for Anaconda. It is different again in Virginia where, as V. O. Key shows in *Southern Politics,* the setup of the state constitution favors control by the old courthouse crowd. In view of these divergences, rooted in local legal niceties as well as in major social and economic factors, it is apparent that any discussion of class and power on the national scene can at best be only an approximation. Yet I would venture to say that the United States is on the whole more like California in its variety—but without its veto boss—than like Montana and Virginia in their particularity. The vaster number of veto groups, and their greater power, mean that no one man or small group of men can amass the power nationally that Artie Samish and, in earlier days, Huey Long, have held locally.

Rather, power on the national scene must be viewed in terms of issues. It is possible that, where an issue involves only two or three veto groups, themselves tiny minorities, the official or unofficial broker among the groups can be quite powerful—but only on that issue. However, where the issue involves the country as a whole, no individual or group leadership is likely to be very effective, because the entrenched veto groups cannot be budged: unlike a party that may be defeated at the polls, or a class that may be replaced by another class, the veto groups are always "in."

One might ask whether one would not find, over a long period of time, that decisions in America favored one group or class—thereby, by definition, the ruling group or class—over others.

Does not wealth exert its pull in the long run? In the past this has been so; for the future I doubt it. The future seems to be in the hands of the small business and professional men who control Congress, such as realtors, lawyers, car salesmen, undertakers, and so on; of the military men who control defense and, in part, foreign policy; of the big business managers and their lawyers, finance-committee men, and other counselors who decide on plant investment and influence the rate of technological change; of the labor leaders who control worker productivity and worker votes; of the black belt whites who have the greatest stake in southern politics; of the Poles, Italians, Jews, and Irishmen who have stakes in foreign policy, city jobs, and ethnic, religious and cultural organizations; of the editorializers and storytellers who help socialize the young, tease and train the adult, and amuse and annoy the aged; of the farmers—themselves a warring congeries of cattlemen, corn men, dairymen, cotton men, and so on —who control key departments and committees and who, as the living representatives of our inner-directed past, control many of our memories; of the Russians and, to a lesser degree, other foreign powers who control much of our agenda of attention; and so on. The reader can complete the list. Power in America seems to me situational and mercurial; it resists attempts to locate it the way a molecule, under the Heisenberg principle, resists attempts simultaneously to locate it and time its velocity.

But people are afraid of this indeterminacy and amorphousness in the cosmology of power. Even those intellectuals, for instance, who feel themselves very much out of power and who are frightened of those who they think have the power, prefer to be scared by the power structures they conjure up than to face the possibility that the power structure they believe exists has largely evaporated. Most people prefer to suffer with interpretations that give their world meaning than to relax in the cave without an Ariadne's thread.

20

THE SOCIAL CLASS BACKGROUND OF U. S. SENATORS

Donald R. Matthews

The fact that an extraordinarily large proportion of American political leaders spring from upper-middle- or upper-class origins does not, in itself, mean that conservative policies inevitably prevail. One cannot always predict a man's political views solely from his social class origins. After all, a great number of the leaders of the Russian Revolution sprang from middle-class backgrounds and few of them were genuine proletarians. And, on the American scene, men of wealth often differ markedly in their political views. Compare, for example, a Franklin Roosevelt or a Robert Kennedy with a Barry Goldwater.

Nevertheless, as economist Robert Heilbroner has reminded us in a seminal essay on the prospects for social change under capitalism in America, the main sources of resistance to social change "are to be found in the structure of privilege inherent in all social systems." * And the fact that so much of American political leadership stems from relatively privileged social classes tends on the whole to establish certain broad limits, biased in a conservative direction, within which the political dialogue takes place.

We include here a section of political scientist Donald R. Matthews' meticulous study of 180 U. S. senators who held office between 1947 and 1957. His findings, as the reader shall observe, are generally that U. S. senators do not represent a cross section of the American class structure, but are concentrated near the top, both with regard to their social origins and their present position.

In an earlier study, Matthews analyzed the social class background of others in the federal government and found that of the presidents, vice-presidents, and cabinet members who have held office in this country during the period from the beginning of the Republic until the mid-1930's, only 4 percent came from working-class or lower-class backgrounds.** More recently, G. William Domhoff studied the social class

* Robert Heilbroner, "The Future of Capitalism," *Commentary*, 41 (April 1966), pp. 23–35.

** Donald R. Matthews, *The Social Background of Political Decision-Makers* (New York: Random House, 1954).

SOURCE: Donald R. Matthews, *U. S. Senators and Their World* (Chapel Hill, N. C.: University of North Carolina Press, 1960), pp. 17–21, 23–25, and 44–46. Reprinted by permission of the publisher.

background of those men who between 1932 and 1964 occupied key power positions in American society.* In brief, he claimed that although the upper class comprises only one half of one percent of the population, they honeycomb strategic positions of political and economic power. At the federal level, the Congress was actually one of the institutions least dominated by the upper class. The upper class proper was far more important in the presidents' cabinet,** among presidential advisors, as members of the diplomatic corps assigned to major countries, and so forth. Besides their lobbying power and their influence with the regulatory agencies, the upper class was found to play a key role in the financing of both the Democratic and Republican parties.

When we analyze the class background of American political leaders, we see in operation that strange social sieve that, working from the raw material of universal suffrage and theoretical equality of political opportunity, strains and sifts out the working class from the seats of political power. The mechanism by which this occurs has been rehearsed many times: the great costs of election campaigns ($300 million for the campaigns of 1968 alone), the possession by the well-to-do of the political skills, the time, the resources, the connections, the interest, and the prestige that their ideas command by virtue of their position.

Moreover, this pattern is not uniquely American. Examining data from England, France, Germany, and Japan, in addition to the United States, Ralph Miliband states:

> What the evidence conclusively suggests is that in terms of social origin, education and class situation, the men who have manned all command positions in the state system have largely, and in many cases overwhelmingly, been drawn from the world of business and property, or from the professional middle classes. Here as in every other field, men and women born into the subordinate classes, which form of course the vast majority of the population, have fared very poorly. . . . In an epoch when so much is made of democracy, equality, social mobility, classlessness and the rest, it has remained a basic fact of life in advanced capitalist countries that the vast majority of men and women in these countries has been governed, represented, administered, judged, and commanded in war by people drawn from other, economically and socially superior and relatively distant classes.†

In a society that is nominally democratic and in which each man has one vote, what is important to bear continually in mind are the *political* implications of *economic* inequality.

Class Origins

Despite a widespread preference not to talk about such matters, few observant Americans would deny that individuals in the United States are ranked or "stratified" on generally accepted scales of social inferiority and superiority. Moreover, most would agree that individuals sharing roughly equal positions in this system of invidious distinctions tend to group into "classes."

But there is still much legitimate confusion about the American class sys-

---

* G. William Domhoff, *Who Rules America?* (Englewood Cliffs, New Jersey: Prentice-Hall, 1967).

** For example, between 1932 and 1964, 5 of the 8 secretaries of state were members of the upper class (as defined by Domhoff), 8 of 13 secretaries of defense or war, 4 out of 7 secretaries of the treasury, and 4 of the 11 attorneys-general.

† Ralph Miliband, *The State in Capitalist Society* (New York: Basic Books, 1969), pp. 66–67.

tem.[1] Many different criteria of ranking are used—family reputation, occupation, race and ethnic origins, income, religious affiliation, education, power and authority, group and association memberships, style of life, and so on—and an individual may rank high on some and relatively low on others. The relative significance of the various criteria, the number of classes and their boundaries are uncertain, vague, and changeful. Upward and downward mobility are so common that class consciousness and identification are relatively weak. As a result, there is not a very close correspondence between the classes people think they and others belong to (subjective class) and the classes in which an impartial observer would place them on the basis of objective criteria (objective class). Yet despite all these ambiguities and

difficulties of analysis, the evidence is overwhelming that classes of some sort exist and have substantial impact on how Americans behave and think and on what their opportunities are. Where do American senators fit into this unsystematic system? What influence has the class system had upon their recruitment? What are the senators' class origins?

The most important single criterion of ranking in the United States seems to be occupation. While it is by no means a certain index to social standing, it is the closest approach to such an infallible guide. Thus information on the occupations of the senators' fathers should provide a reasonably accurate picture of the senators' class origins. Table 1 shows the senators were sons, with only a handful of exceptions, of men possessing upper- and middle-

TABLE 1. Occupational Class Distribution of Fathers Compared with Labor Force in 1900

Occupational Class	Fathers of Senators	Labor Force in 1900	Index of Over-representation *
Professional	24%	6%	4.0
Proprietors & Officials	35	7	5.0
Farmers	32	22	1.5
Low-salaried Workers	2	5	0.4
Industrial Wage Earners	5	39	0.1
Servants	0	5	0.0
Farm Laborers	0	17	0.0
Unknown	2	0	
	100% (180)	100%	

* The "index of overrepresentation" is a way of expressing numerically the relationship between an actual and an expected proportion. If the senators' fathers' occupations had been represented in perfect proportion to their percentages of the 1900 labor force, the index for each occupation would be 1.0. Where the index is greater than 1.0, the occupation is overrepresented; where less than 1.0, underrepresented. See Appendix D.

SOURCE: T. M. Sogge, "Industrial Classes in the United States in 1930," *Journal of the American Statistical Association*, XXVIII (June, 1933), 199–203.

[1] For a good survey of the literature see R. M. Williams, Jr., *American Society* (New York: Alfred A. Knopf, 1951), Ch. 4.

class occupations.[2] The children of low-salaried workers, wage earners, servants, and farm laborers, which together comprised 66 per cent of the gainfully employed in 1900, contributed only 7 per cent of the postwar senators.[3] Only two of the 180 men, Senators Wagner and O'Daniel, were the sons of unskilled, urban wage earners. Wagner's father was a janitor in a New York City tenement; O'Daniel's father was a construction worker.[4] Senator Purtell was the son of a cigarmaker; McNamara, of a shipfitter; Daniel (S.C.), of a millwright; Welker, of a carpenter; Pastore, of a tailor; Cordon and Dirksen, of painters; Payne and Dworshak, of printers; Anderson, of a salesman; Myers, of a bookkeeper; Lennon, of a clerk; Margaret Chase Smith was the daughter of a barber. The remaining senators from urban backgrounds were sons of professional men, proprietors, or officials. Among the sons of farmers, some were born in relative poverty, yet it is virtually impossible to ascertain this in specific cases. It is still possible to conclude that very few senators were born in working-class and lower-class families. Moreover, the differences in occupational-class origins of Democrats and Republicans are small. Fifty-eight per cent of each party were the sons of either professionals, proprietors, or officials; the remainder, sons of farmers, low-salaried workers, or wage earners.

Within these necessarily broad categories, important differences exist in the occupational origins of the members of the two parties (Table 2). The Democrats were more often the sons of lawyers, doctors, professors, and journalists than were the Republicans; the GOP senators were more often the sons of ministers. Among the sons of proprietors and officials, the Democrats mostly came from families headed by merchants, insurance and real estate agents, construction contractors, and bankers. All the sons of manufacturing executives and publishers were Republicans. Finally, among the group of senators born to industrial wage earners, the Republicans tended to be sons of men with quasi-middle-class occupations—printers, carpenters, barbers, and painters—while the Democratic sons of industrial wage earners were born to fathers of somewhat lower status.

. . . . .

Education

It would be a mistake to assume that senators are "born," not "made." In the race for senatorial office most of the senators began with a considerable headstart. Yet American society is a *relatively* open and competitive society, both in fact and in ideology, and the senators had to display considerable ability, ambition, and achievement to get where they are.

Senators are among the most ed-

---

[2] The occupational-class categories used in this study were first developed by A. H. Hansen, "Industrial Class Alignments in the United States," *Journal of the American Statistical Association*, XVII (December, 1920), 416–25. The criteria of inclusion and exclusion from these categories are presented in this article.

[3] The validity of this comparison assumes, of course, that the birthrates of the different occupational classes are the same. Since, as a general rule, the lower the occupational class the higher the birthrate, the disparity in political life-chances was actually greater than these figures indicate.

[4] O'Daniel's father was killed in an accident while the future senator was still a small child. His stepfather was a farmer.

TABLE 2. Occupations of Fathers, by Party and "Class"

Fathers' Occupations, by "Class"	Democrats	Republicans
Professional	(28%)	(19%)
Lawyer	16%	7%
MD	5	2
Minister	1	6
Professor	1	0
Engineer	1	1
Journalist	1	0
Teacher	1	1
Poet	0	1
Government official	0	1
Proprietor and Official	(30%)	(39%)
Manufacturing executive	0%	3%
Publisher	0	6
Merchant	14	17
Banker	3	3
Insurance—Real estate agent	7	3
Construction contractor	3	1
Railroad official	1	2
Other	1	2
Farmers	(33%)	(31%)
Low Salaried Workers	(3%)	(0%)
Salesman	1%	0%
Clerk	2	0
Industrial Wage Earners	(5%)	(7%)
Printer	0%	2%
Carpenter	0	1
Painter	0	2
Barber	0	1
Cigar Maker	0	1
Tailor	1	0
Shipfitter	1	0
Millwright	1	0
Janitor	1	0
Construction laborer	1	0
Unknown	(0%)	(3%)
TOTALS	100%	100%
	(92)	(88)

ucated—in the formal sense of the word—of all occupational groups in the United States.[5] Almost 85 per cent of them attended college, a level of education achieved by only 14 per cent of the adult population in 1950 (Table 3).

The educational gap between the people and the members of the Senate is actually much wider than these figures indicate: 45 per cent of the senators attended both undergraduate college and law school, and 8 per cent of them per-

[5] See J. R. Shannon and M. Shaw, "Education of Business and Professional Leaders," *American Sociological Review*, V (June, 1940), 381–83.

TABLE 3. Educational Attainment Compared with White Population Twenty-five Years or over in 1950

Highest Level of Schooling	Democrats	Republicans	All Senators	White Population over 25 (1950)	Index of Overrep- resentation
Grade School	1%	1%	1%	48%*	0.2
High School	7	22	14	38	0.4
College	91	77	84	14	6.0
Law School	(10)	(7)	(8)		
College	(22)	(25)	(23)		
College & Law	(48)	(41)	(45)		
Postgraduate	(11)	(5)	(8)		
Unknown	1	0	1	0	
	100%	100%	100%	100%	
	(93)	(88)	(180)		

* Includes those with no formal education.

SOURCE: *Statistical Abstract of the United States,* 1954, p. 121, Table 135.

formed some other form of postgraduate work.

This high level of education can be accounted for, in part, by the senators' relatively high class origins. Numerous studies show that while the American educational system is one of the most equalitarian in the world, substantial differences in educational opportunities exist between social classes. Financial pressure, lack of motivation for academic success, the unconscious preference of middle-class teachers for middle-class children, and so on, place the child from working- or lower-class families at a distinct disadvantage even when his intelligence is the same as that of the middle-class child.[6] This is far from a total explanation of the su-

perior educational attainments of the senators, for, regardless of their class origins, more senators attended college than the other members of the white adult population (Table 4). Thus the high educational level of senators is not just the result of their greater opportunities but also reflects exceptional academic interest, ability, and achievement.

There are interesting party-line differences in educational levels, too. The Democrats are more educated than the Republicans (Table 3). Again, this is not the result of different class origins, for, when the level of education of Democratic and Republican senators with roughly the same class origins are compared (Table 4), the Democrats

[6] E. Sibley, "Some Demographic Clues to Stratification" in L. Wilson and W. Kolb (eds.), *Sociological Analysis* (New York: Harcourt, Brace and Co., 1949), pp. 642–50; W. L. Warner, R. J. Havighurst, and M. B. Loeb, *Who Shall Be Educated?* (New York: Harper and Brothers, 1940); C. A. Anderson, "Social Class Differentials in the Schooling of Youth Within the Region and Community Sized Groups of the United States," in K. Davis, M. Levy, and H. C. Bredemeier, *Modern American Society* (New York: Rinehart and Company, 1949), pp. 421–31; R. A. Mulligan, "Socio-Economic Background and College Enrollment," *American Sociological Review*, XVI (April, 1951), 188–96; A. B. Hollingshead, *Elmtown's Youth* (New York: John Wiley and Sons, 1949).

come out well ahead, especially among the senators with the lower-class origins. This evidence of the Democrats' greater concern with, or ability for, formal study is supported by several other pieces of evidence. Seventy-two per cent of the Democrats, but only 65 per cent of the Republicans, who entered undergraduate colleges graduated. Of those who did graduate, 24 per cent of the Democrats, but only 14 per cent of the Republicans, were elected to Phi Beta Kappa, the national scholastic honorary society.[7]

What kinds of schools did the senators attend? As undergraduates, the known Eastern colleges graduated more than their share of the senators. The other Ivy League universities and the Big Ten universities can claim only one-third the number of senators among their alumni one would expect on the basis of chance. The less well-known colleges and universities graduated just about their proportional share of future senators.

Again, we find some significant differences between Democrats and Republicans. Four times as many Republicans as Democrats graduated from "The Big Three" and half again as many from the smaller (but still expen-

TABLE 4. Percentage Attending College, by Occupational Levels of Fathers

Occupational Class of Father	Democrats	Republicans	All Senators
Professional	93%	100%	96% (43)
Proprietors and Officials	96%	82%	84% (61)
Farmers	87%	74%	81% (51)
All Lower Occupations	75%	24%	53% (15)

senators studied in 104 different educational institutions. State universities were the most popular type of undergraduate institution—about half of the senators attending undergraduate schools went to a state university at one time or another—but a very large share of all college graduates in the United States attended these uniquely American institutions. What type of college graduated the largest share of senators, taking into account the size of its alumni body? The answer—as clearly as we are able to supply one—is to be found in Table 5. Harvard, Yale, Princeton, and the smaller but well-

sive and prestige-laden) Eastern colleges. The senators from Big Ten universities—concentrated in the heavily Republican Midwest—were Republicans three to one, and a great many more Democrats than Republicans attended the less well-known institutions of the South and West. While the Democrats are more highly educated and seem to have done better work in undergraduate college, they did not as often attend the nationally known, expensive institutions of the Northeast.

A similar picture emerges from a close look at the fifty-one law schools the senators attended. On the basis of a

[7] The magnitude of this achievement is underscored by the fact that a large number of senators attended undergraduate colleges not accredited by Phi Beta Kappa and not more than 10 per cent of a graduating class is elected to the society.

thorough survey of legal education in 1920 (about the time most senators went to law school), A. Z. Reed found four levels of excellence in the nation's law schools.[8] These were:

1. High-entrance-requirement, full-time law schools which were parts of recognized colleges and universities and which required at least two years of undergraduate work before admis-

different and preoccupied with local law, and the students were exhausted from the strain of combining their legal studies with a full-time job.

4. Short-course law schools which were little more than glorified cram schools whose sole purpose was to prepare their students within a year or two for the bar examination. In 1920 these schools were concentrated in the

TABLE 5. Types of Colleges Attended Compared with Male College Graduates in 1940

Type of Undergraduate College	Democrats	Republicans	All College Graduate Senators	All Male College Graduates 1940	Index of Overrep- resentation
Harvard-Yale-Princeton	5%	19%	10%	5%	2.0
Other Ivy League*	2	2	2	6	0.3
20 Outstanding Eastern Schools**	9	14	11	5	2.2
Big Ten***	4	12	6	12	0.5
All Other	81	52	69	72	1.0
	100%	100%	100%	100%	
	(54)	(42)	(96)		

* Dartmouth, Cornell, Pennsylvania, Columbia.
** Amherst, Bates, Bowdoin, Brown, Clark (Maine), Colby, Franklin and Marshall, Hamilton, Haverford, Hobart, Lafayette, Lehigh, Middlebury, Rutgers, Swarthmore, Trinity (Conn.), Tufts, Union (N.Y.), Wesleyan, Williams.
*** Chicago, Illinois, Indiana, Iowa, Michigan, Minnesota, Northwestern, Ohio State, Purdue, Wisconsin.
SOURCE: F. C. Babcock, *The U.S. College Graduate* (New York: The Macmillan Company, 1941), p. 42, Table DD.

sion plus a three-year course of study for the LL.B.

2. Low-entrance-requirement schools which offered a full-time course of standard length but required only one year of study, or none at all, for admission.

3. Part-time law schools, often not connected with any university, which offered their courses at night or late afternoon. Often the instruction was in-

South, Indiana, and the District of Columbia, where bar entrance requirements were low.

Almost half the law schools attended by the senators were high-entrance requirement schools (at a time when only one-fifth of all American law schools belonged to that category) and another 30 per cent attended the second-ranking type (Table 6). Note also the con-

[8] A. Z. Reed, *Training for the Public Profession of Law* (New York: Carnegie Foundation for the Advancement of Teaching, Bulletin No. 15, 1921).

siderably greater percentage of Republicans than Democrats attending the first ranking schools. This may be explained in part by the fact that the best law schools were located in the strongly Republican areas of New England and the Middle West. The Democratic South simply had fewer first-rate law schools for her young men to attend.

thirteen as teachers, twelve as journalists, six as professors, six as merchants, five as executives in manufacturing concerns. On the other hand, a few of the senators began work in less desirable jobs. Eight senators, for example, started out as farmers, another eight as clerks, four as salesmen, two as common laborers, three as printers, one each as an electrician, machinist, pipe-

TABLE 6. Types of Law Schools Attended Compared with All Law Schools in 1920 (in percentage of all schools attended)

Type of School	Democrats	Republicans	All Legally Trained Senators	Percentage of All Law Schools in Category, 1920	Index of Overrepresentation
High Entrance, Full-Time	31%	68%	47%	21%	2.2
Low Entrance, Full-Time Standard Length	38	20	30	29	1.0
Part-Time	23	12	18	39	0.5
Short Course	8	0	5	11	1.5
	100%	100%	100%	100%	
	(61)	(49)	(109)	(142)	

SOURCE: A. Z. Reed, *Training for the Public Profession of Law* (N.Y.: Carnegie Foundation for the Advancement of Teaching, Bulletin No. 15, 1921), pp. 414–44.

Occupation

As might be expected from a group of highly educated men, most of the senators started work near the top of America's occupational hierarchy.[9] Eighty-eight—almost exactly one-half—of the senators began working as lawyers, fitter, factory worker, and farm laborer.

When all the senators' first occupations are lumped into occupational classes, it is clear that the "log-cabin-to-Capitol-Hill" myth of American politics needs considerable revision. Eighty-one per cent of the senators *started work* in the two highest classes.[10]

By the time the senators settled into their main nonpolitical occupations, a good deal of job shifting had occurred

[9] Part-time employment while in school is not included in this analysis. The senator's "first job" has been defined as his first full-time job after completion of schooling. If a senator's education was interrupted for more than one year, the employment followed during this hiatus is counted as his "first job."

[10] Those senators—about one in five—who started work in relatively menial occupations tended to have relatively low class origins and to have obtained relatively little formal educa-

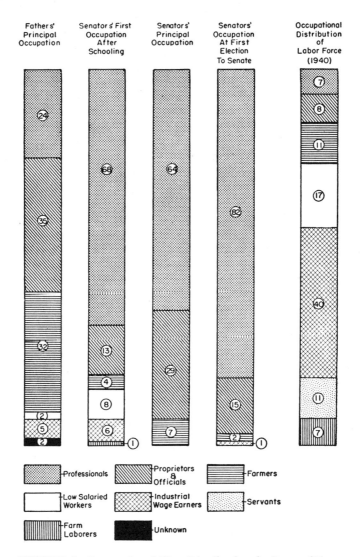

FIGURE 1. Occupational Class Distribution, by Stage of Career

tion. As the table below indicates, their lack of education was by far the more important of these two reasons for their relatively slow start.

Percentage Starting Work Either as Low-Salaried Workers, Industrial Wage Earners, Servants, or Farm Laborers, by Father's Occupation and Level of Education

Father's Occupational Class	Attended College	Did Not Attend College	Totals
Professional	0%	0%	0% (43)
Proprietors and Officials	9%	33%	12% (60)
Farmers	7%	60%	16% (56)
All lower	0%	43%	20% (15)
Totals	5% (149)	44% (25)	

314

(Figure 1).[11] All save one of the teachers had abandoned their original jobs for more rewarding endeavors—mostly law (four Southern Democrats) and business (six Republicans). All the men who started out as low-salaried employees, industrial wage earners, or farm laborers had moved up the status ladder. The number of lawyers, farmers, merchants, manufacturing executives, publishers, insurance and real estate agents, contractors, and oil-gas producers had noticeably increased. The net result of these occupational changes was a considerable increase in the class positions of the senators. By this stage of their careers, all the senators are to be found in the top quarter of the labor force.

By the time our subjects became senators, they had bettered their lot even more. Almost 60 per cent of them were serving in political office at the time of their election or appointment to the Senate.[12] Of those elected to the upper house from "civilian" occupations, the lawyers were most numerous (38), followed at a considerable distance by merchants (6), publishers (3), and manufacturing executives (3). All told, 82 per cent of the prospective senators were professionals (including public officials) and 15 per cent proprietors and officials at the time of their election. Only four of the 180 men were full-time farmers [13] and one was a factory worker when elected to the Senate. Senators, quite obviously, are elected from, or near, the top of the nation's occupational class system. In getting there, a head start helps.

THE LAWYERS

The second most striking feature of the occupational histories of the senators is the number of them who at one time or another were lawyers. The legal profession comprises about 0.1 per cent of the American labor force, and yet about half of the senators were lawyers. No other occupational group even approaches the lawyers' record. Why this predominance of lawyers? Obviously they meet what seems to be one test of top-level leadership—they are a high prestige profession. But why are not other equally highly esteemed occupations equally represented among the senators?

A partial answer to these questions can be found in the skills of the lawyer and in the nature of the legal profession in America. The skills of the lawyer in America tend to give him an advantage in the race for office if not actual training for filling the office once it is achieved. With the erosion of the historic view that a lawyer is an officer of the court, the modern Ameri-

---

[↑] The determination of a senator's principal, nonpolitical occupation is not without its arbitrary aspects for those senators who have followed numerous callings or who have had more than one occupation at a time. In making the relatively few difficult decisions required, the following rules have been followed: If a senator had pursued a number of occupations either the last or the one followed for the longest period of time was selected. The choice here was made in favor of the more time-consuming occupation. For example, if a senator had been a lawyer and a farm owner or a corporation director, he is defined as a lawyer. When two or more occupations were followed simultaneously the same criteria were considered controlling.

[12] Occupation at the time of election or appointment to office was defined as the last occupation held within one year of election or appointment.

[13] A large number of senators owned farm land, however. This merely strengthens the conclusion of this section, for the ownership of farm land is a mark of upper-middle- and upper-class standing in much of America.

can conception developed that the lawyer is a paid servant of his client, justified in using any weapon that the law supplies in his client's interest.[14] His job is primarily one of making the best possible case from the point of view of his clients. In filling this new role, the lawyer has become "a mediator of forces," a "specialist in human relations."[15] The lawyer, in his everyday occupational role, develops not only ability in interpersonal mediation and conciliation but also skill in verbal manipulation. Lasswell and McDougal do not exaggerate when they say: ". . . the lawyer is today . . . the one indispensable advisor of every responsible policy-maker of our society—whether we speak of the head of a government department or agency, of the executive of a corporation or labour union, of the secretary of a trade or other private association, or even of the humble independent enterpriser or professional man. As such an advisor the lawyer, when informing his policy-maker of what he can or cannot legally do, is in an unassailably strategic position to influence, if not create, policy . . . For better or worse our decision-makers and our lawyers are bound together in a relation of dependence or identity."[16] With the development of these skills in the normal course of a legal career, the lawyer has a substan-

tial advantage over the average layman who decides to enter politics.

The professional skills developed by lawyers do not alone explain their dominance in the political leadership groups of America. Unlike many European countries, the United States has never had a landed aristocracy with a tradition of political participation. Relatively few senators are the possessors of inherited wealth. In a highly competitive society, where occupational success is the most highly valued goal for the ambitious, who can, with the least danger, leave their jobs for the tremendous risks of a political career? Among the high-prestige occupations it seems to be the lawyers. Certainly, other professional men find the neglect of their careers for political activity extremely hazardous. To those in professions where the subject matter is rapidly changing, a few years of neglect of their vocations and their skills would be either lost or outmoded.[17] The active businessman, be he an individual entrepreneur or a member of a corporate bureaucracy,[18] would find the neglect of his vocation for politics no asset to his primary occupational interest. Politics demands more and more time from its practitioners: the farmer, under these conditions, finds it difficult to indulge a taste for politics while still keeping the farm going. These barriers

[14] A. A. Berle, Jr., "Modern Legal Profession," *Encyclopedia of the Social Sciences* (New York: The Macmillan Company, 1930), IX, 343.

[15] J. W. Hurst, *The Growth of American Law* (Boston: Little, Brown and Company, 1950), p. 335.

[16] H. D. Lasswell and M. S. McDougal, "Legal Education and Public Policy," in Lasswell, *Analysis of Political Behavior* (London: Routledge and Paul, 1948), p. 27.

[17] B. Barber, "'Mass Apathy' and Voluntary Social Participation in the United States" (Ph.D. dissertation, Harvard University, 1948), p. 118.

[18] The rise of a salaried "new middle class" seems likely to place even greater restrictions on the political activities of middle-class Americans. See C. W. Mills and M. J. Ulmer, *Small Business and Civic Welfare*, Report of the Smaller War Plants Corporation to the Special Committee to Study Problems of American Small Business, Senate Document 135, 79th Congress, 2nd Session, Part IV, p. 27.

to political participation either do not exist or are decreased in significance for the lawyer. The law changes relatively slowly, and a politician is in a position to keep up with many of the changes in the law while active in politics. The lawyer, either in individual practice or in a law firm of a few members, is "dispensable." [19] He can most easily combine his occupation, on a part-time basis, with political activity. Moreover, this activity can be a positive advantage to his occupational advancement—free and professionally legitimate advertising, contacts, and an opportunity to meet important lawyers of his region result from his political activities. The politician must be prepared for at least an occasional defeat at the polls: the lawyer has an insurance policy against this inescapable risk in his professional skill, reputation, and practice.

Finally, lawyers possess a monopoly of public offices relating to the administration of law and the court system.[20] Since in America "every political question tends to become a legal question," the offices of judge and prosecuting attorney provide lawyers (and lawyers alone) relatively easy entry into the political world and important springboards to higher offices. Almost half of the lawyers in the Senate (and therefore about one-quarter of all the senators) began their political careers by serving in law-enforcement offices open only to the legally trained. Twenty-five per cent of the senators held such offices at the time of their election to the Senate. . . .[21]

The new look in senators can be quickly summarized. The "typical" senator during the postwar years was a late-middle-aged or elderly, white, Protestant, native-born man with rural or small-town and upper-middle-class origins, a college-educated lawyer, and a "joiner." This collective portrait is probably what most informed observers would have guessed without charts, graphs, and statistics, but the analysis performed in this chapter tells us much which even the best guesswork will not.

[19] M. Weber, "Politics as a Vocation," in H. Gerth and C. W. Mills (eds. and trans.), *From Max Weber: Essays in Sociology* (New York: Oxford University Press, 1946), p. 84 ff. for the classic analysis.

[20] J. A. Schlesinger, "Lawyers and Politics: A Clarified View," *Midwest Journal of Political Science*, I (May, 1957), 26–39.

[21] The legal profession is a large and heterogeneous one. To discover that most senators are lawyers and to point out some of the reasons why this is so does not advance our understanding as far as we might like. What kind of lawyers are the senators? A few bits and pieces of information provide some insight on this subject.

The lawyers in the Senate have practiced law mostly in the nation's small towns and medium-sized cities while the profession as a whole is heavily concentrated in a few metropolitan areas. W. Weinfeld, "Incomes of Lawyers," *Survey of Current Business*, XXIX (August, 1949), 22, Table 8, reports that 46 per cent of all nonsalaried lawyers in 1947 practiced in cities of a quarter of a million or more in population. Only 20 per cent of the senator-lawyers practiced in cities that large. The most successful lawyers are members of the larger firms. *Ibid.*, Table 7, reports that 88 per cent of all nonsalaried lawyers were in practice alone in 1947, 11 per cent were in firms with from two to five members, and 1 per cent belonged to firms of five or more. The corresponding figures for the lawyer-senators are 40, 47, and 13 per cent—with the Republican lawyers coming in far greater numbers than the Democrats from the larger firms. One reason the lawyer-senators—and again especially the Republicans—came in disproportionate numbers from the larger and presumably more prosperous law firms is their exceptionally good legal training. The better the law school the lawyer-senator attended, the more likely he was to belong to a sizeable firm.

1. We have been able to see how far the "typical" senator differs from the "typical" American. Probably less than 5 per cent of the American people have any significant chance of ever serving in the Senate as long as the present informal "requirements" for the office hold. While these barriers seem rapidly to be weakening, huge blocs of Americans still have little chance for service in the Senate. Many of the factors which so heavily influence the political life-chances of Americans seem to have little if any relationship to political ability.

2. We have been able to see why the typical senator is such an atypical American. One reason, certainly, is the constitutional requirements for Senate membership. The constitution requires that senators be at least thirty years of age, that they be citizens of at least nine years' standing, and that they be residents of the states they represent. The first of these legal requirements explains why the senators are older than the average American, but it does not tell us why they are so much older than they are required to be. The nine-year citizenship requirement may account for the fact that few immigrants are senators, but it does not tell us why some groups of second-generation Americans are discriminated against. The requirement that senators live in the states they represent, when combined with the equal representation of the large and small states, may help explain the bias in favor of Amer-

icans from the nation's smaller towns and cities, although we saw that this was not a total explanation of this bias. If we are to understand the "typical" senator, we must look well beyond the legal formalities to the structure of American society.

The senators were selected, with only rare exceptions, from near the top of the society's class system. While many more studies of this nature are necessary before conclusions can be definite, this study and others like it indicate that governmental offices are class ranked—the more important the office, the higher the social status of its normal incumbent.[22] While this conclusion rings harsh in many an American democrat's ear, it should not be a particularly surprising conclusion. A stratified society places different evaluation on various social positions, and the prestige of the office or position tends to be transferred to the person who fills it. Thus the bank president or lawyer is a "better" man than the janitor or policeman. As long as the system of stratification in a society is generally accepted, one must expect people to look for political leadership toward those who have met the current definition of success and hence are considered worthy individuals. Voters seem to prefer candidates who are not like themselves but are what they would like to be.[23]

Of course, the existence of this class bias in the recruitment of senators may not be solely the result of popular con-

[22] See D. R. Matthews, *The Social Background of Political Decision-Makers* (Garden City: Doubleday and Company, Inc., 1954).

[23] Ironically enough, in a society with a relatively rigid class system like that of Great Britain the class bias in the recruitment of top-level public officials is less than in the United States. Evidently, in class systems with substantial mobility, such as America's, individuals tend to identify with higher strata and accept it as their standard of value. In a less open society, this identification does not exist, and there is a tendency to look to one's own class for political leadership.

sent. Those with high status positions in American society tend to have more money (and easier access to still more) than the ordinary American, and as we shall see, it takes a good deal of money to become a senator. They tend to have more leisure and more flexible work schedules, too. Members of the upper and upper-middle classes in America are more politically aware than the average American and may be more prone to enter politics.[24] As a general rule, they are likely to possess the relevant skills—verbal ability, ability at inter-personal conciliation and manipulation, "functional" and "substantial" rationality [25]—for politics in a democratic land.

3. We have been able to account for many of the differences in background found among the senators. The collective portrait of the United States senator presented in this chapter is a useful fiction, but like other fictions it has its limitations. While most of the senators studied fit the picture, a minority does not. The analysis in this chapter helps explain why.

The two major parties, for instance, recruit somewhat different types of men for the Senate. The Democrats were elected at an earlier age and were born and live in larger towns and cities than the Republicans. Their fathers, as a group, possessed somewhat higher occupational class positions but were also more often immigrants, Catholics, Jews, and members of relatively low prestige Protestant denominations. The Democrats obtained more education than the Republicans, but less often at the well-known schools. They were more often lawyers, but they practiced in smaller towns and as members of smaller law firms than the Republicans. The Republicans were more often businessmen and came from industries different from those of the Democratic businessmen in the Senate.

Party is not the only factor, however, which helps account for differences in the senators' careers. Different constituencies tend to elect different types of men to the Senate. Rural states incline toward senators with rural origins; states with large concentrations of foreign-born or Roman Catholic voters more often elect members to the Senate with these social characteristics; the more competitive a state's party system, the less often lawyers are chosen as senators; and businessmen tend to be elected from mixed urban-rural states. As we shall see, these differences among senators are just as significant as their similarities.

---

[24] That the upper classes are more concerned with politics is clear. See J. L. Woodward and E. Roper, "Political Activity of American Citizens," *American Political Science Review*, XLIV (December, 1950), 872–85. But the higher status groups in American society are also the most biased against a political career [See H. Cantril, ed., *Public Opinion: 1935–46* (Princeton: Princeton University Press, 1951), p. 534.] and have the best opportunities in other lines of endeavor.

[25] The distinction between functional and substantial rationality was originated by Karl Mannheim. In his terminology, functional rationality is the ability to coordinate means so as to obtain most efficiently a given end, while substantial rationality is made up of individual insight and understanding of complex situations.

21

SOCIAL CLASS VOTING IN THE ANGLO-AMERICAN COUNTRIES

Robert R. Alford

"God must have loved the common man," said Abraham Lincoln, "because he made so many of them." And the fact that they are so numerous has had crucial political implications since the advent of universal suffrage and political democracy.* In countries where there is a two-party political system and in which the two parties can be generally identified as either liberal or conservative, the mass of common men *generally* (with numerous exceptions) tend to prefer the left-wing party.** The reason for this is that insofar as economic issues are important in political elections (taxes, education, social security, housing, medical care, labor legislation, and so forth), the liberal party usually is more favorable than the conservative party to the economic interests of the "common man."

This distribution of allegiances poses certain problems for conservative parties in terms of winning votes and elections. What have they tried to do to undercut the appeal which liberal parties have for the vote of the common man? First of all, conservative parties have been obliged to move toward liberal economic policies in order, so to speak, to steal the thunder on the left. Paradoxically we now see conservative parties, in order to stay politically alive, endorsing a whole array of liberal economic legislation that they once opposed. The Tory party in Great Britain has learned to live with—and even claim some credit for—socialized medicine, the welfare state, nationalization of a sector of the British economy, and the like. And Republicans in this country have come to terms with, and have even extended, aspects of the welfare state to which they were originally opposed.

As conservative parties shift left to gain the votes of the common man, the liberal parties tend to move further to the left to distinguish themselves from their conservative colleagues. Thus, over the last century we have had what might be called a secular drift to the left in democratic politics, simply because of the workings of popular suffrage, the emergence of the common man and his generally liberal economic proclivities, and the desire of political parties to win elections. Think, for example, how the definition of the term liberalism has changed since the nineteenth century. Nineteenth-century liberalism was associated primarily with the doctrine of laissez-faire. Today we have moved politically to the left so that this doctrine is considered ultra-

---

* I am indebted to the lectures and writings of S. M. Lipset for much of the material in this section.

** For example, in the late 1960's, 46 percent of American voters considered themselves Democrats, 27 percent Republicans, and the remainder, independent.

SOURCE: Robert R. Alford, *Party and Society* (Chicago: Rand McNally & Company, 1963), pp. 94–104 and 219–27. Reprinted by permission of the publisher and the author.

conservative. And many nineteenth- and twentieth-century socialist demands have been incorporated into the political mainstream. It should be noted, however, that this secular drift to the left involves economic issues alone, not necessarily foreign policy, civil rights, or civil liberties in which the great mass of the electorate has no consistent liberal interest.

While liberal parties have the general advantage of seeming to favor the economic interests of Lincoln's common man, conservatives have other techniques and advantages, as Lipset has pointed out.* (1) Conservatives attempt to turn the attention of the electorate to nonclass issues (because on class issues they are usually outnumbered). Thus, they play down class divisions and stress instead issues which unite the country such as patriotism or foreign policy, or they may attempt to run a war hero such as Eisenhower who symbolizes national unity. In addition, while the American working class is economically liberal, it is racially conservative. Thus, as racial issues become more important, conservative candidates are favored, as demonstrated by the defection of normally Democratic voters in the 1968 presidential election. White working-class backlash is turning liberals into conservatives. (2) Upper-class values tend to have higher status than lower-class values; insofar as upper-class values are politically conservative, the conservative party is aided. (3) The major disseminators of values in society, such as the mass media and the schools, generally propagate middle- and upper-class, rather than working- or lower-class, values. (4) The basic inertia and resistance to change of most people work against a liberal party seeking social reform. (5) Middle- and upper-class persons are more sophisticated than others about their political interests, are more politically involved, are much more apt to vote and to remain loyal to their party. This also aids the conservative cause.

Although the generalization mentioned at the outset is valid—that the lower strata tend to prefer the liberal parties and the higher strata the conservative parties—there are variations from country to country and over time. In this selection, political sociologist Robert Alford discusses the differences in the level of class-voting in the four Anglo-American countries with two-party traditions, attempts to account for the national differences in the levels of class-voting, and finally, treats the United States in somewhat greater detail, addressing himself to trends in class-voting since the 1930's.

To follow Alford's argument, it is necessary to understand his index of class-voting. The index that he uses is computed simply by taking the percentage of manual workers voting for left parties and subtracting from it the percentage of nonmanual workers voting for left parties. Thus, if 60 percent of manual workers voted Democratic as compared to 40 percent of nonmanual workers, the index of class-voting would be 20. If 70 percent of manual, but only 30 percent of nonmanual workers voted Democratic, the index would be 40. Obviously, the higher the number, the greater the magnitude of class-voting.

Since Alford's analysis of American data ends in 1962, we have brought things somewhat more up to date by including here Gallup poll findings on the 1964 and 1968 presidential elections.

In general, class-voting continued strong in the 1964 election. It then dropped considerably in 1968, in what may be portentous for the future of American politics, as the racial struggle, law and order, student unrest, and other nonclass issues drew traditional working-class support away disproportionately from the Democrats and distributed it among Republicans and supporters of George C. Wallace. What seems to be happening is that the American working-class vote, long in the Democratic column,

* See S. M. Lipset, *Revolution and Counterrevolution: Change and Persistence in Social Structures* (New York: Basic Books, 1968), pp. 159 ff.

Presidential Vote by Occupational Class, 1968 and 1964 Elections, (in percent)

	1968		
Occupation of Voter	Democratic	Republican	American Independence (Wallace)
Professional and Business	34%	56%	10%
Other White Collar	41	47	12
Blue Collar	50	35	15
Farmers	29	51	20
TOTAL	43.0	43.4	13.6
	1964		
Professional and Business	54	46	
Other White Collar	57	43	
Blue Collar	71	29	
Farmers	53	47	
TOTAL	61.3	38.7	

is now up for grabs. Politically schizophrenic, capable of alternately supporting a Robert Kennedy and a George Wallace, of beating up student demonstrators one day and picketing the president on his economic policies the next, possessed at once of both left-wing liberal and right-wing hard-hat instincts, the working class can now go either way. And which way it does go depends partly upon whether liberal or conservative politicians can better tap the underlying working-class mood, and partly on objective developments in American society, especially with regard to the economy, the course of race relations, domestic dissent, and our international involvements.

Why Class Voting Should Be Higher in Great Britain and Australia

Considerable historical and institutional evidence indicates that the association of class and vote should be higher in Great Britain and Australia than in the United States and Canada. In particular, the explicit links of the trade unions with the Labor parties of Great Britain and Australia might seem to be prima facie evidence that manual workers are far more likely to support the Labor party than non-manual workers. But this is not a necessary connection. The links of a class organization with a party bearing the name of "labor" do not guarantee that the actual character of the support of the party is sharply differentiated from that of the other party. Particularly in this historical period, when, according to authors already cited, class lines are blurring and the working class in advanced industrial societies is losing its distinctive identity and consciousness as it takes on middle-class values and aspirations, there is no reason to assume that working-class and middle-class persons are still sharply divided in their political loyalties.

Before presenting the actual evidence, the views of political scientists on a few of the historical differences between these four political systems which probably affect the level of class voting should be noted. Since this is a

large topic in itself, only a few representative and current works will be
cited. The point is obvious: class organizations and class ideologies have been
much more explicitly linked to the political parties in Great Britain and Australia than in the United States and
Canada.

The Labour party of Great Britain
was from the first an instrument of
class organizations—the trade unions.

> The Labour party was founded by the
> trade unions to secure Labour represen-
> tation in Parliament and to support by
> political action the objectives sought by
> the trade unions in the interests of their
> members. . . . What produced that
> party was the discovery by the urban
> workers that they could secure better
> conditions of service by combinations
> among themselves, and the threat by the
> employers to seize the initiative by em-
> ployers' federations which could also act
> as pressure groups in Parliament.[1]

Even today, the trade unions raise most
of the money for the Labour party, and
are officially represented in the "National Council of Labour," composed
of representatives of the Labour party,
the Trades Union Congress, and the
Cooperative party.[2] Although in practice the Labour party has a high degree
of independence, the "constitutional
law" of the party holds that it is bound
by the decisions of the annual Parliamentary Labour Conference, in which
the unions are officially represented.

However, though actual relationships exist between the trade unions
and the Labour party in Great Britain, they are complicated and often
strained, and in no sense do the trade
unions dictate to the Labour party.
The party is not the creature of working-class organizations; the very moderation of British political culture prevents any coincidence of class and
party views. But clearly the trade
unions—unquestioned instruments of
working-class interests—and the Labour party are historically and publicly
linked. On this ground alone, we
might expect that political loyalties in
Great Britain might be explicitly class-
linked.[3]

The Labor party in Australia is
equally solidly linked to working-class
organizations.

> The Labour Party was created by the
> trade unions and their Trades and La-
> bour Councils. The solid core and the
> majority of its membership, as of its
> electoral support, came and have ever
> since come from trade unionists and
> their families. Most of its Parliamentar-
> ians, Federal and State, have risen
> through the trade union ranks. For
> many years it was little more than the
> trade-unions-in-politics—in earlier times,
> in some States at least, it was known as
> the "Labour-in-politics" movement,
> implying just that.[4]

---

[1] Sir Ivor Jennings, *Party Politics, II: The Growth of Parties* (Cambridge: Cambridge University Press, 1961), pp. 235, 237.

[2] *Ibid.*, pp. 256–57; Robert T. McKenzie, *British Political Parties* (London: Heinemann, 1955), p. 529.

[3] A common Conservative accusation against Labour is that it is dominated by "special interests" and therefore cannot represent the nation as well as the Conservative party. McKenzie devotes much of his book on British political parties to a demonstration that the Labour party is no more (and no less) bound to outside pressure groups than the Conservative party. See McKenzie, *op. cit.*, chap. 1.

[4] L. F. Crisp, *The Australian Federal Labor Party: 1901–1951* (London: Longmans, Green, 1955), p. 182. See also Donald W. Rawson, *Australia Votes: The 1958 Federal Election* (Melbourne: Melbourne University Press, 1961), p. 2.

The class-structure of Australia is similar to that of the other countries. From these two factors, we might expect that the level of class voting in Australia is close to that of Britain.

But one feature of Australian history might lead to a level of class voting different from that in Great Britain. The Australian Labor party has always had higher prestige and authority than the British Labour party. From the very beginning of Australian nationhood in 1901, the Labor party has existed as a political force and has shaped the political traditions of its country far more than the Labour party of Great Britain did. The British Labour party arose partly as a means of breaking the dominance in Parliament of the industrial and owning classes and of gaining recognition of the legitimacy of class organizations. The Australian Labor party arose partly as an instrument for the unification of Australia as an independent nation and partly as a representative of strongly organized and militant unions mainly composed of workers in "rural" occupations such as sheep-shearing. Its dominance is noted by American political scientist Louise Overacker:

> The position of the Labor Party, both as to program and actual strength in Parliament, is a determining factor from which the politicians calculate their course, right or left. . . . The matrix of Australian politics is the Labor Party, and Australian politics reflects working-class rather than middle-class thinking.[5]

The dominant role of the Labor party in Australia might produce either higher or lower levels of class voting in Australia than Great Britain. Where the Right party has the halo of tradition and defender of the nation and is supported by widespread values of deference toward the aristocracy as in Great Britain, we might expect that a large minority of the workers would vote Conservative for non-class reasons. Even if middle-class persons voted consistently Conservative in accordance with *their* class interests, Conservative "deferential voting" among workers would reduce the level of class voting. On the other hand, the middle class in Australia might be more likely to vote Labor because of the legitimacy and nationalism associated with the Labor party in that country, reducing the level of class voting there.

Both of these arguments are plausible, and both may be wrong. Actually, the greater legitimacy of the Right in Great Britain and of the Left in Australia may negligibly affect the voting of either social class. This point has been raised simply to underline the difficulty of predicting the level of class voting from information on only the historic links of class organizations to political parties.

But regardless of the differences between Australia and Great Britain, historical and institutional evidence does indicate that class voting is likely to be higher in both of these countries than in the United States and Canada.

Occupational differences in the composition of the lower houses of the parliaments of the countries are consistent with this prediction, as Table 1 shows, for various years. In Britain and Australia, 19 per cent of Members of Parliament were either manual workers or

[5] Louise Overacker, *The Australian Party System* (New Haven: Yale University Press, 1952), p. 81. Part of the quote was taken from C. Hartley Grattan, *Introducing Australia* (New York: John Day, 1942), p. 153. Here, as is the case with the British Labour party, such origins and political role do not mean that the party has a consistent ideological position or that it is not willing to compromise.

TABLE 1. Members of the Lower House from Working-Class Occupations, by Parties

Country	Members from Working Class (Per Cent)		
Great Britain, 1959	Conservative	Labour	Total
	0	47	19
Australia, 1951	Liberal	Labor	Total
	4	45	19
United States, 1949	Republican	Democratic	Total
	—	—	3
Canada, 1945	Conservative	Liberal	Total
	—	—	1

SOURCES: Information was not available for all persons, nor for the parties separately in the United States and Canada, although the differences could not possibly be great.

Great Britain: Computed from D. E. Butler and Richard Rose, *The British General Election of 1959* (London: Macmillan, 1960), p. 127. The percentages given include labor union officials, who hold 12 per cent of the Labour seats in the House of Commons. One Conservative was a manual worker.

Australia: Compiled from the *Australian Parliamentary Handbook, 1952* (Sydney: Angus and Robertson, 1952), pp. 265–300. The percentages given include labor union officials, who hold 15 per cent of the Labor seats in the House of Representatives.

United States: From Donald R. Matthews, *The Social Background of Political Decision-Makers* (New York: Random House, 1954). The percentage given refers to either wage-earners or low-salaried workers. It may be noted that of the state legislators in thirteen states (including most of the highly urbanized states, where trade unions are most likely to be politically active), 7 per cent in this period were wage-earners or low-salaried workers.

Canada: From Norman Ward, *The Canadian House of Commons: Representation* (Toronto: University of Toronto Press, 1950), p. 132. Each member was classified according to as many as three "occupations and economic interests." Ward notes also that "in no single province has there been a serious and continuing difference of occupational structure between the major groups composing each party in the legislature" (pp. 135–36).

trade union officials, while in the United States and Canada, only 3 per cent and 1 per cent, respectively, came from such occupations. The class composition of the lower house in the latter two countries is like the composition of the Right parties in Britain and Australia.[6]

The Left political parties in the United States and Canada do not have public and historic links with trade unions and other class organizations which might repel the middle class and attract the working class, producing a high level of class voting. As R. M. MacIver has put it:

> party government can under certain conditions operate with considerable indifference to class stratification. Thus for long periods and over large areas in the

[6] Middle-class professionals comprise almost equal proportions of the Left and Right parliamentarians in both Australia and Britain (between 35 and 40 per cent), despite the dominance of class groupings in the parties. Presumably such groups should be a moderating influence upon class conflicts, having less of a direct stake in the struggle. Lawyers are more highly represented in the British than in the Australian parliament.

United States and in Canada there was little relation between class and party, the struggle between parties being essentially a contest of the "ins" and the "outs" for the spoils of office. When this happens, however, parties are hardly distinguishable from one another with respect to principles or to objectives.

MacIver infers that when, as in the 1930's, "both in Canada and the United States, one or another party came to propose important economic changes," the tendency of the more well-to-do to support one party and the poorer to support another showed again.[7]

That the political parties in the United States and Canada historically have been competing political elites—the "ins" and the "outs"—and not the direct representatives of class organizations does not clearly distinguish them from the parties of Australia and Great Britain, however. In all four societies, each party has in practice consented to whatever legislation has been passed and has even adopted some policies likely to be favored by the class base of the other party in order to win over support. In Australia, "Labor's political opponents have accepted many of Labor's policies," and in Great Britain, most markedly in recent years, the policies of the parties have been well-nigh indistinguishable.[8] Thus it cannot be maintained that the actual policies of the parties in Australia and Great Britain are so different from those in the

other two countries—aside from historic traditions and organizational links—that we may expect sharp differences in the level of class voting.

There is another ground on which class voting may not be expected to be sharply higher in Australia and Great Britain—at least higher than in the United States. The public images of the two parties in the United States sharply define them as representatives of distinctive class bases:

a consistent majority—at times as high as two-thirds to three-quarters—of the adult population of the United States perceives a clear distinction in ideological and interest-group propensity between the two major parties. The polls tend to verify the commonly accepted caricature that the Democratic Party is the party of the poor and of labor and the Republican Party is the party of business and of the rich. . . . These stereotypes may be less important as accurate descriptions of party differences than as reflections of the public's belief that the parties actually provide meaningful alternatives in many areas of policy, even though there are important areas of consensus.[9]

Thus, even though there are no explicit links of class organizations to particular parties, and regardless of the degree to which the parties *actually* represent distinctive class interests, American political parties are viewed by voters as representing different social classes. A much higher level of

---

[7] Robert M. MacIver, *The Web of Government* (New York: Macmillan, 1947), p. 123. MacIver offers no evidence for his assertion that when the parties differ in their objectives class voting is likely to increase, although it is certainly a plausible inference.

[8] Overacker, *op. cit.*, p. 81; and Jennings, *op. cit.*, chap. 9 ("Sham Fight"), pp. 327–42.

[9] Stephen K. Bailey, *The Condition of Our National Political Parties* ("An Occasional Paper of the Center for the Study of Democratic Institutions" [New York, 1959]), p. 22. Evidence for this statement was provided by the Roper Public Opinion Research Center, Williamstown, Massachusetts, which tabulated every question in American public opinion polls since 1946 that dealt with public images of the two parties.

class voting in Australia and Great Britain than in the United States may not therefore be expected.

In Canada, on the other hand, none of these factors favoring a high level of class voting exists. Except for the New Democratic party, one of the minor parties, no political party has any explicit links with class organizations, and such links are, in fact, sedulously avoided. The parties are not ideologically linked with any distinctive class interests historically, and are not identified with specific class bases at present. Therefore, class voting might be low. But, again, this need not be true. Class interests exist in Canada as they do in the United States, and certainly the political parties represent them to some degree. A complete absence of class voting is not, therefore, to be expected. It is also true that the class bases of Canadian politics need not be much different from those of other countries in the British tradition. Since much of its population originated in Great Britain, similar kinds of political expectations and loyalties might exist among Canadians, shaping the parties around specific class bases.

The Liberal party in Canada has not been linked historically to class organizations in the way that the Labor parties of Australia and Great Britain have. This is partly due to the frontier character of Canada (and the frontier has had similar effects upon American politics) since class struggles were vitiated by the availability to dissatisfied workers of land to the West. The continual expansion of Canada and the domination of certain regions by agriculture has emphasized sectional con-

flicts of East and West based on urban-financial versus rural-agricultural conflicts rather than on the classical struggle between industrialists and workers. Therefore, working-class organizations have been relatively weak and relatively irrelevant politically.

The Conservative party took the lead in the policy of national development and in the unification of Canada —while the Labor party led in those matters in Australia—and therefore has historically benefitted from this identification with the national interest. The Liberal party has been the defender of provincial autonomy, mainly due to its long association with the French-Catholic minority in Quebec, and this link has further deterred its identification as the party of the working class.[10]

The parties in Canada have therefore not been identified as class parties, but not for the reason that class interests do not exist or receive political expression in Canada. Class interests have been cross-cut by so many other politically relevant cleavages— sectional, religious, ethnic—that they have not emerged as the chief basis for political loyalties. We may expect that class voting is lower in Canada than in Great Britain and Australia but not necessarily lower than in the United States, where so many diverse cleavages have also determined the strategies and appeals of the political parties.

We may now turn to the evidence on the relation between social-class position and voting in these four countries derived from a large number of public opinion surveys and summarized by means of the index of class voting.

[10] For general descriptions of the links of the Canadian political parties to sectional, class, and urban-rural interests, see R. McGregor Dawson, *The Government of Canada* (2nd ed.; Toronto: University of Toronto Press, 1954), pp. 500–30; and H. M. Clokie, *Canadian Government and Politics* (Toronto: Longmans, Green, 1944), pp. 75–95.

Differences in Class Voting: Survey Results

A number of public opinion surveys taken between 1952 and 1962 indicate that class voting is consistently higher in Australia and Great Britain than in Canada and the United States. The countries may be ranked in the following order: Great Britain, Australia, the United States, and Canada. Table 2 and Figure 1 summarize these results.

cept for one 1958 Canadian survey, and has a mean index of 16 and a range of 13 to 23. Canada always has the lowest level of class voting, with the single exception mentioned.[11]

Particular shifts in each country and the contribution of each social stratum to class voting will be discussed in the chapters on each country, but it must be stressed that no particular figure has any great significance. It is probable, however, that the over-all patterns of differences from country to country

TABLE 2. Class Voting, 1952–1962

Country	Index of Class Voting *			Based on Number of Surveys
	Mean	Lowest	Highest	
Great Britain	40	35	44	8
Australia	33	27	37	10
United States	16	13	23	5
Canada	8	−1	17	10

* The index of class voting was computed by subtracting the percentage of non-manual workers voting for "Left" parties from the percentage of manual workers voting for "Left" parties. For Great Britain, the Labour party was used; for Australia, the Australian Labor party; for the United States, the Democratic party; for Canada, the CCF (or NDP) and Liberal parties. Where two parties were classified as "Left," their votes among each strata were combined. The surveys were taken at various times between 1952 and 1962. All questions referred to voting intention or past vote in a national election.

Class voting is almost always above zero; only one Canadian survey falls below that mark. Great Britain is consistently higher than Australia in the 1952–1962 period; it has a mean index of 40 and a range of 35 to 44. Australia is consistently higher than the United States and has a mean index of 33 and a range of 27 to 37. The United States is consistently higher than Canada, ex-

override any possibilities of sampling error.

The "true" level of class voting may actually have shifted, as Figure 1 indicates. Given the lack of tight integration of social groups, whether they be social classes or others, and the lack of close correspondence of class and party, a rather high level of shifting back and forth of the social bases of the parties is

[11] Table 2 includes only the 1952–1962 period for summary purposes. Prior data are more unreliable for the various countries because of greater sampling variability and the unavailability of really comparable British data prior to 1955.

FIGURE 1. Class Voting in the Anglo-American Countries, 1936–1962

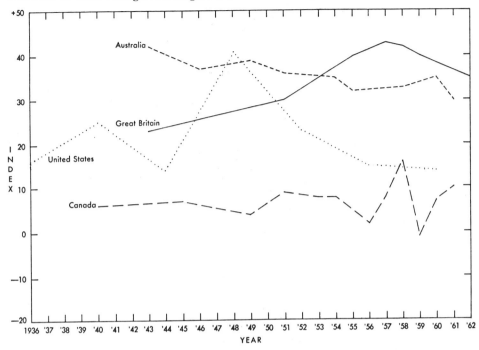

likely, as different issues both class and non-class become salient, and as the parties jockey for support from various groups. But what is striking here is not the variation within the countries, but that, regardless of that variation, the differences in class voting between the countries are so sharp and consistent.

· · · · ·

The United States: the Politics of Diversity

Social class and political behavior are not as closely associated in the United States as they are in Australia and Great Britain.

As was suggested earlier, the parties in the United States are not explicitly linked to class organizations and do not appeal for support on the basis of class. However, voters do see the parties as linked to specific class interests, and probably many people vote in accordance with an image of the parties as representing their economic interests. These are perhaps the most important reasons why class voting is relatively low and yet still exists.

A number of characteristics of American society and its political system undoubtedly reduce the level of class voting further. The enormous size of the country, its division into fifty states with real degrees of sovereignty, tremendous ethnic and religious diversity, and a decentralized party structure, all reduce the salience of *national* class divisions as the main bases for party cleavages. The decentralized, undisciplined character of American parties makes them difficult to distinguish from pressure groups or from combinations of interest groups. The party system thus reflects the federal, plural character of both American society and the governmental system. As the author of a recent study of American federalism put it, "a powerful 'pressure group' at the national level may be very closely identified with a State or local party in one or more States, yet prefer to remain aloof from the national party battle in order to maintain freedom to exert pressure upon both parties when tactics require it." [12] That national class divisions exist and divide the parties even as distinctly as they do, is a measure of the degree of economic and political integration the United States has achieved.

The diversity of support for the political parties has been shown by a series of studies of voting—more studies than for any of the other countries considered—and this chapter will not reiterate their findings in detail. The initial study, which set a pattern for subsequent research in both the United States and Great Britain, was *The People's Choice;* this was a survey of voting behavior in Erie County, Ohio, in the 1940 presidential election.[13] Since it embraced only one northern city and its environs, the regional economic and political diversity of the United States presumably did not affect voting behavior. Still, social class, religion, and rural-urban differences were found crucially to affect the political loyalties of voters. Having a low income, being a Catholic, or living in an urban environment, all predisposed voters toward the Democrats; having a high income, being a Protestant, or living in a rural environment predisposed voters toward the Republicans. The study focused on the consequences of "contradictory" social characteristics that presumably pushed people in opposite political directions—the now classic notion of "cross-pressures." A relatively high proportion of persons in Erie County was under cross-pressures, indicating that the diversity of sources of political loyalties is great in the United States.[14]

The main problem of this chapter will be not to explain the class or religious or regional bases for party support in the United States but to determine whether class voting has declined

---

[12] M. J. C. Vile, *The Structure of American Federalism* (London: Oxford University Press, 1961), p. 92.

[13] P. Lazarsfeld, B. Berelson, and H. Gaudet, *The People's Choice* (New York: Columbia University Press, 1948).

[14] Other such voting studies are: B. Berelson, P. Lazarsfeld, and W. McPhee, *Voting* (Chicago: University of Chicago Press, 1954), and a series of studies done by the Survey Research Center at the University of Michigan beginning with the presidential election of 1948. These are reported in A. Campbell, G. Gurin, and W. E. Miller, *The Voter Decides* (Evanston: Row, Peterson, 1954); Angus Campbell and Homer C. Cooper, *Group Differences in Attitudes and Votes* (Ann Arbor: Survey Research Center, The University of Michigan, 1956), and A. Campbell *et al., The American Voter* (New York: Wiley, 1960). For a summary of the findings of many voting studies, see S. M. Lipset, *Political Man* (New York: Doubleday, 1960), chaps. vii, viii, ix.

Systematic comparative study would be necessary to prove that the American electorate is under more cross-pressures than, say, the British electorate, and that this produces more shifting and more apathy. The British voting studies (cited in Chapter 6) show that the effects of cross-pressures are the same in both countries, but their relative magnitude and intensity remain to be analyzed.

since the 1930's, and in which religious or regional groups.

Despite their diversity of support and their ambiguous class base (compared to the British and Australian parties), American political parties are both perceived as supported by, and actually are supported by, persons at different occupational, educational, and income levels, although, as in the other countries, a sizable minority votes for the "other" party. Since voting studies have also made this point clearly, there is no need to go into details. The authors of a study of the 1954 congressional election summarized their results as follows:

> Our data make it evident that a number of the major population categories have a persistent inclination toward one or the other of the two parties. The major theme of this group orientation in voting is social class. The prestige groups —educational, economic—are the most dependable sources of Republican support while the laborers, Negroes, unemployed, and other low-income and low-education groups are the strongest sources of the Democratic vote.[15]

And the parties can be distinguished as representing Left and Right positions. According to Max Beloff:

> If we take the simple view that there is, other things being equal, likely to be one party of the rich and one party of the poor, the Republicans fill the bill for the former, and outside the South the Democrats fill it for the latter. The former accept roughly the justice of the present distribution of worldly goods be-

tween classes and regions; the latter by and large welcome government intervention to alter it.[16]

The phrases "by and large" and "other things being equal" hide a multitude of contradictions in the policies and voting patterns of Democratic and Republican legislators, but if that statement is accepted as substantially correct, the class bases of the major American parties are understandable. Another compilation of poll data from seven national polls conducted from 1944 to 1952 found that two-and-one-half times as many business and professional people thought the Republicans best served their interests as thought the Democrats did, and that seven times as many unskilled workers and four times as many skilled workers thought the Democrats best served their interests as thought the Republicans did. Whether or not the parties actually served their interests better is, of course, not proved by these images of the parties, but this evidence at least shows that American voting behavior is roughly in line with voters' conceptions of their own interests.[17]

Ideologically, party leaders in the United States are even more divided than voters. A recent study of Democratic and Republican leaders (delegates to national conventions) and followers (a national sample of voters) compared opinions on a number of issues. Republican and Democratic leaders were much farther apart than their followers on issues related to class. The ideology of Republican leaders re-

[15] Campbell and Cooper, op. cit., p. 35.

[16] Max Beloff, The American Federal Government (New York: Oxford University Press, 1959), pp. 157–58.

[17] Harold Orlans, "Opinion Polls on National Leaders," Series 1953, Report No. 6 (Philadelphia and Washington: Institute for Research in Human Relations), pp. 71–73. The author points out that almost exactly as many white-collar workers pick the Democrats as pick the Republicans, and that this corresponds to their "middle" position.

flected their managerial, proprietary, and high-status connections; the ideology of Democratic leaders, their labor, minority, low-status, and intellectual connections.[18]

But, regardless of the current situations, has the association of class and vote declined since the 1930's? It is by now a commonplace notion that the salience of class for voting was less in the prosperous 1950's than it was in the depressed 1930's.[19] A recent study found a decline of class voting in the period 1948 to 1956, which appears to document the decreasing importance of social class for voting behavior. The authors of *The American Voter* computed an index of "status polarization" which showed that the correlation between the occupational status of respondents and their partisan vote in three separate national surveys in 1948, 1952, and 1956 dropped from 0.44 to 0.26 to 0.12.[20] According to the authors:

> The most striking feature of the polarization trend in the recent past has been the steady and rapid depolarization between 1948 and 1956. This decline occurred in a post-war period when the nation was enjoying a striking ascent to prosperity and a consequent release from the pressing economic concerns that had characterized the Depression.[21]

The way that this decline of "status polarization" is explained is also relevant here, because the authors infer that changes have taken place since the 1930's, although they have no specific evidence of such changes. A substitute for this is evidence on the status polarization (or class voting, the term which will be used henceforth to avoid confusion) among different age-groups. In their 1948 and 1952 surveys, a marked "depression-effect" was found. Persons in their twenties and thirties during the depression of the 1930's (presumably those most affected by it) exhibited the highest level of class voting. In 1956, this was not evident, and the authors conclude that this illustrates the "fading effects of the Depression."[22]

This finding of highest class voting among the depression generation does not contradict the usual inference that persons in such a generation should be more similar in their political attitudes and behavior than persons not sharing this common experience. Another study of American voting behavior which specifically focused upon the problem of generational differences found that the depression generation (those who were born in the period 1913–1922) was likely to be more Democratic—regardless of sex, occupation, income, or other social differences.[23] In spite of the Michigan finding that manual and non-manual strata in the depression generation are farther apart in their voting patterns than any other age groups, political consensus is

[18] H. McClosky, P. J. Hoffman, and R. O'Hara, "Issue Conflict and Consensus among Party Leaders and Followers," *American Political Science Review*, LIV (June, 1960), 406–27. The finding holds when various demographic factors are controlled.

[19] See, for example, V. O. Key, Jr., *Politics, Parties and Pressure Groups* (4th ed.; New York: Crowell, 1958), p. 274.

[20] Campbell *et al.*, *The American Voter*, *op. cit.*, p. 347. The method of computing the index of status polarization is identical to that used for my index of class voting.

[21] *Ibid.*, p. 357.

[22] *Ibid.*, p. 359.

[23] Jane O'Grady, "Political Generations: An Empirical Analysis" (Master's thesis, Department of Sociology, University of California, 1960).

still present. Both strata were affected similarly by the Democratic political currents. These two findings reflect the relative independence of the absolute level of vote for a party from the level of class cleavage.

But the Michigan results may not reflect the actual voting patterns in the 1930's. Their results are for persons interviewed in the 1940's and 1950's, divided by age. That age differences at one point in time truly reflect past behavior and the differential impact of a historical crisis is an inference which may or may not be justified. Data to be presented may clarify the real patterns of class voting and the change in those patterns since the 1930's.

The decline of class voting between 1948 and 1956 is linked by the authors of *The American Voter* to "increasing prosperity and fading memories of the Great Depression of the 1930's." These two factors should imply a continuing decrease of class voting since the 1930's. But the authors must account for another of their own empirical findings— that class-voting was lower in 1944 than in 1948, after which it dropped almost linearly. They suggest that variations in the importance of domestic economic versus foreign policy issues account for this change: When economic issues are important, class voting tends to rise; when non-economic issues, such as foreign policy, are important, class voting tends to drop. ". . . war is a basic public concern that may eclipse those problems of domestic economics leading to cleavage among status interest groups." [24] The authors thus infer what the patterns of class voting *might* have been during the 1930's. Presumably class voting should

have been high in the elections of 1932 and 1936, when class issues were dominant. With World War II, "national" issues superseded class ones, and class voting should have been lower in 1940 and 1944. As Campbell *et al.* put it, "Polarization tendencies carrying over from the Great Depression may have been dampened as a result of the national crisis posed by the Second World War, rebounding upward after that conflict was concluded." Domestic economic issues again became important, resulting in the rise of class voting in 1948. After this peak, "the renewal of the threat of global war and the outbreak of hostilities in Korea may have acted, in concert with increasing prosperity, to depress the level of status polarization [class voting] once again." [25]

These inferences are logical ones from the standpoint of the data available to the authors of that study and are relevant to the main problem of this chapter: whether class voting has declined since the 1930's. As was mentioned in Chapter 4, this particular problem is not of primary concern to these authors, since they are focusing upon "short-term" fluctuations. These inferences as to declining class voting certainly imply that a long-term decline of the importance of social class in the support of the American parties has taken place. But has it?

Trends in Class Voting Since the 1930's

Although fluctuations in the level of class voting have occurred in the period 1936 to 1960, there is some evidence that no consistent decline has

[24] Campbell *et al., The American Voter, op. cit.,* pp. 360–61.
[25] *Ibid.,* p. 361.

taken place. Before the evidence for this conclusion is presented, a brief recapitulation of the assumptions upon which the measure of class voting is based is in order.

In estimating the importance of the class bases of politics, shifts to the Right or to the Left should be minimized because they blur the differences between social strata. In such political systems as the Anglo-American ones, shifts usually occur in the same direction in all politically relevant social groups. A shift to the Right such as the Eisenhower victories in 1952 and 1956 could conceivably be regarded as a decline in the importance of social class as a determinant of political behavior. It is probably true that a large vote for Eisenhower among workers meant that class identifications were less important in those elections than in that of 1948, for example. But it is contended here that only if the *gap* between manual and non-manual support of a party has

lessened can one speak meaningfully of a decline of class voting. The data presented in *The American Voter* show without question that not only did all social groups vote more Republican in 1952 and 1956 than they did in 1948, but that *in addition* social classes moved closer together. But, was this part of a long-term decline of the importance of the class bases of politics? Or (and this is the thesis of this chapter) was this only a fluctuation within the "normal range" of change of the class bases of American politics, given the social and political structure of American society in this historical period?

Figure 2 shows the level of Democratic voting among manual and non-manual occupational groups from 1936 to 1960. (The gap between the two lines is the level of class voting, portrayed in Figure 1.) Considerable shifting in the Democratic vote is evident, although class voting was not sharply

FIGURE 2. Class Voting in the United States, 1936–1960

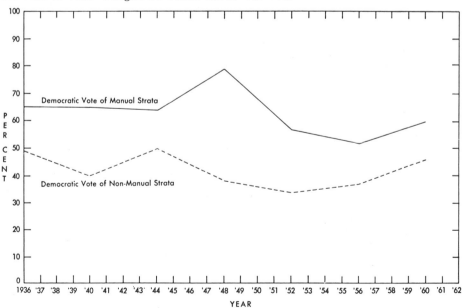

different in the 1950's from the 1930's. About two-thirds of the manual workers voted Democratic in the three elections between 1936 and 1944; their Democratic vote rose sharply in 1948, dropped just as sharply in 1952 and 1956, then rose back to about 60 per cent in 1960. Among the middle class, the Democratic vote stayed between 40 and 50 per cent between 1936 and 1944, dropped below 40 per cent in the following three elections, and rose again to 46 per cent in 1960. The only election in which both strata moved in sharply opposite directions was 1948, which might be termed a "non-consensual election." If that election had been chosen as the beginning of a time-series, the end of class voting might have been predicted, but data for the longer period indicate that 1948 was exceptional.

No pattern of consistent decline of class voting is thus evident, and its level reached that of Britain and Australia only in the 1948 election. Nor has the level of class voting dropped to the average Canadian level in any election. It may be concluded from the evidence presented in Figure 2 that there has been no substantial shift in the class bases of American politics since the 1930's, despite the prosperity since World War II and despite the shifts to the Right in the Eisenhower era.[26]

[26] The figures for middle-class and working-class voting patterns given in Heinz Eulau, *Class and Party in the Eisenhower Years* (New York: Free Press of Glencoe, 1962), p. 2, are not comparable to those presented here because Eulau utilized a measure of class based upon a combination of the occupation, income, and education of the respondent. The percentage-point difference in Democratic preferences of the middle class and working class, defined in this way, was 24 in 1952 and only 4 in 1956. Eulau's study was a secondary analysis of the two Michigan election surveys. Actually, for 1956, he dropped income as a component of the class index with the rather curious justification that "it proved so variable as an indicator that it seriously undermined the stability of the index and interfered with the comparability of results" (p. 45). One might ask how results can be comparable if different procedures are used to compute a major index. The variability of the effect of income may reflect the varying effect upon political behavior from election to election of different *components* of stratification.

22

WORKING-CLASS AUTHORITARIANISM

Seymour Martin Lipset

For Marx, as the reader is by now well aware, the proletariat was that class in modern society which stood in the vanguard of progressive social change, the only social force capable of liberating itself and society from capitalism and ushering in a more advanced social system.

There has been a strong reaction in America against the Marxian vision of the worker, and in many circles today, Marx's heroic proletarian is viewed more as an antihero, a demon. There are at least two reasons for this, one having to do with the general repudiation of Marxism in America, the other with labor's recent political record. Of key importance in the general rejection of Marxian categories has been the Cold War and the anti-Communist crusade in this country which dates most recently from 1945 but which, with a break during World War II when the Soviet Union was America's ally, goes back to 1917 when the Soviet regime was established. American society has been anti-Soviet for half a century and anti-Marxist for a good deal longer. American sociology is part of American society and, therefore, cannot really be understood outside of it. Partly for this reason, it, too, has been primarily anti-Soviet and anti-Marxist.

Probably even more important than the political milieu is the disappointment over what has become of the labor movement as an instrument for progressive social change. The position of the labor movement in the 1930's was analogous to that of the civil rights movement in the early 1960's: it was active, growing, militant, and leading the way for a more egalitarian society. Today, labor's numerical growth has been slowed. Business unionism predominates, which is often low on social idealism and high on materialistic values (as is the rest of American society). Fat and happy, labor has become to many people merely another pressure group, a prosperous and complacent part of the Establishment selfishly pursuing its own interests, no longer a force for social betterment. To many, labor seems to have been sidetracked and left out of the mainstream of social reform of the postwar period, symbolized by liberal and left-wing disenchantment with labor's record on civil rights and the Vietnam War.

This disillusionment with the contemporary working class was best anticipated and brought to a focus in the present selection in which sociologist S. M. Lipset attempts to sever the last vestiges of faith in the working class as a forward-looking force for social change in modern society. Whereas Marx saw the proletariat as a repository of progressive revolution, Lipset and others now see it as a repository of society's most dangerous and backward political instincts.

Basic to Lipset's discussion is the view that there are at least two dimensions to liberalism, one economic and the other noneconomic; and, as suggested earlier, while workers are usually liberal on economic issues, they may at the same time be illiberal

SOURCE: Seymour Martin Lipset, *Political Man* (Garden City, N.Y.: Doubleday, 1960), pp. 97–130. Reprinted by permission of the author.

or even authoritarian on noneconomic issues such as race, civil liberties, tolerance of personal nonconformity, and the like. If the Republican party can put together a new majority in this country in the 1970's, it will be based partly on the final defection of the South to the GOP, plus that party's ability to tap the conservative roots of the American working class, Democratic for so many decades.

There is a paradox to the argument of working-class authoritarianism which must be noted and which Lipset himself discusses toward the end of his essay. On the one hand, there is the unmistakable evidence of working-class and lower-class authoritarian predispositions. But, on the other hand, there is the historical example of working-class organizations such as trade unions and labor parties. Here, in spite of what might be the authoritarian psychology of their members, these organizations have generally, throughout their history in the nineteenth and twentieth centuries, adhered to doctrines of liberalism, tolerance, and democracy. Trade unions, after all, were in the forefront of struggles for universal suffrage, free compulsory education, freedom of organization, freedom of speech, of press, and so forth. In Hitler's Germany, the trade unions were the one significant force which attempted to oppose his rule. And after the war, the allies quickly reorganized the trade unions and recognized in them one of the few remaining hopes for democracy in a reconstituted Germany. Today in the United States, authoritarian and bigoted right-wing organizations receive no support whatsoever from the organized labor movement. In fact, organized labor continues to push, less dramatically than in the 1930's to be sure, for social reforms in the noneconomic as well as the economic sphere. Indeed, the record of labor unions and labor parties is better with respect to liberalism, toleration, extension of civil liberties, and civil rights than that of conservative, business, or elite-oriented organizations or parties which traditionally opposed the extension of democratic rights and liberties to all.

One must conclude, therefore, that the general opinions and psychological predispositions of workers are no infallible guide in predicting the policies of the organizations that speak for them. That is, though workers may often express undemocratic opinions, the organizations and parties that represent them usually have been found to champion democratic rights and causes. It is, in a sense, all the more to the credit of trade unions and labor parties that in spite of these tendencies on the part of many of their members, they have been able to channel these propensities toward democratic rather than authoritarian ends.

The gradual realization that extremist and intolerant movements in modern society are more likely to be based on the lower classes than on the middle and upper classes has posed a tragic dilemma for those intellectuals of the democratic left who once believed the proletariat necessarily to be a force for liberty, racial equality, and social progress. The Socialist Italian novelist Ignazio Silone has asserted that "the myth of the liberating power of the proletariat has dissolved along with that other myth of progress. The recent examples of the Nazi labor unions, like those of Salazar and Peron . . . have at last convinced of this even those who were reluctant to admit it on the sole grounds of the totalitarian degeneration of Communism."[1]

[1] "The Choice of Comrades," *Encounter*, 3 (December 1954), p. 25. Arnold A. Rogow writing in the Socialist magazine *Dissent* even suggests that "the liberal and radical approach has always lacked a popular base, that in essence, the liberal tradition has been a confined minority, perhaps elitist, tradition." "The Revolt Against Social Equality," *Dissent*, 4 (1957), p. 370.

Dramatic demonstrations of this point have been given recently by the southern workers' support of White Citizens' Councils and segregation in the United States and by the active participation of many British workers in the 1958 race riots in England. A "Short Talk with a Fascist Beast" (an eighteen-year-old casual laborer who took part in the beating of Negroes in London), which appeared in the left socialist *New Statesman*, portrays graphically the ideological syndrome which sometimes culminates in such behavior. "Len's" perspective is offered in detail as a prelude to an analytical survey of the authoritarian elements of the lower-class situation in modern society.

'That's why I'm with the Fascists,' he says. 'They're against the blacks. That Salmon, he's a Communist. The Labour Party is Communist too. Like the unions.' His mother and father, he says, are strict Labour supporters. Is he against the Labour Party? 'Nah, I'm for them. They're for y'know—us. I'm for the unions too.' Even though they were dominated by Communists? 'Sure,' he says. 'I like the Communist Party. It's powerful, like.' How can he be for the Communists when the fascists hate them?

Len says, 'Well, y'know, I'm for the fascists when they're against the nigs. But the fascists is really for the rich people y'know, like the Tories. All for the guv'nors, people like that. But the Communists are very powerful.' I told him the Communist Party of Britain was quite small.

'But,' he says, 'they got Russia behind them.' His voice was full of marvel. 'I admire Russia. Y'know, the people. They're peaceful. They're strong. When they say they'll do a thing, they do it. Not like us. Makes you think: they got a

weapon over there can wipe us all out, with one wave of a general's arm. Destroy us completely and totally. Honest, those Russians. When they say they'll do a thing, they do it. Like in Hungary. I pity those people, the Hungarians. But did you see the Russians went in and stopped them. Tanks. Not like us in Cyprus. Our soldiers get shot in the back and what do we do? The Communists is for the small man.' [2]

Such strikingly visible demonstrations of working-class ethnic prejudice and support for totalitarian political movements have been paralleled in studies of public opinion, religion, family patterns, and personality structure. Many of these studies suggest that the lower-class way of life produces individuals with rigid and intolerant approaches to politics.

At first glance the facts of political history may seem to contradict this. Since their beginnings in the nineteenth century, workers' organizations and parties have been a major force in extending political democracy, and in waging progressive political and economic battles. Before 1914, the classic division between the working-class left parties and the economically privileged right was not based solely upon such issues as redistribution of income, status, and educational opportunities, but also rested upon civil liberties and international policy. The workers, judged by the policies of their parties, were often the backbone of the fight for greater political democracy, religious freedom, minority rights, and international peace, while the parties backed by the conservative middle and upper classes in much of Europe tended to favor more extremist political forms, to resist the extension of the suffrage, to back

[2] Clancy Sigal in the *New Statesman*, October 4, 1958, p. 440.

the established church, and to support jingoistic foreign policies.

Events since 1914 have gradually eroded these patterns. In some nations working-class groups have proved to be the most nationalistic sector of the population. In some they have been in the forefront of the struggle against equal rights for minority groups, and have sought to limit immigration or to impose racial standards in countries with open immigration. The conclusion of the anti-fascist era and the emergence of the cold war have shown that the struggle for freedom is not a simple variant of the economic class struggle. The threat to freedom posed by the Communist movement is as great as that once posed by Fascism and Nazism, and Communism, in all countries where it is strong, is supported mainly by the lower levels of the working class, or the rural population. No other party has been as thoroughly and completely the party of the working class and the poor. Socialist parties, past and present, secured much more support from the middle classes than the Communists have.

Some socialists and liberals have suggested that this proves nothing about authoritarian tendencies in the working class, since the Communist party often masquerades as a party seeking to fulfill the classic Western-democratic ideals of liberty, equality, and fraternity. They argue that most Communist supporters, particularly the less educated, are deceived into thinking that the Communists are simply more militant and efficient socialists. I would suggest, however, the alternative hypothesis that, rather than being a source of strain, the intransigent and intolerant aspects of Communist ideology attract members from that large stratum with low incomes, low-status occupations, and low education, which in modern industrial societies has meant largely, though not exclusively, the working class.

The social situation of the lower strata, particularly in poorer countries with low levels of education, predisposes them to view politics as black and white, good and evil. Consequently, other things being equal, they should be more likely than other strata to prefer extremist movements which suggest easy and quick solutions to social problems and have a rigid outlook.

The "authoritarianism" of any social stratum or class is highly relative, of course, and often modified by organizational commitments to democracy and by individual cross-pressures. The lower class in any given country may be more authoritarian than the upper classes, but on an "absolute" scale all the classes in that country may be less authoritarian than any class in another country. In a country like Britain, where norms of tolerance are well developed and widespread in every social stratum, even the lowest class may be less authoritarian and more "sophisticated" than the most highly educated stratum in an underdeveloped country, where immediate problems and crises impinge on every class and short-term solutions may be sought by all groups.[3]

Commitments to democratic proce-

[3] See Richard Hoggart, *The Uses of Literacy* (London: Chatto and Windus, 1957), pp. 78–79 and 146–48, for a discussion of the acceptance of norms of tolerance by the British working class. E. T. Prothro and Levon Melikian, in "The California Public Opinion Scale in an Authoritarian Culture," *Public Opinion Quarterly*, 17 (1953), pp. 353–63, have shown, in a study of 130 students at the American University in Lebanon, that they exhibited the same association between authoritarianism and economic radicalism as is found among workers in America. A

dures and ideals by the principal organizations to which low-status individuals belong may also influence these individuals' actual political behavior more than their underlying personal values, no matter how authoritarian.[4] A working class which has developed an early (prior to the Communists) loyalty to democratic political and trade-union movements which have successfully fought for social and economic rights will not easily change its allegiance.

Commitments to other values or institutions by individuals (cross-pressures) may also override the most established predispositions. For example, a French, Italian, or German Catholic worker who is strongly anticapitalist may still vote for a relatively conservative party in France, Italy, or Germany, because his ties to Catholicism are stronger than his resentments about his class status; a worker strongly inclined toward authoritarian ideas may defend democratic institutions against fascist attack because of his links to anti-fascist working-class parties and unions. Conversely, those who are not inclined toward extremist politics may back an extremist party because of certain aspects of its program and political role. Many persons supported the Communists in 1936 and 1943 as an anti-fascist internationalist party.

The specific propensity of given social strata to support either extremist or democratic political parties, then, cannot be predicted from a knowledge of their psychological predispositions or from attitudes inferred from survey data.[5] Both evidence and theory suggest, however, that the lower strata are relatively more authoritarian, that (again, other things being equal) they will be more attracted to an extremist movement than to a moderate and democratic one, and that, once recruited, they will not be alienated by its lack of democracy, while more educated or sophisticated supporters will tend to drop away.[6]

Democracy and the Lower Classes

The poorer strata everywhere are more liberal or leftist on economic issues; they favor more welfare state measures, higher wages, graduated income taxes, support of trade-unions, and so forth. But when liberalism is defined in noneconomic terms—as support of civil liberties, internationalism, etc.—

survey in 1951–52 of 1,800 Puerto Rican adults, representative of the entire rural population, found that 84 per cent were "somewhat authoritarian," as compared to 46 per cent for a comparable U.S. population. See Henry Wells, "Ideology and Leadership in Puerto Rican Politics," *American Political Science Review*, 49 (1955), pp. 22–40.

[4] The southern Democrats were the most staunch opponents of McCarthy and his tactics, not because of any deep opposition to undemocratic methods, but rather because of an organizational commitment to the Democratic party.

[5] For a detailed discussion of the fallacy of attempting to suggest that political behavior is a necessary function of political attitudes or psychological traits, see Nathan Glazer and S. M. Lipset, "The Polls on Communism and Conformity," in Daniel Bell, ed., *The New American Right* (New York: Criterion Books, 1955), pp. 141–66.

[6] The term "extremist" is used to refer to movements, parties, and ideologies. "Authoritarian" refers to the attitudes and predispositions of individuals (or of groups, where a statistical aggregate of *individual* attitudes, and not group characteristics as such, are of concern). The term "authoritarian" has too many associations with studies of attitudes to be safely used to refer also to types of social organizations.

the correlation is reversed. The more well-to-do are more liberal, the poorer are more intolerant.[7]

Public opinion data from a number of countries indicate that the lower classes are much less committed to democracy as a political system than are the urban middle and upper classes. In Germany, for example, a study conducted by the UNESCO Institute at Cologne in 1953 asked a systematic sample of 3,000 Germans: "Do you think that it would be better if there were one party, several parties, or no party?" The results analyzed according to occupational status indicate that the lower strata of the working class and the rural population were less likely to support a multi-party system (a reason-

able index of democratic attitudes in Westernized countries) than the middle and upper strata. (See Table I.)

Comparable results were obtained in 1958 when a similar question was asked of national or regional samples in Austria, Japan, Brazil, Canada, Mexico, West Germany, the Netherlands, Belgium, Italy, and France. Although the proportion favoring a multi-party system varied from country to country, the lower classes within each nation were least likely to favor it.[8]

Surveys in Japan, Great Britain, and the United States designed to secure general reactions to problems of civil liberties, or the rights of various minorities, have produced similar results. In Japan, the workers and the rural popu-

TABLE I. Responses of Different German Occupational Groups to Preferred Party System in Percentages * (Males Only)

Occupational Group	Several Parties	One Party	No Party	No Opinion	Total Number of Persons
Civil Servants	88	6	3	3	111
Upper White-collar	77	13	2	8	58
Free Professionals	69	13	8	10	38
Skilled Workers	65	22	5	8	277
Artisans	64	16	9	11	124
Lower White-collar	62	19	7	12	221
Businessmen (small)	60	15	12	13	156
Farmers	56	22	6	16	241
Semiskilled Workers	49	28	7	16	301
Unskilled Workers	40	27	11	22	172

* Computed from IBM cards supplied to author by the UNESCO Institute at Cologne.

[7] See two articles by G. H. Smith, "Liberalism and Level of Information," *Journal of Educational Psychology*, 39 (1948), pp. 65–82; and "The Relation of 'Enlightenment' to Liberal-Conservative Opinions," *Journal of Social Psychology*, 28 (1948), pp. 3–17.

[8] Based on as yet unpublished data in the files of the World Poll, an organization established by International Research Associates which sponsors comparable surveys in a number of countries. The question asked in this survey was: "Suppose there was a political party here which corresponds to your own opinions—one you would more or less consider 'your' party. Would you wish this to be the only party in our country with no other parties besides, or would you be against such a one-party system?" Similar correlations were found between low status and belief in the value of a strong leader.

lation were more authoritarian and less concerned with civil liberties than the middle and upper classes.[9]

In England, the psychologist H. J. Eysenck found comparable differences between people who were "tough-minded" and those who were "tender-minded" in their general social outlook. The first group tended to be intolerant of deviations from the standard moral or religious codes, to be anti-Negro, anti-Semitic, and xenophobic, while the "tender-minded" were tolerant of deviation, unprejudiced, and internationalist.[10] Summing up his findings, based on attitude scales given to supporters of different British parties, Eysenck reported that "middle-class Conservatives are more tender-minded than working-class Conservatives; middle-class Liberals are more tender-minded than working-class Liberals; middle-class Socialists are more tender-minded than working-class Socialists; and even middle-class Communists are more tender-minded than working-class Communists."[11]

The evidence from various American studies is also clear and consistent—the lower strata are the least tolerant.[12] In the most systematic of these, based on a national sample of nearly 5,000 Americans, Samuel A. Stouffer divided his respondents into three categories, "less tolerant, in-between, and more tolerant," by using a scale based on responses to questions about such civil liberties as the right of free speech for Communists, critics of religion, or advocates of nationalization of industry, and the like. As the data presented in Table II demonstrate, tolerance increases with moves up the social ladder. Only 30 per cent of those in manual occupations are in the "most tolerant" category, as contrasted with 66 per cent of the professionals, and 51 per cent of the proprietors, managers, and officials. As in Germany and Japan, farmers are low in tolerance.

The findings of public opinion surveys in thirteen different countries that the lower strata are less committed to democratic norms than the middle classes are reaffirmed by the research of more psychologically oriented investigators, who have studied the social correlates of the "authoritarian

---

[9] See Kotaro Kido and Masataka Sugi, "A Report of Research on Social Stratification and Mobility in Tokyo" (III), *Japanese Sociological Review*, 4 (1954), pp. 74–100; and National Public Opinion Institute of Japan, Report No. 26, *A Survey Concerning the Protection of Civil Liberties* (Tokyo, 1951).

[10] See H. J. Eysenck, *The Psychology of Politics* (London: Routledge and Kegan Paul, 1954), p. 127.

[11] *Ibid.*, p. 137: for a critique of the methodology of this study which raises serious questions about its procedures see Richard Christie, "Eysenck's Treatment of the Personality of Communists," *Psychological Bulletin*, 53 (1956), pp. 411–30.

[12] See Arnold M. Rose, *Studies in Reduction of Prejudice* (Chicago: American Council on Race Relations, 1948), for a review of the literature bearing on this point prior to 1948. Several studies have shown the key importance of education and the independent effect of economic status, both basic components of low status. See Daniel J. Levinson and R. Nevitt Sanford, "A Scale for the Measurement of Anti-Semitism," *Journal of Psychology*, 17 (1944), pp. 339–70, and H. H. Harlan, "Some Factors Affecting Attitudes toward Jews," *American Sociological Review*, 7 (1942), pp. 816–27, for data on attitudes toward one ethnic group. See also James G. Martin and Frank R. Westie, "The Tolerant Personality," *American Sociological Review*, 24 (1959), pp. 521–28. For a digest of recent research in the field of race relations in the U.S.A., see Melvin M. Tumin, *Segregation and Desegregation* (New York: Anti-Defamation League of B'nai B'rith, 1957).

personality." [13] Many studies in this area, summarized recently, show a consistent association between authoritarianism and lower-class status.[14] One survey of 460 Los Angeles adults reported that "the working class contains a higher proportion of authoritarians than either the middle or the upper class," and that among workers, those who explicitly identified themselves as "working class" rather than "middle class" were more authoritarian.[15]

Recent research further suggests the possibility of a *negative* correlation between authoritarianism and neuroticism within the lower classes. In general, those who deviate from the standards of their group are more likely to be neurotic than those who conform, so if we assume that authoritarian traits are more or less standard among low-status people, then the more liberal members of this group should also be the more neurotic.[16] As two psychologists, Anthony Davids and Charles Eriksen, point out, where the "standard of reference on authoritarianism is quite high," people may be well adjusted *and* authoritarian.[17] And the fact that this is often the case in lower-class groups fits the hypothesis that authoritarian attitudes are "normal" and expected in such groups.[18]

TABLE II. Proportion of Male Respondents Who Are "More Tolerant" with Respect to Civil Liberties Issues*

Professional and Semiprofessional	66%	(159)
Proprietors, Managers, and Officials	51	(223)
Clerical and Sales	49	(200)
Manual Workers	30	(685)
Farmers or Farm Workers	20	(202)

* Samuel A. Stouffer, *Communism, Conformity and Civil Liberties* (New York: Doubleday & Co., 1955), p. 139. The figures for manual and farm workers were calculated from IBM cards kindly supplied by Professor Stouffer.

[13] See Theodore Adorno, *et al.*, *The Authoritarian Personality* (New York: Harper & Bros., 1950). This, the original study, has less consistent results on this point than the many follow-up studies. The authors themselves (p. 178) point to the inadequacy of their sample.

[14] Richard Christie and Peggy Cook, "A Guide to Published Literature Relating to the Authoritarian Personality," *Journal of Psychology*, 45 (1958), pp. 171–99.

[15] W. J. McKinnon and R. Centers, "Authoritarianism and Urban Stratification," *American Journal of Sociology*, 61 (1956), p. 618.

[16] Too much of contemporary psychological knowledge in this area has been gained from populations most convenient for the academic investigator to reach—university students. It is often forgotten that personality and attitude syndromes may be far different for this highly select group than for other segments of the total population.

[17] See Anthony Davids and Charles W. Eriksen, "Some Social and Cultural Factors Determining Relations Between Authoritarianism and Measures of Neuroticism," *Journal of Consulting Psychology*, 21 (1957), pp. 155–59. This article contains many references to the relevant literature.

[18] The greater compatibility of the demands of Communist party membership and working-class background as indicated by Almond's finding that twice as many of the middle-class party members as of the working-class group in his sample of Communists had neurotic problems hints again at the normality and congruence of extremist politics with a working-class background. Gabriel Almond, *The Appeals of Communism* (Princeton: Princeton University Press, 1954), pp. 245–46.

Extremist Religions and the Lower Classes

Many observers have called attention to a connection between low social status and fundamentalist or chiliastic religion. This suggests that extremist religion is a product of the same social forces that sustain authoritarian political attitudes. The liberal Protestant churches, on the other hand, have been predominantly middle class in membership. In the United States, this has created a dilemma for the liberal Protestant clergy, who have tended to be liberal in their politics as well as their religion and, hence, have often wanted to spread their social and religious gospel among the lower strata. But they have found that these classes want ministers who will preach of hell-fire and salvation rather than modern Protestant theology.[19]

In the early period of the Socialist movement, Engels observed that early Christianity and the revolutionary workers' movement had "notable points of resemblance," particularly in their millennial appeals and lower-class base.[20] Recently, Elmer Clark, a student of small sects in contemporary America, has noted that such sects, like early Christianity, "originate mainly among the religiously neglected poor." He writes that when "the revolts of the poor have been tinged with religion, which was nearly always the case until recent times, millennial ideas have appeared, and . . . these notions are prominent in most of the small sects which follow the evangelical tradition. Premillenarianism is essentially a defense mechanism of the disinherited; despairing of obtaining substantial blessings through social processes, they turn on the world which has withheld its benefits and look to its destruction in a cosmic cataclysm which will exalt them and cast down the rich and powerful."[21]

Ernst Troeltsch, the major historian of sectarian religion, has characterized the psychological appeal of fundamentalist religious sects in a way that might as appropriately be applied to extremist politics: "It is the lower classes which do the really creative work, forming communities on a genuine religious basis. They alone unite imagination and simplicity of feeling with a nonreflective habit of mind, a primitive energy, and an urgent sense of need. On such a foundation alone is it possible to build up an unconditional authoritative faith in a Divine Revelation with simplicity of surrender and unshaken certainty. Only within a fellowship of this kind is there room for those who have a sense of spiritual need, and who have not acquired the habit of intellectual reasoning, which always regards everything from a relative point of view."[22]

[19] See Liston Pope, *Millhands and Preachers* (New Haven: Yale University Press, 1942), pp. 105–16.

[20] See Friedrich Engels, "On the Early History of Christianity," in K. Marx and F. Engels, *On Religion* (Moscow: Foreign Languages Publishing House, 1957), pp. 312–20.

[21] Elmer T. Clark, *The Small Sects in America* (New York: Abingdon Press, 1949), pp. 16, 218–19. According to Bryan Wilson, "insecurity, differential status, anxiety, cultural neglect, prompt a need for readjustment which sects may, for some, provide. The maladjusted may be communities, or occupational groups, or dispersed individuals in similar marginal positions." See "An Analysis of Sect Development," *American Sociological Review*, 24 (1959), p. 8, and the same author's *Minority Religious Movements in Modern Britain* (London: Heinemann, 1960).

[22] Ernst Troeltsch, *The Social Teaching of the Christian Churches* (London: George Allen and Unwin, 1930), Vol. 1, p. 44.

Jehovah's Witnesses, whose membership in the United States runs into the hundreds of thousands, is an excellent example of a rapidly growing sect which "continues to attract, as in the past, the underprivileged strata." [23] The Witnesses' principal teaching is that the Kingdom of Heaven is at hand: "The end of the age is near. Armageddon is just around the corner, when the wicked will be destroyed, and the theocracy, or rule of God, will be set up upon the earth." [24] And like the Communists, their organization is "hierarchical and highly authoritarian. There is little democratic participation in the management or in the formation of policies of the movement as a whole." [25]

Direct connections between the social roots of political and of religious extremism have been observed in a number of countries. In Czarist Russia, the young Trotsky recognized the relationship and successfully recruited the first working-class members of the South Russian Workers' Union (a revolutionary Marxist organization of the late 1890's) from adherents to religious sects.[26] In Holland and Sweden, recent studies show that the Communists are strongest in regions which were once centers of fundamentalist religious re-

vivalism. In Finland, Communism and revivalist Christianity often are strong in the same areas. In the poor eastern parts of Finland, the Communists have been very careful not to offend people's religious feelings. It is reported that many Communist meetings actually begin with religious hymns.[27]

This is not to imply that religious sects supported by lower-class elements necessarily or usually become centers of political protest. In fact, such sects often drain off the discontent and frustration which would otherwise flow into channels of political extremism. The point here is that rigid fundamentalism and dogmatism are linked to the same underlying characteristics, attitudes, and predispositions which find another outlet in allegiance to extremist political movements.

In his excellent study of the sources of Swedish Communism, Sven Rydenfelt analyzed the differences between two socially and economically comparable northern counties of Sweden—Vasterbotten and Norrbotten—in an attempt to explain the relatively low Communist vote in the former (2 per cent) and the much larger one in the latter (21 per cent). The Liberal party, which in Sweden gives much more support than any other party to religious

---

[23] See Charles S. Braden, *These Also Believe. A Study of Modern American Cults and Minority Religious Movements* (New York: Macmillan, 1949), p. 384.

[24] *Ibid.*, p. 370.

[25] *Ibid.*, p. 363. It may be suggested that, as in authoritarian political movements, the intolerant character of most of the sects is an attractive feature and not a source of strain for their lower-class members. Although no systematic evidence is available, this assumption would help account for the lack of tolerance for factionalism within these sects, and for the endless schisms, with the new groups as intolerant as the old, since the splits usually occur over the issue of *whose* intolerant views and methods shall prevail.

[26] See Isaac Deutscher, *The Prophet Armed, Trotsky, 1879–1921* (London: Oxford University Press, 1954), pp. 30–31.

[27] See Sven Rydenfelt, *Kommunismen i Sverige. En Samhallsvetenskaplig Studie* (Kund: Glerupska Universitetsbokhandeln, 1954), pp. 296, 336–37; Wiardi Beckman Institute, *Verkiezingen in Nederland* (Amsterdam, 1951, mimeographed), pp. 15, 93–94; Jaako Novsiainen, *Kommunism Kuopion lää nisssä* (Helsinki: Joensuu, 1956).

extremism, was strong in Vasterbotten (30 per cent) and weak in Norrbotten (9 per cent). Since the total extremist vote in both was almost identical—30 and 32 per cent—he concluded that a general predisposition toward radicalism existed in both counties, containing some of the poorest, most socially isolated, and rootless groups in Sweden, but that its expression differed, taking a religious form in one county, and a Communist in the other: "The Communists and the religious radicals, as for instance, the Pentecostal sects, seem to be competing for the allegiance of the same groups." [28]

The Social Situation of the Lower Classes

A number of elements contribute to authoritarian predispositions in lower-class individuals. Low education, low participation in political or voluntary organizations of any type, little read-

ing, isolated occupations, economic insecurity, and authoritarian family patterns are some of the most important. These elements are interrelated, but they are by no means identical.

There is consistent evidence that degree of formal education, itself closely correlated with social and economic status, is also highly correlated with undemocratic attitudes. Data from the American sociologist Samuel Stouffer's study of attitudes toward civil liberties in America and from the UNESCO Research Institute's survey of German opinion on a multi-party system (Tables III and IV) reveal this clearly.

These tables indicate that although higher occupational status within each educational level seems to make for greater tolerance, the increases in tolerance associated with higher educational level are greater than those related to higher occupational level, other factors being constant. [29] Inferior education and low occupational position are of course closely connected, and both are

TABLE III. The Relationship Between Occupation, Education, and Political Tolerance in the United States, 1955*

	Percentage in the Two "Most Tolerant" Categories			
	Occupation			
Education	Low Manual	High Manual	Low White Collar	High White Collar
Grade School	13 (228)	21 (178)	23 (47)	26 (100)
Some High School	32 (99)	33 (124)	29 (56)	46 (68)
High School Grad	40 (64)	48 (127)	47 (102)	56 (108)
Some College	— (14)	64 (36)	64 (80)	65 (37)
College Grad	— (3)	— (11)	74 (147)	83 (21)

* Computed from IBM cards kindly supplied by Samuel A. Stouffer from his study, *Communism, Conformity and Civil Liberties* (New York: Doubleday & Co., Inc., 1955).

[28] See W. Phillips Davison's extensive review of Sven Rydenfelt, *op. cit.*, which appeared in the *Public Opinion Quarterly*, 18 (1954–55), pp. 375–88. Quote is on p. 382.

[29] A study based on a national sample of Americans reported that education made no difference in the extent of authoritarian responses on an "authoritarian personality" scale among work-

TABLE IV. The Relationship Between Occupation, Education, and Support of a Democratic Party System in Germany—1953*

| | Per Cent Favoring the Existence of Several Parties | |
| | Educational Level | |
Occupation	Elementary School	High School or Higher
Farm Laborers	29 (59)	—
Manual Workers	43 (1439)	52 (29)
Farmers	43 (381)	67 (9)
Lower White Collar	50 (273)	68 (107)
Self-employed Business	53 (365)	65 (75)
Upper White Collar	58 (86)	69 (58)
Officials (Govt.)	59 (158)	78 (99)
Professions	56 (18)	68 (38)

* Computed from IBM cards supplied to author by the UNESCO Institute at Cologne.

part of the complex making up low status, which is associated with a lack of tolerance.[30]

Low-status groups are also less apt to participate in formal organizations, read fewer magazines and books regularly, possess less information on public affairs, vote less, and, in general, take less interest in politics. The available evidence suggests that each of these attributes is related to attitudes toward democracy. The 1953 UNESCO analysis of German data found that, at every occupational level, those who belonged to voluntary associations were more likely to favor a multi-party system than a one-party one.[31] American findings, too, indicate that authoritarians "do not join many community groups" as compared with nonauthoritarians.[32] And it has been discovered that people poorly informed on public issues are more likely to be both *more liberal* on economic issues and *less liberal* on noneconomic ones.[33] Nonvoters and those less interested in political matters are much more intolerant and xenophobic than those who vote and have political interests.[34]

The "hard core" of "chronic know-

ers, but that higher educational attainment reduced such responses among the middle class. The well-educated upper-middle class were least "authoritarian." Morris Janowitz and Dwaine Marvick, "Authoritarianism and Political Behavior," *Public Opinion Quarterly*, 17 (1953), pp. 195–96.

[30] The independent effect of education even when other social factors are least favorable has special long-range significance in view of the rising educational level of the population. Kornhauser and his associates found that auto workers with an eighth-grade education were more authoritarian than those with more education. See A. Kornhauser, A. L. Sheppard, and A. J. Mayer, *When Labor Votes* (New York: University Books, 1956), for further data on variations in authoritarianism *within* a working-class sample.

[31] Data computed for this study.

[32] F. H. Sanford, *Authoritarianism and Leadership* (Philadelphia: Stevenson Brothers, 1950), p. 168. See also Mirra Komarovsky, "The Voluntary Associations of Urban Dwellers," *American Sociological Review*, 11 (1946), p. 688.

[33] G. H. Smith, *op. cit.*, p. 71.

[34] G. M. Connelly and H. H. Field, "The Non-Voter, Who He Is, and What He Thinks," *Public Opinion Quarterly*, 8 (1944), p. 179; Samuel A. Stouffer, *op. cit., passim*, and F. H. Sanford, *op. cit.*, p. 168. M. Janowitz and D. Marvick, *op. cit.*, p. 200.

nothings" comes disproportionately from the less literate, lower socioeconomic groups, according to a study by two American social psychologists, Herbert Hyman and Paul Sheatsley. These people are not only uninformed, but "harder to reach, no matter what the level or nature of the information." Here is another hint of the complex character of the relationship between education, liberalism, and status. Non-economic liberalism is not a simple matter of acquiring education and information; it is at least in part a basic attitude which is actively discouraged by the social situation of lower-status persons.[35] As Genevieve Knupfer, an American psychiatrist, has pointed out in her revealing "Portrait of the Underdog," "economic underprivilege is psychological underprivilege: habits of submission, little access to sources of information, lack of verbal facility . . . appear to produce a lack of self-confidence which increases the unwillingness of the low-status person to participate in many phases of our predominantly middle-class culture . . ."[36]

These characteristics also reflect the extent to which the lower strata are *isolated* from the activities, controversies, and organizations of democratic society —an isolation which prevents them from acquiring the sophisticated and complex view of the political structure which makes understandable and necessary the norms of tolerance.

In this connection it is instructive to examine once again, as extreme cases, those occupations which are most isolated, in every sense, from contact with the world outside their own group. Manual workers in "isolated occupations" which require them to live in one-industry towns or areas—miners, maritime workers, forestry workers, fishermen, and sheepshearers—exhibit high rates of Communist support in most countries.[37]

Similarly, as all public opinion surveys show, the rural population, both farmers and laborers, tends to oppose civil liberties and multi-party systems more than any other occupational group. Election surveys indicate that farm owners have been among the strongest supporters of fascist parties, while farm workers, poor farmers, and

---

[35] See Herbert Hyman and Paul B. Sheatsley, "Some Reasons Why Information Campaigns Fail," *Public Opinion Quarterly*, 11 (1947), p. 413. A recent survey of material on voluntary association memberships is contained in Charles L. Wright and Herbert Hyman, "Voluntary Association Memberships of American Adults: Evidence from National Sample Surveys," *American Sociological Review*, 23 (1958), pp. 284–94.

[36] Genevieve Knupfer, "Portrait of the Underdog," *Public Opinion Quarterly*, 11 (1947), p. 114.

[37] The greatest amount of comparative material is available on the miners. For Britain, see Herbert G. Nicholas, *British General Election of 1950* (London: Macmillan, 1951), pp. 318, 342, 361. For the United States, see Paul F. Brissenden, *The IWW: A Study of American Syndicalism* (New York: Columbia University Press, 1920), p. 74, and Harold F. Gosnell, *Grass Roots Politics* (Washington, D.C.: American Council on Public Affairs, 1942), pp. 31–32. For France, see François Goguel, "Geographie des élections sociales de 1950–51," *Revue française de science politique*, 3 (1953), pp. 246–71. For Germany, see Ossip K. Flechtheim, *Die Kommunistische Partei Deutschlands in der Weimarer Republik* (Offenbach am Main: Bollwerk-Verlag Karl Drott, 1948), p. 211. Data are also available for Australia, Scandinavia, Spain, and Chile.

Isolation has also been linked with the differential propensity to strike of different industries. Violent strikes having the character of a mass grievance against society as a whole occur most often in isolated industries, and probably have their origins in the same social situations as those which produce extremism. See Clark Kerr and Abraham Siegel, "The Interindustry Propensity to Strike: An International Comparison," in *Industrial Conflict*, eds., A. Kornhauser, R. Dubin, and A. M. Ross (New York: McGraw-Hill Book Co., 1954), pp. 189–212.

share-croppers have given even stronger backing to the Communists than has the rest of labor in countries like Italy, France, and India.[38]

The same social conditions are associated with middle-class authoritarianism. The groups which have been most prone to support fascist and other middle-class extremist ideologies have been, in addition to farmers and peasants, the small businessmen of the smaller provincial communities— groups which are also isolated from "cosmopolitan" culture and are far lower than any other non-manual-labor group in educational attainment.[39]

A second and no less important factor predisposing the lower classes toward authoritarianism is a relative lack of economic and psychological security. The lower one goes on the socioeconomic ladder, the greater economic uncertainty one finds. White-collar workers, even those who are not paid more than skilled manual workers, are less likely to suffer the tensions created by fear of loss of income. Studies of marital instability indicate that this is related to lower income and income insecurity. Such insecurity will of course affect the individual's politics and attitudes.[40] High states of tension require immediate alleviation, and this is frequently found in the venting of hostility against a scapegoat and the search for a short-term solution by support of extremist groups. Research indicates that the unemployed are less tolerant toward minorities than the employed, and more likely to be Communists if they are workers, or fascists if they are middle class. Industries which have a high rate of Communists in their ranks also have high economic instability.

The lower classes' insecurities and tensions which flow from economic instability are reinforced by their particular patterns of family life. There is a great deal of direct frustration and aggression in the day-to-day lives of mem-

---

[38] According to Carl Friedrich, agricultural groups are more emotionally nationalistic and potentially authoritarian politically because of the fact that they are more isolated from meeting people who are different than are urban dwellers. See "The Agricultural Basis of Emotional Nationalism," *Public Opinion Quarterly*, 1 (1937), pp. 50–51. See also Rudolf Heberle, *From Democracy to Nazism: A Regional Case Study on Political Parties in Germany* (Baton Rouge, Louisiana: Louisiana State University Press, 1945), pp. 32 ff., for a discussion of the appeal of Nazism to the German rural population, and K. Kido and M. Sugi, *op. cit.*, for similar survey findings in Japan.

[39] Statistical data indicate that German and Austrian Nazism, French Poujadism, and American McCarthyism have all drawn their heaviest nonrural support from the small businessmen of provincial small communities, particularly those with little education.

[40] In addition to the insecurity which is normally attendant upon lower-class existence, special conditions which uproot people from a stable community life and upset the social supports of their traditional values make them receptive to extremist chiliastic ideologies which help to redefine their world. I have already discussed some of the evidence linking the *discontinuities* and rootlessness flowing from rapid industrialization and urbanization on the politics of workers in different countries in Chap. II. Rydenfelt in his study of Swedish Communism suggests that "rootlessness" is a characteristic of individuals and occupations with high Communist voting records. See W. Phillips Davison, *op. cit.*, p. 378. Engels also called attention in the 1890's to the fact that chiliastic religions and social movements, including the revolutionary socialist one, attracted all the deviants or those without a place in society: "All the elements which had been set free, i.e., at a loose end, by the dissolution of the old world came one after the other into the orbit of [early] Christianity . . . [as today] all throng to the working-class parties in all countries." F. Engels, *op. cit.*, pp. 319–20. See also G. Almond, *op. cit.*, p. 236, and Hadley Cantril, *The Psychology of Social Movements* (New York: John Wiley & Sons, 1941), Chaps. 8 and 9.

bers of the lower classes, both children and adults. A comprehensive review of the many studies of child-rearing patterns in the United States completed in the past twenty-five years reports that their "most consistent finding" is the "more frequent use of physical punishment by working-class parents. The middle class, in contrast, resorts to reasoning, isolation, and . . . 'love-oriented' techniques of discipline. . . . Such parents are more likely to overlook offenses, and when they do punish they are less likely to ridicule or inflict physical pain." [41] A further link between such child-rearing practices and adult hostility and authoritarianism is suggested by the finding of two investigations in Boston and Detroit that physical punishments for aggression, characteristic of the working class, tend to increase rather than decrease aggressive behavior.[42]

Lower-class Perspectives

Acceptance of the norms of democracy requires a high level of sophistication and ego security. The less sophisticated and stable an individual, the more likely he is to favor a simplified view of politics, to fail to understand the rationale underlying tolerance of those with whom he disagrees, and to find difficulty in grasping or tolerating a gradualist image of political change.

Several studies focusing on various aspects of working-class life and culture have emphasized different components of an unsophisticated perspective. Greater suggestibility, absence of a sense of past and future (lack of a prolonged time perspective), inability to take a complex view, greater difficulty in abstracting from concrete experience, and lack of imagination (inner "reworking" of experience), each has been singled out by numerous students of quite different problems as characteristic of low status. All of these qualities are part of the complex psychological basis of authoritarianism.

The psychologist Hadley Cantril considered suggestibility to be a major psychological explanation for participation in extremist movements.[43] The two conditions for suggestibility are both typical of low-status persons: either the lack of an adequate frame of

---

[41] See Urie Bronfenbrenner, "Socialization and Social Class Through Time and Space," in E. E. Maccoby, T. M. Newcomb, and E. L. Hartley, eds., *Readings in Social Psychology* (New York: Henry Holt, 1958), p. 419. The sociologist Allison Davis has summarized in a similar vein research findings relating to intra-family relations in different classes: "The lower classes not uncommonly teach their children and adolescents to strike out with fists or knife and to be certain to hit first. Both girls and boys at adolescence may curse their father to his face or even attack him with fists, sticks, or axes in free-for-all family encounters. Husbands and wives sometimes stage pitched battles in the home; wives have their husbands arrested, and husbands try to break in or burn down their own homes when locked out. Such fights with fists or weapons, and the whipping of wives occur sooner or later in many lower-class families. They may not appear today, nor tomorrow, but they *will* appear if the observer remains long enough to see them." Allison Davis, "Socialization and Adolescent Personality," in Guy E. Swanson, *et al.*, eds., *Readings in Social Psychology* (New York: Henry Holt, 1954), p. 528. (Emphasis in original.)

[42] Some hint of the complex of psychological factors underlying lower-class authoritarianism is given in one study which reports a relationship between overt hostility and authoritarianism. See Saul M. Siegel, "The Relationship of Hostility to Authoritarianism," *Journal of Abnormal and Social Psychology*, 52 (1956), pp. 368–72.

[43] See Hadley Cantril, *op. cit.*, p. 65.

reference or general perspective, or a fixed, rigid one. A poorly developed frame of reference reflects a limited education, a paucity of the rich associations on a general level which provide a basis for evaluating experience. A fixed or rigid one—in a sense the opposite side of the same coin—reflects the tendency to elevate whatever general principles are learned to absolutes which even experience may fail to qualify and correct.

The stimulating book by the British journalist Richard Hoggart, *The Uses of Literacy,* makes the same point in another way. Low-status persons without rich and flexible perspectives are likely to lack a developed sense of the past *and* the future. "Their education is unlikely to have left them with any historical panorama or with any idea of a continuing tradition. . . . A great many people, though they may possess a considerable amount of disconnected information, have little idea of an historical or ideological pattern or process. . . . With little intellectual or cultural furniture, with little training in the testing of opposing views against reason and existing judgments, judgments are usually made according to the promptings of those group apothegms which come first to mind. . . . Similarly, there can be little real sense of the future. . . . Such a mind is, I think, particularly accessible to the temptation to live in a constant present." [44]

This concern with the present leads to a concentration on daily activities, without much inner reflection, imaginative planning of one's future, or abstract thinking unrelated to one's daily activities. One of the few studies of lower-class children which used projective techniques found that "these young people are making an adjustment which is orientated toward the outside world rather than one which rests on a developing acquaintance with their own impulses and the handling of these impulses by fantasy and introspection. . . . They do not have a rich inner life, indeed their imaginative activity is meagre and limited. . . . When faced with a new situation, the subjects tend to react rapidly, and they do not alter their original impressions of the situation which is seen as a crude whole with little intellectual discrimination of components." [45]

Working-class life as a whole emphasizes the concrete and immediate. As Hoggart puts it, "if we want to capture something of the essence of working-class life . . . we must say that it is the 'dense and concrete' life, a life whose main stress is on the intimate, the sensory, the detailed and the personal. This would no doubt be true of working-class groups anywhere in the world." [46] Hoggart sees the concrete-

---

[44] Richard Hoggart, *op. cit.,* pp. 158–59.

[45] B. M. Spinley, *The Deprived and the Privileged* (London: Routledge and Kegan Paul, 1953), pp. 115–16. These conclusions were based on Rorschach tests given to 60 slum-area children. The last point is related to that made by another British scholar, that working-class people are not as likely as those with middle-class backgrounds to perceive the *structure* of an object, which involves thought on a more abstract level of relationships, but have an action-oriented reaction to the *content* of an object. For more discussion of this point, see B. Bernstein, "Some Sociological Determinants of Perception," *The British Journal of Sociology,* 9 (1958), pp. 160 ff.

[46] Richard Hoggart, *op. cit.,* p. 88. This kind of life, like other social characteristics of human beings, has different consequences for different areas of society and social existence. It may be argued, though I personally doubt it, that this capacity to establish personal relationships, to

ness of working-class perceptions as the main difference between them and middle-class people, who more easily meet abstract and general questions. The sharp British working-class distinction between "Us" and "Them," he notes, is "part of a more general characteristic of the outlook of most working-class people. To come to terms with the world of 'Them' involves, in the end, all kinds of political and social questions, and leads eventually beyond politics and social philosophy to metaphysics. The question of how we face 'Them' (whoever 'They' are) is, at last, the question of how we stand in relation to anything not visibly and intimately part of our local universe. The working-class splitting of the world into 'Us' and 'Them' is on this side a symptom of their difficulty in meeting abstract or general questions." [47] Hoggart is careful to emphasize that probably most persons in *any* social class are uninterested in general ideas, but still "training in the handling of ideas or in analysis" is far more characteristic of the demands of middle-class parents and occupations.[48]

A recent analysis by the British sociologist Basil Bernstein of how differences in ways of perceiving and thinking in the different classes lead to variations in social mobility also underlines the manner in which different family patterns affect authoritarianism. The middle-class parent stresses "an

awareness of the importance between means and long-term ends, cognitively and affectually regarded . . . [and has] the ability to adopt appropriate measures to implement the attainment of distant ends by a purposeful means-end chain. . . . The child in the middle classes and associative levels grows up in an environment which is finely and extensively controlled; the space, time and social relationships are explicitly regulated within and outside the family group." [49] The situation in the working-class family is quite different:

The working-class family structure is less formally organized than the middle-class in relation to the development of the child. Although the authority within the family is explicit, the values which it expresses do not give rise to the carefully ordered universe spatially and temporally of the middle-class child. The exercise of authority will not be related to a stable system of rewards and punishments but may often appear arbitrary. The specific character of long-term goals tends to be replaced by more general notions of the future, in which chance, a friend or a relative plays a greater part than the rigorous working out of connections. Thus present, or near-present, activities have greater value than the relation of the present activity to the attainment of a distant goal. The system of expectancies, or the time-span of anticipation, is shortened and this creates different sets of preferences, goals, and dissatisfactions. The en-

live in the present, may be more "healthy" (in a strictly medical, mental-health sense) than a middle-class concern with status distinctions, one's own personal impact on one's life situation, and a preoccupation with the uncertain future. But on the political level of consequences, the problem of concern here, this same action-oriented, nonintellectualistic aspect of working-class life seems to prevent the realities of long-term social and economic trends from entering working-class consciousness, simply because such reality can enter only through the medium of abstractions and generalizations.

[47] *Ibid.*, p. 86.
[48] *Loc. cit.*
[49] B. Bernstein, *op. cit.*, pp. 161, 165.

vironment limits the perception of the developing child of and in time. Present gratifications or present deprivations become absolute gratifications or absolute deprivations, for there exists no developed time continuum upon which present activity can be ranged. Relative to the middle-classes, the postponement of present pleasure for future gratifications will be found difficult. By implication *a more volatile patterning of affectual and expressive behavior will be found in the working-classes.*[50]

This emphasis on the immediately perceivable and concern with the personal and concrete is part and parcel of the short time perspective and the inability to perceive the complex possibilities and consequences of actions which often result in a general readiness to support extremist political and religious movements, and a generally lower level of liberalism on noneconomic questions.[51]

Even within extremist movements these differences in the perceptions and perspectives of working-class as against middle-class persons affect their experiences, readiness to join a "cause," and reasons for defecting. The American political scientist Gabriel Almond's study of 221 ex-Communists in four countries provides data on this point. He distinguishes between the "exo-teric" (simple, for mass consumption) and "esoteric" (complex, for the inner circle) doctrines of the party. In contrast to middle-class members "relatively few working-class respondents had been exposed to the esoteric doctrine of the party before joining, and . . . they tended to remain unindoctrinated while in the party."[52] The middle-class recruits "tended to come to the party with more complex value patterns and expectations which were more likely to obstruct assimilation into the party. . . . The working-class member, on the other hand, is relatively untroubled by doctrinal apparatus, less exposed to the media of communication, and his imagination and logical powers are relatively undeveloped."[53]

One aspect of the lower classes' lack of sophistication and education is their anti-intellectualism (a phenomenon Engels long ago noted as a problem faced by working-class movements). While the complex esoteric ideology of Communism may have been one of the principal features attracting middle-class people to it, the fundamental anti-intellectualism which it shares with other extremist movements has been a source of strain for the "genuine" intellectuals within it. Thus it has been the working-class rank and file

---

[50] *Ibid.*, p. 168 (my emphasis).

[51] This hypothesis has suggestive implications for a theory of trade-union democracy, and possible strains within trade-union organizational life. Working-class union members may not be at all as concerned with dictatorial union leadership as are middle-class critics who assume that the rank and file would actively form factions, and critically evaluate union policies if not constrained by a monolithic structure imposed by the top leadership. On the other hand, the more educated, articulate staff members (on a union newspaper, for example) may want to include more literate and complex discussions of issues facing the union but feel constrained by the need to present simple, easily understood propagandistic slogans for rank-and-file consumption. The "house organ" type of union newspaper may not be due entirely to internal political necessities.

[52] G. Almond, *op. cit.*, p. 244.

[53] *Ibid.*, p. 177.

which has been least disturbed by Communism's ideological shifts, and least likely to defect.[54] Their commitment, once established, cannot usually be shaken by a sudden realization that the party, after all, does not conform to liberal and humanistic values.

This helps to explain why socialist parties have been led by a high proportion of intellectuals, in spite of an original ideological emphasis on maintaining a working-class orientation, while the Communists have alienated their intellectual leaders and are led preponderantly by those with working-class occupations.[55] Almond's study concluded that ". . . while the party is open to all comers, working-class party members have better prospects of success in the party than middle-class recruits. This is probably due both to party policy, which has always manifested greater confidence in the reliability of working-class recruits, and to the difficulties of assimilation into the party generally experienced by middle-class party members."[56]

Making of an Authoritarian

To sum up, the lower-class individual is likely to have been exposed to punishment, lack of love, and a general atmosphere of tension and aggression since early childhood—all experiences which tend to produce deep-rooted hostilities expressed by ethnic prejudice, political authoritarianism, and chiliastic transvaluational religion. His educational attainment is less than that of men with higher socioeconomic status, and his association as a child with others of similar background not only fails to stimulate his intellectual interests but also creates an atmosphere which prevents his educational experience from increasing his general social sophistication and his understanding of different groups and ideas. Leaving school relatively early, he is surrounded on the job by others with a similarly restricted cultural, educational, and family background. Little external influence impinges on his limited environment. From early childhood, he has sought immediate gratifications, rather than engaged in activities which might have long-term rewards. The logic of both his adult employment and his family situation reinforces this limited time perspective. As the sociologist C. C. North has put it, isolation from heterogeneous environments, characteristic of low status, operates to "limit the source of information, to retard the development of efficiency in judgment and reasoning abilities, and to confine the attention to more trivial interests in life."[57]

---

[54] *Ibid.*, pp. 313 ff., 392.

[55] For French data from 1936 to 1956 see Mattei Dogan, "Les Candidats et les élus," in L'Association Française de science politique, *Les Elections du 2 janvier* (Paris: Librairie Armand Colin, 1956), p. 462, and Dogan, "L'origine sociale du personnel parlementaire français," in *Parties politiques et classes sociales en France,* edited by Maurice Duverger (Paris: Librairie Armand Colin, 1955), pp. 291–329. For a comparison of German Social Democratic and Communist parliamentary leadership before Hitler see Viktor Engelhardt, "Die Zusammensatzung des Reichstage nach Alter, Beruf, und Religionsbekenntnis," *Die Arbeit,* 8 (1931), p. 34.

[56] G. Almond, *op. cit.,* p. 190. This statement was supported by analysis of the biographies of 123 Central Committee leaders of the Party in three countries, as well as by interviews with 221 ex-Communists (both leaders and rank-and-file members) in four countries, France, Italy, Great Britain, and the United States.

[57] C. C. North, *Social Differentiation* (Chapel Hill: University of North Carolina Press, 1926), p. 247.

All of these characteristics produce a tendency to view politics and personal relationships in black-and-white terms, a desire for immediate action, an impatience with talk and discussion, a lack of interest in organizations which have a long-range perspective, and a readiness to follow leaders who offer a demonological interpretation of the evil forces (either religious or political) which are conspiring against him.[58]

It is interesting that Lenin saw the character of the lower classes, and the tasks of those who would lead them, in somewhat these terms. He specified as the chief task of the Communist parties the leadership of the broad masses, who are "slumbering, apathetic, hidebound, inert, and dormant." These masses, said Lenin, must be aligned for the "final and decisive battle" (a term reminiscent of Armageddon) by the party which alone can present an uncompromising and unified view of the world, and an immediate program for drastic change. In contrast to "effective" Communist leadership, Lenin pointed to the democratic parties and their leadership as "vacillating, wavering, unstable" elements—a characterization that is probably valid for any political group lacking ultimate certainty in its program and willing to grant legitimacy to opposition groups.[59]

The political outcome of these predispositions, however, is not determined by the multiplicity of factors involved. Isolation, a punishing childhood, economic and occupational insecurities, and a lack of sophistication are conducive to withdrawal, or even apathy, and to strong mobilization of hostility. The same underlying factors which predispose individuals toward support of extremist movements under certain conditions may result in total withdrawal from political activity and concern under other conditions. In "normal" periods, apathy is most frequent among such individuals, but they can be activated by a crisis, especially if it is accompanied by strong millennial appeals.[60]

---

[58] Most of these characteristics have been mentioned by child psychologists as typical of adolescent attitudes and perspectives. Werner Cohn, in an article on Jehovah's Witnesses, considers youth movements as a prototype of all such "proletarian" movements. Both "adolescence fixation and anomie are causal conditions" of their development (p. 297), and all such organizations have an "aura of social estrangement" (p. 282). See Werner Cohn, "Jehovah's Witnesses as a Proletarian Movement," *The American Scholar*, 24 (1955), pp. 281–99.

[59] The quotes from Lenin are in his *Left Wing Communism: An Infantile Disorder* (New York: International Publishers, 1940), pp. 74–75. Lenin's point, made in another context, in his pamphlet, *What Is to Be Done?* that workers left to themselves would never develop socialist or class consciousness, and that they would remain on the level of economic "day to day" consciousness, unless an organized group of revolutionary intellectuals brought them a broader vision, is similar to the generalizations presented here concerning the inherent limited time perspective of the lower strata.

[60] Various American studies indicate that those lower-class individuals who are nonvoters, and who have little political interest, tend to reject the democratic norms of tolerance. See Samuel A. Stouffer, *op. cit.*, and G. M. Connelly and H. H. Field, *op. cit.*, p. 182. Studies of the behavior of the unemployed in countries in which extremist movements were weak, such as the United States and Britain, indicate that apathy was their characteristic political response. See E. W. Bakke, *Citizens Without Work* (New Haven: Yale University Press, 1940), pp. 46–70. On the other hand, German data suggest a high correlation between working-class unemployment and support of Communists, and middle-class unemployment and support of Nazis. In France, Italy, and Finland today, those who have been unemployed tend to back the large Communist

Extremism as an Alternative:
A Test of a Hypothesis

The proposition that the lack of a rich, complex frame of reference is the vital variable which connects low status and a predisposition toward extremism does not necessarily suggest that the lower strata will be authoritarian; it implies that, other things being equal, they will choose the least complex alternative. Thus in situations in which extremism represents the more complex rather than the less complex form of politics, low status should be associated with *opposition* to such movements and parties.

This is in fact the case wherever the Communist party is a small party competing against a large reformist party, as in England, the United States, Sweden, Norway, and other countries. Where the party is small and weak, it cannot hold out the promise of immediate changes in the situation of the most deprived. Rather, such small extremist parties usually present the

fairly complex intellectual argument that in the long run they will be strengthened by tendencies inherent in the social and economic system.[61] For the poorer worker, support of the Swedish Social Democrats, the British Labour party, or the American New Deal is a simpler and more easily understood way of securing redress of grievances or improvement of social conditions than supporting an electorally insignificant Communist party.

The available evidence from Denmark, Norway, Sweden, Canada, Brazil, and Great Britain supports this point. In these countries, where the Communist party is small and a Labor or Socialist party is much larger, Communist support is stronger among the better paid and more skilled workers than it is among the less skilled and poorer strata.[62] In Italy, France, and Finland, where the Communists are the largest party on the left, the lower the income level of workers, the higher their Communist vote.[63] A comparison of the differences in the relative income position of workers who vote Social Demo-

---

parties of those countries. See Chap. VII and Erik Allardt, *Social Struktur och Politisk Aktivitet* (Helsingfors: Söderstrom Förlagsaktiebolag, 1956), pp. 84–85.

[61] Recent research on the early sources of support for the Nazi party challenges the hypothesis that it was the apathetic who came to its support prior to 1930, when it still represented a complex, long-range alternative. A negative rank-order correlation was found between the per cent increase in the Nazi vote and the increase in the proportion voting in the German election districts between 1928 and 1930. Only after it had become a relatively large party did it recruit the previously apathetic, who now could see its immediate potential.

[62] For Denmark, see E. Høgh, *Vaelgeradfaerdi Danmark* (Ph.D. thesis, Sociology Institute, University of Copenhagen, 1959), Tables 6 and 9. For Norway, see Allen Barton, *Sociological and Psychological Implications of Economic Planning in Norway* (Ph.D. thesis, Department of Sociology, Columbia University, 1957); and several surveys of voting behavior in Norway conducted by Norwegian poll organizations including the 1949 FAKTA Survey, and the February 1954 and April 1956, NGI Survey, the results of which are as yet unpublished. Data from the files of the Canadian Gallup Poll for 1945, 1949, and 1953 indicate that the Labor-Progressive (Communist) party drew more support from the skilled than the unskilled sections of the working class. For Brazil, see A. Simao, "O voto operario en São Paulo," *Revista Brasileras estudos politicos,* 1 (1956), pp. 130–41.

[63] For a table giving precise statistics for Italy and France, see Chap. VII. See also Hadley Cantril, *The Politics of Despair* (New York: Basic Books, 1958), pp. 3–10. In pre-Hitler Germany, where the Communists were a large party, they also secured their electoral strength much more from the less skilled sections of the workers than from the more skilled. See Samuel

cratic and those who back the Communists in two neighboring Scandinavian countries of Finland and Sweden shows these alternative patterns clearly (Table V). In Finland, where the Communists are very strong, their support is drawn disproportionately from the poorer workers, while in Sweden, where the Communists are a minor party, they have considerably more success with the better paid and more skilled workers than they do with the unskilled and lowly paid.[64]

This holds true in all countries for which data exist.[65] One other country, India, offers even better evidence. In

TABLE V. The Income Composition of the Working-Class Support of the Social Democratic and Communist Parties in Finland and Sweden *

Finland–1956			Sweden–1946		
Income Class in Markkaa	Social Democrats	Communists	Income Class in Kroner	Social Democrats	Communists
Under 100	8%	13%	Under 2,000	14%	8%
100–400	49	50	2,001–4,000	40	38
400–600	22	29	4,001–6,000	32	30
600+	21	8	6,001+	14	24
(N)	(173)	(119)		(5176)	(907)

* The Finnish data were secured from a special run made for this study by the Finnish Gallup Poll. The Swedish statistics were recomputed from data presented in Elis Hastad, *et al.*, eds., *"Gallup" och den Svenska Valjarkaren* (Uppsala: Hugo Gebers Forlag, 1950), pp. 175–76. Both studies include rural and urban workers.

Pratt, *The Social Basis of Nazism and Communism in Urban Germany* (M.A. thesis, Department of Sociology, Michigan State College, 1948), pp. 156 ff.

An as yet unpublished study by Dr. Pertti Pesonen, of the Institute of Political Science of the University of Helsinki, of voting in the industrial city of Tampere reports that the Communist voters were more well to do than the Social Democrats. On the other hand, Communists were much more likely to have experienced unemployment during the past year (21 per cent) or in their entire work history (46 per cent) than Social Democrats (10 per cent and 23 per cent). This study suggests that the experience of recent unemployment in the family is the most important determinant of a Communist vote in Tampere.

[64] Or to present the same data in another way, in Finland, 41 per cent of all workers earning less than 100 markkaa a month vote Communist, as compared with only 12 per cent among those earning over 600 markkaa. In Sweden, 7 per cent of the workers earning less than 2,000 kroner a year vote Communist, as compared with 25 per cent among those earning over 8,000.

[65] It may be noted, parenthetically, that where the Socialist party is small and/or new, it also represents a complex alternative, and attracts more middle-class support proportionately than when it is a well-established mass party which can offer immediate reforms. On the other hand, when a small transvaluational group does *not* offer an intellectually complex alternative, it should draw disproportionate support from the lower strata. Such groups are the sectarian religions whose millennial appeals have no developed rationale. Some extremely slight evidence on this point in a political contest is available from a recent Norwegian poll which shows the composition of the support for various parties. Only eleven persons supporting the Christian party, a party which appeals to the more fundamentalist Lutherans who are comparable to those discussed earlier in Sweden, were included in the total sample, but 82 per cent of these came from lower-income groups (less than 10,000 kroner per year). In comparison, 57 per cent of the 264 Labor party supporters, and 39 per cent of the 21 Communist supporters earned less than 10,000 kroner. Thus the small Communist party as the most complex transvaluational alternative drew its backing from relatively high strata, while the fundamentalist

India, the Communists are a major party, constituting the government or the major opposition (with 25 per cent or more of the votes) in two states, Kerala and Andhra. While they have substantial strength in some other states, they are much weaker in the rest of India. If the proposition is valid that Communist appeal should be substantially for the lower and uneducated strata where the Party is powerful, and for the relatively higher and better educated ones where it is weak, the characteristics of Party voters should vary greatly in different parts of India, and this is in fact precisely what Table VI below shows.[66]

Where the Indian Communist party is small, its support, like that of the two small moderate socialist parties, comes from relatively well-to-do and better educated strata. The picture shifts sharply in Kerala and Andhra, where the Communists are strong. The middle class provides only 7 per cent of Communist support there, with the working class supplying 74 per cent.[67] Educational differences among party supporters show a similar pattern.

Historical Patterns and Democratic Action

Despite the profoundly antidemocratic tendencies in lower-class groups, workers' political organizations and movements in the more industrialized demo-

TABLE VI. Communist and Socialist Preferences in India, by Class and Education *

	Communist Party Kerala and Andhra	Preferences in Rest of India	Preferences for Socialist Parties in All-India
Class			
Middle	7%	27%	23%
Lower-middle	19	30	36
Working	74	43	41
Education			
Illiterate	52%	43%	31%
Under-matric.	39	37	43
Matric. plus	9	20	26
(N)	(113)	(68)	(88)

* These figures have been computed from tables presented in the *Indian Institute of Public Opinion, Monthly Public Opinion Surveys*, Vol. 2, Nos. 4, 5, 6, 7 (Combined Issue), New Delhi, January–April, 1957, pp. 9–14. This was a pre-election poll, not a report of the actual voting results. The total sample was 2,868 persons. The Socialist party and the Praja-Socialist party figures are combined here, since they share essentially the same moderate program. The support given to them in Andhra and Kerala was too small to be presented separately.

Christians had the economically poorest social base of any party in the country. See the February 1954 NGI Survey, issued in December 1956 in preliminary mimeographed form.

[66] These data were located after the hypothesis was formulated, and thus can be considered an independent replication.

[67] The hypothesis presented here does not attempt to explain the growth of small parties. Adaptations to major crisis situations, particularly depressions and wars, are probably the key factors initially increasing the support for a small "complex" party. For an analysis of the change in electoral support of a Socialist party as it moved up to major party status see S. M. Lipset, *Agrarian Socialism* (Berkeley: University of California Press, 1950), esp. pp. 159–78.

cratic countries have supported *both* economic and political liberalism.[68] Workers' organizations, trade-unions and political parties played a major role in extending political democracy in the nineteenth and early twentieth centuries. However, these struggles for political freedom by the workers, like those of the middle class before them, took place in the context of a fight for economic rights.[69] Freedom of organization and of speech, together with universal suffrage, were necessary weapons in the battle for a better standard

[68] There have been many exceptions to this. The Australian Labor party has been the foremost supporter of a "white Australia." Similarly, in the United States until the advent of the ideological New Deal in the 1930's, the lower-class-based Democratic party has always been the more anti-Negro of the two parties. The American labor movement has opposed nonwhite immigration, and much of it maintains barriers against Negro members.

When the American Socialist party was a mass movement before World War I, its largest circulation newspapers, such as the Milwaukee *Social Democratic Herald* and the *Appeal to Reason* opposed racial integration. The latter stated explicitly, "Socialism will separate the races." See David A. Shannon, *The Socialist Party of America* (New York: Macmillan, 1955), pp. 49–52. Even the Marxist Socialist movement of Western Europe was not immune to the virus of anti-Semitism. Thus, before World War I there were a number of anti-Semitic incidents in which Socialists were involved, some avowedly anti-Semitic leaders connected with different socialist parties, and strong resistance to committing the socialist organizations to opposition to anti-Semitism. See E. Silberner, "The Anti-Semitic Tradition in Modern Socialism," *Scripta Hierosolymitana*, III (1956), pp. 378–96. In an article on the recent British race riots, Michael Rumney points out the working-class base of the anti-Negro sentiment and goes so far as to predict that "the Labour party will become the enemy of the Negro as time goes on." He reports that "while the Conservative party has been able to stand behind the police and take any means it feels necessary to preserve the peace, the Labour party has been strangely silent. If it speaks it will either antagonize the men who riot against West Indians, or forfeit its claim to being the party of equal rights." See "Left Mythology and British Race Riots," *The New Leader* (September 22, 1958), pp. 10–11.

British Gallup Poll surveys document these judgments. Thus in a survey completed in July 1959, the poll asked whether Jews "have more or less power than they should really have," and found, when respondents were compared according to party choice, that the anti-Semitic response of "more power" was given by 38 per cent of the Labor voters, 30 per cent of the Tories, and 27 per cent of the Liberals. Seven per cent of the Laborites, 8 per cent of the Conservatives, and 9 per cent of the Liberals thought that Jews have too little power. The same organization has reported a 1958 survey in which fewer Laborites and lower class people said that they would vote for a Jew if their party nominated one than did upper class and Conservative voters. But in all fairness it must also be noted that almost every Jew in the House of Commons represents the Labor party, and that almost all of the approximately two dozen Jews represent overwhelmingly non-Jewish constituencies.

[69] Actually there are some striking similarities between the behavior of various middle-class strata when they constituted the lower strata within a predominantly aristocratic and feudal society, and the working class in newly industrialized societies who have not yet won a place in society. The affinities of both for religious and economic "radicalism," in the same sense, are striking. Calvin's doctrine of predestination, as Tawney points out, performed the same function for the eighteenth-century *bourgeoisie* as did Marx's theory of the inevitability of socialism for the proletariat in the nineteenth. Both "set their virtue at their best in sharp antithesis with the vices of the established order at its worst, taught them to feel that they were a chosen people, made them conscious of their great destiny in the Providential and resolute to realize it." The Communist party, as did the Puritans, insists on "personal responsibility, discipline and asceticism," and although the historical contents differ, they may have the same sociological roots: in isolated, status-deprived occupational groups. See R. H. Tawney, *Religion and the Rise of Capitalism* (New York: Penguin Books, 1947), pp. 9, 99. For a similar point see Donald G. MacRae, "The Bolshevik Ideology," *The Cambridge Journal*, 3 (1950), pp. 164–77.

of living, social security, shorter hours, and the like. The upper classes resisted the extension of political freedom as part of their defense of economic and social privilege.

Few groups in history have ever voluntarily espoused civil liberties and freedom for those who advocate measures they consider despicable or dangerous. Religious freedom emerged in the Western world only because the contending powers each found themselves unable to destroy the other without destroying the entire society, and because in the course of the struggle itself many men lost faith and interest in religion, and consequently the desire to suppress dissent. Similarly, universal suffrage and freedom of organization and opposition developed in many countries either as concessions to the established strength of the lower classes, or as means of controlling them—a tactic advocated and used by such sophisticated conservatives as Disraeli and Bismarck.

Once in existence, however, and although originating in a conflict of interests, democratic norms became part of the institutional system. Thus the Western labor and socialist movement has incorporated these values into its general ideology. But the fact that the movement's ideology is democratic does not mean that its supporters actually understand the implications. The evidence seems to indicate that understanding of and adherence to these norms are highest among leaders and lowest among followers. The general opinions or predispositions of the rank and file are relatively unimportant in predicting behavior as long as the organization to which they are loyal continues to act democratically. In spite of the workers' greater authoritarian propensity, their organizations which are anti-Communist still function as better defenders and carriers of democratic values than parties based on the middle class. In Germany, the United States, Great Britain, and Japan, individuals who support the democratic left party are more likely to support civil liberties and democratic values than people *within* each occupational stratum who back the conservative parties. Organized social democracy not only defends civil liberties but influences its supporters in the same direction.[70]

Conservatism is especially vulnerable in a political democracy since, as Abraham Lincoln said, there are always more poor people than well-to-do ones, and promises to redistribute wealth are difficult to rebut. Consequently, conservatives have traditionally feared a thoroughgoing political democracy and have endeavored in most countries—by restricting the franchise or by manipulating the governmental structure through second chambers or overrepresentation of rural districts and small towns (traditional conservative strongholds)—to prevent a popular

[70] A striking case in point occurred in Australia in 1950. During a period of much agitation about the dangers of the Communist party, a Gallup Poll survey reported that 80 per cent of the electorate favored outlawing the Communists. Shortly after this survey, the Conservative government submitted a proposal to outlaw the party to referendum. During the referendum electoral campaign, the Labor party and the trade-unions came out vigorously against the proposal. Considerable shifting took place after this, to the point that the measure to outlaw the Communists was actually defeated by a small majority, and Catholic workers who had overwhelmingly favored the outlaw measure when first questioned by the Gallup Poll eventually followed the advice of their party and unions and voted against it. See Leicester Webb, *Communism and Democracy in Australia: A Survey of the 1951 Referendum* (New York: Frederick A. Praeger, 1955).

majority from controlling the government. The ideology of conservatism has frequently been based on elitist values which reject the idea that there is wisdom in the voice of the electorate. Other values often defended by conservatives, like militarism or nationalism, probably also have an attraction for individuals with authoritarian predispositions.[71]

It would be a mistake to conclude from the data presented here that the authoritarian predispositions of the lower classes necessarily constitute a threat to a democratic social system; nor should similar conclusions be drawn about the antidemocratic aspects of conservatism. Whether or not a given class supports restrictions on freedom depends on a wide constellation of factors of which those discussed here are only a part.

The instability of the democratic process in general and the strength of the Communists in particular, as we have seen, are closely related to national levels of economic development, including national levels of educational attainment. The Communists represent a mass movement in the poorer countries of Europe and elsewhere, but are weak where economic development and educational attainment are high. The lower classes of the less developed countries are poorer, more insecure, less educated, and relatively more underprivileged in terms of possession of status symbols than are the lower strata of the more well-to-do nations. In the more developed, stable democracies of Western Europe, North America, and Australasia the lower classes are "in the society" as well as "of it"—that is, their isolation from the rest of the culture is much less than the social isolation of the poorer groups in other countries, who are cut off by abysmally low incomes and very low educational levels, if not by widespread illiteracy. This incorporation of the workers into the body politic in the industrialized Western world has reduced their authoritarian tendencies greatly, although in the United States, for example, McCarthy demonstrated that an irresponsible demagogue who combines a nationalist and antielitist appeal can still secure considerable support from the less educated.[72]

While the evidence as to the effects

[71] A study of the 1952 elections in the United States revealed that at every educational level (grammar school, high school, and college) individuals who scored high on an "authoritarian personality" scale were much more likely to vote for Eisenhower rather than Stevenson. Robert Lane, "Political Personality and Electoral Choice," *American Political Science Review*, 49 (1955), pp. 173–90. In Britain, a study of working-class anti-Semitism found that the small group of Conservatives in the sample were much more anti-Semitic than the Liberals and the Laborites. See James H. Robb, *Working-class Anti-Semite* (London: Tavistock Publications, 1954), pp. 83–94.

[72] "The history of the masses, however, has been a history of the most consistently anti-intellectual force in society . . . It was the American lower classes, not the upper, who gave their overwhelming support to the attacks in recent years on civil liberties. It is among the working people that one finds dominant those sects and churches most hostile to the free spirit." Lewis S. Feuer, *Introduction to Marx and Engels, Basic Writings on Politics and Philosophy* (New York: Doubleday Anchor Books, 1959), pp. xv–xvi. And in another wealthy country, white South Africa, Herbert Tingsten points out that "industrialization and commercialization . . . have formed that social class now constituting the stronghold of Boer nationalism: workers, shop assistants, clerks, lower grades of civil servants. Here, as in the United States, these 'poor whites'—more correctly, whites threatened by poverty—are the leading guardians of prejudice and white supremacy." *The Problem of South Africa* (London: Victor Gollancz, Ltd., 1955), p. 23.

of rising national standards of living and education permits us to be hopeful about working-class politics and behavior in those countries in which extremism is weak, it does suggest pessimistic conclusions with regard to the less economically developed, unstable democracies. Where an extremist party has secured the support of the lower classes—often by stressing equality and economic security at the expense of liberty—it is problematic whether this support can be taken away from it by democratic methods. The Communists, in particular, combine the two types of a chiliastic view of the world. Whether democratic working-class parties, able to demonstrate convincingly their ability to defend economic and class interests, can be built up in the less stable democracies is a moot question. But the threat to democracy does not come solely from the lower strata. And in the next chapter we will turn from working-class authoritarianism to an examination of the different varieties of fascism, which is usually identified with the middle class.

VII

THROUGH THE
LIFE CYCLE

23

TRENDS IN CLASS FERTILITY IN WESTERN NATIONS

Dennis H. Wrong

24

SOCIALIZATION AND SOCIAL CLASS THROUGH TIME AND SPACE

Urie Bronfenbrenner

Someone once remarked tongue in cheek that sociology courses might be taught using nothing but proverbs, folk sayings, and the words from Broadway show tunes.* While this is of course an exaggeration, many old maxims contain substantial sociological truth. The expression "the rich get richer and the poor get children" is old and hackneyed, yet it expresses an important fact: that as a general rule fertility is—with certain exceptions—inversely associated with social class. That is, as we descend the social class gradient, family size increases.

In the selection on fertility, sociologist Dennis Wrong surveys data from a number of Western countries, sketches the trends in class fertility since the nineteenth century, and speculates on the future of the traditional relationship between social class and fertility.

Wrong indicates that throughout most of this century class fertility-differences have been declining and, in light of this, he predicts the eventual disappearance of the usual inverse relationship between class and fertility. However, it should be noted that the traditional pattern still held firm by the mid-1960's, as the table on the following page clearly reveals, using family income as an indicator of social class.

Once children *are* born, regardless of social class, parents are confronted with the need to socialize them, to begin the long, slow process of molding and shaping patterns of values and behavior out of the inchoate, anarchistic infant mass.

What provided the impetus for the comprehensive survey of child-rearing studies by Urie Bronfenbrenner was an apparent contradiction among some of the investigations. Some studies seemed to conclude

* For example: on the etiology of juvenile delinquency: the Officer Krupke song from *West Side Story;* on cultural theories of prejudice: "You've Got to Be Carefully Taught" from *South Pacific;* on the importance of extended family ties: blood is thicker than water, and so forth.

Children Ever Born Per 1,000 Married Women, By Family Income, United States, 1964

	Women 15–44 yrs. old (still in child-bearing period) *	Women 45 yrs. old and over (completed family)
Total	2,534	2,577
Under $2,000	3,323	3,531
$2,000–$2,999	3,155	2,827
$3,000–$3,999	2,981	2,652
$4,000–$4,999	2,691	2,463
$5,000–$7,499	2,494	2,397
$7,500–$9,999	2,276	2,353
$10,000 and over	2,075	2,213

* standardized for age

SOURCE: U.S. Bureau of the Census, *Current Population Reports*, Series P-20, No. 147 (Washington, D.C.: U.S. Govt. Printing Office, 1966), p. 17.

that the middle class was stricter with regard to early feeding, weaning, toilet training, and the like; other studies seemed to show just the reverse, that the working class or lower class was more severe toward its children.

Bronfenbrenner ingeniously resolved the apparent contradiction by observing that these studies had been conducted at different periods of time and that middle-class parents who originally *had* been more strict eased up as they gradually fell under the influence of government pamphlets on child care, advice in women's magazines, and child-rearing experts like Dr. Spock, all of which urged, under Freudian or neo-Freudian influences, greater permissiveness in confronting the infants' early impulses.

What unites these two essays on birth rates and child-rearing patterns is not merely their concern with new members of society. Both essays, in addition, say something about the nature of *innovations,* how they enter the social structure, and how they diffuse.

In both cases, the authors discuss innovation as being introduced at the top of the class structure and only later filtering downward. Upper- and middle-class birth rates have been low because these groups were the first and most consistent users of the innovations of family planning and birth control. Only now are these reaching the lower class. And the middle class now seems more permissive in many of its child-rearing techniques because they are more likely to read about and adopt innovations in child-rearing based on new developments in psychological theory.

Indeed, in most societies, innovations are introduced at the top and only later drift downward. This seems to be true for several reasons. First, the adoption of innovations, especially technological innovations, is often expensive and at first can be afforded only by the well-to-do. A contemporary example is air travel, which was adopted first by the higher classes and is only gradually sifting downward. To this day, the majority of Americans has never flown in an airplane. Secondly, the upper classes, being generally more educated, are more likely to be aware of new innovations and thus more ready to adopt them. Finally, in a stable society, upper- and middle-class values typically have higher standing than working- and lower-class values. As Herbert Gans says later in this volume, the hierarchy of values follows the hierarchy of classes. Thus, it is to be expected that the lower classes will imitate upper-class practices rather than vice versa. It might, in fact, be taken as a crude indicator of the breakdown of values and a crisis of legitimacy in a society when the upper and middle classes begin adopting behavior and values that have entered at the bottom of the class structure. In certain areas of American society just this is happening. Standards of fashion, for example (as well as speech, music, and even world-view), are being set, not so much by the upper or even the middle class, but by the dé-classé, anticlass, antisystem youth. Long hair, head bands, beads, pretie-dyed apparel, vests, miscellaneous leather, carefully neglected dungarees, and all the other para-phernalia of the counterculture costume, not only mock the materialistic values of established classes, but have successfully spread into the enemy camp, Fifth Avenue and Main Street, U.S.A. When values and behavior are no longer established by the top or even the middle of a society, its traditional ways are clearly in trouble.

■ Dennis H. Wrong [1]

Although the birth-rate has declined in all Western nations since the middle of the nineteenth century, the decline has not been equal among the various groups that compose their population. Measures of fertility for national units conceal differences in the fertility of the many distinct groups in urban-industrial societies. Changes in the pattern of these differences are of particular significance in the later stages of the demographic transition from high to low birth-rates and death-rates which the Western world has undergone in the past century. Changes in the birth-rate rather than in the death-rate are the main determinants of growth in societies where mortality has been brought under control by modern medicine and public health practices.

Demographers have often treated differential fertility as a special, virtually autonomous subject instead of viewing it in the broad historical context of the Western demographic transition. In fact, as J. W. Innes has pointed out, few studies have been made of *trends* in differential fertility by comparison with the numerous studies which simply establish the existence of group differences in fertility at a single point in time.[2] The present paper is concerned with class differences—probably the most pervasive of all group differences in advanced societies. The attempt is made to gather together by historical period the available data on trends in class differences in fertility for several Western countries in order to present a systematic picture of the way in which these differences have evolved in modern times.

The problem of dividing a population into socio-economic classes that are genuinely distinct from one another in a sociologically meaningful sense has been widely discussed by sociologists. Demographers, however, usually work

[1] This paper is the concluding chapter, somewhat revised, of a larger study in which statistics on socio-economic fertility-differences in Western nations are intensively analysed. I am indebted to Kingsley Davis for valuable advice and to the Canadian Social Science Research Council for financial assistance.

[2] J. W. Innes, *Class Fertility Trends in England and Wales, 1876–1934* (Princeton: 1938), v.

SOURCE: *Canadian Journal of Economics*, 24 (May 1958), 216–29. Reprinted by permission of the author and publisher.

with official data which provide only limited information on the characteristics of populations. They are, therefore, unable to employ the more refined indices of class developed by sociologists and are forced to use as indices such relatively simple objective attributes as income, occupation, or education. Censuses provide data on the occupational distribution of the population and their ready-made categories can easily be combined to form broad stratified groups. Occupation is by no means a perfect index of class, for within an occupation there is a good deal of variation in income and education, and neither of these attributes can be ignored in arriving at an adequate, objective measure of class. Nevertheless, most contemporary sociologists agree that, if defined with sufficient specificity, occupation is probably the best *single* index which it is feasible to use in large-scale statistical inquiries.

Since different nations use different systems of occupational classification, precise international comparisons are usually impossible. The systems vary widely both with respect to the number of groups distinguished and the criteria on the basis of which the classification is constructed. Moreover, few nations use systems of classification that correspond with classes or with a socioeconomic scale of status. Frequently only broad industrial groups are distinguished or the labour force is subdivided solely according to work status—that is, into employers, self-employed, salaried employees, and wage-workers. For all these reasons, changes that may have been taking place are sometimes obscured.

What is true of measures of class is also true of measures of fertility. Current fertility-rates, both crude and refined, fertility-ratios, and cumulative birth-rates based on retrospective reporting of births in response to census questions asking the numbers of children ever born to women in specified categories of the population—all these familiar but different measures have been used in studies of differential fertility. The present study makes greatest use of cumulative rates,[3] particularly for women whose years of childbearing are over. Such rates are especially useful to the student of trends for they permit comparisons of the childbearing performance of successive groups or cohorts of women who were born or married at different dates.

The nations included in the survey have been selected primarily because they possessed the most adequate data on trends in class differences in fertility. Both primary and secondary sources have been used for Great Britain, the United States, Norway, Sweden, France, and Australia. Germany, Switzerland, Denmark, and Canada have been treated more cursorily, reliance being placed largely on secondary sources. The trend and pattern of class differences in fertility are reviewed for each of the three broad periods into which the data have been grouped, and the agencies—delayed marriage, birth control, and so on—that apparently account for group differences in fertility are briefly discussed.

---

[3] Cumulative birth-rates are the total numbers of births before a specified age or date per 1,000 women surviving to that age or date.

First Period: From the Beginning of the Decline in the Birth-Rate to 1910 [4]

Before the general decline in the birth-rate, fertility in Western Europe and the United States varied among classes and tended to be inversely correlated with class, but the relative stability of the differences paralleled the stability of national levels of fertility. Fertility began to decline sharply in most Western countries in the 1870's or 1880's and the general trend of class differences from this period until about the First World War is well defined.

As national birth-rates turned downward, class fertility-differentials increased greatly. The inverse association between fertility and socio-economic status which before the downturn of the birth-rate was clearcut only for groups at the upper and lower ends of the socio-economic scale—the higher non-manual urban occupations on the one hand, and agricultural and unskilled industrial workers on the other —became deeper and more consistent as groups occupying intermediate positions in the class structure began to conform to it as well. Rural—urban and agricultural—nonagricultural differentials also widened in most countries. While all occupational and economic groups were affected by the general decline in fertility, the evidence that the groups of highest socio-economic status were the leaders of the decline is altogether decisive, though the reduced fertility of the more numerous agricultural population and urban lower classes had a greater quantitative effect on the drop in national fertility.

There is very little evidence that the rate of increase in class differentials in England, the United States, or the many European cities for which data on the birth-rates of residential areas are available, or even in France, was slowing down before the First World War, which in this as in so many other features of modern life seems to mark a crucial watershed of historical transition. There is some evidence to suggest that in Australia class fertility-differentials did not begin to increase until the first two decades of the twentieth century rather than in the final decades of the nineteenth, but the evidence is far from conclusive.

The inverse correlation of fertility and socio-economic status was probably more marked in the period considered in this section of the paper than it has ever been before or since in Western civilization. Yet even as the more rapid decline in fertility of the less fertile upper classes enhanced the relation, exceptions to it emerged. Data on the cumulative fertility of women born and married before 1910 in the United

---

[4] The conclusions for this period are based on the following sources. Innes, *Class Fertility Trends in England and Wales*. Great Britain, Census of England and Wales, 1911, XIII, *Fertility of Marriage* (London, 1917). United States Bureau of the Census, Sixteenth Census of the United States (1940), *Population: Differential Fertility, 1940 and 1910* (5 vols., Washington, D.C., 1943–47). Edgar Sydenstricker and Frank W. Notestein, "Differential Fertility According to Social Class," *Journal of the American Statistical Association*, XXV, no. 30, March, 1930. France, Bureau de la Statistique Générale, *Statistique des familles en 1906* (Paris, 1912); *Statistique des familles en 1911* (Paris, 1918). Joseph J. Spengler, *France Faces Depopulation* (Durham, N.C., 1938). *Census of the Commonwealth of Australia*, 1911, II, Part x (Melbourne, 1921). Jacques Bertillon, "La Natalité selon le degré d'aisance," *Bulletin de l'Institut Internationale de Statistique*, XI, 1899.

States are tabulated by the most detailed socio-economic categories used in studies made during this period; they show that within the infertile, higher occupations, the group composed of clerical, sales, and kindred workers was somewhat less fertile than either the group of professionals and semi-professionals or the group composed of proprietors, managers, and officials though both these last two groups were generally higher in status than the white-collar employees of the first group.

Differences in income within broad groups of non-manual occupations may have been to some degree positively correlated with fertility. The lower fertility of wage-earners and salaried employees as compared with employers in Australia, and of salaried employees as compared with proprietors in France, suggests this possibility. Unfortunately, adequate data on differences in fertility by income are not widely available for this period, although data for later periods have indicated that the familiar inverse pattern is, in urban populations, more marked for income groups than for occupational classes. A 1906 study of differences in fertility by income among French salaried employees in the public service showed that above a certain level of income, family size and income were positively correlated,[5] but it is not known whether this same pattern existed in the general population or in other countries at that time. Since fertility began to decline earlier in France than in other Western nations, French differential fertility may

have deviated from the inverse pattern before the First World War, resembling the pattern that developed at a later date in other Western countries.

British textile workers, American service workers, Australians engaged in domestic service, and French domestic servants are other occupational groups whose fertility was lower than that of groups of equal or higher socio-economic status. The reason may probably be found in the special circumstances associated with the environment of these occupations—the British textile industry employed large numbers of women, and personal and domestic service necessitates frequent contacts with people of higher status.

A partially positive relation between fertility and status also existed in the farm populations of several Western countries. The American South, Australia, and probably rural French Canada, which as late as 1941 did not exhibit the usual inverse pattern, showed a direct relation between fertility and class within their farm or rural populations before 1910. In all these areas the direct pattern was associated with relatively high levels of fertility. A direct relation between fertility and status has often been observed in the agricultural areas of under-developed countries such as India and China,[6] so good grounds exist for concluding that it is to some degree characteristic of economically backward and semi-industrialized rural populations. Its presence fifty years ago in the American South, rural Australia, and French Canada, therefore, is not surprising.

[5] France, Bureau de la Statistique Générale, *Statistique des familles en 1906*, 46.

[6] Kingsley Davis, *The Population of India and Pakistan* (Princeton, 1950), 76–79; Herbert D. Lamson, "Differential Reproduction in China," *Quarterly Review of Biology*, X, no. 3, Sept., 1935; Frank W. Notestein, "A Demographic Study of 38,256 Families in China," *Milbank Memorial Fund Quarterly*, XVI, no. 1, Jan., 1938, 68–70; Ta Chen, *Population in Modern China* (Chicago, 1946), pp. 30–31 and Table 19, p. 93.

Differences in age at marriage by class continued to contribute to socio-economic fertility-differentials after the beginning of the general decline in the birth-rate. The average age at marriage in the upper classes was higher than in the lower classes, as it evidently had been for a long time in Western history, and a direct relation between age at marriage and socio-economic status held from the top to the bottom of the social scale.[7] Yet the trend and pattern of class differences in fertility were not substantially altered when cumulative birth-rates were standardized for age at marriage in England and Wales and for duration of marriage in the United States; class differences in the fertility of marriage were evidently the major immediate cause of class differences in average family size. The spread of family limitation throughout the population during this period is strongly indicated, for by the turn of the century all socio-economic groups were declining in fertility in the nations for which data are available. It was, of course, in the last decades of the nineteenth century that public opinion became more receptive to family limitation throughout the Western world.[8]

Class differences in the incidence of celibacy undoubtedly created greater class differences in *total* as distinct from *marital* fertility. A later age at marriage is usually associated with a lower proportion of ultimate marriages,[9] so low-status groups must have exceeded high-status groups in total fertility by an even larger amount than in marital fertility.

Second Period: From 1910 to 1940 [10]

Data on class fertility-differentials reveal trends and patterns that are by no means as uniform after 1910, either within or between nations, as in the

---

[7] Frank W. Notestein, "Differential Age at Marriage According to Social Class," *American Journal of Sociology*, XXXVII, no. 1, July, 1931.

[8] A. M. Carr-Saunders, *World Population* (Oxford, 1936), chaps. VIII, IX; D. V. Glass, *Population Policies and Movements* (Oxford, 1940), chap. 1; James A. Field, *Essays on Population and Other Papers* (Chicago, 1931), chaps. VI, XII.

[9] Kingsley Davis, "Statistical Perspective on Marriage and Divorce," *Annals of the American Academy of Political and Social Science*, CCLXXII, Nov., 1950, 9–17.

[10] The conclusions for this period are based on the following sources. Innes, *Class Fertility Trends in England and Wales*. D. V. Glass and E. Grebenik, *The Trend and Pattern of Fertility in Great Britain*, Part I, Papers of the Royal Commission on Population, VI (London, 1954). Great Britain, Census, 1951, *One Per Cent Sample Tables*, Part 2 (London, 1953). U.S. Bureau of the Census, Sixteenth Census, *Population: Differential Fertility, 1940 and 1910*. Frank W. Notestein, "Differential Fertility in the East North Central States," *Milbank Memorial Fund Quarterly*, XVI, no. 2, April, 1938. Clyde V. Kiser, *Group Differences in Urban Fertility* (Baltimore, 1942). Paul H. Jacobson, "The Trend of the Birth Rate among Persons on Different Economic Levels, City of New York, 1929–1942," *Milbank Memorial Fund Quarterly*, XXIII, no. 2, April, 1944. Bernard D. Karpinos and Clyde V. Kiser, "The Differential Fertility and Potential Rates of Growth of Various Income and Education Classes of Urban Populations in the United States," *Milbank Memorial Fund Quarterly*, XVII, no. 4, Oct., 1939. Evelyn M. Kitagawa, "Differential Fertility in Chicago, 1920–1940," *American Journal of Sociology*, LIII, no. 5, March, 1953. France, Bureau de la Statistique Générale, *Statistique des familles en 1926* (Paris, 1932); *Statistique des familles en 1936* (Paris, 1946); Résultats statistiques de recensement général de la population, effectué le 10 mars 1946, IV, *Familles* (Paris, 1954). Spengler, *France Faces Depopulation*. Folketellingen i Norge, 1. desember 1930, Niende hefte, *Barnetallet i norske ekteskap* (Oslo, 1935), Statistika Centralbyran, Sarskilda Folkraknin-

decades immediately following the downturn of national birthrates. No doubt this appearance of greater diversity is in part merely a result of the fact that vastly more data are available for the more recent period. The findings of later studies also reflect improvements in the techniques of demographic measurement as well as actual changes in the conditions observed by earlier investigators. More careful control of the demographic variables that influence fertility-rates, the use of a greater number of indices of socio-economic status, and the development of more sociologically meaningful indices, were the chief methodological improvements. Yet certain general features can be discerned which broadly differentiate trends and patterns in the period under consideration from trends and patterns in the earlier period.

Some contraction of the relative differences in fertility among socio-economic groups occurred. This contrasts with the progressive increase in differentials during the latter part of the nineteenth century. The fertility-levels of non-manual groups in Great Britain, the United States, France, and Norway converged. In Great Britain the fertility-differential between manual and non-manual groups remained remarkably stable from the beginning of the century until the 1930's, when it narrowed slightly but unmistakably. The differential also ceased to widen in the United States, although it did not contract to any appreciable degree. It was also fairly stable in France from 1906 to 1946.

Before 1910, the upper classes everywhere led the decline in fertility, but after 1910 intermediate groups assumed the lead. In Great Britain all groups declined more slowly after the turn of the century, but the non-manual groups of low status declined most rapidly. Small business men, farmers and farm managers, and salaried employees were the leaders from 1890 to 1925. After 1925, non-manual wage-earners and manual wage-earners—the manual group of highest status—exhibited higher rates of decline than the high-status non-manual groups and the low-status manual groups. In the United States between 1910 and 1940, proprietors, managers, and officials showed the greatest decline, but wage-workers of all degrees of skill declined slightly more rapidly than the other non-manual groups and agriculturalists. In Norway, three white-collar salaried groups, factory workers, and small business men showed the greatest relative declines in cumulative fertility between 1920 and 1930. In Sweden, where no direct data on trends exist, comparison of the fertility of marriages of different durations indicates that leadership in the decline in fertility had passed by the 1930's to salaried employees and to the middle-income groups. In France, a stabilization of average family size in the upper socio-economic strata was apparently reached as early as 1911; the fertility of people engaged in industrial

gen 1935/1936, VI, Partiella Folkrakningen Mars 1936, *Barnantal och Doda Barn i Aktenska-pen* (Stockholm, 1939), Karl A. Edin and Edward P. Hutchinson, *Studies of Differential Fertility in Sweden* (London, 1935). *Census of the Commonwealth of Australia*, 1921, Part xxviii (Melbourne, 1927); *Census of the Commonwealth of Australia, 1947*, Part xi (Canberra, 1952). Danmarks Statistik, *Statistik Arbog 1952* (Copenhagen, 1952). Enid Charles, *The Changing Size of the Family in Canada*, Eighth Census of Canada (1942), Census Monograph, no. 1 (Ottawa, 1948).

occupations declined most rapidly from 1911 to 1926, and from 1926 to 1936 average family size in all groups except the most fertile (fishermen) remained fairly stable. Australia alone may have been an exception to the general trend; there is no clear evidence that the least fertile occupational groups were declining less rapidly than the more fertile groups from 1911 to 1921. Australian employers, however, declined more rapidly than wage- and salary-earners, although they continued to have larger families.

It can be concluded, then, that leadership in rate of decline tended to pass in this period to the low-status non-manual workers, urban wage-workers, and the middle-income groups. Of those in the non-manual occupations who had previously led the decline, only white-collar workers and small business men—those with the lowest socio-economic status in the non-manual group—continued to take the lead in several nations. The relatively rapid decline shown by small business men in both Great Britain and Norway suggests that small business men in the American "proprietors, managers, and officials" group may have been responsible for that group's leadership in rate of decline in the United States.

The fertility of an occupational class continued on the whole to be inversely correlated with its socio-economic status, but by 1940 a larger number of exceptions to this relation existed than in the late nineteenth and early twentieth centuries. In Great Britain, salaried employees had smaller families than large employers in all marriage cohorts after 1890, and in the 1910–14 cohort they fell below members of the professions in average size of family to become the least fertile class in British so-

ciety. In the United States, clerical and sales workers continued to be the least fertile occupational group. In Norway in 1930, white-collar clerks in business and commerce had smaller families than factory owners and merchants, and factory workers had smaller families than artisans. In Sweden in 1936, employers and entrepreneurs in non-agricultural occupations had larger families than salaried employees and officials. In France, where the census classifications fail to differentiate occupations by socio-economic status, people engaged in personal-service occupations had smaller families than those in the liberal professions in 1926 and 1936, proprietors had by 1936 increased the margin by which their average family size exceeded that of both salaried employees and wage-workers in 1911, and in 1946 white-collar employees in commerce and public service were less fertile than a combined high-status group of large employers, the liberal professions, and high officials. In Denmark, salaried employees in manufacturing, construction, and commerce were less fertile in 1940 than proprietors in these occupations.

Agricultural workers, miners, fishermen, and unskilled labourers were the most fertile occupational groups in all countries. In Great Britain and France, miners were more fertile than farmers and agricultural workers, but in all the other countries agricultural owners and labourers were more fertile than any of the non-agricultural groups. In the United States in particular, the differential between agricultural and non-agricultural workers was wide and continued to increase from 1910 to 1940.

Clearly the degree to which fertility was inversely correlated with social class diminished between 1900 and

1940. In general, clerical and sales workers, subordinate officials in both government and business, and small business men were the least fertile groups in the Western world and constituted the major exceptions to the inverse pattern of fertility and status. Their exceptionally low fertility, which was already evident in some nations shortly after the beginning of the decline in the Western birth-rate, became more conspicuous in the present century. Only in Canada, where a third of the total population is composed of French-speaking Catholics, traditionally highly fertile, was there no evidence of any break in the inverse pattern. In Australia, on the other hand, the inverse pattern may not yet have fully developed· occupational classes seemed in general to conform to it, but employers and workers on their own account had larger families than wage- and salary-earners within most of the occupational groups.

Studies of differences in the birth-rates of urban areas classified by various indices of economic status also showed a reduction of the inverse relation in the 1920's and 1930's. In New York, London, Paris, Edinburgh, Glasgow, Hamburg, and Vienna the differ-ences in birth-rates between upper-class and lower-class city districts diminished, while in Dresden, Königsberg, Stockholm, and Oslo the differences had disappeared by the late 1920's. In Berlin, Bremen, and Zürich lower-class districts still had the highest crude birth-rates in the 1930's, but upper-class districts had higher birth-rates than middle-class districts.[11]

When we examine variations in family size by income rather than by occupation, several variant patterns of differential fertility can be identified.

a) The most common pattern was for family size to decrease as income increased, until a fairly high income was reached, and then family size increased slightly. French public-service employees conformed to this reverse J-shaped pattern in 1906. In the 1930's it was observed in numerous cities and urban areas of the United States, and (using average monthly rental as an index of income), in the urban population of the entire nation in 1940.[12] Most of the American studies showed that only the highest or the two or three highest income groups, amounting to a relatively small percentage of the total population, deviated from the usual inverse pattern. This pattern was

---

[11] For New York, see Jacobson, "The Trend of the Birth Rate, City of New York, 1929–1942." For London, see Innes, *Class Fertility Trends in England and Wales*, chaps. IV, V; Glass, *Population Policies and Movements*, 76–82; Frank Lorimer and Frederick Osborn, *Dynamics of Population* (New York, 1934), 79–82; K. Mitra, "Fertility and Its Relation to Social Conditions," *Journal of Hygiene*, XXXVII, no. 1, Jan., 1937. For Paris, see Spengler, *France Faces Depopulation*, 98–100; Adolphe Landry, *Traité de démographie* (Paris, 1945), 307. For Edinburgh, Glasgow, Hamburg, Dresden, Königsberg, and Berlin, see Roderich von Ungern-Sternberg, *The Causes of the Decline of the Birth Rate within The European Sphere of Civilization* (Cold Spring Harbor, N.Y., 1931), 115–116. For Vienna, see Alexander Stevenson, "Some Aspects of Fertility and Population Growth in Vienna," *American Sociological Review*, VII, no. 4, Aug., 1942. For Stockholm, see Edin and Hutchinson, *Studies of Differential Fertility in Sweden*. For Oslo, see Folketellingen i Norge, *Barnetallet i norske ekteskap*. For Bremen, see A. Grotjahn, "Differential Birth Rate in Germany" in Margaret Sanger, ed., *Proceedings of the World Population Conference* (London, 1927), 153–154. For Zürich, see Kurt B. Mayer, *The Population of Switzerland* (New York, 1952), 109–110.

[12] U.S. Bureau of the Census, Sixteenth Census, *Population: Differential Fertility 1940 and 1910: Women by Number of Children Ever Born* (1945), Tables 57–62, pp. 173–206.

also observed in Melbourne, Australia, in 1942, in urban Sweden in 1936 among all occupations and among employers and entrepreneurs not in agriculture for marriages of from fifteen to thirty-five years duration; and in Canada in 1941 in several high educational groups and two urban occupational groups of English-speaking Canadians.[13]

b) In several countries deviation from the inverse correlation of family size to income had developed somewhat further. Among marriages of ten years duration in Greater Oslo in 1930, the highest income group equalled the lowest in average family size.[14] The smallest families were located in the middle of the income range. The distribution of family size by income conformed to a U-shaped curve, suggesting that this pattern represented a later stage of development of the reverse J-shaped curve which was observed in countries and cities where fertility had not yet fallen to the uniformly low level of the Norwegian capital. A somewhat similar pattern also characterized families of less than fifteen years duration in urban Sweden among employers and entrepreneurs not in agriculture, and among salaried employees and officials, although the older marriages in these groups conformed more closely to the reverse J-shaped pattern. Among salaried employees and officials, however, an exceptionally infer-

tile group in most Western countries, there was in Sweden no well-defined relation between average family size and income for the majority of both the older and the younger marriages, and group differences were very slight. They had almost vanished in the two groups of shortest marriage-duration and their disappearance may possibly have indicated the completion of a process of transition to a final stage in which differential fertility ceases to exist.

c) However, the studies of Stockholm by Edin and Hutchinson showed that there was a direct relation in the 1920's between family size and income for marriages of incomplete fertility. Moberg also found a direct relation between family size and income among students taking the Swedish matriculation examinations in 1910, 1920, and 1930.[15] Several American studies of differences in fertility by income within highly educated groups have also reported a direct pattern.[16]

Possibly these three different types of relation between fertility and income represent different stages in a process of transition from the inverse pattern. The "straight line" inverse pattern yields first to a reverse J-shaped curve which is then succeeded by a U-shaped pattern. A final equilibrium, characterized either by the complete disappearance of group fertility-differentials or by the emergence of a positive correla-

---

[13] For Melbourne, see W. D. Borrie, *Population Trends and Policies* (Sydney, 1948), 120. For urban Sweden, see Statistika Centralbyran, *Barnantal och Doda Barn i Aktenskapen*. For Canada, see Charles, *The Changing Size of the Family in Canada*, 112.

[14] Folketellingen i Norge, *Barnetallet i norske ekteskap*. Table 9.

[15] Sven Moberg, "Marital Status and Family Size among Matriculated Persons in Sweden," *Population Studies*, IV, no. 1, June, 1950.

[16] John C. Phillips, "Success and the Birth Rate," *Harvard Graduates Magazine*, XXXV, no. 160, June, 1927; John J. Osborn, "Fertility Differentials among Princeton Alumni," *Journal of Heredity*, XXX, no. 12, Dec., 1939; Ernest Havemann and Patricia Salter West, *They Went to College* (New York, 1952), 46; Frederick Osborn, *Preface to Eugenics* (New York, 1952), 175–176.

tion between fertility and status, may ultimately be attained in relatively stationary populations with uniformly low birth- and death-rates. However, there are not enough data on differences in fertility by income and occupation combined to justify a conclusion that class differentials in the Western world as a whole are following such a process of evolution. The possibility that such a trend is occurring may be regarded as a major hypothesis for future investigation arising out of the present study.

The trends and patterns described above are indirect evidence strongly supporting the view that the practice of family limitation has gradually diffused from the upper to the lower socio-economic strata. Indeed, descriptive studies of differential fertility provided the initial empirical support for this view before there was much direct evidence pertaining to class differences in the use of birth-control. Alternative explanations can hardly account for the divergence of class fertility-rates followed by their convergence, the low fertility in occupations such as clerical and sales work and minor government employment, which are characterized by a combination of "bourgeois" standards of living with incomes lower than those of professional people, employers, and even some groups of manual workers, and the greater modification of the inverse pattern in the countries of lowest over-all fertility. The study of Indianapolis by Whelp-

ton and Kiser and Lewis-Fanings' study of the contraceptive practices of English wives supplied the first massive direct evidence that family planning was both more frequent and more effective in the groups at the upper end of the socio-economic scale, and had been adopted earliest by these groups.[17] Whelpton's and Kiser's demonstration that socio-economic fertility-differentials are greatly reduced and the inverse pattern modified and partly reversed when only successful users of birth-control in the different classes are compared, strikingly confirms the class-diffusion-gradient theory of the causation of differential fertility.[18]

It is quite apparent, however, that the process of diffusion was not yet complete in the United States by the 1940's or even in Norway and Sweden by the 1930's. It remains uncertain whether its final result will be the disappearance of group fertility-differentials, the persistence of differentials varying in an almost random manner with socio-economic status in a context of universally low fertility, or, as many demographers contend,[19] the emergence of a direct relation completely reversing the former inverse relation. Whatever group differentials do survive will clearly not be as great in populations of uniformly low fertility where all groups successfully limit the size of their families as they were during the period of transition from high to low fertility.

Discussions of the future of differen-

[17] P. K. Whelpton and Clyde V. Kiser, *Social and Psychological Factors Affecting Fertility* (3 vols., New York, 1946, 1950, 1953); E. Lewis-Faning, *Family Limitation and Its Influence on Human Fertility During the Past Fifty Years*, Papers of the Royal Commission on Population, I (London, 1949).

[18] Whelpton and Kiser, *Social and Psychological Factors Affecting Fertility*, II, Part IX.

[19] See, e.g., Rudolph Heberle, "Social Factors in Birth Control," *American Sociological Review*, VI, no. 5, Oct., 1941, 800; Margaret Jarman Hagood, "Changing Fertility Differentials among Farm-Operator Families in Relation to Economic Size of Farm," *Rural Sociology*, XIII, no. 4, Dec., 1948, 373; Charles F. Westoff, "Differential Fertility in the United States: 1900 to 1952," *American Sociological Review*, XIX, no. 5, Oct., 1954, 561.

tial fertility often overlook the fact that most of the available data deal only with differences in marital fertility. The few studies which take into account group differences in proportions of marriages show larger fertility-differentials and a more consistent inverse correlation of fertility to socio-economic status. In countries such as Norway and Sweden where the rate of illegitimacy is high, the greater frequency of births out of wedlock in the lower classes may help perpetuate the older pattern of differential fertility with respect to differences in total fertility. Later marriage in the upper classes is also likely to persist in view of the time needed for higher education and the later achievement of peak earning-power in high-status occupations. The report on the 1946 family census of Great Britain, however, demonstrates more fully than earlier family censuses that class differences in average age at marriage make only a minor contribution to differences in marital fertility.[20]

Third Period: The Baby Boom after 1940 [21]

The main difference between trends in differential fertility before and after 1940 arises from the fact that after 1940 the decline in the birth-rate which had continued since the second half of the nineteenth century was reversed in most of the Western world. Increases in the proportions of marriages, a decline in the average age at marriage, a reduction in the numbers of women remaining childless, and a slight increase in the average size of completed families appear to have been the major demographic trends underlying the general rise in indices of current fertility.[22] The rise has occurred too recently to permit definitive conclusions about its long-range significance. It remains to be seen whether the cohorts who contributed to the wartime and post-war baby boom will have given birth to more children by the time they reach the end of the reproductive period than the cohorts who preceded them. Forecasts made in the 1930's that fertility would continue to decline and that ultimately there would be actual decreases in the populations of Western countries were clearly mistaken, but few demographers today are of the opinion that recent increases in current fertility represent a long-term renewal of rapid growth in the West.

The long-run effects on differential fertility of the rise in birth-rates that occurred after 1940 are even more debatable. Apparently spectacular reversals of earlier trends may turn out to be of transitory significance when rates of cumulative complete fertility for

---

[20] Glass and Grebenik, *The Trend and Pattern of Fertility in Great Britain*, 113–128.

[21] The conclusions for this period are based on the following sources: Glass and Grebenik, *The Trend and Pattern of Fertility in Great Britain;* Great Britain, Census, 1951, *One Per Cent Sample Tables;* Kiser, "Fertility Trends and Differentials in the United States"; Westoff, "Differential Fertility in the United States, 1900 to 1952"; U.S. Bureau of the Census, *Current Population Characteristics,* Series P-20, no. 46 (Washington, D.C., Dec. 31, 1953); John Hajnal, "Differential Changes in Marriage Patterns," *American Sociological Review,* XIX, no. 2, April, 1954, and "Analysis of Changes in the Marriage Pattern by Economic Groups," *ibid.,* no. 3, July, 1954.

[22] John Hajnal, "The Analysis of Birth Statistics in the Light of the Recent International Recovery of the Birth Rate," *Population Studies,* I, no. 2, Sept., 1947; Clyde V. Kiser, "Fertility Trends and Differentials in the United States"; P. K. Whelpton, "Future Fertility of American Women," *Eugenics Quarterly,* I, no. 1, March, 1954.

baby-boom mothers are finally available.

Data for Great Britain and the United States indicate that the narrowing of class fertility-differentials already evident in the 1930's was accelerated by the baby boom. Differential rates of increase in fertility replaced the differential rates of decline of the previous period. There is, of course, no reason in principle why different socio-economic groups might not exhibit opposite trends—some increasing in fertility, others declining. But national societies seem to have responded as wholes to new conditions influencing childbearing and this is as true of the period after the Second World War as it was of the previous long period of declining fertility. Just as all intra-national groups participated in the decline, so did all groups contribute to the increase in the 1940's.

In both Great Britain and the United States, the less fertile high-status groups increased their fertility by greater amounts after 1940 than the more fertile low-status groups. The converging of socio-economic fertility-differentials was thus accelerated. In Great Britain non-manual and manual groups were already converging somewhat in the 1940's when fertility was still declining, and Evelyn Kitagawa observes that trends in differential fertility in the city of Chicago point to "the conclusion that the so-called 'postwar' developments in earlier age at marriage and the convergence of fertility differentials may have started about two decades ago. . . ." [23]

Rates of current fertility and of cumulative incomplete fertility for non-manual workers showed a greater increase in the United States than in

Great Britain. Moreover, in Great Britain the earlier pattern of greater increases among non-manual workers was reversed towards the end of the 1940's when manual workers showed greater increases at low marriage-durations.

Greater participation of the less fertile high-status groups in the baby boom has clearly increased the deviation from the inverse relation of fertility to status. In Great Britain non-manual workers remain less fertile than manual workers, but within these broad groups a direct relation between fertility and social class partially replaced the inverse pattern among marriages of less than fifteen years duration in 1951. Data on cohorts by socio-economic group are not yet available for the United States, but fertility-ratios for married women indicate sharp reversals of the inverse relation; the non-manual occupational groups of highest status show higher ratios than some manual groups.

In the past, planned families have invariably been smaller than unplanned families and continuously declining fertility has been associated with the spread of family planning. No inherent reason exists, however, why social and economic conditions favourable to childbearing might not induce married couples to decide to have slightly larger families. Certainly the capacity to "move ahead" one's reproductive schedule is a consequence of planning and has played a large part in the recent rise of current fertility-rates for high-status groups and in cumulative rates for cohorts of incomplete fertility. Changes in the scheduling of births may lead to changes in the ultimate size of family desired. Slightly larger families in the

---

[23] Kitagawa, "Differential Fertility in Chicago, 1920–1940," 493.

middle classes may be a consequence of the baby boom which has been incorporated into the middle-class concept of the standard of living.

The narrowing of class fertility-differentials since 1940 has also been effected by a relatively greater increase in the rate of marriage among the less fertile, later-marrying, upper classes. Greater lowering of the average age at marriage and of the proportions married at given ages in the high-status groups have undoubtedly resulted in as marked a narrowing of socio-economic differences in total fertility as in marital fertility.

The Future of Class Fertility-Differences

The view that the trend of class fertility-differences reflects the gradual spread of family limitation to all intranational population groups does not go much beyond the descriptive level of statement. Some strata exhibit greater susceptibility to family limitation than others, and the studies by Whelpton and Kiser and Lewis-Faning demonstrate the need for more intensive inquiries into the motivational and ideological predispositions towards family limitation and into their class distribution.

American sociologists have given considerable attention to the relative "openness" of class structures, conducting numerous studies of social-mobility rates and of the complex of attitudes associated with mobility aspirations. Demographers since Arsène Dumont have often suggested that the exceptionally low fertility of mobile persons may account for the persistence in Western societies of the inverse correlation of fertility and status. Westoff, for example, has advanced the hypothesis that "social class differences in fertility planning and differential fertility itself are related to the differential frequency of socio-economic ambitions and social mobility within and between class levels—the middle classes exhibiting the clearest manifestations of this type of 'atmosphere' and having the lowest fertility." [24] An increase in the frequency of mobility aspirations in low-status groups would, on this assumption, lead to an increase in the practice of family limitation and accelerate the contraction of class fertility-differentials.

Whether or not an actual increase in the amount of upward social mobility in Western urban-industrial societies has taken place in the past two decades is subject to dispute.[25] Certainly, increases in agricultural and industrial productivity have changed the occupational composition of the labour force and reduced the number of low-status occupations in proportion to those of high status.[26] On the other hand, the narrowing of both absolute and relative class fertility-differences restricts

[24] Charles F. Westoff, "The Changing Focus of Differential Fertility Research: The Social Mobility Hypothesis," *Milbank Memorial Fund Quarterly*, XXXI, no. 1, Jan., 1953, 31.

[25] William Petersen, "Is America Still the Land of Opportunity?" *Commentary*, XVI, no. 5, Nov., 1953; S. M. Lipset and Natalie Rogoff, "Class and Opportunity in Europe and the U.S." *Commentary*, XVIII, no. 6, Dec., 1954; Ely Chinoy, "Social Mobility Trends in the United States," *American Journal of Sociology*, XX, no. 2, April, 1955; Herbert Luethy, "Social Mobility Again—and Elites," *Commentary*, XX, no. 3, Sept., 1955.

[26] Nelson Foote and Paul K. Hatt, "Social Mobility and Economic Advancement," *American Economic Review*, XLIII, May, 1953.

upward mobility by reducing the population "surpluses" of the lower classes and rural areas.[27] The recent increases in the fertility of high-status groups enable them to supply a larger number of candidates for high-status occupations than formerly.

Trends in social mobility, however, are not the only or necessarily the most important feature of the class system related to differential fertility. If mobility and mobility aspirations are associated with low fertility, they can hardly be invoked to explain the *increases* in fertility shown by all socio-economic groups since 1940. Changes in mobility between occupational classes on the one hand, and the upgrading of entire classes as a result both of a redistribution of incomes and of a general rise in the standard of living on the other, are two distinct social processes which may affect fertility in different ways.

Significantly, before the baby boom of the 1940's, the contraction of class fertility-differences had proceeded furthest in the Scandinavian countries. They were the first Western nations where trade unions and co-operatives became powerful pressure groups favouring reduction of the economic inequalities of unregulated capitalism and succeeded in electing to power reformist socialist governments by secure majorities. Since 1940 a marked levelling of incomes has taken place in most Western countries, the result of a sustained period of prosperity during which the lower strata have benefited from increases in productivity, steep progressive taxation of income, and the social policies associated with the rise of the welfare state.

What is of crucial importance so far as the effects of these changes on fertility is concerned, is that "middle-class" standards of living have been brought within the reach of the least privileged strata and made popular by the new mass media. Accordingly, it is not surprising to find that class fertility-differences have diminished in the past thirty years or that, since 1940, all intra-national groups have responded similarly to conditions favourable to higher rates of childbearing.

It is the writer's belief that class fertility-differences are destined to disappear as a feature of the demographic structure of Western populations. This seems a more probable outcome of present trends than the emergence of the positive correlation of fertility to status predicted by several demographers. Yet within the general context of a growing uniformity of behaviour on the part of all classes and groups, some significant differences in standards of living and styles of life are likely to persist, and it is possible that a positive correlation of family size to income will develop within homogeneous occupational and educational groups which are small enough to serve as psychological reference groups for their members.[28] Indeed, studies of differential fertility within high-status groups in the United States and Sweden indicate that this development has already taken place.

Much research and analysis remains to be done before we shall fully understand the changes in fertility that are

[27] Elbridge Sibley, "Some Demographic Clues to Stratification," *American Sociological Review,* VII, no. 3, June, 1942.

[28] A similar hypothesis has been advanced by Albert Mayer and Carol Klapprodt, "Fertility Differentials in Detroit: 1920–1950," *Population Studies,* IX, no. 2, Nov., 1955, 15.

now taking place. The most useful type of inquiry into the underlying causes of trends in differential fertility must address itself primarily to the relation between fertility-trends and secular economic growth in Western industrial society, or, more accurately, to the changes in class structure and in the styles of life of the various classes that are a consequence of rapid and sustained economic expansion.[29] Inquiries into the individual psychological attributes associated with high or low fertility, such as the Indianapolis study by Whelpton and Kiser are of undoubted value, but they are supplementary to analysis of the effects on fertility of the historical transformations which have so profoundly altered the class structures and cultural outlooks of Western populations in the past half-century.

■ Urie Bronfenbrenner *

I. Background and Resources

During the past dozen years, a class struggle has been taking place in American social psychology—a struggle, fortunately, not *between* but *about* social classes. In the best social revolutionary tradition the issue was joined with a manifesto challenging the assumed superiority of the upper and middle classes and extolling the neglected virtues of the working class. There followed a successful revolution with an overthrow of the established order in favor of the victorious proletariat, which then reigned supreme—at least for a time. These dramatic changes had, as always, their prophets and precursors, but they reached a climax in 1946 with the publication of Davis and Havighurst's influential paper on "Social Class and Color Differences in Child Rearing." [1] The paper cited impressive statistical evidence in support of the thesis that middle-class parents "place their children under a stricter regimen, with more frustration of their impulses than do lower-class parents." For the next eight years, the Davis-Havighurst conclusion was taken as the definitive statement of

[29] Heberle ("Social Factors in Birth Control," 805) makes a similar general point, although, writing in 1941, he forecast a continuing decline in fertility to levels below replacement requirements—a trend he regarded as an inevitable result of structural changes in the economic system in the era of "late capitalism."

* This article was made possible only by the work of others; for, in effect, it is a synthesis of the contribution of a score of investigators over a score of years. The author is particularly grateful to Nancy Bayley, Melvin L. Kohn, Richard A. Littman, Daniel R. Miller, Fred L. Strodtbeck, Guy E. Swanson, and Martha S. White, who made available copies of their research reports prior to publication. For their invaluable suggestions, he is also indebted to John E. Anderson, Wesley Allinsmith, Alfred L. Baldwin, John A. Clausen, Robert J. Havighurst, Harry Levin, Eleanor E. Maccoby, and Theodore M. Newcomb.

[1] A. Davis and R. J. Havighurst, "Social Class and Color Differences in Child Rearing," *Am. Sociol. Rev.*, 1948, XI, 698–710.

SOURCE: E. E. Maccoby, T. M. Newcomb, and E. L. Hartley, eds., *Readings in Social Psychology*, 3rd ed. (New York: Holt, Rinehart and Winston, 1958), pp. 400–25. Copyright 1947, 1952, ©1958 by Holt, Rinehart and Winston, Inc. Reprinted by permission of the publisher.

class differences in socialization. Then, in 1954, came the counterrevolution; Maccoby and Gibbs published the first report [2] of a study of child-rearing practices in the Boston area which, by and large, contradicted the Chicago findings: in general, middle-class parents were found to be "more permissive" than those in the lower class.

In response, one year later, Havighurst and Davis [3] presented a re-analysis of their data for a subsample more comparable in age to the subjects of the Boston study. On the basis of a careful comparison of the two sets of results, they concluded that "the disagreements between the findings of the two studies are substantial and large" and speculated that these differences might be attributable either to genuine changes in child-rearing practices over time or to technical difficulties of sampling and item equivalence.

A somewhat different view, however, was taken by Sears, Maccoby, and Levin [4] in their final report of the Boston study. They argued that Davis and Havighurst's interpretation of the Chicago data as reflecting greater permissiveness for the working-class parent was unwarranted on two counts. First, they cited the somewhat contrasting results of still another research—that of Klatskin [5] in support of the view that class differences in feeding, weaning, scheduling, and toilet training "are not very stable or customary." Second, they contended that the Chicago findings of

greater freedom of movement for the lower-class child were more properly interpreted not as "permissiveness" but as "a reflection of rejection, a pushing of the child out of the way." Such considerations led the Boston investigators to conclude:

This re-examination of the Chicago findings suggests quite clearly the same conclusion that must be reached from Klatskin's study and from our own: the middle-class mothers were generally more permissive and less punitive toward their young children than were working-class mothers. Unfortunately, the opposite interpretation, as presented by Davis and Havighurst, has been widely accepted in education circles during the past decade. This notion of working-class permissiveness has been attractive for various reasons. It has provided an easy explanation of why working-class children have lower academic achievement motivation than do middle-class children—their mothers place less restrictive pressure on them. It has also provided a kind of compensatory comfort for those educators who have been working hard toward the goal of improving educational experiences for the noncollege-oriented part of the school population. In effect, one could say, lower-class children may lack the so highly desirable academic motivation, but the lack stems from a "good" reason —the children were permissively reared. [6]

It would appear that there are a number of unresolved issues between

---

[2] E. E. Maccoby, P. K. Gibbs, and the staff of the Laboratory of Human Development at Harvard University, "Methods of Child Rearing in Two Social Classes," in W. E. Martin and C. B. Standler (eds.), *Readings in Child Development* (New York: Harcourt, Brace & Co., 1954).

[3] Havighurst and Davis, "A Comparison of the Chicago and Harvard Studies of Social Class Differences in Child Rearing," *Am. Sociol. Rev.*, 1955, XX, 438–442.

[4] R. R. Sears, Maccoby, and H. Levin, *Patterns of Child Rearing* (Evanston, Ill.: Row, Peterson & Co., 1957).

[5] E. H. Klatskin, "Shifts in Child Care Practices in Three Social Classes under an Infant Care Program of Flexible Methodology," *Am. J. Orthopsychiat.*, 1952, XXII, 52–61.

[6] Sears, Maccoby, and Levin, *op. cit.*, pp. 446–447.

the protagonists of the principal points of view—issues both as to the facts and their interpretation. At such times it is not unusual for some third party to attempt a reappraisal of events in a broader historical perspective with the aid of documents and information previously not available. It is this which the present writer hopes to do. He is fortunate in having at his disposal materials not only from the past and present, but also seven manuscripts unpublished at the time of this writing, which report class differences in child-rearing practices at four different places and five points in time. To begin with, Bayley and Schaefer [7] have reanalyzed data from the Berkeley Growth Study to provide information on class differences in maternal-behavior ratings made from 1928 to 1932, when the children in the study were under three years old, and again from 1939 to 1942, when most of them were about ten years old. Information on maternal behavior in this same locale as of 1953 comes from a recent report by Martha Sturm White [8] of class differences in child-rearing practices for a sample of preschoolers in Palo Alto and environs. Miller and Swanson have made available relevant data from their two comprehensive studies of families in Detroit, one based on a stratified sample of families with children up to 19 years of age,[9] the other a specially selected sample of boys, ages 12 to 14 years.[10] Limited information on another sample of adolescent boys comes from Strodtbeck's investigation of "Family Interaction, Values, and Achievement." [11] Also, Littman, Moore, and Pierce-Jones [12] have recently completed a survey of child-rearing practices in Eugene, Oregon for a random sample of parents with children from two weeks to 14 years of age. Finally, Kohn [13] reports a comparison of child-training values among working and middle-class mothers in Washington, D.C.

In addition to these unpublished sources, the writer has made use of nine published researches.[14] In some

[7] N. Bayley and E. S. Schaefer, "Relationships between Socioeconomic Variables and the Behavior of Mothers toward Young Children," unpublished manuscript, 1957.

[8] M. S. White, "Social Class, Child Rearing Practices, and Child Behavior," Am. Sociol. Rev. 1957, XXII, 704–712.

[9] D. R. Miller and G. E. Swanson, The Changing American Parent (New York: John Wiley & Sons, Inc., in press).

[10] Miller and Swanson, Inner Conflict and Defense (New York: Henry Holt & Co., Inc., 1960).

[11] F. L. Strodtbeck, "Family Interaction, Values, and Achievement," in A. L. Baldwin, Bronfenbrenner, D. C. McClelland, and F. L. Strodtbeck, Talent and Society (Princeton, N.J.: D. Van Nostrand Co., 1958).

[12] R. A. Littman, R. A. Moore, and J. Pierce-Jones, "Social Class Differences in Child Rearing: A Third Community for Comparison with Chicago and Newton, Massachusetts," Am. Sociol. Rev., 1957, XXII, 694–704.

[13] M. L. Kohn, "Social Class and Parental Values," paper read at the Annual Meeting of the American Sociological Society, Washington, D.C., August, 27–29, 1957.

[14] H. E. Anderson (Chrmn.), The Young Child in the Home, report of the Committee on the Infant and Preschool Child, White House Conference on Child Health and Protection (New York: D. Appleton-Century, 1936); A. L. Baldwin, J. Kalhorn, and F. H. Breese, Patterns of Parent Behavior, Psychol. Monogr., 1945, LVIII, No. 3 (Whole No. 268); W. E. Boek, E. D. Lawson, A. Yankhauer, and M. B. Sussman, Social Class, Maternal Health, and Child Care (Albany: New York State Department of Health, 1957); Davis and Havighurst, op. cit.; E. M. Duvall, "Conceptions of Parenthood," Am. J. Sociol., 1946–1947, LII, 190–192; Klatskin, op. cit.; E. E. Maccoby and P. K. Gibbs, op. cit.; D. C. McClelland, A. Rindlisbacher, and R. De-

instances—notably for the monumental and regrettably neglected Anderson report—data were reanalyzed and significance tests computed in order to permit closer comparison with the results of other investigations. A full list and summary description of all the studies utilized in the present review appear in Table 1. Starred items designate the researches which, because they contain reasonably comparable data, are used as the principal bases for analysis.

II. Establishing Comparable Social-class Groupings

Although in most of the studies under consideration the investigators have based their classification of socioeconomic status (SES) explicitly or implicitly on the criteria proposed by Warner,[15] there was considerable variation in the number of social class categories employed. Thus, in the Anderson report data were analyzed in terms of seven SES levels, the New York survey distinguished five, the second Chicago and the two Detroit studies each had four, and Klatskin used three. The majority, however, following the precedent of Havighurst and Davis, differentiated two levels only—middle vs. lower or working class. Moreover, all of these last studies have been reanalyzed or deliberately designed to facilitate comparison with each other. We have already mentioned Havighurst and

Davis' efforts in this regard, to which the Boston group contributed by recalculating their data in terms of medians rather than means.[16] Both White and Littman et al. were interested in clarifying the contradictions posed by the Chicago and Boston studies and hence have employed many of the same indices. As a result, both necessity and wisdom called for dropping to the lowest common denominator and reanalyzing the results of the remaining researches in terms of a two-level classification of socioeconomic status.

In most instances, the delicate question of where to establish the cutting point was readily resolved. The crux of the distinction between middle and working class in all four of the studies employing this dichotomous break lies in the separation between white- and blue-collar workers. Fortunately, this same differentiation was made at some point along the scale in each of the other researches included in the basic analysis. Thus, for the several studies [17] using four levels of classification (upper and lower middle, upper and lower lower), the split occurred, as might be expected, between the two middle categories. For the New York State sample an examination of the occupations occurring at each of the five class levels used pointed to a cutting point between Classes III and IV. Klatskin, in comparing the social-class groupings of the New Haven study with the middle and lower classes of the original Chicago research, proposed a division be-

Charms, "Religious and Other Sources of Parental Attitudes toward Independence Training," in McClelland (ed.), *Studies in Motivation* (New York: Appleton-Century-Crofts, Inc., 1955); Sears, Maccoby, and Levin, *op. cit.*

[15] W. L. Warner, M. Meeker, and others, *Social Class in America* (Chicago: Science Research Associates, 1949).

[16] Sears, Maccoby, and Levin, *op. cit.*, p. 427.

[17] Duvall, *op. cit.*, Miller and Swanson, *Inner Conflict and Defense* and *The Changing American Parent, op. cit.*

TABLE 1. Description of Samples

Sample	Principal investigator source	Date of field work	Age	No. of cases Total	No. of cases Middle class	No. of cases Working class	Description of sample
National Cross Section,* I II III IV	Anderson	1932	0–1 1–5 6–12 1–12	494 2420 865 3285	217 1131 391 1522	277 1289 474 1763	National sample of white families "having child between 1 and 5 years of age" and "representing each major geographic area, each size of community and socioeconomic class in the United States." About equal number of males and females. SES (seven classes) based on Minnesota Scale for Occupational Classification.
Berkeley, Cal., I–II	Bayley and Schaefer	1928–32 1939–42	1–3 9–11	31 31	Information not available		Subjects of both sexes from Berkeley Growth Study, "primarily middle class but range from unskilled laborer, relief, and three-years education to professional, $10,000 income and doctoral degrees." SES measures include education, occupation (Taussig Scale), income, home and neighborhood rating, and composite scale.
Yellow Springs, Ohio	Baldwin	1940	3–12	124	Information not available		Families enrolled in Fels Research Institute Home Visiting Program. "Above average" in socioeconomic status but include "a number of uneducated parents and from the lower economic levels." No SES index computed but graphs show relationships by education and income.
Chicago, Ill., I*	Davis and Havighurst	1943	5 (approx.)	100	48	52	Middle-class sample "mainly" from mothers of nursery-school children; lower class from "areas of poor housing." All mothers native born. Two-level classification SES following Warner based on occupation, education, residential area, type of home, etc.

* Denotes studies used as principal bases for the analysis.

TABLE 1. (Cont.)

Sample	Principal investigator source	Date of field work	Age	No. of cases			Description of sample
				Total	Middle class	Working class	
Chicago, Ill., II	Duvall	1943–44	5 (approx.)	433	230	203	Negro and white (Jewish and non-Jewish) mothers. Data collected at "regular meetings of mothers' groups." SES classification (four levels) following Warner.
New Haven, Conn., I*	Klatskin	1949–50	1 (approx.)	222	114	108	Mothers in Yale Rooming-in Project returning for evaluation of baby at one year of age. SES classification (three levels) by Hollingshead, following Warner.
Boston, Mass.*	Sears, *et al.*	1951–52	4–6	372	198	174	Kindergarten children in two suburbs. Parents American born, living together. Twins, adoptions, handicapped children, and other special cases eliminated. Two-level SES classification follows Warner.
New Haven, Conn., II	Strodtbeck	1951–53	14–17	48	24	24	Third-generation Jewish and Italian boys representing extremes of under- and over-achievement in school. Classified into three SES levels on basis of occupation.
Detroit, Mich., I*	Miller and Swanson	1953	12–14	112	59	53	Boys in grades 7–8 above borderline intelligence within one year of age for grade, all at least third-generation Americans, Christian, from unbroken, nonmobile families of Northwest European stock. SES (four levels) assigned on basis of education and occupation.
Detroit, Mich., II*	Miller and Swanson	1953	0–18	479	Information not available		Random sample of white mothers with child under 19 and living with husband. Step-children and adoptions eliminated. SES (four levels) based primarily on U.S. census occupation categories.

TABLE 1. (Cont.)

Sample	Principal investigator source	Date of field work	Age	No. of cases			Description of sample
				Total	Middle class	Working class	
Palo Alto, Cal.*	White	1953	2½–5½	74	36	38	Native-born mothers of only one child, the majority expecting another. Unbroken homes in suburban area. SES (two levels) rated on Warner scale.
Urban Connecticut	McClelland et al.	1953–54	6–18	152	Information not available		Parents between 30–60 having at least one child between six and eighteen and representing four religious groups. "Rough check on class status" obtained from educational level achieved by parent.
Upstate New York	Boek, et al.	1955–56	3–7 months	1432	595	837	Representative sample of N.Y. state mothers of newborn children, exclusive of unmarried mothers. SES classification (five levels) as given on Warner scale.
Eugene, Oregon*	Littman, et al.	1955–56	0–14	206	86	120	Random sample of children from preschool classes and school rolls. Two SES levels assigned on same basis as in Boston study.
Washington, D.C.	Kohn and Clausen	1956–57	10–11	339	174	165	Representative samples of working- and middle-class mothers classified by Hollingshead's index of social position.

tween the first and second of her three SES levels, and we have followed her recommendation. Finally, for the seven-step scale of the Anderson report, the break was made between Classes III and IV, placing major clerical workers, skilled mechanics and retail business men in the middle class, and farmers, minor clerical positions, and semiskilled occupations in the working class.

In all of the above instances it was, of course, necessary to compute anew percentages and average scores for the two class levels and to calculate tests of significance (almost invariably X^2, two-tailed test, with Fisher-Yates correction for continuity). These computations, the results of which appear in the tables to follow, were performed for the following samples: National I–IV, New Haven I, Detroit I and II, and Upstate New York. All other figures and significance tests cited are taken from the original reports.

The effort to make the division between middle and working class at similar points for the basic samples, however successful it may have been, does not eliminate many other important sources of difference among the several researches. We now turn briefly to a consideration of these.

III. Problems of Comparability

The difficulties involved in comparing the results of more than a dozen studies conducted at different times and places for somewhat different purposes are at once formidable, delicate, and perilous. First of all, even when similar areas are explored in the interview, there is the problem of variation in the wording of questions. Indeed, however marked the changes may be in child-

rearing practices over time, they are not likely to be any more dramatic than the contrasts in the content and, above all, connotation of the queries put to mothers by social scientists from one decade to the next. Thus, the comprehensive report from the first White House Conference which covered the gamut from the number of children having rattles and changing their underwear to the number of toothbrushes by age, and the times the child was frightened by storms (analyzed by seven SES levels), says not a murmur about masturbation or sex play. Ten years later, in Chicago, six questions were devoted to this topic, including such items as: "How did you frighten them out of the habit?" and "What physical methods did you use (such as tight diaper, whipping them, tying their hands, and so forth)?" In the next decade the interviewer in the Boston study (perhaps only a proper Bostonian) was more restrained, or simply less interested. He asked only two questions: first, whether the mother noticed the child playing with himself; then, "How important do you feel it is to prevent this in a child?" Nor is the difficulty completely eliminated in those all-too-few instances when a similar wording is employed in two or more studies, for there is the very real possibility that in different contexts the same words have different meanings.

Serious problems arise from the lack of comparability not only in the questions asked but also in the character of the samples employed. Havighurst and Davis, for example, point out that the Chicago and Boston samples had different proportions of cases in the two bottom categories of the Warner scale of occupations. According to the investigators' reports, the Palo Alto and Eugene studies deviated even further in both directions, with the former containing few families from the lowest occupational categories, and the Oregon group exceeding previous studies in representation from these same bottom levels. The authors of several studies also call attention to the potential importance of existing differences in ethnicity, religious background, suburban vs. urban residence, and strength of mobility strivings.

A source of variation perhaps not sufficiently emphasized in these and other reports is the manner in which cases were selected. As Davis and Havighurst properly pointed out in their original publication, their sample was subject to possible bias "in the direction of getting a middle-class group which had been subjected to the kind of teaching about child rearing which is prevalent among the middle-class people who send their children to nursery schools." Equally important may be the relatively high proportion in the Chicago lower-class sample of mothers coming from East European and Irish background, or the four-year discrepancy in the average ages of the mothers at the two-class levels. The first New Haven sample consisted entirely of mothers enrolled in the Yale Rooming-in Project who were sufficiently interested to bring the baby back for a check-up a year after mother and child had left the hospital. As Klatskin recognized, this selectivity probably resulted in a "sample composed of the families most sympathetic to rooming-in ideology," a fact which, as she noted, was reflected in her research results. White's Palo Alto group consisted solely of mothers of only one child, most of whom were expecting a second offspring; cases were recruited from a variety of sources including friends, neighbors, personnel managers, nursery

school teachers, Public Health nurses, and maternal prenatal exercises classes. In short, virtually every sample had its special eccentricities. For some of these, one could guess at the extent and direction of bias; in others, the importance or effect of the selective features remains a mystery. Our difficulties, then, derive as much from ignorance as from knowledge—a fact which is underscored by the absence, for many of the samples, of such basic demographic information as the distribution of subjects by age and sex.

It is clear that many factors, some known and many more unknown, may operate to produce differences in results from one sample to the next. It is hardly likely, however, that these manifold influences will operate in a consistent direction over time or space. The possibility of obtaining interpretable findings, therefore, rests on the long chance that major trends, if they exist, will be sufficiently marked to override the effects of bias arising from variations in sampling and method. This is a rash and optimistic hope, but—somewhat to our own surprise—it seems to have been realized, at least in part, in the analyses that follow.

IV. Social Class Differences in Infant Care, 1930–1955

In interpreting reports of child-rearing practices it is essential to distinguish between the date at which the information was obtained and the actual period to which the information refers. This caution is particularly relevant in dealing with descriptions of infant care for children who (as in the Eugene or Detroit studies) may be as old as 12, 14, or 18 at the time of the interview. In such instances it is possible only to guess at the probable time at which the practice occurred by making due allowances for the age of the child. The problem is further complicated by the fact that none of the studies reports SES differences by age. The best one can do, therefore, is to estimate the median age of the group and from this approximate the period at which the practice may have taken place. For example, the second Detroit sample, which ranged in age from birth to 18 years, would have a median age of about nine. Since the field work was done in 1953, we estimate the date of feeding and weaning practices as about 1944.[18] It should be recognized, however, that the practices reported range over a considerable period extending from as far back as 1935 to the time of the interview in 1953. Any marked variation in child-rearing practices over this period could produce an average figure which would in point of fact be atypical for the middle year 1944. We

shall have occasion to point to the possible operation of this effect in some of the data to follow.

If dates of practices are estimated by the method outlined above, we find that the available data describe social-class differences in feeding, weaning, and toilet training for a period from about 1930 to 1955. The relevant information appears in Tables 2 through 4.

It is reasonable to suppose that a mother's reports of whether or not she employed a particular practice would be somewhat more reliable than her estimate of when she began or discontinued that practice. This expectation is borne out by the larger number of statistically significant differences in tables presenting data on prevalence (Tables 2 and 3) rather than on the timing of a particular practice (Tables 4–6). On the plausible assumption that the former data are more reliable, we shall begin our discussion by considering the results on frequency of breast feeding

TABLE 2. Frequency of Breast Feeding

1.	2.	No. of cases reporting			Percentage breast fed			9.
		3.	4.	5.	6.	7.	8.	
	Approx.	Total		Work-	Total		Work-	
	date of	sam-	Middle	ing	sam-	Middle	ing	Dif-
Sample	practice	ple	class	class	ple	class	class	ference *
National II	1930	1856	842	1014	80	78	82	−4†
National I	1932	445	201	244	40	29	49	−20†
Chicago I	1939	100	48	52	83	83	83	0
Detroit I	1941	112	59	53	62	54	70	−16
Detroit II	1944	200	70	130	Percentages not given			+
Eugene	1946–47	206	84	122	46	40	50	−10
Boston	1947–48	372	198	174	40	43	37	+6
New Haven I	1949–50	222	114	108	80	85	74	+11†
Palo Alto	1950	74	36	38	66	70	63	+7
Upstate New York	1955	1432	594	838	24	27	21	+6†

* Minus sign denotes lower incidence for middle class than for working class.
† Denotes difference significant at 5-percent level of confidence or better.

[18] It is true that because of the rising birth rate after World War II the sample probably included more younger than older children, but without knowledge of the actual distribution by age we have hesitated to make further speculative adjustments.

TABLE 3. Scheduled versus Self-demand Feeding

1. Sample	2. Approx. date of practice	No. of cases reporting			Percentage fed on demand			
		3. Total sample	4. Middle class	5. Working class	6. Total sample	7. Middle class	8. Working class	9. Difference *
National I	1932	470	208	262	16	7	23	−16†
Chicago I	1939	100	48	52	25	4	44	−40†
Detroit I	1941	97	52	45	21	12	53	−41†
Detroit II	1944	205	73	132	55	51	58	−7
Boston	1947–48	372	198	174	Percentages not given			−
New Haven I	1949–50	191	117	74	65	71	54	+17
Palo Alto	1950	74	36	38	59	64	55	+9

* Minus sign denotes lower incidence of self-demand feeding in middle class.

† Denotes difference significant at 5-percent level of confidence or better.

and scheduled feeding, which appear in Tables 2 and 3.

GENERAL TRENDS

We may begin by looking at general trends over time irrespective of social-class level. These appear in column 6 of Tables 2 and 3. The data for breast feeding are highly irregular, but there is some suggestion of decrease in this practice over the years.[19] In contrast, self-demand feeding is becoming more common. In both instances the trend is more marked (column 8) in the middle class; in other words, it is they especially who are doing the changing. This fact is reflected even more sharply

TABLE 4. Duration of Breast Feeding (for those breast fed)

Sample	Approx. date of practice	No. of cases ††			Median duration in months			
		Total sample	Middle class	Working class	Total sample	Middle class	Working class	Difference **
National II *	1930	1488	654	834	6.6	6.2	7.5	−1.3†
Chicago I	1939	83	40	43	3.5	3.4	3.5	−.1
Detroit I *	1941	69	32	37	3.3	2.8	5.3	−2.5
Eugene	1946–47	95	34	61	3.4	3.2	3.5	−.3
Boston	1947–48	149	85	64	2.3	2.4	2.1	+.3
New Haven I *	1949–50	177	97	80	3.6	4.3	3.0	+1.3
Upstate New York	1955	299	145	154	1.2	1.3	1.2	+.1

* Medians not given in original report but estimated from data cited.

† Denotes difference significant at 5-percent level of confidence or better.

** Minus sign denotes shorter duration for middle class than for working class.

†† Number of cases for Chicago, Eugene, Boston, and Upstate New York estimated from percentages cited.

[19] As indicated below, we believe that these irregularities are largely attributable to the highly selective character of a number of the samples (notably, New Haven I and Palo Alto) and that the downward trend in frequency and duration of breast feeding is probably more reliable than is reflected in the data of Tables 2 and 4.

TABLE 5. Age at Completion of Weaning (either breast or bottle)

Sample	Approx. date of practice	Total sample	Middle class	Working class	Total group	Middle class	Working class	Difference *
		No. of cases			Median age in months			
Chicago I	1940	100	48	52	11.3	10.3	12.3	−2.0†
Detroit I	1942	69	32	37	11.2	10.6	12.0	−1.4†
Detroit II	1945	190	62	128	—Under 12 months—			−
Eugene	1947–48	206	85	121	13.6	13.2	14.1	−.9
Boston	1948–49	372	198	174	12.3	12.0	12.6	−.6
New Haven I	1949–50	222	114	108	—Over 12 months—			−
Palo Alto	1951	68	32	36	13.1	14.4	12.6	+1.8

* Minus sign denotes earlier weaning for middle than for working class.
† Denotes difference significant at 5-percent level of confidence or better.

in column 9 which highlights a noteworthy shift. Here we see that in the earlier period—roughly before the end of World War II—both breast feeding and demand feeding were less common among the middle class than among the working class. In the later period, however, the direction is reversed; it is now the middle-class mother who more often gives her child the breast and feeds him on demand.

The data on duration of breast feeding (Table 4) and on the timing of weaning and bowel training (Tables 5 and 6) simply confirm, somewhat less reliably, all of the above trends. There is a general tendency in both social classes to wean the child earlier from the breast but, apparently, to allow him to suck from a bottle till a somewhat later age. Since no uniform reference points were used for securing information on toilet training in the several studies (i.e., some investigators report percentage training at six months, others at ten months, still oth-

TABLE 6. Toilet Training

Sample	Approx. date practice begun	Bowel training	Bladder training	Beginning bowel training	End bowel training	Beginning bladder training	End bladder training
		No. of cases		Direction of relationship			
National II	1931	2375	2375		−†		−*
National I	1932	494	494		−	−	
Chicago I	1940	100	220†	−†	−	−†**	+†
Detroit I	1942	110	102	−	−	+	−
Detroit II	1945	216	200	+†	−		
Eugene	1947–48	206	206	+	−	+	+
Boston	1948–49	372		−	+†		
New Haven I	1950–51	214		+†			
Palo Alto	1951	73		+†			

* Minus sign indicates that middle class began or completed training earlier than lower class.
† Denotes difference significant at 5-percent level of confidence or better.
** Based on data from 1946 report.

ers at 12 or 18 months), Table 6 shows only the direction of the difference between the two social classes. All these figures on timing point to the same generalization. In the earlier period, middle-class mothers were exerting more pressure; they weaned their children from the breast and bottle and carried out bowel and bladder training before their working-class counterparts. But in the last ten years the trend has been reversed—it is now the middle-class mother who trains later.

These consistent trends take on richer significance in the light of Wolfenstein's impressive analysis [20] of the content of successive editions of the United States Children's Bureau bulletin on *Infant Care*. She describes the period 1929–38 (which corresponds to the earlier time span covered by our data) as characterized by:

> . . . a pervasive emphasis on regularity, doing everything by the clock. Weaning and introduction of solid foods are to be accomplished with great firmness, never yielding for a moment to the baby's resistance. . . . bowel training . . . must be carried out with great determination as early as possible. . . . The main danger which the baby presented at this time was that of dominating the parents. Successful child training meant winning out against the child in the struggle for domination.

In the succeeding period, however,

> . . . all this was changed. The child became remarkably harmless. . . . His main active aim was to explore his world. . . . When not engaged in exploratory undertakings, the baby needs care

and attention; and giving these when he demands them, far from making him a tyrant, will make him less demanding later on. At this time mildness is advocated in all areas: thumbsucking and masturbation are not to be interfered with; weaning and toilet training are to be accomplished later and more gently.[21]

The parallelism between preachment and practice is apparent also in the use of breast feeding. Up until 1945, "breast feeding was emphatically recommended," with "warnings against early weaning." By 1951, "the long-term intransigence about breast feeding is relaxed." States the bulletin edition of that year: "Mothers who find bottle feeding easier should feel comfortable about doing it that way."

One more link in the chain of information completes the story. There is ample evidence that both in the early and the later period, middle-class mothers were much more likely than working-class mothers to be exposed to current information on child care. Thus Anderson cites table after table showing that parents from higher SES levels read more books, pamphlets, and magazines, and listen to more radio talks on child care and related subjects. This in 1932. Similarly, in the last five years, White, in California, and Boek, in New York, report that middle-class mothers are much more likely than those in the working class to read Spock's best-seller, *Baby and Child Care* [22] and similar publications.

Our analysis suggests that the mothers not only read these books but take

---

[20] M. Wolfenstein, "Trends in Infant Care," *Am. J. Orthopsychiat.*, 1953, XXIII, 120–130. Similar conclusions were drawn in an earlier report by Stendler surveying 60 years of child-training practices as advocated in three popular women's magazines. *Cf.* C. B. Stendler, "Sixty Years of Child Training Practices," *J. Pediatrics*, 1950, XXXVI, 122–134.

[21] Wolfenstein, *op. cit.*, p. 121.

[22] Benjamin Spock, *Baby and Child Care* (New York: Pocket Books, Inc., 1957).

them seriously, and that their treatment of the child is affected accordingly. Moreover, middle-class mothers not only read more but are also more responsive; they alter their behavior earlier and faster than their working-class counterparts.

In view of the remarkably close parallelism in changes over time revealed by Wolfenstein's analysis and our own, we should perhaps not overlook a more recent trend clearly indicated in Wolfenstein's report and vaguely discernible as well in the data we have assembled. Wolfenstein asserts that, since 1950, a conservative note has crept into the child-training literature; "there is an attempt to continue . . . mildness, but not without some conflicts and misgivings. . . . May not continued gratification lead to addiction and increasingly intensified demands?" [23] In this connection it is perhaps no mere coincidence that the differences in the last column of Tables 2 to 4 show a slight drop after about 1950; the middle class is still more "relaxed" than the working class, but the differences are not so large as earlier. Once again, practice may be following preachment—now in the direction of introducing more limits and demands—still within a permissive framework. We shall return to a consideration of this possibility in our discussion of class differences in the training of children beyond two years of age.

Taken as a whole, the correspondence between Wolfenstein's data and our own suggests a general hypothesis extending beyond the confines of social class as such: *child-rearing practices are likely to change most quickly in those segments of society which have closest access and are most receptive to the* *agencies or agents of change (e.g., public media, clinics, physicians, and counselors).* From this point of view, one additional trend suggested by the available data is worthy of note: rural families appear to "lag behind the times" somewhat in their practices of infant care. For example, in Anderson's beautifully detailed report, there is evidence that in 1932 farm families (Class IV in his sample) were still breast feeding their children more frequently but being less flexible in scheduling and toilet training than nonfarm families of roughly comparable socioeconomic status. Similarly, there are indications from Miller and Swanson's second Detroit study that, with SES held constant, mothers with parents of rural background adhere to more rigid techniques of socialization than their urban counterparts. Finally, the two samples in our data most likely to contain a relatively high proportion of rural families—Eugene, Oregon and Upstate New York—are also the ones which are slightly out of line in showing smaller differences in favor of middle-class permissiveness.

The above observations call attention to the fact that the major time trends discerned in our data, while impressive, are by no means uniform. There are several marked exceptions to the rule. True, some of these can be "explained" in terms of special features of the samples employed. A case in point is the New Haven study, which —in keeping with the rooming-in ideology and all that this implies—shows the highest frequency and duration of breast feeding for the postwar period, as well as the greatest prevalence of feeding on demand reported in all the surveys examined. Other discrepancies

[23] Wolfenstein, *op. cit.*, p. 121.

may be accounted for, at least in part, by variations in time span encompassed by the data (National 1930 vs. 1932), the demonstrated differential rate in breast feeding for first vs. later children (Palo Alto vs. National 1930 or Boston), ethnic differences (Boston vs. Chicago), contrasting ages of mothers in middle- vs. working-class samples (Chicago), etc. All of these explanations, however, are "after the fact" and must therefore be viewed with suspicion.

SUMMARY

Despite our inability to account with any confidence for all departures from the general trend, we feel reasonably secure in our inferences about the nature of this trend. To recapitulate, over the last 25 years, even though breast feeding appears to have become less popular, American mothers—especially in the middle class—are becoming increasingly permissive in their feeding and toilet-training practices during the first two years of the child's life. The question remains whether this tendency is equally apparent in the training of the child as he becomes older. We turn next to a consideration of this issue.

V. Class Differences in the Training of Children beyond the Age of Two

Once we leave the stage of infancy, data from different studies of child training become even more difficult to compare. There are still greater variations in the questions asked from one research to the next, and results are reported in different types of units (e.g., relating scales with varying numbers of steps diversely defined). In some instances (as in the Chicago, Detroit II, and, apparently, Eugene surveys) the questions referred not to past or current practices but to the mother's judgment about what she would do at some later period when her child would be older. Also, when the samples include children of widely varying ages, it is often difficult to determine at what period the behavior described by the mother actually took place. Sometimes a particular age was specified in the interviewer's question and when this occurred, we have made use of that fact in estimating the approximate date of the practice. More often, however, such information was lacking. Accordingly, our time estimates must be regarded as subject to considerable error. Finally, even though we deal with substantially the same researches considered in the analysis of infant care, the total period encompassed by the data is appreciably shorter. This is so because the mothers are no longer being asked to recall how they handled their child in infancy; instead they are reporting behavior which is contemporary, or at least not far removed, from the time of the interview.

All of these considerations combine to restrict severely our ability to identify changes in practices over time. Accordingly, the absence of evidence for such changes in some of the data is perhaps more properly attributed to the limitations of our measures than to the actual course of events.

PERMISSIVENESS AND RESTRICTION ON FREEDOM OF MOVEMENT

The areas of impulse expression documented in Table 7 reflect a continuity in treatment from babyhood into early childhood. With only one minor, statistically insignificant exception, the re-

TABLE 7. Permissiveness Toward Impulse Expression

Sample	Approx. date of practice	No. of cases reported	Direction of trend for middle class				
			Oral behavior	Toilet accidents	Sex	Aggression
National I	1932	470			More infants allowed to play on bed unclothed.*	
Chicago	1943	100		Treated by ignoring,* reasoning or talking, rather than scolding,* slapping* or showing disgust.*		More children allowed to "fight so long as they don't hurt each other badly."*
Detroit II	1946	70–88	Less often disciplined for thumb sucking.		Less often disciplined for touching sex organs.	
New Haven	1949–50	216	Less often disapproved for thumb sucking, eating habits, mannerisms, etc.*			
Eugene	1950	206		Less often treated by spanking or scolding.	More permissive toward child's sexual behavior.*	Fewer children allowed "to fight so long as they don't hurt each other badly." More permissiveness toward general aggression.

* Indicates difference between classes significant at the 5-percent level or better.
† The difference between percentages is not significant but the difference between ratings is significant at the 5-percent level or better.

TABLE 7. (*Cont.*)

Sample	Approx. date of practice	No. of cases reported	Direction of trend for middle class			
			Oral behavior	Toilet accidents	Sex	Aggression
Boston	1951–52	372	Less restriction on use of fingers for eating.*	Less severe toilet training.*	Higher sex permissiveness (general index).*	More permissive of aggression toward parents,* children† and siblings. Less punishment of aggression toward parents.*
Palo Alto	1953	73		Less severe toilet training.*		More permissive of aggression toward parents.* Less severe punishment of aggression toward parents.

sults depict the middle-class parent as more permissive in all four spheres of activity: oral behavior, toilet accidents, sex, and aggression. There is no suggestion of a shift over the somewhat truncated time span. The now-familiar trend reappears, however, in the data on restriction of freedom of movement shown in Table 8.

In Table 8 we see a gradual shift over time with the middle class being more restrictive in the 1930's and early 1940's but becoming more permissive during the last decade.

Training for Independence and Achievement

Thus far, the trends that have appeared point predominantly in one direction—increasing leniency on the part of middle-class parents. At the same time, careful consideration of the nature of these data reveals that they are, in a sense, one-sided: they have been concerned almost entirely with the parents' response to the expressed needs and wishes of the child. What

TABLE 8. Restriction on Freedom of Movement

Sample	Approx. date of practice	No. of cases reported	Age	Item	Direction of relationship *
National II	1932	2289	1–5	Play restricted to home yard	−
				Play restricted to block	+
				Play restricted to neighborhood	+†
				No restriction on place of play	+†
National III	1932	669	6–12	Child goes to movie with parents	+
				Child goes to movie with other children	+
National IV	1932	2414	1–12	Child goes to bed earlier	+
Chicago	1943	100	5	Age at which child is allowed to go to movie alone or with other children	+†
				Age at which child is allowed to go downtown	−†
				Time at which children are expected in at night	+†
New Haven I	1949–50	211	1	Definite bed time	−†
Boston	1951–52	372	5	Restriction on how far child may go from home	−
				Frequency of checking on child's whereabouts	−**
				Strictness about bed time	−†
				Amount of care taken by persons other than parents	−†
Detroit II	1953	136	0–18	Child supervised closely after 12 years of age	−†
Palo Alto	1953	74	2½–5½	Extent of keeping track of child	0

* Plus sign denotes greater restriction for middle class.
† Denotes difference significant at 5-percent level or better.
** The difference between percentages is not significant but the difference between mean ratings is significant at the 5-percent level or better.

about the child's response to the needs and wishes of the parent, and the nature of these parental demands? The results presented in Table 9 are of especial interest since they shed light on all three aspects of the problem. What is more, they signal a dramatic departure from the hitherto unchallenged trend toward permissiveness.

Three types of questions have been asked with respect to independence training. The first is of the kind we have been dealing with thus far; for example, the Boston investigators inquired about the mother's reaction to the child's expression of dependence (hanging on to the mother's skirt, demanding attention, etc.). The results for this sort of query, shown in column 6 of Table 9, are consistent with previous findings for the postwar period; middle-class mothers are more tolerant of the child's expressed needs than are working-class mothers. The second type of question deals with the child's progress in taking care of himself and assuming responsibility (column 7). Here no clear trend is apparent, although there is some suggestion of greater solicitousness on the part of the middle-class mother. For example, in the 1932 material the middle-class child excelled in dressing and feeding himself only "partially," not "completely." In the 1935 Palo Alto study, the middle-class mother viewed her child as more dependent even though he was rated less so by the outside observer. It would appear that the middle-class mothers may be on the alert for signs of dependency and anxious lest they push too fast.

Yet, as the data of column 8 clearly indicate, they push nevertheless. By and large, the middle-class mother expects more of her child than her working-class counterpart. All five of the statistically significant differences support this tendency and most of the remaining results point in the same direction. The conclusion is further underscored by the findings on class differences in parental aspirations for the child's academic progress, shown in column 9. The only exception to the highly reliable trend is in itself noteworthy. In the Boston study, more middle-class mothers expected their children to go to college, but they were less likely to say that it was important for their child to do well in school. Are these mothers merely giving what they consider to be the socially acceptable response, or do they really, as Sears and his colleagues suggest, have less cause for concern because their children are living up to expectations?

The preceding question raises an even broader and more significant issue. Our data indicate that middle-class parents are becoming increasingly permissive in response to the child's expressed needs and desires. Yet, these same parents have not relaxed their high levels of expectations for ultimate performance. Do we have here a typical instance of Benedict's "discontinuity in cultural conditioning," [24] with the child first being encouraged in one pattern of response and then expected to perform in a very different fashion? If so, there are days of disappointment ahead for middle-class fathers and mothers. Or, are there other elements in the parent-child relationship of the middle-class family which impel the child to effort despite, or, perhaps, even because of, his early experiences of relatively

[24] R. Benedict, "Continuities and Discontinuities in Cultural Conditioning," *Psychiat.*, 1938, I, 161–167.

TABLE 9. Training for Independence and Academic Achievement

1. Sample	2. Approx. date of practice	3. No. of cases reported	4. Age	5. Item	Direction of relationship			
					6. Parents' response to child's dependency	7. Child's behavior *	8. Parental demands and expectations	9. Academic aspirations for child *
National II	1932	2380	1–5	Dress self not at all		+		
				Dress self partially		+		
				Dress self completely		–		
		2391		Feed self not at all		–		
				Feed self partially		+		
				Feed self completely		–		
		2301		Children read to by parents				+
National III	1932	865	6–12	Runs errands		0		
				Earns money		–		
				Receive outside lessons in music, art, etc.				+†
National IV	1932	2695	1–12	Books in the home				+†
Chicago I	1943	100	5	Age child expected to dress self			0	
				Expected to help at home by age 5			+†	
				Expected to help with younger children			+†	
				Girls expected to begin to cook			+	
				Girls expected to help with dishes			+	
				Child expected to finish high school only				+†
				Child expected to finish college				+†
				Father teaches and reads to children				+†
Detroit II	1946	128	0–18	All right to leave three-year-old with sitter			0	
	1947	128		Expected to pick up own toys			+	
	1948	127		Expected to dress self by age 5			+	
	1948	126		Expected to put away clothes by age 5			+†	
				Children requested to run errands at age 7			0	
				Agree child should be on his own as early as possible			+	

* Plus sign denotes greater independence or achievement required for middle-class child.
† Difference between classes significant at the 5-percent level or better.
** This is the entire high-school sample which Strodtbeck surveyed in order to select his experimental and control group.

400

TABLE 9. (Cont.)

1. Sample	2. Approx. date of practice	3. No. of cases reported	4. Age	5. Item	6. Parents' response to child's dependency behavior*	7. Child's behavior*	8. Parental demands and expectations	9. Academic aspirations for child*
					Direction of relationship			
Urban Connecticut	1950	152	6–18	Age of expected mastery (Winterbottom scale)			+†	
Eugene	1950	206	0–18	Household rules and chores expected of children			+	
Boston	1951–52	372	5	Parent permissive of child dependency	−†			
				Punishment, irritation for dependency	−†			
				Parents give child regular job around house			0	
				Importance of child's doing well at school				−†
				Expected to go to college				+†
New Haven II	1951–53	48	14–17	Father subscribes to values of independence and mastery			+†	
		1151**	14–17	Expected to go to college				+†
				Family checks over homework				+†
Palo Alto	1953	74	2½–5½	M's report of child's dependency		−		
				Amount of attention child wants		+		
				Child objects to separation		−		
				Judge's rating of dependency		+		
Upstate New York	1955	1433	0–1	Mother's educational aspirations for child				+†

401

uninhibited gratification? The data on class differences in techniques of discipline shed some light on this question.

TECHNIQUES OF DISCIPLINE

The most consistent finding documented in Table 10 is the more frequent use of physical punishment by working-class parents. The middle class, in contrast, resort to reasoning, isolation, and what Sears and his colleagues have referred to as "love-oriented" discipline techniques.[25] These are methods which rely for their effect on the child's fear of loss of love. Miller and Swanson referred to substantially the same class of phenomena by the term "psychological discipline," which for them covers such parental behaviors as appeals to guilt, expressions of disappointment, and the use of symbolic rather than direct rewards and punishments. Table 10 shows all available data on class differences in the use of corporal punishment, reasoning, isolation, and "love-oriented" techniques. Also, in order to avoid the risks, however small, involved in wearing theoretical blinders, we have listed in the last column of the table all other significant class differences in techniques of discipline reported in the studies we have examined.

From one point of view, these results highlight once again the more lenient policies and practices of middle-class families. Such parents are, in the first place, more likely to overlook offenses, and when they do punish, they are less likely to ridicule or inflict physical pain. Instead, they reason with the youngster, isolate him, appeal to guilt,

show disappointment,—in short, convey in a variety of ways, on the one hand, the kind of behavior that is expected of the child; on the other, the realization that transgression means the interruption of a mutually valued relationship.

These consistent class differences take on added significance in the light of the finding, arrived at independently both by the Boston and Detroit investigators, that "love-oriented" or "psychological" techniques are more effective than other methods for bringing about desired behavior. Indeed, both groups of researchers concluded on the basis of their data that physical punishment for aggression tends to increase rather than decrease aggressive behavior. From the point of view of our interest, these findings mean that middle-class parents, though in one sense more lenient in their discipline techniques, are using methods that are actually more compelling. Moreover, the compelling power of these practices, rather than being reduced, is probably enhanced by the more permissive treatment accorded to middle-class children in the early years of life. The successful use of withdrawal of love as a discipline technique implies the prior existence of a gratifying relationship; the more love present in the first instance, the greater the threat implied in its withdrawal.

In sum, to return to the issue posed in the preceding section, our analysis suggests that middle-class parents are in fact using techniques of discipline which are likely to be effective in evoking the behavior desired in the child. Whether the high levels of expectation held by such parents are actually

---

[25] These investigators also classify "isolation" as a love-oriented technique, but since this specific method is reported on in several other studies as well, we have tabulated the results separately to facilitate comparison.

TABLE 10. Techniques of Discipline

Sample	Approx. date of practice	No. of cases reporting	Age	Direction of relationship*				Nature of love-oriented technique	Other significant trends for middle class
				Physical punishment	Reasoning	Isolation	Love-oriented technique		
National II	1932	1947	1–5	–†					
National III	1932	839	6–12			+†			Infractions more often ignored†
National IV	1932	3130	1–12		+†				More children deprived of pleasure as punishment
Chicago I	1943	100	5	+		–	+†	Praise for good behavior	Soiling child more often ignored,† rather than spanked† or shown disgust
Detroit I	1950	115	12–14	–†			+†	Mother expresses disappointment or appeals to guilt	
Detroit II	1950	222	0–19	–			+	Mother uses symbolic rather than direct rewards and punishments	
Eugene	1950	206	0–18	–	0	+†	0	No difference in overall use of praise or withdrawal of love	
Boston	1951–52	372	5	–†	+	+			Less use of ridicule,† deprivation of privileges** or praise for no trouble at the table†

* Plus sign indicates practice was more common in middle class than in working class.
† Denotes difference between classes significant at 5-percent level or better.
** The difference between percentages is not significant but the difference between mean ratings is significant at the 5-percent level or better.

achieved is another matter. At least, there would seem to be some measure of functional continuity in the way in which middle-class parents currently treat their children from infancy through childhood.

Before we leave consideration of the data of Table 10, one additional feature of the results deserves comment. In the most recent study reported, the Boston research, there were three departures from the earlier general trend. First, no class difference was found in the over-all use of praise. Second, working-class parents actually exceeded those of the middle class in praising good behavior at the table. Third, in contrast to earlier findings, the working-class mother more frequently punished by withdrawing privileges. Although Sears *et al.* did not classify "withdrawal of privileges" as a love-oriented technique, the shift does represent a change in the direction of what was previously a method characteristic of the middle-class parent. Finally, there is no clear trend in the differential use of love-oriented techniques by the two social classes. If we view the Boston study as reflecting the most recent trends in methods of discipline, then either middle-class mothers are beginning to make less use of techniques they previously relied upon, or the working class is starting to adopt them. We are inclined toward the latter hypothesis in the belief that the working class, as a function of increasing income and education, is gradually reducing its "cultural lag." Evidence from subsequent studies, of course, would be necessary to confirm this speculative interpretation, since the results cited may merely be a function of features peculiar to the Boston study and not typical of the general trend.

OVERALL CHARACTER OF THE PARENT-CHILD RELATIONSHIP

The material considered so far has focused on specific practices employed by the parent. A number of researches document class differences as well in variables of a more molar sort—for example, the emotional quality of the parent-child relationship as a whole. These investigations have the additional advantage of reaching somewhat further back in time, but they also have their shortcomings. First of all, the results are not usually reported in the conventional form of percentages or means for specific social-class levels. In some studies the findings are given in terms of correlation coefficients. In others, social status can only be estimated from educational level. In others still, the data are presented in the form of graphs from which no significance tests can be computed. Partly to compensate for this lack of precision and comparability, partly to complete the picture of available data on class differences in child rearing, we cite in Table 11 not only the results from these additional studies of molar variables but also all other statistically significant findings from researches considered previously which might have bearing on the problem at hand. In this way, we hope as well to avoid the bias which occasionally arises from looking only at those variables in which one has a direct theoretical interest.

The data of Table 11 are noteworthy in a number of respects. First, we have clear confirmation that, over the entire 25-year period, middle-class parents have had a more acceptant, equalitarian relationship with their children. In many ways, the contrast is epitomized in Duvall's distinction between

TABLE 11. Overall Character of Parent-child Relationship

Sample	Approx. date of practice	No. of cases reported	Age	Middle-class trend	Working-class trend
Berkeley I	1928–32	31	1–3	Grants autonomy Cooperative Equalitarian	Expresses affection Excessive contact Intrusive Irritable Punitive Ignores child
National I	1932	494	0–1		Baby picked up when cries†
National IV	1932	3239	1–12	Higher percentage of children punished†	Nothing done to allay child's fears†
Yellow Springs, Ohio	1940	124	3–12	Acceptant-democratic	Indulgent Active-rejectant
Berkeley II	1939–42	31	9–11	Grants autonomy Cooperative Equalitarian Expresses affection	Excessive contact Intrusive Irritable Punitive Ignores child
Chicago I	1943	100	5		Father plays with child more†
Chicago II	1943–44	433	1–5	"Developmental" conception of "good mother" and "good child"†	"Traditional" conception of "good mother" and "good child"†
New Haven I	1949–50	219	1	More necessary discipline to prevent injury or danger†	More prohibitive discipline beyond risk of danger or injury
Boston	1951–52	372	5	Mother warmer toward child† Father warmer toward child* Father exercises more authority* Mother has higher esteem for father† Mother delighted about pregnancy† Both parents more often share authority*	Father demands instant obedience† Child ridiculed† Greater rejection of child† Emphasis on neatness, cleanliness, and order† Parents disagree more on child-rearing policy*
New Haven II	1951–53	48	14–17	Fathers have more power in family decisions† Parents agree in value orientations†	
Palo Alto	1953	73	2½–5½	Baby picked up when cries†	Mother carries through demands rather than dropping the subject†
Eugene	1955–56	206	0–18	Better relationship between father and child†	
Washington, D.C.	1956–57	400	10–11	Desirable qualities are happiness,* considerateness,* curiosity,* self-control*	Desirable qualities are neatness and cleanliness,* obedience*

* Trend significant at 5-percent level or better.
† The difference between percentages is not significant but the difference between mean ratings is significant at the 5-percent level or better.

the "developmental" and "traditional" conceptions of mother and child. Duvall asked the mothers in her sample to list the "five things that a good mother does" and the "five things that a good child does." Middle-class mothers tended to emphasize such themes as "guiding and understanding," "relating herself lovingly to the child," and making sure that he "is happy and contented," "shares and co-operates with others," and "is eager to learn." In contrast, working-class mothers stressed the importance of keeping house and child "neat and clean," "training the child to regularity," and getting the child "to obey and respect adults."

What is more, this polarity in the value orientation of the two social classes appears to have endured. In data secured as recently as 1957, Kohn [26] reports that working-class mothers differ from those of the middle class in their choice of characteristics most desired in a child; the former emphasize "neatness, cleanliness, and obedience," while the latter stress "happiness, considerateness, and self-control."

Yet, once again, it would be a mistake to conclude that the middle-class parent is exerting less pressure on his children. As the data of Table 11 also show, a higher percentage of middle-class children are punished in some manner, and there is more "necessary" discipline to prevent injury or danger. In addition, though the middle-class father typically has a warmer relationship with the child, he is also likely to have more authority and status in family affairs.

Although shifts over time are difficult to appraise when the data are so variable in specific content, one trend is sufficiently salient to deserve com-

ment. In the early Berkeley data the working-class parent is more expressive of affection than his middle-class counterpart. But in the follow-up study of the same children eight years later the trend is reversed. Perhaps the same mothers behave differently toward younger and older children. Still, the item "Baby picked up when cries" yields a significant difference in favor of the working-class mother in 1932 and a reliable shift in the opposite direction in 1953. *Sic transit gloria Watsoniensis!*

Especially with terms as heavily value laden as those which appear in Table 11, one must be concerned with the possibility that the data in the studies examined document primarily not actual behavior but the middle-class mother's superior knowledge of the socially acceptable response. Undoubtedly, this factor operates to inflate the reported relationships. But there are several reassuring considerations. First, although the items investigated vary widely in the intensity of their value connotations, all show substantially the same trends. Second, four of the studies reported in Table 11 (Berkeley I and II, Yellow Springs, and New Haven II) are based not on the mother's responses to an interview but on observation of actual interaction among family members. It seems highly unlikely, therefore, that the conclusions we have reached apply only to professed opinions and not to real behavior as well.

VI. Retrospect and Prospect

It is interesting to compare the results of our analysis with the traditional view of the differences between the

---

[26] Kohn, *op. cit.*

middle- and lower-class styles of life, as documented in the classic descriptions of Warner,[27] Davis,[28] Dollard,[29] and the more recent accounts of Spinley,[30] Clausen,[31] and Miller and Swanson.[32] In all these sources the working class is typically characterized as impulsive and uninhibited, the middle class as more rational, controlled, and guided by a broader perspective in time. Thus Clausen writes:

> The lower class pattern of life . . . puts a high premium on physical gratification, on free expression of aggression, on spending and sharing. Cleanliness, respect for property, sexual control, educational achievement—all are highly valued by middle class Americans—are of less importance to the lower class family or are phrased differently.[33]

To the extent that our data even approach this picture, it is for the period before World War II rather than for the present day. The modern middle class has, if anything, extended its time perspective so that the tasks of child training are now accomplished on a more leisurely schedule. As for the lower class the fit is far better for the actual behavior of parents rather than for the values they seek to instill in their children. As reflected in the data of Tables 10 and 11, the lower-class parent—though he demands compliance and control in his child—is himself more aggressive, expressive, and impulsive than his middle-class coun-

terpart. Even so, the picture is a far cry from the traditional image of the casual and carefree lower class. Perhaps the classic portrait is yet to be seen along the skid rows and Tobacco Roads of the nation, but these do not lie along the well-trodden paths of the survey researcher. He is busy ringing doorbells, no less, in the main section of the lower-class district, where most of the husbands have steady jobs and, what is more important, the wife is willing to answer the door and the interviewer's questions. In this modern working-class world there may be greater freedom of emotional expression, but there is no laxity or vagueness with respect to goals of child training. Consistently over the past 25 years, the parent in this group has emphasized what are usually regarded as the traditional middle-class virtues of cleanliness, conformity, and control, and although his methods are not so effective as those of his middle-class neighbors, they are perhaps more desperate.

Perhaps this very desperation, enhanced by early exposure to impulse and aggression, leads working-class parents to pursue new goals with old techniques of discipline. While accepting middle-class levels of aspiration he has not yet internalized sufficiently the modes of response which make these standards readily achievable for himself or his children. He has still to learn to wait, to explain, and to give and with-

---

[27] W. L. Warner and P. S. Lunt, *The Social Life of a Modern Community* (New Haven: Yale University Press, 1942); Warner, Meeker, and Others, *op. cit.*

[28] A. Davis, B. Gardner, and M. R. Gardner, *Deep South* (Chicago: University of Chicago Press, 1941).

[29] J. Dollard, *Caste and Class in a Southern Town* (New Haven: Yale University Press, 1937).

[30] B. M. Spinley, *The Deprived and the Privileged: Personality Development in English Society* (London: Routledge & Kegan Paul, Ltd., 1953).

[31] J. A. Clausen, "Social and Psychological Factors in Narcotics Addiction," *Law and Contemporary Problems*, 1957, XXII, 34–51.

[32] Miller and Swanson, *The Changing American Parent, op. cit.*

[33] Clausen, *op. cit.*, p. 42.

hold his affection as the reward and price of performance.

As of 1957, there are suggestions that the cultural gap may be narrowing. Spock has joined the Bible on the working-class shelf. If we wish to see the shape of the future, we can perhaps do no better than to look at the pages of the newly revised edition of this ubiquitous guide-book. Here is a typical example of the new look—a passage not found in the earlier version:

> If the parent can determine in which respects she may be too permissive and can firm up her discipline, she may, if she is on the right track, be delighted to find that her child becomes not only better behaved but much happier. Then she can really love him better, and he in turn responds to this.[34]

Apparently "love" and "limits" are both watchwords for the coming generation of parents. As Mrs. Johnson, down in the flats, puts away the hairbrush and decides to have a talk with her unruly youngster "like the book says," Mrs. Thomas, on the hill, is dutifully striving to overcome her guilt at the thought of giving John the punishment she now admits he deserves. If both ladies are successful, the social scientist may eventually have to look elsewhere in his search for ever larger *F*'s and *t*'s.

Such speculations carry us beyond the territory yet surveyed by the social scientist. Perhaps the most important implication for the future from our present analysis lies in the sphere of method rather than substance. Our attempt to compare the work of a score of investigators over a score of years will have been worth the labor if it but convinces future researchers of the wastefulness of such uncoordinated ef-

forts. Our best hope for an understanding of the differences in child rearing in various segments of our society and the effects of these differences on personality formation lies in the development of a systematic long-range plan for gathering comparable data at regular intervals on large samples of families at different positions in the social structure. We now have survey organizations with the scientific competence and adequate technical facilities to perform the task. With such hopes in mind, the author looks ahead to the day when the present analysis becomes obsolete, in method as well as substance.

VII. Recapitulation and Coda

A comparative analysis of the results of studies of social-class differences in child rearing over a 25-year period points to the following conclusions.

A. TRENDS IN INFANT CARE

1. Over the past quarter of a century, American mothers at all social-class levels have become more flexible with respect to infant feeding and weaning. Although fewer infants may be breast fed, especially over long periods of time, mothers are increasingly more likely to feed their children on demand and to wean them later from the bottle.

2. Class differences in feeding, weaning, and toilet training show a clear and consistent trend. From about 1930 till the end of World War II, working-class mothers were uniformly more permissive than those of the middle class. They were more likely to breast feed, to follow a self-demand schedule, to

---

[34] Spock, *op. cit.*, p. 326.

wean the child later both from breast and bottle, and to begin and complete both bowel and bladder training at a later age. After World War II, however, there has been a definite reversal in direction; now it is the middle-class mother who is the more permissive in each of the above areas.

3. Shifts in the pattern of infant care —especially on the part of middle-class mothers—show a striking correspondence to the changes in practices advocated in successive editions of U.S. Children's Bureau bulletins and similar sources of expert opinion.

4. In addition to varying with social-class level, methods of infant care appear to differ as a function of cultural background, urban vs. rural upbringing, and exposure to particular ideologies of child rearing.

5. Taken together, the findings on changes in infant care lead to the generalization that socialization practices are most likely to be altered in those segments of society which have most ready access to the agencies or agents of change (e.g., books, pamphlets, physicians, and counselors).

B. Trends in Child Training

6. The data on the training of the young child show middle-class mothers, especially in the postwar period, to be consistently more permissive toward the child's expressed needs and wishes. The generalization applies in such diverse areas as oral behavior, toilet accidents, dependency, sex, aggressiveness, and freedom of movement outside the home.

7. Though more tolerant of expressed impulses and desires, the middle-class parent, throughout the period covered by this survey, has higher expectations for the child. The middle-class youngster is expected to learn to take care of himself earlier, to accept more responsibilities about the home, and—above all—to progress further in school.

8. In matters of discipline, working-class parents are consistently more likely to employ physical punishment, while middle-class families rely more on reasoning, isolation, appeals to guilt, and other methods involving the threat of loss of love. At least two independent lines of evidence suggest that the techniques preferred by middle-class parents are more likely to bring about the development of internalized values and controls. Moreover, the effectiveness of such methods, should, at least on theoretical grounds, be enhanced by the more acceptant atmosphere experienced by middle-class children in their early years.

9. Over the entire 25-year period studied, parent-child relationships in the middle class are consistently reported as more acceptant and equalitarian, while those in the working class are oriented toward maintaining order and obedience. Within this context, the middle class has shown a shift away from emotional control toward freer expression of affection and greater tolerance of the child's impulses and desires.

In the past few years, there have been indications that the gap between the social classes may be narrowing. Whatever trend the future holds in store, let us hope that the social scientist will no longer be content to look at them piecemeal but will utilize all the technical resources now at his command to obtain a systematic picture of the changes, through still more extended space and time, in the way in which humanity brings up its children.

25

SOCIAL CLASS AND EDUCATION

Burton R. Clark

The role of education in the social-class system of modern society is changing. Prior to the twentieth century, education was often merely a correlate of social class, a byproduct of high social position, rather than a means of achieving a particular social-class position. Thus, an upper-class family secured for its sons an education at a prestigious institution in order to conform to the manners and morals of upper-class life. In short, education was not so much a means for *achieving* a particular social-class position as it was a technique for *displaying* a social position that one already occupied.

However, the structure of economic opportunities has dramatically shifted in the twentieth century and the main avenues to economic and social success today have become large-scale bureaucratic organizations—private corporations or public institutions at all levels. The old middle-class self-made man, who started and ran his own business, did not need a great deal of education to succeed simply because he was on his own, and his success or failure depended upon his native business acumen rather than a college diploma. Today, however, large-scale bureaucratic organizations with their formal hierarchy and rules inevitably establish strict educational and training requirements for each position. In this changed economic setting education becomes a prerequisite for success and is not, as previously, simply an upper-class luxury.

In this sense, education is becoming a crucial determinant of one's occupation and income, and thus one's social class position. This has led to the tremendous burgeoning of educational institutions of which we are all aware. Although the exact figures are not known for sure, it is estimated that for the generation of Americans born in the 1860's, somewhere between 2.5–13.1 percent were graduated from high school, and between 1.3–2.6 percent were graduated from college. For the generation born in the early 1940's, on the other hand, some 65 percent were graduated from high school and 20 percent from college.*

In every stratification system there is what has been called a "strain toward aristocracy," that is, a natural tendency for fathers to attempt to pass on their wealth, positions, opportunities, privileges, and motivation to their sons. This phenomenon tends to make the system more rigid, strengthening the forces of inheritance and restricting mobility according to achievement. Working against this principle in modern society is a "strain toward equality"—a goal of economic productivity and efficiency that depends in part upon recruiting the best and most able man for the job, regardless of

---

* Christopher Jencks and David Riesman, "On Class in America," *The Public Interest*, 10 (Winter 1968), 76.

SOURCE: Burton R. Clark, *Educating the Expert Society* (San Francisco: Chandler Publishing Co., 1962), pp. 58–62 and 64–84. Copyright © 1962 by Chandler Publishing Co. Reprinted by permission of the publisher.

his social origins. Considerations of economic efficiency would tend to break down inheritance of social position and substitute status according to achievement.

As education becomes a primary vehicle for social mobility, and as success in education presumably depends upon individual achievement regardless of social class, the strain toward equality would seem to gain advantage over the strain toward aristocracy. However, this assumption ignores the fact that there is social class inequality built into the educational system itself that undermines equal opportunity. Whether a boy goes on to college and from there to a business or professional career depends, not only upon his talent, but upon his social origins. Thus, one national survey revealed that of young people graduating from high school in the mid-1960's, less than 20 percent of those who came from families where the income was less than $3,000 went on to college, as compared to 87 percent of those who came from families where total income exceeded $15,000.*

But perhaps this is not social class discrimination at all; perhaps the higher strata have a near-monopoly on talent, and it is this which explains their high rates of college attendance. This is simply not true; and I have chosen but one recent study to illustrate this point, which will serve to enlarge and bring more up-to-date Burton Clark's own discussion of this issue. In 1957 William Sewell and Vimal Shah conducted an ambitious study of all the high school seniors in the state of Wisconsin.** Among other things, they recorded the students' intelligence test scores and ascertained their socioeconomic status. In 1964–65, Sewell and Shah contacted approximately 10,000 of the original sample of young people in order to assess how many of them had gone on to college in the intervening seven years. The figures on college attendance and college graduation were then related to the students' socioeconomic status and their intelligence test levels, with the results shown on p. 412.

What these data clearly demonstrate is that educational opportunity is still based to a very large degree on class background. Upper-class males here are nearly six times as likely to graduate from college as lower-class males (42.1 percent vs. 7.5 percent), and at even the highest level of intelligence, chances of college graduation are largely determined by socioeconomic position. Besides affecting individuals, this pattern has larger social and economic consequences. In line with Tumin's arguments presented earlier, one can see how a stratification system can be dysfunctional in the sense that a poor man's intelligent son may often be relegated to a position far below his capacities, while a rich man's dull or average son may be elevated to a position far above his abilities. Social class discrimination, like racial discrimination, by keeping many of the "right" people from the right jobs, is, from the point of view of human resources, socially and economically wasteful.

In this excerpt from his book, *Educating the Expert Society,* Burton Clark discusses these and other aspects of the relationship of social class to education. Since this book was published (1962), some effort has been made to increase the educational opportunity for blacks, other minorities, and the poor. Nevertheless, in spite of these efforts, Clark's discussion is still extremely relevant.

* U.S. Bureau of the Census, *Current Population Reports,* Series P-20, No. 185 (Washington, D.C.: U.S. Government Printing Office, 1969).
** William H. Sewell and Vimal P. Shah, "Socioeconomic Status, Intelligence, and the Attainment of Higher Education," *Sociology of Education,* 40 (Winter 1967), 1–23. For national data with similar conclusions, based on Project Talent research, see Willard Wirtz, "Income and College Attendance," in Robert E. Will and Harold G. Vatter, eds., *Poverty in Affluence* (New York: Harcourt, Brace & World, 1965), pp. 135–9; *Project Talent News,* 5 (University of Pittsburgh, October, 1966), 2.

Percentage of 1957 High School Seniors Who Had Graduated from College by 1964–65, by Socioeconomic Status and Intelligence, Separately for Males and Females*

Socioeconomic Status Levels	Males Intelligence Levels					Females Intelligence Levels				
	Low	Lower Middle	Upper Middle	High	Total	Low	Lower Middle	Upper Middle	High	Total
Low	0.3	7.9	10.9	20.1	7.5	0.2	1.3	2.5	13.8	2.7
	(363)	(267)	(193)	(149)	(972)	(411)	(316)	(236)	(138)	(1,101)
Lower Middle	2.3	7.4	16.7	34.4	14.2	0.9	5.3	8.9	20.8	7.9
	(300)	(324)	(275)	(253)	(1,152)	(335)	(342)	(291)	(226)	(1,194)
Upper Middle	4.4	9.8	24.4	46.7	21.7	2.4	9.3	12.1	24.9	12.4
	(273)	(277)	(316)	(289)	(1,155)	(250)	(324)	(332)	(289)	(1,195)
High	10.5	23.3	38.5	64.0	42.1	7.9	15.3	36.4	51.1	35.0
	(134)	(232)	(299)	(442)	(1,107)	(126)	(223)	(324)	(458)	(1,131)
Total	3.2	11.5	23.9	47.2	21.8	1.8	7.1	16.1	33.5	14.5
	(1,070)	(1,100)	(1,083)	(1,133)	(4,386)	(1,122)	(1,205)	(1,183)	(1,111)	(4,621)

* All x²'s for each column and row in this table are significant beyond the 0.05 level.

Effect parameters: Males: Socioeconomic Status .081   Intelligence: .123
                    Females: Socioeconomic Status .077   Intelligence: .083

SOURCE: Sewell and Shah, p. 15.

Education and Life Chances

The chance to get ahead in the modern world depends in considerable part on education. This is a new link in an old chain. It has always been true that opportunities in life are shaped by social background, especially the social station of one's family. This was most likely when status was largely *ascribed,* assigned to persons according to the family, tribe, and class into which they were born. The extreme case of ascribed status is membership from birth to death in a particular caste. Where status in part is *achieved,* as in modern industrial nations, the determination of one's life chances by socio-economic background is not so complete. But social origins are still influential, primarily through affecting how far the young go in their schooling, which in turn so strongly affects their later occupational opportunity. Socio-economic level, or socio-educational level as we shall call it, affects interest and aspiration and the capacity to use the schools for an education.

SOCIAL BACKGROUND AND EDUCATION

Everyone knows that students come to school with widely varying interests and aspirations, but the social categories to which these differences are generally linked are less well known. The most important of these background differences, leaving race and ethnicity aside, is the socio-educational level of the family—a combination of father's (and mother's) occupation, income, and education.

The constraint on education that may be exercised by the social setting within which the young are reared is reflected, in the extreme, in the estimated 150,000 children of migratory agricultural workers, now the greatest single source of illiteracy in the United States. Consider the following conditions and their effect on schooling: [1]

> Whether the child is a Negro, moving from Florida to New York on a truck with the other members of his crew; a Spanish-American, picking cotton in Texas or Arizona, sugar beets in Colorado, berries in Michigan; an Indian child moving out from the reservation with other members of his tribe to pull carrots or pick lettuce; or an Anglo, like the Kentucky mountain white children who were described by a woman who had worked with them as "chawing tobaccy and using strong language at the age of two," they are children who grow up in a very different context from other American children. Though they move so often, they move from one migratory camp to another, and a migrant camp in one state looks very much like one in another, though the states be as remote as Florida and New York. Their travels are what little they can see of a road uncoiling, glimpsed from the cramped middle of a crowded truck. . . . There often is no single spot conceived of as "home," or if there is, it is simply a shack in a camp where the group stays longer than at other places. There are almost no possessions; little can be taken with a family that moves in a truck.

These children do not easily find their way into the schools, nor remain long once they get there. Their geographical mobility cuts into school attendance; family income is very low—migrant

---

[1] Esther P. Edwards, "The Children of Migratory Agricultural Workers in the Public Elementary Schools of the United States: Needs and Proposals in the Area of Curriculum," *Harvard Educational Review,* Vol. 30 (Winter, 1960), pp. 12–52.

workers averaged $961 in 1958—and the family needs the child as an additional field hand or as babysitter so that the mother can go out and work. The parents, themselves illiterate or nearly so, can do little to add to their children's education. Most migrant families possess no books and there is no background for learning in the home. The children generally feel out of step and rejected when they do enter school. In addition, from New Jersey to California, the farmers who employ the migratory workers are not anxious to see the young go off to school, for then they are lost to the work and education will ruin them as stoop-laborers. "When a migrant goes to school beyond the seventh grade, you've ruined a good bean picker." [2] The communities where the migrants are employed also encourage them to move on when the harvest is in. The net result is that state laws compelling school attendance up to a certain age, commonly 15 or 16, are widely blinked in the case of the migrants. Most of their children quit school by the fourth grade and few complete high school, let alone enter college. Their background and the encompassing institutional structure restrain their education to the degree that it is difficult to break out of the vicious cycle of unskilled labor to little education to unskilled labor. Illiteracy or near illiteracy in the young condemns them to repeat the life of their parents.

The case of the migrant child illustrates the low end of a general relationship between socio-educational background and education. Broadly, children from the lower class do not have as much interest in education nor opportunity to obtain it as those from upper strata; because of lowered motivation and financial pressure, some drop out of school as soon as they can. However, compulsory attendance laws, and increased interest, now hold almost all students in the high school up through age 15. Ninety-seven per cent of the 14- and 15-year-olds were enrolled in school in 1958; and, the same year, 81 per cent of the 16- and 17-year-olds were also in school, an increase of 10 per cent in eight years (1950–1958).[3] Clearly the trend toward completion of high school is running deep and promises soon to bracket all classes. The important locus of the relation between the socio-economic status of the family and the education of the son and daughter now lies at entry to college. Let us look in detail at some recent findings.

The plans of high-school seniors for going to college reflect the connection between social position and education. Table 1 is based on a 1955 nation-wide survey of over 35,000 seniors in 500 public high schools. Each student was rated on *scholastic ability* (as indicated by a special 20-item test) and *"socio-educational" status of family,* an index based on father's occupation, father's education, and whether older brothers and sisters had gone to college. The students were classified into four categories of ability and five status groupings that ranged from well-educated professional and managerial families to poorly educated, unskilled manual and farm families. The share of students in each of the five status categories who planned to attend college varied from 72 per cent at the top to 24 per cent at the bottom, or a difference of 48 per

[2] *Time,* August 8, 1960, p. 66.

[3] *A Fact Book on Higher Education* (Washington, D.C.: American Council on Education, n.d.), p. 65.

TABLE 1. Going to College (Percentage of High-School Seniors Planning to Attend College, According to Scholastic Ability and Socio-Educational Status of the Family)*

| Scholastic Ability | Family Socio-Educational Status | | | | | All Students of Given Ability Level |
| | (High) | | | | (Low) | |
	5	4	3	2	1	
(High) 4	83	66	53	44	43	61
3	70	53	37	29	29	44
2	65	41	31	20	21	33
(Low) 1	53	30	22	16	18	24
All students of given family status	72	47	35	26	24	40

* Based on a study of over 35,000 American high-school seniors who constituted the entire senior class of 500 public secondary schools. The schools were a fairly representative sample of the 20,000-odd senior public high schools in the country, 1955.

SOURCE: Natalie Rogoff, "College, Careers, and Social Contexts," paper presented at the Fifty-Fourth Annual Meeting of the American Sociological Association, September, 1959.

cent; the share of *all* students expecting to go to college was 40 per cent. (See the last row of the table.) The variation in plans for college over the four levels of ability was from 61 per cent among the top ability to 24 per cent among those of lowest ability, a range of 37 per cent. (See the last column of the table.) Note that social status produced greater variation than did ability, 48 compared to 37 per cent, although this may be partly an artifact of having grouped ability only in four categories while status was split into five levels.

. . . . .

How do we account for these "class" differences in college-going expectations? One group of reasons lies in objective differentials; higher education costs money and lower-status families do not have much of it. Easily the most important reason given by parents for not expecting their children to go to college is: "Can't raise the money." [4] This reason can be an easy excuse, of course, but it undoubtedly reflects cold reality for most families below the average economic level. Other reasons lie in beliefs; often a lower-class person, compared to those higher in status, "doesn't want as much success, knows he couldn't get it even if he wanted to, and doesn't want what might help him get success." [5] In brief, formal education is differently valued and pursued. A nation-wide survey in 1947 asked the question: "About how

[4] Elmo Roper, "College Ambitions and Parental Planning," *The Public Opinion Quarterly*, 25:2 (Summer, 1961), pp. 159–166.

[5] Herbert H. Hyman, "The Value Systems of Different Classes: A Social Psychological Contribution to the Analysis of Stratification," in Reinhard Bendix and S. M. Lipset (eds.), *Class, Status, and Power* (Glencoe, Illinois: The Free Press, 1953), p. 427. The material immediately following is adapted from Hyman.

much schooling do you think most young men need these days to get along well in the world?" Responses varied by economic level and education of the respondents:

Economic level (Interviewer's rating):	Per cent recommending college education
Wealthy	68
Middle class	52
Lower class	39
Highest education achieved:	
Attended college	72
Attended high school	55
Attended grammar school	36

A more direct question, one on parents' *desire* for their own children to go on to college, was put in a 1945 national survey: "After the war, if you had a son (daughter) graduating from high school would you prefer that he (she) go on to college, or would you rather have him (her) do something else, or wouldn't you care one way or the other?" (See tabular matter below.) Whenever such questions are asked, similar gradations by socio-economic strata are found in the orientation of parents to higher education; it is also known that children of the different

On the other hand, too much can be made of these background differences, and the growing urge throughout the population to obtain more education thereby underplayed. The last set of figures above showed that 68 per cent, or over two out of three, of the adults in the lowest class *preferred* that their son or daughter go to college. The absolute number is as important as the comparison; it indicates that even in the lowest category most parents want their children to be educated. Too, this national response was 15 years ago, and the sentiment and opportunity for higher education has increased rapidly since then. In 1959, when a national survey asked 5,000 heads of households whether they actually *expected* (not *preferred*) their own children to go to

Class level	Per cent preferring college
Prosperous	91
Upper middle	91
Lower middle	83
Poor	68

classes show values parallel to their parents.[6] Thus class-related definitions of what is valuable and possible connect objective social status and amount of education desired.

college, the *percentage of children* expected to go was 44 per cent in the lowest of four economic categories.[7] No social or economic class is immune from academic aspirations.

[6] Hyman, "The Value Systems of Different Classes," pp. 431–432.
[7] Roper, "College Ambitions and Parental Planning," p. 160.

The democratizing of education in respect to income restriction is now moving rapidly in this country, chiefly through public junior colleges, state colleges, and state universities. The percentage of the 18 through 21 year olds who were enrolled in college was less than 2 per cent in 1870, only 4 per cent in 1900, 12 per cent in 1930, 30 per cent in 1950.[8] The American labor force had, on the average, gone as far as the freshman year of high school in 1940; half-way through the sophomore year in 1948; and about all the way through high school by 1957.[9]

This schooling trend is moving with amazing speed. *One generation has seen an advance of four years in the median number of years of schooling completed.* The average young adult in urban areas today has completed high school; his rural counterpart has gone almost as far. In contrast, their fathers and mothers had not advanced much

beyond the eighth grade.[10] Clearly this schooling trend will increasingly affect the college-going tendencies of the lower classes, as diversified systems of higher education develop to provide colleges that are near home and have low tuition as well as colleges that are costly and out of town.

College-going in one such diversified system shows where the lower-income students will appear in great numbers. Table 2 reports that 43.1 per cent of the graduates of California high schools in 1955 went to college in California. However, less than 5 per cent went to private colleges and universities and less than 5 per cent went directly to the state university (more later transferred to the university). All the rest went to state colleges and junior colleges, which for most students are home-town institutions or colleges to which they can commute from home. How did students from different so-

TABLE 2. Public High-School Graduates Continuing Their Education in California *

Type of College	Proportion of High-School Graduates Who Enter
Private college	4.7
State university	4.4
State college	9.4
Junior college	24.6
All California Colleges	43.1

* Based on data from 41 selected California counties, 1955; the 41,423 graduates included were more than half of the total number in the state.

SOURCE: *A Study of the Need for Additional Centers of Public Higher Education in California* (Sacramento: California State Department of Education, 1957), pp. 130–131.

[8] *Historical Statistics of the United States, Colonial Times to 1957* (Bureau of the Census, 1960), pp. 210–211.

[9] "Average" here means the median number of school years completed for the labor force, 18 to 64 years old. The shift in the median reflects the retiring of less-well-educated older persons as well as the entry into the labor force of the better-educated young. *Statistical Abstract of the United States, 1960* (Bureau of the Census, 1960).

[10] Sloan Wayland and Edmund de S. Brunner, *The Educational Characteristics of the American People* (Bureau of Applied Social Research, Columbia University, 1958), pp. 1–3.

cio-economic backgrounds distribute among the types of colleges? Table 3 compares four institutions in the San Jose–San Francisco sector as to the socio-economic status of students who came to them from the city of San Jose. For Stanford University, a selective, high-cost private university located only 15 miles from this city, nearly nine out of ten San Jose students (87 per cent) came from families of professional men, business owners, and business officials ("upper white-collar"),

between the *private* university and the leading public institution (87 compared to 69, or 18 per cent). The dotted line in the table, drawn at the point of greatest difference in each column, shows that the break-point lies between the state university and the state college. With conveniently located public colleges, most students remain at home; the principal socio-economic cleavage is then likely to occur between the colleges of local draw and the colleges with state and national recruit-

TABLE 3. Comparison of Backgrounds (Comparison of Four Colleges, Students Classified by Socio-Economic Background, in Per Cent) *

College	Upper White-Collar	Lower White-Collar	Upper Blue-Collar	Lower Blue-Collar	Total
Stanford University	87	7	6	0	100
University of California	69	14	11	6	100
San Jose State College	38	17	29	16	100
San Jose Junior College	23	15	45	17	100
[Total work force of city of San Jose]	26	17	38	19	100

* Based on freshman students from city of San Jose, 1955; socio-economic background determined by father's occupation.
SOURCE: Burton R. Clark, *The Open Door College: A Case Study* (New York: McGraw-Hill Book Co., Inc., 1960), p. 54.

with about one in sixteen (6 per cent) from families of blue-collar workers.

At the other extreme, the junior college had a spread of students whose status was distributed similar to the city's total work force, with nearly two out of three (45 and 17, or 62 per cent) from blue-collar families. The difference in the proportion of students from the families of highest social standing between the *state university* (Berkeley campus, approximately 50 miles from San Jose) and the *state college* in the home town (69 compared to 38, or 31 per cent), is greater than the difference

ment. In brief, free, local colleges increase educational opportunity; at the same time they contribute to a socioeconomic differential between those who go away from home to the more expensive and generally more selective colleges and those who attend schools at home which are less expensive and usually less selective academically. This cleavage among colleges promises to be as important in the future as the better-understood difference between those who go to college and those who do not attend any kind of college at all.

EDUCATION AND OCCUPATIONAL
ATTAINMENT

We have now reviewed briefly the first half of the chain stretching from social station of parents *to* education *to* future social position. Let us now look at the last half, the extent to which education shapes the possibilities of occupational and social attainment. Again we are talking about what is true of a large number of persons, not necessarily the destiny of any particular individual.

as to obscure some important groups. The category of "proprietors and managers" includes the small shop owner as well as the corporation executive. The small businessman need not have advanced education but the corporation man generally does. The change that has taken place in the education of top business leaders is shown in Table 5. The businessmen referred to hold top executive positions in the largest firms in each type of business and industry

TABLE 4. Occupation and Education

People Who Work in These Occupations	Have This Kind of Education (In per cent)		
	Less Than High-School Graduation	High-School Graduation	Some College Education
Professional and technical workers	6	19	75
Proprietors and managers	38	33	29
Clerical or sales workers	25	53	22
Skilled workers	59	33	8
Semi-skilled workers	70	26	4
Service workers	69	25	6
Unskilled workers	80	17	3
Farmers and farm workers	76	19	5

SOURCE: *Manpower: Challenge of the 1960s* (U.S. Department of Labor, 1960), p. 17.

First, education strongly relates to occupational achievement. Table 4 shows the extent to which the higher occupations are composed of the fairly well-educated. Professional and technical workers are in a world by themselves in this regard, for three-fourths of them have had some college whereas no more than a fourth to a third of any other *major* occupational group has had that much education.

These categories are useful for the broad picture but each is so inclusive

in America. As can be seen, the business leaders of 1952 were much better educated than the leaders of 1928. In 1952, only 4 per cent had less than a high-school education, but 27 per cent did in 1928, or roughly seven times as many. About one-third were college graduates in the earlier group, compared with 57 per cent in 1952. The situation is changing rapidly; today's young men who will be the business leaders of tomorrow will be even more highly educated.

If education relates strongly to occupational attainment, so does it connect

TABLE 5. Education of Business Leaders of 1928 and 1952 (in Per Cent)

Highest Stage of Schooling Completed	1928 Business Leaders	1952 Business Leaders
Less than high school	27	4
High school	28	20
Some college	13	19
College graduation	32	57
Total	100	100

SOURCE: W. Lloyd Warner and James C. Abegglen, *Occupational Mobility in American Business and Industry, 1928–1952* (Minneapolis: University of Minnesota Press, 1955), p. 108.

to future income. The average annual income in 1958 of American men, age 45–54—the prime of life—differed widely according to the amount of education they had received: [11]

with high-school graduation. The differences in annual and lifetime income among men with these different levels of education is increasing, not decreasing; the largest increase between 1949

some elementary schooling	$3,008 *
completed elementary school	$4,337
some high school	$4,864
completed high school	$6,295
some college	$8,682
completed college	$12,269

* The comparable income figures for 1968 are as follows: some elementary school, $4,973; completed elementary school, $6,566; some high school, $7,601; completed high school, $9,106; some college, $11,072; completed college, $15,465. *Editor.*

Thus a college graduate is likely to earn almost twice as much each year as a high-school graduate and almost three times as much as someone whose education ended with eight years of elementary school. The differences in *lifetime* income are almost equally great: as of 1958, total income from age 18 to death was estimated as $182,000 for those who had completed only grammar school; $258,000 for high-school graduates; and $435,000 for those with four or more years of college. The man with a college degree would thus receive approximately $175,000 more income during his life than a man whose education stopped

and 1958 was made by college-educated men.

We can also guess that the kind of school attended makes some difference in later rewards, with wealthier high-prestige schools leading to greater financial success. Such is the case, for if we divide male graduates into groups by type of school attended we get the differences in median incomes shown in Table 6. The different financial rewards still are there even when we take into account the family backgrounds of the students. Poor boys who go to rich schools do much better financially than poor boys who go to the more obscure colleges.

[11] Herman P. Miller, "Annual and Lifetime Income in Relation to Education: 1939–1959," *The American Economic Review*, 50:5 (December, 1960), pp. 962–986.

These figures make clear what level and type of education mean for occupational and status attainment on the average. The educational ladder leads to the higher occupations, the upper social statuses, the prestigeful styles of life, and membership in the subsociety of the "educated." It is true in growing degree that without education one has lowered horizons—occupationally, socially, culturally; with education, many doors are open, perhaps even some doors in the mind.

The educational system moves individuals from one social station to another; it may also move whole groups. The "lower class," for example, may have considerable turnover, if many of the sons and daughters of one cultural group move up a notch or two, replaced by unskilled immigrants of another background who provide the

TABLE 6. Types of Colleges and Financial Success *

Type of College	Annual Income of Graduates, 1947
The Big Three (Harvard, Yale, Princeton)	$7,365
Other Ivy League (Columbia, Cornell, Dartmouth, Pennsylvania)	$6,142
Seventeen Technical Schools (California, Carnegie, Case, Detroit, Drexel, Georgia, Illinois, Massachusetts, and Stevens Institutes of Technology; Rensselaer, Rose, Virginia, and Worcester Polytechnic Institutes; Clarkson College of Technology, Cooper Union, Polytechnic Institute of Brooklyn, Tri-State College)	$5,382
Twenty Famous Eastern Colleges (Amherst, Bates, Bowdoin, Brown, Clark, Colby, Franklin and Marshall, Hamilton, Haverford, Hobart, Lafayette, Lehigh, Middlebury, Rutgers, Swarthmore, Trinity, Tufts, Union, Wesleyan of Connecticut, Williams)	$5,287
The Big Ten (Chicago, Illinois, Indiana, Iowa, Michigan, Minnesota, Northwestern, Ohio State, Purdue, Wisconsin)	$5,176
All Other Midwest Colleges	$4,322
All Other Eastern Colleges	$4,235

* Based on questionnaire replies from over 9,000 college graduates, 1947.

SOURCE: Ernest Havemann and Patricia Salter West, *They Went to College* (New York: Harcourt, Brace and Co., 1952), pp. 178–179.

floor of the occupational structure in the next generation. The United States has seen numerous Yankees, Irish, Italians, and others start at the bottom and move right on up the occupational ladder. Education has played an important role in providing the necessary acculturation and training. Then, too, the lower class can be denuded, in a sense, as the number of unskilled jobs decreases and more persons take on the skills, earn the money, and gain the trappings that lead to and symbolize middle-class status. In short, whole strata as well as individuals can be in motion. Such shifts are especially likely to happen in the modern technological society, where improved technique and the trend toward service industry lead to a general upgrading of jobs, in level of skill and thus also in education required. Other reasons aside, the technological society must enourage mass education in order to meet its occupational needs; then education functions to move the lower strata upwards.

When education operates to any considerable degree in this way, it can lead to a pervasive sense of opportunity; with this, it functions to keep the lower classes "in society" as well as "of it." Lower classes become resentful and alienated, in societies where achievement is a value, when low status appears permanent and son follows father in menial labor unto the sixth generation. Resentment is lowered and alienation abated where achievement of the "better life" is thought possible, if not always probable. If the chance to achieve is considered somewhat available, then nonachieving is a *personal* failure rather than the fault of the society. The chance to participate in the general society, through such means as education, also reduces the inclination to extremist politics. "It is in the advanced industrial countries, principally the United States, Britain, and Northwestern Europe, where national income *has* been rising, where mass expectations of an equitable share in that increase are relatively fulfilled, and where social mobility affects ever greater numbers, that extremist politics have least hold." [12] The stability of the democratic process in general is closely related to national levels of economic development, including degrees of educational attainment.[13] In brief, the open society of modern times is likely to remain open and democratic only if, among other conditions, its lower classes have some reasonable degree of access to the educational avenue and other roads leading to social rewards.

We need at this point to resolve a conflict that has gradually built up in this chapter's discussion: What determines life chances to the *greatest* extent—social position or education, ascription or achievement? On the one hand, children from the higher social strata are likely to receive more and better education than their lower-class counterparts. The higher-level education then, in turn, provides access to the better positions. In short, education is a mechanism whereby social-class positions are stabilized across the generations,[14] and is thereby a barrier to the social mobility of those who start from lower rungs. This is one general tendency. Another and contradic-

[12] Daniel Bell, "The Theory of Mass Society," *Commentary*, Vol. 22 (July, 1956), p. 80.
[13] Seymour Martin Lipset, *Political Man* (Garden City, N.Y.: Doubleday & Company, Inc., 1960), p. 129.
[14] See Bernard Barber, *Social Stratification* (New York: Harcourt, Brace and Co., 1957), p. 395.

tory tendency is for a considerable number of the young to be mobile upward from the lower strata by virtue of the availability of schooling, their persistence and success once in school, and then their entry into some higher-status occupation to which their education has admitted them. Here education is a mechanism whereby social positions are changed rather than stabilized. What is the balance? Until the twentieth century, education's role in providing for mobility was everywhere largely secondary to its role in assigning *similar* social positions across generations. Father's status counted more than the classroom; and mobile individuals were often mobile without education. But the role of the school and college in social mobility grows stronger as (a) education becomes more available to all and (b) men are judged by the universal criteria of scholastic achievement and technical competence—when the question asked is, what do you know, rather than who do you know or what did your father do. In the United States in the middle of the twentieth century, increasing numbers in lower social strata now have the high-school habit; the time is approaching when they, like the middle and upper class, will have the college habit to a considerable degree. Especially in an expanding economy, where there is more room at the top, these habits can lead to the very highest positions; a higher proportion of the American business elite now comes from the lower social ranks than a quarter of a century ago. The gigantic business organizations are particularly open: "The larger the firm the smaller the proportion of men with fathers in the same firm. . . . The stronghold of inherited position today in America is in the smaller enterprises; the larger enterprises are more open to competition for men rising from lower occupational levels." [15] What matters now for social mobility is that one travel the educational road; and access to this highway, despite the handicaps of dirt-road entrances for some, is increasingly open. The lower-class boy majoring in engineering at the state university is a case in point.

For society, the extending and especially the equalizing of opportunity is a necessary part of a fuller use of talent for trained manpower. When for various economic, ethnic, and motivational reasons, high-ability children leave education early and in large numbers, considerable talent goes undeveloped. A technological society has an insatiable appetite for competence, especially in engineering and allied fields; a bureaucratic society needs trained experts for the myriad specialized positions of the large organization; and on top of this, societies competing internationally also look upon trained men as essential to national vigor. These triple pressures of technology, bureaucracy, and world tension promote the effort in the United States to open wider the doors of educational agencies, train more persons, uncover hidden talent, and draw to higher levels those of obvious ability who otherwise would leave early.

The extending of *larger* amounts of education to *larger* numbers and *larger* proportions of the population in modern society has all kinds of consequences, deeply affecting the nature of

[15] W. Lloyd Warner and James C. Abegglen, *Occupational Mobility in American Business and Industry, 1928–1952* (Minneapolis: University of Minnesota Press, 1955), p. 32.

education in the lower and the higher grades. One problem raised by the extension of educational opportunity [16] to ever larger numbers is that the upper grades of the school must then face many students who are ill-equipped; when formerly selective schools become unselective, as happened in the American high school, the schools naturally handle more young people of low to average ability. Increased quantity, without quality control, puts pressure on standards, and the derivative problem thus becomes one of maintenance of quality. American secondary education has been plagued with this problem since shortly after the turn of the century, with the schools adapting their programs to a wide range of abilities and the critics of the schools pressing for greater rigor.

Greater schooling for greater numbers also has brought with it, and evidently implies, a greater practicality in what the schools teach and what they do for students. The existence of children of diverse ability and destiny in the schools calls forth the comprehensive school, or the multischool comprehensive structure, within which some students receive a broad, general education but others take primarily a technical or commercial training. In short, increased quantity means greater vocationalism. This tendency hit the American high school around the beginning of the century, changing its character from the strictly academic. It has played a growing role in higher education ever since higher education began seriously to slip out of the liberal-arts-college mold in the last quarter of the nineteenth century. As indicated ear-

lier, the growth in enrollment in higher education in America in recent decades has been in the applied fields, especially business, engineering, and education. Part of the impetus for this growth has come from students of lower social origins entering college intent on a "realistic" training for higher occupations without academic or collegiate frills.

Democratization in the sense of throwing open the doors of educational agencies without regard to *ability* also causes the sorting processes of education to take somewhat different form than was the case, and is the case, when schools are selective. Sorting must take place at some point in the educational structure. If, at that level, it does not take place *at* the door, the time of entry, it must occur *inside* the doors, in the classroom and counseling office. The problem of sorting within the school and classroom is faced acutely at the level in the educational structure where the staff must say to the student, in effect: "From here on, it is ability and not automatic promotion. If you want to be an engineer, you must be able to pass in mathematics and physics. If you can't, then you can no longer kid yourself." This situation is found in the high school, but it is now most critical in the first year of public colleges and universities that unselectively take all high-school graduates. Those who have little or no promise for college are let in to have a try; most of these unpromising recruits are quickly selected out in the first year.

This selecting-out-after-entry means that sorting must become a major internal consideration, affecting the work

---

[16] *Extending* opportunity should be distinguished from *equalizing* opportunity. To extend means to offer to a larger number; to equalize means to offer on grounds of ability without regard to such "irrelevant" criteria as race, creed, or ancestry. Extension often implies equalization but need not, as when more education is given to more white children but not to Negroes.

of the teacher, the counselor, and the administrator. Special procedures arise, for example, for sidetracking or getting rid of the failures, with the procedures leading the student into a counseling orbit. The procedures in some cases lead to quick dismissal, as in state universities where students numbering in the thousands are dropped in the freshman year, or to a change in major to an easy field. In other colleges, the procedures lead to an alternative track, as in junior colleges where students are eased from four-year to two-year programs, to become an "engineering aide" instead of an engineer.[17] Democracy encourages aspiration, and generous admission allows the student whose hopes outrun his capabilities to carry his hopes into the school or now principally the college. But there his desires run into the standards necessary for the integrity of programs and the training of competent workers. The college offers the opportunity to try, but the student's own ability and his accumulative record of performance finally insist that he be sorted out. It is everywhere a problem of democratic institutions that encouragement to achieve runs up against the realities of fewer successes at ascending levels of training and work. With this, situations of opportunity are also inherently situations of denial and failure. Some succeed and some do not.

Thus as ascription has given way to achievement in this country in the very recent past, sorting for adult role has moved considerably from class origin to the classroom. In some democratic countries—England, for example—the sorting through achievement has taken place through national examination and careful selection at a certain level. But in the American educational system, sorting through achievement has become a drawn-out, subtle process. Selection takes place in less formal and less obvious ways. Compared to sorting at the door, selection within the school or college often leads to a somewhat masked and cushioned rearranging of the fate of individuals.

The Transference of Status

Part of the ever closer connection between education and the occupational structure is the interesting phenomenon of the status of one rubbing off on the other. Let us first consider the transference of prestige that takes place from occupations to schools and colleges. The decisive feature in the assignment of status to levels and types of schools and colleges, broadly, is their relationship to occupations. The university prepares students in its professional and graduate schools for occupations of high social status, such as the established professions, science, business management. The four- or five-year college relates *directly* to occupations of somewhat lower status for the most part, in which neither advanced graduate nor prolonged professional-school training is needed, such as teaching, engineering, lower management positions in business and government. The two-year junior college prepares semiprofessionals and technicians.

The high school now provides relatively little occupational training other than elementary clerical work and, where vocational schools still exist, some training for the building trades

---

[17] Burton R. Clark, "The 'Cooling-out' Function in Higher Education," *The American Journal of Sociology*, Vol. 65 (May, 1960), pp. 569–576.

and the machine shop. The differential status of the occupations inevitably attaches to the preparatory agencies. Despite the efforts of educators to erase invidious status distinctions among schools, it is unrealistic to expect equality of status for schools when they are differentially geared into the basic outside hierarchy of social status. This is fundamental to the general tendency to rank the university over the state college, the state college in turn over the two-year college, and any level of college over the high school.

This principle of status transference has been observed in the relationship of education to occupations in Britain, even within the limits of secondary education alone.[18] English secondary education contains three types of public schools primarily (public in the American definition of public and private): the Grammar school, the Technical school, and the Secondary Modern school. In keeping with democratic principles, many citizens and government officials would like a parity of prestige for these schools. Yet this is impossible given the encompassing social structure. The several schools relate to occupations of differential status and hence vary considerably in prestige. The Grammar schools, which are selective, lead to the university and the top-status occupations; the Technical school is also somewhat selective, and its graduates typically go into "the new middle class of technologists and industrial managers"; the Secondary Modern school is unselective and leads to all the work of lesser status, from bookkeeper to dressmaker to laborer. A central consideration in this tripartite structure is how to raise the status of the Secondary Modern school, which handles the majority of students, in the face of the selective schools which have better students on the average and lead typically to the better-paying fields.

In the United States a similar status differential has been attached to the several major programs or curricula *within* the comprehensive high school, with the vocational and the commercial tagged by most teachers, students, and parents as inferior to the academic or college-preparatory major which leads to more education and higher things. Here again efforts to assign a parity of status have largely failed because of the linkage of levels and kinds of education to the general occupational-status hierarchy. Yet Americans have been more "successful" than the English in this matter; the comprehensive school blurs the distinction between curricula more than does a structure composed of three kinds of schools.

An especially interesting feature of the education-occupation connection is the way that status rubs off the other way around, from schools to fields of work. This transference is especially noticeable in the case of occupations that are becoming, or are attempting to become, professions. To be defined as a high-status field, an occupation must usually have high-status educational preparation; a profession must have professional schools in the universities. Entry into the field through training in a university professional program is now one of the several basic hallmarks of a profession, along with licensing or certification of practitioners and a professional association organized for control and protection. Thus it is not solely for reasons of increasing com-

---

[18] Olive Banks, *Parity and Prestige in English Secondary Education* (London: Routledge & Kegan Paul, Ltd., 1955), Chapter 16.

plexity of knowledge and training that some fields come knocking at the door of the university, seeking advanced programs.

The push is on in many fields in the United States today to become known as a profession. Law and medicine long ago arrived; now struggling up the slope and trailing in various degrees come agriculture, business administration, dentistry, education, engineering, forestry, librarianship, nursing, optometry, pharmacy, public health, social welfare, and so on. Fields are being so rapidly upgraded in skill requirements that a very large number of them can claim some degree of "professionalization." The desire for professional status encourages attempts to speed up the already rapid evolution, so that in many cases those in the field attempt a bootstrap operation. An essential part of this professionalization is to get universities to institute professional schools for the field, from which subsequently the field will receive status as well as trained recruits.

We should emphasize in closing this chapter how much the making of the individual's destiny has changed since the days of old. In simple societies, young people are allocated to adult positions and statuses by custom and heritage of the family, clan, and community. Many statuses are ascribed according to birth; for example, the son of a chief is destined to be the ruler after his father. Often only one or two major occupations are available, and the young know quite early whether they will be fisherman or hunter or farmer.

In the complex society, with its elaborate division of labor, one's occupational future is more open and much more likely to be won by dint of individual achievement. The processes of allocating young people to adult positions become complicated and heavily intwined with formal education and training. The more advanced the technology and the state of organization, the more occupational (and social) achievement depend on the possession of special knowledge and skills. The work of the business manager becomes more complicated and specialized, for example, requiring training and perspectives not to be gained by working one's way up from a factory hand. The "self-made man" of the middle twentieth century typically makes himself through four years of college and very probably through additional work in a graduate or professional school. Mobility through education is a core element of the twentieth-century society.

26

ALIENATED LABOR

Karl Marx

Alienation is a term much in vogue today, and, as with much of Freudian terminology, it has become part of the everyday vocabulary of college-educated laymen. One of Marx's most lasting contributions to the understanding of industrial society was his analysis of the phenomenon of the alienation of labor. As he was to do with other ideas, Marx borrowed the concept of alienation from the nineteenth-century philosopher, Hegel, and moved it from the world of philosophy to the realm of sociology.

While today the term is used broadly—everyone is said to be alienated from something—Marx focused primarily upon the alienation of the modern working class from its own industrial labor. And it is a measure of the continuing relevance of the idea that industrial sociologists have been able to use and operationalize the concept of work alienation in contemporary studies of life in the modern factory. The alienating character of work continues, a century and a quarter after the twenty-six-year-old Marx sketched his *Economic and Philosophical Manuscripts,* from which this selection is taken. And although we in the Western world have come far closer to overcoming the poverty suffered by the nineteenth-century working class of whom Marx wrote, are we really any closer to the achievement of fulfilling, creative, enjoyable work for the mass of men than we were in Marx's day?

From the selection included here and other passages from Marx, we can isolate the following general elements in his theory of alienation.

1. Under conditions of modern factory labor, work is repetitive, routine, fragmented, unsatisfying, and unfulfilling. The worker becomes, as Marx said in the *Manifesto,* merely an "appendage of the machine." Thus, the worker becomes alienated from his own creative potential, from what he might be as a man, and from himself. Work is not an end in itself, nor an inherent source of satisfaction, but merely a means to other ends.

2. Under capitalist production, work is for someone else, not for oneself. Further, the conditions of work are undemocratic and thus constricting. Even if the government is democratically constituted, when the worker enters the shop or the factory, he enters an institutional system which is essentially authoritarian, where the employer is not responsible to his workers for his decisions, and where the worker must obey orders he has had no part in formulating.

3. The modern worker is separated or alienated from the ownership of the factory and the tools with which he works. In contrast to the medieval craftsman who owned his shop and his tools, the modern worker's only possession is his "labor power" which he is forced to sell daily for his wage.

SOURCE: Karl Marx, *Economic and Philosophical Manuscripts* in Erich Fromm, ed., *Marx's Concept of Man,* trans. T. B. Bottomore (New York: Frederick Ungar, Publishing Co., 1961), pp. 93–109. Reprinted by permission of C. A. Watts and Co., Ltd.

4. Finally, the worker is separated from the product of his labor when he is finished making it. He pours his labor into the object, but when finished he cannot dispose of it as he likes. The men upstairs in the office decide where and how it will be sold, at what prices, and the like. And so the worker is again deprived of a sense or a pride of ownership and participation.

Marx was vague on just how communism would reduce the alienating quality of industrial labor under capitalism. To a degree, he apparently believed that work, because it lay in the realm of necessity and because of technological imperatives in which man must necessarily struggle with nature in order to win his bread, could never be completely liberating and fulfilling. But, as he implied toward the end of his life in the third volume of *Capital,* production based on communal ownership and democratic control could go far to mitigate the alienated labor found under capitalism. "Freedom in this field," Marx wrote, "cannot consist of anything else but of the fact that socialized man, the associated producers, regulate their interchange with nature rationally, bring it under their common control, instead of being ruled by it as by some blind power. . . ."

As mentioned, contemporary research in what might be called the work alienation area has been extensive. Where workers have simply been asked whether or not they are satisfied with their jobs, the results point to a uniformly high level of job contentment cutting across occupational lines. Such studies are apt to be very misleading, however, because of general social pressures toward expressing satisfaction to interviewers in important areas of life. Slightly more subtle inquiries, however, which seek to discover whether workers would want their sons to enter their occupation or whether, if they had a chance to start all over again, they would enter the same field, are more highly revealing, as the table below indicates. Job satisfaction is clearly dependent upon social class, or, more accurately, occupational class: the higher the posi-

The Proportion of Men in Various Occupations Who Would Choose a Similar Type of Job if They Could Start Over Again

Professional and Lower White-Collar Occupations	Percent
Urban University Professors	93
Mathematicians	91
Physicists	89
School Superintendents	85
Lawyers	83
White-Collar Workers, age 21–29	46
White-Collar Workers, age 30–55	43
Working-Class Occupations	
Skilled Printers	52
Paper Workers	52
Skilled Auto Workers	41
Skilled Steelworkers	41
Blue-Collar Workers, age 30–55	24
Blue-Collar Workers, age 21–29	23
Unskilled Steelworkers	21
Unskilled Auto Workers	16

SOURCE: Adapted from Harold L. Wilensky, "Work as a Social Problem," in Howard S. Becker, ed., *Social Problems* (New York: John Wiley, 1966), p. 134.

tion, the greater the likelihood of satisfaction in work. This is explained by a number of things: the prestige of higher occupations, their superior compensation, the intrinsically more satisfying kinds of work involved, and the like. So important are social-class influences that many writers hold it to be the single most decisive element in determining job satisfaction.

We have begun from the presuppositions of political economy. We have accepted its terminology and its laws. We presupposed private property, the separation of labor, capital and land, as also of wages, profit and rent, the division of labor, competition, the concept of exchange value, etc. From political economy itself, in its own words, we have shown that the worker sinks to the level of a commodity, and to a most miserable commodity; that the misery of the worker increases with the power and volume of his production; that the necessary result of competition is the accumulation of capital in a few hands, and thus a restoration of monopoly in a more terrible form; and finally that the distinction between capitalist and landlord, and between agricultural laborer and industrial worker, must disappear and the whole of society divide into the two classes of property *owners* and propertyless *workers*.

Political economy begins with the fact of private property; it does not explain it. It conceives the *material process* of private property, as this occurs in reality, in general and abstract formulas which then serve it as laws. It does not *comprehend* these laws; that is, it does not show how they arise out of the nature of private property. Political economy provides no explanation of the basis of the distinction of labor from capital, of capital from land. When, for example, the relation of wages to profits is defined, this is explained in terms of the interests of cap-

italists; in other words, what should be explained is assumed. Similarly, competition is referred to at every point and is explained in terms of external conditions. Political economy tells us nothing about the extent to which these external and apparently accidental conditions are simply the expression of a necessary development. We have seen how exchange itself seems an accidental fact. The only moving forces which political economy recognizes are *avarice* and the *war between the avaricious, competition*.

Just because political economy fails to understand the interconnections within this movement it was possible to oppose the doctrine of competition to that of monopoly, the doctrine of freedom of the crafts to that of the guilds, the doctrine of the division of landed property to that of the great estates; for competition, freedom of crafts, and the division of landed property were conceived only as accidental consequences brought about by will and force, rather than as necessary, inevitable and natural consequences of monopoly, the guild system and feudal property.

Thus we have now to grasp the real connection between this whole system of alienation—private property, acquisitiveness, the separation of labor, capital and land, exchange and competition, value and the devaluation of man, monopoly and competition—and the system of *money*.

Let us not begin our explanation, as does the economist, from a legendary primordial condition. Such a primordial condition does not explain anything; it merely removes the question into a gray and nebulous distance. It asserts as a fact or event what it should deduce, namely, the necessary relation between two things; for example, between the division of labor and exchange. In the same way theology explains the origin of evil by the fall of man; that is, it asserts as a historical fact what it should explain.

We shall begin from a *contemporary* economic fact. The worker becomes poorer the more wealth he produces and the more his production increases in power and extent. The worker becomes an ever cheaper commodity the more goods he creates. The *devaluation* of the human world increases in direct relation with the *increase in value* of the world of things. Labor does not only create goods; it also produces itself and the worker as a *commodity,* and indeed in the same proportion as it produces goods.

This fact simply implies that the object produced by labor, its product, now stands opposed to it as an *alien being,* as a *power independent* of the producer. The product of labor is labor which has been embodied in an object and turned into a physical thing; this product is an *objectification* of labor. The performance of work is at the same time its objectification. The performance of work appears in the sphere of political economy as a *vitiation* of the worker, objectification as a *loss* and as *servitude to the object,* and appropriation as *alienation.*

So much does the performance of work appear as vitiation that the worker is vitiated to the point of starvation. So much does objectification appear as loss of the object that the worker is deprived of the most essential things not only of life but also of work. Labor itself becomes an object which he can acquire only by the greatest effort and with unpredictable interruptions. So much does the appropriation of the object appear as alienation that the more objects the worker produces the fewer he can possess and the more he falls under the domination of his product, of capital.

All these consequences follow from the fact that the worker is related to the *product of his labor* as to an *alien* object. For it is clear on this presupposition that the more the worker expends himself in work the more powerful becomes the world of objects which he creates in face of himself, the poorer he becomes in his inner life, and the less he belongs to himself. It is just the same as in religion. The more of himself man attributes to God the less he has left in himself. The worker puts his life into the object, and his life then belongs no longer to himself but to the object. The greater his activity, therefore, the less he possesses. What is embodied in the product of his labor is no longer his own. The greater this product is, therefore, the more he is diminished. The *alienation* of the worker in his product means not only that his labor becomes an object, assumes an *external* existence, but that it exists independently, *outside himself,* and alien to him, and that it stands opposed to him as an autonomous power. The life which he has given to the object sets itself against him as an alien and hostile force.

Let us now examine more closely the phenomenon of *objectification,* the worker's production and the *alienation* and *loss* of the object it produces, which is involved in it. The worker can create nothing without *nature,* without the *sensuous external world.*

The latter is the material in which his labor is realized, in which it is active, out of which and through which it produces things.

But just as nature affords the *means of existence* of labor in the sense that labor cannot *live* without objects upon which it can be exercised, so also it provides the *means of existence* in a narrower sense; namely the means of physical existence for the *worker* himself. Thus, the more the worker *appropriates* the external world of sensuous nature by his labor the more he deprives himself of *means of existence,* in two respects: first, that the sensuous external world becomes progressively less an object belonging to his labor or a means of existence of his labor, and secondly, that it becomes progressively less a means of existence in the direct sense, a means for the physical subsistence of the worker.

In both respects, therefore, the worker becomes a slave of the object; first, in that he receives an *object of work,* i.e., receives *work,* and secondly that he receives *means of subsistence.* Thus the object enables him to exist, first as a *worker* and secondly, as a *physical subject.* The culmination of this enslavement is that he can only maintain himself as a *physical subject* so far as he is a *worker,* and that it is only as a *physical subject* that he is a worker.

(The alienation of the worker in his object is expressed as follows in the laws of political economy: the more the worker produces the less he has to consume; the more value he creates the more worthless he becomes; the more refined his product the more crude and misshapen the worker; the more civilized the product the more barbarous the worker; the more powerful the work the more feeble the worker; the more the work manifests intelligence the more the worker declines in intelligence and becomes a slave of nature.)

Political economy conceals the alienation in the nature of labor insofar as it does not examine the direct relationship between the worker (work) and production. Labor certainly produces marvels for the rich but it produces privation for the worker. It produces palaces, but hovels for the worker. It produces beauty, but deformity for the worker. It replaces labor by machinery, but it casts some of the workers back into a barbarous kind of work and turns the others into machines. It produces intelligence, but also stupidity and cretinism for the workers.

The direct relationship of labor to its products is the relationship of the worker to the objects of his production. The relationship of property owners to the objects of production and to production itself is merely a *consequence* of this first relationship and confirms it. We shall consider this second aspect later.

Thus, when we ask what is the important relationship of labor, we are concerned with the relationship of the *worker* to production.

So far we have considered the alienation of the worker only from one aspect; namely, *his relationship with the products of his labor.* However, alienation appears not only in the result, but also in the *process,* of *production,* within *productive activity* itself. How could the worker stand in an alien relationship to the product of his activity if he did not alienate himself in the act of production itself? The product is indeed only the *résumé* of activity, of production. Consequently, if the product of labor is alienation, production itself must be active alienation—the alienation of activity and the activity of alienation. The alienation of the object of labor merely summarizes the alienation in the work activity itself.

What constitutes the alienation of labor? First, that the work is *external* to the worker, that it is not part of his nature; and that, consequently, he does not fulfill himself in his work but denies himself, has a feeling of misery rather than well being, does not develop freely his mental and physical energies but is physically exhausted and mentally debased. The worker therefore feels himself at home only during his leisure time, whereas at work he feels homeless. His work is not voluntary but imposed, *forced labor*. It is not the satisfaction of a need, but only a *means* for satisfying other needs. Its alien character is clearly shown by the fact that as soon as there is no physical or other compulsion it is avoided like the plague. External labor, labor in which man alienates himself, is a labor of self-sacrifice, of mortification. Finally, the external character of work for the worker is shown by the fact that it is not his own work but work for someone else, that in work he does not belong to himself but to another person.

Just as in religion the spontaneous activity of human fantasy, of the human brain and heart, reacts independently as an alien activity of gods or devils upon the individual, so the activity of the worker is not his own spontaneous activity. It is another's activity and a loss of his own spontaneity.

We arrive at the result that man (the worker) feels himself to be freely active only in his animal functions—eating, drinking and procreating, or at most also in his dwelling and in personal adornment—while in his human functions he is reduced to an animal. The animal becomes human and the human becomes animal.

Eating, drinking and procreating are of course also genuine human functions. But abstractly considered, apart from the environment of other human activities, and turned into final and sole ends, they are animal functions.

We have now considered the act of alienation of practical human activity, labor, from two aspects: (1) the relationship of the worker to the *product of labor* as an alien object which dominates him. This relationship is at the same time the relationship to the sensuous external world, to natural objects, as an alien and hostile world; (2) the relationship of labor to the *act of production* within *labor*. This is the relationship of the worker to his own activity as something alien and not belonging to him, activity as suffering (passivity), strength as powerlessness, creation as emasculation, the *personal* physical and mental energy of the worker, his personal life (for what is life but activity?) as an activity which is directed against himself, independent of him and not belonging to him. This is *self-alienation* as against the above-mentioned alienation of the *thing*.

We have now to infer a third characteristic of *alienated labor* from the two we have considered.

Man is a species-being [1] not only in the sense that he makes the community (his own as well as those of other things) his object both practically and

---

[1] The term "species-being" is taken from Feuerbach's *Das Wesen des Christentums* (The Essence of Christianity). Feuerbach used the notion in making a distinction between consciousness in man and in animals. Man is conscious not merely of himself as an individual but of the human species or "human essence."—*Tr. Note*

theoretically, but also (and this is simply another expression for the same thing) in the sense that he treats himself as the present, living species, as a *universal* and consequently free being.

Species-life, for man as for animals, has its physical basis in the fact that man (like animals) lives from inorganic nature, and since man is more universal than an animal so the range of inorganic nature from which he lives is more universal. Plants, animals, minerals, air, light, etc. constitute, from the theoretical aspect, a part of human consciousness as objects of natural science and art; they are man's spiritual inorganic nature, his intellectual means of life, which he must first prepare for enjoyment and perpetuation. So also, from the practical aspect they form a part of human life and activity. In practice man lives only from these natural products, whether in the form of food, heating, clothing, housing, etc. The universality of man appears in practice in the universality which makes the whole of nature into his inorganic body: (1) as a direct means of life; and equally (2) as the material object and instrument of his life activity. Nature is the *inorganic body* of man; that is to say, nature excluding the human body itself. To say that man *lives* from nature means that nature is his *body* with which he must remain in a continuous interchange in order not to die. The statement that the physical and mental life of man, and nature, are interdependent means simply that nature is interdependent with itself, for man is a part of nature.

Since alienated labor: (1) alienates nature from man; and (2) alienates man from himself, from his own active function, his life activity; so it alienates him from the species. It makes *species-life* into a means of individual life. In the first place it alienates species-life

and individual life, and secondly, it turns the latter, as an abstraction, into the purpose of the former, also in its abstract and alienated form.

For labor, *life activity, productive life,* now appear to man only as *means* for the satisfaction of a need, the need to maintain his physical existence. Productive life is, however, species-life. It is life creating life. In the type of life activity resides the whole character of a species, its species-character; and free, conscious activity is the species-character of human beings. Life itself appears only as a *means of life.*

The animal is one with its life activity. It does not distinguish the activity from itself. It is *its activity.* But man makes his life activity itself an object of his will and consciousness. He has a conscious life activity. It is not a determination with which he is completely identified. Conscious life activity distinguishes man from the life activity of animals. Only for this reason is he a species-being. Or rather, he is only a self-conscious being, i.e. his own life is an object for him, because he is a species-being. Only for this reason is his activity free activity. Alienated labor reverses the relationship, in that man because he is a self-conscious being makes his life activity, his *being,* only a means for his *existence.*

The practical construction of an *objective world,* the *manipulation* of inorganic nature, is the confirmation of man as a conscious species-being, i.e. a being who treats the species as his own being or himself as a species-being. Of course, animals also produce. They construct nests, dwellings, as in the case of bees, beavers, ants, etc. But they only produce what is strictly necessary for themselves or their young. They produce only in a single direction, while man produces universally. They produce only under the compulsion of direct physical need, while man produces when he is free from physical need and only truly produces in freedom from such need. Animals produce only themselves, while man reproduces the whole of nature. The products of animal production belong directly to their physical bodies, while man is free in face of his product. Animals construct only in accordance with the standards and needs of the species to which they belong, while man knows how to produce in accordance with the standards of every species and knows how to apply the appropriate standard to the object. Thus man constructs also in accordance with the laws of beauty.

It is just in his work upon the objective world that man really proves himself as a *species-being*. This production is his active species life. By means of it nature appears as *his* work and his reality. The object of labor is, therefore, the *objectification of man's species life;* for he no longer reproduces himself merely intellectually, as in consciousness, but actively and in a real sense, and he sees his own reflection in a world which he has constructed. While, therefore, alienated labor takes away the object of production from man, it also takes away his *species life,* his real objectivity as a species-being, and changes his advantage over animals into a disadvantage in so far as his inorganic body, nature, is taken from him.

Just as alienated labor transforms free and self-directed activity into a means, so it transforms the species life of man into a means of physical existence.

Consciousness, which man has from his species, is transformed through alienation so that species life becomes only a means for him.

(3) Thus alienated labor turns the *species life of man,* and also nature as his mental species-property, into an *alien* being and into a *means* for his *individual existence*. It alienates from man his own body, external nature, his mental life and his *human* life.

(4) A direct consequence of the alienation of man from the product of his labor, from his life activity and from his species life is that *man is alienated* from other *men*. When man confronts himself he also confronts *other* men. What is true of man's relationship to his work, to the product of his work and to himself, is also true of his relationship to other men, to their labor and to the objects of their labor.

In general, the statement that man is alienated from his species life means that each man is alienated from others, and that each of the others is likewise alienated from human life.

Human alienation, and above all the relation of man to himself, is first realized and expressed in the relationship between each man and other men. Thus in the relationship of alienated labor every man regards other men according to the standards and relationships in which he finds himself placed as a worker.

We began with an economic fact, the alienation of the worker and his production. We have expressed this fact in conceptual terms as *alienated labor,* and in analyzing the concept we have merely analyzed an economic fact.

Let us now examine further how this concept of alienated labor must express and reveal itself in reality. If the product of labor is alien to me and confronts me as an alien power, to whom does it belong? If my own activity does not belong to me but is an alien, forced activity, to whom does it belong? To a being *other* than myself. And who is this being? The *gods?* It is apparent in the earliest stages of advanced production, e.g., temple building, etc. in Egypt, India, Mexico, and in the service rendered to gods, that the product belonged to the gods. But the gods alone were never the lords of labor. And no more was *nature*. What a contradiction it would be if the more man subjugates nature by his labor, and the more the marvels of the gods are rendered superfluous by the marvels of industry, he should abstain from his joy in producing and his enjoyment of the product for love of these powers.

The *alien* being to whom labor and the product of labor belong, to whose service labor is devoted, and to whose enjoyment the product of labor goes, can only be *man* himself. If the product of labor does not belong to the worker, but confronts him as an alien power, this can only be because it belongs to *a man other than the worker*. If his activity is a torment to him it must be a source of enjoyment and pleasure to another. Not the gods, nor nature, but only man himself can be this alien power over men.

Consider the earlier statement that the relation of man to himself is first realized, objectified, through his relation to other men. If therefore he is related to the product of his labor, his objectified labor, as to an *alien*, hostile, powerful and independent object, he is related in such a way that another alien, hostile, powerful and independent man is the lord of this object. If he is related to his own activity as to unfree activity, then he is related to it as activity in the service, and under the domination, coercion and yoke, of another man.

Every self-alienation of man, from himself and from nature, appears in the relation which he postulates between other men and himself and nature. Thus religious self-alienation is necessarily exemplified in the relation between laity and priest, or, since it is here a question of the spiritual world, between the laity and a mediator. In the real world of practice this self-alienation can only be expressed in the real, practical relation of man to his fellowmen. The medium through which alienation occurs is itself a *practical* one. Through alienated labor, therefore, man not only produces his relation to the object and to the process of production as to alien and hostile men; he also produces the relation of other men to his production and his product, and the relation between himself and other men. Just as he creates his own production as a vitiation, a punishment, and his own product as a loss, as a product which does not belong to him, so he creates the domination of the non-producer over production and its product. As he alienates his own activity, so he bestows upon the stranger an activity which is not his own.

We have so far considered this relation only from the side of the worker, and later on we shall consider it also from the side of the non-worker.

Thus, through alienated labor the worker creates the relation of another man, who does not work and is outside the work process, to this labor. The relation of the worker to work also produces the relation of the capitalist (or whatever one likes to call the lord of labor) to work. *Private property* is therefore the product, the necessary result, of *alienated labor*, of the external relation of the worker to nature and to himself.

Private property is thus derived from the analysis of the concept of *alienated labor;* that is, alienated man, alienated labor, alienated life, and estranged man.

We have, of course, derived the concept of *alienated labor (alienated life)* from political economy, from an analysis of the *movement of private property*. But the analysis of this concept shows that although private property appears to be the basis and cause of alienated labor, it is rather a consequence of the latter, just as the gods are *fundamentally* not the cause but the product of confusions of human reason. At a later stage, however, there is a reciprocal influence.

Only in the final stage of the development of private property is its secret revealed, namely, that it is on one hand the *product* of alienated labor, and on the other hand the *means* by which labor is alienated, the *realization of this alienation*.

This elucidation throws light upon several unresolved controversies:

(1) Political economy begins with labor as the real soul of production and then goes on to attribute nothing to labor and everything to private property. Proudhon, faced by this contradiction, has decided in favor of labor against private property. We perceive, however, that this apparent contradiction is the contradiction of *alienated labor* with itself and that political economy has merely formulated the laws of alienated labor.

We also observe, therefore, that *wages* and *private property* are identical, for wages, like the product or object of labor, labor itself remunerated, are only a necessary consequence of the alienation of labor. In the wage system labor appears not as an end in itself but as the servant of wages. We shall develop this point later on and here only bring out some of the consequences.

An enforced *increase in wages* (disregarding the other difficulties, and especially that such an anomaly could only be maintained by force) would be nothing more than a *better remuneration of slaves,* and would not restore, either to the worker or to the work, their human significance and worth.

Even the *equality of incomes* which Proudhon demands would only change the relation of the present day worker to his work into a relation of all men to work. Society would then be conceived as an abstract capitalist.

(2) From the relation of alienated labor to private property it also follows that the emancipation of society from private property, from servitude, takes the political form of the *emancipation of the workers;* not in the sense that only the latter's emancipation is involved, but because this emancipation includes the emancipation of humanity as a whole. For all human servitude is involved in the relation of the worker to production, and all the types of servitude are only modifications or consequences of this relation.

As we have discovered the concept of *private property* by an *analysis* of the concept of *alienated labor,* so with the aid of these two factors we can evolve all the categories of political economy, and in every category, e.g., trade, competition, capital, money, we shall discover only a particular and developed expression of these fundamental elements.

However, before considering this structure let us attempt to solve two problems.

(1) To determine the general nature of *private property* as it has resulted from alienated labor, in its relation to *genuine human and social property*.

(2) We have taken as a fact and analyzed the *alienation of labor*. How does it happen, we may ask, that *man alienates his labor*? How is this alienation founded in the nature of human development? We have already done much

to solve the problem in so far as we have *transformed* the question concerning the *origin of private property* into a question about the relation between *alienated labor* and the process of development of mankind. For in speaking of private property one believes oneself to be dealing with something external to mankind. But in speaking of labor one deals directly with mankind itself. This new formulation of the problem already contains its solution.

(1) *The general nature of private property and its relation to genuine human property.*

We have resolved alienated labor into two parts, which mutually determine each other, or rather constitute two different expressions of one and the same relation. *Appropriation* appears as *alienation* and *alienation* as *appropriation,* alienation as genuine acceptance in the community.

We have considered one aspect, *alienated* labor, in its bearing upon the *worker* himself, i.e., *the relation of alienated labor to itself.* And we have found as the necessary consequence of this relation the *property relation* of the *non-worker* to the *worker* and to *labor. Private property* as the material summarized expression of alienated labor includes both relations; *the relation of the worker to labor, to the product of his labor and to the non-worker,* and the relation of the *non-worker to the worker and to the product of the latter's labor.*

We have already seen that in relation to the worker, who *appropriates* nature by his labor, appropriation appears as alienation, self-activity as activity for another and of another, living as the sacrifice of life, and production of the object as loss of the object to an alien power, an alien man. Let us now consider the relation of this *alien* man to the worker, to labor, and to the object of labor.

It should be noted first that everything which appears to the worker as an *activity of alienation,* appears to the non-worker as a *condition of alienation.* Secondly, the *real, practical* attitude of the worker in production and to the product (as a state of mind) appears to the non-worker who confronts him as a *theoretical* attitude.

Thirdly, the non-worker does everything against the worker which the latter does against himself, but he does not do against himself what he does against the worker.

Let us examine these three relationships more closely.[2]

2 The manuscript breaks off unfinished at this point.—*Tr. Note*

27

THE WORKINGMAN'S WIFE: DAY IN, DAY OUT

Lee Rainwater, Richard P. Coleman, and Gerald Handel

The perceptive study from which this selection is taken is based largely on interviews and psychological tests of some 480 white working-class married women between the ages of 20 and 44, living in Chicago; Louisville; Tacoma, Washington; and Trenton, New Jersey. To this was added a contrast group of 120 white middle-class wives living in the same cities. The picture that emerges is enough to fuel the fires of the women's liberation movement; with few exceptions, the life of the typical young working-class wife and mother here is a constant round of bleak, unrelieved drudgery, day after day.

It should be noted, however, that this study was primarily designed as a marketing survey, and all the working-class women interviewed were, by design, either subscribers or newsstand purchasers of the so-called Family Behavior Group magazines: *True Story, True Romance, True Experience,* and *True Love Stories.* The reader may legitimately ask whether the readers of these magazines are representative of working-class women in general, or whether they perhaps represent a group lower in intellectual or educational achievement. Another study of working-class women reached somewhat more optimistic conclusions about the lives and marriages of this group, especially those with higher levels of education.* In fact, a distinction is commonly made between two types of working-class families, *traditional* and *modern.*** In contrast to the latter, traditional families are poorer and less mobile, and members have less education and fewer job skills. The women discussed in this study are primarily members of more traditional working-class families.

Here are not the alert, active, sophisticated American mothers portrayed by television, movies, and popular magazines; instead we see women who are isolated, passive, submissive, incredibly parochial, and, to cite A. E. Housman's much-quoted lines: "Lonely and afraid/In a world they never made." The television set is a paramount aspect of their daily lives, and it is frequently their only window on the outside world. Their personal contacts are pathetically narrow, outside of their children, their husbands, and a small circle of relatives.

These women generally felt insignificant and helpless before the world, lacking the personal resources to understand or improve the quality of their lives. Many feared that the delicate equilibrium of their lives was in constant danger of being upset.

---

* Mirra Komarovsky, *Blue Collar Marriage* (New York: Random House, 1962).
** See Arthur B. Shostak, *Blue-Collar Life* (New York: Random House, 1969), ch. 8.

SOURCE: Lee Rainwater, Richard P. Coleman, and Gerald Handel, *Workingman's Wife: Her Personality, World and Life Style* (New York: Oceana Publications, 1959), Chapter 2. Reprinted by permission of Social Research, Inc., and Oceana Publications, Inc.

For most of these women, life had an overriding elemental quality, a preoccupation with the fundamental processes of life: birth, nurturing the young, health, physical comfort, illness, and death. While everyone must be concerned with these matters to some extent, what distinguishes the working-class woman in this study from others is that these things almost exclusively dominate her life and consciousness.

Unlike middle-class housewives, these working-class women were not great joiners. Partly it was due to a lack of time and money (for baby sitters or dues), but largely it was a consequence of their pervasive sense of not being sophisticated, poised, or acceptable enough for the formidable universe of clubs and organizations. Even religion, which offers them solace, hope, and strength to see life's struggles through, is a very personal experience and is not reflected in widespread participation in or attendance at church.

The ideal of marriage in our society is perhaps embodied in the notion of "total communication" between husband and wife, both physical and psychological, so that there is almost a psychic fusion of the two people while each retains his own individuality at the same time. Unfortunately, this ideal is not often realized in these working-class homes (it is probably not realized in most middle- or upper-class homes either, although the failures are probably not as frequent nor as thoroughgoing).

The traditional (much more than modern) working-class marriage is often characterized by a rigorous "role segregation," in which the husband and wife function within two separate social worlds, with little overlap. This segregation is manifested in many ways. Unlike the middle-class wife, who has often helped, encouraged, or pushed her husband into his career, the working-class wife in this study often knows little about and takes little interest in her husband's job. Many women did not know exactly what their husbands did on the job, or did not know exactly where their husbands worked. There is relatively little sharing of recreational activity, as the men often went off by themselves on hunting or fishing vacations while the wives remained at home. There is, in addition, relatively little sharing and cooperation between husband and wife of child care and housework; each has his own separate sphere of responsibilities. There were great deficiencies in emotional interchange and disclosure between husband and wife, due partly to working-class masculine inarticulateness. Finally, in their sexual life, the popular cliché was frequently verified, with the husband making physical demands upon his wife but not reciprocating with needed affection and emotional tenderness.

As a result of her tremendous household responsibilities, her isolation from the world of clubs, her limited education and sparce intellectual resources, her early marriage and motherhood, the working-class wife lives a very sheltered existence, completely cut off from the larger world outside. Although she is an urban dweller alive in a century in which the means of communicating ideas and information are greater than ever before in human history, she remains in the backwash of society, often benighted, superstitious, and fearful.

We have discussed briefly the social position in the American social hierarchy which is called "working class," and have noted that the women whose lives are being described belong to this class by virtue of their husbands' blue collar jobs, their own and their husbands' modest educational attainments (mostly high school graduation, sometimes less) and their similarly modest housing and residential acquisitions. In this chapter we shall concern ourselves with the way in which these women live their daily lives within such a social context. In our research, we have asked working class women to tell us what their day-to-day activities are and how they feel about these by asking: "What is a typical day like?", "How does the week go?", "How are the weekends different from weekdays?", "What happens at vacation time?", "Which holidays are celebrated?", and "How does winter differ from summer, or spring from fall?"

The way working class and middle class women talk in response to such questions provides us with insight into the variety of activities in which they engage, and indicates the hierarchy or importance of time consumption for them. We learn about the "daily rhythm" in these women's lives and come to some understanding of the "annual round of life"—the adjustments made to the changing seasons and the ways holidays and vacations interrupt the normal routine. Finally, we gain insight into their emotional response to the content of their daily lives.

The working class wife's daily life is centered upon the tasks of homemaking, child-rearing, and husband-servicing. When these women describe a "typical day" they devote most of their reportorial attention to three aspects of the day: their housework, their children, and their husbands. The attention devoted to their children is only partially affected by the age of these children—the mothers of very young children quite naturally believe their "typical days" are consumed by both nurturant and policeman-like attention to these children; however, the mothers of older children seem to be equally wrapped up in the activities of these not-so-necessarily-dependent children. The working class women whose lives seem to contain any other important foci are those who hold jobs. In the following description we occasionally differentiate between the "working

women" and the "homemakers only." And, of course, we also find it useful to separate the mothers of older children from those of very young children. However, it is this latter group which we have taken as our main model.

We will let some of these women speak for themselves about their days. These samples are rather typical in the range and kind of daily activity mentioned even though these particular women are more articulate than many in the richness of detail they provide. The first description was given by a 24-year old woman from Trenton, New Jersey. She lives in one of Levittown's modest new houses:

> Well, naturally, I get up first, make breakfast for my husband and put a load of clothes in my washer while breakfast cooks. Then I wake him up, give him his breakfast and he's off to work. Then I make breakfast for the children. After the children eat I dress them and they go out to play. Then I hang the clothes up and clean lightly through the house. In between times I do the dishes—that's understood, of course. Then I make lunch for the children and myself and I bring them in, clean them up, and they eat. I send them out to play when they're done and I do the dishes, bring the clothes in, and iron them. When I'm done ironing it's usually time to make supper, or at least start preparing it. Sometimes I have time to watch a TV story for half an hour or so. Then my husband comes home and we have our meals. Then I do the dishes again. Then he goes out to work again—he has a part-time job—at his uncle's beverage company. Well, he does that two or three nights a week. If he stays home he watches TV and in the meantime I get the kids ready for bed. He and I have a light snack, watch TV awhile and then go to bed.

A 22-year old housewife from Tacoma tells much the same story:

Ye Gods—what do I do. Well, I get up and out of bed at 6 A.M. I get my son dressed and then get breakfast. After breakfast I wash dishes then bathe and feed my baby. She's 3 months old. Then I start the procedure of house cleaning. I make beds—dust, mop, sweep, vacuum. Then I do my baby's wash. Then I get lunch for the three of us. Then I put my baby to bed, and the little boy to bed for his nap. Then I usually sew or mend or wash windows or iron and do the things I can't possibly get done before noon. Then I cook supper for my family. After supper my husband usually watches TV while I wash dishes. I get the kids to bed. Then—if I'm lucky—I'm able to sit down, watch TV or read a magazine. Then I set my hair and go to bed.

Here is a story of harassment told by a 23-year old Louisville mother of two young children:

Well, I fight with the children to eat for one thing. They don't want to eat. The little girl—she's 4—is hungry and then she won't eat. They usually go on outside after breakfast. I feed the baby and give him a bath and then I put him on the floor. Then I make the bed up, dust the floors and dust the furniture and by that time it's time for dinner. Then I fix dinner and do the dishes. In between time I have to feed him and give him a bath and put him to bed. Then it's time to fix supper and Daddy comes home. After supper we just sit here and watch TV or I visit one of the neighbors. We very seldom go out during the week because he works. My husband may wash the car or something like that. Other than that he just watches TV or goes to sleep. He putters around the yard or reads maybe. He is usually too tired after he comes home from work. The children just spend the whole day playing and getting messed up. Then they watch TV after supper with me. Then they get washed and go to bed about 9 o'clock.

And finally, we have a daily-tale by a 29-year old Trenton woman in which a mode of relaxation other than TV is mentioned:

I get up and do the dishes and make the beds and sweep the floors. I scrub the kitchen once a day, wash and iron, and then towards evening I get dinner. I do just what most everybody does. In the afternoons—well, my husband works nights—so I get his meal about 2 o'clock, and clean up after him. Then I usually have a couple of hours I spend at the neighbors yaking. This backyard takes a lot of work too because we are going to seed it over. This place was a mess when we moved in here a year ago. I usually go to the store once a day and my little boy takes a nap too. Usually I sit and sew half the evening and read the rest of the evening.

These four accounts of "my day" illustrate quite clearly how extremely busy the woman is with her housework. She fixes breakfast, washes clothes, dresses children, cleans the house, does the dishes, makes lunch, irons the clothes, makes supper, makes light snacks, makes beds, dusts, mops, sweeps, mends old clothes, washes windows, scrubs the kitchen, works out in the yard, shops for groceries, and sews on new clothes or curtains. She has no maid to help her with any of these tasks. Her children are too young to be of assistance. Her husband often has an extra income job or has his own responsibilities (such as washing the car or seeding the yard), so that he cannot be counted on to help her.

It is no wonder that with all these homemaking activities to perform, she is sometimes tempted to describe her daily life as one in which:

I wash or iron or clean up the house or sew and that just about covers my days. I haven't ever caught up with myself since the twins were born four years ago.

or where,

> By the time I get breakfast and dishes done my morning's gone and by the time the canning I'm doing this summer is over the whole day's gone. And it's been just housework all day long.

She also views her children as a source of considerable concern in her daily life. She must feed them, clothe them, bathe them, and put them to bed, and she must keep a continual weather-eye out for them, even when she is not immediately ministering to their habitual wants and needs, lest "I spend half of my day kissing all their little hurts and bruises." Or, as another said, "What with hunting for the kids I'm running in and out most of the day."

These women frequently find that "life around little children" is one perpetual battle—either with them, or between them. When they are asked how the children spend their time—and hers, many chorused: "The children—they fight," or "The kids get up in the morning and they don't do anything but fuss all day," or "In between fights, the children play and eat and sleep." And sometimes, "They don't want to eat," so that the mother must "fight with the children to get them to eat."

Time and again working class women express the feeling that their responsibilities toward their children preclude many expeditions into the outside world of clubs or parties or travels. To these women the presence of small children in a home is an automatic definition for the busy woman: "I have three boys so you can imagine I'm busy all right."

In these descriptions of daily routines, the husbands seem to come in a poor third in the attention they get. The wives serve them breakfast, sometimes fix their lunch, prepare their suppers, wash and mend their clothes—but don't "waste" nearly as many words on them, as on the house and children. Perhaps this is because the presence of the husband is only a part-time phenomenon, while the children are a "full-time nuisance."

The principal effect of the husband's activities on these daily routines seems to be in setting the hour for breakfast, supper, and bedtime. If a husband does not work the standard eight-hour day (between 8:00 and 5:00), the working class woman regards this as upsetting her time schedule. She may have to fix her big meal at 2:00 in the afternoon, instead of at noon or in the early evening. If the husband has an extra job in the evening or on the weekends, this enlarges the amount of home and yard responsibilities she must undertake. If the husband drives the car to work, she finds herself isolated in her own immediate neighborhood while he's gone.

By the time she fulfills the tasks which arise from these three important roles as homemaker, child-rearer, and husband-servicer, she finds herself with little time for, or interest in, any other kind of activity. She rarely attends a club meeting or goes to a party—at least she doesn't mention this as being a part of her typical day. She may get time for reading, "while the children are napping," or "before going to bed." She almost never mentions playing games, such as bridge or canasta, or spending time at sports, such as bowling or swimming.

The "daily routine" of a working class wife typically includes only two activities beyond the big three of house, children, and husband. These "other two" activities are TV watching and neighbor or relative visiting. However, "casual visiting" as a daily activity is not mentioned by a majority of these women. Television, in contrast, ranks very high in their devotion: well over a majority of working class women consider their television sessions important enough aspects of their days to be included in their descriptions. Very few of these women, however, work in any TV time until the evening when they are able to sit down in front of the set with either their husbands or children. Occasionally a young housewife mentions that her family takes daily car rides in the evening, or that she chauffeurs the children to a nearby swimming pool in the summer. But such adventures beyond the realm of homemaking or TV watching are distinct exceptions.

The only "adventurers" among these young housewives are those with jobs which take them out of their homes every day. This kind of "adventure" however does not change their daily life much, except to confine it to a quadrangle instead of a triangle: the job becomes a fourth point of energy output. They do not use their jobs as an avenue toward additional adventure. Perhaps this report of "her day" from a 39-year old Chicago working wife will illustrate the typical effect of a job upon the daily routine.

> I just run from one day to the next. I get up at six, eat breakfast and fix lunch for myself and my husband. We get up at the same time, but he leaves a half-hour before me. He takes the bus to work and then later on at five I pick him up in the car and we drive home. I drive if he is tired, or else he does the driving. You see, we both work near each other—it's really only a few blocks away. I let mother keep care of my

youngest daughter, and then I send Carol, who is 3, to nursery school. In the evenings I just get the supper and then do the dishes, plus maybe some ironing or cleaning. There's always enough to do: too much in fact. Mostly we just watch TV in the evening, or if it's hot like yesterday we go out and sit on the lawn. But mostly we're both tired. Our jobs just knock us out and in the evenings we just plop down.

Where the wife has no children around her house—because she is still a "young bride," or has become a "deserted mother," or was never anything other than a "childless wife," a slight increase is noted in the extent of her "visiting" or "movie going." However, the evidence leans in the direction of indicating a relatively "empty" existence for these women rather than one of equal "busyness" directed elsewhere. When asked how their days went, these women were singularly non-verbal, as if their days were not as full of meaningful activity.

A young bride related the events of her typical day in the following fashion:

> We get up at 5:45. I make my husband's breakfast and pack his lunch. I have coffee and straighten up the house, then I go to work at 8:45. Both my husband and I work all day long. My husband gets home at 4. I get home an hour later and I start supper. Afterwards, I clean the dishes. We spend our evenings either visiting or going to movies. We watch television when we get home and then retire at 10 or 11.

And a deserted mother describes her "deserted day" with these comments:

> I get up at 5:30 in the morning and make breakfast. I get my husband off to work by 6:30. He comes home about 4 o'clock and I make dinner. In between times I do some household chores and

look at television maybe an hour or so. In the evening we visit friends for several hours in the neighborhood and then go to bed about 11 o'clock.

One suspects that her television set is left on for more than "an hour or so," and that she has not reported the amount of time she spends in magazine reading.

At the other extreme from the daily boredom implied by this woman's report of her day, is that given us by a "school-age mother" who is trying to expand her mental and social horizons.

First of all I fix breakfast for everybody—We have six people in the house—then I start the wash—when there is enough to bother with. That's about three times a week. Then right away I fix my husband's lunch to take to work. I get up at 5:45 in order to get everything done. After breakfast I get the wash out and put it in the dryer, clean the dishes and fix lunch for myself and my children. They have come home from school, and I keep them home for a full hour so they will rest. Then I send them back at 1 o'clock. After lunch I straighten things up around the home and do some sewing—you see I make my own dresses and a lot of other things. I'm not a TV watcher like some people. I'd rather sew or read. By 5:45 it's time to start supper so we can all eat around 6:00. In the evenings I just read or sew or I visit with the neighbors. A lot of the time I show them how to sew. I have classes, sort of—I taught it to myself, you know. I'm not a professional dressmaker—what I want to do now is to take some evening course so that I'll learn to sew without a pattern like a real professional.

This woman is an exception: as a rule, working class housewives whose children are of school age do not get out of the house much more than the younger mothers. A minority of them, mostly upper working class mothers in new suburbs, mention some PTA activity or work in the scouting movements or attendance at Little League games.

The Working Class Wife Classifies Her Daily Routine as "Dull, Normal"

She characterizes her daily life as "busy," "crowded," "a mess," "humdrum," "dull, just dull." But she feels that this is the lot of most housewives, except, perhaps, "those society leaders you read about in the papers." The general tenor of her attitude toward what a day in her life is like is indicated by the following comments:

Crowded, just crowded—that's what every day is like. They're all busy. They're just dull too. We just don't do much except work. They're all dull compared to those you read about in the newspapers of people who run around all the time.

Oh, it's housework all day long. We really don't do very much—I would like to get out more if I weren't so isolated out here. My husband has the car all day long, so I'm sort of stuck here.

All I ever seem to do is mess around. I get up at 8—I make breakfast, so I do the dishes, have lunch, do some more dishes, and then some more work in the afternoon. Then it's supper dishes and I get to sit down for a few minutes before the children have to be sent to bed. That's it—that's all there is to my day.

My day's just like any other wife's. It's just routine. Humdrum. It's really just what every other housewife does.

We don't do much of anything special. I imagine my day is spent doing what any housewife does. Just cooking and cleaning, washing the dishes and mending clothes. Then the biggest part of the time I am chasing kids.

If she feels that her own life is one of monotony or is a "humdrum" existence, she is consoled by her belief that this does not make her different from most of the other women she knows. She usually does not know many middle class women. Since middle class women and working class women tend to live in different sections of the city, the latter are not sufficiently acquainted with the middle class mode of life to draw comparisons of self or life styles. Even if the working class woman were able to make such comparisons, she might not see her own life as so very different. After all, the "young mothers" among the middle class also spend a considerable amount of time in infant care; they also wash dishes and clothes; they also fix three meals a day for their families (as a rule). Where the middle class woman is really different is not so much in what she does (though this is different in noticeable ways, as will be described shortly), but in her reaction to her life circumstances.

The middle class woman does not see her daily life as "dull, normal." To her one day is not "just like the next." Life is not "routine," or "humdrum"— if anything, it sometimes seems not quite "routine" enough. When middle class women were asked to describe a typical day they reacted with statements such as:

> Are there any typical days? Every day there's something new! How can I possibly describe a typical day?

or,

> Each day is different. I do try to accomplish certain things each day—but my schedule usually gets upset.

or,

> Every day is different when you have two little ones around. I have a teenager

and then this little child, and I can assure you that with them coming up with something new, there are no two days alike. You can't even plan very well.

Where the working class wife finds her children "fighting every day," the middle class woman sees her children "coming up with something new." Undoubtedly both groups of children do their share of squabbling and "coming up with something new." But the working class mother is more conscious of the fights and their wearing effect upon her patience, while the middle class woman is more conscious of the "new," and this engenders pride and wonderment at her children. The difference in these women's days seems as much a matter of viewpoint as behavior.

Middle class women do not believe they have "typical days." The variety which they impute to their "days" is not solely a product of different viewpoint, however. They frequently schedule the days in the week so each has its function. The weekend is assigned its importance as a time when the whole "family can get together and do something as a unit." It is a time specifically laid aside for relaxation. The various seasons are thought of as providing opportunities for exploration of different facets of life: winter is for social pleasures, and summer is for the personal pleasures of swimming or boating or working in the garden. This is the way the middle class woman thinks of her year. When, therefore, she is asked to describe a typical day, her first thought is to ask: "Do you mean a weekday, or a Sunday?"; "Do you mean in summer or winter—we've got a different pattern, you know."

The middle class woman, despite her knowledge that it might not work out as she intends, usually assigns a function to each of her days:

Monday is laundry; Tuesday, I shop for groceries; Wednesday, the cleaning woman comes; Thursday, I buy the meats for the weekend; and Friday, I go to the beauty parlor.

Monday is washing and ironing; Tuesday is club meeting; Wednesday is mending and shopping; Thursday is downstairs day, and Friday is upstairs day.

She obviously homemakes just as does the working class wife. However, she does not appear to be hell-bent on doing everything every single day. Thereby she apparently makes more efficient use of her housekeeping time.

The middle class woman also child-rears and husband-tends. She fixes their meals, sews their clothes frequently, and makes sure they get to work or school on time. But that is not all she does.

I get up at 6:45 A.M. and get every one off—my husband to work, and my daughter to school. Then I get my younger two children dressed for outside so they can play while I do up my dishes and my general housework. In the afternoons I do a lot of sewing—making things for the girls and myself. I have a lot of organizations I belong to and sometimes I attend those if I can find someone to take care of the children. Then my husband comes home—and we have a fairly late dinner, usually, unless he has to run out to attend a couple of his meetings. If he doesn't, he may work around the house, while I read or sew—and then again, we may just watch TV. Right now we're getting ready to have an open house this weekend—so my husband will probably help me get the place in ship-shape.

The middle class woman experiences more variety in her life, and less monotony, because she has a much greater number of personal avocational and outside interests than does the working class wife. Most middle class women have a "meeting" to go to at least twice a month. And they report that every now and then one of their "typical" days might include:

Going out for dinner and a dance,

Getting together with another couple to play mah-jongg,

Having an open house for 40 or 50 people,

Going to a tea today—we'll probably play bridge also,

Doing voluntary work for the Red Cross,

Playing volleyball down at the club with a bunch of the girls,

Doing some backstage work at the Little Theater.

Both groups of women report with fairly considerable frequency that a typical day might include some "visiting." But when the middle class woman speaks of visiting, she is usually referring to the talking she does at one of these meetings or parties, while the working class woman usually refers to visits with a "neighbor," "relatives and in-laws," or "a girl friend" whom she's known since her childhood. Thus, even the visiting a working class wife does during a day might seem monotonous to her (as compared with that done by the middle class woman), inasmuch as she's doing it with the "same old people" she has always known.

Let us conclude this comparison of the "typical" day by noting that time and again the middle class women refused to describe a "typical day." They combined elements from several of their days into their description of one. Perhaps they were afraid a "typical day" would not really do justice to the variety of interests which occupy them during a month. Perhaps they did not want to appear to lead as dull a life as a single day, taken at random, might indicate. On the other hand, the working class women did not seem to mind describing a "typical day," though they were mindful and conscious of how routinely similar the days are.

The Weekend Routine Is Also Dull, Normal

Weekends are "not too much different from the rest of the week" for the working class wives. When these women are asked: "How are the weekends different from the rest of the week?" they are apt to curtly reply, "They're not." They may issue this judgment in a variety of ways: the chorus is different, but the tune is essentially the same.

> Nothing different about them. They're much the same except that I may go for a swim.
>
> There's really not too much to do around this town so they're pretty much the same.
>
> The only thing different about them is that my husband has a different job —he works right through Saturday and Sunday.
>
> The weekend is just the same as the week except the children sometimes go to Sunday School. We're pretty much the home-bodies—we really lead quite dull lives.
>
> Oh well, there's hardly any difference. My husband has to work part of Saturday and Sunday, too.
>
> They are just about the same, except I refuse to do housework on weekends. They're really just like any other day. A day's a day to me.
>
> I'm a lot busier, that's what. I do the same things as I do the rest of the week, but with everybody home, I have less time to do them in.

Let it be noted that "weekend days" are not always the same: the housewife refuses to work, or else she's busier. The children may go to Sunday school, the husband may have a different job,

the wife may go for a swim. But these differences seem less significant to them than the similarities. They seem surprisingly ready to believe that "every day is like every other." Perhaps the worst indictment of the weekend was rendered by a woman who reported:

> Saturday is different from Sunday because my husband brings home all his work clothes and I wash them.

In fact, it is far from true that "the weekends are no different from the rest of the week" for the majority of these women. There is one custom practiced by a great many (on either Saturday or Sunday) which is not paid such regular heed during the week. This is a visit to the relatives. Many echo the statement made by the 32-year old housewife from Tacoma:

> On Sunday we always get the family together; that's just automatic.

For some families, this weekend visit is Sunday dinner at either the mother's home or the mother-in-law's; for others it requires a drive into the country or to a nearby town to visit "the folks" or perhaps a brother and sister-in-law who still live in the "old hometown."

Other activities, which various working class women report as characteristic of their weekends (in contrast to their weekdays), are "taking a ride out into the country," "going to the shore," "my husband goes fishing or hunting," "taking in a movie," or "going out to eat." For many families there is a division between Saturday and Sunday: Saturday is for yard work and shopping, while Sunday is for church and relaxation. However, less than half of the women in our study sample go to church as often as twice a month. They are not church-going women for the most part, just as they are not club members.

Working class women do not actually experience a weekend as it is known by most "white collar" Americans. Many of the husbands have "extra income jobs" on Saturday or Sunday (or perhaps in the evenings during the week). Another large portion of the husbands, particularly those in the transportation industries or in public service as policemen or firemen, are required by the nature of their employment, to serve the public during the weekend as well as on weekdays.

In direct contrast, middle class women think of their weekends as entirely different from the weekdays. The weekend theme is "doing things as a family" and "relaxing from the ardors of mid-week." Middle class women describe their weekends in a strikingly different tone.

> The difference is that I try to do things with my family more than some housework. Sometimes I prepare a lunch or dinner out on the lawn in summertime—and we do a little extra entertaining in the winter.
>
> Sunday is the day we do things together—the whole family goes to church and then we may go visiting. We want to do it all together if we can.
>
> We never have a set routine for the weekend. We do whatever we feel like on the spur of the moment. I don't worry about the work as much. I spend more time with my family—and we just enjoy loafing around the house and get more relaxation out of it. We may have some extra-good things to eat.
>
> We break out of the weekday grind. Our meals are at different times. Sunday, we go to church, and maybe we will shop on Saturday, or my husband will play golf, or sometimes we all go bowling. During the week, when the children are in school, I'm more or less my own

boss. I do as I please—but on the weekends my family is around and we do a lot together.

> We belong to a club of couples—we play cards about once a month. My husband is a Mason and we go to the Shrine Club on Saturday nights quite often. Sometimes we take the children, sometimes we don't. Sunday, after church, it's just 'mess-around.' We may go swimming or out to the beach in the afternoon during the summer. We do just what we want to do and when we want to do it. There is no really set pattern for anything.

Occasionally they visit relatives on the weekend, but most of the instances cited involved a relative who had a "beach cottage" or perhaps a horse farm where the "children can learn how to handle animals." In short, when middle class women say they do "things as a family" during the weekend, they are usually referring to the immediate family circle of their children and husband; whereas, the working class women who say that "getting the whole family together is automatic" every weekend, are talking about the extended clan of in-laws, brothers, and perhaps aunts, uncles or grandparents.

Summer Is Dull, Normal, Just Like Winter

Working class women, generally, believe that their lives are very little influenced by the changing seasons. The biggest change they envision is the invitation from summer weather to stay outside in their yards more often, while winter forbiddingly keeps them "holed up in their houses."

As with their reaction to the "weekend" or the "weekday," working class women are more conscious of the overall similarities in daily events than they are of whatever diversity and variety may be present.

> We're outside more in the summer and inside more in the winter, that's all. My husband remodelled the inside of the house this past winter. He'll paint the outside next summer.

> We stay inside more at night in winter. We usually sit outside in the summer time. I wouldn't really say that the time of the year makes any difference in what we do—when you have three children you've got to stay home a lot the whole year round.

> It's about the same in summer or winter. I'm still sewing. All we do is work no matter what month of the year it is.

> One thing that's different is that summer is cheaper for us. We can eat outdoors quite often, and it doesn't cost us so much. It doesn't use up so much electric power. We're confined to the inside during the winter and we watch TV all the time. (She also said: "The TV relaxes me and gives me a change from reading so many short stories.")

Working class husbands seem to be more affected by the changing of season, thereby eliciting varying reactions from their wives. At times it leaves the wives somewhat less than happy, as when:

> My husband fishes in summer and hunts up in the mountains in winter— but in either case I stay home.

On the other hand, the change in seasons can be a blessing when:

> My husband doesn't fish in the wintertime, so he stays home and I get to enjoy his company.

or,

> He doesn't go off playing sandlot ball in the winter.

But then, there is the woman who wishes the seasons did make a difference in her husband's life, because:

> There's no difference at all in the wintertime—my husband still makes his model cars, boats, and airplanes.

These bleak references to the lack of any difference between the seasons fortunately are not the whole picture. Though a good many of these women take this view, for others the winter is a time when they can go ice-skating, attend church more often, play cards every now and then, go bowling, take part in some of the children's school activities, or spend more time on home improvement projects. And the summer is a time when they can take more drives out into "nature," when they can garden, go on barbecues, swim, take in a baseball game every now and then, go berry picking or clam digging, watch their son's Little League games, or do some outdoor cooking.

Middle class women report many of the same differences between their summertime lives and their winter days. They also view winter as the time for indoor life and summer as the season for outdoor living. However, above and beyond these changes in the details of life, middle class women see the different seasons as having essentially different functions. Winter is the "social season," and summer is "for more purely personal pleasures":

> We do more entertaining in the winter evenings than during the summer. In the summertime so many friends are vacationing at any one time and are out of town that it's simpler to get the group together in the winter than during the summer.

> We have all these social activities in the winter—parties and dances, school affairs, or civic things like Community Chest drives, and then there's football games most every Saturday in the fall, and plays or concerts all through the winter. But in summer, we have our lake cottage, and we go out there more

and get away from people. We just swim
and relax. By the time summer is over,
we're ready to pitch into our winter
schedule once again.

If winter is highly active for the middle class families, then the summer's
function is recuperative.

Working class wives do not usually
have vacations which they can devote
to travel. What they do with their vacation time is strictly influenced by the
wife's age or child-rearing status. Many
of the "young mothers" scoff at the
idea of a "vacation." As one said: "Vacations, what are those? You don't
ever get one when you have three little
kids around." Most "older mothers" are
able to report trips of one kind or another, even if their only purpose is to
visit a relative in a nearby city.

The "young" working class wife is
unlikely to take a vacation either, because her husband is not established
enough in his occupation:

My husband hasn't always worked long
enough or steady enough for a vacation
—but we plan the first one he gets to go
to the beach or camping and fishing.

We don't have vacation time—my
husband never gets a paid vacation.
We're going to plan on it for next year
though.

My husband isn't going to get a vacation this year. Last year he got one—but
it wasn't exactly a vacation. He went out
to visit his sick mother. Sometime I'd
like to leave the children behind and go
to Mexico or Hawaii or Paris and do a
lot of sightseeing.

or because her brood of children would
be "too much trouble carting around
the country."

We visited my relatives in Iowa last
year—but it was a nightmare taking two
children along. I certainly didn't think
I'd had any vacation. I'm waiting till
they get a little older before I try that
again.

Babies are such a mess to bother with
—they don't enjoy it and neither do
you.

Or else, she and her husband choose
to spend any vacation time on home
projects:

Last year we spent it building the
house.

We just stay around the house—he
paints the outside of the house, and I
try to keep the kids out of his way.

or perhaps on extra jobs which will
eventually provide a better "home in
the suburbs."

Middle class women in this same age
group are also quite frequently inclined to "pass up real vacations while
the kids are young." However, instead
of letting the tender age of these children interfere with their own vacations, many manage to persuade for-
bearing grandparents to "take over the
kids for a week or two." They say, in
justification of their behavior, "That
makes everybody happy: we get away
from the kids, they get away from us
. . . and then the grandparents are
tickled to have them for a while, and
for the kids it's a great treat too."

For many working class women the
celebration of one of the big holidays
(Christmas or Easter or Thanksgiving)
is the nearest thing to a vacation.
These holidays are usually celebrated
in family-clan fashion at the grandparents' home. This, again, is somewhat
different and in contrast with the middle class pattern of spending such holidays with the immediate family or with
adult friends of long standing.

Overall, it appears that the lives of
working class wives are relatively more
constricted to the triangle of the home,
children, and husband than is the case
with the middle class families. Many
satisfactions are found within this
triangle, which often expands to in-

clude the whole circle of relatives and the family clan. However, they also respond to the life lived within this triangle by feeling it does not provide them with as much variety or relief from monotony as they might like. They see themselves as "hard working" women. They feel "tied down to the house" by their small children. They are solaced in their sometimes unhappy reaction by the recognition that their "dull" lot in life is shared by many American housewives, including most of the women they know.

The satisfactions which they do find are vested primarily in the people with whom they live so closely, and in the daily occupation of their lives as wives and mothers.

28

SOCIAL CLASS AND POPULAR CULTURE

Herbert J. Gans

The American writer H. L. Mencken once said, "Nobody ever went broke underestimating the taste of the American public." This remark highlights a traditional concern of intellectuals, social critics, sociologists, and others with the level of mass aesthetic taste in modern society. While radical and conservative critics disagree on the causes and the cure of the so-called mass culture phenomenon, they are united by their sorrow over what they believe to be the crude, vulgar, and philistine tastes of much of the public in music, popular literature, magazines, newspapers, films, television and radio programming, art, drama, and the like. Critics of mass culture despair, for example, that the *Readers' Digest* has the largest circulation of any magazine and the *New York Daily News* the largest circulation of any newspaper in the country; that a day's television fare seems to be a horrible window into the mind of the typical American; that books like *Peyton Place* and *Valley of the Dolls* have sold millions of copies and been transposed to other media; that in the last fifteen years Elvis Presley has made more than twenty-five movies and sold eighty-three million records, and that according to a delighted announcement from MGM, Presley has "one of the most heard voices in the history of mankind." Meanwhile, classical music accounts for only 5 percent of all record sales, having dropped from 20 percent only a decade ago.

The issue of mass (or popular) culture is a prominent one today. During periods of economic crisis, social analysts turn their attention to the crucial economic problems of the day and inequities arising therefrom. During periods of prosperity, however, such as the United States has enjoyed during the long era following World War II,

SOURCE: Herbert J. Gans, "Popular Culture in America: Social Problem in a Mass Society or Social Asset in a Pluralist Society?" in Howard S. Becker, ed., *Social Problems: A Modern Approach* (New York: John Wiley & Sons, 1966), pp. 582–98. Reprinted by permission of the author and publisher.

social analysts turn their attention to the quality of life in society. This is perhaps reflected in the recent concern over such issues as alienation, community, the meaninglessness of life in the affluent suburbs, the problems of identity in a society of large-scale bureaucratic organizations, and, as noted, concern over the level of public cultural taste.

Here is a sample of some of the issues frequently joined in the debate over mass culture. Assuming the level of popular taste is lower than the intellectual critics desire, what are the sources of debased popular aesthetics? Does mass culture exist because the public is simply given what it wants, or do the purveyors of popular culture *create* bad taste and impose it upon an essentially passive public simply because it is profitable and easy to sell? Are intellectual pleas for high culture valid or do they represent an elitist, opinionated, authoritarian, and ethnocentric claim to the superiority of their own values? What has been the effect of democracy, universal literacy, and mass communication upon the level of popular taste? Is the level of aesthetic taste today higher or lower than in preindustrial societies? Does mass culture—with its themes of violence, sex, appeals to the irrational as in advertising, the distortion and the simplification of reality—have negative social and psychological consequences? Does the unprecedented extension of modern means of communication atomize the public and render it more susceptible to political demagoguery and manipulation? Does mass culture have deleterious effects on high culture, by borrowing and debasing elements of high culture, by luring serious artists with promises of fame and fortune, by overpowering and driving high culture out? Is a high level of national culture compatible with the profit motive that seeks the largest possible audience for its product and thus tends to fall victim to the "lowest common denominator" principle?

In this selection, taken from a longer and very provocative essay on mass culture, sociologist Herbert Gans takes a somewhat more sanguine view of popular culture than the critics. Gans claims that only in the simplest and most homogeneous societies is there a homogeneous culture. In all complex societies, on the other hand, you are bound to have what he calls "esthetic pluralism," that is, many "taste publics" which partake of various "taste cultures." And Gans argues that the single most important determinant of the diverse taste publics found in America today is not ethnic, racial, religious, or regional background, but social class. In this excerpt, Gans sketches his view of the various social class taste publics in the United States today and discusses the complex interaction of social class factors and cultural taste.

Taste publics and cultures are not official bodies or organized groups but aggregates of similar people making similar choices, and aggregates of similar content chosen by the same people who can be identified through sociological research. Several factors probably determine a person's identification with a taste public and his choice among taste cultures. For the purpose of this analysis, which is primarily to illustrate the diversity of taste publics and cultures, it is possible to oversimplify and stress one factor, *class*. As I noted earlier, aesthetic standards and leisure choices reflect people's backgrounds and in American society, where ethnic, religious, and regional differences are rapidly disappearing, the major source of subcultural variety is increasingly that of age and class, especially the latter.[1]

[1] Herbert J. Gans, "Diversity Is Not Dead: A Report on Our Widening Range of Choice," *The New Republic*, 144 (April 3, 1961), pp. 11–15.

Perhaps the most important criterion for cultural choice is education, for two reasons. First, every item of cultural content carries with it a built-in educational requirement—little for the comic strip, much for the poetry of T. S. Eliot. Second, aesthetic standards and taste are taught in our society both by the home and the school. Thus a person's educational achievement and the kind of school he attended will probably predict better than any other single index that person's cultural choices. Since both of these are closely related to an individual's (and his parents') socioeconomic level, the range of taste cultures and publics follows closely the range of classes in American society.

The following descriptions of publics and cultures have the limitations of thumbnail sketches; I shall describe only American cultures and will even leave out ethnic, religious, and regional variants within them. Moreover, although each taste public culture is stratified by age, containing children, adolescent, young adult, and adult subgroupings, I will deal only with adult publics and their cultures. (Incidentally, this theory questions the existence of a single American "youth culture" and suggests instead the existence of several, with some common elements that reflect the position of adolescents in contemporary society.)

Publics and cultures will be treated as relatively homogeneous and static wholes, even though in reality each has factions that might be called traditional, contemporary, and progres-

sive (or academic, establishment, and avant-garde, as they are referred to in high culture). Undoubtedly age correlates strongly with these factions; the progressives are younger than the traditionalists. Ethnic and religious backgrounds may also be relevant, and I suspect that in each taste public Catholics and Jews are likely to be more progressive, Protestants more traditional. Finally, the descriptions identify tendencies and cannot be used to classify individuals or even individual cultural items.

I will identify six major taste publics and their cultures. For other purposes, such as the formulation of public policy, more specificity would be necessary, and one might identify twenty or more publics and cultures, including the age, ethnic, and other subgroupings just referred to. The decision to describe publics and their cultures rather than the reverse was made because the characteristics and standards of publics are better known and are fairly stable, whereas the cultures shift somewhat over the years as new fashions and ideas replace old ones.

Because taste is a function of class, the six publics are labeled with class terms. Although stylistically poor, these terms have the advantage of being neutral.[2] The six publics and cultures to be described are called creator high culture, consumer high culture, upper-middle culture, lower-middle culture, lower-culture, and lower-lower culture.[3] The distinction between the two high-culture publics is based on the previously made distinction between crea-

---

[2] Edward Shils, who maintains the tripartite division used by [Van Wyck] Brooks and [Russell] Lynes, used the terms refined, mediocre, and brutal, which are hardly neutral. See Shils, "Mass Society and Its Culture," in N. Jacobs, ed., *Culture for the Millions* (Princeton, N.J.: Van Nostrand, 1961).

[3] Another alternative would be to use the model educational level of each public, thus calling them university, collegiate, high school, tenth grade and grade school.

tor orientation and consumer orientation. A creator-oriented public or culture is one whose aesthetic standards have to do with what the creator intended to do, how he did it, what methods he used, and how they relate to the content. Such an evaluation asks the audience to take the creator's role, to look over his shoulder in using the cultural product. The aesthetic standards of a consumer-oriented public or culture stress the content's effect on the audience. Thus the evaluation of the product asks first whether the audience thought it good or bad; whether they liked it or not; and what kind of an impact it had on them, with the creator's aims being secondary.

Since all cultures include both creators and consumers, everyone has creator- and consumer-oriented aesthetic standards. These standards and the people who hold them are often in conflict. In each of the cultures one could therefore describe creator and consumer factions, but I will do so only for high culture, partly because there the conflict is most visible. In the other cultures the conflict is muted, largely because commercially supplied culture is consumer-oriented. Although its creators have their own aesthetics and may oppose the consumer orientation privately, they usually give first priority to satisfying their publics while trying to include content that meets their creator standards as well.[4] When it comes to activities in which the publics themselves function as creators, however, they will have standards different from those of consumers. For example, people who build their own

hot rods reject the standards of people who buy Detroit's high-powered sports cars, just as those who own sailboats are at odds with their neighbors who prefer to be driven through the water by a motor.

Creator-oriented High Culture

This is the taste culture of the "serious" artist, the critic, and the scholar who select and judge cultural content on the basis of creator standards. It is thus principally the culture of a creator public, and also of a noncreator public of highly educated predominantly upper-middle-class people who work largely in academic and professional jobs. The latter is subdivided into a creator-oriented public and a consumer-oriented public.

Although it is difficult to summarize the aesthetic standards of high culture in a few paragraphs, it is fair to say that they stress the relationship between method and content (or form and substance) and the higher priority of the former. These standards, which are formulated by creators and critics rather than by the culture's public, also place high value on subtlety in content and on the careful depiction of mood and feeling. Analysis and abstraction are desirable as long as there is also a final synthesis in which the personal values of the creator are indicated explicitly or implicitly.

In the culture's dramatic content the emphasis is away from plot and toward the emotional and logical developments of the character and his relation-

[4] This content is usually described as "technical effects" and is often not visible to the consumers. For a good illustration of creator and consumer differences and conflicts, see Howard S. Becker, "The Professional Dance Musician and His Audience," *American Journal of Sociology*, 57 (September 1951), pp. 136–144, and also Joan Moore, "The Writer Views the Viewer," unpublished paper delivered at the 1963 meeting of the American Sociological Association.

ships with others. Fictional content stresses basic philosophical and psychological themes, with the heroes often modeled on the creators themselves, emphasizing, for example, the conflict between individual and society and the problems of familial and other relationships (for example, the ability to love) that reflect the marginal role of the high-culture creator in contemporary society.

Because high culture is creator-oriented and dominated, there is much discussion about aesthetic standards, and differences of opinion become major sources of disagreement. These disagreements are often institutionalized, leading to the explicit formation of factions, representing not only academic, establishment, and avant-garde divisions, but also more specialized ones. For instance, at present there are many schools of film making and film criticism, reflecting differences of opinion about appropriate content, techniques of filming, and the role of the director.

Since the culture serves a small public that prides itself on exclusiveness, its products are not intended for distribution by the major media. Its art takes the form of originals distributed through galleries; its books are published by subsidized presses or commercial publishers willing to take a loss for prestige reasons; its journals are the so-called "little magazines"; its theater is concentrated largely in New York's Off-Broadway and occasional university repertory companies, although it may share a few Broadway plays with the upper-middle public. Its movies are either European and shared with upper-middle culture, or American "underground cinema" productions made on a shoestring, which are not so shared;

its radio is limited to a handful of urban or collegiate FM stations; and what little high-culture television exists is shown on big-city and university educational channels.

The desire for exclusiveness is not necessarily shared by the creators, some of whom want larger audiences, and high culture is constantly attacked by other taste publics. Magazines like *Time,* which appeal to upper-middle-culture publics, provide up-to-date coverage of new trends and fashions in high culture, partly to let their readers in on the ways of the "cultural upper classes," and judging by the disparaging tone of much of the coverage, to show that high culture and its public are also given to fads and other normal human foibles. In this manner they seek to debunk the exclusiveness of high culture and its claim to aesthetic and moral superiority.

The creator orientation of high culture means that more status is awarded to creators, such as writers, painters, and directors, than to performers. For example, actors are not viewed as stars but as tools of the director and writer. Critics have almost as high a status as creators, since they determine whether a given item of content deserves to be considered high culture, or whether it is only an example of middle-brow culture.

Consumer-oriented High Culture

The consumer-oriented high-culture public draws on the same content but selects what satisfies it without placing itself in the creator role, or to put it another way, without doing the "work" that high-culture creators demand from their audiences. As a result, conflict develops between this public and the creators, with the latter accusing the former of not being genuinely interested in culture.

The consumer-oriented public is somewhat more concerned with the status and fashionableness of the content, partly because it perceives the content differently from the creators and partly because it seeks to maintain the boundary between itself and upper-middle culture, which is constantly threatening it by borrowing and by debunking press coverage of high-culture fashions. Yet like the upper-middle-culture public, the consumer-oriented high-culture public sometimes relates to creators as fans, in the process making "stars" out of the better-known ones. Most recently, for example, this method of romanticizing the artist has been applied to James Baldwin and Norman Mailer. Partly for this reason, the consumer-oriented public gives higher status to performers than does the creator-oriented.

Although the consumer-oriented public must accept prevailing high-culture content if it is to remain within the culture, and must therefore go along with the creator-oriented, its size and affluence are tempting to the commercial distributors of high culture. As a result, they try to find content that will be acceptable to them and advertise it in consumer-oriented ways. For example, Grove Press, a publisher of avant-garde high-culture literature, has recently begun to advertise its novels by their effect on the reader—sometimes quite luridly so—and seems to be transforming its magazine, *Evergreen Review,* into a high-culture version of *Playboy.* Similarly, Susan Sontag's advocacy of "camp" as a proper taste for high-culture creators has been taken up by the consumer-oriented high-culture public to justify its use of high culture for enjoyment.[5]

As the consumer-oriented public tries to transform creator-oriented culture, the creators and their public escape to new outlets and even new forms of content, for example, by founding new art galleries and magazines, such as the *New York Review of Books.* As abstract expressionism became popular with consumers, some painters began to develop new interest in the human figure, and now that pop art and op art, both of which create an easy effect on museum and gallery visitors, have been taken up by the consumer-oriented public, the creator-ori-

---

[5] Susan Sontag, "Notes on 'Camp,'" *Partisan Review,* 31 (Fall 1964), pp. 515–531. Miss Sontag defines camp as a "disengaged, purely esthetic and unserious vision," "a mode of enjoyment, of appreciation, not judgment," which emphasizes style and "blocks out content" (*passim*). It has a natural appeal to the consumer-oriented public because it values frivolity, rejects the "work" involved in creator-oriented high culture, approves of the ostentatious and the shocking, and provides another source of content which can be used to maintain the boundary with upper-middle culture. Camp also justifies the borrowing from lower taste cultures and, indeed, these are a major source of what Sontag calls naive or pure camp, that is, content which is unintendedly in accord with the aesthetic standards of camp. Interestingly enough, one of the first subclassifications of camp was into high, middle, and low camp, not because the lower taste cultures were also interested in it, but to permit high-culture publics to borrow from these cultures without impairing their own cultural status. For a description of the consumption of camp and an example of how new high-culture trends are reported for upper-middle-class publics, see Thomas Meehan, "Not Good Taste, Not Bad Taste; It's Camp," *New York Times Magazine,* March 21, 1965, pp. 30–31, 113–115. In my analytic scheme, camp is a new subfaction—and fashion—in avant-garde high culture, and especially among its sizable and influential homosexual public.

ented art world is seriously concerned about how to maintain some distance between itself and the demands of the audience.[6]

These issues are on the whole limited to avant-garde high culture, and since it, as well as the majority of the creator-oriented and the consumer-oriented high-culture publics are located in New York City, the conflicts between them take place there. Indeed, the consumer-oriented public could be described as "hanging around" the major social and cultural centers of creator-oriented high culture in that city. The news magazines report the latest events on the New York cultural scene to the rest of the country, but in what New York high-culture publics call the hinterland, high culture exists on a minute scale, is usually traditional or contemporary in form, and is almost entirely consumer-oriented. Avant-garde high culture can also be found at some of the major universities around the country, although it is usually a pale duplication of what is being done and argued in New York.

UPPER-MIDDLE CULTURE

This is the taste culture of America's upper-middle class, the professionals, executives, and managers, people who have attended the better colleges and universities. Although well-educated, they were not trained as creators, intellectuals, or even humanists, and therefore they neither see themselves in

these roles nor share the interests associated with them. Like the consumer-oriented public of high culture, they shy away from the critical analysis of ideas and feelings, but unlike this public, they do not wish to participate in a creator-oriented milieu. They are consumers of culture, and for them substance is more important than method. As a result, the culture's dramatic content places more stress on plot than on character and mood. This public wants content that contains the ideas and feelings relevant to their own endeavors, for example, their active social and civic life. Since they are economically and politically influential, their dramatic heroes are more concerned with power and the ability to achieve their goals vis-à-vis other power blocs than with problems of relating to the larger society; more interested in the conflict of familial and occupational responsibilities than in the ability to love.

Because this public values being "cultured," it makes selective use of high-culture content, for example, the less subtle films of Bergman or Fellini. Its affluence and its rapid growth as a result of the boom in college attendance encourage distributors of high culture to seek it out to increase their audience. Moreover, distributors of upper-middle content look over high culture to see what can be borrowed, thus incurring the wrath of that culture's creators and critics. In fact, some of high culture's opposition to popular

[6] I do not mean to suggest that painters change their styles and methods either to satisfy or to escape from the consumers, but that those who are experimenting with new approaches are brought to the attention of other painters and they are then encouraged to experiment also. There are, however, many high-culture creators whose work imitates that of their leading peers, and there are also those who want to do something different when a current fashion becomes popular with consumers. As a result, high culture goes through the same process that is called a "cycle" in popular culture, for example, the monster situation comedy cycle in television, or the war movie cycle that took hold in Hollywood in 1964.

culture represents displeasure and disappointment over the failure of well-educated people to choose high culture.

Despite the borrowing, most of this culture's content is from its own creators, and they have little contact with high culture or high-culture creators, except perhaps at publishers' parties. Upper-middle-culture creators have attained added prominence in recent years by being invited to the White House for cultural ceremonies and performances.

Upper-middle culture is distributed through the so-called quality mass media. Its public reads magazines such as *Harper's,* the *New Yorker,* and the *Saturday Review;* it purchases most of the new books and determines which are to be best-sellers; it supports the Broadway theater, goes to see foreign film comedies, and provides the major audience for television documentaries and Sunday afternoon "cultural ghetto" programing. It finds its art in museums and is responsible for the popularity of modern furniture and architecture, although its conservative faction fights to preserve eighteenth- and nineteenth-century architectural landmarks.

This public pays considerable attention to creators as "stars." It relies extensively on critics, especially those of the *New York Times,* to differentiate between high- and upper-middle-culture content when both are served by the same media.[7] They carry out this function by disapproving of content which is too philosophical, pessimistic, difficult, enthusiastic about sexual and political deviance, or critical of upper-middle-culture values.

LOWER-MIDDLE CULTURE

This is America's dominant taste culture and public today. It attracts middle- and lower-middle-class people in the lower-status professions, such as accountancy and public school teaching, and all but the lowest-level white-collar jobs. Although older members of this public have only a high school diploma, many of its younger ones have attended and graduated from state universities, community colleges, and the many small private schools that dot the American landscape.

This public is not interested in what it calls "culture," by which it means both high and upper-middle culture and standards, although some of its women have long been interested in being "cultured." The culture it seeks is traditional, often adopted from the upper-middle culture of the late nineteenth and early twentieth centuries, and it rejects the intellectual and the cosmopolitan sophistication of today's upper-middle culture. For example, it dislikes abstract art and condemns satire as "sick" comedy.[8] This public obtains some of its content from high and upper-middle culture, but accepts it only in simplified and bowdlerized form as in the altered film versions of Broadway dramas and best-selling novels.[9]

[7] The *New York Times* Sunday edition is probably the major organ of upper-middle culture in the United States, especially its book review, entertainment section, and magazine.

[8] For an example of this rejection, see David E. Scherman, "Alienated Hero, Please Go Home," *Life,* 57 (July 24, 1964), pp. 8–9.

[9] Lester Asheim, "From Book to Film," *Quarterly of Film, Radio and Television,* 5 (1950), pp. 289–304, 334–349; 6 (1951), pp. 54–68, 258–273. See also George Bluestone, *Novels into Film* (Baltimore: Johns Hopkins Press, 1957).

The aesthetics of lower-middle culture emphasize substance; form must serve to make substance more intelligible or gratifying. Dramatic materials express and reinforce the culture's own ideas and feelings, and although some questioning is permitted, doubts must be resolved at the conclusion of the drama. Its heroes are ordinary people, or extraordinary ones who turn out to be ordinary in that they accept the validity of traditional virtues, such as wholesomeness, and traditional institutions, such as the church. For example, familial dramas deal primarily with the problem of upholding tradition and maintaining order against sexual impulses and other upsetting influences. Unlike high culture, lower-middle culture never makes unresolvable conflicts explicit.

The lower-middle-culture public provides the major audience for today's most popular mass media; it is the group for which these media program most of their content. This public reads *Life, Look,* the *Reader's Digest,* the *Saturday Evening Post,* and *McCall's.* It also supplies the book buyers who make the big best-sellers. It attends Hollywood's "spectaculars" and watches the situation comedies, popular dramas, and adult westerns that constitute the staple of television. It finds its art in *Life* and buys reproductions of representational paintings at department store art counters. Its architectural and furniture tastes are conservative, as reflected in the prevalence of "colonial" styles in the suburban single-family houses where this public lives. Given its consumer orientation, this culture's public pays little attention to writers or directors, concentrating on performers. It prefers the word-of-mouth judgment of friends and neighbors to the views of published critics.

Aside from high culture, where factional differences are sharp and highly visible, this culture displays perhaps the greatest internal differentiation between its "traditional" and "progressive" wings. For example, although Norman Rockwell and Grandma Moses are the favored artists of the former, the latter has begun to buy reproductions of nineteenth-century Impressionists, such as Cézanne and Van Gogh, and is much more receptive to the discussion of resolvable social problems and the depiction of erotic encounters (as in the novels of Irving Wallace) than the conservative, and probably older, members of this culture.[10] The current search for new formats and types of content by the *Saturday Evening Post* and *Life* is a reflection of the growing importance of the progressive faction in lower-middle culture, and in the case of *Life,* of its incipient interest in some forms of upper-middle culture.

LOWER CULTURE

Lower culture was America's dominant taste culture until the end of World War II, when it was replaced by lower-middle culture. It probably still has the largest public of all, even though the size of the public has been shrinking steadily, partly because of longer school attendance. This is the culture of the older lower-middle class, especially the working class: the people with low-status white-collar jobs and skilled or semiskilled blue-collar and

[10] Herbert J. Gans, "The Rise of the Problem Film," *Social Problems,* 11, 4 (Spring 1964), pp. 327–336.

service jobs, those who obtained their education at working-class high schools and often dropped out after the tenth grade.

Like the lower-middle culture public, this one also rejects "culture," but it does so with more hostility. It finds culture not only dull but also effeminate, immoral, and sacrilegious; it supports vigorously church and police efforts at censorship.

The aesthetic standards of lower culture stress substance, form being totally subservient. There is no concern with ideas per se. Thus there is almost no contact with high- or upper-middle-culture content, even in bowdlerized versions. The standards emphasize dramatization of values; much of the culture's content consists of modern forms of the morality play, in which traditional values win out over temptation, conflicting behavior, and impulses. The culture's dominant values are not only expressed, as in lower-middle culture, but also dramatized and sensationalized, with strong emphasis on demarcating good and evil. The drama is melodramatic, and its world is divided clearly into heroes and villains, with the former always winning out eventually over the latter.

Working-class society practices sexual segregation in social life: male and female roles are sharply differentiated, and there is relatively little social contact between men and women, even within the family.[11] These patterns are reflected in lower culture. There are male and female types of content, rarely shared by both sexes. Sexual segregation and working-class values are well expressed in the Hollywood "action" film and television program, and in the confession magazine, the staples of male and female lower culture respectively. The action film insists on a rigid distinction between hero and villain; the only social problems that are explicitly considered are crime and related violations of the moral order. These are dealt with by an ostensibly classless hero with such working-class characteristics as masculinity and shyness toward women in all nonsexual relationships. He works either alone or with peers of the same sex, depends partly on luck and fate for success, and is distrustful of government and all institutionalized authority. Clark Gable and Gary Cooper were the prototypes of this hero, and that they have not been replaced is indicative of low culture's loss of dominance. Conversely, the confession magazine features the working-class girl's conflict between being sexually responsive to be popular with men and remaining virginal until marriage. Familial drama that deals sympathetically with the problems of both sexes at once is rare.

In this culture the performer is not only paramount but is revered as a "star," and contact is sought with him, for example, through the fan clubs that are peopled by younger members of the lower-culture public. Moreover, this public does not distinguish between performers and the characters they play; it wants its stars to play "themselves," that is, their public images. Writers and other creators receive little attention.

Lower culture is provided through the mass media, but despite the size of this public, it must share much of its content with lower-middle culture. Often it does so by questioning lower-

[11] Herbert J. Gans, *The Urban Villagers* (New York: The Free Press of Glencoe, 1962), Chapters 3 and 11.

middle-class content, or by reinterpreting it to fit working-class values. For example, in a working-class population that I studied, people watching a detective serial questioned the integrity of the policeman-hero and identified instead with the working-class characters who helped him catch the criminal. They also protested or made fun of the lower-middle-class heroes and values they saw depicted in other programs and commercials.[12]

Exclusively lower-culture content exists as well, but has little status on Madison Avenue.[13] For one thing, this public reads very little because of its low educational level. It buys tabloid newspapers that stress dramatic happenings among ordinary people and entertainers; the men also read sports and adventure magazines, the women fan and confession magazines.

Most Hollywood films once were made for this taste public, but this is no longer true. Lower-culture people now watch television. Although they share this medium with lower-middle publics, they probably constitute the major audience for westerns, mysteries, comic action such as Red Skelton's, the acrobatic vaudeville of the Ed Sullivan show, and situation comedies such as "Beverly Hillbillies" and "McHale's Navy" (which describe how working-class people outwit the more sophisticated and powerful middle class). Much of this public's need for dramatic content is also met by women's soap operas and televised sports programs. It is served by independent radio stations, especially in the major cities, which feature rock and roll as well as country music and brief news

broadcasts that use various sound effects to duplicate the attention-getting device of the tabloid newspaper headlines.

Lower-culture art reflects the sexual segregation of its public. The men choose pinup pictures (more overtly erotic than those featured in the upper-middle-culture *Playboy*), which they hang in factories and garage workshops at home. The women like religious art and secular representational pictures with vivid colors. Home furnishings reflect the same aesthetic; they must be solid, overstuffed, with bright floral or "colorful" slipcovers. While high- and upper-middle-culture publics value starkness and simplicity, lower-culture publics prefer ornateness— either in traditional, almost rococo, forms, or in the contemporary style often described as "Hollywood modern."

LOWER-LOWER CULTURE

This taste culture serves the lower-class public, people who work in unskilled blue-collar and service jobs, and whose education ended in grade school. Today, much of this public is rural or nonwhite. Although large, its low status and low purchasing power mean that its cultural needs receive little attention from the mass media; by and large, it must get along with the content aimed at lower culture.

Data about lower-lower culture are scarce, but it seems primarily a simpler version of lower culture, with the same sexual segregation, with the same stress on morality, and with almost the total content emphasis on melodrama and

---

[12] *Ibid.*, Chapter 9.

[13] One indication of this is the frequent appearance of advertisements by the MacFadden Publications, a major publisher of lower-culture magazines, reminding manufacturers to advertise to their large, if low-status, audience.

morality play. This public's reading matter is probably tabloids and comic books; its films are old westerns and adventure stories now shown only in side-street movie houses in the slums, and for Spanish-speaking audiences the simple action films and soap operas made in Mexico. Television and radio fare is that of lower culture. Because its culture is almost entirely ignored by the mass media, this public probably has retained more elements of folk culture than any other. This culture is re-created at church festivals and other social gatherings.

The Social Structure of Taste Cultures

Despite the preceding categorization, taste cultures and publics are not entirely separate or independent groupings. To begin with, there is multicultural choice. Although most people restrict their content choices to one culture or to two "adjacent" ones, there is some wider spread, as when members of high-culture publics choose detective stories for their light reading and follow a major league baseball team. People who are creator-oriented in one field of high culture may be consumer-oriented in another, and will even prefer middle-culture choices outside their specialty. As Susan Sontag points out, "one of the facts to be reckoned with is that taste tends to develop unevenly. It's rare that the same person has good visual taste and good taste in people and good taste in ideas." [14] Finally, higher-culture publics sometimes take up popular culture that has been dropped by its audience, currently, for

example, the Hollywood musicals of the 1930's and the films of Humphrey Bogart. Although cultural straddling of various kinds takes place among all publics, it is most prevalent in the higher ones.

In addition, there is mobility of choice, for some people are upwardly mobile culturally as well as socially and economically. Usually, this mobility occurs during the school years, with college a major agent of the shift to upper-middle culture. It generally ceases with parenthood, when reading and "going out" are cut drastically. In old age there may even be downward mobility, as the content that people found gratifying in their youth becomes too difficult or upsetting.

Content also moves between cultures. They borrow from one another, often transforming the content to make it acceptable to different publics. Content may also be shared. Thus a book written for a high-culture public may be made available to the upper-middle one through an article in *Harper's*, which is then cut and edited to appear in the *Reader's Digest*. Eventually, the central thesis of the book might even receive passing mention in a lower-culture publication.

Occasionally, a specific cultural product or a performer may appeal to several cultures and publics at once and thus become extraordinarily successful; for example, the comic strips "Li'l Abner" and "Pogo," or performers such as Charlie Chaplin, Frank Sinatra, and Marilyn Monroe. Generally speaking, the multicultural appeal is possible because the content is complex enough to allow every culture to see something in it to meet its needs. Thus Charlie

[14] Sontag, *op. cit.*, p. 516. I am indebted to David Riesman for calling my attention to this quotation.

Chaplin was seen as a slapstick comic and clown by the lower cultures, and the higher ones perceived him as a satirical critic of society. Once in a while, a product is accepted by all cultures because it conforms to aesthetic standards that are shared by all of them, but this is rare because there is so little agreement about what is beautiful or desirable.

Finally, and in some ways most important, content is shared because several of the taste cultures are served by the same medium. For example, television fare, which is provided by three networks, must serve all cultures. In practice, it serves primarily lower-middle- and lower-culture publics, offering higher-culture content mainly to meet the public service requirements of the Federal Communications Commission. Much of the effort and anxiety of television programing executives stems from their attempt to find content that will be acceptable to the major taste cultures and their age groupings, and much of the conflict between executives and creators follows from the need to alter content so that this will happen. Similarly, when Hollywood makes high-budget films, it plans for content that will appeal to several publics, for example, by including characters that can be played by stars who appeal to diverse cultures and age groups.

Taste cultures and publics, especially those served by the mass media, may also be seen as participants in a societal taste structure, where the creators and industries providing content attempt to obtain the attention of as many publics as possible, and the publics use what veto power they have as ticket buyers or purchasers of sponsored goods to try to get the content they want. The overall structure is not unlike that of party politics, in that it consists of executives and creators who, like politicians, offer alternatives, and of audiences who, like voters, choose among them. Networks compete with each other like political parties, and the careers of network executives, like those of politicians, ride on their ability to guess what the public will accept. They are aided by the fact that taste, like party preference, is related to socioeconomic background and is therefore relatively stable, so that Ed Sullivan and "Ozzie and Harriet" have been "in office" longer than most senators from one-party states. Even so, the media's need to appeal to several taste publics at once forces them to act like political parties whose constituencies cut across class lines and include opposing interest groups.

The publics themselves can be conceived as interest groups, for they are competing with others to make sure that the content they want is created. When resources are scarce, as with television channels, or when values are contradictory, as with high culture's espousal of sexual or political deviance and low culture's hostility to it, there is likely to be conflict among publics. Since these do not exist as organized groups, however, the conflict usually takes place among creators and decision makers. Since mass-media creation is a group process, it can be shown that group members often function as self-appointed representatives of conflicting taste publics.[15]

Like all structures that deal with profits and power, the taste structure is

[15] Herbert J. Gans, "The Creator-Audience Relationship in the Mass Media: An Analysis of Movie Making," in Bernard Rosenberg and David M. White, eds., *Mass Culture: The Popular Arts in America* (Glencoe, Ill.: The Free Press, 1957).

hierarchical. Economic dominance is today located in the lower-middle public since it has the largest purchasing power. This dominance is naturally accompanied by some political power, as may be seen by the failure of the Federal Communications Commission to enforce the legislative requirement for public service programing of interest primarily to upper-middle publics. Upper-middle culture has political power over public allocations for culture, because the civic leaders who plan and support national or local art centers such as New York's Lincoln Center for the Performing Arts are usually drawn from the upper-middle public, much to the chagrin of high culture. They tend to emphasize the performing arts at the expense of such nonperforming ones as musical composition; and when they support high-culture ventures, they prefer traditional or establishment ones, shunning the avant-garde. The latter are supported by private foundations or individual sponsors, if they are subsidized at all.

When it comes to prestige, however, the cultural hierarchy follows the stratification pattern, with high culture at the top and lower-lower culture at the bottom, thus reflecting the social statuses of their publics. Consequently, when a culture of lower status borrows the content of a higher one, the latter usually drops this content from its repertoire. For example, when Ingmar Bergman's films became popular with upper-middle-culture moviegoers, he lost much of his standing among high-culture "film buffs," and when prints of Picasso's Impressionist paintings began to be sold in department stores, the high-culture public and its galleries turned to other of his paintings that had not yet become popular.

There is an important difference between the conflict that exists among taste publics and the conflict among socioeconomic strata. Although poor people would like to have the income and power that is available to the upper income groups, low taste publics do not feel deprived by their inability to participate in high culture. The antagonism and public conflict between taste publics are therefore much milder than those between socioeconomic strata.

The prestige of high culture derives not only from the status of its public but also from its historical alignment with the elite and its occasional alliance with "Society" in America. This culture, like all others, insists that its standards are universally valid and that the standards of other cultures are inferior. But because of the influence and occupational roles of its public, this insistence makes high-culture standards more overt and powerful. They are constantly applied in the literary journals, discussed by scholars and critics, and taught in the most prestigeful universities. The standards of the other cultures are more covert and less publicized. As a result, high culture has more influence than the relative size of its public suggests.

This influence is even felt in the mass media, because most of the critics of film, theater, and television are conscious of high-culture standards, although in their evaluations they tend to apply upper-middle-culture standards. Moreover, even when the publications in which they appear are circulated primarily among lower-middle-culture publics, their criticism is concentrated on high- and upper-middle-culture content, so that, for example, the critics of the *New York Daily News,* which has a principally low-culture readership, regularly review the plays and the serious foreign films that their readers probably never see.[16] On the other hand, the content seen by most people—the weekly installments of popular television series—receives no public criticism at all.

For this reason publics in the lower taste cultures become their own critics, developing their criticism in conversation among family members, friends, and fellow workers. This criticism is called "word of mouth" in the mass media and is more influential than that of the published critics in determining which popular novels, films, and even television programs become hits.[17]

Nevertheless, the public dominance of high- and upper-middle culture criticism encourages obeisance to the aesthetic standards of these two cultures, especially among people who place some value on being "cultured" or who are upwardly mobile in the class structure. Such obeisance is also encouraged by the status implications of cultural choice, so that people in all cultures are loath to admit they use content popular among people of lower status than their own. Consequently, they often make distinctions between what they publicly think is good and what they privately choose. The advocates of high culture interpret the existence of this distinction as evidence of the universality of their standards and conclude either that people want more high culture than they actually get, or that they prefer to choose what they think is bad rather than what they say is good. Both interpretations are inaccurate, however, and reflect the invisibility of the aesthetic standards of the other taste cultures.

The invisibility of the standards has other implications. For one thing, it hides the fact that these standards, like those of high culture, include criteria for bad content as well as good. Although some critics of popular culture have argued that only high culture can choose between good and bad content, the publics in other cultures make similar qualitative judgments. The people whose favorite type of drama is the western can and do distinguish between good and bad ones in the same way as theatergoers distinguish between good and bad plays. The theatergoer's judgment may be more sophisticated, and more explicitly related to his standards, but this is only because his standards are public and explicit, because he has been trained in making judgments based on these standards, and because his judgments are supported by professional critics. The viewer of television westerns lacks the explicit standards, and therefore the training to apply them, and he cannot resort to published criticism to test and sharpen his own views.

The difference between the two publics is in the amount of aesthetic training, but this does not justify assuming a difference in aesthetic concern. Thus low-culture publics may think calendar art and overstuffed furniture as beautiful as upper-culture publics consider abstract expressionist paintings and Danish modern furniture; the difference between them is in their ability to put their feelings into the proper aesthetic vocabulary. High-culture housewives may have learned interior design in school or may be able to hire pro-

[16] However, when critics review the offerings of a higher taste culture not shared by their readers, they are often negative and use their reviews to demonstrate the cultural inferiority and the moral deviancy of the higher culture.

[17] The popular evaluation of popular culture content has been studied tangentially by sociologists interested in the flow of influence. See Elihu Katz and Paul Lazarsfeld, *Personal Influence* (Glencoe, Ill.: The Free Press, 1955).

fessional decorators, but every housewife of every taste culture who can afford to buy furniture seeks to make her rooms into a work of beauty expressing her standards. In this process she chooses form, color, and relationships between individual pieces, as does the trained decorator. Differences among house-wives are in the amount of training in their standards, in the skill with which they can put their standards into action, perhaps, as well as in verbal fluency with which they justify their choices and, of course, in what they think is beautiful.

29

SOCIAL CLASS, LIFE EXPECTANCY AND OVERALL MORTALITY

Aaron Antonovsky*

A moment's reflection will convince the reader that the rich not only live better than the poor, but longer as well. In his definition of class, Max Weber invoked the term "life chances," and although he did not mean that phrase in a strictly literal sense, it can be taken so, for one's chances of remaining alive depend, in part, upon one's class position. Because of the high accessibility of the data, let us for a moment take *race* as a crude index of *class*. Knowing that blacks as a group are poorer than whites, we can very readily observe the impact of socioeconomic position upon mortality.

In the late 1960's, white men in this country could expect to live seven full years longer than nonwhite men (67 years for whites as compared to 60 for nonwhites). The infant mortality rate (deaths under one year of age) for nonwhites was virtually double the white rate, and the maternal death rate (maternal deaths due to complications of pregnancy and childbirth) were over three-and-a-half times higher for nonwhites than for whites.

Consider for a moment how the life styles at the extremes of the class structure account for mortality differences. During pregnancy, the upper-class woman receives the best medical care, enjoys a proper diet, and has sufficient leisure, all of which enhance the probability of a successful and incident-free delivery. During the first years after birth, all infants are extremely susceptible to adverse environmental conditions, and poor sanitation, diet, crowding, inadequate medical care, or faulty medical knowledge

* Work on this study was conducted while the writer was attached to the Social Science Unit of the Department of Public Health Practice, Harvard University School of Public Health, under a Special Research Fellowship from the National Institute of Mental Health, U.S. Public Health Service (1-F3-MH-29, 642-01, BEH). My gratitude is hereby expressed to my hosts and colleagues, Profs. Sol Levine, Norman Scotch, Sidney Croog and Lenin Baler.

SOURCE: *Milbank Memorial Fund Quarterly*, 45 (April 1967), pp. 31–39 and 49–73. Reprinted by permission of the publisher.

are inevitably reflected in high infant mortality rates. During youth, to take but one example, lower-class children are exposed to all the risks and accidents of crowded urban streets, while the isolated avenues of the well-to-do, with their rigorously enforced speed and traffic laws, protect their children.

The draft laws in this country and the operation of the military have always discriminated against the poor, and this is reflected in higher combat deaths in wartime for lower-class soldiers.* The inherent risks and strains of lower-class manual occupations inevitably take their toll. Social disorganization among the lower class results in higher rates of crimes of violence. Finally, and perhaps most important, are the cumulative debilitating effects upon health of a life of struggle, want, and economic deprivation.

In this comprehensive review of data from many countries, Aaron Antonovsky surveys the historical trends in social class mortality differentials and attempts to answer the question of whether class differences in mortality are narrowing as life expectancy for the population as a whole continues to increase.

> *. . . recalling what happened when an "unsinkable" trans-Atlantic luxury liner, the* Titanic, *rammed an iceberg on her maiden voyage in 1912. . . . The official casualty lists showed that only 4 first class female passengers (3 voluntarily chose to stay on the ship) of a total of 143 were lost. Among the second class passengers, 15 of 93 females drowned; and among the third class, 81 of 179 female passengers went down with the ship.*[1]

Death is the final lot of all living beings. But, as the tragic experience of the *Titanic* passengers dramatically illustrates, the time at which one dies is related to one's class. The intent of this paper is to examine the evidence which bears upon the closeness of this relationship, ranging as far back as the data will allow. It will first focus on the question of life expectancy at birth, and subsequently turn to that of overall mortality.

Studies of Life Expectancy

The average infant born today in the Western world can look forward, barring unforeseen events and radical changes in present trends, to a life span of about 70 years. That this has not always been the case for the human infant—and still is not for by far most infants born today—is well known. Whatever the situation prior to the era of recorded history, for the greater part of this era, that is, until the nineteenth century, most men lived out less than half their Biblical span of years.

In what is probably the first study of a total population, Halley, using data for the city of Breslau, Germany, for 1687 to 1691, calculated an average life expectancy at birth of 33.5 years.[2] Henry's estimate for the expectation of life of Parisian children born at the beginning of the eighteenth century was 23.5 years.[3] Half a century later, in the Vi-

* On the Korean War, see Albert Mayer and Thomas Haught, "Social Stratification and Combat Survival," *Social Forces*, 34 (1955), pp. 155–9. During the Vietnam War, overrepresentation in the armed forces by the poor and especially by blacks led to a major national drive to reform the draft. See Maurice Zeitlin, "A Note on Death in Vietnam," in Zeitlin (ed.), *American Society, Inc.* (Chicago: Markham, 1970), pp. 174–75.

enna of 1752 to 1755, of every 1,000 infants born alive, only 590 survived their first year, 413 their fifth year, and 359 their fifteenth year.[4] Henry further cites an estimate, which he regards as "too pessimistic," of 28.8 years for the total French population toward the end of the Ancien Regime.[5]

In the nineteenth century, Villerme, in a careful first-hand study, reported a life expectancy at birth for the total population of the city of Mulhouse, France, of seven years and six months, based on the period 1823 to 1834. However, he also cites Penot's data for Mulhouse, from 1812 to 1827, which show an average life expectancy of 25 years.[6] Ansell found a life expectation at birth for the total British population in 1874 of about 43 years.[7] At about the same time, the reported figures for Italy were somewhat lower: 35 years (1871 to 1880); 36.2 years for males, 35.65 years for females (1881–1882).[8]

Whatever the discrepancies and unreliabilities of these various sets of data, they consistently paint a picture of the Western world up to recent centuries which is quite similar to that of the world of presently "developing" societies until the last decade or two. Moreover, in the period of recorded history prior to the eighteenth century, no sizable increment had been added to the average life span. But if, from Greco-Roman times through the eigh-

teenth or perhaps even the nineteenth century, the mythical "average" infant could anticipate living some 20 to 30 years, does any evidence indicate that dramatic class differences existed? Though the evidence is perforce limited, the answer would seem to be no.

Two studies of male property owners in England of the generation born before 1276, and of a population born between 1426 and 1450, show average lengths of life being 35.3 and 33 years, respectively. Dublin, et al., who report these studies, also cite a study by Peller of men in the "ruling classes of Europe" from 1480 to 1579 in which a life span of 30 years is given as the average.[9] In Peller's paper, the average life expectancy of males at birth in a population of "Europe's ruling families," which included a total of 8,500 individuals, was 32.2 years in the sixteenth century, declined to 28.1 in the seventeenth century, rose considerably to 36.1 in the next century and, from 1800 to 1885 was 45.8 years. (In each case the female figure was higher.) [10]

A somewhat similar study, covering 1,908 individuals born between 1330 and 1954 as legitimate offspring of British kings, queens, dukes or duchesses, shows a corresponding increase in the eighteenth century, as can be seen in the data below.[11]

At the opposite end of the social scale, the reported life expectancy at

| Period of birth | Expectation of life at birth (years) | |
	Males	Females
1330–1479	24	33
1480–1679	27	33
1680–1729	33	34
1730–1779	45	48
1780–1829	48	55
1830–1879	50	62
1880–1954	55	70

birth for a British Guiana slave population between 1820 and 1832 was 22.8 years.[12] A reasonable assumption, keeping in mind that the life expectancy at birth of countries such as India, Burma and Cambodia in the late 1950's ranged from 35 to 44 years,[13] is that class differences prior to the eighteenth century were relatively limited. In other words, given a society which, though it manages to survive, does so at or near what might be called a rock-bottom level of life expectancy, one is not likely to find great differences among the strata of that society.

The data suggest the possibility that the trend in the nineteenth century, and perhaps even earlier, was toward a substantial widening of class differences. No report is available comparing the life expectancies of social strata of the population prior to the nineteenth century. Titmuss quotes Milne as saying, in 1815, that "There can . . . be no doubt but that the mortality is greater among the higher than the middle classes of society." [14] Villerme's study of Mulhouse, which was based on an analysis of the occupation of the head of household of 5,419 deceased out of a total of 6,085 registered deaths from 1823 to 1834, shows a life expectancy at birth which ranges from 28.2 years for "manufacturers, merchants, directors, etc." through 17.6 years for "factory workers, unspecified" and 9.4 years for day laborers, to 1.3–1.9 years for spinners, weavers and locksmiths. (Consideration of the life expectancy at age one of the same occupations indicates far smaller occupational differences.) Villerme concludes that "One sees here that most infants reach adulthood or die at a young age depending upon the condition or occupation to which they belong . . ." [15] At about the same time (1832), an observer of the British scene remarked that members of the peerage had a lower expectation of life than the general population.[16]

Morris cites Gavin's analysis of the average age at death of 1,632 deceased in Bethnal Green (a suburb of London) in 1839 by social strata. "Gentlemen, professional men and their families" died, on the average, at age 45; "tradesmen and their families," at age 26; and "mechanics, servants, labourers and their families," at age 16. Very similar data are quoted by Titmuss for the years 1839 to 1841 for the city of York. For near-identical social groups, the average ages at death were: 48.6, 30.8 and 23.8. Morris also refers to Clay's report for the 1840's on chances of survival in the town of Preston, Lancashire, among 1,000 infants born into each of the families of gentry, tradesmen and operatives. Among the gentry, not until well past the fortieth year did more than one-half of those infants die. The average infant of families of tradesmen survived until just past his twentieth year. Among operatives' families, however, more than half of those born had died by their fifth year. Titmuss also reports, for this period, that a "gentleman" in London lived, on the average, twice as long as a "labourer." The corresponding figures for Leeds were 44 and 19 years, and for Liverpool 35 and 15.[17]

A study by Bailey and Day, published in 1861, is referred to in the same context by Titmuss, though their data are not cited. Collins, however, does cite the data, which show a narrower gap than the aforementioned studies. Bailey and Day studied the life tables of 7,743 members of families of British peers from 1800 to 1855, and compared them with deaths in the total population from 1838 to 1844.

The mean duration of life for the two groups was 52 and 40.4 years, respectively.[18]

A further cautionary note on the class gap is sounded by William Farr, the great pioneer of English mortality statistics. In his discussion of the life expectancy of laborers employed by the East India Company compared with that of English peers over the course of centuries, using data for the latter published by Edmonds in 1838, Farr notes little difference in annual average mortality between the two groups, especially after age 50. "Are we," Farr comments, "to infer that the mortality among peers is now higher than among labourers, crowded within the metropolis? Should we not rather infer, that as the investigation extends far back into the centuries of bloodshed and pestilence, that the lives of peers were then shorter, and are now longer, than the lives of labourers? The plague, which was born in huts, and nursed by famine, rioted in luxurious halls, and smote the highborn." [19]

In the same cautionary direction, Ansell found that "the expectation of life at birth in the upper and professional classes was 53 years indicating an advantage of about 10 years over the expectation for the general population [in 1874]." [20]

Very few later investigators have dealt with class differences in life expectancy, preferring to concentrate on differences in mortality rates. A search of the literature has revealed only four such studies, whose data are presented in Table 1. The published data for Chicago refer only to the two extreme groups of census tracts with the highest and lowest median rentals. Because, after World War I, Chicago witnessed a tremendous influx of Negroes, most of whom were lower class, the available data for whites only has also been presented. From 1920 to 1940, the difference between the extreme groups seesawed, but did decline to a difference in life expectancy for whites, in both sexes, of 7.6 years. In England and Wales of about 1930, a direct gradient between class and life expectancy of males is evident, the extreme groups being separated by 7.4 years. Just about the same number of years separates the highest and lowest groups in Buffalo in 1939–1941. Although this is also true for white males in Baltimore in 1949–1951, the difference among white females in that city is only 4.7 years. In both cities, the direct gradient is clear.[21]

Can any conclusion be drawn from these data, most of which are admittedly tenuous and not overly reliable? A crude picture, as represented in Figure 1, could be inferred which indicates the following. The bulk of recorded history was one of high birth and high death rates, which offset each other and led to at most a very small increase in population. During the first 16 centuries of the Christian era, world population increased from about one-quarter to one-half billion people, an annual growth rate of about .005 per cent. Conceivably, throughout this period, no substantial differentials in life expectancy could be found among different social strata of the population. From 1650 to 1850 world population again doubled, most of the increase being in the Western world, representing an average annual increase of .05 per cent. These two centuries would seem to mark the emergence of an increasing class gap in life expectancy, starting slowly but gathering increasing momentum and reaching its peak about the time Malthus made his observations. On the one hand, the life

TABLE 1. Life Expectancy at Birth for Selected Populations, by Sex and Social Class, in the Twentieth Century [21]

Population, Place and Time	Class *					Difference Between I and V (years)
	I (highest)	II	III	IV	V (lowest)	
England and Wales, 1930–32						
all males	63.1	60.8	60.0	57.3	55.7	7.4
Chicago, 1920						
all males	60.6	—	—	—	49.6	11.0
Chicago, 1930						
all males	63.0	—	—	—	49.5	13.5
white males	63.0	—	—	—	51.3	11.7
Chicago, 1935						
all males	60.9	—	—	—	53.5	7.4
Chicago, 1940						
all males	65.4	—	—	—	56.5	8.9
white males	65.4	—	—	—	57.8	7.6
Buffalo, 1939–41						
all males	65.7	65.5	63.4	62.2	58.2	7.5
Baltimore, 1949–51						
white males	68.5	66.4	65.4	63.9	61.4	7.1
Chicago, 1920						
all females	62.9	—	—	—	52.5	10.4
Chicago, 1930						
all females	67.1	—	—	—	54.5	12.6
white females	67.1	—	—	—	56.2	10.9
Chicago, 1935						
all females	66.6	—	—	—	58.3	8.3
Chicago, 1940						
all females	70.3	—	—	—	61.0	9.3
white females	70.3	—	—	—	62.7	7.6
Buffalo, 1939–41						
all females	69.6	68.3	66.4	64.8	61.8	7.8
Baltimore, 1949–51						
white females	73.1	72.4	71.2	69.8	68.4	4.7

* "Class" in the British data refers to the Registrar-General's system of classification based on occupation, into which Tietze introduced a number of modifications. In the three American cities, "class" refers to the division of the city census tracts into quintiles based on the median rental in each tract.

expectancy of the middle and upper strata of the population increased at a rapid rate. On the other, the lowest strata's life expectancy may have increased much more slowly or, conceivably, even declined as an industrial proletariat emerged. At some time during the nineteenth century, probably in the latter half, this trend was reversed, and the class gap began to diminish. This is reflected in the doubling of the world's population, again mostly in the West, this time in the 80 years from 1850 to 1930. In recent decades, the

FIGURE 1. Model of Class Differences in Life Expectancy at Birth in Various Populations

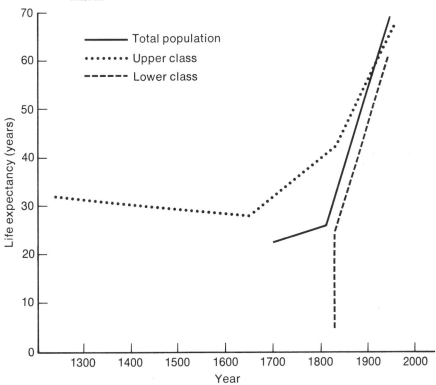

Data are derived from specific studies cited in the text and are plotted at the mid-year of each time period. The values for the last five years for the total United States population are from *The Facts of Life and Death,* Public Health Service publication no. 600, revised 1965, p. 21.

class gap has narrowed to what may be the smallest differential in history, but evidence of a linear gradient remains, with a considerable differential, given man's life span.

This supposition—not claimed to be more than that, since Figure 1 is no more than a very crude representation —seems to be of more than historical interest. It is, for two important reasons, most germane to the concern of this paper. In the first place, the scientist, no less than the lay person, often seems, in considering the question of the relationship between class and health, to be beset by a nineteenth cen-

tury notion of perpetual progress. Ideologically committed, in this area, to the desirability of the disappearance of the class gap, he tends to assume, with or without data, that the historical picture is unilinear; the history of mankind, in his view, shows steady progress in this respect. The realization that this may well be an inaccurate image, that the relationship is more complex, suggests a more cautious orientation. Such an orientation would suggest various possibilities: a narrowing gap being transformed into one which is widening; differing positions, on any given index of health, of different strata of the population at various times.

The second reason for stressing the possibility of a curvilinear relationship between class and life expectancy over time is that such a relationship may help in forming an adequate idea of the relationship between class and health, and, more broadly, an adequate theory of disease. Once the search begins for explanations of why, in a given period, one stratum seems to be making more health progress than another, and less so in another period, factors are uncovered which must be integrated into a theory of disease.

Thus, for example, McKeown and Brown, arguing that the increase in the population of England in the eighteenth century was overwhelmingly due to the decline in mortality, attribute that decline to improvements in the environment (housing, water supply, refuse disposal, nutrition) rather than to any advances in medical care.[22] Supposedly, such improvements first appeared in the upper strata of society, and only slowly percolated downward. This would explain the increasing class differences in life expectancy. Once the environmental sanitation gap began to narrow, some reversal in the trend could be expected which, however, might soon be offset by other factors;

e.g., the malnutrition of poverty. The point is that a very careful collection of data over time and the search for ups and downs may serve to pinpoint the various factors, and their modes of interaction, which influence overall mortality or the course of any specific disease.

. . . . .

World War II to the Present

Altenderfer[23] divided the 92 United States cities with a population of 100,000 or more in 1940 into three equal-sized groups on the basis of per capita income. The mean incomes for the three groups of cities were $918, $789, and $668. The age-adjusted death rates per thousand people, using 1939–1940 data, were, respectively, 10.9, 11.0 and 12.1 (100:100:111). Thus, in what is probably the crudest kind of ecological comparison, in that the groupings are quite heterogeneous, the poorest third of the cities showed a higher death rate, though the magnitude of the difference hardly approaches that found in more detailed studies, while the other two thirds, as groups, do not differ from each other.

Following the model set by Coombs in her earlier study of Chicago, Ye-

TABLE 2. **Age-standardized Annual Death Rates per 1,000 Persons, and Ratios, Buffalo, 1939–41, by Census Tracts Grouped on Basis of Median Rentals**[24]

Rental Group	Males		Females	
	Death Rate	Ratio *	Death Rate	Ratio
1 (highest)	9.4	100	7.2	100
2	9.9	105	8.1	112
3	11.4	121	9.0	125
4	12.2	130	10.0	139
5 (lowest)	14.9	158	12.4	172

* Highest rental group=100.

racaris [24] divided the 72 census tracts in the city of Buffalo into five levels on the basis of the 1940 median rentals. Death rates were calculated for each of the five levels, using 1939–1941 data. As Table 2 shows, an inverse gradient is found for both sexes. Though female death rates are consistently below those for males, the actual spread between the tract groups is larger for females. With each successively lower step in the rental ladder, the differential between the tract groups increases, so that the largest gap appears between the lowest and next lowest groups, whereas a relatively small difference appears between the two top groups.

Yeracaris notes that, if the death rate of the highest tract group had prevailed throughout Buffalo, 19.1 per cent of the deaths would not have oc-

curred. Had this rate prevailed in the second highest tract group, 6.8 per cent of its deaths would have been avoided. This percentage increases to 17.3 in the intermediate level, 24.5 in the fourth level and 38.5 in the lowest level.

Patno's analysis of Pittsburgh mortality data followed the same pattern.[25] The 1940 census tracts were ranked by using either the median value of owner-occupied units or the median monthly rental. The tracts were then grouped into three levels, each containing about one-third of the city's white population. Data for 1950 were also employed, using median family income in each tract as a third criterion for classification.

With few exceptions, the data, shown in Table 3, indicate an inverse gradient of mortality with economic

TABLE 3. Mortality Ratios * Among White Residents of Pittsburgh, by Census Tracts, Age and Sex [25]

	Economic Level					
	1940			1950		
Sex and Age	High	Middle	Low	High	Middle	Low
Males						
All ages **	93	97	111	88	99	113
Under 10	84	98	114	73	105	119
10–29	102	86	113	90	116	95
30–39	73	88	143	64	83	148
40–49	67	114	117	85	85	131
50–59	93	89	123	75	104	123
60–69	98	97	108	92	98	108
70 and over	103	98	99	97	98	104
Females						
All ages **	93	100	114	91	105	106
Under 10	107	103	91	116	85	101
10–29	80	114	107	87	112	100
30–39	88	102	113	77	96	127
40–49	81	101	127	68	121	118
50–59	79	92	165	84	99	123
60–69	93	99	120	87	103	113
70 and over	100	100	103	95	109	97

* Rate in each age-sex category = 100.
** Age-standardized.

level of the tract grouping in the age-sex categories. This is true for both 1940 and 1950. The largest differentials are found in the 30 to 59 age group, particularly in the first of these decades. For females under ten, the gradient is direct, and in both sexes the 70 and over category shows no clear difference among the economic levels. No indication is given that economic differentials are any greater among males than among females.

Mortality rates in the Netherlands are among the lowest in the world. In this context, determination of social class differences becomes of particular interest. DeWolff and Meerdink [26] studied the mortality rates of gainfully employed males, aged 15–64 in Amsterdam in 1947–1952, using the 1947 census to provide denominator information. The population was divided into six occupational levels. The annual, average, age-adjusted death rates per thousand persons were: liberal professions, civil service, etc., 3.6; independent businessmen, 3.9; clerical workers, 5.1; managers, foremen, higher technical staff, 3.3; skilled workers, 4.2; unskilled labor, 4.2. The difference between the most favored group and the workers (117:100) barely reaches statistical significance. In contrast to the findings of all other studies, unskilled workers do not differ from skilled workers. Only the clerical group is relatively high (though a death rate of 5.1 is, as such, quite low). The authors suggest two reasons for this rate. First, the clerical workers do not reach the standards of physical fitness required to obtain civil service employment, which would have placed them in the top level. Second, many are probably children of manual workers and are not sufficiently fit to work.

By the 1950's, the number of studies of socioeconomic mortality differentials had increased considerably. Szabady's review of the Hungarian data,[27] which had pointed to a higher rate among non-manual earners in 1941, shows a relatively small difference, though in the direction to be expected, for 1948–1949. Manual workers had a rate of 10.4 per thousand compared to 8.6 for non-manual workers (not age-adjusted). By 1959–1960 the difference had narrowed slightly, with rates of 10.5 and 9.0, respectively. Age-standardization reduces this gap somewhat, to 11.7 and 10.9 (107:100).

Tayback [28] divided Baltimore's 168 census tracts on the basis of the 1950 median tract rentals, grouping them into equal-sized population quintiles. The 1949–1951 death rates for the socioeconomic levels, excluding the non-white population, are shown in Table 4. In overall terms, a clear inverse class gradient is seen, the male slope being somewhat steeper than the female slope, with very few figures being out of line. The gap tends to be quite large in the younger age groups, where the death rate is low. Class differences in middle age (35–54) are very sizable. At this age, the major differences seem to be at the top and bottom, between the highest and next-highest and between the lowest and second-lowest economic levels. Differences remain considerable at ages 55–64, but tend to become much smaller thereafter.

Ellis conducted a very similar study in Houston.[29] The index used to rank census tracts was a modification of the index of social rank developed by Shevky and Williams, which utilizes measures of education, occupation and median family income. Tracts were grouped into quintiles, each of which contained 12 or 13 tracts. The 1949–1951 age-standardized, annual,

TABLE 4. Annual Death Rates Per 1,000 White Population, by Age and Sex, in Five Economic Levels, Baltimore City, 1949–51[28]

Economic Level	15–24 Rate	15–24 Ratio *	25–34 Rate	25–34 Ratio	35–44 Rate	35–44 Ratio	45–54 Rate	45–54 Ratio	55–64 Rate	55–64 Ratio	65–74 Rate	65–74 Ratio	75+ Rate	75+ Ratio
White Males														
Highest	0.8	100	0.8	100	3.2	100	6.8	100	24.1	100	57.0	100	128.2	100
2	1.0	125	1.5	188	4.3	134	10.9	160	26.6	110	57.2	100	135.2	105
3	1.3	162	1.6	200	4.1	128	12.7	187	29.5	122	56.5	99	124.1	97
4	1.3	162	1.7	212	4.8	150	13.8	203	32.9	136	61.9	108	137.3	107
Lowest	1.4	175	2.2	275	6.4	200	17.6	259	40.5	168	72.8	128	142.3	111
White Females														
Highest	0.4	100	1.1	100	1.8	100	4.8	100	13.4	110	34.2	100	110.2	100
2	0.4	100	0.8	73	2.7	150	5.7	119	13.4	110	36.8	108	106.7	97
3	0.4	100	1.2	109	2.6	144	6.3	131	16.8	125	38.3	112	118.5	108
4	0.7	175	1.3	118	3.1	172	7.6	158	16.1	120	42.4	124	132.8	120
Lowest	0.8	200	2.1	191	3.4	189	7.9	164	21.9	163	42.8	125	123.8	112

* Highest economic level in each group=100.

average death rates per thousand persons for the white population of Houston by socioeconomic level are shown in Table 5. Although class differentials do appear, they differ from those in other studies. The range of differences is smaller, though still substantial. The two top groups of tracts, for males, and the three top, for females, are quite similar in their death rates. Most puzzling, perhaps, is the fact that males in the lowest tract level have a lower rate

also used a modified form of the Shevky-Williams index, studied deaths in 1949–1951, and included about one-fifth of the number of tracts in each socioeconomic level. Stockwell's data pertain to Providence and Hartford. The class differentials in these two cities are quite similar to those in Houston. In Providence, little difference is found among the top three levels of males or the top two levels of females. Hartford females do not differ among all five

TABLE 5. Age-standardized Average, Annual Death Rates per 1,000 Population for Five Social Rank Areas, by Sex, 1949–51, in Houston,[29] Providence and Hartford [30]

Socioeconomic Level	Houston		Providence		Hartford	
	Rate	Ratio *	Rate	Ratio	Rate	Ratio
White Males						
1 (highest)	7.5	100	10.8	100	9.3	100
2	7.9	105	11.8	109	10.3	111
3	9.1	121	11.2	104	11.2	120
4	11.1	148	12.7	118	11.8	127
5 (lowest)	9.9	132	14.0	130	12.5	134
White Females						
1 (highest)	5.4	100	7.3	100	6.6	100
2	5.3	98	7.6	104	7.5	114
3	5.6	104	8.9	122	7.5	114
4	7.1	131	9.4	129	8.2	124
5 (lowest)	7.5	139	10.4	142	8.3	126

* Highest economic level in each group=100.

than do those in the adjacent level. Ellis suggests as a possible explanation the availability of free medical treatment for the lowest group. Group 4, not having such an advantage but having a limited income, may utilize funds for the females, who do have a lower rate than the females in group 5, whereas the males go on working and refrain from using such funds for themselves.

Stockwell, whose concern was methodological as well as substantive, presents data exactly parallel to the above. These data also appear in Table 5. He

strata; levels 2 and 3 and levels 4 and 5 have almost identical rates.

Stockwell proceeded to compute rank order correlation coefficients between the census tracts in each city ranked by age-sex-standardized death rates and each of eight socioeconomic variables (occupation, two education variables, two income variables, two rent variables, crowding). In all cases, the correlation coefficients were significant.[30]

Since the British Registrar General system of social classification is the richest source of data on mortality differences over time among different socioeconomic levels, a number of attempts have been made to construct a comparable ranking in the United States. Breslow and Buell,[31] using the 1950 census for denominator data, classified all deaths of California males, aged 20–64, from 1949 to 1951, in one of five occupational classes. Class I includes professionals and kindred workers; class II is an intermediate group; class III includes sales, clerical and skilled workers; class IV includes semiskilled workers; and class V includes unskilled workers. Data for farmers and farm laborers are presented separately, differing from the British system, because the data on death certificates for these men were thought to be unreliable. All data are presented in terms of the standardized mortality ratio which is a ratio of the observed deaths in an occupation to the age-standardized expected number of deaths, as determined by the age-specific rates for men in all occupations. The standardized mortality ratio for all men is equal to 100. The California data are presented in Table 6.

For the entire age group, a rough inverse gradient is seen between class and mortality. To all intents and purposes, however, classes I and II do not differ,

nor do III and IV, though the latter two have a somewhat higher rate than the former. Class V has a strikingly higher rate. A smoother gradient appears at ages 20–34, and is most strikingly regular at ages 35–44, though in both cases class V is set off from the others by its high rate. Class differences begin to be attenuated at ages 45–54, with the exception of class V. This is even more true for the 55–59 group, and in the 60–64 group almost no class differences exist.

A more ambitious attempt along the same lines was conducted by Guralnick, who analyzed all male deaths in age group 20 to 64 in the United States in 1950.[32] In view of the fact that one primary purpose was to compare the United States data with the British, Guralnick collapsed classes II to IV to make this intermediate group comparable in the two countries. The data are presented in Table 7. For the entire age group, the picture is quite similar to that presented in the California study: a linear inverse gradient, with the intermediate occupational level being closer to class I, and the major gap occurring between class V and the intermediate group. Another publication by Guralnick,[33] in which standard mortality ratios are given separately for

TABLE 6. Mortality Ratios, California Men, Ages 20 to 64, by Social Class, 1949 to 1951 [31]

Age Group	Social Class				
	I	II	III	IV	V
20–64 *	87	85	94	98	132
20–34 *	62	66	77	91	183
35–44	69	76	86	105	171
45–54	90	81	94	102	141
55–59	99	88	99	99	115
60–64	95	96	101	91	107

* Age-standardized.

TABLE 7. Annual Death Rates per 1,000, and Ratios, Males,
by Age and Social Class, United States, 1950 [32]

Age Group		All Occupations	Social Class *		
			I	II–IV	V **
20–64	Death rate	8.1	6.4	7.6	10.6
	Ratio ***	100	79	94	131
20–24	Death rate	2.0	0.9	1.6	2.6
	Ratio	100	45	80	130
25–34	Death rate	2.2	1.1	1.8	3.2
	Ratio	100	50	82	145
35–44	Death rate	4.4	2.9	4.0	6.5
	Ratio	100	66	91	148
45–54	Death rate	10.9	9.3	10.5	14.2
	Ratio	100	85	96	130
55–64	Death rate	24.7	23.2	24.8	26.9
	Ratio	100	94	100	109

* See text for definition of class.
** White only.
*** Rate for all occupations in each age category=100.

the five classes, presents figures almost identical with the California figures. The standardized mortality ratios for all United States males aged 20–64, in 1950, from class I to class V, are: 83, 84, 96, 97, 120. These ratios are for whites only, except for class I, which contains a few nonwhites. Once again classes I and II do not differ, nor do classes III and IV.

Examination of the age-specific rates in Table 7 shows the largest class gap to lie in the 25 to 44 age group, with classes II to IV being closer to class I than to class V. A considerable gap remains at ages 45–54, but it is substantially narrowed by ages 55–64.

Guralnick also analyzed the same 1950 data along more traditional American lines, using the occupational classification developed by Edwards for the United States Census.[34] This scheme seeks to rank occupations by socioeconomic levels. The standardized mortality ratios presented in Table 8, for white males aged 25–59, shows an inverse gradient, but one which does not distinguish among all of the eight occupational groups. The lowest ratios are found among the top three groups; they are followed closely by sales, skilled and semiskilled workers, whose ratios are identical. Service workers fare substantially poorer, and, finally, laborers have a considerably higher mortality ratio.

This pattern does not hold in all age groups. Prior to age 30, only the roughest gradient appears, though laborers fare markedly worse. A clear gradient appears in the 30–34 groups, which is maintained in the next ten year cohort. In both cases, the ratios of the top three occupational groups are nearly identical. This pattern holds in ages 45–54 and 55–59 in part. Three mortality levels can be distinguished in these groups, which do not conform to the socioeconomic ranking: non-manual workers except sales workers; sales, skilled and semiskilled workers; and service and unskilled workers. In the

TABLE 8. Annual Death Rates per 1,000, and Ratios, White Males, by Age and Major Occupation Group, United States, 1950 [34]

Major Occupation Group	25–29 SMR**	20–24 X	20–24 Y*	25–29 X	25–29 Y	30–34 X	30–34 Y	35–44 X	35–44 Y	45–54 X	45–54 Y	55–59 X	55–59 Y	60–64 X	60–64 Y
All occupations	93	1.7	100	1.6	100	2.0	100	3.9	100	10.1	100	19.4	100	28.8	100
Professional, technical, kindred	82	1.2	73	1.2	70	1.5	76	3.2	81	9.4	93	18.9	98	29.2	101
Managers, officials, proprietors, nonfarm	85	1.5	86	1.3	79	1.5	76	3.3	85	9.5	94	18.9	98	28.9	100
Clerical, kindred	83	0.9	54	1.3	78	1.5	76	3.3	86	9.6	95	18.2	94	26.9	93
Sales	94	1.1	62	1.1	66	1.7	82	3.6	94	11.0	109	21.7	112	31.8	110
Craftsmen, foremen, kindred	94	1.8	103	1.6	97	2.0	99	4.0	102	10.1	100	20.8	107	32.1	111
Operatives, kindred	94	1.8	106	1.8	108	2.2	107	4.1	106	10.3	102	19.4	100	28.6	99
Service, except private household	116	1.2	72	1.6	98	2.4	117	5.1	133	13.8	136	22.4	116	29.2	101
Laborers, except farm and mine	131	2.6	149	2.8	171	3.6	178	6.5	167	14.5	144	23.8	123	34.9	121

* X = death rate per 1,000. Y = ratio, computed on the basis of rate for all occupations in each age category = 100.
** Standardized mortality ratios are computed on the basis of the entire population. Since non-white are excluded in this table, SMRs can fall below 100.

481

oldest age category, only laborers continue to differ from all other groups.

A state-wide ecological study merits mention in passing. Hamilton [35] analyzed the age-adjusted 1950 death rates in the 100 counties of North Carolina. Three of the eight variables used in the multiple correlation analysis may be regarded as socioeconomic measures: percentage of families owning own homes; percentage of homes with modern plumbing and not dilapidated; mean number of grades completed by adults. Only the first of these, with a correlation of -0.69 with mortality, makes a statistically significant contri-

classes IV and V in the 28 London boroughs, continue to show highly significant correlations. For these three variables, the correlations were: 0.36, 0.80 and 0.90.[36]

Hansluwka's review of Austrian mortality data [37] begins with reference to a number of early studies which were based upon workers covered by social insurance, reflecting only a very small part of the population. He does, however, present data for the entire employed population for 1951–1953. Table 9 presents these rates for males in different age groups. For the very gross categories of "middle and upper

TABLE 9. Annual Death Rates per 1,000 Employed Males, by Age and Socioeconomic Category, Austria, 1951–53 [37]

Age Group	Middle and Upper Class Occupations (1)	Working Class Occupations (2)	Ratio of (2) to (1) *
14–17	2.0	1.3	68
18–29	1.7	1.8	110
30–49	3.4	3.8	112
50–59	12.6	13.4	106
60–64	15.8	24.4	154
65 and over	65.1	73.9	114

* Rate of (1) = 100.

bution toward explaining the inter-county mortality variation. Home condition and education measures have almost a zero correlation with mortality rates. Of far greater importance are variables such as percentage of whites and ratio of hospital beds to the population.

Despite the tremendous shifts in the London population and the overall decline of about one million persons during the two decades following 1930, Martin's data for 1950–1952, correlating age-standardized death rates with percentage of two or more persons per room, average number of persons per room and percentage of employed in

class" and "working class" occupations, few sizable differences emerge, though the latter's rates are higher. At ages 14–17, the former's rate is appreciably higher. At ages 60–64, however, the working class has a much higher death rate. Hansluwka also presents a bar chart showing mortality in Vienna in 1951–1953. The city's 23 districts were classified on the percentage of workers of the labor force in each district and grouped into four categories. The data, he concludes, show "a clearcut pattern of social grading of mortality."

A problem which has consistently bedevilled those who seek to study socioeconomic differentials on mortality by use of death certificates and census records is the frequent noncomparability of data in the two sources, which leads to overestimation of the denominator in some occupations and underestimation in others, or difficulty in making any calculations. The nature of the problem has been explored, theoretically and empirically, by several writers.[38] Among these, Kitagawa and Hauser have sought to overcome the difficulties by individual matching of 340,000 death certificates from deaths occurring in the United States from May through August, 1960, with census information recorded for these individuals in the 1960 census. In addition, personal interviews were conducted with individuals knowledgeable about 94 per cent of a sample of 9,500 of the descendents.

A preliminary analysis of the data using education and family income for white persons has been reported, though not yet published.[39] Consideration of the education variable, which is broken down into four levels of completed education by persons 25 and older, shows an inverse gradient of mortality rates by amount of education for both sexes in ages 25 to 64. Interestingly enough, this gradient disappears for males 65 and over, but remains quite strong for females of this age.

The latest mortality study available is Tsuchiya's presentation of standardized mortality ratios for an occupational-industrial categorization of Japanese males, age 15 and over, in 1962.[40] No clear occupational gradient emerges from the data. The ratios, ranked from low to high, are: "management," 58; "clerks," 67; "mechanics and simple," 88; "sales," 89; "professional and technical," 92; "transporting and communicating," 135.

Class Mortality Differentials in England and Wales

Since William Farr initiated the systematic study of occupational mortality statistics in 1851, the decennial reports of the British Registrar General for England and Wales have served as the outstanding source of information on the relationship of social class and mortality. For many years, the focus was on differential mortality risks of specific occupations. In the analysis of the 1910–1912 data, the various occupations were, for the first time, grouped together into five social classes, which excluded textile workers, miners and agricultural laborers, for whom separate statistics were presented. This classification was, in large part, industrial. Substantial changes were introduced in the following decade, making the classification more properly occupational.

In 1930–1932 a further step was taken in moving from a concern with occupational hazards toward one with comparison of mortality risks of people sharing a given social environment: the mortality of married women classified according to husband's occupation was introduced as a systematic part of the data analysis. Since this time, despite reclassification of various occupations, the five-class scheme of the Registrar General has been maintained. During the war years, no census was taken. Moreover, a number of technical difficulties have arisen in the analysis of the data based on the 1961 census, hence nothing has yet been published for the latest period.

The Registrar General identifies 586 occupational unit groups to which every occupation in the country is assigned. Each of these groups is assigned as a whole to one of five social classes, on the basis of the predominant characteristics of the majority of persons in the unit group. "The basic common factor of all groups is the kind of work done and the nature of the operation performed. . . . The occupations included in each category [of the five social classes] have been selected so as to secure that, so far as is possible in practice, the category is homogeneous in relation to the basic criterion of *the general* standing within the community of the occupations concerned." [41]

The five social classes are described as follows (the proportion of occupied and retired men aged 15 and over in 1951 is given in brackets):

Class I. Higher administrative and professional occupations and business directorships (3.3 per cent).

Class II. Other administrative, professional and managerial, and shopkeepers: persons responsible for initiating policy and others without this responsibility, but with some responsibility over others (15 per cent).

Class III. Clerical workers, shop assistants, personal service, foremen, skilled workers: skilled workers with a special name, special responsibility and adaptability (52.7 per cent).

Class IV. Semiskilled workers: persons who are doing manual work which needs no great skill or training but who are doing it habitually and in association with a particular industry (16.2 per cent).

Class V. Unskilled workers: laborers, cleaners and other lowly occupations (12.8 per cent).

Farmers and farm managers are included in class II and agricultural workers in class IV. Also, class III, which includes more than half the population, is composed of both manual and non-manual workers.

From the great amount and variety of data available in the reports of the Registrar General and papers based on these reports, those that seem to be the most important have been selected for present purposes. These are presented in Table 10. Collins' analysis of the 1910–1912 data for occupied and retired males aged 15 and over, which refers to classes I, III and V and excludes textile workers, miners and agricultural laborers, shows a regular inverse gradient, with the largest gap being between class III and class V.[42] Stevenson's figures for the same period,[43] which also exclude the same three occupational categories, but refer to males aged 25–64 in the five social classes, show a similar gradient. The ratios for classes II, III and IV, however, are nearly identical, and not very much higher than for class I. Stevenson argued that about ten per cent of the laborers on the census are misclassified as class IV rather than class V, which tends to lower the rates for the former and increase those for the latter. Changing the denominators to this extent would, he notes, produce a smoother gradient, as shown in Table 10. Collins also took the 1900–1902 and 1890–1892 data for 100 specific occupations and classified them as they had been classified in 1910, adjusting the death rates for age. "The results," he comments, "need not be presented here since they merely confirm the findings for 1910–1912." Collins proceeded to analyze the age-specific rates, which show that class differentials were largest in the 25–54 age groups. This is supported by Stevenson's analysis.

A similar picture emerges from the data for 1921–1923, despite the significant changes in classification. The gap between classes I and II is somewhat

TABLE 10. Standardized Death Rates per 1,000 and Standardized Mortality Ratios, England and Wales, for Selected Age-sex Groups and Time Periods, by Social Class

Time Period	I	II	III	IV	V	Population Group
1910–12						
Death rate per 1,000	12.0	—	13.6	—	18.7	Occupied and retired
Ratio (I=100)	100	—	114	—	156	males, age 15+, ex-cludes textile workers, miners, agricultural laborers.[18]
Standardized mortality ratio	88	94	96	93	142	Males, age 25–64, excludes textile, miners, agricultural laborers.[43]
Standardized mortality ratio	88	94	96	107	128	As immediately above, modified by Stevenson.[43]
1921–23						
Death rate per 1,000	7.4	8.6	8.7	9.2	11.5	Males [44]
Ratio (I=100)	100	116	117	124	155	
Standardized mortality ratio	82	94	95	101	125	Males, 20–64*
1930–32						
Standardized mortality ratio	90	94	97	102	111	Males, 20–64*
	81	89	99	103	113	Married women, 20–64*
1949–53						
Standardized mortality ratio	98	86	101	94	118	Males, 20–64*
	96	88	101	104	110	Married women, 20–64*
	100	90	101	104	118	Occupied males, 20–64, adjusted to control for occupational changes since 1930–32.
Death rate per 1,000	6.6		6.4		9.5	Males, 20–64, excludes
Ratio (I=100)	100		97		144	agricultural workers.[45]

* See reference 61 (Registrar General, page 20). Logan (ref. 61, p. 204) gives only figures for 1950.

greater than in the previous decade. Classes II and III have near-identical ratios and class IV a somewhat higher ratio, while class V is still widely distinct from the others. Britten's analysis [44] of the age-specific rates compares class I to class III and class III to class V. For the former comparison, the greatest gap is at ages 16–19, and declines with regularity at each succeed-ing age. The pattern of the class V:III ratio, however, is different. Here the greatest gap is at ages 35–44 and, though a bit less so, at 45–54.

By 1930, class differentials, though now presenting a regular inverse gradient, had narrowed, with standardized mortality ratios of 90 for class I and 111 for class V, for males, aged 20–64. The innovation introduced in the data analysis for these years shows that general socioeconomic differences rather than specific occupational hazards were crucial in the relationship between class and mortality. This is seen in the data for married women classified by husband's occupation, in which the gradient is somewhat more steep than for the males.

The latest available data, for 1949–1953, show a rather different picture than that of previous decades. Class V still has a substantially higher ratio than the other classes; for the males, it is even higher than in 1930. Class II, however, now has the lowest ratio, followed by classes IV, I and III, in that order. For married women, the inverse gradient persists, except that here too, as among the males, class II has a lower ratio than class I. The relatively low ratio of class IV may well be an artifact of classificational changes from one social class to another. Adjustment of the data for occupied males to take account of these changes "has had the important effect of raising the SMR of Social Class IV from 94, where it was second lowest, to 104, where it occupies the second highest position, as it did in 1921–1923 and 1930–1932." [45] Guralnick's analysis of the British data,[46] excluding all gainfully employed in agriculture, and collapsing classes II–IV, shows that this latter group had a very slightly lower death rate than class I, while class V remains very much higher.

Moriyama and Guralnick,[47] in their attempt to compare data for males from the United States and England and Wales, present age-specific ratios for the latter, combining the three middle classes and excluding all engaged in agriculture, for 1950 only. For most age groups, little difference is seen between class I and classes II–IV; this is particularly true from age 45 upwards. Class V has consistently higher rates; but whereas this is the case to a moderate degree at ages 20–24, the differential increases thereafter, reaching a peak at ages 35–44, after which it declines again and nearly disappears at ages 60–64. (The respective ratios of the three class groups I, II–IV and V, taking the rate of all occupations as 100, are: at ages 20–24, 102, 94, 122; at ages 25–34, 90, 95, 138; at ages 35–44, 83, 96, 143; at ages 45–54, 98, 97, 129; at ages 55–59, 99, 99, 115; and at ages 60–64, 100, 101, 106.)

Viewing the data for England and Wales in overall terms, class differentials in mortality in the twentieth century both have and have not declined. On the one hand, the differentials between the middle levels (among whom mortality rates differed little even in the earlier years) and class I have more or less disappeared. On the other hand, class V is still strikingly worse off than the rest of the population. Though indications are that its relative position improved in the earlier decades of the century, this does not seem to be the case between 1930 and 1950.

Conclusions

This statistical examination clearly provides no basis to reject the inference drawn from the figures of the *Titanic* disaster. Despite the multiplicity of methods and indices used in the 30-odd studies cited, and despite the variegated populations surveyed, the inescapable conclusion is that class influences one's chance of staying alive. Almost without exception, the evidence shows that classes differ on mortality rates. Only three such exceptions were found, indicating no or almost no class difference. Altenderfer, comparing 1939–1940 mortality rates of 92 United States cities classified into three mean income groups, shows a relatively small difference among them. Szabady, comparing nonagricultural manual and non-manual workers in Hungary in 1959–1960, shows the same. In both cases, the classification is so gross as to minimize differences which a finer analysis might reveal. Only DeWolff and Meerdink's study in Amsterdam in 1947–1952 can legitimately be regarded as strongly contradictory of the link between class and mortality. Their data, however, must be seen in the context of a population which has just about the lowest death rate ever recorded. This is not to dismiss the importance of their findings. On the contrary, it suggests the extremely important hypothesis that as the overall death rate of a population is lowered, class differentials may similarly decline.

This hypothesis finds support in an overall trend reflected in the studies reported. In the earlier studies, the differential between the mortality rates of extreme class groups is about a 2:1 ratio, but later studies show a narrowing of this differential, so that by the 1940's, a 1.4:1 or 1.3:1 ratio is much more typical. As can be seen from studying the death rates, these years witnessed a progressive decline in the overall death rate. At the same time, a cautionary note must be exercised. Despite an undoubted overall decline in mortality in the past three decades, the trend in the earlier decades of the century toward the closing of the class gap has been checked, if not halted.

This indication focuses on the differences between mortality rates of the lowest class and other classes. A more accurate picture of the overall pattern would be to suggest that what has happened is a blurring, if not a disappearance, of a clear class gradient, while class differences remain. On the basis of the existent data—using, for the sake of convenience, a five-fold class distinction, this being the most popular —it is difficult to conclude whether classes I to IV now no longer differ in their mortality rates, or whether classes I and II have the lowest rates, and III and IV have higher rates, though not necessarily substantially so. What seems to be beyond question is that, whatever the index used and whatever the number of classes considered, almost always a lowest class appears with substantially higher mortality rates. Moreover, the differential between it and other classes evidently has not diminished over recent decades.

At this point discussion of the complex question of explanations for such patterns would not be appropriate. A possibility could be suggested, however. The truly magnificent triumphs over infectious diseases have been crucial in both narrowing the overall class differentials and in nearly eliminating differentials among all but the lowest class. In recent decades, however, access to good medical care, preventive medical action, health knowledge, and limitation of delay in seeking treatment have become increasingly important in combating mortality, as chronic diseases have become the chief health enemy in the developed world. In these areas, lower class people may well be at a disadvantage. As such factors become more and more important, as the historical supposition presented in the first pages of this paper suggests, increasing class differentiation may occur. This approach does not necessarily preclude consideration of genetic selection and what has commonly come to be called "the drift hypothesis."

The data reviewed lead to a further conclusion. With amazing consistency, the class differentials are largest in the middle years of life. This is no less true in the latest than in the earliest studies. Over and over again, the greatest gap is found in young and middle adulthood. The predominant pattern characterizing class differentials by age is that in which class differences are moderately high in the younger ages, rise to a peak at ages 30 to 44, begin to decline at that point and tend to disappear beyond age 65. Where a given set of data varies from this pattern, it is in one of two directions: in the former cases, class differentials are lowest in the younger and older groups; in the latter, the decline in class differentials only begins in late middle age.

This pattern of greatest class differences in middle adulthood may be linked to the two historical suppositions which have heretofore been pre- sented. To hypothesize in more general terms, when mortality rates are extremely high or extremely low, class differences will tend to be small. In other words, when men are quite helpless before the threat of death, or when men have made great achievements in dealing with this threat, life chances will tend to be equitably distributed. On the other hand, when moderate progress is being made in dealing with this threat, differential consequences are to be expected. The crucial idea that may be involved here is that of preventable deaths, at any given level of knowledge, technique and social organization. Where and/or when such deaths are concentrated, class differentials will be greatest, unless appropriate social action is taken. This differential is not inevitable.

Much more, of course, could be said in summary, with reference to both substantive and methodological issues. Needless to say, consideration of patterns of class differences by cause of death is essential for a full understanding of this relationship. But this would have extended the paper into a book.

REFERENCES

1. Hollingshead, August B. and Redlich, Frederick C., *Social Class and Mental Illness,* New York, John Wiley & Sons, Inc., 1958, p. 6, citing Lord, Walter, *A Night to Remember,* New York, Henry Holt, 1955, p. 107.

2. Cited in Dublin, Louis I., Lotka, Alfred J. and Spiegelman, Mortimer, *Length of Life,* revised edition, New York, Ronald Press, 1949, pp. 34, 30–43. The book as a whole is one of the most detailed treatments of the subject of life expectancy.

3. Henry, Louis, "The Population of France in the 18th Century," in Glass, David V. and Eversley, D. E. C. (Editors), *Population in History,* London, Edward Arnold, 1965, p. 444.

4. Peller, Sigismund, "Births and Deaths Among Europe's Ruling Families Since 1500," in Glass and Eversley, *op. cit.,* p. 94.

5. Henry, *op. cit.,* pp. 445–446.

6. Villerme, Louis R., *Tableau de L'Etat Physique et Moral des Ouvriers,* Vol. 2, Paris, Jules Renouard et Cie., 1840, pp. 249, 376–385.

7. Ansell, C., "Vital Statistics of Families in the Upper and Professional Classes," *Journal of the Royal Statistical Society,* 37, 464, 1874, cited in Titmuss, Richard, *Birth, Poverty and Wealth,* London, Hamish Hamilton Medical Books, 1943, p. 19.

8. Cipolla, Carlo M., "Four Centuries of Italian Demographic Development," in Glass and Eversley, *op. cit.*, pp. 578, 582.

9. Dublin, Lotka and Spiegelman, *op. cit.*, pp. 31–32.

10. Peller, *op. cit.*, p. 95.

11. Hollingsworth, T. H., "A Demographic Study of the British Ducal Families," in Glass and Eversley, *op. cit.*, p. 358.

12. Roberts, G. W., "A Life Table for a West Indian Slave Population," *Population Studies*, 5, 242, March, 1952.

13. United Nations Department of Economic and Social Affairs, *1963 Report on the World Social Situation*, New York, United Nations, 1963, p. 13.

14. From Milne's *Treatise on Annuities*, quoted in Titmuss, *op. cit.*, p. 17.

15. Villerme, *op. cit.*, pp. 251, 376–385.

16. Farren, *Observations on the Mortality Among the Members of the British Peerage*, cited in Titmuss, *op. cit.*, p. 17.

17. Morris, Jeremy N., *Uses of Epidemiology*, second edition, Edinburgh and London, E. and S. Livingstone, 1964, pp. 161–162; Titmuss, *op. cit.*, p. 18.

18. Bailey, A. H. and Day, A., "On the Rate of Mortality Prevailing Amongst the Families of the Peerage During the 19th Century," *Journal of the Institute of Actuaries*, 9, 305; cited in Collins, Selwyn D., *Economic Status and Health*, Washington, United States Government Printing Office, 1927, p. 14.

19. Farr, William, *Vital Statistics: A Memorial Volume of Selections from the Reports and Writings of William Farr*, Humphreys, N. A. (Editor), London, The Sanitary Institute, 1885, pp. 393–394. Also cited in Titmuss, *op. cit.*, pp. 17–18. Titmuss notes that even when Farr excluded from the peer's mortality those deaths due to violence, the laborers had the lower mortality.

20. Ansell, C., cited in Titmuss, *op. cit.*, p. 19.

21. Mayer, Albert J. and Hauser, Philip, "Class Differentiations in Expectation of Life at Birth," in Bendix, Reinhard and Lipset, Seymour M. (Editors), *Class, Status and Power*, Glencoe, Illinois, Free Press, 1953, pp. 281–284; Tietze, Christopher, "Life Tables for Social Classes in England," *Milbank Memorial Fund Quarterly*, 21, 182–187, April, 1943; Yeracaris, Constantine A., "Differential Mortality, General and Cause-Specific, in Buffalo, 1939–41," *Journal of the American Statistical Association*, 50, 1235–1247, December, 1955; Tayback, Matthew, "The Relationship of Socioeconomic Status and Expectation of Life," *Baltimore Health News*, 34, 139–144, April, 1957.

22. McKeown, Thomas and Brown, R. G., "Medical Evidence Related to English Population Changes in the Eighteenth Century," *Population Studies*, 9, 119–241, 1955 (reprinted in Glass and Eversley, *op. cit.*, pp. 285–307).

23. Altenderfer, Marion E., "Relationship Between Per Capita Income and Mortality, in the Cities of 100,000 or More Population," *Public Health Reports*, 62, 1681–1691, November, 1947.

24. Yeracaris, *op. cit.*, pp. 1235–1247.

25. Patno, Mary E., "Mortality and Economic Level in an Urban Area," *Public Health Reports*, 75, 841–851, September, 1960.

26. DeWolff, P. and Meerdink, J., "Mortality Rates in Amsterdam According to Profession," *Proceedings of the World Population Conference*, 1954, Vol. I, New York, United Nations (E/Conf. 13/413), pp. 53–55.

27. Szabady, Egon, "Recent Changes in the Socio-Economic Factors of Hungary's Mortality," in *International Population Conference, Ottawa, 1963*, Liège, International Union for the Scientific Study of Population, 1964, pp. 401, 403.

28. Tayback, *op. cit.*, p. 142.

29. Ellis, John M., "Socio-Economic Differentials in Mortality from Chronic Diseases," *Social Problems*, 5, 30–36, July, 1957. Reprinted in expanded form in Jaco, E. Gartly (Editor), *Patients, Physicians and Illness*, Glencoe, Illinois, Free Press, 1958, p. 32.

30. Stockwell, Edward G., *Socio-Economic Mortality Differentials in Hartford, Conn. and Providence, R. I.: A Methodological Critique*, unpublished doctoral dissertation, Brown University, 1960. Relevant papers published by Stockwell based on his dissertation include: ———, "A Critical Examination of the Relationship Between Socioeconomic Status and Mortality," *American Journal of Public Health*, 53, 956–964, June, 1963; ———, "Socioeconomic Status and Mortality," *Connecticut Health Bulletin*, 77, 10–13, December, 1963.

   Stockwell investigated the difference made in the analysis of socioeconomic mortality data when different indices of class are used. He notes that the precise conclusions one draws will "vary considerably with the methodological conditions characterizing a particular study," however the overall patterns are sufficiently similar so that, for present purposes, it is adequate to refer to only one or two of his measures. Since many studies reported in the present paper used median rental, however, it is important to note that Stockwell's data indicate that, of all eight variables, this is the poorest predictor of mortality rates.

31. Breslow, Lester and Buell, Philip, "Mortality from Coronary Heart Disease and Physical Activity of Work in California," *Journal of Chronic Diseases*, 11, 421–444, April, 1960.

32. Guralnick, Lillian, "Socioeconomic Differences in Mortality by Cause of Death: United States, 1950 and England and Wales, 1949–1953," in *International Population Conference, Ottawa*, 1963, *op. cit.*, p. 298.

33. ———, "Mortality by Occupation Level and Cause of Death Among Men 20 to 64 Years of Age, U.S., 1950," *Vital Statistics, Special Reports*, 53, 452–481, September, 1963. For an earlier paper reporting provisional death rates in the same population by the five classes and seven age categories, see Moriyama, Iwao M. and Guralnick, Lillian, "Occupational and Social Class Differences in Mortality," in *Trends and Differentials in Mortality*, New York, Milbank Memorial Fund, 1956, p. 66.

34. Guralnick, Lillian, "Mortality by Occupation and Industry Among Men 20 to 64 Years of Age, U.S., 1950," *Vital Statistics, Special Reports*, 53, 59, 61, 84–86, September, 1962.

35. Hamilton, Horace C., "Ecological and Social Factors in Mortality Variation," *Eugenics Quarterly*, 2, 212–223, December, 1955.

36. Martin, W. J., "Vital Statistics of the County of London in the Years 1901 to 1951," *British Journal of Preventive and Social Medicine*, 9, 130, July, 1955, p. 130.

37. Hansluwka, Harold, "Social and Economic Factors in Mortality in Austria," in *International Population Conference, Ottawa*, 1963, *op. cit.*, pp. 315–344.

38. Buechley, Robert, Dunn, John E., Jr., Linden, George and Breslow, Lester, "Death Certificate Statement of Occupation: Its Usefulness in Comparing Mortalities," *Public Health Reports*, 71, 1105–1111, November, 1956; Kitagawa, Evelyn M. and Hauser, Philip M., "Methods Used in a Current Study of Social and Economic Differentials in Mortality," in *Emerging Techniques of Population Research*, New York, Milbank Memorial Fund, pp. 250–266; and ———, "Social and Economic Differentials in Mortality in the U.S., 1960: A Report on Methods," in *International Population Conference, Ottawa*, 1963, *op. cit.*, pp. 355–367.

39. Kitagawa, Evelyn M. and Hauser, Philip M., "Social and Economic Differentials in Mortality, United States, 1960." Paper presented at the 1966 annual meeting of the Population Association of America.

40. Tsuchiya, Kenzaburo, "The Relation of Occupation to Cancer, Especially Cancer of the Lung," *Cancer*, 18, 136–144, February, 1965.

41. Quote is from the Registrar General's *Decennial Supplement, England and Wales, 1951, Occupational Mortality*, Part II, Vol. 1, *Commentary*, London, Her Majesty's Stationery Office, 1958, pp. 12–13. This system of classification is also described in Logan, W. P. D., "Social Class Variations in Mortality," in *Proceedings of the World Population Conference, op. cit.*, pp. 185–188; and Brockington, Fraser C., *The Health of the Community*, third edition, London, J. & A. Churchill Ltd., 1965, pp. 325–334. The percentage distribution of the social classes is taken from Logan, p. 201. For further discussions of the antecedents and development of the Registrar General system of classification, see Greenwood, Major, *Medical Statistics from Graunt to Farr*, Cambridge, University Press, 1948; and ———, "Occupational and Economic Factors of Mortality," *British Medical Journal*, 1, 862–866, April, 1939.

42. Collins, *op. cit.*, p. 15.

43. Stevenson, T. H. C., "The Social Distribution of Mortality from Different Causes in England and Wales, 1910–1912," *Biometrika*, 15, 384–388, 1923; Logan, *op. cit.*, p. 204. Logan's paper was also published, with variations, under the same title, in *British Journal of Preventive and Social Medicine*, 8, 128–137, July, 1954, and in *Public Health Reports*, 69, 1217–1223, December, 1954.

44. Britten, Rollo H., "Occupational Mortality Among Males in England and Wales, 1921–1923," *Public Health Reports*, 43, 1570, June, 1928.

45. Registrar General, *op. cit.*, p. 20.

46. Guralnick, *op. cit.* (International Population Conference), p. 298.

47. Moriyama and Guralnick, *op. cit.*, p. 69.

VIII

SOCIAL MOBILITY

30

THE AMERICAN OCCUPATIONAL STRUCTURE: PATTERNS OF MOVEMENT

Peter M. Blau and
Otis Dudley Duncan

Social mobility is usually defined as movement up or down the social class hierarchy. Societies are judged as more or less "fluid" or "open" depending upon how much mobility they permit. For example, a caste system such as India's with hereditary ranks permits little mobility and would be judged, therefore, closed. It has been argued that built into a social class system is the incentive to move upward, to be socially mobile, as the values underlying the system clearly instruct us that it is in fact good to "make good." And although most people undoubtedly prefer upward to downward mobility, a small but growing group of Americans—dropouts from the system —rejects the prevailing values, and can be said actually to be downwardly mobile. Perhaps the beat-hip poet Lawrence Ferlinghetti spoke for this group as he urged:

> *Let us go then you and I*
> *leaving our neckties behind on lampposts*
> *take up the full beard*
> *of walking anarchy*
> *looking like Walt Whitman*
> *a homemade bomb in the pocket.*
> *I wish to descend in the social scale.*
> *High society is low society.*
> *I am a social climber*
> *climbing downward*
> *and the descent is difficult.*
> *The Upper Middle Class Ideal*
> *is for the birds*
> *but the birds have no use for it*
> *having their own kind of pecking order*
> *based upon birdsong.*
> *Pigeons on the grass alas. . . .*[*]

Although sociologists talk and write about *social* mobility, they have most often studied *occupational* mobility. This for

[*] From Ferlinghetti's poem, "Junkman's Obligato," in *A Coney Island of the Mind* (New York: New Directions, 1958), pp. 62–3.

SOURCE: Peter M. Blau and Otis Dudley Duncan, *The American Occupational Structure* (New York: John Wiley & Sons, 1967), pp. 23–38. Reprinted by permission of the publisher.

495

two reasons: occupational changes are fairly easy to measure; and occupation is really the kingpin of social class, playing a crucial role in the determination of one's level of income, style of life, and status.

In general, two types of mobility have been studied: (1) intergenerational mobility in which, for example, the occupational position of sons is compared with their fathers in order to assess how much mobility has taken place between the generations; and (2) intragenerational (or career) mobility in which the amount of mobility a man experiences within the course of his own lifetime is assessed.

We present here a detailed excerpt from the most ambitious study of occupational mobility ever conducted in any country. Each month the U.S. Census Bureau carries out its current population survey based on interviews with thousands of persons in order to gather data on characteristics of the labor force, employment, and the like. In the early 1960's Peter M. Blau and Otis Dudley Duncan were able to append to the *Current Population Survey* a questionnaire dealing primarily with the occupational and educational backgrounds of the respondents and their fathers. In all, over 20,000 men from all parts of the country supplied the data on which the tables presented here are based. These tables demand and deserve careful study. From them we see that there is an enormous *amount* of mobility—sons moving into different occupations from their fathers—but we also see that mobility is most often limited in *extent*. That is, occupational movement from father to son is frequent, but great leaps, either up or down the occupational ladder, are rare.*

What are the causes of all this turbulence, this movement from position to position over the generations which, as the authors point out, is more upward than downward? Most would ascribe it to the traditional virtues associated with success: personal ambition, initiative, and hard work. While on an individual basis this is important, it overlooks some basic structural features of American society which permit, even require, the movement upward of individuals within the system. Among the important structural features contributing to mobility are: (1) long-term changes in the occupational structure reflecting developments in the economy, with expansion at the top (high level white-collar jobs) and contraction at the bottom (unskilled labor, farming occupations, and so on); (2) differential fertility; the relatively low birth rates of the upper strata mean that these groups are unable to reproduce themselves sufficiently to continue to fill the demand for high-level positions, which therefore requires the movement upward of persons from lower strata to fill the vacuum; (3) large-scale immigration of unskilled workers into the United States pushing those already here into higher level jobs; (4) the in-migration of large numbers of persons, black and white, from rural areas into the cities, again permitting the rise of already urbanized groups. Of all these factors, changes in the occupational structure are by far the most important; mobility due to immigration from abroad is today nearly negligible, having been replaced by the continuing streams of internal migrants from the rural South and elsewhere; and mobility due to differential fertility is a minor, declining factor, but still worthy of note.**

Among the many myths of the American class structure are two concerning social mobility which should be dispelled. It is commonly believed, first of all, that there is considerably more social mobility in the United States than in other Western societies. Now, Blau and Duncan's data reveal that 37 percent of those men whose fathers were manual workers "rose" into white-collar occupations. Surprisingly, however, national

* For this distinction between the amount and the extent of mobility, see Kurt Mayer and Walter Buckley, *Class and Society*, 3d ed. (New York: Random House, 1970), chap. 8.
** For estimates of the relative importance for social mobility of these factors, see Joseph Kahl, *The American Class Structure* (New York: Rinehart & Co., 1957), chap. 9.

surveys in Sweden, Great Britain, Denmark, Norway, France, Germany, Japan, Italy, and other countries indicate a reasonable similarity to the United States and to each other in the amount of intergenerational mobility.* According to Lipset and Bendix, rates of upward mobility are similar in industrialized countries because (1) structural factors, inherent in industrial societies, tend to promote comparable amounts of mobility, and (2) the individual quest for upward mobility is common to all social class systems, and is not peculiar to the United States. It should be noted, however, that while rates of intergenerational mobility from blue-collar to white-collar occupations are similar in many industrial countries, there is undoubtedly more movement in the United States among sons of manual workers into professional jobs, because more persons here of working-class background have access to higher education—a prerequisite for professional positions—than elsewhere.**

A second important myth of the American class system holds that the equality of opportunity which exists here is such that any man with sufficient ambition can work his way to the top, regardless of social origins, proved by the fact that the American business elite is dominated by those who by their own efforts have risen from humble origins to the pinnacle of power, wealth, and prestige.

Innumerable studies have demonstrated that this myth is not and never was accurate. To cite only one example, in the early 1950's *Fortune* magazine studied the social origins of the 900 highest paid executives of 300 of our largest corporations and found that fully 75 percent of these men came from homes where the father was either a businessman himself or a professional.† Less than 8 percent of the business leaders came from working-class homes. And of the younger executives (those under 50 years of age), only 2.5 percent had working-class backgrounds. Finally, Reinhard Bendix, studying the trends in elite mobility, found that it is just about as difficult today for a poor man to rise to the top as it ever was.‡ Although this is a subject of continuing controversy, Bendix concluded that the system is apparently becoming neither more rigid nor more flexible. Surveying the social backgrounds of prominent U.S. businessmen born as early as 1770 and as late as 1920, he found that throughout the entire period of American history, about 70 percent of the business elite have come from what might be deemed upper-class homes, about 20 percent from middle-class homes, and only approximately 10 percent from working or lower-class homes.

The study of social mobility may be approached from various perspectives. We can focus on changes in socioeconomic status, whatever the particular occupational base on which the status rests, or on movements between occupational groups (clerks, farmers), ignoring status differences within each group. Concern may be with the opportunities for success of individuals or with the occupational structure of the society. In subsequent chapters atten-

---

* See S. M. Lipset and Reinhard Bendix, *Social Mobility in Industrial Society* (Berkeley: University of California Press, 1959); S. M. Miller, "Comparative Social Mobility," *Current Sociology*, 9 (1960); Thomas Fox and S. M. Miller, "Intra-Country Variations: Occupational Stratification and Mobility," *Studies in Comparative International Development*, I, No. 1 (1965); Gerhard Lenski, *Power and Privilege* (New York: McGraw-Hill, 1966), pp. 416 ff.

** Blau and Duncan, *op. cit.*, p. 434.

† The Editors of *Fortune*, *The Executive Life* (Garden City, N.Y.: Doubleday Dolphin Books, 1956), pp. 34–5. The sample of executives was drawn from the 250 largest industrial corporations, the 25 largest railroads, and the 25 largest utilities.

‡ Lipset and Bendix, *op. cit.*, chap. 4.

tion centers largely on socioeconomic status, and the investigation deals with the factors associated with individual opportunity and achievement. This first substantive chapter on our research findings, in contrast, presents an analysis of the American occupational structure at large, specifically, of the movements of manpower among occupational groups.

The occupational structure is conceived of as consisting of the relations among its constituent subgroups; and these occupational subgroups, not the individuals composing them, are the units of analysis. The labor force has been divided for the purpose of this analysis into 17 occupational categories, an extension of the 10 major occupational groups of the U.S. Bureau of the Census. The seven additional categories represent simple subdivisions of Census categories; self-employed "professional, technical, and kindred workers" are distinguished from salaried ones. Similarly, "managers, officials, and proprietors" are separated into the self-employed ("proprietors") and the salaried ("managers"). "Sales workers" are divided into retail and other salesmen. Finally, three groups of manual workers have been partitioned by industry: there are three categories of "craftsmen, foremen, and kindred workers"—in manufacturing, in construction, and in other industries—two categories of "operatives and kindred workers"—in manufacturing and in other industries—and the same two categories of "laborers, except farm and mine."

The structure of relations among these occupational groupings is defined in terms of the flow of manpower between them through time, either intergenerationally or intragenerationally. Each occupation is characterized by the inflow or recruitment of its manpower from various origins, on the one hand, and by the outflow or supply of sons to various destinations, on the other. For example, farmers are disproportionately recruited from their own ranks and from farm laborers, but they supply sons to a large variety of occupations in the next generation. This procedure of describing an occupation on the basis of its relations to the others in the social structure is analogous to the sociometric method, which also describes individuals in a group on the basis of their relations to the rest, and which also usually employs two criteria of relations: choices made and choices received. The analogy is intended to indicate that concern is with a structure of relations among units in a larger whole, but it must not be pressed too far. The units are large occupational groupings in our case, not individuals; and whereas self-choice is usually not considered in sociometric studies, self-recruitment and occupational inheritance occur, of course, and must be taken into account.

The flow of manpower among occupational groups reveals the dynamics of the occupational structure. To be sure, the 17 occupational categories used are not social groups in the conventional sense of the term. Most members of an occupational category are not in direct social contact and may not even share a common identification, because their occupational identification may be either broader ("professional") or narrower ("accountant") than the category delimited by the social scientist. Nevertheless, the occupational classes are meaningful social groupings and not entirely arbitrary categories. Their members share life chances and social experiences, and many of the direct social contacts of men at work and even at play are with others in a similar, if not necessarily the same, occupational category. The term "occupational grouping" might best convey the fact that although these are not corporate groups with distinct boundaries and pervasive social interaction among members, neither are they arbitrary categories, but they are meaningful social aggregates that affect the formation of many face-to-face groups.

The classification by father's occupation, however, raises additional problems. Whereas the occupational classification of sons represents actual groupings of individuals in 1962, the generation of fathers never existed at any one time. Many of these fathers still pursued their occupations in 1962, that is, are part of the labor force that has been sampled. The occupational distribution of fathers is not an actual distribution of men existing at any earlier period. Even if all fathers had been in the labor force at some one time, they provide a sample of that universe biased by differential fertility. Thus a farmer has more weight in the generation of fathers than a professional because the farmer's higher fertility gives him a greater probability of falling into the sample through his sons. However, although origin categories do not refer to distinctive groupings of fathers, they do refer to distinctive groupings of sons: those who have similar occupational backgrounds and home environments. What is under consideration, therefore, is the movement of manpower from groupings that have common social origins, defined by father's occupation, to occupational groupings in 1962.[1]

The occupational structure constitutes the framework of social mobility within which individuals must achieve occupational success or suffer failure.[2] Changes in the size of the various occupations reflect changes in the demand for different occupational services, which, in turn, often have their source in technological advances, as exemplified by the declining demand for farm workers consequent to improved farming methods and higher farm productivity. These structural changes require a redistribution of manpower. But the actual amount of occupational mobility observed far exceeds that necessary to effect the redistribution of manpower. Some of this additional mobility results from educational improvements that alter the quality of the manpower supplied, and some of it results from indirect repercussions of changes in demand. For example, a need for professionals is most likely to be met by those men who have acquired in their early environments the social skills and habits appropriate to professional pursuits, those aware of various professional careers and able to afford the prolonged education requisite to professional status, that is, by sons of other white-collar workers. If the need for these other white-collar workers does not decline at the same time as that for professionals is increasing, the outflow of sons will create a demand in the lower white-collar occupations, a secondary product of the demand for professionals. Moreover, a high de-

---

[1] The same applies to first occupation in respect to intragenerational mobility. Classification by first occupation refers to groupings of men with common early career experiences, not to occupational groupings that actually existed at any one time, since different times are involved for men of different ages.

[2] This analysis is not concerned with the question of the socioeconomic mobility achieved by whole occupational groupings.

mand for professionals may lead to the lowering of previously existing barriers to entry—for instance, by no longer restricting admission to professional schools to whites—with the result that more qualified men from lower strata can now move up into this level.

The flow of manpower in the occupational structure, rather than merely the net redistribution necessitated by shifts in demand, delineates the existential conditions governing the individual's chances of socioeconomic success. The analysis of this pattern of movement provides a baseline for the investigation, in subsequent chapters, of historical trends, the process of social mobility, and the factors associated with individual achievements.

The Flow of Manpower

In order to determine whether movement from an occupational origin to an occupational destination entails upward or downward mobility, it is necessary to rank the occupations. Table 1 presents a rank order of the 17 occupational groupings and the data on which this ranking is based. The criteria are median income and median education. The percentage increase in income or education is indicated as one moves up the ranks. Only five of these percentage differences are not in the same direction. In these cases the two are equally weighted, which means that the larger percentage difference determines the rank. The one exception is the placement of retail salesmen above craftsmen, which has been made to maintain the nonmanual-manual distinction.

Differences between manufacturing and other craftsmen, and between manufacturing and other laborers, are not

available, and the mean difference across the same industry line for operatives is small. Hence, in considering upward and downward mobility, the industry partition of these three major occupational groups is treated as a horizontal one. To wit, movement between manufacturing and other industry within each of the three manual groups is considered to be horizontal and counted neither as upward nor as downward mobility.

This ranking differs in a few respects from the customary ranking of the ten major occupational groups. Nonretail salesmen fall between the two subgroups of "managers, officials, and proprietors" of the Census classification, so that only salaried managers remain above these other salesmen. Proprietors have descended to a point that may confound, or possibly delight, doctrinaire Marxists, though by virtue of their income levels they are still above clerks and retail salesmen (who are nevertheless their educational superiors). Retail sales is the lowest white-collar occupation.

Table 2 presents the transition matrix of intergenerational mobility; that is, the movements between father's occupation and respondent's 1962 occupation. These movements can be considered to consist of two steps, from social origin to entry into the labor market, and from the latter to present occupation. The pattern of movement from father's to first occupation is shown in Table 3, and intragenerational mobility from first to present occupation is shown in Table 4. The percentages in the tables, computed horizontally, reveal the outflow from occupational origins to occupational destinations. The total row in Table 2 indicates the per cent of men in the various occupational destinations. It is

TABLE 1. Ranking of Seventeen Occ. Categories by Socioeconomic Status, for Males 14 and Over Employed in 1962

Occ.	Income Median (dollars)	Income Percentage Difference	Years of Schooling Median	Years of Schooling Percentage Difference
Professionals				
Self-Empl.	$12,048		16.4	
		76.1		
Salaried	6,842			
		−5.5		28.1
Managers	7,238		12.8	
		20.5		−1.5
Salesmen, Other	6,008		13.0	
		8.3		7.4
Proprietors	5,548		12.1	
		7.2		−3.2
Clerical	5,173		12.5	
		69.9		1.6
Salesmen, Retail	3,044		12.3	
		−44.5		9.8
Craftsmen				
Mfg. / Other	5,482 [a]		11.2	
		4.1		9.8
Construction	5,265		10.2	
		13.6		2.0
Operatives				
Mfg.	4,636		10.0	
		10.2		−3.8
Other	4,206		10.4	
		30.1		1.0
Service	3,233		10.3	
		47.7		15.7
Laborers				
Mfg. / Other	2,189		8.9	
		9.9		1.1
Farmers	1,992		8.8	
		308.2		6.0
Farm Laborers	488		8.3	

[a] Excludes foremen, who are concentrated in manufacturing and whose median income is $7073.

SOURCE: *Current Population Reports*, P-60, #41, Consumer Income: "Income of Family and Persons in the United States: 1962," October 21, 1963, and *Special Labor Force Report*, #30, "Educational Attainment of Workers, March, 1962," May, 1963. (Some figures include minor estimates entailed in combining detailed occupation groups. All data subject to sample error and to distortion due to inclusion of men outside age range 25–64.)

TABLE 2. Mobility from Father's Occ. to 1962 Occ., for Males 25 to 64 Years Old: Outflow Percentages

Father's Occupation	Respondent's Occupation in March, 1962																	Total[a]
	1	2	3	4	5	6	7	8	9	10	11	12	13	14	15	16	17	
1 Professionals (Self-Empl.)	16.7	31.9	9.9	9.5	4.4	4.0	1.4	2.0	1.8	2.2	2.6	1.6	1.8	.4	2.2	2.0	.8	100.0
2 Professionals (Salaried)	3.3	31.9	12.9	5.9	4.8	7.6	1.7	3.8	4.4	1.0	6.9	5.2	3.4	1.0	.6	.8	.2	100.0
3 Managers	3.5	22.6	19.4	6.2	7.9	7.6	1.1	5.4	5.3	3.1	4.0	2.5	1.5	1.1	.8	.5	.1	100.0
4 Salesmen (Other)	4.1	17.6	21.2	13.0	9.3	5.3	3.5	2.8	5.4	1.9	2.6	3.7	1.7	.0	.8	1.0	.3	100.0
5 Proprietors	3.7	13.7	18.4	5.8	16.0	6.2	3.3	3.5	5.2	3.9	5.1	3.6	2.8	.5	1.2	1.1	.4	100.0
6 Clerical	2.2	23.5	11.2	5.9	5.1	8.8	1.3	6.6	7.1	1.8	3.8	4.6	5.6	1.0	1.8	1.3	.0	100.0
7 Salesmen (Retail)	.7	13.7	14.1	8.8	11.5	6.4	2.7	5.8	3.4	3.1	8.8	5.1	4.6	.1	3.1	2.2	.0	100.0
8 Craftsmen (Mfg.)	1.0	14.9	8.5	2.4	6.2	6.1	1.7	15.3	6.4	4.4	10.9	6.2	4.6	1.7	2.4	.4	.1	100.0
9 Craftsmen (Other)	.9	11.1	9.2	3.9	6.5	7.6	1.5	7.8	12.2	4.4	8.2	9.2	4.6	1.2	2.8	.9	.3	100.0
10 Craftsmen (Constr.)	.9	6.7	7.1	2.6	8.3	7.9	.8	10.4	8.2	13.9	7.5	6.2	5.2	1.1	4.3	.8	.6	100.0
11 Operatives (Mfg.)	1.0	8.6	5.3	2.7	5.6	6.0	1.4	12.2	7.3	3.2	17.9	6.9	5.1	4.0	3.5	.8	.6	100.0
12 Operatives (Other)	.6	11.5	5.1	2.5	6.6	6.3	1.4	7.1	9.3	4.9	10.4	12.5	5.9	2.1	4.2	.9	1.1	100.0
13 Service	.8	8.8	7.4	3.5	6.0	9.0	1.9	8.0	6.4	5.4	11.7	8.1	10.5	2.7	3.3	1.0	.2	100.0
14 Laborers (Mfg.)	.0	6.0	5.3	.7	3.3	4.4	.7	10.7	6.0	2.8	18.1	9.4	9.4	7.1	5.8	1.7	.9	100.0
15 Laborers (Other)	.4	4.9	3.5	2.5	3.5	8.7	1.7	7.7	8.2	5.7	12.7	10.6	8.1	3.4	9.9	.9	1.1	100.0
16 Farmers	.6	4.2	4.1	1.2	6.0	4.3	1.1	5.6	6.7	5.8	10.2	8.6	4.8	2.4	5.4	16.4	3.9	100.0
17 Farm Laborers	.2	1.9	2.9	.6	4.0	3.5	1.2	6.4	6.6	5.8	13.1	10.8	7.5	3.2	9.2	5.7	9.4	100.0
Total[b]	1.4	10.2	7.9	3.1	7.0	6.1	1.5	7.2	7.1	4.9	9.9	7.6	5.5	2.1	4.3	5.2	1.7	100.0

[a] Rows as shown do not total 100.0, since men not in experienced civilian labor force are not shown separately.
[b] Includes men not reporting father's occupation.

TABLE 3. Mobility from Father's Occupation to First Job, for Males 25 to 64 Years Old: Outflow Percentages

Father's Occupation	First Job																	Total[a]
	1	2	3	4	5	6	7	8	9	10	11	12	13	14	15	16	17	
1 Professionals (Self-Empl.)	10.5	27.6	2.2	4.4	.8	17.9	4.4	2.6	3.2	.0	4.6	6.7	2.0	1.0	2.8	1.2	1.6	100.0
2 Professionals (Salaried)	1.2	29.5	3.7	2.1	.0	12.3	6.0	3.9	4.7	1.6	9.7	7.6	3.4	3.1	5.3	.5	2.0	100.0
3 Managers	1.9	18.2	2.8	3.5	.8	20.8	5.9	2.9	4.4	1.7	10.0	11.5	1.8	2.5	6.7	.5	1.1	100.0
4 Salesmen (Other)	2.6	17.0	2.6	11.4	1.0	17.2	8.9	1.4	2.8	1.4	9.0	9.5	1.8	1.2	3.7	.0	2.3	100.0
5 Proprietors	1.9	14.0	3.9	5.1	4.4	12.5	11.0	3.7	3.8	2.5	10.1	9.4	3.4	2.4	5.9	.3	2.2	100.0
6 Clerical	.4	18.0	2.3	1.7	.2	21.9	4.3	2.8	5.7	1.0	13.2	9.4	3.1	4.8	5.7	.7	1.3	100.0
7 Salesmen (Retail)	1.5	10.0	2.5	2.1	1.8	19.3	11.8	3.3	3.0	.1	15.5	8.0	2.1	3.9	8.0	.7	4.3	100.0
8 Craftsmen (Mfg.)	.1	6.5	.8	.5	.1	14.4	5.2	9.6	3.6	2.6	25.3	8.9	4.4	8.5	4.8	.2	1.8	100.0
9 Craftsmen (Other)	.5	6.1	.4	.8	.3	13.9	6.0	3.9	10.1	1.6	15.0	13.6	3.6	3.9	10.9	.5	4.3	100.0
10 Craftsmen (Constr.)	.1	5.7	.8	.6	.0	12.5	5.5	4.1	5.2	10.4	17.0	11.0	6.0	3.1	9.2	1.1	5.7	100.0
11 Operatives (Mfg.)	.3	4.1	.4	1.0	.1	11.1	3.9	4.1	2.6	1.7	35.9	7.7	5.1	8.6	6.1	.2	3.0	100.0
12 Operatives (Other)	.3	5.5	2.2	.3	.1	10.9	4.6	3.4	4.1	1.6	13.2	28.6	3.5	4.6	8.7	.4	3.9	100.0
13 Service	.2	4.4	1.4	1.2	.3	13.8	4.2	2.8	6.0	2.2	18.2	12.9	10.1	6.7	8.4	.7	4.1	100.0
14 Laborers (Mfg.)	.0	3.8	.1	.0	.0	5.3	4.8	1.1	4.1	1.1	23.2	9.1	4.1	22.2	7.5	.3	7.7	100.0
15 Laborers (Other)	1.1	3.2	.2	.5	.1	9.4	4.4	2.5	3.1	1.0	16.0	12.8	6.5	6.8	21.9	.7	6.3	100.0
16 Farmers	.2	3.3	.4	.4	.3	4.1	2.3	1.9	2.0	1.8	9.7	8.5	2.2	4.0	7.5	10.2	37.8	100.0
17 Farm Laborers	.2	.7	.2	.2	.3	2.4	1.1	.6	3.1	1.0	10.6	7.0	2.9	5.5	5.9	1.5	54.5	100.0

[a]Rows as shown do not total 100.0, since men not reporting first job are not shown separately.

TABLE 4. Mobility from First Job to 1962 Occupation, for Males 25 to 64 Years Old: Outflow Percentages

First Job	Respondent's Occupation in March, 1962																	Total[a]
	1	2	3	4	5	6	7	8	9	10	11	12	13	14	15	16	17	
1 Professionals (Self-Empl.)	53.5	25.5	1.8	4.7	2.5	1.5	.0	1.5	.7	.0	.7	.0	.0	.0	2.5	.0	.7	100.0
2 Professionals (Salaried)	6.5	54.5	12.3	2.8	5.5	4.9	.4	1.6	2.0	.4	1.2	1.2	1.0	.1	.3	1.0	.1	100.0
3 Managers	1.2	20.4	35.7	4.3	9.1	6.6	2.3	2.3	4.1	2.9	2.1	1.4	1.2	.6	1.2	.6	.4	100.0
4 Salesmen (Other)	.6	8.5	25.1	23.7	12.4	5.0	2.8	.6	3.3	1.3	5.4	3.9	2.8	.0	.0	.4	.0	100.0
5 Proprietors	.9	6.8	19.2	6.4	36.3	2.6	2.6	1.7	2.1	.4	4.3	4.3	3.0	.9	2.1	3.8	.0	100.0
6 Clerical	1.6	13.0	17.3	7.3	5.4	17.6	1.8	4.6	4.3	2.6	5.6	4.2	4.4	1.0	1.8	1.2	.2	100.0
7 Salesmen (Retail)	2.1	10.0	15.6	7.4	11.6	11.6	5.1	4.5	4.8	2.9	6.1	7.4	3.1	1.1	1.9	1.0	.1	100.0
8 Craftsmen (Mfg.)	.9	8.7	7.8	2.5	12.2	4.1	.7	22.5	7.5	4.3	9.1	3.5	3.7	.8	4.0	2.3	.0	100.0
9 Craftsmen (Other)	.3	9.0	6.6	1.9	10.3	4.1	3.4	10.9	21.3	4.7	7.1	5.5	3.6	1.4	1.7	1.2	.7	100.0
10 Craftsmen (Constr.)	.3	5.6	3.4	1.6	11.1	3.1	.2	8.8	13.2	26.2	5.0	4.3	2.4	1.0	3.1	2.1	.8	100.0
11 Operatives (Mfg.)	.4	6.1	5.3	2.0	7.0	6.2	1.7	13.4	6.7	4.6	18.8	7.6	4.7	3.2	3.5	2.0	.6	100.0
12 Operatives (Other)	.5	5.0	6.1	3.0	8.7	4.3	1.1	7.3	1C.8	6.9	9.6	15.0	6.0	1.4	4.3	1.8	1.0	100.0
13 Service	.5	7.1	4.9	1.4	6.2	5.0	1.2	3.4	6.4	6.2	13.3	7.7	19.8	2.5	5.8	.4	.5	100.0
14 Laborers (Mfg.)	.3	5.5	3.9	1.5	2.9	6.2	1.2	10.5	5.3	3.9	18.1	8.8	7.3	8.2	6.3	1.6	1.7	100.0
15 Laborers (Other)	.2	5.5	5.4	2.4	6.7	4.1	1.3	6.1	9.6	6.8	10.5	10.8	6.3	2.4	11.5	2.1	.9	100.0
16 Farmers	.2	2.3	2.6	1.8	3.8	3.0	1.2	4.2	5.9	5.4	8.3	5.0	4.6	1.4	3.6	30.0	5.0	100.0
17 Farm Laborers	.2	1.7	2.4	.8	4.7	2.7	1.1	5.3	6.3	5.5	10.4	9.3	5.8	2.8	6.7	19.3	7.0	100.0

[a] Rows as shown do not total 100.0, since men not in the experienced civilian labor force are not shown separately.

evident that the 17 occupational categories were not equal in size in 1962, ranging from 1⅓ per cent of the total labor force for self-employed professionals to 10 per cent each for salaried professionals and operatives in manufacturing.

By and large the percentages are highest in the major diagonal and decrease with movement away from it, a reflection of a prevailing tendency toward self-recruitment and occupational inheritance. But the pattern is by no means entirely consistent. Fewer sons of retail salesmen become retail salesmen than become clerks, proprietors, other salesmen, managers, or salaried professionals. Sons of operatives outside manufacturing have a greater chance of becoming salaried professionals than the higher-status (hence closer to the diagonal) sons of craftsmen outside manufacturing, and nearly as good a chance as sons of proprietors. The intragenerational matrix (Table 4) shows that the likelihood of rising to the status of independent businessman is better for workers who begin their careers as either skilled craftsmen or semiskilled operatives than for men whose first jobs are as clerks, even though the latter are only one step below business owners in the socioeconomic status hierarchy. Perhaps manual workers are more likely than clerks to start working for self-employed fathers whose business they later inherit.

Although percentages within the same column can be compared, tables in this form do not permit meaningful direct comparisons across columns. Thus sons of self-employed professionals are nearly twice as likely to become salaried professionals as they are

to become self-employed professionals (Table 2, row 1). But this is in part because of the fact that there are today seven times as many salaried as self-employed professionals, a fact indicated in the total row at the bottom of the table. Whereas the ratio of self-employed to salaried professionals for the entire sample is 1:7, the ratio among sons of self-employed professionals is 1:2. These sons exceed the chance all sons have of becoming self-employed professionals even more than they exceed the chance all sons have of becoming salaried professionals. The sons of self-employed professionals who follow in their father's footsteps, though fewer in number than those who go into salaried professions, pre-empt a proportionately larger share of the positions in the free professions.

The influence of social origins on occupational destinations finds expression in the relative, not the absolute, proportion of men with the same origin who end up in a certain occupation, specifically, in the ratio of the per cent from a given origin in one occupation to the per cent of the total labor force in this occupation. The last row in Table 2, which presents the percentage distribution of the total labor force in the several occupations, serves as the standard against which all percentages in the body of the matrix are compared, the divisor in the desired ratio. By dividing each value in the matrix by the corresponding figure in the total row at the bottom of its column, we obtain an index of the influence of occupational origins on occupational destinations. This ratio, which has been termed the "index of association" or "social distance mobility ratio," [3] mea-

---

[3] For previous use of this index, see David V. Glass (Ed.), *Social Mobility in Britain*, Glencoe: Free Press, 1956, pp. 177–217; and Natalie Rogoff, *Recent Trends in Occupational Mobility*, Glencoe: Free Press, 1953.

sures the extent to which mobility from one occupation to another surpasses or falls short of "chance"; that is, a value of 1.0 indicates that the observed mobility is equal to that expected on the assumption of statistical independence.

The model of "perfect" mobility, defined by statistical independence of origins and destinations, serves as a baseline for comparison, departures from it being reflected in the mobility ratios. In the case of perfect mobility each destination group has the same distribution of origins as the total population, each origin group has the same distribution of destinations as the total population, and all indices are 1.0. The actual mobility ratios for intergenerational movements, corresponding to Table 2, are presented in Table 5; those for mobility from father's to first occupation are presented in Table 6; and the intragenerational flow patterns from first to present occupation are shown in Table 7. In order to convey a visual impression of the over-all flow of manpower, values greater than 1.0 are underlined.

These three tables bring the main characteristics of the American occupational structure into high relief. First, occupational inheritance is in all cases greater than expected on the assumption of independence; note the consistently high values in the major diagonal. Second, social mobility is nevertheless pervasive, as revealed by the large number of underlined values off the diagonal. Third, upward mobility (to the left of the diagonal) is more prevalent than downward mobility (to the right), and short-distance movements occur more often than long-distance ones.

If occupational inheritance and fixed careers were dominating the stratification system, all excess manpower would be concentrated in the 17 cells in the major diagonal and the values in all other cells would fall short of theoretical expectation. In fact an excess flow of manpower is manifest in 101 cells of the father's-to-1962-occupation matrix, also 101 cells in the father's-to-first-job matrix, and 78 cells in the first-to-1962-job matrix. This indicates much movement among occupational strata. A rough indication of the prevailing direction of mobility is the number of such cells lying on either side of the major diagonal. For the intergenerational flow of manpower, as Table 5 shows, the underlined values to the lower left of the diagonal, which indicate disproportionate upward mobility, outnumber by more than three to one (64:20) those to the upper right, which indicate disproportionate downward mobility. Excessive upward movements outnumber excessive downward movements in the intragenerational flow five to two (44:17), as can be seen in Table 7. Table 6 shows, however, that the excessive flow of manpower from father's to first occupation is hardly more likely to go to higher than to lower occupations (46:38), undoubtedly because career beginnings often entail a temporary drop in status.[4]

Short-distance movements exceed long-distance ones. Most of the underlined values are concentrated in the area adjacent to the major diagonal, denoting short-distance mobility, and there are few in the areas surrounding the upper right and the lower left corners, which would be evidence of long-distance mobility. The values of the mobility ratios tend to be highest in

---

[4] These patterns hold also if the cells indicative of horizontal movement are omitted.

TABLE 5. Mobility from Father's Occupation to Occupation in 1962, for Males 25 to 64 Years Old: Ratios of Observed Frequencies to Frequencies Expected on the Assumption of Independence

Father's Occupation	Respondent's Occupation in March, 1962																
	1	2	3	4	5	6	7	8	9	10	11	12	13	14	15	16	17
1 Professionals (Self-Empl.)	11.7	3.1	1.2	3.0	.6	.7	.9	.3	.3	.5	.3	.2	.3	.2	.5	.4	.5
2 Professionals (Salaried)	2.3	3.1	1.6	1.9	.7	1.2	1.1	.5	.6	.2	.7	.7	.6	.5	.1	.2	.1
3 Managers	2.5	2.2	2.5	2.0	1.1	1.2	.7	.8	.7	.6	.4	.3	.3	.5	.2	.1	.1
4 Salesmen (Other)	2.9	1.7	2.7	4.1	1.3	.9	2.2	.4	.8	.4	.3	.5	.3	.0	.2	.2	.2
5 Proprietors	2.6	1.3	2.3	1.9	2.3	1.0ᵃ	2.1	.5	.7	.8	.5	.5	.5	.2	.3	.2	.2
6 Clerical	1.6	2.3	1.4	1.9	.7	1.4	.8	.9	1.0ᵃ	.4	.4	.6	1.0ᵃ	.2	.4	.2	.0
7 Salesmen (Retail)	.5	1.3	1.8	2.8	1.6	1.0ᵃ	1.7	.8	.5	.6	.9	.7	.8	.5	.7	.4	.0
8 Craftsmen (Mfg.)	.7	1.5	1.1	.8	.9	1.0	1.1	2.1	.9	.9	.9	.8	.8	.1	.6	.1	.1
9 Craftsmen (Other)	.6	1.1	1.2	1.2	.9	1.2	1.0	1.1	1.7	.9	1.1	1.2	.8	.8	.6	.2	.2
10 Craftsmen (Constr.)	.6	.7	.9	.8	1.2	1.3	.5	1.4	1.1	2.8	.8	.8	.9	.5	1.0	.2	.4
11 Operatives (Mfg.)	.7	.8	.7	.9	.8	1.0	.9	1.7	1.0ᵃ	.6	1.8	.9	.9	1.9	.8	.2	.4
12 Operatives (Other)	.4	1.1	.6	.8	.9	1.0ᵃ	.9	1.0	1.3	1.0	1.0ᵃ	1.7	1.1	1.0	1.0	.2	.7
13 Service	.5	.9	.9	1.1	.9	1.5	1.2	1.1	.9	1.1	1.2	1.1	1.9	1.3	.8	.2	.1
14 Laborers (Mfg.)	.0	.6	.7	.2	.5	.7	.5	1.5	.8	.6	1.8	1.2	1.7	3.3	1.4	.3	.5
15 Laborers (Other)	.3	.5	.4	.8	.5	1.4	1.1	1.1	1.1	1.2	1.3	1.4	1.5	1.6	2.3	.2	.7
16 Farmers	.4	.4	.5	.4	.9	.7	.7	.8	.9	1.2	1.0ᵃ	1.1	.9	1.1	1.3	3.2	2.3
17 Farm Laborers	.1	.2	.4	.2	.6	.6	.8	.9	.9	1.2	1.3	1.4	1.4	1.5	2.1	1.1	5.5

ᵃ Rounds to unity from above (other indices shown as 1.0 round to unity from below).

TABLE 6. Mobility from Father's Occupation to First Job, for Males 25 to 64 Years Old: Ratios of Observed Frequencies to Frequencies Expected on the Assumption of Independence

Father's Occupation	Respondent's First Job																
	1	2	3	4	5	6	7	8	9	10	11	12	13	14	15	16	17
1 Professionals (Self-Empl.)	15.2	3.8	1.8	3.3	1.4	1.7	.9	.8	.8	.0	.3	.6	.5	.2	.4	.4	.1
2 Professionals (Salaried)	1.8	4.1	3.0	1.6	.0	1.2	1.3	1.2	1.2	.7	.6	.7	.9	.6	.7	.2	.1
3 Managers	2.8	2.5	2.3	2.6	1.5	2.0	1.2	.9	1.2	.8	.7	1.0a	.5	.5	.8	.2	.1
4 Salesmen (Other)	3.7	2.3	2.1	8.5	1.8	1.6	1.9	.4	.7	.7	.6	.9	.5	.2	.5	.0	.2
5 Proprietors	2.8	1.9	3.2	3.7	7.6	1.2	2.3	1.1	1.0	1.1	.7	.9	.9	.5	.7	.1	.2
6 Clerical	.6	2.5	1.9	1.2	.3	2.1	.9	.9	1.5	.4	.9	.7	.8	.9	.7	.2	.1
7 Salesmen (Retail)	2.2	1.4	2.1	1.5	3.1	1.8	2.5	1.0a	.8	.1	1.0a	.7	.5	.8	1.0	.2	.3
8 Craftsmen (Mfg.)	.1	.9	.7	.4	.2	1.4	1.1	3.0	1.0	1.2	1.7	.8	1.2	1.7	.6	.1	.1
9 Craftsmen (Other)	.7	.8	.3	.6	.5	1.3	1.3	1.2	2.7	.7	1.0a	1.2	1.0	.8	1.4	.2	.3
10 Craftsmen (Constr.)	.2	.8	.7	.4	.0	1.2	1.2	1.3	1.4	4.8	1.1	1.0a	1.6	.6	1.1	.3	.4
11 Operatives (Mfg.)	.4	.6	.3	.7	.1	1.0	.8	1.3	.7	.8	2.4	.7	1.3	1.7	.8	.1	.2
12 Operatives (Other)	.4	.8	1.8	.2	.1	1.0	1.0	1.1	1.1	.8	.9	2.6	.9	.9	1.1	.1	.3
13 Service	.3	.6	1.2	.9	.5	1.3	.9	.9	1.6	1.0a	1.2	1.2	2.7	1.3	1.0a	.2	.3
14 Laborers (Mfg.)	.0	.5	.1	.0	.0	.5	1.0a	.4	1.1	.5	1.6	.8	1.1	4.4	.9	.1	.5
15 Laborers (Other)	1.6	.4	.1	.4	.2	.9	.9	.8	.8	.5	1.1	1.2	1.7	1.4	2.7	.2	.4
16 Farmers	.3	.5	.3	.3	.5	.4	.5	.6	.5	.8	.7	.8	.6	.8	.9	3.3	2.7
17 Farm Laborers	.3	.1	.2	.1	.5	.2	.2	.2	.8	.4	.7	.6	.8	1.1	.7	.5	3.8

aRounds to unity from above (other indices shown as 1.0 round to unity from below).

TABLE 7. Mobility from First Job to Occupation in 1962, for Males 25 to 64 Years Old: Ratios of Observed Frequencies to Frequencies Expected on the Assumption of Independence

First Job	Respondent's Occupation in 1962																
	1	2	3	4	5	6	7	8	9	10	11	12	13	14	15	16	17
1 Professionals (Self-Empl.)	37.3	2.5	.2	1.5	.4	.2	.0	.2	.1	.0	.1	.0	.0	.0	.6	.0	.4
2 Professionals (Salaried)	4.5	5.4	1.6	.9	.8	.8	.2	.2	.3	.1	.1	.2	.2	.0	.1	.2	.1
3 Managers	.9	2.0	4.5	1.4	1.3	1.1	1.5	.3	.6	.6	.2	.2	.2	.3	.3	.1	.2
4 Salesmen (Other)	.4	.8	3.2	7.6	1.8	.8	1.8	.1	.5	.3	.5	.5	.5	.0	.0	.1	.0
5 Proprietors	.6	.7	2.4	2.0	5.2	.4	1.7	.2	.3	.1	.4	.6	.5	.4	.5	.7	.0
6 Clerical	1.1	1.3	2.2	2.3	.8	2.9	1.2	.6	.6	.5	.6	.6	.8	.5	.4	.2	.1
7 Salesmen (Retail)	1.4	1.0	2.0	2.3	1.7	1.9	3.3	.6	.7	.6	.6	1.0	.6	.5	.4	.2	.0
8 Craftsmen (Mfg.)	.6	.9	1.0	.8	1.7	.7	.5	3.1	1.0[a]	.9	.9	.5	.7	.4	.9	.4	.4
9 Craftsmen (Other)	.2	.9	.8	.6	1.5	.7	2.2	1.5	3.0	1.0	.7	.7	.7	.6	.4	.2	.4
10 Craftsmen (Constr.)	.2	.5	.4	.5	1.6	.5	.2	1.2	1.8	5.3	.5	.6	.4	.5	.7	.4	.5
11 Operatives (Mfg.)	.3	.6	.7	.6	1.0	1.0[a]	1.1	1.9	.9	.9	1.9	1.0	.9	1.5	.8	.4	.3
12 Operatives (Other)	.3	.5	.8	.9	1.3	.7	.7	1.0[a]	1.5	1.4	1.0	2.0	1.1	.7	1.0[a]	.4	.6
13 Service	.3	.7	.6	.4	.9	.8	.8	.5	.9	1.3	1.3	1.0[a]	3.6	1.2	1.4	.1	.3
14 Laborers (Mfg.)	.2	.5	.5	.5	.4	1.0[a]	.8	1.5	.7	.8	1.8	1.2	1.3	3.8	1.5	.3	1.0
15 Laborers (Other)	.2	.5	.7	.8	1.0	.7	.8	.8	1.4	1.4	1.1	1.4	1.1	1.1	2.7	.4	.6
16 Farmers	.2	.2	.3	.6	.5	.5	.8	.6	.8	1.1	.8	.7	.9	.7	.8	7.0	3.0
17 Farm Laborers	.1	.2	.3	.2	.7	.4	.7	.7	.9	1.1	1.0	1.2	1.1	1.3	1.6	3.7	4.1

[a]Rounds to unity from above (other indices shown as 1.0 round to unity from below).

the diagonal and decrease gradually with movement away from it. In general, the closer two occupations are to one another in the status hierarchy, the greater is the flow of manpower between them.

There are, however, numerous exceptions to this basic tendency for the flow of manpower to occur predominantly between occupations similarly ranked, as revealed by the blank cells in areas that have predominantly underlined values and the underlined values in predominantly blank areas. The majority of these discrepancies in all three tables reflect industrial lines. Hence another distinctive pattern to which the tables call attention is that industrial lines constitute stronger barriers to mobility than do skill levels within an industry. Indeed, the expectation that industrial differences would affect the flow of manpower, partly because industries are concentrated in different geographical areas, was what prompted the decision to subdivide manual occupations by industry.

Finally, exceptional cases that are not covered by any of the above general patterns should be mentioned. Looking first at movements from father's to 1962 occupation (Table 5), we note that sons of craftsmen are more likely to move into higher than into lower white-collar occupations. This possibly reflects a reluctance on the part of men reared in the most affluent blue-collar homes to accept the lower income levels of the more menial nonmanual occupations. By and large, sons of manual workers outside manufacturing are more apt to be upwardly mobile than those in manufacturing. Lastly, service occupations contain relatively few sons of farmers.

The flow from father's to first occupation (Table 6), which often entails a temporary drop in status, reveals more discontinuities than that from father's to 1962 occupation. Sons of nonmanufacturing operatives and of service workers disproportionately often find first jobs as managers. The unexpectedly large movement of sons of nonmanufacturing laborers to first jobs as self-employed professionals may be due to sampling error resulting from the small number of cases involved—approximately six, possibly even fewer.[5] Even with a sample as large as this one, some cells have frequencies too low to assure reliable results. Sons of service workers start their careers in an unusually large variety of occupations, ranging from other laborers to salaried managers. Downward mobility to first job is most marked for those in the highest white-collar groups and for skilled craftsmen, and upward mobility to the first job is most common among both lower nonmanual and lower manual workers. This observation suggests that movements within the white-collar and within the blue-collar class are more prevalent than movements between these two classes.

Intragenerational movements (Table 7) also reveal a few deviations from the main trends. First, men who start their careers as farmers, in sharp contrast to those starting as farm laborers, do not move in proportionate numbers to any nonfarm occupation, with the sole exception of skilled construction work. Second, proprietors are disproportionately recruited from skilled and semiskilled manual workers (except manufacturing operatives). Third, men who enter the labor force on higher white-collar levels and later move

---

[5] These might be men in such unusual "professions" as boxing.

downward drop in excessive numbers down to retail sales, skipping the slightly higher status of clerk. Indeed, whereas men are recruited to clerical work from a wide variety of social origins, few move into clerical work after having started their careers (compare the columns for clerks in the three tables).

31

from
AUTOMOBILE WORKERS AND THE
AMERICAN DREAM

Ely Chinoy

The open society is constantly given unstinting praise for offering persons the opportunity to improve their social position and escape from humble origins. According to the traditional mythology of the American dream, any man who possesses ambition, drive, foresight, and intelligence can achieve economic success. And popular literature is so replete with rags to riches stories that in the popular mind most successful men have sprung from poverty and built empires from shoestrings.

The American *reality*, however, is somewhat different, and reflects the impact of social class. Although the proverbial Horatio Alger tale is not complete mythology—it occurs often enough to sustain belief in it and is publicized so that it appears to be an everyday occurrence—nevertheless, the classic American success story is more the exception than the rule. Putting aside the myth for a moment, it must be reiterated that the great majority of America's economic elite has come from business and professional, not working- or lower-class, homes. Furthermore, as Blau and Duncan's data reveal, most sons of manual workers become manual workers themselves.

While much attention has been given to the relative handful of men who have experienced spectacular careers, *what of the millions of men—the vast majority—who don't make it?* For the typical factory worker, the American dream can be a nightmare and the myth of unlimited mobility can serve only to mock and haunt him. On every hand, he is urged to achieve, to build, to climb; but factory work is often a dead-end street.

In his study of a group of workers in a midwestern automobile factory, Ely Chinoy carefully explores the dilemma in which factory workers often find themselves. Work your way up to higher levels in the company? But in the modern corporation, management never recruits its junior executives from among workers on the factory floor. Careers that begin on the assembly line do not end in carpeted private offices. Well,

SOURCE: Ely Chinoy, *Automobile Workers and the American Dream* (New York: Random House, 1955), Chapter 10. Copyright © 1955 by Random House, Inc. Reprinted by permission of the publisher.

if this is impossible, then work your way up in the factory itself, through hard work, diligence, sobriety, and the other traditional virtues. But these qualities are meaningless and impossible to demonstrate in the context of assembly-line production and standardized work routines. Furthermore, with the advent of unionization, wage scales between the highest and lowest paid factory workers are compressed, thus limiting the scope and opportunity for upward mobility. Movement up from semiskilled to skilled work often collides with restrictions of apprenticeship programs. The ultimate to many in the factory is the job of foreman, but this position is a mixed blessing, as many studies have indicated.

There is, however, another possibility: start your own business to achieve success. But factory workers rarely have sufficient savings and know-how to launch a substantial business, and with the growing size and concentration of economic enterprise in this country, the fate of the small enterpriser, never very secure, is becoming increasingly precarious. A recent study of small business ventures launched by former manual workers in Providence, Rhode Island, found that of 92 new businesses begun, 45 had closed down after only two years. Of those remaining, only 8 were classed as either potentially profitable or profitable, the remainder being either marginal survivors in which the owner had to take on other work to survive, or limited successes, with the owner barely eeking out a living, putting in long hours for what was comparable to working-class pay.*

The dilemma, therefore, is this: according to the American dream, opportunity for success is unlimited, but for a great many manual workers, the structure of economic opportunity in which they find themselves is very limited indeed. What, then, are the social and psychological *reactions* to this contradiction between the dream of unlimited mobility and the everyday reality of working-class life? Are workers able to save face, to avoid corrosive feelings of defeat and self-hatred; and if so, how? In this final chapter from *Automobile Workers and the American Dream,* Chinoy discusses the ways in which a group of factory workers attempts some kind of reconciliation between the heralded tradition of opportunity and the mundane facts of their workaday lives.

The tradition of opportunity imposes heavy burdens upon workers who must repeatedly reconcile desire, stimulated from diverse sources, with the realities of working-class life. Since each individual is assigned full responsibility for his economic fate, failure can be due only to limited ability or defects in character—lack of ambition or determination or initiative, for example—and not to the absence of opportunity. Self-regard and self-esteem are challenged by this assumption that failure to rise from the level of wage labor is "one's own fault." Since large ambitions and unremitting persistence are sanctioned not only as prerequisites for success, but also as intrinsically desirable traits whose absence testifies to a lamentable weakness of character, feelings of guilt may also be generated when men cease to strive for the rich rewards ostensibly available to all.

As we have noted earlier, workers may try to maintain the illusion of persisting ambition by defining their jobs in the factory as "temporary" and by incessantly talking of their out-of-the-

---

* Kurt B. Mayer and Sidney Goldstein, "Manual Workers as Small Businessmen," in Arthur B. Shostak and William Gomberg, eds., *Blue-Collar World* (Englewood Cliffs, New Jersey: Prentice-Hall, 1964).

shop goals and expectations. As long as workers can sustain this illusion, they can escape from the problems of self-justification created by their inability to rise and their low level of aspiration. But these expedients are themselves at best temporary, at worst only a public demonstration that one is ambitious— which may convince others without assuaging inner feelings of guilt and self-blame. No matter what public image of plans and prospects workers can create, they still live in a world in which they have manifestly gained no substantial advancement. Eventually they may have to face up to the fact that they are likely to remain factory workers for the rest of their lives.

Since men do not readily reveal self-doubt and self-blame, it is difficult to gauge the extent to which workers find the reasons for their failure to rise out of the ranks of factory labor in their own actions, habits, or personality. Occasionally some of the men interviewed did give evidence of self-depreciation, guilt, and lowered self-regard. "I guess I'm just not smart enough," said a thirty-eight-year-old machine-operator who had never worked at anything except a factory job, laughing gently at himself as if to ease this self-evaluation. A thirty-two-year-old worker in parts and service who had never been employed anywhere except in the A.B.C. plant commented:

> It's my own fault. I was going to work here for a year after I graduated from high school and then be a printer's apprentice. But then I bought a car and that was my downfall. I couldn't afford to leave if I was going to have the car. Then I got married—and I certainly couldn't afford to quit.

And a thirty-year-old machine-operator who had also gone directly into the A.B.C. plant from high school exclaimed bitterly:

> Sometimes I look at myself in the mirror and I say to myself, Pat, you dumb so-and-so, you could have been somebody if you'd only set your mind to it and not been so interested in the almighty dollar.

(Pat could have gone to college with the assistance of a well-to-do relative, but had instead gone to work in the factory where he could earn high wages immediately.)

But most workers, it appears, frequently try to rationalize their status as factory employees and to justify their small ambitions. Despite the fact that their aspirations are controlled by a relatively objective appraisal of what is possible rather than by the unreliable image of America projected by the tradition of opportunity, most workers do not explain their failure to rise in terms of forces beyond their control. Nor do they feel that under the circumstances they could not be expected to pursue larger goals. Instead they try to maintain their self-regard by redefining advancement to include the goals and interests with which they are actively concerned, by projecting their hopes and aspirations upon their children, and, to a lesser extent, by minimizing success and emphasizing alternative values.

In order to convince themselves that they are getting ahead and that they are not without ambition, workers apply to the ends they pursue the vocabulary of the tradition of opportunity. They extend the meaning of ambition and advancement to include the search for security, the pursuit of small goals in the factory, and the constant accumulation of personal possessions.

Security, it has been frequently asserted, is replacing advancement as the major objective of most industrial workers. It seems highly probable that the automobile workers studied in this investigation *are* actually more interested in security than in traditional patterns of advancement. Workers' attitudes toward specific aspects of their job world reveal clearly their intense concern with security. They value a steady job over one that is not steady, even if the latter pays higher wages. They are unwilling to assume the risks inherent in small business despite their desire to leave the factory and be independent. They want to save as much as they can, not in order to be able eventually to strike out for themselves, but to provide protection against a "rainy day." They place great emphasis upon seniority, with its protection against arbitrary layoffs and its assurance of recall if one is laid off temporarily. The union's fight for a company pension plan drew strong support from these men because it articulated deep-seated concerns. And it seems likely that the union's increasing interest in the guaranteed annual wage will elicit a similar response.

But workers do not see security, thus concretely exemplified, as an alternative to advancement. Questions which were designed to elicit the relative importance assigned to security and opportunities for advancement frequently proved meaningless; the respondents could see no difference between them. "If you've got security, if you've got something you can fall back on, you're still getting ahead," said a twenty-eight-year-old truck-driver with three children. "If you can put away a couple of hundred dollars so you can take care of an emergency, then you're get-

ting ahead," declared a forty-year-old nonskilled maintenance worker with four children. "If you work during a layoff, like back in the depression, that's my idea of working up," commented a thirty-two-year-old fender-wrapper who had been in the plant since 1935. And a thirty-nine-year-old oiler summed it up: "If you're secure, then you're getting ahead."

The small goals workers pursue in the factory resemble the prevailing cultural definition of advancement only in the case of small wage increases gained individually through promotion (although usually on the basis of the seniority rule). The more significant wage increases are now secured collectively through the union. And the other goals in the factory embody hitherto distinct values which are now assimilated to the idea of advancement. "Getting ahead," explained a machine-operator with ten years of seniority, "is working up to a job where you don't get kicked around." "I'll be getting ahead all right," declared a discontented line-tender, "if I can just get off the line." Upward movement in the informal hierarchy is equated with advancement even though it may mean no economic gain, no greater demands on skill, and no increase in responsibility.

In their efforts to reconcile their own ambitions and achievements with the tradition of opportunity, workers have also transformed what was once a symbol of economic success into a significant form of personal progress in itself. Advancement has come to mean the progressive accumulation of things as well as the increasing capacity to consume. A nonskilled maintenance worker who had been in the plant for fourteen years commented:

A lot of people think getting ahead means getting to be a millionaire. Not for me though. If I can just increase the value of my possessions as the years go by instead of just breaking even or falling behind and losing, if I can keep adding possessions and property—personal property too—and put some money away for when I can't work, if I happen to own two or three houses like this one [which had cost $1,600 in 1940, of which he still owed eight hundred dollars] and have five thousand dollars put away in the bank, I'll figure I got ahead quite a lot.

The achievement which most clearly betokens advancement by purchase is home ownership, a goal already sanctioned and supported by a complex set of values.[1] A thirty-nine-year-old welder living in one of the city's two slum areas remarked:

> We're all working for one purpose, to get ahead. I don't think a person should be satisfied. My next step is a nice little modern house of my own. That's what I mean by bettering yourself—or getting ahead.

If one manages to buy a new car, if each year sees a major addition to the household—a washing machine, a refrigerator, a new living-room suite, now probably a television set—then one is also getting ahead.

American culture encourages men to seek both occupational advancement and the acquisition of material possessions. But workers who respond to both of these admonitions use the second to rationalize their failure to achieve the first. As long as possessions continue to pile up, the worker can feel that he is moving forward; as long as his wants do not give out, he can feel that he is ambitious.

Workers may also attempt to cushion the impact of failure and to maintain an identification with the tradition of opportunity by projecting their unfulfilled ambitions upon their children—their extended ego, as it were. The hope that one's child may succeed where one has failed may make that personal failure seem less important; ambition for a child may substitute for ambition for oneself. "What sustains us as a nation," wrote Eleanor Roosevelt in one of her daily columns, "[is] the feeling that if you are poor you still see visions of your children having the opportunities you missed." Further, as we have already seen, the burden of family responsibilities, which includes concern for the future of one's children, serves as an acceptable justification for remaining in the factory rather than risking savings and security in business.

Sons of twenty-eight of the workers interviewed were not yet old enough to work. Among the fathers there was an almost universally expressed desire that their sons not go into the factory, that they "do better than that." The occasional intensity of this desire is suggested by the assertion of a forty-year-old line repairman whose sixteen-year-old son was talking of dropping out of high school: "If he goes into the factory I'll beat the hell out of him—except if he just goes in for a visit or if he goes to engineering school or learns a trade first."

Since most workers felt that they could not and should not dictate their children's occupational choices, their positive aspirations usually focussed upon education rather than upon specific occupations or professions, although a few did have definite occupational hopes—doctor, musician, artist, engineer. Thirteen of these twenty-eight workers hoped that their sons would go to college, seven wished that they would at least secure some kind of technical training after graduating from high school, and three merely insisted that their children should finish high school. The remaining five did not have any positive desires or hopes for their children.

The significance of these aspirations for children as a possible substitute for personal achievement emerged in the comment of a thirty-two-year-old machine-operator who had taken his first job in the depths of the Great Depression: "I never had a chance, but I want my kids to go to college and do something better than factory work." The direct relationship which may exist between the hopes men have for their children and their own unfulfilled interests and desires is suggested by a worker who, having once played an instrument in a high-school band, hoped that his son might become a professional musician, and by the would-be cartoonist who hoped that his four-year-old son would become an artist—seeing in his childish scribbling signs of some artistic capacity and interest.

Finally, workers may try to protect themselves from guilt and self-blame by stressing other values as substitutes for success, minimizing the importance of wealth. In a few instances, for example, workers asserted that what mattered was "happiness—and you don't need a lot of money for that," that what counted was "the kind of person you are and not how much money you have." Such assertions do not represent a radical rejection of American values. The importance of moral integrity, the happiness to be found in humble surroundings, the spuriousness of the single-minded search for fortune when human values are neglected are all familiar, though usually minor, themes

in American culture. In emphasizing these themes, workers have not denied the desirability of economic success, but have sought to relegate it to a lesser position in the hierarchy of values.

Only in the occasional instances of men who could be defined in Marx's terms as *lumpenproletariat* or in W. L. Warner's terms as "lower-lower class" could one find workers who had totally rejected American success values. (No such workers were interviewed, although several were pointed out or identified.) But this solution to the problems imposed on workers by the disparity between their goals and achievements on the one hand and the tradition of opportunity on the other was in effect no solution. Such men offered no alternative values to replace those which they had rejected; they were in a state of anomy.

The efficiency with which these defensive rationalizations protect workers from the cultural attack upon the stability and integrity of their personalities is, of course, difficult to appraise. It does seem unlikely that they can be totally effective. In the immediate context of the factory and of a working-class community, small gains in the factory and security may represent important achievements. But when men move into a larger social context these gains may seem insignificant, and men are forced again to face the fact that they have not been able to get on in the world. In a society which emphasizes economic achievement as strongly as ours, it seems unlikely that workers can get away with their deprecation of success values. Indeed, the few men who tried to minimize the importance of economic achievement and to stress other values also felt it necessary to defend themselves in other ways which did not deny the importance of success.

There are serious and more obvious limits on the long-run efficacy of aspirations for children as a protection against the impact of failure. Lacking knowledge of occupational alternatives and possessing few resources with which to aid their children financially, most workers can only encourage and exhort, they cannot offer effective guidance or practical assistance. If their sons finally become factory workers, as a substantial proportion usually do,* not only must they surrender whatever ego-protection they have derived from their hopes, they may also be forced to bear a new burden: a sense of responsibility for their children's failure stemming from their own inability to provide guidance or assistance.

Workers can only succeed in the acquisition of possessions, even if they do not suffer from recurrent hard times, if they have mastered what Wesley Mitchell once called "the backward art of spending money." [2] That they, together with most Americans, may not yet have mastered that art is suggested, for example, by John Dean's analysis of the risks inherent in buying a house. Ignorant of many of the problems of home ownership and unprotected against error and exploitation by institutional safeguards, workers—and others—may be defenseless against the "organized pressure to buy." [3]

Since these defensive measures are only partially effective, it seems probable that there remains among these workers a deep and substantial undercurrent of guilt and self-depreciation. The inability and failure to live up to the demands of the tradition of opportunity generate a process of self-justification in which frustration, guilt, and defensive rationalization follow one another in disorderly, almost endless, sometimes painful succession.

Both self-blame and the defensive rationalizations against self-blame, however, contribute to the maintenance of both existing economic institutions and the tradition of opportunity itself. To the extent that workers focus blame for their failure to rise above the level of wage labor upon themselves rather than upon the institutions that govern the pursuit of wealth or upon the persons who control those institutions, American society escapes the consequences of its own contradictions.

The measures by which workers try to maintain their self-regard serve in various ways to reinforce the belief that America is still a land of promise. The felt need to sustain hope for their children encourages workers to believe that there will be opportunities available to them, indeed, in some cases, that there will be even greater opportunities in the future than in the past. This belief gains particular support from the obvious and unceasingly reported progress of science and technology. For ex-

* There were nine adults among the male children of the workers interviewed. Four of these held nonskilled factory jobs. Two held minor white-collar jobs which might eventually be exchanged for factory work because of the low wages they paid. One was completing an apprentice course as a pattern-maker. One was studying engineering at the state university located nearby. One, the son of a skilled worker and grandson of a doctor, was a commercial photographer. In their study of occupational mobility in San Jose, California, P. E. Davidson and H. D. Anderson found that 58.2% of the sons of unskilled workers and 43.4% of the sons of semiskilled workers became either unskilled or semiskilled workers, as did 23.4% of the sons of skilled workers. *Occupational Mobility in an American Community*, Stanford University, Stanford University Press, 1937, p. 20. Table 4. These figures are comparable to those reported in other studies.

ample, a machine-operator with three young children commented: "There's better opportunities now than when I started. There are more things being created, like diesel engine work, things that weren't thought of when we were children. Science is growing greater every day. Children now have a better opportunity to get in on the ground floor." In the urgent search for grounds for hope, the fact that success in new industrial fields built on scientific research requires either capital or education and training which their children may have difficulty in acquiring passes unnoticed.

If they have redefined advancement in terms closer to the realities of their own experience, workers may continue to feel that there are still real opportunities to get ahead. Security and small gains in the factory are within reach. Since Americans live on an escalator standard of living which offers an ever-growing array of things to buy and to have, there must always be new opportunities for advancement by purchase.

The social order is thus protected, however, only at the psychological expense of those who have failed. The destructive character of guilt and self-blame is obvious. But workers' attempts to avoid self-depreciation also strip much of their lives of positive significance in more subtle ways.

The justification for the universal pursuit of success has been in part the assertion that men can best realize their individual potentialities by seeking to get ahead in the world. The pursuit of success not only tests one's character, it has been argued, it also strengthens and ennobles it. Since the welfare of society rests upon the self-seeking of individuals, each man can feel that he is contributing to the progress of his country by his efforts to gain personal advancement. But the defenses which workers erect against the guilt and self-blame generated by limited aspirations and failure to get ahead tend to strip their jobs of meaning and significance and to inhibit rather than stimulate personal growth and self-development.

Both security and small goals in the factory (except for wage increases) are essentially defensive in character. The concern with security is based upon fear and uncertainty; sought-for job improvements (again except for wage increases) entail primarily escape from difficulties. As goals, therefore, they constitute patterns of avoidance rather than of creative activity. Once gained, they offer workers no positive gratifications, no meaningful experience. Some measure of security is undoubtedly necessary as the basis for the pursuit of other ends. But security, however labeled, cannot in itself substitute for the process of personal growth and enrichment which is assumed to be inherent in the pursuit of advancement.

Workers, as we have seen, also try to maintain the illusion of persisting ambition by extending the meaning of advancement to include the acquisition of personal possessions. This extension of the meaning of advancement is part of the shift from concern with getting ahead in the occupational world to concern with leisure time and leisure activities which we have noted earlier. This changing emphasis, which plays down the values of production and stresses the values of consumption, is both a consequence and a completion of workers' alienation from their labor. Since leisure is becoming the major area of self-fulfillment, the job becomes increasingly instrumental, and workers are tied to their jobs primarily by the cash nexus. Work in the factory, as a fifty-year-old machine-operator put it, is "just bread and butter," a necessary evil to be endured because of the weekly pay check.

But men cannot spend eight hours per day, forty hours each week, in activity which lacks all but instrumental meaning. They therefore try to find some significance in the work they must do. Workers may take pride, for example, in executing skillfully even the routine tasks to which they are assigned. "When I put up a pile of doors or fenders and it's a good job, I appreciate it," said a fender-wrapper. "I have an appreciation of myself when I do a good job." They may derive a moral satisfaction from doing "an honest day's work," even if they feel, as some do, that they are being exploited by management. They may try to squeeze out some sense of personal significance by identifying themselves with the product, standardized though it may be, and with the impersonal corporation in which they are anonymous, easily replaceable entities. A line repairman in his late thirties commented: "A lot of fellows like to work in the plant. They take pride in the product they turn out. A lot of them, even if they only do a little operation, they look at a finished car and seem to think they had some part in it. I've thought about that myself. I was up north fishing once and I ran into a couple of guys— I didn't know them but they work in the plant—and when we met one of them said to me, 'You an A.B.C.- maker too?' "

We know little of the deeper consequences of such makeshift substitutes for full-bodied emotional satisfaction on the job, but it does not seem likely that workers can derive much real satisfaction from these attenuated meanings in a context in which individual economic advancement is of central concern.

Since workers do not deny the validity of the tradition of opportunity or reject the legitimacy of economic or other institutions because of their inability to rise from the level of wage labor, it is easy to overlook these more subtle consequences of the disparity between tradition and reality. Lack of explicit dissatisfaction, of rebelliousness or radicalism, is taken as evidence of positive satisfaction. But not only may workers be experiencing psychological travail because of their failure, they may also be losing whatever desire they once possessed for a positive and creative work life. Chronic absence of rewarding experience, as Lewis Mumford has reminded us, produces lack of desire for such experience.

In a real sense, the idea that the goal of everyone should be unlimited personal advancement has been an historical accident. It emerged in large part because of the unusual opportunities offered in a new society which was being built across an empty continent rich in resources. But in no society is it possible for everyone to move up. In every society there must be those who perform the lesser tasks, those who "hew wood and draw water," or in an industrial society, those who man the machines. In a complex modern society, access to the top positions becomes more and more identified with extended training and unusual personal ability. To persist in the belief that everyone should strive to achieve individual economic success is to maintain values which, in some degree, are no longer appropriate.

If we are to continue to give self-development and self-fulfillment, values which underlie the belief in the desirability of universal striving for advancement, any significant content in this modern world, we must redefine them in terms of the realities of a complex industrial society. The extension of opportunities for advancement to those now laboring under disabilities not of their own making, desirable though it is, hardly touches what are perhaps the more important—and more difficult—problems: How shall we enable those who do the routine, humble tasks in our society to find meaning and satisfaction in their work? How shall we provide them with opportunities for personal growth and enrichment?

We need to explore the ways in which a complex society can solve these problems. Such an exploration might well begin with the following hypotheses suggested by some of our observations in Autotown.

As we have already seen, those men who do routine jobs will seek their major satisfactions in "the things I do when I get home from work," as one man remarked. Part of the answer to these problems, therefore, lies in the progressive enrichment of leisure activities. But we cannot deal with the problem of leisure without taking into account the nature of the work men do. The needs men try to satisfy in recreation may, in part, be generated by their experience on the job. One worker who was interviewed, for example, reported that he had usually felt it necessary to drop into a tavern for a few beers after a day spent on the assembly line; since being transferred to a job in parts and service, the after-work beer habit had disappeared. A job that leaves men physically or psychologically overfatigued, as does the assembly line, according to the consistent testimony of many workers, destroys the possibility of a lively and creative pattern of recreation.

Without more systematic analysis it is difficult to judge the adequacy of the recreational pursuits of industrial workers. The American approach to leisure, on the whole, has been casual and unorganized. The provision of opportunities for recreation has been left largely in the hands of those intent primarily on reaping a profit rather than satisfying human needs. The assertion that the businessmen of recreation are merely providing the public with what they want neglects the fact that most people, as J. L. Hammond notes in his discussion of "common enjoyment" in England, "have leisure without the tradition of leisure." [4] "The average citizen," Mannheim has said, "is unable to invent new uses for his leisure," [5] and since he has no traditional patterns to fall back upon, he is largely dependent upon what is made available to him. In a society largely dominated by success values, many leisure pursuits, as Lundberg and his colleagues point out in their detailed study of leisure, may tend to "lose their unique and primary value as recreation and become merely another department of activity devoted to the achievement of prestige or status." [6]

Even if leisure does become the workers' major source of personal satisfaction, work, which is still the largest single activity in men's lives, cannot remain purely instrumental in character. We have already described how men try to derive a significant sense of self on their jobs by taking pride in the (standardized, mass-produced) product, in efficient (even if routine) work, and in the knowledge that they have done an "honest day's work." But these values can only become substantially rewarding if there exists a corporate purpose which gives significant meaning to their jobs. Several workers remarked approvingly, for example, that during the war "things were different. You knew what you were working for—to bring the boys back home."

Elton Mayo and his colleagues and followers have found that sense of corporate purpose in the small work group.[7] The existence of informal groups in the factory characterized by shared sentiments and stable social relationships, they have argued, provides the common values and group goals which give work and life their meaning and significance. But men need more than the satisfactions derived from predictable patterns of social interaction on the job and from working with a "good bunch of guys." They seek in their jobs to satisfy desires derived not only from their co-workers but also from family and friends and from their experience as members of the community and the larger society. If workers find it difficult to realize the values they have acquired from the larger culture, as they do in the case of success and advancement, then the solution to the problems of the meaning and purpose of their labor lies not merely in reorganization of the job situation but in changes in the values of the larger society or in institutional changes which give them a greater degree of control over their fate.

It would seem from our observations that workers have already begun, however tentatively, to shuffle the hierarchy of values which govern their behavior. In their defensive efforts to prevent frustration and self-depreciation they assign to success a less prominent, less overriding place in their scheme of things. Since the universal search for individual success can result, in our society, only in widespread failure and frustration, this is probably a desirable change in values, although it contains the danger of sharply differentiated class ideologies which would sustain and justify a rigid, highly stratified class structure.

But if workers have relegated success to a more reasonable place in their hierarchy of values, they have not given up the ideal of advancement. They have begun to redefine advancement in realistic and effective, as well as defensive, terms. They have come to see that their future well-being lies in a collective effort to achieve common goals, for example, general wage increases, rather than in the private pursuit of success. Their work in usually dead-end jobs can have new meaning if they continue to redefine advancement as a quantitative increase of things within the reach of everyone, that is, as a rise in the general standard of living, a goal achieved together rather than apart. The common good would then become an explicit aim rather than the accidental product of each individual's search for self-advancement. Changes in economic institutions and organization might be necessary to enhance workers' sense of participation in this collective effort, but the existence of a common objective would give meaning and significance to both great achievements and the faithful performance of humble tasks.

FOOTNOTES

1. For an analysis of the values basic to home ownership, see J. P. Dean: *Home Ownership*, New York, Harper & Brothers, 1945, Chapter 2.
2. See "The Backward Art of Spending Money," in *The Backward Art of Spending Money and Other Essays*, New York, McGraw-Hill Book Company, Inc., 1937, pp. 3–19.
3. Dean, *op. cit.*

4. J. L. Hammond: *The Growth of Common Enjoyment*, London, Oxford University Press, 1948, L. T. Hobhouse Memorial Lecture No. 3, p. 19.

5. K. Mannheim: *Man and Society in an Age of Reconstruction*, p. 317.

6. G. Lundberg, M. Komarovsky, and M. A. McInerny: *Leisure: A Suburban Study*, New York, Columbia University Press, 1934, p. 17.

7. See E. Mayo: *Human Problems of an Industrial Civilization* and *Social Problems of an Industrial Civilization;* F. J. Roethlisberger and W. J. Dickson: *Management and the Worker;* and T. N. Whitehead: *Leadership in a Free Society*, Cambridge, Harvard University Press, 1936.

32

from
THE RISE OF THE MERITOCRACY: 1870–2033

Michael Young

Imagine a society in which perfect equality of opportunity was a reality, not just a goal, where no man could unfairly inherit his father's social class position, but where all were free to rise as far as their talents and energies carried them, without being obstructed by barriers of poverty, racial discrimination, or social origins of any kind. Imagine, in short, a society where one's social class position depended upon merit and merit alone. Is this not, after all, a central dream of the free and open society?

The British sociologist Michael Young has imagined such a society, and in his book, *The Rise of the Meritocracy,* has written a brilliantly satiric sketch of an imaginary "utopian" Britain in the year 2033. Extrapolating from contemporary trends, Young traces the origins and development of a society in which all our hopes for a perfectly open society have been realized. In the Britain of the twenty-first century, social origins count for nothing: the son of a banker may become a shoeshiner; the shoeshiner's son may become a scientist. Inscribed on the banners of civilization is the equation $I+E=M$ (IQ+Effort=Merit). The entire operation of the society is based on rigorous intelligence testing, and on its basis people are appropriately placed. Here at last, intelligence is all, and for the first time in history one's class position is based simply on measurable, intellectual superiority. In terms of ability and achievement, the people at the top really *deserve* to be there.

A society based solely on merit may seem to be an admirable one. However, Young asks us to pause and examine it closer, and, in so doing, he finds such a society to be

SOURCE: Michael Young, *The Rise of the Meritocracy: 1870–2033* (Baltimore, Md.: Penguin Books, 1962), pp. 103–15 and 143–45. Copyright © 1958 by Thames and Hudson, Ltd. Reprinted by permission of Random House and Thames and Hudson, Ltd.

quite antihumanistic and unjust. First of all, Young's meritocracy is very highly stratified, with enormous chasms between classes. Equality of opportunity is not at all synonymous with equality. The fact that classes were now based on intelligence rather than, say, wealth, did not at all mitigate the fact that tremendous social inequality remained. This was aggravated by the circumstance that the lower classes were not only beneath the other classes socially, but they were, because of complete equality of opportunity and the precision of the mobility selection process, actually and inescapably inferior to the higher classes. The frustrations of failure and the feelings of self-hatred were now multiplied many times because failure could only be due to personal inadequacies, not, as in previous societies, to the faulty workings of an unjust order.

Also, because the more intelligent members of the working and lower classes were selected out of the lower classes, the lower strata were then completely denuded of whatever talent they previously had. Instead of as in the old days when intelligence was more or less distributed equally among all the classes, now the lower class was peopled only by dolts. This meant, among other things, that the lower class was deprived of intelligent economic and political leadership.

We present two brief selections from the book. Writing in the first person as a sociologist of the twenty-first century, Young describes some of the *disadvantages* of a society which is obsessed with equality of opportunity.

What Young seems to be saying is that there is perhaps today too great stress upon intelligence and achievement, and that a society based solely on merit can lead to an aristocracy as unjust and inequitable as other aristocracies. What he seems to be arguing for is not so much a ruthless equality of opportunity based on intelligence and merit that will only once again stratify society, but rather for a kind of restructuring of human values which will mitigate the effects of social stratification altogether and begin to recognize the unique value of every human being. Quoting a "revolutionary document" of the twenty-first century which resurrects the old idea of equality itself and not simply equality of opportunity, Young writes:

The classless society would be one which both possessed and acted upon plural values. Were we to evaluate people, not only according to their intelligence and their education, their occupation, and their power, but according to their kindliness and their courage, their imagination and sensitivity, their sympathy and generosity, there would be no classes. Who would be able to say that the scientist was superior to the porter with admirable qualities as a father, the civil servant with unusual skill at gaining prizes superior to the lorry-driver with unusual skill at growing roses? The classless society would also be the tolerant society, in which individual differences were actively encouraged as well as passively tolerated, in which full meaning was at last given to the dignity of man. Every human being would then have equal opportunity, not to rise up in the world in the light of any mathematical measure, but to develop his own special capacities for leading a rich life.

Status of the Worker

GOLDEN AGE OF EQUALITY

I have in the first part of this book reviewed the means by which our modern élite has been established, and what a splendid result it is! No longer is it just the brilliant individual who shines forth; the world beholds for the first time the spectacle of a brilliant class, the five per cent of the nation who know what five per cent means. Every member is a tried specialist in his own sphere. Mounting at a faster and faster rate, our knowledge has been cumulative from generation to generation. In the course of a mere hundred years we have come close to realizing at one stroke the ideal of Plato, Erasmus, and Shaw. But, if sociology teaches anything, it teaches that no society is completely stable; always there are strains and conflicts. In the first part of this essay I have mentioned some of the tensions—between family and community, between different parts of the educational structure, between young and old, between the *déclassé* and the other members of the proletariat—incident to the rise of the meritocracy. Now I turn, in this second part, to consider from the same point of view, the consequences of progress for the lower class, and, as I have said, particularly for those born into it.

My method of analysis is historical; the comparison I draw once more with a century ago. Taylor has called that time the golden age of equality.[1] A sort of egalitarianism flourished then because two contradictory principles for legitimizing power were struggling for mastery—the principle of kinship and the principle of merit—and nearly everyone, in his heart of hearts, believed in both. Everyone thought it proper to advance his son and honour his father; everyone thought it proper to seek out ability and honour achievement. Individuals were riven as much as society. The consequence was that anyone who had reached privilege behind the shield of only one of these principles could be attacked with the sword of the other—the man born great was criticized because, by another reckoning, he did not deserve his fortune; and the base-born achieving greatness could be charged half impostor. The powerful were, by this whirligig, unfailingly unseated.

Many people were catapulted forward by their parents' riches and influence; not only did they benefit from the culture festooning their homes, they were sent to the best schools and colleges, dispatched on trips abroad and given expensive training for Bar, counting-house, or surgery —all the advantages, in short, which we in our day try to keep for the deserving. But since such treatment was sanctioned by only half the moral code, the beneficiaries were only half at home in their station in life. They could not say to themselves with complete conviction 'I am the best man for the job' because they knew that they had not won their place in open competition and, if they were honest, had to recognize that a dozen of their subordinates would have been as good, or perhaps better. Although they sometimes sought to deny self-doubt by too brassy an assertion of self-confidence, such denial was hard to sustain when it plainly ran against the facts. The upper-class man had to be insensitive in-

---

[1] Taylor, F. G. *The Role of Egalitarianism in Twentieth-century England.* 2004.

deed not to have noticed, at some time in his life, that a private in his regiment, a butler or 'charlady' in his home, a driver of taxi or bus, or the humble workman with lined face and sharp eyes in the railway carriage or country pub—not to have noticed that amongst such people was intelligence, wit, and wisdom at least equal to his own, not to have noticed that every village had its Jude the Obscure. If he had so observed, if he had so recognized that his social inferiors were sometimes his biological superiors, if the great variety of people in all social classes had made him think in some dim way that 'a man's a man for a' that,' was he not likely to respond by treating them with a kind of respect? [2]

Even if the superiors deceived themselves, they could not their subordinates. These knew that many bosses were there not so much because of what they knew, as who they knew, and who their parents were, and went on, with wanton exaggeration, to denounce all bosses on like account. Some men of talent took pains (if contemporary novels are to be relied on) to make it known in the factory, if not in the golf club, that they had 'come up the hard way.' But who could tell for certain how far success had been accident, or lack of scruples offset lack of brains? The workmen had their doubts. They let fly with their criticism of the powers-that-be, and so kept even the able under restraint. The energy wasted on criticism and counter-criticism was colossal.

An even more important consequence of the conflict in values was that the workers could altogether dissociate their own judgements of themselves from the judgement of society. Subjective and objective status were often poles apart. The worker said to himself: 'Here I am, a workman. Why am I a workman? Am I fit for nothing else? Of course not. Had I had a proper chance I would have shown the world. A doctor? A brewer? A minister? I could have done anything. I never had the chance. And so I am a worker. But don't think that at bottom I am any worse than anyone else. I'm better.' Educational injustice enabled people to preserve their illusions, inequality of opportunity fostered the myth of human equality. Myth we know it to be; not so our ancestors.

GULF BETWEEN THE CLASSES

This evocation of the past shows how great the change has been. In those days no class was homogeneous in brains: clever members of the upper classes had as much in common with clever members of the lower classes as they did with stupid members of their own. Now that people are classified by ability, the gap between the classes has inevitably become wider. The upper classes are, on the one hand, no longer weakened by self-doubt and self-criticism. Today the eminent know that success is just reward for their own capacity, for their own efforts, and for their own undeniable achievement. They deserve to belong to a superior class. They know, too, that not only are they of higher calibre to start with, but that a first-class education has been built upon their native gifts. As a result, they can come as close as anyone

[2] In an earlier age the sumptuary laws passed by Henry VII to force lords to eat in the same great hall as their retainers were not only for the benefit of the retainers. In modern times there is nothing to be gained from social mixing, in school, in residence, or at work, because the upper class now have little or nothing to learn from the lower.

to understanding the full and ever-growing complexity of our technical civilization. They are trained in science, and it is scientists who have inherited the earth. What can they have in common with people whose education stopped at sixteen or seventeen, leaving them with the merest smattering of dog-science? How can they carry on a two-sided conversation with the lower classes when they speak another, richer, and more exact language? Today, the élite know that, except for a grave error in administration, which should at once be corrected if brought to light, their social inferiors are inferiors in other ways as well—that is, in the two vital qualities, of intelligence and education, which are given pride of place in the more consistent value system of the twenty-first century. Hence one of our characteristic modern problems: some members of the meritocracy, as most moderate reformers admit, have become so impressed with their own importance as to lose sympathy with the people whom they govern, and so tactless that even people of low calibre have been quite unnecessarily offended. The schools and universities are endeavouring to instil a more proper sense of humility—what does even modern man count beside the wonders which Nature has wrought in the universe?—but for the moment the efficiency of public relations with the lower classes is not all that it might be.

As for the lower classes, their situation is different too. Today all persons, however humble, know they have had every chance. They are tested again and again. If on one occasion they are off-colour, they have a second, a third, and fourth opportunity to demonstrate their ability. But if they have been labelled 'dunce' repeatedly they cannot any longer pretend; their image of themselves is more nearly a true, unflattering, reflection. Are they not bound to recognize that they have an inferior status—not as in the past because they were denied opportunity; but because they *are* inferior? [3] For the first time in human history the inferior man has no ready buttress for his self-regard. This has presented contemporary psychology with its gravest problem. Men who have lost their self-respect are liable to lose their inner vitality (especially if they are inferior to their own parents and fall correspondingly in the social scale) and may only too easily cease to be either good citizens or good technicians. The common man is liable to sulk for his fig-leaf.

The consequences of so depressing the status of the inferior and elevating that of the superior have naturally engaged the full attention of social science. We cannot pretend that its path has always been smooth. Dr. Jason's 'tadpole' argument which amounted, when stripped of verbiage, to saying that on the whole all tadpoles were happier because they knew that some of them would turn into frogs, was at best a half-truth. The young might be happier; but what of the many older tadpoles who knew they would never become frogs? The tadpoles only confused counsel. Since Lord Jason himself became a 'frog,' research has proceeded more steadily.

The situation has been saved by five things. First, by the philosophy under-

[3] This is not entirely a new realization. My colleague, Mr. Fallon, has drawn my attention to an old cartoon in the *New Yorker,* an ostensibly humorous American periodical, *circa* 1954. It showed a large psychiatrist confronting a small patient, saying, 'You haven't got an inferiority complex. You *are* inferior.'

lying teaching in secondary modern schools. When these were started, no one quite knew what to do about the content of education for the lower classes. Children were taught the three R's as well as how to use simple tools and to measure with gauges and even micrometers. But this was only the formal skeleton of a course without an ideology to guide it. The schools had a far more important function than to equip their pupils with a few elementary skills; they also had to instil an attitude of mind which would be conducive to effective performance of their future tasks in life. The lower classes needed a *Mythos,* and they got what they needed, the Mythos of Muscularity. Luckily they already had this in a rudimentary form, which the modern schools have been able to promote into the modern cult of physical (as distinct from mental) prowess. The English love of sport was traditional, and nowhere stronger than in the lower classes. The modern schools were not breaking with the past, they were building on it, when they encouraged their pupils to value physical strength, bodily discipline, and manual dexterity. Handicrafts, gymnastics, and games have become the core of the curriculum. This enlightened approach has achieved a double purpose. Appreciation of manual work has been cultivated, and leisure made more enjoyable. Of the two, education for leisure has been the most important. More capable pupils have been trained to participate in active games which they can continue to play when they leave school; and the others who form the great majority have been given heightened appreciation of boxing, football, and other sports displayed before them nightly on the screens in their own homes. They esteem physical achieve-

ment almost as highly as we of the upper classes esteem mental.

Secondly, the adult education movement has, in its maturity, not only maintained and enlarged the regional centres but has arranged for everyone, irrespective of previous results, to attend there for a periodic intelligence check at intervals of five years. Tests can be even more frequent at the behest of the individual. A few remarkable changes of I.Q. both up and down, have occurred in middle life. Widely publicized in the popular newspapers, the reports have given new heart to many an ambitious technician. Now that psychiatric treatment is freely available in every workplace, many people with emotional blocks to the realization of their potential have been fully cured.

Thirdly, even when they have abandoned hope themselves, all parents have been solaced by the knowledge that, however low their own I.Q., their child (or grandchild) will have the chance to enter the meritocracy. The solace is a real one. Psychologists have shown that parents, whose own ambitions are thwarted, invariably displace those ambitions on to their children. They are satisfied if they think that their own child may achieve what they could not achieve themselves. 'Do as I wish, not as I do,' they say. The relationship can even be expressed in quantitative terms: according to the well-known principle of compensating aspirations, the greater the frustrations parents experience in their own lives, the greater their aspirations for their children. Almost from the moment when they fail their first intelligence tests at school, children can comfort themselves that one day they will have offspring who will do better; and even when it is dismally clear from teachers' reports that the offspring too are dull, there are still the grandchildren.[4] Personal failings are not so painful if there is a vision of vicarious triumph. As long as all have opportunity to rise through the schools, people can believe in immortality: they have a second chance through the younger generation. Also, the more children, the more second chances, which helps to account for the higher birth-rate in the second half of last century, after the reforms.

The fourth saving feature has been the very stupidity which has assigned the lower classes to their present status. A common mistake of some sociologists is to impute to the lower orders the same capacity as themselves—a way of thinking akin to anthropomorphism. Sociologists would naturally be aggrieved were they to be denied their proper status. But the lower classes are the objects of study, not the students. The attitude of mind is quite different. People of low intelligence have sterling qualities: they go to work, they are conscientious, they are dutiful to their families. But they are unambitious, innocent, and incapable of grasping clearly enough the grand design of modern society to offer any effective protest. Some are sulkily discontented, without being too sure what to do about it, and find their way to the psychologist or the priest. Most are not, for they know not what is done to them.

PIONEERS OF DIRTY WORK

The fifth, and most important, saving feature has been the application of scientific selection to industry. In the previous chapter I showed how promotion by merit gradually replaced promotion by seniority—how the grammar school and university streams were eventually extended into working life. I will now deal with the treatment of the secondary modern stream.

The modern schools have been reproduced in industry just as surely as the grammar schools, and with consequences just as far-reaching. The starting-point is again the Hitler war. In the early years of that war the methods of distributing recruits were almost as haphazard as in industry. Only after several disasters was a more sensible practice adopted, described as follows in the words of a leading Command Psychiatrist in one of the official histories of the war: *"In allocating personnel, the basic principle should be that no man is to be employed on work which is definitely above, or, on the other hand, definitely below his ability. Any other method of allotment is wasteful of ability, or destructive of unit efficiency."* [5]

What wise and far-sighted words!

By the end of the war the instruction was obeyed and very few men entering the Forces were assigned to any branch until their intelligence and aptitudes had been ascertained as accurately as the crude methods of the time allowed. Much greater efficiency was obtained in the utilization of manpower when the stupid were kept together, and the lesson was not lost on some of the better brains in civilian industry. This was long before advertisers began to include 'State I.Q.' (soon shortened to S.I.Q.) in their copy; and longer still before H.Q. (at Eugenics House) sup-

---

[4] Three-generation interlocking of aspirations in the extended family was discussed in an interesting way by Michael Young in 'The Role of the Extended Family in Channeling Aspirations,' *British Journal of Sociology*, March 1967. Note the earliness of the date.

[5] F. A. E. Crew, F.R.S. *The Army Medical Services.* H.M.S.O., 1955.

plied I.Q. certificates to authorized inquirers by teleprinter. The flower of that experiment of the 1940's was the Pioneer Corps. When this indispensable body of hewers and drawers was confined to men with I.Q.s below the line required to get them into the Intelligence Corps, the rise in efficiency was spectacular. The morale of these dull-witted men was better. They were no longer daunted by having superior people to compete with. They were amongst their equals—they had more equal opportunities since they had more limited ones—and they were happier, had fewer mental breakdowns, *and* were harder working. The Army had learnt the lesson of the schools: that people can be taught more easily, and get on better, when they are classed with people of more or less equal intelligence, or lack of it.

Not until the 1960's did this same lesson strike home in civil life. Intelligent people used to ask themselves what they thought was a profound poser: 'Who,' they asked, 'will do the dirty work in the future commonwealth?' Those who knew the right answer apparently said: 'Machines, of course; they will be the robots of the future.' It was a good answer as far as it went, but, in view of the many jobs which can never be taken over by machinery, at best a partial one. Then as they became aware of the new and revolutionary developments in intelligence testing, aptitude testing, and vocational selection, managements realized that a permanent peace-time Pioneer Corps was a practical possibility. At first tentatively, they suggested the correct answer to the old question: 'Who will do the dirty work?' The correct answer was: 'Why, men who like doing it, of course.'

They could see the need for a kind of permanent civilian Pioneer Corps, men with large muscles and small brains (selected by other men with small muscles and large brains) who were not only good at emptying dustbins and heaving loads but liked doing it. They were never to be asked to do more than they were proved to be fit for. They were never to be forced to mix with anyone who made them feel foolish by emptying dustbins more quickly or, what was worse at that time, by consigning all dustbins to the rubbish-heap—a sure sign either of mental deficiency or genius. As I say, progressive managements were very tentative and even a little shamefaced. They were easily put off by references to Mr. Huxley's gammas and Mr. Orwell's proles. The managers did not see that these two gentlemen had both been attacking not equal opportunity, but the effects of conditioning and propaganda. By these means even intelligent people were to be brought to accept their fate as manual workers. We know that in the long run this is impossible, and in the short run absurdly wasteful and frustrating. The only good manual workers, we know, are those who have not the ability for anything better. Enlightened modern methods have nothing in common with these brave new worlds. But at first not all managers realized that so signally to square efficiency with justice, and order with humanity, was nothing less than a new stage in the ascent of man, brought within his reach by the early advances in the social sciences.

The Pioneer Corps was the essential counterpart of the administrative class in the civil service; its historical significance is as great as that. The success of open competition in government employment established the principle that the most responsible posts should be filled by the most able people; the Pioneers that the least responsible jobs should be filled by the least able people. In other words, a society in which power and responsibility were as much proportioned to merit as education. The civil service won acceptance far more easily—no one wanted to be blown up by hydrogen bombs or starved of foreign exchange because something less than the finest brains were ensconced in Whitehall. The Pioneers encountered far more opposition. The community of principle governing the civil service and the Pioneers was not at once recognized. The objectors, amongst them a growing number of socialists, complained of 'indignity.' A vague word, to conceal a vague concept. The brute fact is that the great majority of minds were still thinking in pre-merit terms.

In the dark England of the distant past it made the best of sense to plead for equality. In the main way that counts, in their brain-power, the industrial workers, or the peasantry, or whoever it might be, were as good as their masters. What the anti-Pioneers did not realize was that the gradual shift from inheritance to merit as the ground of social selection was making (and has finally made) nonsense of all their loose talk of the equality of man. Men, after all, are notable not for the equality, but for the inequality, of their endowment. Once all the geniuses are amongst the élite, and all the morons amongst the workers, what meaning can equality have? What ideal can be upheld except the principle of equal status for equal intelligence? What is the purpose of abolishing inequalities in nurture except to reveal and make more pronounced the inescapable inequalities of Nature?

                    .   .   .   .   .

Fall of the Labour Movement

ADJUSTMENT IN THE UNIONS

To appreciate how far we have come, cast your mind back to a meeting of the tripartite National Joint Council for Industry, say, in 1950. There sat Ministers of the Crown with representatives of the T.U.C., the F.B.I., and the public corporations.* Did any group have more ability than another? Were the trade unionists outmanoeuvred in argument because they left school at thirteen or fourteen while the leaders of private industry had been to Cambridge and the chiefs of the public corporations to Sandhurst? Were the trade union leaders at a disadvantage because they were shoved into a factory at an age when the others were still in short trousers? Obviously not—if anything the advantage was the other way round. The trade unionists not only spoke from longer experience. They included some of the ablest men in the country. The sharing of power between the classes was the natural consequence of sharing the intelligence. These leaders commanded the confidence of the followers from whose ranks they came, and deserved to. Many of them were Ministers in the first, second, third, and fourth Labour Cabinets, before the decline set in. The ability of the miners' leaders was especially high, for in colliery villages there were no other jobs for young men to take and little prospect of promotion to the middle class. It was not fully appreciated in the 1950's and 1960's that these folk-heroes were not being succeeded by others equally able; the children of top trade unionists and Labour Ministers, and of other outstanding working men, were not becoming manual workers them-

* T.U.C.: Trades Union Congress; F.B.I.: Federation of British Industry. *Editor.*

selves. They were in attendance at grammar schools and universities, training for commerce and the professions, very large numbers of them even going to public schools. The children of the Labour leaders were the augurs of the future.

Contrast the present—think how different was a meeting in the 2020's of the National Joint Council, which has been retained for form's sake. On the one side sit the I.Q.s of 140, on the other the I.Q.s of 99. On the one side the intellectual magnates of our day, on the other honest, horny-handed workmen more at home with dusters than documents. On the one side the solid confidence born of hard-won achievement; on the other the consciousness of a just inferiority. The trade unionists' ponderous, carefully rehearsed reflections have no more influence upon their colleagues, if we are frank with ourselves, than a pea-shooter upon an astro-rocket. Primed with their sociological surveys the civil servants know more about the state of opinion in the factories than the stewards who work in them. The union leaders seldom have the insight to see that the courtesy with which they are treated is pure formality. They do not know that instead of the substance of power, they are being flattered by its shadow.

We do not need to ask why. The schools have begun to do their proper job of social selection—that is all. Once the long-called-for reforms were made, none of the ablest children in the country, unless by an unfortunate mistake, had to take up manual work. They were trained by something better than the 'Workers Educational Association (sic).' Twenty years after 1944 the brilliant children of manual workers automatically went to the best grammar schools in their district, from there on to Oxford and Cambridge, and, when they came down, they were eligible for travelling scholarships and grants for the Imperial College of Science, the Inns of Court, and the Administrative Staff College. The Keir Hardies of later generations have been the star civil servants, physicists, psychologists, chemists, business executives, and music critics of their day.

Amongst children who left school for manual jobs in the 1940's one in twenty still had I.Q.s over 120; in the 1950's—after the Act was working—there was one in fifty, by the 1970's only one in a thousand. By the last quarter of the century, the supply of really capable working men to fill the top union posts had dried up completely, and long before that, the fall in quality amongst Union M.P.s and branch and workshop officials, especially amongst the younger men, had become very marked indeed. I should say that the rule of promotion by seniority, to which the unions remained attached, was not such a brake as it was in industry because the older officials were on the whole more able. Intelligence is, of course, by no means the only quality required by a union leader; they also need belligerence, doggedness, and capacity for hard work. But although intelligence is not the only quality, it is a necessary one, and the new leaders have been dreadfully handicapped by its absence.

INDEX